22-23
46 ✓
60
99
166 ✓
172-3
174-7 ←
217-18 (also 211) ✓
296-300 ✓
324 — 333. ✓
399- 400
436-37 ←
466
547-58
613-19 ✓
645 ← For Gene ✓
664 — 670

# ALSO BY MORDECAI RICHLER

*Novels*
The Acrobats
A Choice of Enemies
Son of a Smaller Hero
The Apprenticeship of Duddy Kravitz
The Incomparable Atuk
Cocksure
St. Urbain's Horseman
Joshua Then and Now
Solomon Gursky Was Here

*Stories*
The Street

*Essays*
Hunting Tigers Under Glass
Shovelling Trouble
Home Sweet Home
Broadsides

*Children's Books*
Jacob Two-Two Meets the Hooded Fang
Jacob Two-Two and the Dinosaur

*Anthologies*
The Best of Modern Humor (editor)

# WRITERS ON WORLD WAR II

# WRITERS ON WORLD WAR II

## AN ANTHOLOGY

■

Edited by

## MORDECAI RICHLER

ALFRED A. KNOPF

NEW YORK 1991

THIS IS A BORZOI BOOK
PUBLISHED BY ALFRED A. KNOPF, INC.

Library of Congress Cataloging-in-Publication Data

Writers on World War II: an anthology/edited by Mordecai Richler—1st ed.
p.    cm.
ISBN 0-394-57258-0
1. World War, 1939–1945—Literary collections.   I.  Richler, Mordecai.
II.  Title: Writers on World War 2.   III.  Title: Writers on World War Two.
PN6071.W75W7   1991
808.8′0358—dc20                          91-52723
CIP

Manufactured in the United States of America
FIRST EDITION

In memory of Jack Newcombe
1923–1990

# Contents

■

## ▪ 1944 ▪

▪ 1945 ▪

# *Foreword*

## by MORDECAI RICHLER

1.

ARGUABLY, it was no more than a second act. Some second act. Over 78 million people were killed or wounded in World War II, the majority of them civilians.

Seventy-eight thousand perished in just one instant, the instant that yielded that noiseless flash over Japan. "At exactly fifteen minutes past eight in the morning, on August 6, 1945, Japanese time, at the moment when the atomic bomb flashed above Hiroshima," wrote John Hersey in *Hiroshima*, "Miss Toshiko Sasaki, a clerk in the personnel department of the East Asia Tin Works, had just sat down at her place in the plant office and was turning her head to speak to the girl at the next desk." Seven hundred miles away, in a sports stadium in Shanghai, where Japanese troops had assembled prisoners, ". . . a flash of light filled the stadium," wrote J. G. Ballard in his novel *The Empire of the Sun*, "flaring over the stands in the southwest corner of the football field, as if an immense American bomb had exploded somewhere to the northeast of Shanghai. The sentry hesitated, looking over his shoulder as the light behind him grew more intense. It faded within a few seconds, but its pale sheen covered everything within the stadium: the looted furniture in the stands, the cars behind the goalposts, the prisoners on the grass. They were sitting on the floor of a furnace heated by a second sun."

One of the American B-29 bomber pilots flying over Japan with General Curtis LeMay's Twentieth Air Force was the poet John Ciardi. "We were playing a lottery," he told Studs Terkel. "A certain number of planes had to be lost. You were just hoping that by blind chance yours would not be. When news of that atom bomb came—we didn't know what it was—we won the lottery. Hey, we're gonna get out of here! We may survive this after all."

Thirty-five thousand died in the 1944 incendiary bombing of Dresden, a firestorm that Kurt Vonnegut, Jr., experienced as an American prisoner of war. In his novel *Slaughterhouse-Five*, he wrote that prior to the raid which virtually destroyed the city, "The Americans arrived in Dresden at five in the afternoon. The boxcar doors were opened, and the doorways framed the loveliest city that most of the Americans had ever seen. The skyline was intricate and voluptuous and enchanted and absurd. It looked like a Sunday school picture of Heaven to Billy Pilgrim.

"Somebody behind him in the boxcar said, 'Oz.' That was I. That was me. The only other city I'd ever seen was Indianapolis, Indiana."

When the siege of Leningrad, the longest ever endured by a city, came to an end after 880 days, wrote Harrison E. Salisbury in *The 900*

*Days*, it was estimated that not less than 800,000 had died of starvation. "In the worst days of the siege," a survivor noted, "Leningrad was in the power of the cannibals. God alone knows what terrible scenes went on behind the walls of the apartments."

Nearly 6,000,000 Jews were murdered in the Holocaust.

Twenty years after the Warsaw Ghetto was annihilated, the diary of Chaim Kaplan was found intact on a farm outside of Warsaw, preserved in a paraffin tin. On June 3, 1942, he had written: ". . . the deportees are transported as prisoners in tightly sealed freight cars under the supervision of Nazi oppressors. They are in the care of those angels of destruction until they come to the place of execution, where they are killed. Many of the deportees, among them mothers and their infants, are put to death along the way; the remainder are brought to some secret place, unknown even to the hawk, and there killed in satanic fashion, by the thousands and tens of thousands. . . ."

We know how these events happened and what happened to the people who were part of them because all these writers and the many more whose works follow bore witness to the war, to its horrors and to the daily details of life in a time of total turmoil and destruction. They have recorded for us, the readers, the second cataclysm of our century. Possibly, just possibly, had the victors in World War I—or the Great War, as it was once known—not imposed the vengeful Treaty of Versailles on the defeated, demanding reparations that it would be impossible for the Germans to pay, it is conceivable that Hitler might never have risen to power. Certainly after the treaty was finally signed, the perspicacious Marshal Ferdinand Foch, savior of Paris, hero of the Battle of the Marne, declared: "It is not peace, it is an armistice for twenty years."

Not quite. For a case can be made that World War II actually began with the Japanese invasion of Manchuria in 1931, escalating through Mussolini's venture into Ethiopia in 1935, and the outbreak of the Spanish Civil War a year later, followed by Hitler's occupation of the Sudetenland in 1938.

Preparing this anthology, this book of witness, I did once consider beginning with a long thirties prelude, including an excerpt from Malraux's *Man's Fate* and chunks out of Orwell's *Homage to Catalonia* and Koestler's *Spanish Testament*, leaning on W. H. Auden's poem "Spain 1937," a salute to those "premature anti-fascists" who fought for the Republic in the International Brigades:

They clung like burrs to the long expresses that lurch
Through the unjust lands, through the night, through
       the alpine tunnel;

   They floated over the oceans;
They walked the passes: they had come to present their lives.

Sifting through novels, journals, and diaries about the thirties I did stumble on passages, previously unknown to me, that were either chilling or mind-boggling with hindsight.

In 1934, American newspaper columnist Dorothy Thompson drove through the German town of Murnau, passing a Hitler Youth camp that had been built to accommodate six thousand boys between the ages of ten and sixteen. "They were beautiful children," she wrote to a friend. "I did not think they would ever grow up to be thickset beer drinkers with rubber-tire necks. They sang together, and no people sing in unison as the Germans do, thousands of them, in the open air, young voices, still soprano, and the hills echoing! It made one feel sentimental.

"An enormous banner stretched across the hillside [and] dominated the camp. It was so huge that you could see it from the farthest point. It was so prominent that every child could see it many times a day. It was white, and there was a swastika painted on it, and besides that only seven words, seven immense black words: YOU WERE BORN TO DIE FOR GERMANY!"

The same year, H. G. Wells, then one of the most famous writers in the English-speaking world, was received by Stalin in Moscow. "I have never met a man more candid, fair or honest," he wrote in *An Experiment in Autobiography*, "and to these qualities it is, and to nothing occult or sinister, that he owes his tremendous undisputed ascendancy in Russia. I had thought before I saw him that he might be where he was because men were afraid of him, but I realize that he owes his position to the fact that no one is afraid of him and everybody trusts him. . . ."

But, tempting as so many of the thirties items were, I finally decided to confine myself in this collection to what are generally accepted to be the years of World War II, 1939–1945, beginning with the Auden poem "1st September 1939," which paid homage, as it were, to the thirties:

> I sit in one of the dives
> On Fifty-second Street
> Uncertain and afraid
> As the clever hopes expire
> Of a low dishonest decade:
> Waves of anger and fear
> Circulate over the bright
> And darkened lands of the earth,
> Obsessing our private lives;
> The unmentionable odor of death
> Offends the September night.

For those who fought on the Allied side during World War II it was, in Herbert Mitgang's phrase, "The Good War," and for those who were too young to fight in it, but lived through it—my generation—it remains, quite simply, *the* war. Say "the war" to anybody born before 1935 and he or she knows you don't mean the Korean War or Vietnam, but that world conflict in which civilization was at risk. It was the forces of darkness that were being engaged, and that were, furthermore, terrifyingly triumphant for too long a time.

"Then came Dunkirk," wrote Richard Hillary in *The Last Enemy*, "tired, ragged men who had once been an army, returning now with German souvenirs but without their own equipment; and the tendency of the public to regard it as almost a victory.

"After days on the beaches without sight of British planes these men were bitter, and not unnaturally. They could not be expected to know that, had we not for once managed to gain air superiority behind them, over Flanders, they would never have left Dunkirk alive."

On June 14, 1940, Paris fell. The Germans, wrote George Kennan, had in their embrace its pallid corpse. "They will now perhaps deceive themselves into believing the city never had a soul."

In Jean-Paul Sartre's novel *Troubled Sleep (Iron in the Soul)*, Gomez, a survivor of the Spanish Civil War wandering the streets of New York, imagines himself in occupied Paris: "The Rue Royale is deserted; the Place de la Concorde is deserted; a German flag is flying over the Chamber of Deputies, an S.S. regiment is marching under the Arc de Triomphe, the sky is dotted with airplanes."

A week later George Orwell wrote a letter to the editor of *Time and Tide*. "Sir," it began, "It is almost certain that England will be invaded within the next few days or weeks, and a large-scale invasion by seaborne troops is quite likely. At such a time our slogan should be ARM THE PEOPLE."

The Battle of Britain began in the autumn.

"The house about 30 yards from ours," wrote Virginia Woolf in her diary on September 10, "struck at one in the morning by a bomb. Completely ruined. Another bomb in the square still unexploded."

Then, on December 7, 1941, the United States was brought into the war.

"I first heard the news from the elevator man in the National Press Building," wrote I. F. Stone in *The War Years*. "The ticker tape at the Press Club, normally shut off on a Sunday, carried the first flash telling of the Japanese attack on Pearl Harbor. It was a beautiful late-autumn Sunday, the sky clear and the air crisp. At the entrance to the White House a small crowd had gathered to watch Cabinet members arrive."

James Jones was at Pearl Harbor, of course, and wrote of that day in his novel *From Here to Eternity*:

". . . a big tall thin red-headed boy who had not been there before was running down the street toward them, his red hair flapping in his self-induced breeze, and his knees coming up to his chin with every step. He looked like he was about to fall over backwards.

" 'Whats up, Red?' Warden hollered at him. 'Whats happening? Wait a minute! What's going on?'

"The red-headed boy went on running down the street concentratedly, his eyes glaring whitely wildly at them.

" 'The Japs is bombing Wheeler Field!' he hollered over his shoulder. 'The Japs is bombing Wheeler Field! I seen the red circles on the wings!'

"He went on running down the middle of the street, and quite suddenly right behind him came a big roaring, getting bigger and bigger; behind the roaring came an airplane, leaping out suddenly over the trees."

For poet George MacBeth, author of *A Child of the War*, there was the terror that came after darkness, once German bombers began to patrol over England.

"Sometimes I would hear them, or think I did, on the brink of going to sleep. Often, I was wrong. What I would really hear first, if there was to be a raid, or a warning, was the sound of the sirens.

"I don't think any child who survived the Second World War could ever again hear that awesome rising and falling sound without experiencing a chill of fear. As with all wartime sources of terror, it was joked away as moaning Minnie, but moaning Minnie was a dark lady like the witch in *Snow White*, who dragged me half-awake out of a warm bed, and had me carried downstairs night after night to lie on a cold floor and listen to a remote, frightening droning interspersed with the dull, repeated thud of anti-aircraft guns."

But for contemporaries of George MacBeth, E. L. Doctorow, say, who survived the war across a sheltering sea, there was no terror. "I did not think the war was anything but far away. I did not feel personally threatened," he wrote in *World's Fair*, his forties memoir.

2.

I WAS a mere eight-year-old when war broke out in 1939, fourteen when it ended, still too young to serve, but shaped by the war all the same. The headlines, the battles, the casualties, the atrocities, but, above all, the guilt. The guilt, because for those of us who sprang to adolescence in the forties in Montreal's St. Urbain Street area, the war years were incomparably good. Our fathers, who had survived the Depression, were earning reasonable salaries at last and the drift out of the cold-water flats of St. Urbain into the tree-lined streets of Outremont began.

Life was also looking up for me and my bunch. Tricked out in our Boy Scout uniforms, we went door to door collecting old aluminum kettles to be forged into Spitfires for "The Few," sometimes turning our haul in at the depot, but more often than not selling it to a junkyard, splitting the take. We sang:

> Goebbels has only got one ball,
> Goering has two, but they are small,
> Himmler has something similar,
> but Hitler has no balls at all.

The war dragged on. We took to drifting downtown after dark, nudging each other whenever we espied an obvious pair of V for Victory Girls, who went the limit with men in uniform. Unfortunately, our Baron Byng High School cadet uniforms met with sneers. We didn't qualify.

Far away, across the sheltering seas, dive bombers were terrorizing cities, refugees were clogging the roads, battles were being fought in the air and on the land and at sea. We knew because we saw the newsreels at the local Rialto, applauding every appearance of King George VI, Churchill or Monty, before settling into a double feature starring Mickey Rooney as Andy Hardy followed by another knee-slapper, this one featuring Bob Hope, Bing Crosby, and Dorothy Lamour on the road to somewhere or other. John Wayne was taking it to the Japs in *Back to Bataan*, Errol Flynn was running wild in *Objective, Burma!*, while Noel Coward, poor chap, was torpedoed in *In Which We Serve*. The closest the film war came to us was in an unintentionally hilarious movie that I still cherish, *Forty-ninth Parallel*, in which Laurence Olivier, of all people, played a French Canadian trapper, thwarting dirty Nazi submariners who had the effrontery to land on our shores. Actually, the majority of French Canadians were supporters of Vichy France. Camillien Houde, the mayor of Montreal, was interned for four years after urging Quebecers not to register for military service. Thousands took to the woods.

Coffee was rationed, as were tea and sugar. My older brother, and other university students, went out west to bring in the grain harvest, singing, "I lost my fingers in a threshing machine." We actually had air raid drills in Montreal, roly-poly men wearing steel helmets and blue zippered Churchill suits, members of the Canadian Provost Corps, patrolling St. Urbain Street, searching for telltale chinks of light showing through blackout blinds. I tacked a map of the world to my bedroom wall, inking in every Allied advance, learning surprising new place-names: Dunkirk, Pearl Harbor, Corregidor . . . ("I still remember my terror as a nine-year-old when, running in from playing in the street after school," wrote Philip Roth in *The Facts*, "I saw the banner headline CORREGIDOR FALLS on the evening paper in our doorway and understood that the United States actually could lose the war it had entered only months before") . . . Tobruk, El Alamein, Stalingrad, Iwo Jima. . . .

Fiddling with the shortwave band of our huge RCA radio, my brother and I tried to catch Hitler's speeches. Instead we picked up Ed

Murrow and J. B. Priestley broadcasting from London. We sent Bundles to Britain. My aunts, their knitting needles constantly clicking, made sweaters for the troops that were bound to unravel within a week. Holt Renfrew, a posh department store, appealed to our better instincts in a widely published advertisement:

> HOLT RENFREW has taken ANOTHER STEP in aid of the government's all-out effort to defeat aggression!
> Beginning July 15 no deliveries will be made on Wednesdays. This will enable HOLT RENFREW to save many gallons of gasoline . . . and many a tire . . . for use by the government.
> However, will it not THRILL you to think that non-delivery of your dress on Wednesday will aid in the delivery of a "block-buster" over the Ruhr . . . Naples . . . Berlin. . . .
> During the past months, thousands of our patrons have been proudly willing to carry packages bearing HOLT RENFREW'S red-white-and-blue label:
> "I AM CARRYING FOR VICTORY"

The real war also came home to St. Urbain Street. One Saturday morning Mr. Fox's firstborn son turned up for services at the Young Israel synagogue wearing a first lieutenant's uniform and old men wept at the sight of him. The Kugelmass boy, one of the first to join up, was killed when his Harvard Trainer crashed not far from Montreal. A cousin of mine volunteered for the Commandos but failed their intelligence test, venturing the original notion that "A.D." stood for "After the Depression." However, he did manage to get into the merchant marine. He was torpedoed in the North Atlantic and survived for ten days in a lifeboat before being picked up.

In 1945, once victory seemed assured, our magazines began to feature "thought-provoking" articles by learned psychiatrists warning us that when the boys came home they would be trained killers and would need time to adjust. We were also instructed never to ask them what things had been like over there. When the boys did come home, however, they adjusted to peacetime life in a jiffy and were visibly upset only when we tried to change the subject each time they started in on a story about their adventures in the war.

A month after Japan surrendered, I happened to stop in at my father's scrap yard on the day he received a railroad carload of brand-new Lancaster bomber engines that were being attacked with sledgehammers, after which they were to be resold for a pittance as scrap iron. Five years later I was living in a hotel on the Boulevard St-Michel in Paris. Among my drinking companions there was a Korean painter. "During the Japanese occupation," he told me, "they showed us a film of American prisoners they had taken in the Philippines. We had never seen a white man in our village and we couldn't believe people could be so ugly. We were convinced that the film was a fake, more Japanese propaganda."

3.

ONE OF THE aims of this anthology was to illuminate what it was like for the other side, yesterday's enemies, to see the war in its totality. Look at it this way. So far as the triumphant American navy was concerned the Battle of the Marianas, in which the Japanese lost three aircraft carriers, was a turkey shoot, but that wasn't the case for novelist Hiroyuki Agawa, who describes the battle as seen by a young naval lieutenant called Kuki, who is floating in seas thick with fuel oil after his ship has been torpedoed:

". . . the carrier, still listing to port, red hull exposed, was about to sink, its stern in the air. An officer stood on the sloping deck waving his cap in farewell. The battle flag, which should have been lowered, still flew at the mast. . . .

"The actual sinking was over quickly. The 44,000-ton vessel thrust its stern up into space and slipped beneath the waves in the twinkling of an eye. . . .

"Kuki once again began to drift into unconsciousness, overcome by a not-unpleasant drowsiness. One hour after the *Taiho* went to the bottom, as the colors of evening deepened in the waters west of the Marianas, devoid now of ships, Kuki's body also disappeared quietly beneath the huge swells. He was 26."

While we cheered the saturation bombings of Germany from the safety of Montreal—carrying for victory, as it were—it was not quite the same thing for Austrian novelist and playwright Thomas Bernhard, who was a schoolboy in Salzburg at the time.

"What I studied in class was forced into the background," he wrote in *Gathering Evidence*, "on the one hand by my fear of the National Socialist Grünkranz, on the other by my fear of war, in the shape of hundreds and thousands of droning, menacing aircraft which daily darkened the cloudless sky; for the greater part of our time was no longer spent working at our lessons . . . but in the air-raid shelters, which we had seen being driven, over a period of months, into the two hills of the city by forced labor from abroad, mainly Russian, French, Polish, and Czech prisoners working under inhuman conditions. These shelters were enormous tunnels, hundreds of yards long, into which the populace streamed every day, at first hesitantly and out of curiosity but later, after the first air-raids on Salzburg, in their thousands out of fear and terror. In these dark caverns we witnessed the most terrible scenes, very often of death, for the air supply was inadequate, and I often found myself sharing these dark, wet tunnels first with dozens and then gradually with hundreds of men, women, and children who had fainted. I can still see the thousands of people who had taken refuge in them anxiously stand-

ing, squatting, or lying there, pressed close together. The shelters underneath the hills afforded protection from the bombs, but many people
died there of suffocation or fright, and I saw many of the victims being
dragged out dead."

I did not get to Germany myself until 1955, at a time when those
cities that had been devastated by Allied bombers were still being rebuilt,
Munich reverberating day and night to the sound of pneumatic drills. I
had only been in town for a week when a Texan girl I met invited me to
the American army service club, domiciled in what had once been Hitler's Haus der Kunst, a showplace for Nazi art. A poster in the entry hall
announced that there would be a barn dance on Saturday night. But it
was another poster, this one tacked to the wall behind the reception
desk, that caught my eye.

BUS LEAVES FOR DACHAU
2 P.M. SATURDAY
VISIT THE CASTLE AND THE CREMATORIUM
DON'T FORGET TO BRING YOUR CAMERAS

Four years later I was in Germany again, this time with my wife,
bound for Rome. We had to allow that the Rhine, castles soaring out of
the mist, was enchanting, and that the country inns we stopped at served
splendid soups, the innkeepers unfailingly kind. Then one night, as we
were taking our dinner in a charming old guesthouse, we were startled
by the outbreak of singing from behind closed doors. When a waiter,
lugging a tray of overflowing beer steins, slid open the doors to the private
dining room a reunion of old soldiers was revealed. Sturdy, good-natured
fellows they seemed, rosy-cheeked country folk. They were singing the
Horst Wessel song:

Raise high the flags!
Stand rank on rank together.
Storm troopers march
with steady, quiet tread. . . .

Elie Wiesel, a survivor of Buchenwald and the author of *Night*,
among other books, has written: "I cry out with all my heart against
forgiveness, against forgetting, against silence. Every Jew, somewhere in
his being, should set apart a zone of hate—healthy, virile hate—for what
the German personifies, and for what persists in the German. To do
otherwise would be a betrayal of the dead." But Wiesel, who returned to
Germany on a visit in 1962, found it difficult to sustain such hatred. And
so, understandably, did the men of RCAF 4 (F) Wing at Baden-Soellin-
gen, although many of them were veterans of World War II. When I was
in Germany yet again, this time in 1973, and spent a week on the Canadian air base, a flying officer said to me, "There might be some Germans
who thought the Nazi party was a good thing but I never met any."

"They want to leave their past behind them," a schoolteacher said.

My first night on the base I interrupted a tangle of teenagers at a dance in the social center to chat with them about their life in Europe. "What have you seen?" I asked.

"Venice!"

"A bullfight in Barcelona."

"Dachau."

The boy was only fourteen. His parents had taken him there when he was twelve, and most of the other kids, it turned out, had also toured the camp. "What do you know about Dachau?" I asked.

"They used to punish people there."

"Naw. Like it was extermination."

"No, no. They just hung guys there. They never used the gas chambers."

"Who told you that?" I asked.

"The Germans."

"Did you find Dachau a frightening place?" I asked.

"It's not used anymore."

"Yeah, it was only during the war. They used to torture guys there."

"Why?" I asked.

"Um, there were too many prisoners so they had to kill some off."

"What else?" I asked.

"It's an unusual place to visit."

### 4.

WHEN I put together *Writers on World War II*, I had in mind not only those who had lived through the conflict but also those who came after, a few of whom may even now think of Dachau only as an unusual place to visit. My original impulse had been to limit this collection to the writings of novelists and poets, but, looking to fill in gaps in the story, I soon found myself leaning on diarists and journalists as well. Mind you, I make no apology for including such a superb stylist as A. J. Liebling or such a splendid military historian as John Keegan in what I prefer to think of as a mosaic rather than an anthology.

*The Oxford English Dictionary* defines mosaic as "The process of producing pictures or patterns by cementing together small pieces of stone, glass, etc., of various colours," and that is exactly what I was after in editing this book. I had hoped that by assembling the works of novelists and poets who had been through World War II, not necessarily as combatants, I could put together the big picture, something like a group novel that would tell the story from the invasion of Poland to the signing of the peace treaty on board the battleship *Missouri* in Tokyo Bay, a drunken Allied delegate making rude faces at the Japanese and the Canadian delegate signing on the wrong line. I have not been entirely successful. However, I have managed to bring together writers from many countries: the U.S.A., the United Kingdom, Russia, France, Germany, Japan, Austria, Italy, Holland, Poland, Canada, Australia, New Zealand, Rhodesia as it then was, and Czechoslovakia.

My criteria for selection were shifty. Wherever possible, of course, I opted for excellence. Next I settled for what I took to be the best writing available to describe a crucial event of the war. I also called upon witnesses, several of them plucked from Studs Terkel's *"The Good War,"* to illuminate what it was like, for example, to be a black soldier in the segregated American army of World War II.

*Writers on World War II* makes no claim to being definitive. In the end I had collected sufficient material to fill three volumes and there were some hard choices to be made. Friends were enormously helpful, reminding me of novels and poems I had forgotten, but the selections were mine alone and I take responsibility for the many omissions that are bound to be pointed out by the partisans of one writer or another.

Finally I would like to thank my daughter Martha. Drafted as my researcher on this project, she was sent out again and again to libraries to search for out-of-print books, and performed other chores without complaint. Her help was invaluable.

■ **1939** ■

# W(YSTAN) H(UGH) AUDEN

THE MOST GIFTED POET of his generation, Auden was part of a group of new British voices—among them Christopher Isherwood, C. Day Lewis, Louis MacNeice, and Stephen Spender—that were first heard in the 1930s. In the years just before and after Hitler's rise to power, Auden lived in Germany, and in 1935 married Thomas Mann's daughter Erika to provide her with a British passport and thus a means of escaping from Germany. He was much criticized in England for quitting the country in 1939—gone, along with Isherwood, to sit out the war in America. However, on his return to England in 1956, he was elected professor of poetry at Oxford.

■

## 1st September 1939

I sit in one of the dives
On Fifty-second Street
Uncertain and afraid
As the clever hopes expire
Of a low dishonest decade:
Waves of anger and fear
Circulate over the bright
And darkened lands of the earth,
Obsessing our private lives;
The unmentionable odor of death
Offends the September night.

Accurate scholarship can
Unearth the whole offense
From Luther until now
That has driven a culture mad,
Find what occurred at Linz,
What huge imago made
A psychopathic god:
I and the public know
What all schoolchildren learn,

Those to whom evil is done
Do evil in return.

Exiled Thucydides knew
All that a speech can say
About Democracy,
And what dictators do,
The elderly rubbish they talk
To an apathetic grave;
Analyzed all in his book,
The enlightenment driven away,
The habit-forming pain,
Mismanagement and grief:
We must suffer them all again.

Into this neutral air
Where blind skyscrapers use
Their full height to proclaim
The strength of Collective Man,
Each language pours its vain
Competitive excuse:
But who can live for long
In an euphoric dream;
Out of the mirror they stare,
Imperialism's face
And the international wrong.

Faces along the bar
Cling to their average day:
The lights must never go out,
The music must always play,
All the conventions conspire
To make this fort assume
The furniture of home;
Lest we should see where we are,
Lost in a haunted wood,
Children afraid of the night
Who have never been happy or good.

The windiest militant trash
Important Persons shout
Is not so crude as our wish:
What mad Nijinsky wrote
About Diaghilev
Is true of the normal heart;
For the error bred in the bone

Of each woman and each man
Craves what it cannot have,
Not universal love
But to be loved alone.

From the conservative dark
Into the ethical life
The dense commuters come,
Repeating their morning vow;
"I *will* be true to the wife,
I'll concentrate more on my work,"
And helpless governors wake
To resume their compulsory game:
Who can release them now,
Who can reach the deaf,
Who can speak for the dumb?

Defenseless under the night
Our world in stupor lies;
Yet, dotted everywhere,
Ironic points of light
Flash out wherever the Just
Exchange their messages:
May I, composed like them
Of Eros and of dust,
Beleaguered by the same
Negation and despair,
Show an affirming flame.

# WILLIAM L. SHIRER

ONE OF the most famous World War II correspondents, William L. Shirer reported, most notably for CBS radio, from Nazi Germany from 1934 until 1940, when censorship made his job impossible. In 1960, he published his definitive and still widely read *The Rise and Fall of the Third Reich: A History of Nazi Germany. Berlin Diary,* Shirer's day-to-day account of Germany in the 1930s and Hitler's early conquests, appeared in 1941.

■

FROM *Berlin Diary*

BERLIN, *September 1, later*

It's a "counter-attack"! At dawn this morning Hitler moved against Poland. It's a flagrant, inexcusable, unprovoked act of aggression. But Hitler and the High Command call it a "counter-attack." A gray morning with overhanging clouds. The people in the street were apathetic when I drove to the *Rundfunk* for my first broadcast at eight fifteen a.m. Across from the Adlon the morning shift of workers was busy on the new I. G. Farben building just as if nothing had happened. None of the men bought the Extras which the newsboys were shouting. Along the east-west axis the Luftwaffe were mounting five big anti-aircraft guns to protect Hitler when he addresses the Reichstag at ten a.m. Jordan and I had to remain at the radio to handle Hitler's speech for America. Throughout the speech, I thought as I listened, ran a curious strain, as though Hitler himself were dazed at the fix he had got himself into and felt a little desperate about it. Somehow he did not carry conviction and there was much less cheering in the Reichstag than on previous, less important occasions. Jordan must have reacted the same way. As we waited to translate the speech for America, he whispered: "Sounds like his swan song." It really did. He sounded discouraged when he told the Reichstag that Italy would not be coming into the war because "we are unwilling to call in outside help for this struggle. We will fulfill this task by ourselves." And yet Paragraph 3 of the Axis military alliance calls for immediate, automatic Italian support with "all its military resources on land, at sea, and in the air." What about that? He sounded desperate when, referring to Molotov's speech of yesterday at the Russian ratification of the Nazi-Soviet accord, he said: "I can only underline every word of Foreign Commissar Molotov's speech."

Tomorrow Britain and France probably will come in and you have your second World War. The British and French tonight sent an ultimatum to Hitler to withdraw his troops from Poland or their ambassadors will ask for their passports. Presumably they will get their passports.

LATER. *Two thirty a.m.*—Almost through our first black-out. The city is completely darkened. It takes a little getting used to. You grope around the pitch-black streets and pretty soon your eyes get used to it. You can make out the whitewashed curbstones. We had our first air-raid alarm at seven p.m. I was at the radio just beginning my script for a broadcast at eight fifteen. The lights went out, and all the German employees grabbed their gas-masks and, not a little frightened, rushed for the shelter. No one offered me a mask, but the wardens insisted that I go to the cellar. In the darkness and confusion I escaped outside and went down to the studios, where I found a small room in which a candle was burning on a table. There I scribbled out my notes. No planes came over. But with the English and French in, it may be different tomorrow. I shall then be in the by no means pleasant predicament of hoping they bomb the hell out of this town without getting me. The ugly shrill of the sirens, the rushing to a cellar with your gas-mask (if you have one), the utter darkness of the night—how will human nerves stand that for long?

One curious thing about Berlin on this first night of the war: the cafés, restaurants, and beer-halls were packed. The people just a bit apprehensive after the air-raid, I felt. Finished broadcasting at one thirty a.m., stumbled a half-mile down the Kaiserdamm in the dark, and finally found a taxi. But another pedestrian appeared out of the dark and jumped in first. We finally shared it, he very drunk and the driver drunker, and both cursing the darkness and the war.

The isolation from the outside world that you feel on a night like this is increased by a new decree issued tonight prohibiting the listening to foreign broadcasts. Who's afraid of the truth? And no wonder. Curious that not a single Polish bomber got through tonight. But will it be the same with the British and French?

BERLIN, *September 2*

The German attack on Poland has now been going on for two days and Britain and France haven't yet honored their promises. Can it be that Chamberlain and Bonnet are going to try to sneak out of them? Hitler has cabled Roosevelt he will not bomb open towns if the others don't. No air-raid tonight. Where are the Poles?

BERLIN, *September 3*

Hitler's "counter-attack" on Poland has on this Sabbath day become a world war! To record the date: September 3, 1939. The time: eleven a.m. At nine o'clock this morning Sir Nevile Henderson called on the

German Foreign Minister and handed him a note giving Germany until eleven o'clock to accept the British demand that Germany withdraw her troops from Poland. He returned to the Wilhelmstrasse shortly after eleven and was handed the German reply in the form of a memorandum. The extras are out on the streets now. The newboys are giving them away. The *D.A.Z.* here. Its headlines:

BRITISH ULTIMATUM TURNED DOWN
ENGLAND DECLARES A STATE OF WAR
WITH GERMANY
BRITISH NOTE DEMANDS WITHDRAWAL
OF OUR TROOPS IN THE EAST
THE FÜHRER LEAVING TODAY FOR THE FRONT

A typical headline over the official account:

GERMAN MEMORANDUM PROVES
ENGLAND'S GUILT.

I was standing in the Wilhelmplatz about noon when the loud-speakers suddenly announced that England had declared herself at war with Germany. Some 250 people were standing there in the sun. They listened attentively to the announcement. When it was finished, there was not a murmur. They just stood there as they were before. Stunned. The people cannot realize yet that Hitler has led them into a world war. No issue has been created for them yet, though as this day wears on, it is plain that "Albion's perfidy" will become the issue as it did in 1914. In *Mein Kampf* Hitler says the greatest mistake the Kaiser made was to fight England, and Germany must never repeat that mistake.

It has been a lovely September day, the sun shining, the air balmy, the sort of day the Berliner loves to spend in the woods or on the lakes nearby. I walked in the streets. On the faces of the people astonishment, depression. Until today they have been going about their business pretty much as usual. There were food cards and soap cards and you couldn't get any gasoline and at night it was difficult stumbling around in the black-out. But the war in the east has seemed a bit far away to them— two moonlight nights and not a single Polish plane over Berlin to bring destruction—and the papers saying that German troops have been advancing all along the line, that the Polish air force has been destroyed. Last night I heard Germans talking of the "Polish thing" lasting but a few weeks, or months at the most. Few believed that Britain and France would move. Ribbentrop was sure they wouldn't and had told the Führer, who believed him. The British and French had been accommodating before. Another Munich, why not? Yesterday, when it seemed that London and Paris were hesitating, everyone, including those in the Wilshelmstrasse, was optimistic. Why not?

In 1914, I believe, the excitement in Berlin on the first day of the

World War was tremendous. Today, no excitement, no hurrahs, no cheering, no throwing of flowers, no war fever, no war hysteria. There is not even any hate for the French and British—despite Hitler's various proclamations to the people, the party, the East Army, the West Army, accusing the "English warmongers and capitalistic Jews" of starting this war. When I passed the French and British embassies this afternoon, the sidewalk in front of each of them was deserted. A lone *Schupo* paced up and down before each.

At lunch-time we gathered in the courtyard of the Adlon for drinks with a dozen members of the British Embassy staff. They seemed completely unmoved by events. They talked about *dogs* and such stuff. Some mystery about the French not acting in concert with the British today, Coulondre's ultimatum not running out until five p.m., six hours after Britain was at war. But the French tell us this was due to faulty communications with Paris.[1]

The High Command lets it be known that on the western front the Germans won't fire *first* against the French.

LATER.—Broadcast all afternoon and evening. Third night of the blackout. No bombs, though we rather expected the British and French. The newspapers continue to praise the decree against listening in to foreign broadcasts! What are they afraid of?

BERLIN, *September 4*
After midnight and no air-raid, even with the British and French in the war. Can it be that in this new World War they're not going to bomb the big cities, the capitals, the civilians, the women and children at home, after all? The people here breathing easier already. They didn't sleep much the first couple of nights.

On the feedback from New York tonight I heard the story of the sinking of the *Athenia* with 1,400 passengers, including 240 Americans, aboard. The English said it was a German U-boat. The Germans promptly denied it, though the German press and radio have been forbidden to mention the matter until tomorrow. I felt lousy talking from here at all tonight after that story and went out of my way to explain my personal position as an American broacaster—that I had been assigned to give the news from Germany, that official statements such as the denial that a German submarine had torpedoed the *Athenia* were part of that news, and that my orders from home were to refrain from expressing my personal opinions. The High Command has installed military censorship of everything I say, but fortunately the chief censor is a naval officer, an honorable and decent man. I have had some warm words with

---

[1] Actually Bonnet boasted after the Franco-German armistice that he had refused the plea of Halifax for a simultaneous declaration of war. He played for peace at any price until the very end.

him the last couple of days, but within the limits of his job he has been reasonable.

The war is starting to hurt the average man. Tonight a decree providing for a surtax on the income tax of a straight fifty per cent and a big increase in the tax on beer and tobacco. Also a decree fixing prices and wages.

The staffs of the French and British embassies got away today in two big Pullman trains. I was a little struck by the weird fact that while the killing goes on, all the diplomatic niceties were strictly observed by both sides to the very last.

The faces of the Germans when word came in late tonight that the British had bombed Cuxhaven and Wilhelmshaven for the first time! This was bringing the war home, and nobody seemed to like it.

BERLIN, *September 5*

Very strange about that western front. The Wilhelmstrasse assured us today that not a single shot has been fired there yet. Indeed, one official told me—though I doubt his word—that the German forces on the French border were broadcasting in French to the poilus: "We won't shoot if you don't." Same informant claimed the French had hoisted a streamer from a balloon saying the same thing. Today the RRG[2] gave its first broadcast from the front, and it sounded plenty realistic. It was of course a recording. The Germans say they will let me do radio recordings at the front, but American networks won't permit the broadcasting of recordings—a pity, because it is the only way radio can really cover the war from the front. I think we're throwing away a tremendous opportunity, though God knows I have no burning desire to die a hero's death at the front. The fortress of Graudenz fell today and the Germans have smashed through the Corridor. After a slow start they seem to be going awfully fast. In the south Cracow is surrounded.

BERLIN, *September 6*

Cracow, second town of Poland, was captured this afternoon. The High Command also states that Kielce has fallen. Looking for it on my map, I was amazed to find that it lies way to the east of both Lodz and Cracow, almost due south of Warsaw. Nobody had any idea the German army had got that far. In one week the Germans have pushed far beyond their 1914 frontiers. It begins to look like a rout for the Poles.

I learned tonight that the liner *Bremen* has succeeded in evading the British blockade and today put in at Murmansk on the northern coast of Russia after a dash from New York. I'm pretty sure I'm the only one in town who knows it and I led off my broadcast with the yarn. At the last minute the military censor rushed in and cut it out; said I couldn't mention it.

[2] *Reichs Rundfunk Gesellschaft*—the German State Broadcasting Company.

LATER.—Joe [Barnes] and I met in my room at one a.m. to talk things over. We have an idea that Britain and France will not shed much blood on the western front, but will maintain an iron blockade and wait for Germany to collapse. In the meantime Poland will of course be overrun.

BERLIN, *September 7*

Have heard much talk today about peace! Idea is that after Germany's victory over Poland Hitler will offer the West peace. I wrote this rather carefully for my broadcast this evening, but the censor wouldn't allow a word of it.

It's just a week since the "counter-attack" began and tonight I learn from an army friend that the Germans are within twenty miles of Warsaw. A new decree today providing the death penalty for anyone "endangering the defensive power of the German people"—a term which will give Gestapo chief Himmler plenty of leeway. Another decree forces workers to accept new jobs even if they pay lower wages than jobs previously held.

BERLIN, *September 8*

The German High Command announces that at five fifteen p.m. today German troops reached Warsaw. The radio broadcast the news at seven fifteen p.m. Immediately afterwards a band played *Deutschland über Alles* and the *Horst Wessel* song. Even our military attachés were stunned by the news. There was no wild rejoicing in the streets of Berlin tonight. In the subway going out to the radio studio I noted the strange indifference of the people to the big news. And while Poland is being overrun, not a shot yet—so the Germans say—on the western front! The first person to be executed under yesterday's decree—Himmler has lost no time—is one Johann Heinen of Dessau. He was shot, it's announced, "for refusing to take part in defensive work."

NBC and Mutual have stopped their European broadcasts. Ed Klauber cables we shall continue alone. Smart we were to build up a staff of American radio reporters. Home early tonight at one a.m. for the first time since the war started and shall get a night's sleep for once. Heard Ed broadcasting from London tonight. He sounded dead tired, as am I after being on the air night and day with practically no sleep for a month.

BERLIN, *September 9*

The second air-raid alarm of the war at four a.m. today, but I did not hear it, being engulfed in my first good night's sleep in ages. No more news of the German army's entry into Warsaw and I begin to suspect yesterday's announcement was premature. O.W., back from the front, told me this noon that he'd seen some of the horribly mutilated bodies of Germans killed by Poles. He described also how he'd seen the Germans rounding up Polish civilians—men, women, boys—and marching them into a building for a summary court-martial and then out into the back yard against a wall, where they were disposed of by German firing squads. Our military attaché says you can do that, that that's the way cricket is played with franc-tireurs, but I don't like it, even if they are snipers, and I doubt from what O. W. says that the court-martial makes any great effort to distinguish actual franc-tireurs from those whose only guilt is being Poles.

Göring broadcast today—from a local munitions factory. He warned the people it might be a long war. He threatened terrible revenge if the British and French bombed Germany. He said seventy German divisions now in Poland would be released within a week for service "elsewhere." Apparently the war in Poland is all but over. Most of the correspondents a bit depressed. Britain and France have done nothing on the western front to relieve the tremendous pressure on Poland. It begins to look as though in Hitler we have a new Napoleon who may sweep Europe and conquer it.

# WILFRID SHEED

BRITISH-BORN and -educated Wilfrid Sheed, a novelist and literary journalist, has been rooted in America for years, a resident of Sag Harbor, New York. In the following excerpt, taken from one of his most recent satirical novels, *Transatlantic Blues,* the middle-aged protagonist, Chatworth, reflects on his British boyhood.

■

FROM *Transatlantic Blues*

The only thing that rivaled myself in interest was the coming of World War II. That would be super. The barrage balloons against a blue London sky (the summer of '39 was a beauty) looked like ads for a coming circus. Inside the shop window, once I got my mind off that fascinating face, was a panoply of war toys: miniature Hawker Hurricanes and Blenheim bombers, the latest in tanks and field guns, and the deluxe of the day, the H.M.S. *Rodney*, to complete my collection of capital ships. All my pocket money went into armaments. At home my room was zoned into air strips, deep-water ports, and a front line somewhere in France: the Somme, the Marne, I assumed we'd fight at all the same places again, like a series of football stadiums. Presiding over all this, my father's cap and bayonet from World War I, hanging above the bed.

It was an answer of sorts to my mother's room, which was crammed with holy pictures, knickknacks, bones of a saint. World War II was my first religious commitment, and, of course, my first betrayal. Wartime propaganda was cranking up and it was perfectly designed for an eight-year-old. No one was too small to tote a sandbag or douse an incendiary bomb. We had exhilarating drills at school, charging down fire escapes and flinging ourselves to the cellar floor; even digging a trench and wrestling contentedly in it. The face on the shop window was cannon fodder: gallantly missing in action, Group Captain Chatworth. Enough said.

My fear that the war might somehow be avoided at the last minute was triumphantly laid to rest that Sunday morning in September. There were long faces on the grownups of course, for the sake of form. But I could tell they were as happy as larks inside. The pastor said, "Well, it's a relief, isn't it?" and we all trooped down the street like late-night revelers: old people, young people, all in this together. I also remember the street as gray and empty except for us. Is that possible? My Irish mother was as excited as anybody, crying great boisterous tears. Although she hated the small group of Protestants that ran England, she loved the Crown, which she thought of as basically Catholic, and the real English people. My father, whose moods (except for irritation) I never bothered to analyze—didn't think he had moods, didn't care—stroked his mustache and said, "I'll be needing that hat, Pen."

Ah, yes. Air raid warden. Me trotting at his side looking for chinks of light. In hog heaven . . . God knows the English later made fun of this period, and then with that wonderful derision of theirs made fun of the next period too, the serious one, and of everything any good about themselves; but I missed the evolution of these jokes and do not really understand them now, though I make them with ease. I secretly still admire Mrs. Miniver.

# K. S. KAROL

ON AUGUST 23, 1939, Hitler and Stalin struck a demonic bargain, signing a pact that allowed Hitler a free hand in western Poland and Stalin control of eastern Poland. The pact also included a secret protocol which gave the Soviets the right to swallow the three independent Baltic republics of Lithuania, Latvia, and Estonia.

When war broke out just over a week later, K. S. Karol was a fifteen-year-old student in Lodz, Poland. Within two years, however, Hitler turned on Stalin, invading Russia on June 22, 1941, and the USSR ordained that the Poles—yesterday's enemies—were now free to join the Red Army. And that is what Karol did.

After the war Karol settled in Paris, where he is now an editor of *Le Nouvel Observateur.* Following, an excerpt from his memoir, *Between Two Worlds.*

■

## FROM *Between Two Worlds*

On September 1, 1939, my classmates and I were just finishing up a month in the countryside, in Wlodzimierzow on the Pilica, in a military training camp. It had been a boring time but, all things considered, almost like a holiday. The course was compulsory for baccalaureat candidates. We were due to return to Lodz that day, but it was also the day that the Germans chose to attack Poland—and to launch the Second World War. I remember that we were all indignant but certain of Poland's quick victory.

The camp's commander—a lieutenant—thought differently. He announced that the war would be a long one and that we would have a chance to fight when we reached eighteen or even twenty-one years of age. For now, however, he wanted some volunteers to protect public buildings, perhaps in Warsaw, thereby freeing a company of the regular army for duty on the front. Every one of us a patriot, we all took a step forward. I imagine that we resembled closely those schoolboys of the Kaiser's Germany, described so well by Erich Maria Remarque in *All Quiet on the Western Front.* Just as with them, patriotic ardor glazed over our eyes. For Jurek, Rysiek, and myself—Stefan Wegner's three protégés—enthusiasm consisted above all of antifascist élan. I also promised myself that in the Hour of Victory, after crushing the Germans, I would redirect my gun at the oppressor regime in Poland. But guarding public buildings would do until then: our army at the front had to have its rear guard well secured.

The only problem was that the front seemed to be everywhere, beginning with the road we took to Warsaw. In undisputed command of the air, the Luftwaffe bombed everything that moved, at least in western Poland. In the beginning, we were terrified. During the first raid, Sergeant Major Bartczak, a stupid and cruel man, even ordered a peasant woman to strangle her baby so that it would stop exposing us to risk with its crying. Fortunately the brave woman refused. Slowly we became used to the Luftwaffe; it had claimed no victims among our little troop, which comprised a hundred "auxiliary soldiers" and ten or so regular soldiers who flanked us. The real problems were slow progress in marching and the palpable lowering of morale, prompted by the fear that perhaps we weren't on the winning side after all.

Where were *our* planes? Did Poland have any planes? Some of us took comfort from pretending that our air force was active on the front, unlike the Luftwaffe, which was being used against civilians, including women and children. But this explanation, based on trust in the moral superiority of our pilots, collapsed when, on September 5, we at last reached the suburbs of the capital. Muffled rumblings of artillery fire convinced us that the front couldn't be very far away; and, alas, there wasn't a Polish plane in sight. Worse still, nourished by the myth of the combined might of France and Great Britain, we half expected to see their squadrons flying above our country. Instead, they were conspicuous by their absence.

Things were bad—much worse than our most pessimistic fears. The weary eyes of our camp commander betrayed fatigue and confusion; in Warsaw they hadn't any need of us, and it was too late to send us back to Lodz, which was now occupied by the Germans. Our leader recovered his verve only after meeting a group of officers among whom was a major who agreed to speak to him, to help him, to help us. I remember that after their conversation they separated on a perky note: "See you again, after another miracle on the Vistula." I too was sure that the Polish Army still had the capacity to wage a victorious battle on the outskirts of the capital. Hadn't my mother told me that in the hour of danger our people were capable of surpassing themselves, of revealing unsuspected reserves of heroism?

Nevertheless, our small troop was not supposed to contribute to this exploit. Our leader, after assembling our supplies and receiving his instructions, ordered us to march—singing!—in the direction of Lublin. In our song, even the trees were supposed to salute us, because it was "for our Poland" that we were going into combat.

In reality, neither man nor beast nor any other living thing paid us any honor, and we didn't have the opportunity to fire a single shot. The

enemy always came from the air, and even when they flew very low, they
were still beyond the range of our old Mausers. The spectacle of the war
therefore rapidly became monotonous; day after day we saw the same
scenes: civilians running to save themselves from air raids, convoys dis-
persing, trucks or carts on fire. The smell along the road was unchang-
ing, too. It was the smell of dead horses that no one had bothered to
bury and that stank to high heaven. We moved only at night and we
learned to sleep while marching; smoking was forbidden out of fear that
the glow of a cigarette could bring down on us the all-powerful Luftwaffe.

It was a marvelous month, that September of 1939: mild, sunny,
worthy of the end of an Italian summer, and we weren't cold.

Two weeks after our departure from Warsaw, when we had already
gone well beyond Lublin, our leader suddenly ordered us to make an
about-face. We were going back toward the west, toward Chelm. What
had happened? Had the miracle on the Vistula materialized? Were we
finally going to protect the public buildings of Warsaw? In an army,
orders are never explained—and the Polish Army was no exception to
the rule. But along the roads, day or night, we were never alone; other
soldiers and civilians were also on the march, and, thanks to the ubiqui-
tous rumor mill called in some parts of the West the "Arab telephone"
and in the USSR "Radio Yerevan," we learned that no miracle had taken
place. We were heading west because the Russians were arriving from
the east. And not to come to our aid, either, to fight "in a consistent
manner against the Nazis" as my Communist brother's old formula had
it! "Stalin and his loyal comrades" were coming quite simply to gobble
up their share of Poland.

Rysiek, Jurek, and I were seized with consternation. If the Bolshe-
viks had become friends with the Nazis, then principles no longer mattered; there was no longer any hope for our poor Poland. On the other
hand, why should we go to meet the Germans, who had attacked us first,
rather than toward the Russians, who, as far as one could tell, were
neither bombing nor destroying everything in their way? Should we talk
to our leader about his decision? Such a step would certainly have yielded
nothing and would have marked us as Communist sympathizers—
which, in Poland, even at this moment of total disarray, could only lead
to unfortunate results. What, then, if all three of us took off to try to join
up with the Russians? But this solution didn't have much to recommend
it, either. After much discussion, we decided that if there was a way out
of the trap that enclosed us, it was still our commander who had some
hope of finding it. So we followed him to the end, but we were bitterly
disappointed at having been betrayed by all sides: by the Western powers,
by the Russians, and by our own government, which had already bolted
to Romania.

While still marching, I began to sleep more and more deeply. I began to dream as if I were in bed. One night I saw the sky fill with countless Soviet squadrons. They were coming to deliver us from the Nazis, and our commander thanked them, as a comrade-in-arms who knows how to appreciate fraternal bravery and help. Even Sergeant Major Bartczak, a vitriolic anti-Bolshevik who never missed an opportunity to curse the Reds, ignoring the fact that it was the Germans who had attacked us, embraced the Russian tank drivers as they rolled down the road in their powerful armored vehicles. Bartczak cried out, "We are all part of the same Slav family." Our Soviet liberators also had an enormous tank of fresh cream, which they were distributing generously, as if to show just how wrong my father had been to think that there wasn't any to be had under the Bolshevik regime.

"Are you crazy or what?" Jurek asked, pulling me toward a gully as some Luftwaffe planes roared over our heads. According to Jurek, I replied that they were Soviet squadrons, but I don't remember anything of this. Ever since this rudely interrupted dream of the great Russo-Polish antifascist reconciliation, however, I have talked in my sleep, and I even reply, apparently, to questions, just as if I were awake.

We marched around in circles for one week more. Warsaw surrendered on September 27, but we continued our march until October 5, when we found ourselves encircled, along with some detachments of the regular army, by the Germans, near the village of Krzywda (Injustice). The Wehrmacht, for its own amusement or to encourage us to lay down our arms more quickly, sprayed us copiously with bursts of machine-gun fire and bombarded us with grenades. I caught something in the eye almost without noticing it, and without feeling any pain. My right eye simply closed and I could no longer open it except with the help of my fingers, by forcing the eyelid. I didn't make a fuss about it, believing that it would pass, and I took part in all of the farewell ceremonies. A high-ranking Polish officer, a colonel or perhaps even a general, had been authorized by our German captors to make a speech to us in which he said that the war was not over, that the Polish Army, under the command of General Sikorski, fought on in France, and that our powerful Western allies were more than ever at our side. Our camp commander also came to say good-bye; the Germans were separating the officers from the NCOs and the rank-and-file troops.

We were taken to Demblin Fortress, on the Vistula. I would spend ten days there before being sent to a hospital in Radom. It wasn't a camp like the one I had seen in Jean Renoir's film *La Grande Illusion*, replete with barracks, beds, and even a theater. In Demblin we were shut up in a large depot full of racks for arms—emptied, obviously—and were allowed out only to line up, in the rain, in front of an improvised, open-air kitchen. At night we arranged bunks as best we could with boards torn from the partitions and placed on the racks because, without them, there wouldn't even have been enough space for everyone on the ground. Our bunks, however, had an unfortunate tendency to collapse, which often provoked a good deal of stumbling and swearing in the darkness. The Germans would arrive forthwith, hurling abuse and insults, the wealth and variety of which far exceeded anything I had learned at Skorupka High School. Blows struck with rifle butts landed here and there on the heads of these "*polnische Schweinerhunde*" but I was lucky enough to avoid them.

We waited for them to take a census of their prisoners, so that we could explain our peculiar situation as student auxiliaries, but they didn't seem to be in any hurry. Instead, we were subjected to another sort of census altogether. One rainy morning, one of the Wehrmacht loudmouths came into our depot, screaming, "*Alles was Jude ist, aufstehen.*" ("Anyone who is Jewish, stand up.") "These savages only know how to speak the most brutal German," remarked Jurek, who was one-hundred-percent Aryan but who was still more afraid than I, because he had a bronze tint and a flattish nose that had earned him the nickname "golliwog" at the high school.

# JESSICA MITFORD

BRITISH-BORN Jessica Mitford, who now lives in Oak-land, California, is possibly best known for her exposé of the funeral business, *The American Way of Death* (1963). She was a close friend of the London literary critic Philip Toynbee, and three years after his death in 1981 published a memoir about him called *Faces of Philip.* The following anecdote, which quotes another friend of Toynbee's, the screenwriter Ivan Moffat, is taken from that memoir.

■

## FROM *Faces of Philip*

Eventually Colonel Powell summoned Philip for a formal interview to question him about his plans *vis à vis* the war effort.

*Philip said, in typical style, that he thought he'd join the Metropolitan Police; after all, they wore steel helmets like soldiers when they were on duty. Needless to say this idea was, on the face of it, extremely distasteful to Colonel Powell of the Brigade of Guards, former Tory Member of Parliament—his son-in-law a policeman! So the Colonel then said, "Well, Barbara and I had rather thought it would be a good idea if you joined the Army. I've still got some connection with the Brigade of Guards and we might find you a situation there."*

*Philip countered with the idea that he could join up in a notoriously effete battery manned by an odd assortment of writers and painters, incongruously decked out as bombardiers in full battle dress—amongst them, Ben Nicolson who was one of Philip's best friends. At the time it was said—I don't know with what accuracy—that Winston Churchill had established this outfit for people who were patently not soldier types, so they would be less likely to be cannon fodder, thrown into the trenches and mowed down as happened to their counterparts in the First World War.*

The colonel then said to his wife, "Barbara, would you mind leaving the room?" She dutifully did so and the colonel, looking Philip squarely in the eye, said, "Philip, I don't think your mother-in-law would much care for the idea of her son-in-law being a member of a bugger's battery."

# CHAIM KAPLAN

CHAIM KAPLAN, who was born in White Russia, received a classical Talmudic education as well as a secular one. A teacher and writer, he founded a pioneering Hebrew school in Warsaw. His diaries, written in Hebrew, were smuggled out of the ghetto in late 1942 by a man named Rubinsztejn, who worked daily outside the walls and passed the notebooks on singly to Wladyslaw Wojeck, a Pole who was a resident of Liw, a small village near Warsaw. In 1962, when Wojeck emigrated to the United States, he brought the diaries with him, and they were subsequently purchased for the New York University Library of Judaica and Hebraica.

■

## FROM *Scroll of Agony*

*September 2, 1939*

Today there were four air raids in Warsaw. The inhabitants have already grown accustomed to them and know what they have to do. We have indeed entered upon a new era. We feared its coming and greeted it with anxious hearts, but since it has come and assumed a definite shape, this era will become second nature. Even abnormal living becomes normal when it becomes constant. But our nerves are working hard. Almost the entire day is filled with air raids whose results are unknown because the communiqués are delivered in a terse, clipped style, and conceal more than they reveal. As is customary, each side proclaims its victories and conceals its defeats, but it is not hard to understand why Poland's defeats are great, for the full force of war with a cruel and barbaric enemy, armed from head to foot, is directed against her. The aid which will eventually come from her allies will be indirect rather than direct.

My brain is full of the chatterings of the radio from both sides. The German broadcast in the Polish language prates propaganda. Each side accuses the other of every abominable act in the world. Each side considers itself to be righteous and the other murderous, destructive, and bent on plunder. This time, as an exception to the general rule, both speak the truth. Verily it is so—both sides are murderers, destroyers, and plunderers, ready to commit any abomination in the world. If you want to know the character of any nation, ask the Jews. They know the character of every nation. . . .

*September 10, 1939*

The streets are sown with trenches and barricades. Machine-guns have been placed on the roofs of houses, and there is a barricade in the doorway of my apartment house, just under my balcony. If fighting breaks out in the street no stone will remain upon another in the wall within which I live. We have therefore fled to my wife's sister's at 27 Nowolipki Street, which is nearby. Her apartment is supposed to be safer, since it faces a courtyard.

The enemy of the Jews attested long ago that if war broke out, Jews would be eliminated from Europe. Now half the Jewish people are under his domination. Why has God embittered our lives so cruelly? Have we indeed sinned more than any nation? We are more disgraced than any people!

# SIMONE DE BEAUVOIR

SIMONE DE BEAUVOIR, author of *The Second Sex* (1949), was the lifelong companion of Jean-Paul Sartre, with whom she edited the periodical *Les Temps Modernes.* In 1954 she won the Prix Goncourt for her novel *The Mandarins,* and between 1957 and 1972 she wrote four volumes of autobiography. The following excerpt is taken from the second volume, *The Prime of Life.*

■

## FROM *The Prime of Life*

*3 September*

Awake at 8:30 to find it raining. My first thought: "It's really true, then." I'm not exactly miserable or unhappy, and I can't discern any feeling of resentment inside *me*; it's the world outside that's so horrible. Someone turns on the radio. No reply to the Final Notes from France and England; fighting still going on in Poland. Unthinkable prospect: another day after this, and another, and another—much worse, too, for then *we* shall be fighting. Only stopped from crying by the feeling that there would be just as many tears left to shed afterwards.

I read Gide's *Journal.* Time passes slowly. Eleven o'clock brings news of last-minute efforts in Berlin. The result will be known today. Hope is non-existent. I can't conceive the joy I would feel if someone told me, "There isn't going to be any war"; perhaps I wouldn't feel anything.

Phone call from Gégé, I go over to see her on foot. This cuts actual distances everywhere considerably: to go half a mile or so still takes about ten minutes of one's time. The police have all got magnificent new tin helmets, and carry their gas masks slung in little snuff-coloured satchels. Some civilians have got the same equipment. Many Métro stations are shut and barricaded, with notices announcing the nearest one available. Car headlights, painted blue, look like large precious stones. I have lunch at the Dôme with Pardo (Gégé's second husband, whom she married after her first marriage was annulled), Gégé herself, and an Englishman who has very striking blue eyes. Pardo takes a bet, against Gégé and me, that there won't be a war, and the Englishman agrees with him. All the same, there's a rumour going around that England has declared war already. Gégé tells us about her trip from Limoges back to Paris: all the way an endless stream of taxis and cars going in the opposite direction, piled high with bedding. Very few cars in the vicinity of Paris: nothing but unaccompanied men, mobilized reservists. Workmen busy blacking out the windows of the Dôme with thick blue curtains. Then the sudden announcement at 3.30 in *Paris-Soir:* "Great Britain declared war at 11 a.m. France to follow suit at five this afternoon." Despite everything, the shock is still tremendous . . .

A scuffle on the Place Montparnasse. Some woman mistook a man for a foreigner, and he slapped her face. Bystanders protested, and a military policeman grabbed the man by his hair. Fresh objections from the crowd. Policeman seemed somewhat confused and told people to move along. By and large they seemed to blame the atmosphere of hostility on the "foreigner."

This evening, with Gégé, at the Flore. People still saying they don't believe in the war, but they look pretty panic-stricken all the same. A man who works for Hachette says all his trucks have been requisitioned and the Métro bookstalls emptied out on the sidewalk, just like that. We walk back along the Rue de Rennes: lovely effect of violet or blue headlights in the darkness. At the Dôme we find a policeman arguing with the manager, who finally has extra-thick blue curtains put over the windows. I catch a glimpse of Pozner, in uniform, and the Hungarian. At eleven o'clock they clear the café. People hang around on the pavement; nobody wants to go home. I spend the night at Gégé's place. Pardo gives me a pill, and I am able to sleep.

# SIR HAROLD GEORGE NICOLSON

HAROLD NICOLSON married Vita Sackville-West in 1913, and with his wife was on terms of intimacy with Virginia Woolf and other members of the Bloomsbury circle. The son of a diplomat, he became one himself and then, less successfully, an MP. He began to keep a diary from the moment he resigned from the Foreign Office in 1929 until October 1964. The three volumes covering the years 1930 to 1962 were edited by his son Nigel.

■

FROM *The Diaries and Letters of Harold Nicolson*

H.N. TO V.S-W.                                           *14th September, 1939*
*4 King's Bench Walk, E.C.4*

The House sits till Friday and I shall therefore come down that evening. The Opposition are getting somewhat restive, especially about the Ministry of Information. The latter has been staffed by duds at the top and all the good people are in the most subordinate positions. The rage and fury of the newspapermen passes all bounds. John Gunther,[1] for instance, told me that he had asked one of the censors for the text of our leaflet which we dropped over Germany. The request was refused. He asked why. The answer was, "We are not allowed to disclose information which might be of value to the enemy." When Gunther pointed out that two million of these leaflets had been dropped over Germany, the man blinked and said, "Yes, something must be wrong there." . . .

*14th September, 1939*

The House is mainly concerned with the evacuation of children. It seems that where children have been evacuated along with their schoolteachers everything has gone well. But when the mothers have come, there has been trouble. Many of the children are verminous and have disgusting habits. This horrifies the cottagers upon whom they have been billeted. Moreover, the mothers refuse to help, grumble dreadfully, and are pathetically homesick and bored. Many of them have drifted back to London. Much ill feeling has been caused. But the interesting thing is that this feeling is not between the rich and the poor but between the

[1]The American writer, then a war correspondent in London.

urban and the rural poor. This is a perplexing social event. One thing that they say is that these children were evacuated at the end of the holidays and were therefore more verminous and undisciplined than if they had been taken in the middle of the term. But the effect will be to demonstrate to people how deplorable is the standard of life and civilization among the urban proletariat.

# W(YSTAN) H(UGH) AUDEN

AUDEN, one of a group of distinguished British poets who first came to prominence in the thirties, spent the war years in the United States. He was, however, constantly and acutely conscious of the multifarious forms of human suffering inflicted by the war on the other side of the Atlantic. The selection that follows deals with the plight of Jewish refugees from Hitler.

■

## XXVIII

Say this city has ten million souls,
Some are living in mansions, some are living in holes:
Yet there's no place for us, my dear, yet there's no place for us.

Once we had a country and we thought it fair,
Look in the atlas and you'll find it there:
We cannot go there now, my dear, we cannot go there now.

In the village churchyard there grows an old yew,
Every spring it blossoms anew:
Old passports can't do that, my dear, old passports can't do that.

The consul banged the table and said;
"If you've got no passport you're officially dead":
But we are still alive, my dear, but we are still alive.

Went to a committee; they offered me a chair;
Asked me politely to return next year:
But where shall we go today, my dear, but where shall we
        go today?

Came to a public meeting; the speaker got up and said:
"If we let them in, they will steal our daily bread";
He was talking of you and me, my dear, he was talking of
        you and me.

Thought I heard the thunder rumbling in the sky;
It was Hitler over Europe, saying: "They must die";
O we were in his mind, my dear, O we were in his mind.

Saw a poodle in a jacket fastened with a pin,
Saw a door opened and a cat let in:
But they weren't German Jews, my dear, but they weren't
    German Jews.

Went down the harbor and stood upon the quay,
Saw the fish swimming as if they were free:
Only ten feet away, my dear, only ten feet away.

Walked through a wood, saw the birds in the trees;
They had no politicians and sang at their ease:
They weren't the human race, my dear, they weren't the
    human race.

Dreamed I saw a building with a thousand floors,
A thousand windows and a thousand doors;
Not one of them was ours, my dear, not one of them was ours.

Stood on a great plain in the falling snow;
Ten thousand soldiers marched to and fro:
Looking for you and me, my dear, looking for you and me.

# MAX BEERBOHM

A BRITISH CRITIC, essayist, and caricaturist, the incomparable Max is probably best known for his delightful novel *Zuleika Dobson,* set in turn-of-the-century Oxford. It should also be noted that when he published his first book of essays at the age of twenty-four, the volume was titled *The Works of Max Beerbohm.* I stumbled on this letter in a collection of Max's correspondence edited by Rupert Hart-Davis. Happily, Ms. Jungmann did become a British subject, and worked for the Foreign Office throughout the war.

■

FROM *Letters of Max Beerbohm, 1892–1956*

## TO THE CHAIRMAN, ALIENS TRIBUNAL
### T.S. REICHMANN

*October 1939*                                      *Abinger Manor Cottage*

Dear Sir, It is about twelve years since my wife and I had the pleasure of meeting, in Italy, Miss Elisabeth Jungmann, who was at that time secretary to the famous German poet and dramatist Gerhart Hauptmann. Since then we have had that pleasure year after year.

She is a woman of high intellectual attainments, and of noble and beautiful character. She is dearly beloved and deeply respected by all her friends.

I was, of course, sorry that owing to the Nazi persecution she was obliged to leave her native country; but not less glad am I that she is in England; and in England I do hope she will be free to remain always.

I am, dear Sir, Yours obediently

MAX BEERBOHM

# DAN VITTORIO SEGRE

---

DAN VITTORIO SEGRE, the son of a wealthy land-owner, was raised as a Fascist in pre–World War II Italy. But when the racial laws against Jews went into effect in 1938, his hitherto secure world was shattered. Although ignorant of Zionism, he became—at the age of sixteen—one of the first Italian Jews to emigrate to Palestine. Segre is now a professor of Zionism and Jewish Political Thought at Haifa University. Following is an excerpt from his autobiography, *Memoirs of a Fortunate Jew.*

---

■

FROM *Memoirs of a Fortunate Jew*

### A FASCIST CADET IN ZION

After so many years I still laugh at the thought of my arrival in Tel Aviv. I was traveling on a small ship carrying a mixed cargo and about thirty passengers. I was sixteen and had a "capitalist" immigration visa, the type of visa that the British issued to immigrants with at least one thousand pounds sterling, which, in my case, my father had deposited in an English bank through the good offices of the Fascist party. I was alone in one of the six or eight first-class cabins. Traveling with me were some priests and a few Palestinian Jews making their precipitous return because of the outbreak of war. I was the only immigrant on board. The British mandatory authorities had by that time practically closed the door to Jews from Europe. With the publication of a white paper limiting Jewish immigration they had put an end to Zionist hopes of having a Jewish state in Palestine, since the percentage of the Jewish population had been fixed at one-third of the Arab inhabitants of the Holy Land.

My situation was thus particularly hybrid. I was a "deluxe" immigrant, due to join a kibbutz; I was the nephew of the owner of the ship on which I was sailing, but the ship had just been confiscated by the Italian government because he was a baptized Jew; I was under the personal care of the ship's captain, at whose table I took my meals, and at the same time abandoned in every sense into the hands of an unknown fate. Nobody, and first and foremost myself, knew exactly who I was.

Among the passengers, a beautiful lady seemed particularly startled by my presence. Wife of the owner of the then-largest textile factory in Palestine, she too was traveling first class, and we quickly became friends.

She could have been about thirty-five years old and told me she had a son not much younger than I. She did not mingle with the other passengers and spent long hours looking at the sea as if oppressed by nightmares. We used to take our afternoon tea together in long, quiet sessions—I too busy with myself to ask her about her troubles, she too plunged into her own thoughts. She must have left most of her family behind in Europe and perhaps had tried in vain to persuade them to follow her to Palestine. A tall, blond, sad woman, she listened to me with a strange look in her eyes, a look of curiosity and compassion. With considerable tact she kept warning me of the illusions I was weaving about the country awaiting me. I would not find anything remotely like Italy, she said, either in the landscape or in the people. It was not the physical toil that I should be afraid of but the cruelty of human relations. In Palestine the differences among people were greater than in other places because of the large number of immigrants. I would probably find myself lonely and misunderstood by other youngsters because of the type of world I was coming from. I would be caught up in a network of abrasive relationships among uprooted people who, because they were uprooted, were now busily engaged in building a world in which to forget their past. I should not expect compassion, pity, or kindness, though I would be able to rely on human solidarity. But it was a type of solidarity that shied away from privacy and individualism. Necessity and ideology privileged the group rather than the individual. For this reason it would be wise of me to find and adhere to a group as quickly as possible. I would suffer less than if I remained aloof. The price to be paid for acceptance would certainly consist of the loss of many of my dreams, not to speak of the tastes and habits I had brought with me from home, but nevertheless I should conform. The only other piece of advice she could give me was to try and develop thick calluses on my soul like those that would very soon harden the palms of my hands. Palestine, she kept telling me, is a land where caresses are made with sandpaper.

Naturally I was not convinced. Stretched out on my deck chair in the morning and the late afternoon, I enjoyed the infinite, changing blue of a bright, glassy sea—an atmosphere of well-being that made it impossible to imagine a future of pain and humiliation. The unreality that had always surrounded me was still there, even if different from before. World War II had broken out, but I was making my first cruise as a private person, free from uniforms, obligations, or discipline. I was a Jew, branded by racial laws, but served in style by Aryan waiters, protected by a captain who was perhaps wondering whether my uncle might not someday again be his boss. I was a refugee, an immigrant, a being in flight from a Europe that was tumbling into hell, but this did not prevent me from feeling free, fortunate, and happy at being able to run away from the war fronts, from college discipline, and from the oppression of Jewish life in Turin. I was full of hopes, without responsibilities, enjoying every minute of my life on board, which kept me busy from morning to night. I slept, I ate, I chatted; I read novels from the ship's library; I roamed freely around the ship, from the captain's bridge to the engine room; I talked to the boatswain, who demonstrated the knots he could make with a piece of string; I discussed the radio bulletins announcing German victories, and I was not—as I had dreaded—seasick!

During the crossing which, even near Crete, where the sea is often rough, was consistently sunny and calm, an abandon-ship exercise was carried out. The first officer called the passengers onto the top deck, checked the correct fastening of our life belts, explained the meaning of the siren blasts in case of danger, and took care to assure us that such danger was highly unlikely. Italy, he said, would remain neutral, thanks to the wisdom of Il Duce. Nobody would dare to provoke her in *mare nostrum*. Just the same, we should not allow ourselves to sink into a comfortable fatalism; not for nothing was England known as *perfide Albion*. Should we find ourselves in danger, we should face it with Italian, Aryan, and Fascist courage. The poor man, destined perhaps to die soon in some naval operation, must have learned his speech by heart. Facing a public composed mainly of Jews, his words sounded like a Marx Brothers' gag.

It was early in the morning when we anchored off Tel Aviv. To the right, clustered on the promontory of Jaffa, was a conglomeration of small houses, the bell tower of a church, and a large, castle-like building. Facing me, rising from an expanse of sand, were lines of flat roofs, colorless cement cubes with a splash of green here and there. A number of barges swayed on the water. The entire harbor consisted of a small jetty from which they shuttled back and forth to the few cargo ships waiting beyond the shallow water. An Italian priest, with whom I had gotten friendly during the trip and with whom I had discussed, for the first time in my life, the dogmas of Judaism and Christianity, explained to me that the only real harbor in the country was further north, at Haifa. The Jews had built the jetty in Tel Aviv and were handling their own cargoes because the Arabs of Jaffa had refused to unload the ships for them. "Jews and Arabs always quarrel," he said, "and they will go on quarreling for a long time to come if somebody does not put an end to the attempts of the Zionists to have a state of their own in Palestine."

# ▪ 1940 ▪

# E(DGAR) L(AURENCE) DOCTOROW

E. L. DOCTOROW, author of *The Book of Daniel* and *Ragtime,* among other novels, won the American Book Award in 1986 for *World's Fair,* from which the following excerpt is taken.

■

FROM *World's Fair*

At home in the evenings earlier now, my father was in the habit of listening to all the news commentators to find out what was going on in Europe. I knew, even before it was discussed in my class during current events, that a terrible war had begun—Hitler and Mussolini against England and France. He listened to every one of those news commentators; they didn't just read the news bulletins, but analyzed them too. Then my father analyzed their analyses. His new theory was that you had to listen to them all to figure out what the truth was. He liked Gabriel Heatter and Walter Winchell because they were antifascist. He detested Fulton Lewis and Boake Carter and H. V. Kaltenborn because they were against the New Deal and against unions and made comments verging on fascist, America First sympathies. He hated Father Coughlin, who said the Jewish bankers were to blame for everything. I grew to recognize the voices of these men and the products that sponsored them. Gabriel Heatter talked about gingivitis, which was a fancy name for bleeding gums; he passionately described the advantages of Forhan's toothpaste for this condition in the same fervent tones with which he described democracy's battle against fascism. If you didn't listen carefully, you might think that fascism and bleeding gums were the same thing.

My father sat in a chair near the radio and the newspapers opened in his lap to news stories with maps about the very same events being discussed by the commentators. He bought most of the papers—the *Times,* the *Herald Tribune,* the *Post,* the *World-Telegram,* even the *Daily Worker.* He would not read the Hearst papers.

In the movies on Saturday afternoons, after the cartoons, the Fox Movietone newsreel showed scenes from the war in Europe: big cannon muzzles afire in the night, German dive-bombers with angled wings coming out of the clouds. You saw the bombs falling. You saw burning buildings in London. You saw people swinging bottles of champagne against the sides of ships and diplomats getting out of cars and walking hurriedly up the steps of palaces for meetings. The war was talked about everywhere and shown in pictures. I liked to draw, I had made up my own comic-book stories and drawn them and colored them with crayon. I had a hero modeled after Smilin' Jack, the comic-strip pilot. I called my man Daring Dave. He had a mustache and wore a leather helmet with goggles and a lumber jacket and he had flown racing planes—like Smilin' Jack. I loved to draw these planes, snub-nosed daring little machines with checkerboard designs on their wings and ailerons. I drew them trailing exhaust in the sky so you could see what looping maneuvers they were capable of. They flew around courses measured by pylons. They flew over hangars decorated with wind socks. I wasn't sure exactly how something as vast and immeasurable as air could be used for a closed race course but I trusted that it could. I drew all sorts of those racing planes, some with cylindrical engine cowlings, some with enclosed cowlings pointed like index fingers. I drew cockpits that were open to the wind and cockpits that were enclosed with Plexiglas covers, but whatever the plane, whatever the design, I always put those streamlined wheel covers on them that were like raindrops coming along the window sideways in a windy rain. I liked streamlining, I liked those Chrysler cars that looked like beetles because their wheels were almost completely covered over and all their surface was rounded to get through the wind more easily, and for the same reason I liked those rear tapered airplane wheel covers. But now that World War Two had come to Europe I decided to get Dave into a fighter plane. I put him into a Spitfire flying over London for the Royal Air Force. The English insignia was a bull's-eye colored red, white and blue. I liked the colors but wondered if it wasn't a mistake to paint brightly colored targets on the wings and fuselage of your planes for the enemy to shoot at. I showed Nazi Messerschmitts going down in smoke.

I did not think the war was anything but far away. I did not feel personally threatened. But my mother talked about the war with worried references to Donald. He had graduated from Townsend Harris High School under a rapid advance program and now, age seventeen, he was enrolled at City College. My mother was afraid Donald would draw a low number in the Selective Service registration and be drafted into the Army and taken off to fight in Europe. This seemed to me an outlandish worry, inasmuch as America wasn't even in the war. I could not quite make the connections adults around me were making. One day I saw a headline in my father's copy of the *Post*: WAR CLOUDS, it read. The article went on to speculate about how and when the United States might have to become involved in the war against Hitler.

In the same Madison Square Garden where I had seen the Ringling Brothers and Barnum & Bailey Circus with that family that rode bicycles on high wires and the little clown who swept the spotlight at his feet, the American Nazis, called the Bund, had held a rally. They had put up a flag with a swastika next to an American flag, and marched in their brown shirts and with belts like Texas Rangers going from their shoulders down slantwise to their waists. They gave the fascist salute. There were thousands of them. Charles Lindbergh and Father Coughlin had spoken to them and they shouted and screamed just as the Germans did when Hitler spoke to them. "They are everywhere, this rabble," my father said one night at dinner. "Two of them came into the store today and I kicked them out. Can you imagine the temerity—coming into my store in their uniforms to try to sell me a subscription to their magazine?"

# GEORGE ORWELL

GEORGE ORWELL was the pen name of Eric Arthur Blair, the novelist, essayist, and critic. Orwell's service with the Indian Imperial Police in Burma, 1922–1927, led to his first novel, *Burmese Days,* as well as to that famous essay, "Shooting an Elephant." Orwell, who fought for the Spanish Republic, went on to write one of the most honest and enduring accounts of that Civil War, *Homage to Catalonia.* His most popular books by far, however, are still his political satires: *1984* and *Animal Farm.*

Four volumes of Orwell's collected essays, journalism, and letters were published in 1968, edited by the author's widow, Sonia Orwell, and Ian Angus. The following review is taken from Volume 2.

■

*Review:*
*Mein Kampf* BY ADOLF HITLER
*(unabridged translation)*

It is a sign of the speed at which events are moving that Hurst and Blackett's unexpurgated edition of *Mein Kampf*, published only a year ago, is edited from a pro-Hitler angle. The obvious intention of the translator's preface and notes is to tone down the book's ferocity and present Hitler in as kindly a light as possible. For at that date Hitler was still respectable. He had crushed the German labor movement, and for that the property-owning classes were willing to forgive him almost anything. Both Left and Right concurred in the very shallow notion that National Socialism was merely a version of Conservatism.

Then suddenly it turned out that Hitler was not respectable after all. As one result of this, Hurst and Blackett's edition was reissued in a new jacket explaining that all profits would be devoted to the Red Cross. Nevertheless, simply on the internal evidence of *Mein Kampf*, it is difficult to believe that any real change has taken place in Hitler's aims and opinions. When one compares his utterances of a year or so ago with those made fifteen years earlier, a thing that strikes one is the rigidity of his mind, the way in which his world-view *doesn't* develop. It is the fixed vision of a monomaniac and not likely to be much affected by the temporary maneuvers of power politics. Probably, in Hitler's own mind, the

Russo-German Pact represents no more than an alteration of time-table. The plan laid down in *Mein Kampf* was to smash Russia first, with the implied intention of smashing England afterwards. Now, as it has turned out, England has got to be dealt with first, because Russia was the more easily bribed of the two. But Russia's turn will come when England is out of the picture—that, no doubt, is how Hitler sees it. Whether it will turn out that way is of course a different question.

Suppose that Hitler's program could be put into effect. What he envisages, a hundred years hence, is a continuous state of 250 million Germans with plenty of "living room" (i.e., stretching to Afghanistan or thereabouts), a horrible brainless empire in which, essentially, nothing ever happens except the training of young men for war and the endless breeding of fresh cannon-fodder. How was it that he was able to put this monstrous vision across? It is easy to say that at one stage of his career he was financed by the heavy industrialists, who saw in him the man who would smash the Socialists and Communists. They would not have backed him, however, if he had not talked a great movement into existence already. Again, the situation in Germany, with its seven million unemployed, was obviously favorable for demagogues. But Hitler could not have succeeded against his many rivals if it had not been for the attraction of his own personality, which one can feel even in the clumsy writing of *Mein Kampf*, and which is no doubt overwhelming when one hears his speeches. I should like to put it on record that I have never been able to dislike Hitler. Ever since he came to power—till then, like nearly everyone, I had been deceived into thinking that he did not matter —I have reflected that I would certainly kill him if I could get within reach of him, but that I could feel no personal animosity. The fact is that there is something deeply appealing about him. One feels it again when one sees his photographs—and I recommend especially the photograph at the beginning of Hurst and Blackett's edition, which shows Hitler in his early Brownshirt days. It is a pathetic, dog-like face, the face of a man suffering under intolerable wrongs. In a rather more manly way it reproduces the expression of innumerable pictures of Christ crucified, and there is little doubt that that is how Hitler sees himself. The initial, personal cause of his grievance against the universe can only be guessed at; but at any rate the grievance is there. He is the martyr, the victim, Prometheus chained to the rock, the self-sacrificing hero who fights single-handed against impossible odds. If he were killing a mouse he would know how to make it seem like a dragon. One feels, as with Napoleon, that he is fighting against destiny, that he *can't* win, and yet that he somehow deserves to. The attraction of such a pose is of course enormous; half the films that one sees turn upon some such theme.

Also he has grasped the falsity of the hedonistic attitude to life. Nearly all western thought since the last war, certainly all "progressive" thought, has assumed tacitly that human beings desire nothing beyond ease, security and avoidance of pain. In such a view of life there is no room, for instance, for patriotism and the military virtues. The Socialist who finds his children playing with soldiers is usually upset, but he is never able to think of a substitute for the tin soldiers; tin pacifists somehow won't do. Hitler, because in his own joyless mind he feels it with exceptional strength, knows that human beings *don't* only want comfort, safety, short working-hours, hygiene, birth-control and, in general, common sense; they also, at least intermittently, want struggle and self-sacrifice, not to mention drums, flags and loyalty-parades. However they may be as economic theories, Fascism and Nazism are psychologically far sounder than any hedonistic conception of life. The same is probably true of Stalin's militarized version of Socialism. All three of the great dictators have enhanced their power by imposing intolerable burdens on their peoples. Whereas Socialism, and even capitalism in a more grudging way, have said to people "I offer you a good time," Hitler has said to them "I offer you struggle, danger and death," and as a result a whole nation flings itself at his feet. Perhaps later on they will get sick of it and change their minds, as at the end of the last war. After a few years of slaughter and starvation "Greatest happiness of the greatest number" is a good slogan, but at this moment "Better an end with horror than a horror without end" is a winner. Now that we are fighting against the man who coined it, we ought not to underrate its emotional appeal.

# JOHN MORTIMER

JOHN MORTIMER is a writer of many parts. A successful novelist *(Paradise Postponed)* and West End playwright *(The Dock Brief, A Voyage Round My Father)*, he is also the author of the immensely popular television series "Rumpole of the Bailey." An excerpt from his charming autobiography, *Clinging to the Wreckage*, follows.

■

## FROM *Clinging to the Wreckage*

The rumblings from Europe grew louder. Sandy Wilson joined our form and took to knitting long khaki objects, socks, mufflers and Balaclava helmets, comforts for the troops. When our form master protested at this click of needles, which recalled, in a somewhat sinister way, the foot of the guillotine, Sandy Wilson rightly said that it was the patriotic duty of all of us to do our bit for the boys at the front. The future composer of *The Boy Friend* also organized trips to London to see a play called *The Women* by Clare Boothe Luce which had not a man in the cast. Oliver and I saw it several times. He hired opera-glasses and took a careful view of the cleavage of the cast, but seemed to come no nearer reassurance.

We practiced for air raids, going down to the cellars and wearing our gas masks while Gracie Fields sang *Wish me luck as you wave me goodbye* on Mr. Lamb's wireless. Our housemaster took a gloomy view of the situation. "War is hell," he said. "I remember the Somme and we never thought we should have to go through that again. Of course we could have nipped this one in the bud, if we'd only fought in Spain. Or even Czechoslovakia."

"You mean, sir," I asked, intolerably, "that war is hell except in Spain or Czechoslovakia?" As a matter of fact I agreed with Mr. Lamb entirely, but I had inherited what my father would call the art of the advocate, or the irritating habit of looking for the flaw in any argument.

"School songs" were a great and proud feature of Harrow life. We would assemble in the Speech Room and sing the compositions of long-dead housemasters and music masters, songs redolent of vanished boys playing cricket in knickerbockers, enjoying romantic friendships on summer evenings and going out to die in Afghanistan or on Majuba Hill:

*Forty Years On; Jerry a Poor Little Fag; Byron lay, lazily lay, Hid from lesson and game away, Dreaming poetry all alone, Up on the top of Peachey stone*. That was the repertoire and then a new boy with a childish treble would pipe,

> "Five hundred faces and all so strange
> Life in front of me, home behind. . . ."

And the gravelly-voiced, hairy-chinned, spotty seniors would trumpet in chorus,

> "But the time will come when your heart will thrill
> And you'll think with joy of your time on the Hill!"

Winston Churchill, then First Lord of the Admiralty, came down to this strange ceremony which he apparently enjoyed. After the songs were over Mr. Churchill climbed with difficulty on to the stage. He cannot have been more than sixty-five years old, but his ancient head emerged from the carapace of his dinner-jacket like the hairless pate of a tortoise, his old hand trembled on the handle of the walking-stick which supported him and his voice, when he spoke, was heavily slurred with brandy and old age. He seemed to us to be about a hundred and three.

"If they ever put *him* in charge of the war," I whispered to Oliver, "God help us all!"

"Oh, they won't do that," he assured me. "They'll never do that. Chap in the Government told my Ma."

# BARBARA PYM

---

BARBARA PYM, daughter of a Shropshire solicitor, wrote satirical novels about middle-class life, among them *Less Than Angels* and *Quartet in Autumn.* There follows an entry from *A Very Private Eye,* her diaries.

---

■

## FROM *A Very Private Eye*

*Friday 10 May. Oswestry.*

Today Germany invaded Holland and Belgium. It may be a good thing to put down how one felt before one forgets it. Of course the first feeling was the usual horror and disgust, and the impossibility of finding words to describe this latest *Schweinerei* by the Germans. Then came the realization that the war was coming a lot nearer to us—airbases in Holland and Belgium would make raids on England a certainty. People one met were either gloomy (Mr. Beauclerk, the electrician, and Mr. Cobb, the wireless shop), slightly hysterical (Miss Bloomer) or just plainly calm like Steele. I think I was rather frightened, but hope I didn't show it, and anyway one still has the "it couldn't happen to us" feeling. Then there is the very real, but impotent, feeling of sympathy for these poor wretches who are the latest victims. In the news the Dutch and Belgian Ministers spoke and the Dutch Minister sent a greeting to his wife and children and grandchildren. Then it was the most difficult thing to control oneself, and I know that if I had been alone I couldn't have done. Later came the news of Mr. Chamberlain's resignation and his speech, in that voice which brings back so many memories mostly of crisis. But even if he has failed, and we can't be sure yet that he has, there is no more courageous man in the government or indeed anywhere, I'm sure of that. But Winston Churchill will be better for this war—as Hilary said, he is such an old beast! The Germans loathe and fear him and I believe he can do it.

It was odd to remember that this day used to be a great anniversary for me. Seven years ago, on May 10th 1933, I first went out with Henry. Imagine a lovely summer evening at the Trout with the wistaria out and the soft murmuring of the water. And my heart so full of everything. And now, emotion recollected in tranquillity. . . . dust and ashes, dry bones. Or are they not so dry as all that? I don't suppose I shall ever know.

# JESSICA MITFORD

JESSICA (DECCA) is one of the extraordinary Mitford girls. Nancy, the eldest, was author of *The Pursuit of Love* and *The Blessing,* among other comic novels. Diana married the English Fascist leader Oswald Mosley, and Unity was smitten with Hitler. But Decca was something else again. A Communist sympathizer, she eloped with Esmond Romilly in 1937 and went on to write an early autobiography, *Hons and Rebels.*

Following is an excerpt from that book, but first a few words about Esmond Romilly are in order. Romilly, a nephew of Churchill's, was one of the first Englishmen to join the International Brigade in the Spanish Civil War. He fought in the defense of Madrid and again at Boadilla del Monte, where the entire English section was killed, except for Romilly and one other man. Romilly and Decca left for America in February 1939. Two years later Romilly joined a bomber station in Yorkshire. He was killed in action in a mission over Hamburg in November 1941.

■

## FROM *Hons and Rebels*

Usually the events which make history seem to take an interminable time when one is living through them. Only years later do the essentials appear in perspective, telescoped and summarized in glib phrases for the history books: "the Thirty Years War," "the Restoration," "the Industrial Revolution." In real life, the maturing of the crisis that leads up to a change in government, the course of international negotiations and conferences that shape the destiny of a generation, the ebb and flow of battles that decide the outcome of a war, unroll in maddening slow-motion fashion, the decisive meaning of each stage often obscured and buried under mountains of newsprint, speculation, rumor, interpretation, "inspired" stories, comment pro and con.

Not so the German offensive against Western Europe, when it was finally unleashed. On the 9th of May, a month after Chamberlain had looked into his clouded crystal ball, there to find that Hitler had "missed the bus" and was no longer capable of waging aggressive war, the Germans struck. The offensive moved with such speed that no newspaper could keep up with it; "extras" were out of date before they appeared on the streets. Once more we stayed glued to the radio. Each hourly news broadcast announced new tragedies, and the regular programs were peppered with special bulletins from the front. Within hours the Germans had swept through Holland, whose much-vaunted system of dikes had proved about as effective a defensive weapon as a child's sand-castle moat, and the French front was reported to be in mortal danger, perhaps already lost.

Out of the wild confusion of those first few days of the attack, one fact emerged: the German rain of fire against these ill-prepared, disunited countries had illuminated in one vast flash the real nature of the danger confronting Europe, had exposed for all to see and understand the criminal stupidity of the years of shabby deals and accommodation to Hitler's ambitions. Overnight, the appeasement policy was buried for ever. The day after the offensive began to roll Chamberlain announced his resignation, and Churchill was summoned to form a National Government.

To Esmond this was the turning-point, the moment when all doubts as to whether or not the war would be fully prosecuted were at an end, and the course of English policy was once and for all clear. As he saw it, Churchill's advent to power, accompanied as it was by an unparalleled display of support from labor, had set the seal on this policy. The fiddling about with civilian gas-masks that didn't work, the ill-conceived leaflets for airplane distribution behind German lines which had marked the first five months after the declaration of hostilities, were at last done with.

In deciding to go back and fight—a decision that was inevitable from the moment the course of the war became clear in those first days of the offensive—Esmond was ruefully conscious of just what he was heading into. This would be no replica of Spain, no thrilling adventure of self-propelled action directed against the oppressors. The machine was rolling, a machine whose every cog was cluttered up with Wellington prefects grown older, dominated at every point by the Old School Tie enemies of *Out of Bounds* days. The upper classes, even the most pro-Hitler of them, would now swing into line to do their duty to King and Empire, and would no doubt find themselves in their ordained role of leadership in all phases of the war. "I'll probably find myself being commanded by one of your ghastly relations," Esmond commented glumly.

There was no doubt it was going to be a dull war, and the absence of the Communists, who announced they were sticking by their characterization of it as an "imperialist war," would make it even duller. Fighting in such a war would be an irksome task, dogged by boredom every step of the way, but none the less essential.

Characteristically, while analyzing and expatiating at length on all the drawbacks and drearier aspects of the war, Esmond was full of optimism. He predicted that the necessary clearing away of the Nazi rubble would open up the way to enormous social change everywhere, that in the course of the war the "spirit of Madrid" would once more emerge.

He was exultant at being in a position to arrange the details of his own participation in the war. Had he been caught up in the English conscription he would have found himself at the mercy of officialdom, with nothing whatsoever to say about what branch of the services he would join. As things stood, he was free to steer as clear as possible of the more tradition-bound centers of the armed forces. He decided to leave immediately for Canada, there to volunteer for the Air Force.

Esmond was of the opinion that the only thing which really mattered in life now was the defeat of the Axis powers. The horrors they were visiting on Europe made it unthinkable to stand aside from the war. If Hitler should win, he reasoned—and, as the days passed, news from the front began to make this look quite probable—it would be unlikely that we or any of our friends would survive. Therefore, in view of all that was involved, it was pointless to dwell on the drabber and more distasteful aspects, the interminable drilling, mastery of neatness, submission to all kinds of meaningless routines administered by a legion of officer class petty tyrants that he anticipated in a war which was basically being run by English Tories. Overriding all this were the issues at stake; exactly the same issues, he felt, as in Spain, only on a much larger scale, for now the survival of the whole of Europe was in the balance.

His attitude towards his own prospects were serious and practical. He was prepared to submit wholeheartedly to whatever lay in store for him in Canada, to suppress for now any temptation that might arise to torment, bait, or in any way harass his superiors in the Air Force. He would of course have to overcome the habits of a lifetime in order to carry out this resolution; but he was convinced that it could be done.

Esmond was a complicated and many-sided person, with an enormous capacity for change and almost none for self-analysis. His reversal of mood at this time was one that he would, no doubt, had he given it any thought, have put down entirely to the practical needs, as he saw them, of the existing situation; just as he would have defended any of his past attitudes on the grounds of necessity in the particular circumstances in which he had found himself at any given time. It would have seemed to him merely logical that his entire outlook should now be colored by a single-minded devotion to the problem of winning the war; for he was above all a person of political action, and this quality, dormant when no action seemed called for, now came to the fore in full force.

Perhaps it is inevitable that, to those who came into his orbit, Esmond appeared in so many different guises, for the personality of a fifteen- to twenty-one-year-old, no matter how strong, is still in a state of flux and development, now one trait and now another emerging as the dominant one. I always thought that my family looked on him as a sort of Struwwelpeter ("There he stands! With his nasty hair and hands!"), a youthful ruffian of uncouth appearance and even less couth ways; in fact, a cousin once remarked, "It seems so strange that you and Esmond should have managed to have such a sweet little baby, I was quite sure it would turn out to be a baby dragon." To his friends among his contemporaries, he appeared as a delightful but formidable figure, always excellent company because so predictably unpredictable, at times a leader, but more often too dangerous to follow. To the Durrs and others who got to know him best after he joined the Air Force, during his frequent visits to the States, he seemed to epitomize all that was best and most hopeful of his generation: "Though there's nothing *sweet* about Esmond," Virginia used to say regretfully, for she rather liked sweetness, a quality much cultivated by her fellow-southerners.

Whichever of these contrasting views of Esmond may have been closest to the objective truth, to me he was my whole world, my rescuer, the translator of all my dreams into reality, the fascinating companion of my whole adult life—three years, already—and the center of all happiness.

Both Esmond and I would have scouted the idea that anything in our conduct was remotely attributable either to heredity or to upbringing, for, like most people, we regarded ourselves as "self-made," free agents in every respect, the products of our own actions and decisions. Yet our style of behavior during much of our life together, the strong streak of delinquency which I found so attractive in Esmond and which struck such a responsive chord in me, his carefree intransigence, even his supreme self-confidence—a feeling of being able to walk unscathed through any flame—are not hard to trace to an English upper-class ancestry and upbringing.

The qualities of patience, forbearance and natural self-discipline that the worker brings to his struggle for a better life, the instinctive respect for the fundamental dignity of every other human being—even his enemy—so often displayed by the Negro or Jew in his own fight for equality, were on the whole conspicuously lacking in us, or only present in the most undeveloped form.

Esmond's strong and perfectly genuine love for his fellow man was hardly of the St. Francis of Assisi type, his hatred of war hardly that of a Gandhi. His brand of socialism was uncluttered by fine Christian sentiments, for, like Boud, he was a gifted hater, although, unlike her, he directed his venom against the enemies of humanity, peace and freedom.

Our childhood surroundings, through which ran a rich vein of lunacy, and in Esmond's case of brutality, were hardly calculated to endow us with an instinct for the highest in humanity and culture. No wonder that much of our rebellion against this past took at times a highly personal turn. "Comrades, Oi bring a message from the grive!" we once heard a Hyde Park Sunday speaker declare. "From the grive of Lenin, Marx and Nietzsche! You see them things be'oind them plite-glass winders in Selfrages. Brike them winders! Tike them things!" We never did find out just what Nietzsche was doing in such company, and although we chortled at this odd speech, we did feel a certain sympathy for the point of view it expressed. "Tike that car! Pocket them cigars!" we might have paraphrased from time to time as these opportunities presented themselves.

In other generations the same heritage no doubt produced its quota of gentlemen racers of horses or cars, gentlemen gamblers with love or money, who so often managed to die eventually horseless, carless, penniless and unloved. Such pursuits held no interest for our generation. The drama that attracted us and so many of our contemporaries was the real-life drama of politics, the vision of organizing a world of plenty and a good life for all. To the diversity of banners offering to lead the way to the new life flocked a tremendous variety of people from all kinds of different backgrounds.

While almost all of them, I think it can truthfully be said, joined the struggle from the highest of motives, and would have gone to any lengths of personal sacrifice to further whatever cause they followed, some, like us, had a number of old scores to settle along the way. Too much security as children, coupled with too much discipline imposed on us from above by force or threat of force, had developed in us a high degree of wickedness, a sort of extension of childhood naughtiness. We not only egged each other on to ever greater baiting and acts of outrage against the class we had left, but delighted in matching wits with the world generally; in fact, it was our way of life. Years later, Philip Toynbee reminded me of the time we had stolen a car-load of top hats from the cloakroom of the Eton Chapel, and of the time we had pilfered the curtains at a rich country house where we were staying to embellish the Rotherhithe Street windows. "Don't you remember?" he kept saying. When I confessed that I remembered only the barest outlines of these particular incidents, Philip rejoined sadly, "It all made an enormous impression on me, but I suppose that to you and Esmond it was just another day's work."

# EVELYN WAUGH

GRAHAM GREENE pronounced Evelyn Waugh the greatest novelist of his generation, and Edmund Wilson adjudged him "the only first-rate comic genius that has appeared in England since Bernard Shaw." Waugh served with the Royal Marines during World War II in both Crete and Yugoslavia and, based on his experiences, wrote that wonderful World War II trilogy *Men At Arms, Officers and Gentlemen, The End of the Battle.* An entry from *The Diaries of Evelyn Waugh* follows.

■

## FROM *The Diaries of Evelyn Waugh*

*Sunday, 19 May 1940*

Mass at 9.15 at Pirbright; afterwards sat in the sun at the Guards' mess, drinking beer, watching croquet, and talking about the extreme gravity of the situation. To camp for a football match which we won. Met the Brigadier at 5th Battalion mess. He said that the French failure is due to aircraft bombing driving gunners from their guns. The French were in the mood to surrender until Churchill went to hearten them. He said, "Can't stop these tanks. The men have to get out sometimes to pee don't they? Shoot 'em then." Apparently this simple precept impressed the French enormously and they decided to postpone surrender. Luncheon in the mess was a most peculiar spectacle. Some time ago Messrs. Bourne & Hollingsworth offered to adopt the Royal Marines and knit comforts for the troops. In thanking them the Brigadier expressed the hope that some of them would come and visit him some day. This was eagerly accepted, with the result that about thirty shopgirls suddenly descended on us for the day. It was inexpressibly painful. By good fortune they greatly overstayed their invitation so the senior officers do not wish to repeat the experiment. At 5 I went to look at training areas with Hedley and his sergeant, Cowan and his girl, Farmer and Sergeant Farrer. Later to dinner at Pirbright.

# MARIE VASSILTCHIKOV

---

EARLY IN 1940 Marie Vassiltchikov, a White Russian princess, found herself on her own in Berlin. She soon found a minor position in the Foreign Office. Many of her friends were involved in the July 20, 1944 plot to assassinate Hitler. After her death in 1978, her brother, George Vassiltchikov, prepared her Berlin diaries for publication.

---

■

## FROM *Berlin Diaries*

*Sunday, 2 June*

Yesterday we went shopping as it was pay day. We never seem to have a cent left at the end of the month, which is not astonishing, considering our salaries. The two of us now earn 450 marks, of which 100 go to the family in Rome, another 100 to repay our debts and about 200 more for food, transportation, etc. This leaves us about 50 marks for our personal expenses, clothes, mail, etc. But this time I had saved and was able to buy a dress I had spotted months ago. I had also had to put aside enough clothing coupons, but the shop forgot to ask me for them!

Tonight a bath. Now that baths are rationed too, this is an event.

*Monday, 3 June*

Paris was bombed for the first time today. The Germans have officially announced their losses in the West to date: 10,000 dead, 8,000 missing and probably also dead. 1,200,000 Allied prisoners have been taken so far.

*Thursday, 6 June*

Aga Fürstenberg's brother Gofi has been granted special leave for bravery. He is being sent to an officers' training school. Apparently, though he had never even done his military service, he behaved like an absolute hero and has been awarded the Iron Cross and the Panzersturmabzeichen [Tank Combat Clasp]. Yet he hates the war; before it broke out lived most of the time in Paris.

*Sunday, 9 June*

P. G. Wodehouse was taken prisoner near Abbeville while playing golf. The German High Command want him to edit a newspaper for British P.O.W.s and have brought him to Berlin.

# NATALIA GINZBURG

A NOVELIST, essayist, and playwright, Natalia Ginzburg
is also a member of the Italian parliament. Following
is an excerpt from her World War II memoir, *All Our
Yesterdays.*

■

FROM *All Our Yesterdays*

Signora Maria related what she had heard in the shops and from the
music-master, whom she still met sometimes on the road by the river.
The Germans were sprinkling a kind of powder that made people stupid,
the Allies were breathing in this powder and were fighting half asleep.
And the French generals were accepting gold coins from the Germans
to make wrong moves. And the Germans were dressing up as French
peasants and fishermen and were cutting the telegraph wires and poisoning the rivers. And the roads of France were full of refugees, women
running away with their children, and the children got lost and the
Germans caught them and sent them off to their laboratories, where
they used them for scientific experiments like frogs or rabbits. Emanuele
put his hands over his ears and besought them for goodness' sake to
make her stop talking; his nerves were all to pieces and he couldn't
control himself, one day perhaps he would strangle Signora Maria.
Emanuele disliked the Belgians, the French, the English, the Russians
who had allied themselves with the Germans, he limped up and down
the room and kicked at the furniture. He disliked Signora Maria who was
spreading panic. In his own home he also had Franz spreading panic, he
wandered about like a ghost and said that the Germans by advancing in
France would overflow into Italy. Emanuele told him he was behaving
as though the Germans were already in Italy; but perhaps Mussolini was
not sticking by the Germans. Franz said he was not afraid of Mussolini,
he was only afraid of the Germans, if he found himself face to face with
German soldiers he would go mad. At night he came to Emanuele's
room and sat on his bed, and made him repeat that the Maginot Line
was impenetrable. But the Germans went on penetrating it. One night
he woke Emanuele to tell him that not only was his mother Jewish but
his father too, he was completely Jewish and it was well known what
the Germans were doing to the Jews, if the Germans came down into
Italy the only thing for him to do would be to put a bullet through his
head. So many times he had been on the point of going to America

but he liked Italy too much, in Italy he felt he was safe even though for some time now there had been laws against the Jews, all you did was to pay a little and the police left you alone. But now he felt the Germans altogether too near, there they were in France behind the mountains and all they had to do was cross the mountains to get to where he was.

# JEAN-PAUL SARTRE

PHILOSOPHER, NOVELIST, and playwright, Jean-Paul
Sartre joined the French army in 1939. He was posted
to an artillery headquarters just behind the front in Al-
sace, and was taken prisoner in 1940. Released soon
after the capitulation of France, he then served in the
resistance movement, writing for the clandestine newspaper *Combat*. The discovery and publication in France
of his hitherto unknown war diaries in 1984 was an
event of major importance. An entry from *The War Diaries* follows.

■

## FROM *The War Diaries*

This evening Klein, the colonel's driver, pays us a visit. He heard
our raised voices—I was explaining to Pieter that he had a feminine
temperament and he was getting angry—and that attracted him: light,
warmth. We offered him a slice of tart and he told stories. He's the first
fellow I've met who has really *seen* the state the evacuated villages are
in. The other day they stopped in a frontier-village, and while the colonel
was going to the gun-emplacements, he asked a sergeant to open one of
the houses for him and show him the state of the furnishings. It was
edifying. Mirrors smashed on the wardrobes; pieces of furniture split by
bayonet-strokes; bed-linen looted—what couldn't be carried away is torn.
The tiles on the roofs are smashed, the silverware has disappeared. In
the cellars, the lads drank what they could and then, when they could
drink no more, went off leaving the spigots of the barrels open; the cellar
is flooded with wine. A sewing-machine is split in two. By axe-blows?
"And yet it was cast-iron," says Klein sadly.

Not long ago, some evacuees returned to this village and its neighbors on a 24-hour pass, to fetch bed-linen. When they left their houses,
most of them were weeping in despair: they'd found nothing left. They
complained to the commandant. But what could be done? The people
responsible don't come from our division, nor in all probability even from
the division which preceded us here. It goes back to the earliest days
of the war. As Pieter rightly said, that was the time when everyone
believed the war would be a cataclysm. The soldiers made haste to loot,
thinking that the first artillery bombardment would wipe out all trace of
looting, along with the very existence of the looted houses. And then, lo

and behold, the war became a long tedium, a long wait, and the looted houses remain—shocking and indiscreet.

"It's not possible," the sergeant was saying, "it's not possible to give them back in that state; it'd cause trouble. They'll have to be told the Boches looted everything. But for that, the Boches would have to attack . . ." It seems that the officers set the example. At Herrlisheim, some wagons supposedly containing damaged ammunition were unsealed: they were stuffed full of underwear, sewing-machines, silverware. It's impossible to know whether the civilians who come to fetch warm clothes don't loot too. They have a free pass and that's all. Impossible to tell whether they really go to their own houses or into their rich neighbor's instead. Only the mayor could say, but the mayor isn't there, he's in the Limousin.

We talk about Strasbourg. He says the police there, by contrast, is well organized and strict. One old eccentric he used to know, an umbrella-merchant, wouldn't allow himself to be evacuated; he hid in his house and let the others go off, then lived alone, feeding himself from tins. In the end, he grew bolder and switched on the lamps of an evening. One night, as the constables were doing their rounds, they saw a light. They called and shouted, but the old man didn't reply. They called three times, but the old man still remained silent, terrified no doubt that he'd be evacuated forcibly. After the third time, they fired through the window and the first volley killed him stone dead.

# RICHARD HILLARY

RICHARD HILLARY was born in Australia and came to England as a small child. He was killed when his plane crashed while landing at an airfield near Berwick on January 7, 1943. *The Last Enemy,* his memoir of the air war, was one of the most famous books to emerge from the Battle of Britain. (In the U.S., it was published under the title *Falling Through Space.*) An excerpt follows.

■

FROM *The Last Enemy*

Then came Dunkirk: tired, ragged men who had once been an army, returning now with German souvenirs but without their own equipment; and the tendency of the public to regard it almost as a victory.

After days on the beaches without sight of British planes these men were bitter, and not unnaturally. They could not be expected to know that, had we not for once managed to gain air superiority behind them, over Flanders, they would never have left Dunkirk alive. For us the evacuation was still a newspaper story, until Noel, Howes, and I got the day off, motored to Brighton, and saw for ourselves.

The beaches, streets, and pubs were a crawling mass of soldiers, British, French, and Belgian. They had no money but were being loyally welcomed by the locals. They were ragged and weary. When Howes suddenly met a blonde and vanished with her and the car for the rest of the day, Noel and I soon found ourselves in various billets acting as interpreters for the French. They were very tired and very patient. It had been so long. What could a few more hours matter? The most frequent request was for somewhere to bathe their feet. When it became obvious that there had been a mix-up, that some billets looked like being hopelessly overcrowded and others empty, we gave up. Collecting two French soldiers and a Belgian dispatch rider, we took them off for a drink. The bar we chose was a seething mass of sweating, turbulent khaki. Before we could even get a drink we were involved in half a dozen arguments over the whereabouts of our aircraft over Dunkirk. Knowing personally several pilots who had been killed, and with some knowledge of the true facts, we found it hard to keep our tempers.

In fairness to the BEF, it must be said that by no means all returned as rabble. A story of the Grenadier Guards was already going the rounds.

In columns of three they had marched on to the pier at Dunkirk with complete equipment, as though going for a route march. A Territorial officer, seeing them standing at ease, advanced and started to distribute spoons and forks for them to deal with the food that was being handed out. His efforts were summarily halted by the acid comment of a young Grenadier subaltern:

"Thank you," he said, "but the Grenadiers always carry their own cutlery."

# OLIVIA MANNING

OLIVIA MANNING spent much of her youth in Ireland. In 1939 she married R. D. Smith, then a British Council lecturer, and traveled with him to Bucharest and then on to Greece, Egypt, and Jerusalem, the setting for her Balkan and Levant trilogies, which form a single narrative entitled *Fortunes of War*. "The finest fictional record of the war produced by a British writer," wrote Anthony Burgess.

Following is an excerpt from the first novel of the Balkan trilogy, *The Great Fortune*.

■

## FROM *The Great Fortune*

Inchcape's servant, Pauli, made a model in a sand-box of the British Expeditionary Force queueing for embarkation on the Dunkirk beaches. The little ships stood in a sea of blue wax. Inchcape put it in the window of the Propaganda Bureau. Though it was skillfully made, it was a sad-looking model. The few who bothered to give it a glance must have thought the British now had nothing to offer but a desperate courage.

In Bucharest the most startling effect of events was the change in the news films. French films ceased to arrive. Perhaps there was no one left with the heart to make them. English-speaking films were blocked by the chaos of Europe. What did come, with triumphant regularity, were the U.P.A. news films.

People sat up at them, aghast, overwhelmed by the fervor of the young men on the screen. There was nothing here of the flat realism of the English news, nothing of the bored inactivity which people had come to expect. Every camera trick was used to enhance the drama of the German machines reaping the cities as they passed. Their destructive lust was like a glimpse of the dark ages. The fires of Rotterdam shot up livid against the midnight sky. They roared from the screen. The camera backed, barely evading a shower of masonry as tall façades, every window aflame, crashed towards the audience. Bricks showered through the air. Cathedral spires, towers that had withstood a dozen other wars, great buildings that had been a wonder for centuries, all toppled into dust.

Clarence, sitting beside Harriet, said in his slow, rich voice: "I bet these films are faked."

People shifted nervously in their seats. Those nearest glanced askance at him, fearful of his temerity.

The cameras moved between the poplars of a Flemish road. On either side stood lorries, disabled or abandoned, their doors ripped open and their contents—bread, wine, clothing, medical supplies, munitions —pulled out and left contemptuously in disarray. In the main streets of towns from which the inhabitants had fled, the invaders sprawled asleep in the sunshine. These were the golden days, the spring of the year. Outside one town, among the young corn, tanks lay about, disabled. Each had its name chalked upon it: *Mimi, Fanchette, Zephyr.* One that stood lopsided, its guns rakishly tilted, was called *Inexorable.*

On the day that news came of the bombing of Paris, a last French film reached Bucharest, like a last cry out of France. It showed refugees trudging a long, straight road; feet, the wheels of perambulators, faces furtively glancing back; children by the roadside drinking in turn from a mug; the wing of a swooping plane, a spatter of bullets, a child spread-eagled on the road. The French film cried: "Pity us"; the German film that followed derided pity.

Out of the smoke of some lost city appeared the German tanks. They followed each other in an endless stream into the sunlight, driving down from Ypres and Ostend. A signboard said: *Lille—5 kilomètres.* There seemed to be no resistance. The Maginot Line was being skirted. The break-through had been so simple, it was like a joke.

And the fair-haired young men standing up in their tanks came unscathed and laughing from the ruins. They held their faces up to the sun. They sang: "What does it matter if we destroy the world? When it is ours, we'll build it up again."

The tanks, made monstrous by the camera's tilt, passed in thousands —or, so it seemed. The audience—an audience that still thought in terms of cavalry—sat watching, motionless, in silence. This might of armor was a new thing; a fearful and merciless thing. The golden boys changed their song. Now, as the vast procession passed, they sang:

> *"Wir wollen keine Christen sein,*
> *Weil Christus war ein Judenschwein.*
> *Und seine Mutter, welch ein Hohn,*
> *Die heisst Marie, gebor'ne Kohn."*

Someone gasped. There was no other noise.

Harriet, alone this time, at a matinée, surrounded by women, felt they were stunned. Yet, as she left in the crowd, she heard in its appalled whispering a twitter of excitement. One woman said: "Such beautiful young men!" and another replied: "They were like the gods of war!"

It was strange to emerge into the streets and see the buildings standing firm. Harriet now had somewhere to go. She went straight to the

Athénée Palace garden, that had become a meeting-place for the English since they were dispossessed of the English Bar.

The bar itself had been occupied by the Germans one morning at the end of May. The move was obviously deliberate. It was a gesture, jubilantly planned and carried out by a crowd of journalists, businessmen and members of the huge Embassy retinue. The English—only three were present at the time—let themselves be elbowed out without a struggle. The Germans had the advantage of their aggressive bad manners, the English the disadvantage of their dislike of scenes.

Galpin was the first of the three to pick up his glass and go. Before he went, he spoke his mind. "Just at the moment," he said, "I can't stomach sight, sound or stench of a Nazi." He walked out and his compatriots followed him.

There were more Germans in the vestibule. Germans were crowding through the public rooms into the dining-room. Some sort of celebratory luncheon was about to take place. Galpin, trying to escape them, marched on, drink in hand, until he found the garden—a refuge for the routed.

The next day the Germans were back again in the bar. Apparently they had come to stay. Galpin returned to the garden: anyone who wanted him was told they could find him there. Most of the people who came in search of news had not known before that the hotel garden existed.

Galpin now spent most of his day there. It was there that his agents brought him news of Allied defeats and an occasional item of Rumanian news, such as the enforced resignation of Gafencu, the pro-British Foreign Minister, whose mother had been an Englishwoman. Other people came and went. As the situation, growing worse, became their chief preoccupation, they began to sit down and wait for news; each day they stayed longer and longer. They were drawn together by the one thing they held in common—their nationality. Because of it, they shared suspense. The waiter, understanding their situation, did not trouble them much.

Clarence, Inchcape, Dubedat and David looked in between work and rehearsals, but not, of course, Guy and Yakimov. It was thought to be a sign of those strange times that the English, the admired and privileged, the dominating influence in a cosmopolitan community, should be meeting in so unlikely a place.

# ANDRÉ GIDE

ANDRÉ GIDE was the author of more than eighty books, among them such novels as *The Immoralist, The Fruits of the Earth,* and *The Counterfeiters.* Gide, who spent the war years in North Africa, was awarded the Nobel Prize in 1947. Three wartime entries from *The Journals of André Gide* follow.

■

## FROM *The Journals of André Gide*

*14 June 1940*

That "important announcement" that Reynaud is holding in store for us, Naville thinks that . . .

Yes, that is it. And one ceases to understand where that "soul" or that "genius" of France may still be that they are claiming to save in spite of everything. Its very support is going to be taken away from it. From now on (and this was clear even the day before yesterday), the struggle is useless; our soldiers are getting killed in vain. We are at the mercy of Germany, which will strangle us as best she can. Despite everything, we shall shout very loud: "Honor is saved!" resembling that lackey in Marivaux who says: "I don't like people to show disrespect for me" while receiving a kick in the rear.

Doubtless there is no shame in being conquered when the enemy forces are so far superior, and I cannot feel any; but it is with an indescribable sorrow that I hear these phrases that exhibit all the shortcomings that have brought us to our ruin: vague and stupid idealism, ignorance of reality, improvidence, heedlessness, and absurd belief in the value of token remarks that have ceased to have credit save in the imagination of simpletons.

How can one deny that Hitler played the game in masterful fashion, not letting himself be bound by any scruple, by any rule of a game that, after all, has none; taking advantage of all our weaknesses, which he had long and skillfully favored. In the tragic light of events there suddenly appeared the deep decay of France, which Hitler knew only too well. Everywhere incoherence, lack of discipline, invoking of fanciful rights, repudiation of all duties.

What will the well-intentioned young men who yesterday were concerned with remaking France do with the miserable ruins that will remain? I am thinking of Warsaw, of Prague. . . . Will it be the same with

Paris? Will the Germans let the best of our energies breathe and recover themselves? They will not limit their attention solely to our material ruin. Today we cannot yet envisage the frightful consequences of the defeat.

We should not have won the other war. That false victory deceived us. We were not able to endure it. The relaxing that followed it brought us to our ruin. (On this subject Nietzsche spoke words of wisdom. *Thoughts out of Season.*) Yes, we were ruined by victory. But shall we let ourselves be taught by defeat? The evil goes so deep that one cannot say whether or not it is curable.

Pétain's speech is simply admirable: "Since the victory, the spirit of enjoyment has won out over the spirit of sacrifice. People claimed more than they served. They wanted to save effort; today they are meeting misfortune." It cannot be better expressed, and these words console us for all the *flatus vocis* of the radio.

*23 June*

The armistice was signed yesterday evening. And now what is going to happen?

*24 June*

Yesterday evening we heard with amazement Pétain's new speech on the radio. Can it be? Did Pétain himself deliver it? Freely? One suspects some infamous deceit. How can one speak of France as "intact" after handing over to the enemy more than half of the country? How to make these words fit those noble words he pronounced three days ago? How can one fail to approve Churchill? Not subscribe most heartily to General de Gaulle's declaration? Is it not enough for France to be conquered? Must she also be dishonored? This breaking of her word, this denunciation of the pact binding her to England, is indeed the cruelest of defeats, and this triumph of Germany the most complete, by getting France, as she hands herself over, to debase herself.

# JEAN-PAUL SARTRE

JEAN-PAUL SARTRE joined the French army in 1939 and was taken prisoner in 1940. On his release, he joined the Resistance movement, writing for its clandestine newspaper *Combat*.

Out of his wartime experiences Sartre forged *The Roads to Freedom,* a trilogy of novels: *The Age of Reason, The Reprieve,* and *Troubled Sleep.* The following excerpt has been plucked from *Troubled Sleep* (also published under the title *Iron in the Soul).*

■

## FROM *Troubled Sleep*

There was nothing in the whole world but *this* heat, *these* stones, nothing at all—save dreams. He turned into Seventh Avenue. The human tide flowed over him, its waves crested with a fine spray of bright, dead eyes. The sidewalk vibrated. Incandescent colors spattered him as he passed; steam rose from the crowd as from a damp sheet laid out in the sun. Eyes and grins everywhere: *not to grin is a sin:* eyes vague or definite, flickering or slow moving, but all of them dead. He did his best to go on pretending that these were real men: no, impossible! Everything was falling apart in his hands; his feeling of happiness ebbed. These eyes were like the eyes of portraits. Do they know that Paris has fallen? Do they give a thought to it? They were all walking with the same hurried concentration, splashing him with the white spume of their looks. They're not real at all, he thought: they're make-believe. Where *are* the real people?—certainly not here. No one here is real; *I'm* not real. A make-believe Gomez had ridden in the bus, read the paper, smiled at Ramon, talked of Picasso, looked at the Mondrians. I am striding through Paris. The Rue Royale is deserted; the Place de la Concorde is deserted; a German flag is flying over the Chamber of Deputies, an S.S. Regiment is marching under the Arc de Triomphe, the sky is dotted with aeroplanes. The brick walls crumbled, the crowd returned to the bowels of the earth, and Gomez walked lonely through the streets of Paris: through Paris, through the Truth, the only Truth, through blood and hate and defeat and death. "French swine!" he muttered, and clenched his fists: "couldn't take it, just ran like rabbits: I knew they would; I knew they were lost."

He turned right into Fifty-fifth Street, and stopped in front of a

French café-restaurant, À La Petite Coquette. He looked at the red and green façade, hesitated a moment, then pushed through the door. He wanted to see what Frenchmen were looking like today. Inside it was dark and almost cool. The blinds were lowered, the lamps lit.

It was a pleasure to find himself in artificial light. At the far end, plunged in silence and shadow, lay the restaurant. A great hulking fellow, with his hair cropped *en brosse*, was seated at the bar, staring fixedly through a pair of pince-nez. Every now and again his head dropped forward, but he recovered himself at once with a great show of dignity. Gomez sat down on one of the bar-stools. He knew the barman slightly.

"Double Scotch," he said in French: "got today's paper?"

The barman pulled a *New York Times* out of a drawer and handed it to him. He was a fair young man, melancholy and precise. But for his Burgundy accent he might have passed for a native of Lille. Gomez made a pretence of glancing through the *Times*, then, suddenly, raised his eyes. The barman was looking at him with a tired expression.

"News not too good, it it?" said Gomez.

The barman shook his head.

"Paris has fallen," said Gomez.

The barman gave a melancholy grunt, poured whisky into a small glass which he emptied into a larger one. He went through the operation a second time, and pushed the large glass in front of Gomez. The American with the pince-nez momentarily fixed them with a glassy stare, then his head dropped gently forward, as though he were bowing.

"Soda?"

"Yes."

Gomez continued unabashed:

"Afraid France is a goner."

The barman sighed but said nothing, and Gomez thought with a stab of cruel joy, that he was probably too unhappy to speak. Nevertheless, he stuck to his point, almost tenderly:

"Don't you think so?"

The barman poured mineral water into Gomez's glass. Gomez's eyes never left the lachrymose moonface. How delicious to choose his moment, to say in quite a different voice, "What did you and your lot do for Spain? It's your turn now to dance on hot bricks!"

The barman looked up with finger raised. Suddenly he began to talk. His voice was thick, slow and peaceable, slightly nasal, and marked by a strong Burgundian accent.

"One pays for everything sooner or later," he said.

Gomez chuckled.

"Yes," he said, "one pays for everything."

The barman stabbed with his finger at the air above Gomez's head —a comet announcing the end of the world. He did not look at all unhappy.

"France," he said, "is going to learn now what it costs to abandon her natural allies."

"And what precisely does that mean?" thought Gomez in sudden astonishment. He had meant to stare the other out of countenance with a look of insolent, rancorous triumph, but it was in the barman's eyes that triumph showed.

He picked his words carefully, feeling his way. "When Czechoslovakia . . ."

The barman broke in with a shrug:

"Oh, Czechoslovakia!" he said, and there was contempt in his voice.

"Well, what about Czechoslovakia?" said Gomez: "It was your fault that it fell."

The barman smiled.

"In the reign of Louis-the-Well-Beloved, sir, France had already committed every fault there was to commit."

"Ah," said Gomez: "you're a Canadian."

"I'm from Montreal," said the barman.

"Are you now?"

Gomez laid the paper down on the counter. After a brief pause he said:

"Don't you ever get any French in here?"

The barman pointed with his finger at a spot behind Gomez's back. Gomez turned. Seated at a table covered with a white cloth, an old man was dreaming over a newspaper, a *real* Frenchman, with a worn, lined, stocky face, hard, bright eyes, and a gray mustache. Compared with the florid cheeks of the American with the pince-nez, his own looked as though they had been carved out of some inferior material. A *genuine* Frenchman, with genuine despair in his heart.

"Ah," said he: "I hadn't noticed him."

# ELIZABETH BOWEN

THE ANGLO-IRISH NOVELIST and short story writer
Elizabeth Bowen was considered one of the great writers about the Blitz. She was born in Dublin but lived
for ten years in London. Her novels include *Eva Trout,
The House in Paris,* and *The Death of the Heart.* The
following excerpt is taken from what was possibly her
most famous novel, *The Heat of the Day.*

■

## FROM *The Heat of the Day*

What the inheritance came to be for Roderick, Robert was for Stella
—a habitat. The lovers had for two years possessed a hermetic world,
which, like the ideal book about nothing, stayed itself on itself by its
inner force. They had first met in London in September 1940, when
Robert, discharged from hospital after a Dunkirk wound, came to the
War Office. The damage was to a knee; it had left its trace on his walk in
an inequality which could be called a limp; he was not likely again to see
active service. That honorable queerness about his gait varied: at times
he could control it out of existence, at others he fairly pitched along with
an impatient exaggeration of lameness further exaggerated by his height.
The variation, she had discovered, had like that in a stammer a psychic
cause—it was a matter of whether he did or did not, that day, feel like a
wounded man. Her awareness, his unawareness of that was so deep a
component of their intimacy that she wondered what, had they met
before 1940, would have taken the place between them of his uncertain
knee. The first few times they met she had not noticed the limp—or, if,
vaguely, she had, she had put it down to the general rocking of London
and one's own mind.

They had met one another, at first not very often, throughout that
heady autumn of the first London air raids. Never had any season been
more felt; one bought the poetic sense of it with the sense of death. Out
of mists of morning charred by the smoke from ruins each day rose to a
height of unmisty glitter; between the last of sunset and first note of the
siren the darkening glassy tenseness of evening was drawn fine. From the
moment of waking you tasted the sweet autumn not less because of an
acridity on the tongue and nostrils; and as the singed dust settled and
smoke diluted you felt more and more called upon to observe the daytime as a pure and curious holiday from fear. All through London, the

ropings-off of dangerous tracts of street made islands of exalted if stricken silence, and people crowded against the ropes to admire the sunny emptiness on the other side. The diversion of traffic out of blocked main thoroughfares into byways, the unstopping phantasmagoric streaming of lorries, buses, vans, drays, taxis, past modest windows and quiet doorways set up an overpowering sense of London's organic power—somewhere here was a source from which heavy motion boiled, surged and, not to be dammed up, forced for itself new channels.

The very soil of the city at this time seemed to generate more strength: in parks the outsize dahlias, velvet and wine, and the trees on which each vein in each yellow leaf stretched out perfect against the sun blazoned out the idea of the finest hour. Parks suddenly closed because of time-bombs—drifts of leaves in the empty deckchairs, birds afloat on the dazzlingly silent lakes—presented, between the railings which still girt them, mirages of repose. All this was beheld each morning more lightheadedly: sleeplessness disembodied the lookers-on.

In reality there were no holidays; few were free however light-headedly to wander. The night behind and the night to come met across every noon in an arch of strain. To work or think was to ache. In offices, factories, ministries, shops, kitchens the hot yellow sands of each afternoon ran out slowly; fatigue was the one reality. You dared not envisage sleep. Apathetic, the injured and dying in the hospitals watched light change on walls which might fall tonight. Those rendered homeless sat where they had been sent; or, worse, with the obstinacy of animals retraced their steps to look for what was no longer there. Most of all the dead, from mortuaries, from under cataracts of rubble, made their anonymous presence—not as today's dead but as yesterday's living—felt through London. Uncounted, they continued to move in shoals through the city day, pervading everything to be seen or heard or felt with their torn-off senses, drawing on this tomorrow they had expected—for death cannot be so sudden as all that. Absent from the routine which had been life, they stamped upon that routine their absence—not knowing who the dead were, you could not know which might be the staircase somebody for the first time was not mounting this morning, or at which street corner the newsvendor missed a face, or which trains and buses in the homegoing rush were this evening lighter by at least one passenger.

These unknown dead reproached those left living not by their death, which might any night be shared, but by their unknownness, which could not be mended now. Who had the right to mourn them, not having cared that they had lived? So, among the crowds still eating, drinking, working, traveling, halting, there began to be an instinctive movement to break down indifference while there was still time. The wall between the living and the living became less solid as the wall between the living and the dead thinned. In that September transparency people became transparent, only to be located by the just darker flicker of their hearts.

Strangers saying "Goodnight, good luck," to each other at street corners, as the sky first blanched, then faded with evening, each hoped not to die that night, still more not to die unknown.

That autumn of 1940 was to appear, by two autumns later, apocryphal, more far away than peace. No planetary round was to bring again that particular conjunction of life and death; that particular psychic London was to be gone forever; more bombs would fall, but not on the same city. War moved from the horizon to the map. And it was now, when you no longer saw, heard, smelled war, that a deadening acclimatization to it began to set in. The first generation of ruins, cleaned up, shored up, began to weather—in daylight they took their places as a norm of the scene; the dangerless nights of September two years later blotted them out. It was from this new insidious echoless propriety of ruins that you breathed in all that was most malarial. Reverses, losses, deadlocks now almost unnoticed bred one another; every day the news hammered one more nail into a consciousness which no longer resounded. Everywhere hung the heaviness of the even worse you could not be told and could not desire to hear. This was the lightless middle of the tunnel. Faith came down to a slogan, desperately re worded to catch the eye, requiring to be pasted each time more strikingly on to hoardings and bases of monuments. . . . No, no virtue was to be found in the outward order of things: happy those who could draw from some inner source.

# KAY BOYLE

THE MINNESOTA-BORN novelist, short story writer, and poet Kay Boyle spent some thirty years in Europe, the setting for a good deal of her fiction. The opening pages of her short story "Defeat," for which she won the O. Henry Memorial Award in 1941, follow.

■

## Defeat

Towards the end of June that year and through July, there was a sort of uncertain pause, an undetermined suspension that might properly be called neither an armistice nor a peace, and it lasted until the men began coming back from where they were. They came at intervals, trickling down from the north in twos or threes, or even one by one, some of them prisoners who had escaped and others merely a part of that individual retreat in which the sole destination was home. They had exchanged their uniforms for something else as they came along—corduroys, or workmen's blue, or whatever people might have given them in secret to get away in—bearded, singularly and shabbily outfitted men getting down from a bus or off a train without so much as a knapsack in their hands and all with the same bewildered, scarcely discrepant story to tell. Once they had reached the precincts of familiarity, they stood there a moment where the vehicle had left them, maybe trying to button the jacket that didn't fit them or set the neck or shoulders right, like men who have been waiting in a courtroom and have finally heard their names called and stand up to take the oath and mount the witness stand. You could see them getting the words ready—revising the very quality of truth—and the look in their eyes, and then someone coming out of the post office or crossing the station square in the heat would recognize them and go toward them with a hand out, and the testimony would begin.

They had found their way back from different places, by different means, some on bicycle, some by bus, some over the mountains on foot, coming home to the Alpes-Maritimes from Rennes, or from Clermont-Ferrand, or from Lyons, or from any part of France, and looking as incongruous to modern defeat as survivors of the Confederate Army might have looked, transplanted to this year and place (with their spurs still on and their soft-brimmed, dust-whitened hats), limping wanly back, half dazed and not yet having managed to get the story of what happened straight. Only, this time, they were the men of that tragically unarmed and undirected force which had been the French Army once but was no longer, returning to what orators might call reconstruction but which they knew could never be the same.

Wherever they came from, they had identical evidence to give: that the German ranks had advanced bareheaded, in short-sleeved summer shirts—young blond-haired men with their arms linked, row on row, and their trousers immaculately creased, having slept all night in hotel beds and their stomachs full, advancing singing and falling singing before the puny coughing of the French machine-guns. That is, the first line of them might fall, and part of the second, possibly, but never more, for just then the French ammunition would suddenly expire and the bright-haired blond demi-gods would march on singing across their dead. Then would follow all the glittering display: the rust-proof tanks and guns, the chromium electric kitchens, the crematoriums. Legends or truth, the stories became indistinguishable in the mouths of the Frenchmen who returned—that the Germans were dressed as if for tennis that summer, with nothing but a tune to carry in their heads, while the French crawled out from under lorries where they'd slept maybe for every night for a week, going to meet them like crippled, encumbered miners emerging from the pit of a warfare fifty years interred with thirty-five kilos of kit and a change of shoes and a tin helmet left over from 1914 breaking them in two as they met the brilliantly nickeled Nazi dawn. They said their superiors were the first to run; they said their ammunition had been sabotaged; they said the ambulances had been transformed into accommodations for the officers' lady friends; they said *Nous avons été vendus* or *On nous a vendu* over and over, until you could have made a popular song of it—the words and the music of defeat. After their testimony was given, some of them added (not the young but those who had fought before) in grave, part embittered, part vainglorious voices, "I'm ashamed to be a Frenchman" or "I'm ashamed of being French today," and then gravely took their places with the others.

# JEAN-PAUL SARTRE

AS A SOLDIER in World War II and then as a member of the Resistance, Jean-Paul Sartre saw the war at firsthand and wrote three novels based on his experiences: *The Age of Reason, The Reprieve,* and *Troubled Sleep.*

■

## FROM *Troubled Sleep*

Outside was the white cascade of the day, the lunatic stammer of machine-guns. The house was dark and cool. He walked over to the door: he'd got to make a plunge into that surf of light. A small square, the church, the war-memorial, piles of manure in front of the houses. Between two blazing buildings the road looked pink under the morning sun. The Germans were there, thirty men or so, all busy, workmen on the job. They were firing on the church with a Schnellfeuerkanon, and being shot at from the tower. The place looked like a builder's yard. In the middle of the square, beneath the cross-fire, a number of French soldiers in shirtsleeves, their eyes red with sleep, were tiptoeing along, with short, hurried steps, like so many competitors filing past the judges at a beauty contest. Their pale hands were raised above their heads. The sun played antics between their fingers. Brunet looked at them. He looked at the church-tower. To his right a large building was in flames: he could feel the heat on his face. "Hell!" he said, and went down the three steps into the street. It was all over: he was taken. He kept his hands in his pockets: they felt as heavy as lead. "Stick 'em up!" There was a German with his rifle pointing straight at him. He flushed. His hands rose slowly until they were in the air above his head: they shall pay for that with blood! He joined the Frenchmen and tripped along with them —it's just like a film, nothing looks real: those bullets won't kill anyone, and the gun's firing blanks. One of the Frenchmen doubled up and fell. Brunet stepped over him. Without hurrying, he turned the corner of a brown house and emerged on to the main road at the same moment as the church-tower collapsed. No more Jerries, no more bullets, the film was over. He was in the open country. He put his hands back in his pockets. All round him were Frenchmen, a crowd of little Frenchmen in khaki; unwashed, unshaved, their faces blackened with smoke, laughing, joking, talking together in low voices, a bobbing sea of bare heads and forage caps—not a helmet among them. There were recognitions and greetings. "Saw you at Saverne in December! Hello, Girard, how goes it? Takes a defeat, don't it, to get one so's one can meet one's pals? Lisa O.K.?" A single German soldier, with a bored look and his rifle slung, was in charge of this herd of the undersized and vanquished, matching his long slow stride to the patter of their progress. Brunet pattered with the rest, though in size he was the Jerry's equal, and was no less well-shaved than him. The pink road wound between stretches of grass. There was not a breath of air, only the stifling stillness of defeat. The men smelt strong. They chattered away and the birds sang. Brunet turned to his neighbor, a large, kindly-looking fellow who was breathing through his mouth. "Where does this lot come from?" "Saverne: we spent the night billeted in the farms." "I came on my own," said Brunet. "All this is a damn' nuisance, I thought the village was deserted." A young, fair-haired chap, with a suntanned face, was walking a couple of files from him. He was stripped to the waist, and had a great bleeding scab between his shoulder-blades. To the rear of the column a vast hubbub had developed, a normal, everyday sound of shouts and laughter and the scrabbling of boots on the surface of the road. It sounded like the noise of wind in the trees. Brunet turned his head. By this time the number of men behind him had run into thousands. Prisoners had been mopped up from here, there, and everywhere; from the fields, from the hamlets, from the farms. Brunet showed head and shoulders above the rest, a solitary landmark in the undulating sea of heads. "I'm Moulu," said the big chap: "from Bar-le-Duc," he added with pride: "know this part of the world like the back of me 'and." At the side of the road a farm was burning. The flames looked black in the sunlight. A dog was howling. "Hear that tyke?" said Moulu to his neighbor: "bin and shut him up in the house." The man he was speaking to hailed, obviously, from the North: he was fair, medium-sized, with a skin like milk, and bore a strong resemblance to the Jerry in charge of them. He frowned and looked at Moulu with large blue eyes. "What's that?" "The dog: he's inside." "Well, what of it?" said the northerner: "it's only a dog" . . . "Ouah! ouah! ouah! ouah!" . . . this time it was not the dog howling, but the young fellow with the naked back. Someone was dragging him along with one hand clamped over his mouth. Brunet had a glimpse of his large, pale, frightened face with its lashless eyes. "Charpin don't seem too good," said Moulu to the northerner. The other stared at him: "Eh?" "I said your pal Charpin don't seem too good." The northerner laughed, displaying very white teeth: "Always has bin a bit odd!" The road began to climb. All about them was a delicious smell of sun-warmed stone and wood smoke. Behind them the dog was still howling. They reached the top of the hill. The road began to descend steeply. Moulu jerked his thumb in the direction of the interminable column. "Where's all this lot come from?" He turned to Brunet: "How many should you say there are?" "Don't know, maybe ten thousand, maybe more." Moulu looked at him incredulously. "Mean to say you can tell that just by looking at 'em?" Brunet thought of the Fourteenth of July, of the First of May, when they used to have chaps posted along the Boulevard Richard-Lenoir, whose job it was to estimate the numbers demonstrating by judging the time it took the columns to pass a given point. The crowd on those occasions had been silent and hot. If one was in the middle of them it was stifling. This one was noisy, but cold and dead. He smiled: "I've got the trick of it." "Where are we going?" asked the northerner. "Search me!" "Where are the Fritzes? Who's in charge of this little lot?" The only Fritzes they saw were the ones they passed along the road, amounting to about ten. The herd slid down the hill as though propelled by its own weight. "Enough to make a bloke proper fed up!" said Moulu. "You bet it is," said Brunet. It *was* enough to make a loke fed up. There were enough of them to overwhelm the Germans, strangle them, and make off across the fields. But what good would that do? On they trudged, straight ahead, as the road took them. A while back they had been at the bottom of the hill, in a kind of cup, now they were climbing, and felt hot. Moulu took from his pocket a bundle of letters held together by an elastic band, and for a while turned it over and over in his great clumsy fingers. Sweat made stains on the paper, causing the violet ink to run. Then he took off the elastic band, and started to tear the letters up. He did this methodically, without re-reading them, and scattered the fragments with the movement of a man sowing seed. Brunet followed their eddying progress with his eyes. Most of them fell, like showers of confetti, on the men's shoulders, and from there to their feet. One there was which fluttered for a moment or two and then settled on a tuft of grass. The blades bent slightly, upholding it like a canopy. There were other pieces of paper all along the road, some torn, some scrabbled up, some crumpled into balls. They lay in the ditches, among the broken rifles and dinted helmets. Where the writing was round and elongated, Brunet could make out an occasional sentence: eat well, don't expose yourself, Hélène has come with the children, all yours, darling. The road was one long, dirtied love-letter. Small flabby monsters crouched low on the ground, watching the gay convoy of defeated men with sightless eyes—gas-masks. Moulu nudged Brunet with his elbow and pointed to one of them. "Lucky we didn't have to use 'em!" Brunet said nothing, and Moulu looked about for someone else to confide in. "Hey! Lambert!" A man in front of Brunet turned his head. Moulu silently pointed to a mask, and they both began to laugh. The others near them joined in. They were filled with hatred of the parasitic grubs of which once they had been so frightened, yet had to care for and keep efficient. Now they lay beneath their feet, smashed, useless, and the sight of them was a further reminder that the war was over. Peasants, who had come as usual to the fields to work, watched the men pass, leaning on their spades. Lambert was in a gay mood, and shouted to them: "Morning, daddy: we're the boys they called up!" Ten voices, a hundred, repeated the words with a kind of defiance: "We're the boys they called up! we're the boys they called up—and we're going home!" The peasants said nothing. It was as though they had not heard. A fair-haired youth with frizzed hair, who looked as though he came from Paris, turned to Lambert. "How long d'you think it'll be?" he asked. "Pretty soon," said Lambert; "pretty soon, Goldilocks." "Really think so? —you sure?" "Look for yerself. Where's the blokes who ought to be guarding us? If we was prisoners good and proper, we'd be regularly hemmed in." "Why did they capture us, then?" asked Moulu. "Capture? —they didn't capture us—they've just put us aside so's we shan't get in the way while they're advancing." "Even so," sighed Goldilocks, "It might be quite a while." "You daft?—why, they can't run fast enough to keep up with our lot!" He was as merry as a cricket, and laughing all the while. Nothing for old Fritz to do: just a pleasure jaunt in the country with a nice little bit o' skirt in Paris, a drink or two at Dijon, and a bowl of bouillabaisse at Marseilles. Marseilles'll be the end: "damn it all, it must be! They can't go no further than Marseilles, 'cos of the sea! When they get there, they'll turn us loose. We shall be home by the middle of August." Goldilocks shook his head—"You're in a thundering hurry: they got to mend the railways, haven't they?—so's they can get the trains running." "They can keep their trains for all I care," said Moulu: "if that's all we're waiting for, I don't mind doing it on me flat feet!" "Hell! —not for this baby! I bin walking for the last fortnight, and I've just about had it. Bit of comfort's what I want!" "How about having a tumble with your girl?" "What'll I use? I've done so much footslogging, I don't seem to have nothing inside me pants. All I want's a bit of sleep, with the bed to meself!" Brunet listened to them. He looked at the backs of their necks, and he thought what a lot of work there was for him to do. Poplars, poplars, a bridge over a stream, more poplars. "Makes a fellow feel thirsty," said Moulu. "It's not the thirst I mind," said the northerner, "so much as the hunger: haven't had a bite since yesterday." Moulu was sweating profusely as he jogged along, and panting. He took off his tunic, put it across his arm, and unbuttoned his shirt. "Any'ow there's no one to stop a bloke from taking off his coat," he said with a grin. There was a sudden halt, and Brunet bumped into the back of the man in front of him, who happened to be Lambert. Lambert turned round. He had a Newgate fringe and sharp little eyes under thick-growing black brows. "Why can't yer look where yer going, clumsy! Haven't you got eyes in yer face?" He looked at Brunet's uniform with an insolent expression. "Non-coms is out—no one's giving orders now—just reglar fellers, that's what we are—all of us!" Brunet returned his look, but without anger, and the man said no more. Brunet found himself wondering what his job in civil life was likely to be: small shopkeeper? clerk?—lower-middle-class, anyhow, that was quite certain. Must be hundreds of thousands like him—with no feeling for authority and no sense of personal cleanliness. There'd have to be iron discipline. "What we stopping for?" asked Moulu. Brunet made no reply. Another lower-middle-class product: not much difference between him and the other, except he was stupider. Not easy material to work on. Moulu heaved a sigh of contentment, and began to fan himself. "P'raps we got time for a sit-down?" He put his haversack by the roadside and squatted on it. The German soldier came up and stood staring at them with his long, handsome, expressionless face. There was a vague look of sympathy in his blue eyes. Speaking slowly and carefully, he said: "Poor French—war over—you go home— home." "What's he say?—that we're going home?—should damn' well think we *are* going home! Hear that, Julien, says we're going home—ask him when!" "Give us the low-down, Fritzy, *when* are we going home?" Their attitude to him was at once servile and familiar. He might represent the army of the victors, but he was only a footslogger after all! The German, still with his blank stare, repeated what he had already said: "You go home—home!" "Yes, but *when*?" "Poor French, you go home!" The column started to move again . . . poplars, poplars . . . Moulu groaned: he was hot, thirsty, and tired: he wanted to stop. No one could check this plodding progress, because there was nobody in command. Somebody grunted, "Me head's splitting," and trudged on. The talk began to flag: there were long spells of silence. The same thought was in every mind: "surely we're not going on walking like this all the way to Berlin?" But no one stopped. Each man followed the man ahead, pushed along by the man behind. A village. On the square was a pile of helmets, gas-masks, and rifles. "Poudroux," said Moulu: "come through it yesterday." "So did I," said Goldilocks, "yesterday evening—in a lorry. Folks were all out on their doorsteps—didn't look too pleased to see us." They were there now, on the doorsteps, their arms folded, silent: women with black hair, black eyes, and black dresses, and old men: all staring. Confronted by these spectators, the prisoners straightened up: their faces became peaky and cynical: they waved their hands, they laughed and shouted, "Hello, ma! Hello, pa!—we're the lads!—war's over!—so long!" They passed in an agitation of greeting, ogling the girls, smiling provocatively. But the spectators said nothing—just looked. Only the grocer's wife, a fat, good-natured creature, murmured—"Poor boys." The man from the North smiled gleefully. "Good thing we're not where I come from!" he said to Lambert. "Why?" "They'd 'a' bin chucking the furniture at us!" . . . A water-trough: ten, a hundred broke from the ranks in their eagerness to drink. Moulu was one of them. He leaned down clumsily, greedily. They slaked their weariness: their shoulders moved spasmodically: the water ran over their faces. The German guard seemed not to notice them. They could have stayed in the village had they been brave enough to face the inhabitants' hostile eyes: but they made no effort to do so. One by one they came back, hurrying, as though they feared to miss their places in the line. Moulu's run was like a woman's—knock-kneed. They jostled one another, laughing and shouting, shameless and provocative as a crowd of nattering washerwomen, their mouths gaping with merriment, their eyes abject like the eyes of beaten dogs. Moulu wiped his lips. "That was good, that was! You not thirsty?" Brunet shrugged his shoulders but said nothing. Pity this mob wasn't surrounded by five hundred soldiers with fixed bayonets, prodding the laggards and bashing the chatterers with their butts! *That'd* take the grins off their faces! He looked to right and left. He turned his head, seeking, in all this forest of lost, hysterical features twisted into masks of irrepressible gaiety, for someone like himself. Where were the Comrades? Not hard to tell a Communist when you see him. Oh, for one face, one hard, calm, controlled face, for something that might have betokened a man! But no: under-sized, nimble, mean, they sloped along, their ferrety muzzles pressing ever onward, the facile mobility of their race showing through the dirt, twitching their mouths like the mouths of puppets, compressing or dilating their nostrils, wrinkling their foreheads, making their eyes sparkle: no good for anything but to appraise, to draw fine distinctions, to argue and judge and criticize, to weigh the pros and cons, to savor objections, to demonstrate, to draw conclusions—an interminable syllogism in which each one of them was a term. On they slouched obedient, argumentative, unworried by their fate. The war was over: they had seen no fighting: the Germans weren't a bad lot: unworried because they fondly imagined that they had summed up their new masters, and were intent on hoarding the fruits of their intelligence—that specifically French *article de luxe*—so that they could later use it to advantage with the Jerries as coin with which to buy a few trivial concessions. Poplars . . . poplars: the sun blazing down on them: noon. "That's them!"—gone suddenly all sign of intelligence from the crowded faces. A groan of delight rose from the vast concourse, not a cry, not even a murmur, but, rather, a sort of wordless, passive reflex of admiration, like the gentle susurration of leaves under a shower of rain. "That's them!" Back and forth the words passed down the line, traveling from man to man like a rumor of good news. The ranks crowded together, jostling into the gutter. A shudder went through the human caterpillar. A column of Germans was moving down the road; Germans in cars and tractors and lorries, freshly shaven, freshly rested, tanned, handsome, calm, remote as Alpine pastures. They had eyes for no one, but sat there staring southward, driving into the heart of France, upright and silent: getting a free trip—foot-slogging on wheels—that's what I *call* a war—look at them machine-guns—and the mobile artillery—all A1 stuff—no wonder we lost the war! They were delighted that the Germans should be so strong, feeling themselves by so much less to blame: "unbeatable—say what you like—unbeatable!" Brunet looked at the defeated mob caught up in a frenzy of wonder and admiration, and he thought: "This is the material I've got to work on—pretty poor stuff, but that can't be helped:

it's all I have. One can always work on what's to hand, and there must be one or two in this little lot who will respond to treatment." By this time the German column had gone by. The human caterpillar had crawled off the road on to what had been a basket-ball ground. The prisoners swarmed over it like an ooze of black pitch. They sat and lay about with old newspapers spread over their faces to keep off the sun. The whole place looked like a racecourse, or the Bois de Vincennes on a Sunday. "What've we stopped for?" "Don't know," said Brunet. The sight of all these men stretched on their backs got on his nerves. He had no wish to sit down, but realized that he was being merely stupid. No use despising them: that was the surest way of bungling his job. Besides, there was no knowing how far they would have to go, and he'd got to husband his strength. He sat down. Behind him, first one German, then another, sauntered past. They grinned at him in friendly fashion, saying with kindly irony: "Where are the English?" He looked at their boots of soft black leather, but said nothing. The Germans took themselves off, all but one lanky Feldwebel who stayed behind and said in tones of reproachful melancholy: "Where are the English?—poor old Frenchies, where you think the English are?" No one answered him, and he stood there, shaking his head. As soon as the Jerries were at a safe distance, Lambert gave his answer between clenched teeth: "Search me! but wherever they are you'll have to run pretty fast to get the English out of your hair!" "Ouais!" said Moulu: "Eh?" "Perhaps," explained Moulu, "the English *will* get in Jerry's hair, but just at the moment he's in theirs, good and proper, and not so very far away, either." "Who says so?" "It's a sure thing, you silly bugger. It's easy for them to talk big when they're tucked away in their island, but just you wait until the Fritzes have got across the Channel. If we French couldn't win the war, it's a damn' sure thing the *English* won't."

# ALUN LEWIS

THE WELSH POET and short story writer Alun Lewis
was killed in Burma in 1944.

■

## Raiders' Dawn

Softly the civilized
Centuries fall,
Paper on paper,
Peter on Paul.

And lovers waking
From the night—
Eternity's masters,
Slaves of Time—
Recognize only
The drifting white
Fall of small faces
In pits of lime.

Blue necklace left
On a charred chair
Tells that Beauty
Was startled there.

# GEORGE BERNARD SHAW

THE *ENCYCLOPÆDIA BRITANNICA* has dubbed GBS "the most significant British playwright since the 17th century," a reputation based on such plays as *Caesar and Cleopatra, Man and Superman, Major Barbara,* and *Saint Joan.* Shaw was awarded the Nobel Prize for Literature in 1925. The following note comes from his *Collected Letters, 1926–1950,* edited by Dan H. Laurence.

■

FROM *Collected Letters,*
*1926–1950*

TO WINSTON S. CHURCHILL

[Ayot St Lawrence. Welwyn]
[T/122]                                                    [Undated: June 1940]
Dear Prime Minister
    Why not declare war on France and capture her fleet (which would gladly strike its colors to us) before A.H. recovers his breath?
    Surely that is the logic to the situation?

tactically
G. Bernard Shaw

# GEORGE ORWELL

---

THE FOLLOWING LETTER, to the editor of the now defunct weekly review *Time and Tide,* appeared in volume 2 of *The Collected Essays, Journalism and Letters of George Orwell.*

---

■

## Letter to the Editor of
## *Time and Tide*

Sir,

It is almost certain that England will be invaded within the next few days or weeks, and a large-scale invasion by sea-borne troops is quite likely. At such a time our slogan should be ARM THE PEOPLE. I am not competent to deal with the wider questions of repelling the invasion, but I submit that the campaign in France and the recent civil war in Spain have made two facts clear. One is that when the civil population is unarmed, parachutists, motor cyclists and stray tanks can not only work fearful havoc but draw off large bodies of regular troops who should be opposing the main enemy. The other fact (demonstrated by the Spanish war) is that the advantages of arming the population outweigh the danger of putting weapons in the wrong hands. By-elections since the war started have shown that only a tiny minority among the common people of England are disaffected, and most of these are already marked down.

ARM THE PEOPLE is in itself a vague phrase, and I do not, of course, know what weapons are available for immediate distribution. But there are at any rate several things that can and should be done *now,* i.e. within the next three days:

1. Hand-grenades. These are the only modern weapon of war that can be rapidly and easily manufactured, and they are one of the most useful. Hundreds of thousands of men in England are accustomed to using hand-grenades and would be only too ready to instruct others. They are said to be useful against tanks and will be absolutely necessary if enemy parachutists with machine-guns manage to establish themselves in our big towns. I had a front-seat view of the street fighting in Barcelona in May 1937, and it convinced me that a few hundred men with machine-guns can paralyze the life of a large city, because of the fact that a bullet will not penetrate an ordinary brick wall. They can be blasted out with artillery, but it is not always possible to bring a gun to bear. On the other

hand, the early street fighting in Spain showed that armed men can be driven out of stone buildings with grenades or even sticks of dynamite if the right tactics are used.

2. Shotguns. There is talk of arming some of the Local Defence Volunteer contingents with shotguns. This may be necessary if all the rifles and Bren guns are needed for the regular troops. But in that case the distribution should be made *now* and all weapons should be immediately requisitioned from the gunsmiths' shops. There was talk of doing this weeks ago, but in fact many gunsmiths' windows show rows of guns which are not only useless where they are, but actually a danger, as these shops could easily be raided. The powers and limitations of the shotgun (with buckshot, lethal up to about sixty yards) should be explained to the public over the radio.

3. Blocking fields against aircraft landings. There has been much talk of this, but it has only been done sporadically. The reason is that it has been left to voluntary effort, i.e. to people who have insufficient time and no power of requisitioning materials. In a small, thickly populated country like England we could within a very few days make it impossible for an airplane to land anywhere except at an aerodrome. All that is needed is the labor. Local authorities should therefore have powers to conscript labor and requisition such materials as they require.

4. Painting out place-names. This has been well done as regards signposts, but there are everywhere shopfronts, tradesmen's vans etc., bearing the name of their locality. Local authorities should have the power to enforce the painting-out of these immediately. This should include the brewers' names on public houses. Most of these are confined to a fairly small area, and the Germans are probably methodical enough to know this.

5. Radio sets. Every Local Defence Volunteer headquarters should be in possession of a radio receiving set, so that if necessary it can receive its orders over the air. It is fatal to rely on the telephone in a moment of emergency. As with weapons, the Government should not hesitate to requisition what it needs.

All of these are things that could be done within the space of a very few days. Meanwhile, let us go on repeating ARM THE PEOPLE, in the hope that more and more voices will take it up. For the first time in decades we have a Government with imagination,[1] and there is at least a chance that they will listen.

I am, etc.<br>George Orwell

Time and Tide, *22 June 1940*

[1] On 10 May the Chamberlain Government had fallen and Winston Churchill became Prime Minister at the head of a Coalition Government.

# STEPHEN SPENDER

THE POET AND CRITIC Stephen Spender, raised in Hampstead, went on to University College, Oxford, where he met W. H. Auden, Louis MacNeice, and Christopher Isherwood. In 1932, they published together in an anthology titled *New Signatures.*

   Spender was a member of the National Fire Service during World War II.

■

## Air Raid Across the Bay at Plymouth

### I

Above the whispering sea
And waiting rocks of black coast,
Across the bay, the searchlight beams
Swing and swing back across the sky.

Their ends fuse in a cone of light
Held for a bright instant up
Until they break away again
Smashing that image like a cup.

### II

Delicate aluminum girders
Project phantom aerial masts
Swaying crane and derrick
Above the sea's just surging deck.

### III

Triangles, parallels, parallelograms,
Experiment with hypotheses
On the blackboard sky,
Seeking that X
Where the raider is met
Two beams cross
To chalk his loss.

### IV

A buzz, felt as ragged but unseen
Is chased by two Excaliburs of light
A thud. An instant gleams
Gold sequins shaken from a black-silk screen.

### V

Round the coast, the waves
Chuckle between rocks.
In the fields, the corn
Rustles with metallic clicks.

# JULIAN MACLAREN-ROSS

---

THAT UNDERESTIMATED and unjustly neglected writer Julian Maclaren-Ross—short story writer, novelist, and critic—was educated in Paris and the south of France and went on to become a legend in his time in Soho, a regular at the Mandrake, the Gargoyle, and other choice watering holes.

---

■

## They Can't Give You a Baby

*A BIG LAKE*

"They can do anything to you in the army bar give you a baby," the old London-Irish porter who'd had varicocele and served in four campaigns told me as I got aboard the train in July 1940. "But keep your trap shut and your bowels open you can't come to no harm."

So I reported as ordered to the Infantry Training camp at Blandford, Essex, and was there enlisted as No. 6027033 Private Ross J.

Further advice was offered me on arrival by an older recruit who said: "Take my tip, mate, when they put you down for the range don't go on the piss the night before and don't go with no woman neither 'cause you can't shoot proper with a shaking hand," but this advice was wasted because the only drink available in the camp was Naafi beer which certainly resembled piss but was not drunk-making enough to send one on it; no women were allowed in; and we for the first fortnight weren't allowed out.

Besides, going on the range was out of the question as none of us had so far been issued with rifles: since Dunkirk, in short supply.

The survivors from Dunkirk had been billeted for a short time in the camp on their return, and the latrine walls were decorated with drawings of a death's head above a grave-mound, underlined with the caption: "HOW D'YOU LIKE THIS YOU ROOKIE BASTARDS? (SIGNED) THE BOYS WHO BEEN THROUGH IT."

There was also a rhyme signed by Spokeshave the Shithouse Poet, a universal figure who seems to have served in every regiment in the British Army:

When apples are ripe
And ready for plucking
Girls of sixteen are ready for . . .

NOT WHAT YOU THINK THEY'RE READY FOR
YOU FILTHY-MINDED FUCKERS.

The camp looked from the air like a big lake, they told us, which
hadn't prevented Jerry from dropping a load on it in the not so distant
past, as craters in the surrounding chalk abundantly testified.

Every time a plane roared overhead, the blokes rushed joyfully to
the barrack hut windows, shouting "Watch out, boys, here comes Hitler!"; they made whistling noises like sticks of bombs falling, followed by
concerted shouts of "BOOM" to represent the explosion. But that summer Hitler seemed to have got sick of coming.

"That's on account of this new camouflage we got," explained our
platoon sergeant, who looked like the soldierly figure depicted on the
labels of Camp coffee bottles and claimed that we resembled not a big
lake but a big bloody shower.

So while we new recruits drilled in shirt sleeve order on the enormous sun baked barrack square, other more seasoned soldiers sprayed
the surface of sheds and buildings round about with camouflage paint
that speckled our bare arms and khaki shirts with almost indelible brown
and green spots as it was blown towards us on the wind.

We drilled at first with broomsticks owing to the dearth of rifles, then
an actual rifle appeared and was handed round the square, though our
platoon hadn't much time to learn its mechanism before a runner came
to attention in front of our sergeant saying: "Please sar'nt our sar'nt in
No. 8 says could we have the rifle for a dekko over there 'cause none of
our blokes so much as seen one yet."

We had none of us seen a steel helmet at close quarters either, they
hadn't been issued to us although a consignment in the stores awaited a
War Office or Command order authorizing distribution.

Then one afternoon, when parades were over and the blokes in our
barrack hut were rattling their mess tins all ready for tea, Hitler came at
last.

His coming was not heralded, as it should have been, by sirens (it
turned out after someone had forgotten to let these off), and a series of
dull detonations from the Artillery Camp across the valley caused little
stir, as things were always going off over there. But this time the hum of
an engine could be heard, the blokes began their whistling and booming
then stopped abruptly, dropping their mess tins, as real whistles and
crumps duplicated outside the sounds they'd made.

Through the window, from the hillside on which the Artillery Camp
was built, a tall brown flower of earth could be seen blossoming while we

watched: it expanded outwards like a firework in all directions and afterwards many swore they had seen swastikas on the wings of the lone raider
that was now heading straight towards us.

There were no NCOs present, still less an officer; we dashed to the
side doorway, got jammed in the entrance, then threw ourselves flat
beneath a whitewashed wall outside as Jerry zoomed over low, chips of
whitewash flew; and we heard for the first time in earnest the DUH-
DUH-DUH of the machine gun that had been so often mimicked in jest.

The plane dived, again the DUH-DUH-DUH, then it banked and
headed toward the Gunner camp while we made crouching for the
trenches: there was no one to lead the way there but we knew that already
since we'd helped, ourselves, to dig them in the chalk, pissing on our
palms to harden them as it was said that navvies did.

More bombs whistled down, one sounding like a direct hit; and the
Nazi plane returned, circling silver and so high above our heads it could
hardly be seen; voices from adjoining trenches shouted: "Where the
bleeding bloody officers?" and "Why'nt we got tin hats?" while somebody
shrilled hysterically: "Shut your row he'll hear us, he'll hear us I tell you
shut your bleeding row."

The Jerry pilot didn't hear them and soon ceased to hear anything
at all, for he flew away to be caught in the Bournemouth barrage and
shot down in flames so we were later told.

Directly he'd gone everyone clambered out of the trenches and
began to utter guffaws of relief and bravado, then suddenly a young
subaltern appeared panting, to mutters of "Bout time too" and "Joy your
tea, mate?," and red in the face ordered us back in until the All Clear
was blown, which happened after we'd stood tealess for another thirty
minutes in the trenches.

There were no casualties in the Artillery Camp, indeed we almost
wished Jerry had chosen us instead, for the direct hit had demolished
the Gunners' empty gym whereas ours remained intact and there were
many who hated PT, above all the Horse.

But the upshot of this baptism by fire was that we were issued with
tin hats and small arms shortly followed. First to be given a rifle was our
barrack room NCO, a lance-corporal who'd been an insurance clerk in
civvy street and now felt the chance had come to show his mettle as a
leader of men.

To demonstrate the efficacy of our new steel helmets and the protection they afforded, he clapped on his own tin hat then handing his
rifle to a huge recruit told this man to strike him with the butt.

The recruit, a gentle timid soul despite his size, demurred. "That's
an order," the lance-jack rapped out. "You either hit me or go on a 252,"
there was a pause while the nature of a 252, the minor offence report,
was explained to the huge recruit who could expect seven days to barracks if he went on one for disobeying an order; then down came the rifle

butt, blood spurted from under the tin hat's brim and the corporal sank slowly down, the sound of his fall swiftly echoed by a heavier thump as the huge recruit followed suit, having fainted at the sight of blood.

It appeared a loose screw inside the corporal's helmet had been driven into his scalp by the blow; we agreed that a screw had also been loose inside the corporal's head, and he was carted off to hospital where the huge contrite recruit visited him every day: being unable, himself, ever to handle a rifle with confidence thereafter.

Meanwhile the barrack room radio played records of Judy Garland singing "Over the Rainbow" or a tune called "I Was Watching a Man Paint a Fence"; and the camp must have ceased to look from above like a big lake, for Jerry took time off from the Battle of Britain to bomb us day and night.

Planes came over in droves, it was no longer necessary for the blokes to whistle and boom, all leave was canceled, and when not a lot of the ITC was left we were abruptly evacuated, destination unknown to all other ranks.

On arrival, after a roundabout train journey so long that we'd believed ourselves bound for Scotland, we were assembled on an enormous desert of asphalt and addressed in pitch darkness by the Commanding Officer of another ITC in Suffolk.

"Now you men have been through a bad time," he told us, "blitzed and strafed right and left by the Hun, and you've stood up to it well. But you'll be glad to hear that Jerry hasn't smelt us out so far ha ha, so you can get on with your training in peace," and at this prospect searchlights suddenly probed the sky, a German engine nosed chugging somewhere overhead, and the sirens started to wail.

# GEORGE KENNAN

THE DISTINGUISHED DIPLOMAT George Kennan was first secretary at the U.S. embassy in Berlin in 1939–1940. The following is an excerpt from his wartime memoirs.

■

FROM *Sketches from a Life*

*July 2, 1940*

BRUSSELS—PARIS

This morning, since offers of free rides were still not forthcoming from the Germans, B. offered me one of his cars, together with the requisite quantity of gasoline; and at exactly 2 P.M. I set forth from his country place near Waterloo in a little Chevrolet bound for Paris. I had with me one of the American ambulance drivers, who was trying to get down to Paris to recover his clothes. Warned that the intervening country had been reduced by the fighting to a state of desolation which made it as uncharitable to travelers as a desert, we were armed with a bottle of drinking-water and some chocolate, to keep us alive in case we broke down on the way.

The devastation, especially south of the old Belgian frontier, was indeed formidable. All the towns were damaged; and certain large ones, particularly Valenciennes and Cambrai, were completely gutted, deserted, and uninhabitable. Here the road led through streets where the house facades were standing on both sides; but back of the facades, visible through the gaping, pane-less windows, there was wreckage and ashes and debris. In spots the odor of decomposing corpses still stole out to the streets to tell its grim message to the outside world. These communities seemed to have been entirely vacated, probably at the insistence of the military authorities, by any inhabitants who might have escaped destruction in the bombardment. They were shut off and guarded by German sentries, probably to prevent pillaging; and it affected me strangely to see these inscrutable, weatherbeaten German sentries, standing guard there over their own handiwork of destruction. As though it mattered now who stood before these shattered homes and these stinking corpses! As though this tangled litter of half-destroyed human belongings had any more value when life and hope had already been destroyed!

Refugees were laboriously making their way back northward, in search of their homes. Most were traveling on the great two-wheeled horse-drawn cart of the French peasant, which could accommodate a whole family and many of its belongings. Some were on bicycles. Some pushed baby buggies with a few parcels of belongings on them. Their faces were unforgettable, stripped of all pretense, of all falseness, of all vanity, of all self-consciousness, seared with fatigue and fear and suffering.

I saw a young girl bouncing along on top of one of the carts. Her dress was torn and soiled. She had probably not had her clothes off, or been able to wash, for days. She was resting her chin in her hand and staring fixedly down at the road. All the youth had gone out of her face. There was only a bitterness too deep for complaint, a wondering too intense for questions. What would be her reaction to life after this? Just try to tell her of liberalism and democracy, of progress, of ideals, of tradition, of romantic love; see how far you get. What is going to be her impression of humanity? Do you think she's going to come out of it a flaming little patriot? She saw the complete moral breakdown and degradation of her own people. She saw them fight with each other and stumble over each other in their blind stampede to get away and to save their possessions before the advancing Germans. She saw her own soldiers, routed, demoralized, trying to push their way back through the streams of refugees on the highways. She saw her own people pillaging and looting in a veritable orgy of dissolution as they fled before the advancing enemy; possibly she had joined in the looting herself. She saw these French people in all the ugliness of panic, defeat, and demoralization.

The Germans, on the other hand, she saw as disciplined, successful, self-confident. Their soldiers were sun-tanned, fit and good-humored. She saw them giving food and water to refugees at the crossroads, establishing camps and first-aid stations, transporting the old and the sick in their great Diesel trucks and trailers, guarding against pillaging. What soil here for German propaganda, what thorough plowing for the social revolution which National Socialism carries in its train.

As we approached Senlis, we went through a section where the road was lined for miles with litter abandoned by the French. It seemed to be mostly paper and clothing. Almost every inch of the ground was covered with it. I could explain the paper, which consisted largely of empty cartridge boxes. The clothing remains a mystery to this time, unless it was taken off of the dead and wounded.

At one place we saw a field where the Germans had corralled hundreds of stray or abandoned horses. They had some Allied prisoners, mounted, guarding them.

In the suburbs of Paris there were a few people; but the streets looked no less normal than those of Brussels. As we drove down the rue Lafayette, the passers-by became fewer and fewer. By the time we reached the Opéra, the streets were practically empty. The city was simply dead. Policemen stood listlessly on the corners, but there was no traffic to direct and no pedestrians to guard. At the Café de la Paix six German officers sat at an outside table. They looked lonely sitting there with the empty café behind them and the empty cold street before them —no passers-by to watch; no other guests to support them; no one but themselves to witness their triumph.

The Place de la Concorde was as dead as a village square at dawn on a rainy Sunday. There was no flag or shield on the American embassy. The big iron gate was closed. I went to the side door and rang. A night watchman, who viewed me with some suspicion, told me that the ambassador and Murphy (his deputy) had left for Clermont, where the new French government was. He helped me to get through a telephone call to B., who was in charge. B. asked me to come over for supper.

I dropped my ambulance driver and my baggage at the Hotel Bristol. This building had been appropriated as a place of refuge for the remaining Americans. Much of the hotel personnel was missing; the whole place had a make-shift atmosphere; but the Americans had succeeded in keeping the Germans out and were pleased enough with the arrangement.

B.'s home was in the Étoile district. The streets around there gave the impression of an abandoned city. Houses were boarded up. The stillness was oppressive. Across from B.'s house the German army had occupied a building; and while we talked in his living room, we could hear the clatter of sentry boots against the pavement, echoing among the houses.

It was after the ten o'clock curfew when I drove the car to the embassy and then walked back through the totally deserted streets to the hotel. The sad Paris policemen and the German sentries stared at the unaccustomed sight of a pedestrian and were too surprised to remonstrate. The individual at the desk in the Bristol was no less amazed to have anyone demanding entrance at that unseasonable hour, and he unbolted his doors with all the ceremony of one opening a besieged citadel.

At the hotel the ambulance driver and I, feeling much too near to the end of the world to think of sleep, cracked out a bottle of rye. We were joined by our next-door neighbor, female and no longer entirely young. She was a true product of Parisian America and was accepting her privations with such excellent good humor that she kept us in gales of laughter with the account of her experiences.

*July 3, 1940*

PARIS

Spent the morning driving around town looking up friends of friends, none of whom were there. I wondered about the reactions of the

Germans. I saw their officers in the restaurants, trying so desperately to be genteel when there was nobody to be genteel before. I heard that Goebbels was at the Ritz and thought how different that forsaken square, the Place Vendôme, must have seemed from the glamour and luxury of that place as he had pictured it. I was told that the Germans were making efforts to reopen the Casino de Paris for the benefit of their troops, but couldn't do so because all the British girls were gone and the French girls, if any could be found, were too individualistic to keep time in a chorus.

I struggled all day to find a metaphor for what had happened. Could one not say to the Germans that the spirit of Paris had been too delicate and shy a thing to stand their domination and had melted away before them just as they thought to have it in their grasp? Was there not some Greek myth about the man who tried to ravish the goddess, only to have her turn to stone when he touched her? That is literally what has happened to Paris. When the Germans came, the soul simply went out of it; and what is left is only stone. So long as they stay (and it will probably be a long time) it will remain stone. Their arrival turned the walls of a living city into the cold stones of historical monuments. And the beauties of the city had already, after a fortnight's disassociation from their own soul, begun to look faintly shabby, useless, and fantastic, like Versailles or Fontainebleau—as though they expected at any moment to be roped off and placarded and shown to tourists by guides for the rest of time.

In short, the Germans had in their embrace the pallid corpse of Paris. They will now perhaps deceive themselves into believing that the city never had a soul. That will be the most comforting conclusion for them to draw.

# RICHARD HILLARY

RICHARD HILLARY went directly from Trinity College, Oxford, into the RAF. His famous account of the Battle of Britain was titled *The Last Enemy*, from which the following is excerpted.

■

FROM *The Last Enemy*

We retired early to bed and slept until, at two o'clock in the morning, a gillie banged on the door. Colin got up, took from the gillie's hand a telegram, opened it, and read it aloud. It said: SQUADRON MOVING SOUTH STOP CAR WILL FETCH YOU AT EIGHT OCLOCK DENHOLM. For us, the war began that night.

At ten o'clock we were back at Turnhouse. The rest of the Squadron were all set to leave; we were to move down to Hornchurch, an aerodrome twelve miles east of London on the Thames Estuary. Four machines would not be serviceable until the evening, and Broody Benson, Pip Cardell, Colin, and I were to fly them down. We took off at four o'clock, some five hours after the others, Broody leading, Pip and I to each side, and Colin in the box, map-reading. Twenty-four of us flew south that tenth day of August 1940: of those twenty-four, eight were to fly back.

We landed at Hornchurch at about seven o'clock to receive our first shock. Instead of one section there were four squadrons at readiness; 603 Squadron were already in action. They started coming in about half an hour after we landed, smoke stains along the leading edges of the wings showing that all the guns had been fired. They had acquitted themselves well although caught at a disadvantage of height.

"You don't have to look for them," said Brian. "You have to look for a way out."

From this flight Don MacDonald did not return.

At this time the Germans were sending over comparatively few bombers. They were making a determined attempt to wipe out our entire fighter force, and from dawn till dusk the sky was filled with Messerschmitt 109s and 110s.

Half a dozen of us always slept over at the dispersal hut to be ready for a surprise enemy attack at dawn. This entailed being up by four-thirty and by five o'clock having our machines warmed up and the oxygen, sights and ammunition tested. The first Hun attack usually came over about breakfast-time and from then until eight o'clock at night we were almost continuously in the air. We ate when we could, baked beans and bacon and eggs being sent over from the mess.

On the morning after our arrival I walked over with Peter Howes and Broody. Howes was at Hornchurch with another squadron and worried because he had as yet shot nothing down. Every evening when we came into the mess he would ask us how many we had got and then go over miserably to his room. His squadron had had a number of losses and was due for relief. If ever a man needed it, it was Howes. Broody, on the other hand, was in a high state of excitement, his sharp eager face grinning from ear to ear. We left Howes at his dispersal hut and walked over to where our machines were being warmed up. The voice of the controller came unhurried over the loud-speaker, telling us to take off, and in a few seconds we were running for our machines. I climbed into the cockpit of my plane and felt an empty sensation of suspense in the pit of my stomach. For one second time seemed to stand still and I stared blankly in front of me. I knew that that morning I was to kill for the first time. That I might be killed or in any way injured did not occur to me. Later, when we were losing pilots regularly, I did consider it in an abstract way when on the ground; but once in the air, never. I knew it could not happen to me. I suppose every pilot knows that, knows it cannot happen to him; even when he is taking off for the last time, when he will not return, he knows that he cannot be killed. I wondered idly what he was like, this man I would kill. Was he young, was he fat, would he die with the Fuehrer's name on his lips, or would he die alone, in that last moment conscious of himself as a man? I would never know. Then I was being strapped in, my mind automatically checking the controls, and we were off.

We ran into them at 18,000 feet, twenty yellow-nosed Messerschmitt 109s, about 500 feet above us. Our squadron strength was eight, and as they came down on us we went into line astern and turned head on to them. Brian Carbury, who was leading the Section, dropped the nose of his machine, and I could almost feel the leading Nazi pilot push forward on his stick to bring his guns to bear. At the same moment Brian hauled hard back on his own control stick and led us over them in a steep climbing turn to the left. In two vital seconds they lost their advantage. I saw Brian let go a burst of fire at the leading plane, saw the pilot put his machine into a half roll, and knew that he was mine. Automatically, I kicked the rudder to the left to get him at right angles, turned the gun-button to "Fire," and let go in a four-second burst with full deflection. He came right through my sights and I saw the tracer from all eight guns thud home. For a second he seemed to hang motionless; then a jet of red flame shot upward and he spun out of sight.

For the next few minutes I was too busy looking after myself to think of anything, but when, after a short while, they turned and made off over the Channel, and we were ordered to our base, my mind began to work again.

It had happened.

My first emotion was one of satisfaction, satisfaction at a job adequately done, at the final logical conclusion of months of specialized training. And then I had a feeling of the essential rightness of it all. He was dead and I was alive; it could so easily have been the other way round; and that would somehow have been right too. I realized in that moment just how lucky a fighter pilot is. He has none of the personalized emotions of the soldier, handed a rifle and bayonet and told to charge. He does not even have to share the dangerous emotions of the bomber pilot who night after night must experience that childhood longing for smashing things. The fighter pilot's emotions are those of the duelist— cool, precise, impersonal. He is privileged to kill well. For if one must either kill or be killed, as now one must, it should, I feel, be done with dignity. Death should be given the setting it deserves; it should never be a pettiness; and for the fighter pilot it never can be.

From this flight Broody Benson did not return.

During that August-September period we were always so outnumbered that it was practically impossible, unless we were lucky enough to have the advantage of height, to deliver more than one squadron attack. After a few seconds we always broke up, and the sky was a smoke trail of individual dog-fights. The result was that the Squadron would come home individually, machines landing one after the other at intervals of about two minutes. After an hour, Uncle George would make a check-up on who was missing. Often there would be a telephone-call from some pilot to say that he had made a forced landing at some other aerodrome, or in a field. But the telephone wasn't always so welcome. It would be a rescue squad announcing the number of a crashed machine; then Uncle George would check it, and cross another name off the list. At that time, the losing of pilots was somehow extremely impersonal; nobody, I think, felt any great emotion—there simply wasn't time for it.

# VIRGINIA WOOLF

THE NOVELIST, critic, and essayist Virginia Woolf was the most celebrated of the Bloomsbury group. In 1941 —depressed by the war and, with a history of mental breakdowns, fearful of suffering another—she committed suicide by drowning.

■

## FROM A *Writer's Diary*

*Saturday, August 31st* [1940]

Now we are in the war. England is being attacked. I got this feeling for the first time completely yesterday; the feeling of pressure, danger, horror. The feeling is that a battle is going on—a fierce battle. May last four weeks. Am I afraid? Intermittently. The worst of it is one's mind won't work with a spring next morning. Of course this may be the beginning of invasion. A sense of pressure. Endless local stories. No—it's no good trying to capture the feeling of England being in a battle. I daresay if I write fiction and Coleridge and not that infernal bomb article for U.S.A. I shall swim into quiet water.

*Monday, September 2nd*

There might be no war, the past two days. Only one raid warning. Perfectly quiet nights. A lull after the attacks on London.

*Thursday, September 5th*

Hot, hot, hot. Record heat wave, record summer if we kept records this summer. At 2:30 a plane zooms: 10 minutes later air raid sounds; 20 later, all clear. Hot, I repeat; and doubt if I'm a poet. H. P. hard labor. Brain w—no, I can't think of the word—yes, wilts. An idea. All writers are unhappy. The picture of the world in books is thus too dark. The wordless are the happy: women in cottage gardens: Mrs. Chavasse. Not a true picture of the world; only a writer's picture. Are musicians, painters, happy? Is their world happier?

*Tuesday, September 10th*

Back from half a day in London—perhaps our strangest visit. When we got to Gower Street a barrier with diversion on it. No sign of damage. But coming to Doughty Street a crowd. Then Miss Perkins at the window. Mecklenburgh Square roped off. Wardens there. Not allowed in.

The house about 30 yards from ours struck at one in the morning by a bomb. Completely ruined. Another bomb in the square still unexploded. We walked round the back. Stood by Jane Harrison's house. The house was still smoldering. That is a great pile of bricks. Underneath all the people who had gone down to their shelter. Scraps of cloth hanging to the bare walls at the side still standing. A looking glass I think swinging. Like a tooth knocked out—a clean cut. Our house undamaged. No windows yet broken—perhaps the bomb has now broken them. We saw Bernal with an arm band jumping on top of the bricks. Who lived there? I suppose the casual young men and women I used to see from my window; the flat dwellers who used to have flower pots and sit in the balcony. All now blown to bits. The garage man at the back—blear eyed and jerky—told us he had been blown out of his bed by the explosion: made to take shelter in a church. "A hard cold seat," he said, "and a small boy lying in my arms. I cheered when the all clear sounded. I'm aching all over." He said the Jerries had been over for three nights trying to bomb Kings Cross. They had destroyed half Argyll Street, also shops in Grays Inn Road. Then Mr. Pritchard ambled up. Took the news as calm as a grig. "They actually have the impertinence to say this will make us accept peace . . . !" he said: he watches raids from his flat roof and sleeps like a hog. So, after talking to Miss Perkins, Mrs. Jackson—but both serene —Miss P. had slept on a camp bed in her shelter—we went on to Grays Inn. Left the car and saw Holborn. A vast gap at the top of Chancery Lane. Smoking still. Some great shop entirely destroyed: the hotel opposite like a shell. In a wine shop there were no windows left. People standing at the tables—I think drink being served. Heaps of blue green glass in the road at Chancery Lane. Men breaking off fragments left in the frames. Glass falling. Then into Lincoln's Inn. To the *New Statesman* office: windows broken, but house untouched. We went over it. Deserted. Wet passages. Glass on stairs. Doors locked. So back to the car. A great block of traffic. The Cinema behind Madame Tussaud's torn open: the stage visible; some decoration swinging. All the Regent's Park houses with broken windows, but undamaged. And then miles and miles of orderly ordinary streets—all Bayswater, and Sussex Square as usual— streets empty—faces set and eyes bleared. In Chancery Lane I saw a man with a barrow of music books. My typist's office destroyed. Then at Wimbledon a siren: people began running. We drove, through almost empty streets, as fast as possible. Horses taken out of the shafts. Cars pulled up. Then the all clear. The people I think of now are the very grimy lodging house keepers, say in Heathcote Street: with another night to face: old wretched women standing at their doors; dirty, miserable. Well—as Nessa said on the phone, it's coming very near. I had thought myself a coward for suggesting that we should not sleep two nights at 37. I was greatly relieved when Miss P. telephoned advising us not to stay, and L. agreed.

*Wednesday, September 11th*

Churchill has just spoken. A clear, measured, robust speech. Says the invasion is being prepared. It's for the next two weeks apparently if at all. Ships and barges massing at French ports. The bombing of London of course preparatory to invasion. Our majestic City—etc., which touches me, for I feel London majestic. Our courage etc. Another raid last night on London. Time bomb struck the Palace. John rang up. He was in Mecklenburgh Square the night of the raid: wants the Press moved at once. L. is to go up on Friday. Our windows are broken, John says. He is lodging out somewhere. Mecklenburgh Square evacuated. A plane shot down before our eyes just before tea: over the racecourse; a scuffle; a swerve; then a plunge; and a burst of thick black smoke. Percy says the pilot bailed out. We count now on an air raid about 8:30. Anyhow, whether or not, we hear the sinister sawing noise about then, which loudens and fades; then a pause; then another comes. "They're at it again" we say as we sit, I doing my work, L. making cigarettes. Now and then there's a thud. The windows shake. So we know London is raided again.

# GEORGE MACBETH

---

THE POET AND NOVELIST George MacBeth was born
in Lanarkshire, Scotland. He worked for many years as
a poetry and arts producer for the BBC. His *Collected
Poems, 1958–1970* was published in 1971, and in 1989
he brought out his memoir of the war years, *A Child
of the War,* from which the following is excerpted.

---

■

## FROM *A Child of the War*

The war now began in earnest. This was the autumn of the Battle
of Britain, and later of the bombing of the English cities. The first of
these events made little direct impact on my day-to-day life. I was too
young to be excited by the ominous and then exhilarating accounts on
the wireless and in the newspapers of how many German airplanes had
been shot down by our fighter pilots.

My fascination with their exploits came later. We had rationing to
contend with, and some weeks of Home Service, when lessons were
conducted in private houses as a protection, soon abandoned as impractical, against the threat of daytime air raids.

In fact, there never were any daytime air raids, despite the endless
precautions taken against them. It was in the cold of October, and after
the fall of darkness, that the German bombers began to patrol over
England.

Sometimes I would hear them, or think I did, on the brink of going
to sleep. Often, I was wrong. What I would really hear first, if there was
to be a raid, or a warning, was the sound of the sirens.

I don't think any child who survived the Second World War could
ever again hear that awesome rising and falling sound without experiencing a chill of fear. As with all wartime sources of terror, it was joked away
as moaning Minnie, but moaning Minnie was a dark lady like the witch
in *Snow White*, who dragged me half-awake out of a warm bed, and had
me carried downstairs night after night to lie on a cold floor and listen to
a remote, frightening droning interspersed with the dull, repeated thud
of anti-aircraft guns.

In the morning, I would walk along Clarkehouse Road with my eyes
glued to the pavement for shrapnel. It became the fashion to make a
collection of this, and there were few days when I came home without a

pocketful of jagged, rusting bits, like the unintelligible pieces from a scattered jigsaw of pain and violence.

Of course we didn't see them as this at the time. They were simply free toys from the sky, as available and interesting as the horse chestnuts in the Botanical Gardens, or the nippled acorns in Melbourne Avenue.

It must have been about this time that the British Restaurants were opening, with their austerity jam roll and meat balls; and our own meals were beginning to rely rather more on rissoles and home-made apple sponge. But my mother was always a good manager, and I have no sense of any sudden period of shortage or of going hungry.

Sweets were the great loss. There was no longer an everlasting, teeth-spoiling fountain of sherbet and liquorice, or of Boy Blue cream whirls, or of Cadbury's Caramello. Sweets were hard to come by, and then limited to a fixed ration.

One of the worst casualties was chocolate. The traditional division into milk and plain disappeared, and an awful intervening variety known as Ration Chocolate was born, issued in semi-transparent grease-proof wrappers, and about as appetizing as cardboard. In spite of a lifelong sweet tooth, I could never eat it.

They say that Sheffield was blitzed twice in December 1940. The first night the Germans had come to bomb the steel-works, but they mistook the main shopping street, the Moor, for that other dead straight street on the way to Rotherham which should have been their target. So the center of the city was badly hit.

Three days later the bombers came back and attacked the steel-works. In later years this has struck me both as a mark of German efficiency and as proof that their first intention was not to attack a civilian target.

However, this was too late to matter much to me. On the Thursday night when the city was bombed we had had a warning from the sirens in good time, and my mother and father had wakened me and taken me down to the hall, which we regarded, rightly or wrongly, as the safest part of the house.

There was no cellar to the house at Southbourne Road, and the long period of freedom from air raids had convinced my father that no under-ground provision against attack would be necessary. So what we did was to group ourselves in the corner of the entrance hall opposite the stairs, in a space between the kitchen and the dining-room doors. This meant that, with the doors shut, we were well away from any windows, and some distance from the potential collapse of any outside wall.

On this particular night we were wrapped up in clothes and blankets. I must have been very tired, because I dropped off to sleep almost immediately. The next thing I remember is waking up and thinking that my head was itchy. My hair seemed to be full of dust.

I was cold, and I could feel a wind blowing in through the front door, which had no glass in it. The glass lay all over the floor of the hall, a scatter of brightly colored art nouveau panels. My father was on his feet, making a crunching sound on the glass, and my mother was lifting me up to make sure I was all right.

I hadn't heard the explosion, or felt the blast. The bomb was in fact a land-mine, of the sort that fell slowly in a parachute and exploded not on contact, but some minutes later, by a time device. It had landed at the end of our garden, and completely destroyed a large stone house about fifty yards away.

The blast had swept through some trees, across our garden, and hit the house at the rear, smashing all the windows, tearing doors off their hinges, and flinging shrubs and flowers into all the rooms. Then, by some curious trick of its own, it had turned and blown out all the windows at the front of the house.

When it was apparent that none of us was hurt, my father knelt down on the glass under the stairs. I was amazed to hear that he was saying a prayer of thanks for our safety.

Nothing else then or since has done more to convince me of how serious the explosion must have been. My father never presented himself as a believer in God, and it was entirely out of character for him to show any public emotion, or make any form of ritual gesture.

After the prayer he stood up and made sure my mother and I were warmly wrapped up. Then he opened the door of the sitting-room—I suppose because the front door in the hall must have been blocked— and helped us over the wreckage of the furniture.

The windows were all blown out, and there was jagged glass in the larger, lower panes. My father helped me through one of these, taking care that I shouldn't get cut.

I noticed that he was carrying something. At first I didn't recognize what it was, and then I saw that it was his miner's safety helmet. He put it on my head. It was much too big, but the straps could be adjusted, and he did his best to make it fit.

Then we all started walking up the road. Once, there was the drone of a bomber, and we all lay down in the gutter, but no bombs fell, and we soon got up and walked on. There was no one else about, and it was very dark.

My father garaged his car about ten minutes' walk away, and his idea was to take us all there, get the car, and drive out into the country, where his boss at Colliery Engineering, Mr. Laurie, had a house. He thought that the Lauries would take us in, and we would be safe.

At this time the air raid was still in progress, and for all we knew, the worst was still to come. So we started to walk on up the road, and through Melbourne Avenue, as fast as we could.

This quiet tree-lined walk was later to become notorious as the place where the Yorkshire Ripper was arrested, but at this date such a sleazy association was unthinkable. It was noted only for the Girls' High School and a number of distinguished stone-built houses.

To the right, as we walked, we could see a wall of bright flame. My father, looking over, speculated that the fire might be at his office, and wondered what he ought to do. Later when we were safe he went back on his own to check, but as it turned out, the office had not been hit.

So we reached the garage, and got the Standard out, and my father drove us to the Lauries'. They were up, and shocked to hear of our disaster, and immediately took us in.

It was only the following day when I combed my hair that my mother told me the itchy dust I had first noticed in it was crumbled stone.

Many years later, when my horoscope was cast, the astrologer indicated that I might one day be under threat from some falling body, possibly a landslide or a fall of rock. Then, upon recalculating the evidence, she suggested, without knowing of the land-mine, that this danger might have menaced me in the past, and proposed a date in the early 1940s.

I wonder if some particle of that shivered stone was still trembling, after all those years, at the roots of my hair. Something, at any rate, whether star or souvenir, or simply the transmitted echoes of an unconscious telepathy, conveyed and preserved the trauma.

# EDITH SITWELL

THE ECCENTRIC DAME EDITH, sister of Osbert and Sacheverell, published her first volume of poetry, *The Mother and Other Poems,* in 1915. She was, for a time, at the very center of London's literary life. Among her friends were W. B. Yeats, Virginia Woolf, Robert Graves, T. S. Eliot, and Dylan Thomas. Her *Selected Letters, 1919–1964* were published in 1970. Following is an excerpt from a letter written to Geoffrey Gorer on October 28, 1940.

■

## FROM *Selected Letters, 1919–1964*

I hear that Willie M[augham] (I do not know if this is true) found himself being reconciled—(One of those air-raid-shelter reconciliations) —with his ex-wife, at a hotel in London the other day. That great woman, who was about to leave for America, said, in an effort to enlist his sympathy: "Oh Willie, I *know* I shall be torpedoed!" "Then," said Willie, true to type as ever, "I have only one piece of advice to offer you. Keep your mouth open, and you will drown the sooner." Mrs. M. began to cry.

# SIMONE DE BEAUVOIR

---

SIMONE DE BEAUVOIR lived through the war years in France, and for part of that time was a teacher in Paris. Between 1957 and 1972, she published four volumes of autobiography. The following excerpt is taken from the second volume, *The Prime of Life*.

---

■

FROM *The Prime of Life*

### CHAPTER 7

No, time had not turned topsy-turvy after all; the seasons continued to revolve, and a new school year was beginning. It began badly, too. At the Lycée Camille-Sée—as was the case in every *lycée*—I was made to sign a document affirming upon oath that I was neither a Freemason nor a Jew. I found putting my name to this most repugnant, but no one refused to do so; the majority of my colleagues, like myself, had no possible alternative.

I left my grandmother's flat and moved back to the Hôtel du Danemark on the Rue Vavin. Paris was a dismal place now. No more petrol, so no cars on the streets; the few buses operating were running on gas. Almost the only means of transport was by bicycle; many Métro stations were still barricaded. The curfew had been extended till midnight, though places of public entertainment still closed at eleven. I no longer went anywhere near a cinema: nothing was being shown except German films and the very worst sort of French features. The Germans had forbidden any applause during the newsreels, on the grounds that such demonstrations were intended to be insulting. A large number of cinemas, including the Rex, had been turned into troops' cinemas, or *Soldaten-Kino*. I took my meals in various little restaurants which still got by quite nicely; but in the markets and food shops there was a real shortage. Ration cards had been brought in toward the end of September, though this step did nothing to improve supplies. At my parents' dinner table I found vegetables served up that had been popular during the previous war, such as swedes and Jerusalem artichokes.

Nevertheless, people came drifting back to town again. I ran into Marco at the Dôme; he had resumed his old job at the Lycée Louis-le-Grand. He told me, mysteriously, "I have Philippe Pétain's ear," which probably meant he knew someone who was very vaguely acquainted with Alibert. Anyway, I thought, it was hardly something to boast about. I was far more pleased to see Pagniez again; he had gone through the retreat as a colonel's driver, and had stayed at the wheel for nearly forty-eight hours without sleep. He disconcerted me by refusing to join in my fulminations against the Vichy Government. To disparage Pétain, he assured me, was to play straight into the hands of those who wanted to put all France under some Gauleiter's heel. "And what about afterwards?" I asked him.

At all events, Vichy did what the Germans commanded. On 2 October a German edict had been promulgated ordering all Jews to declare themselves as such, and all Jewish firms to notify the authorities of their nationality. On 19 October Vichy published its own "Jewish statute," debarring all Jews from public office or the liberal professions. The crawling hypocrisy of the man who had the nerve to assert his loathing for "the lies which have done us such terrible harm" put me in a blazing temper. Under the specious pretext of moral improvement he was preaching a back-to-the-land policy (as my father's friend Monsieur Jeannot had previously done in his sponsored plays), the real point of which was to reduce France, at her conquerors' insistence, to be a mere German granary. They were all lying: these generals and other notabilities who had sabotaged the war because they preferred Hitler to the Popular Front were now proclaiming that it was because of our "frivolous spirit" that we had lost. These ultrapatriotic characters were turning the defeat of France into a sort of pedestal on which they could stand, the better to insult Frenchmen. In a mealy-mouthed way they protested that they were working for the good of France—but which France? They took advantage of the German occupation to impose a really tyrannous program on the people, something that might have been thought up by a bunch of former Cagoulards. The Marshal's "messages" attacked everything which I felt to be of value, liberty in particular. Henceforth the family would be the sovereign unit, the reign of virtue was at hand, and God would be spoken of respectfully in the schools. This was something I knew only too well, the same violent prejudice and stupidity that had darkened my childhood—only now it extended over the entire country, an official and repressive blanket. Hitler and Nazism had been worlds apart from me; I hated them at a distance, almost calmly. But Pétain and the Révolution Nationale aroused my active personal loathing, and the anger they kindled in me flared up afresh daily. The details of what was going on in Vichy, the various transactions and concessions, never aroused my interest at all, since I regarded the whole idea of Vichy as a shameful scandal.

Sartre's leave was soon over. In my diary for 15 February I wrote: *Sartre gets into uniform again. We reach the station just before 9.15. Large notice up announcing that all trains for men going back from leave will depart at 9.25. Crowds of soldiers and their womenfolk making for*

the underground passage. Am reasonably calm, but the idea of this departure as part of a collective move I find distressing. The scene on the
platform brings a lump to my throat—all these men and women with
their awkward handshakes! There are two crowded trains, one on either
side. The right-hand one pulls out, and a long line of women—some
mothers, but mostly wives or girl friends—drift away, eyes glassy and
red-rimmed: some of them are sobbing. A few elderly fathers among
them, a dozen at most: this separation of the sexes is a primitive business,
with the men being carried off and the women returning to town. There
are very few tearful ones among those waiting for the departure of the
second train, though some cling desperately around their lovers' necks;
you can sense a warm, passionate night behind them, and the lack of
sleep, and the nervous exhaustion that morning has brought. The soldiers make joking little remarks like, "Look at the waterworks!" but you
can feel their closeness and solidarity. Just as the train is about to leave,
a crowd of them jam the door of the carriage, and all I can see of Sartre
in a dark corner of the compartment is his garrison cap, and his glasses,
and an intermittently waving hand. The fellow in front at the door steps
back and lets another take his place. The newcomer embraces a woman,
then calls out, "Who's next?" The women line up and each takes her
turn on the step, me among them. Then Sartre vanishes inside again.
Violent feeling of collective tension in the air: this train's departure is
really like a physical severance. Then the break comes, and it's gone. I'm
the first to leave, walking very fast.

# GEORGE ORWELL

GEORGE ORWELL (pen name of Eric Arthur Blair), author of *Animal Farm* and *1984,* among other works, worked for the BBC in London during the war. Here, in an excerpt from his wartime diary, he offers some less-than-complimentary reflections about Jews and other refugees, and what he sees as their state of mind.

■

FROM *War-time Diary: 1940*

*25 October*

The other night examined the crowds sheltering in Chancery Lane, Oxford Circus and Baker Street stations. *Not* all Jews, but, I think, a higher proportion of Jews than one would normally see in a crowd of this size. What is bad about Jews is that they are not only conspicuous, but go out of their way to make themselves so. A fearful Jewish woman, a regular comic-paper cartoon of a Jewess, fought her way off the train at Oxford Circus, landing blows on anyone who stood in her way. It took me back to old days on the Paris Métro.

Surprised to find that D, who is distinctly Left in his views, is inclined to share the current feeling against the Jews. He says that the Jews in business circles are turning pro-Hitler, or preparing to do so. This sounds almost incredible, but according to D they will always admire anyone who kicks them. What I do feel is that any Jew, i.e. European Jew, would prefer Hitler's kind of social system to ours, if it were not that he happens to persecute them. Ditto with almost any Central European, e.g. the refugees. They make use of England as a sanctuary, but they cannot help feeling the profoundest contempt for it. You can see this in their eyes, even when they don't say it outright. The fact is that the insular outlook and the continental outlook are completely incompatible.

According to F, it is quite true that foreigners are more frightened than English people during the raids. It is not their war, and therefore they have nothing to sustain them. I think this might also account for the fact—I am virtually sure it *is* a fact, though one mustn't mention it —that working-class people are more frightened than middle-class.

The same feeling of despair over impending events in France, Africa, Syria, Spain—the sense of foreseeing what must happen and being powerless to prevent it, and feeling with absolute certainty that a British government *cannot* act in such a way as to get its blow in first.

Air raids much milder the last few days.

# BRIAN MOORE

BRIAN MOORE, born and educated in Belfast, emigrated to Canada in 1948 and now lives in California.
He is the author of *The Lonely Passion of Judith
Hearne, The Luck of Ginger Coffey, Catholics,* and
many other novels. The following excerpt is taken from
*The Emperor of Ice-Cream,* a novel set in wartime Belfast.

■

FROM *The Emperor of Ice-Cream*

Far off down the Lough, antiaircraft guns were firing with a noise
like slamming doors. Yet the guns seemed uncertain, aiming into emptiness. For seven hours, attacking in waves, more than one hundred
German bombers had flown in over Cave Hill and the Lough, dropping
incendiaries and heavy explosives. The city was ablaze, the skies above
it visible for miles around in a red, burning glow. But there was no longer
the terrible thump of exploding bombs. And when, in the first light of
dawn, the sirens sounded the thin, exhausted note of the all clear, they
merely confirmed what the guns had said an hour before. The Germans
had gone, at last.

For Gavin, Freddy, and the other A.R.P. stretcher-bearers, the
raid's end brought no change in the routine of work. Ambulance drivers
continued to bring in casualties, reporting, as they did, that whole districts of the city had been wiped out. An injured Heavy Rescue worker
told them he had seen the engines of the Dublin Fire Brigade, pumping
away in the York Street area, their peacetime headlamps blazing. His
story was confirmed by others, and, soon, the hospital nuns, very pleased
by this news, were telling patients how the Dublin Fire Brigade, God
bless them, their headlamps blazing, had driven one hundred and thirteen miles, crossing the border from neutral Eire, to help with the con-
flagration. A loyal pro-British patient countered with the intelligence that
the English had loaded fire engines on ships in Liverpool and that those
ships were already on their way across the Irish Sea. Another patient told
how she had seen a Canadian aircraft carrier, in dock for refitting, blaze
away at the enemy until all its ammunition was spent. There were other
stories too: stories of looting and cowardice. An English naval rating,
who died shortly after Gavin and Freddy carried him to the operating
room, told them that he had heard two men cheering in a pub as Lord

Haw-Haw, the Nazis' English-speaking commentator, reported on the German radio that Belfast would be completely wiped out.

Reports and rumors continued to circulate well into the morning, but, by then, Gavin and Freddy were too exhausted for listening. Their hands had developed blisters, their feet were wet with perspiration, their limbs ached, and each time they sat for a minute, it seemed they would not have the energy to get back on their feet again. Craig, who carried few stretchers but was everywhere in evidence, shouting orders and harrying his staff, behaved in a demented manner if he saw any of the men taking a rest. "Youse have a job, get cracking!" His pale face glistened with the excitement of it all and, despite the grim sights all around him, his uneven teeth were revealed in a constant, pleased grin. Walking beside a stretcher, he would announce loudly, to no one in particular: "There'll be no more laughing now. I said, they'll be laughing on the other side of their faces now." Occasionally, he would frown and declare: "Letting them doctors give my men orders, that's not right, that needs fixing, yes, fixing. Next time, it will be different. You'll see."

Around ten in the morning, one of the post ladies made tea and brought mugs around to all the men. Gavin, drinking the sweet, strong brew, thought he had never tasted anything so wonderful in his life. He lit his first cigarette in several hours and, without warning, fell asleep, tumbling onto the floor, the mug of tea spilling, scalding him.

"God, I'm tired."

"On your feet, there." It was Craig, coming up the corridor, shouting in a high voice. "Go in thon room there, the head doctor wants to talk to youse."

In the room, Big Frank Price, his face gray, sat slumped against a wall. Old Crutt, the stoolie, was beside him, similarly exhausted. Jimmy Lynan came in a few minutes later with his partner, Wee Bates. None of the other men could be found. Craig, closing the door, pompously blew his whistle for attention.

"Day shift has fully taken over now, so youse men can get some sleep. They'll be back the night, they said it on the wireless. I said, the Germans will be back tonight. But, before you go off, the head doctor, I said, the head doctor, wants to speak with youse. Stand to attention."

Gavin and Freddy joined the others in the semblance of men standing to attention. Craig went out and was heard saying: "All right, Doctor. My men is here."

Old Dr. MacLanahan came in. His white coat was smeared with blood, his pajama collar was similarly soiled. "Good morning," he said, in his usual brisk tone. "I know you boys are going off duty now. I know you need sleep. But I wonder if I could have two volunteers for a nasty job?"

He looked around as he spoke, his gaze coming to rest on Freddy Hargreaves. "What job, sir?" Freddy said, on cue.

"The dead. We're jammed up in the back there, no room at all. I've been in touch with the city authorities, and the plan is to put all the dead together in coffins, in a big hall downtown, bring them in from all over. Then identification can be done at one central place. Do you follow?"

Heads nodded, uncertainly.

"So, we've got to get our lot coffined and out of here by tonight. I've lined up three medical students to help our morgue man. But I need at least two more men. Will any of you help us?"

There was silence.

"What about you, Mister Craig?"

Craig's Adam's apple jiggled in his throat. "Well, Doctor, I'd be happy to oblige, only, you see, I'm in charge here, I have to be on duty again, the night."

Dr. MacLanahan's heavy eyebrows lifted expressively, causing Craig to shift his feet and utter an uneasy cough.

"I'll go," Freddy offered.

"Me too," Gavin heard himself say.

"Good lads," Dr. MacLanahan said. "Follow me." Pointedly ignoring Craig, he led them out of the room, across the extern hall, and into the hospital yard. At the far end of the yard, a canvas sheet had been tied from wall to wall, obscuring the entrance to the morgue. A policeman in a heavy black cape saluted as Dr. MacLanahan approached. "I want nobody in here, do you hear?" the doctor said. "Except the men who're working."

"Right, sir."

The policeman lifted a corner of the canvas and they all three ducked under it. At the entrance of the morgue, two young men in tweed jackets and flannels were smoking cigarettes. Medical students, they stiffened into poses of respect at the approach of the hospital superintendent. "Morning, sir."

"Morning, MacReady. And you, what's your name, I'm sorry?"

"Geary, sir."

"Ah, yes, Geary. Where's the other lad?"

MacReady, a tall young man with a wide clown's mouth and a lock of curly black hair falling over his forehead, said, in a Dublin brogue, "He was taken sick, sir. He asked to be excused."

"Hmm. Well that leaves only the four of you, you and these A.R.P. lads. You'll have your work cut out for you, I'd say. Where's Willie?"

One of the students opened the morgue door and bawled: "Willie?" The morgue attendant appeared. He was the same man Gavin had seen the night before, small, chain-smoking, his long rubber apron greasy with blood. "Morning, sir. Ah, it's a shocking mess, a shocking mess."

"Did Sister send over some whisky?"

"Yes, Doctor."

"Good. And the coffins?"

"They just come. They're out the back."

"You'll have to work outside," Dr. MacLanahan said. "I don't want anybody to see you, but the back yard's pretty well screened off. Too bad about the rain, but it'll be easier for all of you to be out in the fresh air. Willie, do you have those antigas suits?"

"Yes, Doctor."

"Good. Give these lads a good jar of whisky to get them started. Remember, we want to identify people if we can. Thank you, gentlemen. I'll be back later to see how you're getting on."

"Okey-dokey," Willie said, when the doctor had disappeared back behind the canvas curtain. "You lads wait here and I'll get your duds. No sense in dirtying yourself."

He went back into the morgue and came out with an armload of Wellington boots and the yellow oilskins Gavin and Freddy had worn so often in Craig's decontamination drills. When they and the medical students had put these things on, Willie beckoned them inside. "Hold your snouts," he said.

Gavin had seen his first corpse when he was eleven years old. Corpses were elderly relatives, dressed sometimes in brown shrouds, more often in their Sunday best. They lay in the downstairs bedroom on white linen sheets, their hands crossed over their breasts, fingers entwined in rosary beads or crucifixes, black-edged Mass cards strewn around them in tribute. People knelt and said prayers or looked silently at the waxy, dead face, before withdrawing to the sitting room for tea, whisky, and praise of the dear departed. The dead he had seen last night had not stiffened into *rigor mortis* and seemed like actors, shamming death. But now, in the stink of human excrement, in the acrid smell of disinfectant, these dead were heaped, body on body, flung arm, twisted feet, open mouth, staring eyes, old men on top of young women, a child lying on a policeman's back, a soldier's hand resting on a woman's thigh, a carter, still wearing his coal sacks, on top of a pile of arms and legs, his own arm outstretched, finger pointing, as though he warned of some unseen horror. Forbidding and clumsy, the dead cluttered the morgue room from floor to ceiling, seeming to stage some mass lie-down against the living men who now faced them in the doorway.

"Jaysus," said the tall medical student. "How many are there?"

"There was eighty-seven the last time I looked in my book," Willie said. "But the ambulance men was shoving them in sometimes when I was out the back. There's more in the yard. Here, have a wet."

He produced a bottle of whisky and passed it around. "Take a good swig," he advised. "It's all buckshee, and there's more where that comes from."

Waiting his turn at the whisky, Gavin gazed on the dead, his attention caught by the bare, callused feet of an old woman, sticking out from the bottom of a pile of bodies.

If her horny feet protrude, they come
To show how cold she is, and dumb.
Let the lamp affix its beam.
The only emperor is the emperor of ice-cream.

"Here," Freddy said, passing the whisky, "have a swig."

The whisky, strong and biting, did not refresh, as had the tea. Gavin swallowed, then, his stomach heaving, threw up, the tea coming up too. The medical student, Geary, was similarly sick. "You'll get used to it," Willie advised. "Now, here's what you have to do."

What they had to do was work in pairs. Two men would drag a corpse out of the morgue and into the back yard. One, using an old-fashioned cutthroat razor, would cut or loosen the corpse's clothes, while the other searched pockets for identification, money, and valuables. These, if found, were placed in a small canvas bag which was tied around the corpse's neck. If the corpse was fouled by excrement, the clothes were cut off. The corpse was then lifted and placed in a coffin and, if stripped, covered with a shroud. The head, unless mutilated, was left exposed. A lid was placed over the coffin but not nailed down. The coffin was then carried to the outer yard to be shipped to the central hall downtown, where casualties would be exhibited for identification.

The first body Gavin and Freddy took hold of was that of a mill girl in her twenties, a body picked because it was nearest to the entrance. Her cold, stiff hand in his, Gavin dragged her behind him out of the door, into the thick, foggy drizzle of rain, dragging her corpse across the cold, wet concrete of the yard. In death, her bowels had loosened, and so, cutthroat razor in hand, he cut away her skirt, sweater, and under-clothes, revealing the first naked body of an adult woman he had ever really looked at in his life. Of course, he had seen female nakedness before, but fleetingly, as in a glimpse of his sister, or women on beaches inexpertly changing out of their clothes. But now, unurgent, cold in death, this woman's nipples sat on her skin like blind, brown eyes, and, sick, he gazed in fascination at the dark clump of pubic hair beneath her belly. He looked at Freddy, but Freddy merely picked up her skirt and threw it into a beginning heap in the corner. Freddy's glasses were misted with rain and sweat. He lit a cigarette. Naked, the woman lay on the cold, wet concrete and, naked, she sagged between Gavin's arms as he dragged her toward a coffin. Freddy helped lift her in and lay her down and Freddy covered the body. "Bloody Comrade MacLarnon," he said, suddenly. "And the other arseholes. So, they think this war is a good idea, do they? Capitalist killing capitalist. Look at this poor bitch, born and brought up on the means test and the dole. Bread and dripping all her bloody days. Some capitalist."

Gavin put the lid on the coffin.

# ▪ 1941 ▪

# SIR HAROLD GEORGE NICOLSON

---

THE DIPLOMAT Harold Nicolson reports on a luncheon meeting with General Charles de Gaulle, leader of the Free French.

---

■

FROM *The Diaries and Letters of
Harold Nicolson*

DIARY                                              *20th January, 1941*

I lunch with General de Gaulle at the Savoy. Attlee[1] and Dalton[2] are there. De Gaulle looks less unattractive with his hat off, since it shows his young hair and the tired and not wholly benevolent look in his eyes. He has the taut manner of a man who is becoming stout and is conscious that only the exercise of continuous muscle-power can keep his figure in shape. I do not like him. He accuses my Ministry of being "Pétainiste." "*Mais non,*" I say, "*Monsieur le Général.*" "*Enfin, Pétaini-sant.*" "*Nous travaillons,*" I said, "*pour la France entière.*" "*La France entière,*" he shouted, "*c'est la France Libre. C'est moi!*" Well, well. I admit he has made a great Boulangiste gesture. But the specter of General Boulanger passes across my mind. He begins to abuse Pétain, saying that once again he has sold himself to Laval,[3] saying that Weygand[4] showed cowardice when bombed at the front. Osusky[5] says that French opinion imagines that de Gaulle and Pétain are at heart as one. "*C'est une erreur,*" he says sharply. I am not encouraged.

To change the subject I say that I have received a letter from occupied France which I was surprised had passed the censor. De Gaulle says that he had received a long letter of the most Gaulliste nature, the writer of which had written on the top, "I am sure the censor will stop this." Underneath in violet ink was written, "*La censure approuve totalement.*" We discuss Darlan.[6] He says that Darlan loves his ships as a race-horse owner loves his horses. It does not matter to him whether he races at Longchamps or on Epsom Downs. What matters is that it should be a great race and that he should win it. "*Mais il manque d'estomac.*" Had

[1] Leader of the Labour Party.
[2] Minister of Economic Warfare.
[3] Deputy head of the Vichy government.
[4] Vichy minister of war.
[5] Czech Ambassador in Paris before the fall of France.
[6] Admiral of the Vichy French Fleet.

he been a strong man, he would either have fought his fleet with us against the Italians or fought with the Germans against us. As it was, he was preserving his race-horses and they would become old, old, old.

I turn on Roosevelt's inaugural address from Washington. I am still young enough to be amazed at hearing a voice from Washington as if it were in my own room. It is a good speech. He recalls the great blows which America has struck for liberty. He reminds them that Washington created the American idea, that Lincoln saved it from disintegration, and that now they must save it from a menace from outside. "We do not retreat," he concludes. "We are not content to stand still." I enjoyed that part very much indeed.

# EDITH SITWELL

DAME EDITH, the eccentric sister of Osbert and Sacheverell, had a circle of distinguished, mostly literary friends. Part of a letter to Merula Guinness, wife of the actor Alec Guinness, follows.

■

FROM *Selected Letters,*
*1919-1964*

## TO MERULA GUINNESS

*Wednesday [Summer 1941]*                                    RENISHAW HALL
My dear Merula,

Osbert is going *again* to stay with Queen Mary next month. She has started "giving lifts" to the forces, and the other day, when out driving with the Princess Royal and Osbert,—seeing a youth in Air Force uniform, trudging along, she stopped the motor, and the youth was propelled into it. It wasn't until he got in that the awful truth of the company he found himself in, dawned upon him. First, he looked at the Princess Royal, and thought: It can't be true. Then he looked at H.M. and saw that it *was*. Osbert says the poor boy threw a fit, and was too frightened to say where he wanted to go, so found himself in Bath when he probably wanted to go in exactly the opposite direction.

Much love to you, dear,

Yours affectionately,

Edith.

# DAVID BRINKLEY

AFTER HIS ARMY SERVICE in World War II, David Brinkley worked for United Press and then NBC radio news, becoming White House correspondent before the end of the war. He has since won ten Emmy Awards and three George Foster Peabody Awards, the most recent of which, in 1987, was for his current television program, "This Week with David Brinkley." *Washington Goes to War* is his memoir of the war years.

■

## FROM *Washington Goes to War*

While the civilian agencies grew, the military was expanding even faster. By early 1941, the army alone had grown from seven thousand civilian employees to forty-one thousand, spread through twenty-three buildings in the District of Columbia and nearby Maryland and Virginia. A new War Department building was already going up on Virginia Avenue, in a dreary part of town known as Foggy Bottom. Stimson hated it, said it was too small, and complained that the façade looked like the entrance to a provincial opera house. He announced he would never move into it. He never did. (The building became, and remains, the Department of State.)

And so began a movement to build a new colossus for the military, a building so enormous there was no room for it in the city. It was to rise across the Potomac River in Virginia on a site near Arlington National Cemetery, and to have three times the floor space of the Empire State Building. It would hold the War Department in a mammoth, five-sided agglomeration of concrete corridors and offices a mile in circumference, filled with the military secretariat, officers and enlisted men and civilian clerks and all their desks, file cabinets, cafeterias, mimeograph machines and mechanical typewriters that, in time, would turn out the notices to families that their sons, brothers and fathers had been killed in battle.

Congress was asked to put up thirty-five million dollars for the monstrous new building but would not do so until it had a good deal of conversation about it. Representative Fritz Lanham of Texas explained the problem on the House floor: "One of the high officers of the War Department testified that his offices are now in four different places in the city and that he loses two hours a day going from one to another.

. . . So, by all means, I say it is feasible to pass this legislation" to spend the money.

But Robert Rich of Pennsylvania still insisted that if the country was sensible it would stay out of war and therefore would not need a new building for the military. "Where are you going? Where are you taking this nation? No place except to national bankruptcy and ruin. . . . I am opposed to it in every way I can be. War in Europe or Asia for us spells ruination of America."

Others wondered how a building so huge could possibly be used after the war. Everett Dirksen of Illinois said, "Here is a building proposed to house thirty thousand people, to stand over across the Potomac River. You can ride [by taxi] to the present War Department for twenty cents. It will cost you at least sixty cents to go over to this new building and sixty cents back. We may not need all that space when the war comes to an end. . . . What will we do with the extra space?"

Clifton Woodrum of Virginia responded that when the war was over the new building could be used to store military records, or some other civilian agencies of government could be moved into it.

August Andresen of Minnesota rose and said, "I understand that the report is quite current around here that they want these big buildings so we can police the world after the war is over. . . ."

After receiving the most solemn assurances that the total cost of the new building would be thirty-five million dollars including all furniture and fixtures, Congress voted the money. The final cost would be eighty-seven million dollars.

Reluctantly, Roosevelt agreed to allow the building of the Pentagon, as it quickly came to be called, but he would not agree to the location. In his view and that of the press and public, it would desecrate a hallowed place, Arlington National Cemetery. Only twenty years after the previous war, with many of its veterans still in hospitals, people were deeply emotional about Arlington, and the outcry was so fervent that the military and its architects could not ignore it. They chose another site, farther from the cemetery, partially occupied by warehouses and a public dump.

Roosevelt agreed to the new site but said he disliked the building. Why not, he asked, build a huge, square, concrete monolith without windows and with entirely artificial light and ventilation? Then, he said, after the war when the military was back down to its peacetime size, the building might be useful for storage. When Stimson heard this, he was appalled and said—out of Roosevelt's hearing—that he would never work in a building designed like a cold-storage warehouse for bananas.

At a press conference in August 1941, a reporter asked, "Mr. President, can you say anything about the new War Department in Arlington?"

Roosevelt recalled that in the fall of 1917 he was assistant secretary of the navy and his department needed more room. He talked with President Woodrow Wilson about a new temporary building across the lawns from the White House. Wilson asked, "Why did you select that place?"

"Because it would be so unsightly right here in front of the White House it would just have to be taken down at the end of the war."

Wilson thought for a moment. "Well, I don't think I could stand all that sawing and hammering right under my front windows. Can't you put it somewhere else?"

Roosevelt had told the 1917 contractor to put it on the Mall about a mile from the White House where Wilson could not hear the hammering and now, twenty-four years later, it still stood and still housed many of the offices of the navy, uglier than ever. "It was a crime. I don't hesitate to say so. It was a crime for which I should be kept out of heaven, for having desecrated the whole plan of, I think, the loveliest city in the world. . . . " He was willing, he said, for the War Department to build something, but what the Pentagon now proposed was too big and would spoil the city planning of a hundred and fifty years.

Two months later, in late September 1941, while Roosevelt still wavered about the location, the army just went ahead. General Somervell, not yet busy fighting Donald Nelson, was a West Point engineering graduate whose previous projects had included New York City's La Guardia Airport. He simply told the contractor to start work. By the time Roosevelt found out about it a month later, the foundations were already in place.

The construction moved ahead with incredible speed. At one point, thirteen thousand men were working around the clock, with enormous banks of arc lights burning through the night. Accident rates were 400 percent higher than average. Three hundred architects worked in a large, abandoned airplane hangar near the construction site. They were trying, and failing, to design the building fast enough to keep up with the workmen. Construction foremen were snatching blueprints off their desks even before they had finished drafting them. Alan Dickey, one of the architects, recalled another architect asking him, "How big should I make that beam across the third floor?"

Dickey answered, "I don't know. They installed it yesterday."

By May 1942, half-a-million square feet were ready for occupancy, and the army began moving in. Military guards lined the route from the old Munitions Building on the Mall, across the Fourteenth Street Bridge and through the muddy fields to the half-finished structure. Armored trucks rolled in with secret files. Movers carried in office furniture so hurriedly that workers the next day deluged their supervisors with complaints about broken lamps and damaged desks. For months more, Pentagon workers had to fight construction barriers, wet cement, noise, and dust so thick, one remembered, "you could write your name on any desk with your finger."

By early 1943, the Pentagon was complete—a building big enough to house forty thousand people and all their accoutrements, the largest building in the world, conceived, funded, designed and constructed in a little more than a year. And on the day it was finished, it was already too small. The army was once again spreading outward over the city, renting office space in hotels, apartments and downtown office buildings.

Jokes about the Pentagon quickly became a staple of bureaucratic humor. It was so huge people were said to spend days and even weeks wandering its endless corridors trying to find their way out. One woman was said to have told a guard she was in labor and needed help in getting to a maternity hospital. He said, "Madam, you should not have come in here in that condition."

"When I came in here," she answered, "I wasn't."

# V(ICTOR) S(AWDON) PRITCHETT

THAT QUINTESSENTIAL and astonishingly prolific British man of letters, V. S. Pritchett—novelist, short story writer, and critic—was born in Ipswich, the son of a traveling salesman, and was knighted in 1975. Sir Victor, who lives in London, is also a foreign honorary member of the American Academy of Arts and Letters. He is probably best known for his short stories, which were collected in two volumes in 1982 and 1983. He has written a biography of Balzac and two volumes of autobiography—*A Cab at the Door* and *Midnight Oil*. His novels include *Mr. Beluncle* and *Dead Man Leading*. *The Living Novel and Later Appreciations* is probably the best known of his books of criticism. Below, a story of the war.

■

## The Voice

A message came from the rescue party, who straightened up and leaned on their spades in the rubble. The policemen said to the crowd: "Everyone keep quiet for five minutes. No talking, please. They're trying to hear where he is."

The silent crowd raised their faces and looked across the ropes to the church which, now it was destroyed, broke the line of the street like a decayed tooth. The bomb had brought down the front wall and roof, the balcony had capsized. Freakishly untouched, the hymnboard still announced the previous Sunday's hymns.

A small wind blew a smell of smoldering cloth across people's noses from another street where there was another scene like this. A bus roared by and heads turned in passive anger until the sound of the engine had gone. People blinked as a pigeon flew from a roof and crossed the building like an omen of release. There was dead quietness again. Presently a murmuring sound was heard by the rescue party. The man buried under the debris was singing again.

At first difficult to hear, soon a tune became definite. Two of the rescuers took up their shovels and shouted down to encourage the buried man, and the voice became stronger and louder. Words became clear. The leader of the rescue party held back the others, and those who were near strained to hear. Then the words were unmistakable:

> "Oh Thou whose Voice the waters heard,
>  And hushed their raging at Thy Word."

The buried man was singing a hymn.

A clergyman was standing with the warden in the middle of the ruined church.

"That's Mr. Morgan all right," the warden said. "He could sing. He got silver medals for it."

The Reverend Frank Lewis frowned.

"Gold, I shouldn't wonder," said Mr. Lewis dryly. Now he knew Morgan was alive, he said: "What the devil's he doing in there? How did he get in? I locked up at eight o'clock last night myself."

Lewis was a wiry, middle-aged man, but the white dust on his hair and eyelashes, and the way he kept licking the dust off his dry lips, moving his jaws all the time, gave him the monkeyish, testy, and suspicious air of an old man. He had been up all night on rescue work in the raid and he was tired out. The last straw was to find the church had gone and that Morgan, the so-called Reverend Morgan, was buried under it.

The rescue workers were digging again. There was a wide hole now and a man was down in it filling a basket with his hands. The dust rose like smoke from the hole as he worked.

The voice had not stopped singing. It went on, rich, virile, masculine, from verse to verse of the hymn. Shooting up like a stem through the rubbish, the voice seemed to rise and branch out powerfully, luxuriantly, and even theatrically, like a tree, until everything was in its shade. It was a shade that came towards one like dark arms.

"All the Welsh can sing," the warden said. Then he remembered that Lewis was Welsh also. "Not that I've got anything against the Welsh," the warden said.

The scandal of it, Lewis was thinking. Must he sing so loud, must he advertise himself? I locked up myself last night. How the devil did he get in? And he really meant: How did the devil get in?

To Lewis, Morgan was the nearest human thing to the devil. He could never pass that purple-gowned figure, sauntering like a cardinal in his skull cap on the sunny side of the street, without a shudder of distaste and derision. An unfrocked priest, his predecessor in the church, Morgan ought in strict justice to have been in prison, and would have been but for the indulgence of the bishop. But this did not prevent the old man with the saintly white head and the eyes half closed by the worldly juices of food and wine from walking about dressed in vestments, like an actor walking in the sun of his own vanity, a hook-nosed satyr, a he-goat significant to servant girls, the crony of the public house, the chaser of bookmakers, the smoker of cigars. It was terrible, but it was just that the bomb had buried him; only the malice of the Evil One would have thought of bringing the punishment of the sinner upon the church as well. And now, from the ruins, the voice of the wicked man rose up in all the elaborate pride of art and evil.

Suddenly there was a moan from the sloping timber, slates began to skate down.

"Get out. It's going," shouted the warden.

The man who was digging struggled out of the hole as it bulged under the landslide. There was a dull crumble, the crashing and splitting of wood, and then the sound of brick and dust tearing down below the water. Thick dust clouded over and choked them all. The rubble rocked like a cakewalk. Everyone rushed back and looked behind at the wreckage as if it were still alive. It remained still. They all stood there, frightened and suspicious. Presently one of the men with the shovels said, "The bloke's shut up."

Everyone stared stupidly. It was true. The man had stopped singing. The clergyman was the first to move. Gingerly he went to what was left of the hole and got down on his knees.

"Morgan!" he said in a low voice.

Then he called out more loudly: "Morgan!"

Getting no reply, Lewis began to scramble the rubble away with his hands.

"Morgan!" he shouted. "Can you hear?" He snatched a shovel from one of the men and began digging and shoveling the stuff away. He had stopped chewing and muttering. His expression had entirely changed. "Morgan!" he called. He dug for two feet and no one stopped him. They looked with bewilderment at the sudden frenzy of the small man grubbing like a monkey, spitting out the dust, filing down his nails. They saw the spade at last shoot through the old hole. He was down the hole widening it at once, letting himself down as he worked. He disappeared under a ledge made by the fallen timber.

The party above could do nothing. "Morgan," they heard him call. "It's Lewis. We're coming. Can you hear?" He shouted for an axe and presently they heard him smashing with it. He was scratching like a dog or a rabbit.

A voice like that to have stopped, to have gone! Lewis was thinking. How unbearable this silence was. A beautiful proud voice, the voice of a man, a voice like a tree, the soul of a man spreading in the air like the cedars of Lebanon. "Only one man I have heard with a bass like that. Owen the Bank, at Newtown before the war. Morgan!" he shouted. "Sing! God will forgive you everything, only sing!"

One of the rescue party following behind the clergyman in the tunnel shouted back to his mates.

"I can't do nothing. This bleeder's blocking the gangway."

Half an hour Lewis worked in the tunnel. Then an extraordinary thing happened to him. The tunnel grew damp and its floor went as soft as clay to the touch. Suddenly his knees went through. There was a gap with a yard of cloth, the vestry curtain or the carpet at the communion rail was unwound and hanging through it. Lewis found himself looking down into the blackness of the crypt. He lay down and put his head and shoulders through the hole and felt about him until he found something solid again. The beams of the floor were tilted down into the crypt.

"Morgan. Are you there, man?" he called.

He listened to the echo of his voice. He was reminded of the time he had talked into a cistern when he was a boy. Then his heart jumped. A voice answered him out of the darkness from under the fallen floor. It was like the voice of a man lying comfortably and waking up from a snooze, a voice thick and sleepy.

"Who's that?" asked the voice.

"Morgan, man. It's Lewis. Are you hurt?" Tears pricked the dust in Lewis's eyes, and his throat ached with anxiety as he spoke. Forgiveness and love were flowing out of him. From below, the deep thick voice of Morgan came back.

"You've been a hell of a long time," it said. "I've damn near finished my whisky."

"Hell" was the word which changed Mr. Lewis's mind. Hell was a real thing, a real place for him. He believed in it. When he read out the word "Hell" in the Scriptures he could see the flames rising as they rise out of the furnaces at Swansea. "Hell" was a professional and poetic word for Mr. Lewis. A man who had been turned out of the church had no right to use it. Strong language and strong drink, Mr. Lewis hated both of them. The idea of whisky being in his church made his soul rise like a angered stomach. There was Morgan, insolent and comfortable, lying (so he said) under the old altar-table, which was propping up the fallen floor, drinking a bottle of whisky.

"How did you get in?" Lewis said sharply from the hole. "Were you in the church last night when I locked up?"

The old man sounded not as bold as he had been. He even sounded shifty when he replied, "I've got my key."

"Your key. I have the only key of the church. Where did you get a key?"

"My old key. I always had a key."

The man in the tunnel behind the clergyman crawled back up the tunnel to daylight.

"O.K.," the man said. "He's got him. They're having a ruddy row."

"Reminds me of ferretting. I used to go ferretting with my old dad," said the policeman.

"You should have given that key up," said Mr. Lewis. "Have you been in here before?"

"Yes, but I shan't come here again," said the old man.

There was the dribble of powdered rubble, pouring down like sand in an hour-glass, the ticking of the strained timber like the loud ticking of a clock.

Mr. Lewis felt that at last after years he was face to face with the devil, and the devil was trapped and caught. The tick-tock of the wood went on.

"Men have been risking their lives, working and digging for hours because of this," said Lewis. "I've ruined a suit of . . ."

The tick-tock had grown louder in the middle of the words. There was a sudden lurching and groaning of the floor, followed by a big heaving and splitting sound.

"It's going," said Morgan with detachment from below. "The table leg." The floor crashed down. The hole in the tunnel was torn wide and Lewis grabbed at the darkness until he caught a board. It swung him out and in a second he found himself hanging by both hands over the pit.

"I'm falling. Help me," shouted Lewis in terror. "Help me." There was no answer.

"Oh, God," shouted Lewis, kicking for a foothold. "Morgan, are you there? Catch me. I'm going."

Then a groan like a snore came out of Lewis. He could hold no longer. He fell. He fell exactly two feet.

The sweat ran down his legs and caked on his face. He was as wet as a rat. He was on his hands and knees gasping. When he got his breath again, he was afraid to raise his voice.

"Morgan," he said quietly, panting.

"Only one leg went," the old man said in a quiet grating voice. "The other three are all right."

Lewis lay panting on the floor. There was a long silence. "Haven't you ever been afraid before, Lewis?" Morgan said. Lewis had no breath to reply. "Haven't you ever felt rotten with fear," said the old man calmly, "like an old tree, infested and worm-eaten with it, soft as a rotten orange? You were a fool to come down here after me. I wouldn't have done the same for you," Morgan said.

"You would," Lewis managed to say.

"I wouldn't," said the old man. "I'm afraid. I'm an old man, Lewis, and I can't stand it. I've been down here every night since the raids got bad."

Lewis listened to the voice. It was low with shame, it had the roughness of the earth, the kicked and trodden choking dust of Adam. The earth of Mr. Lewis listened for the first time to the earth of Morgan. Coarsened and sordid and unlike the singing voice, the voice of Morgan was also gentle and fragmentary.

"When you stop feeling shaky," Morgan said, "you'd better sing. I'll do a bar, but I can't do much. The whisky's gone. Sing, Lewis. Even if they don't hear, it does you good. Take the tenor, Lewis."

Above in the daylight the look of pain went from the mouths of the rescue party, a grin came on the dusty lips of the warden.

"Hear it?" he said. "A ruddy Welsh choir!"

# GEORGE BERNARD SHAW

IN THE FOLLOWING letter to H. G. Wells, the aged Shaw comments on Wells's latest work, *Babes in the Darkling Wood* (described in its preface as a "dialogue novel of contemporary ideas"); offers his views and impressions of Stalin; and discusses education and the war, among other matters.

■

## My dear H.G.

I have just finished The Babes, which was impossible until everyone else had finished it first. You are not dead yet (I am, unfortunately): there are luminosities and subtleties that are newly born as well as the old Wellsian faculty.

I was especially tickled by your onslaught on brass tacks, because I am trying to write a book with the express object of bringing your Declaration of Rights down to these useful articles. Churchill was absolutely right the other day in his broadcast when he said that if he declared his war aims the united nation behind him would split into fifty irreconcilable factions.

My book is a little list of the things a person ought to understand (no matter what his or her conclusions may be) before being trusted with a vote or put on the panel as eligible for public work of this or that grade.

You are less splenetic than you were. The British spleen that broke out occasionally and upset your valuations is mellowing a bit. This is very noticeable in your description of Stalin. I rate him higher than you do. He was equal to two very big opportunities of going wrong. The first was Socialism in a single country versus Trotsky's world revolution. The second was collective farming versus the moujik. His choice and the success with which he carried it out rank him as the greatest living statesman. Collective farming is the only chance for our agriculture; but we stick helplessly to the moujik and the Kulak. Stalin would not have a dog's chance in a British consituency. He made a favorable impression on me when I met him in 1931. The attentive silence in which he listened to us until we had said everything we had to say and the goodhumor with which he laughed at us when his turn came (for he did laugh at us) could not have been improved on in point of pleasant manners and grasping

■ 130 ■

of the situation. Lothian's[1] proposal that he should invite Lloyd George to Moscow with a view to his leading the progressive Liberals to the Left of the Labour Party as a Party of scientific Socialism simply amused him, though he cordially invited Ll.G. to come and see for himself. When Lady Astor told him that the Soviet knew nothing about handling children of five years he was outraged. "In England" he said "you beat children[.]" But Nancy went for him like a steamroller and ordered him to send a sensible woman to London to learn the business. The moment he saw that she knew what she was talking about he made a note of her address, and presently dumped not one but half a dozen sensible women on her doorstep. This trifle impressed me; for I thought his noting the address was mere politeness. I, who had heard nothing of Lothian's proposal until he paid it out to Uncle Joe, had nothing to say; but when Astor, who is by temperament a born Communist, gave him assurances that Russia had many friends in England, I asked him whether he had ever heard of Cromwell, and quoted the refrain of the old song

> So put your trust in God, my boys;
> And keep your powder dry.

He knew all about Cromwell, and intimated that at any rate he would keep his powder dry. He was very friendly; and as I was treated all through as if I were Karl Marx risen from the grave, I did not see the rough side of anybody or anything. But there was no attempt to humbug me. They were too full of their achievements to dream of any need for that, especially as they were convinced that Capitalist England was in comparison a Chamber of Horrors.

I was prepared for Finland, as Ireland is the British Finland, and I have said ever since the Treaty that in the event of a world war England would have to re-occupy Ireland militarily, or at least take over the ports, for the duration. Churchill and Roosevelt may still have to do it if the battle of the Atlantic continues to go against us. The only novelty about Finland was the unprecedented fact that Russia took only what she needed instead of taking back the whole place as any other Power would have done.

Talking of Ireland, were you aware that in 1937, when the ports were given back, the ownership of Eire was formally and explicitly transferred to The Most Holy Trinity? I discovered that a month ago. Had you ever heard of it?

I think you and Benedetto Croce are not civil enough to Karl Marx. I have myself pointed out his purely academic mistakes; but as he was unquestionably an epoch making philosopher who changed the mind of the intellectually conscious world, attempts to belittle him fail and belittle their authors.

[1] The Marquess of Lothian, a newspaper editor and statesman.

To balance it I dismiss Pavlof as a supremely damned fool. But he seems to have been as civil to you as Uncle Joe was to me, for which I give him one good mark. His personal resemblance to me I take as an unpardonable liberty. Your difficulty about him is fundamentally due to the fact that you were educated by your schooling, which you carried to its end by becoming a teacher and crammer. My education was entirely aesthetic: I learnt nothing at school, and loathed it. It kept me from becoming a young gangster; but it did this by imprisoning me; and I have never forgiven it. I have at last come definitely to believe that all effective education is aesthetic, and that the Materialistic Mechanistic science which you had to get up for school purposes was all wrong. As an aesthetic worker I claim to be scientifically a biologist and an economist, my laboratory, or rather my observatory[,] being the whole world in which the events are not put-up jobs (see Love and Mr. Lewisham) and, barring mere accidents, their cause is always in the future and never in the past. In short I understand why we differ; so there is no harm done, as I am careful to say nothing about it; for the idea must not get about that the Wellsians and Shavians have any differences. They are in fact the same body.

We are quiet here. Up to last November we had a searchlight here, with the result that every raid began on us: we have several craters to shew. But I.C.I. took a house here.[2] The searchlight was taken away. Whether the two events were connected I don't know; but since then we have had no bombs. Frank [Wells] is nearer the viaduct, which is a target; but it is of less importance now that there is an alternative line. We presume you are well, as anything happening to you would be in the papers. I haven't been in London for months. My imagination is nearly dead; I forget everything in ten minutes; and my weight has fallen to 9 stone; but I keep up a stage effect of being an upstanding old man. I am not unhappy in spite of this senseless war, though I ought to be dead, and am not in the least troubled by that fact.

always yours<br>GBS

PS I haven't written a play for nearly two years. I am by no means sure that I shall ever write another.

As the Babes was really an exhaustive letter to me, this is an acknowledgment, and need not be acknowledged, as you must have something better to do.

Read my letter in today's *Times* ["A King's Spelling: Letters and Sounds"]. It is not about the war.

---

[2] Imperial Chemical Industries Ltd leased a large house as a refuge for its employees.

# LOVAT DICKSON

LOVAT DICKSON was born in Australia and brought up
in Canada. He lived in London for twenty-two years,
where he was an editor with and director of Macmillan. This passage, from Dickson's autobiography, *The
House of Words,* should be read together with Richard
Hillary's own pieces in the present volume.

■

FROM *The House of Words*

One afternoon in March, when there was a cold wind outside and a
dank leaden sky, someone I knew at Dr. McIndoe's hospital in East
Grinstead, The Royal Victoria, where so many survivors of the Battle of
Britain were undergoing skin-grafting operations, brought to see me a
young airman who wanted to write a book. He and she came to my door
together; I saw them outlined against the dark paneled wall. She was
small and vivacious and in early middle age; he was tall with a fine shaped
head and fair hair with a glint of gold in it. At the distance of the door
from my desk on this winter afternoon, he seemed a gay, debonair figure.
He exuded handsomeness and vitality; something in the shape of his
head, his white teeth, his lithe figure, the way he walked and the proud
way he held himself was as assertive of his masculinity and personality as
though he had called out clearly to me. Yet all he did was to stand shyly
behind the friendly figure of the middle-aged lady leading him in to me
as an animal is led into the ring at a show. As he advanced into the light
I saw that he had no lips; these had been burnt away. He had no eyelashes nor any lids to his eyes; these had been licked off by the flames.
He had lost about four skins, and only the last one, so thin that it was
transparent, held in his blood. His eyes were a vivid blue, but the cold
wind outside had blown straight on them since they had no protective
lids, and what appeared to be tears, though they were belied by his grin,
were running down his ravaged cheeks. It was painful to look at him; he
seemed raw and scraped like an animal that had been skinned by the
hunter's knife, and involuntarily I looked down so that he might not see
how much I was pitying him. I waved him to a seat and then stole a
commiserating glance at him again, only to see that his lipless mouth
was parted still in a derisive grin. I could see against the window the bold
and fascinating outline of his golden head, the fine broad shoulders, the
physical strength of his young body. In outline he was as he must have

been before meeting the flames; and inside, too, he must have been the same, if that insolent grin meant anything. A boy with a sense of humor and a keen intelligence, wearing a face that was a traversty of what a human face should look like, a crude caricature which said from behind that grin, "You bloody well have to look at me, you poor civilian sod."

Patricia Hollander, who had brought him to me, who was acting at that time as a librarian at the East Grinstead Hospital, was very anxious that this boy and I should make a good impression on each other. It was easy to see that in this golden-haired youth she had what is called a "handful." He treated her very mockingly; he seemed anxious to shock me into some sort of statement. It was plain that he was used to having his own way with people, and that he did not propose to make an exception with me. This was all very well, but though my feelings were profoundly moved and he had made a great impression on me, I did not propose to treat him any differently from the way in which I had treated other young R.A.F. survivors, unless by a miracle it turned out that he could write. That was unlikely.

I probed for his background. Name, Richard Hillary, age twenty-one, an undergraduate at Oxford when the war broke out, an oarsman (hence the figure, I thought), son of a civil servant. In how few sentences could you write the biography of a young gentleman like this; and he was now proposing to deliver himself of a book! He hadn't got beyond the first chapter. Probably, I thought to myself, that first chapter has been written and rewritten; so bewitched is he with its beautiful beginning that he can't get on with it, but has to keep going back to read it. How many people must have been made to listen to it!—all his girl friends, and he must have had plenty; and here he was coming with his beautiful face and his burnt stumps of fingers to play on my sensibilities, and read me the damned thing too. How could I tell from a first chapter whether he would be able to write a book? My guess would be that he would never complete it. With a face like that, with that twisted, agonized, supercilious, scornful smile, he would never run out of admirers who would listen to what he had done; he would never be able to get on with the book.

Here he was, taking a dozen pages of typescript with his stumps of fingers out of a file he was carrying with him, and taking it for granted that like some of these silly women I would listen adoringly to him. I would very soon put that matter right. I said a publisher could not judge a manuscript by having a few pages read to him, that I was very busy: if he liked to leave this bit I would write to him and tell him what I thought. . . . My lips might have been moving and saying nothing for all the attention he paid to my protest. He continued to look at me with those watery eyes and with that lipless mouth smiling, patient as though with an animal that resists training. "Oh, very well," I said, "but you are not giving your work its best chance. I absolutely hate being read to," and I did my best to look morose and unreceptive.

He started to read, not very well and in the strained accents young Englishmen always adopt for declamatory purposes. I thought, Oh my God, twelve pages or more! and I felt impatient with this whole business; until suddenly I began to see what he was telling me—not hear it so much as see it—the windswept empty sky, the explosion, the difficulty of opening his canopy, the fall through space as a swinging plummet of fire, the gradual hissing immersion as his parachute settled like a collapsing tent into the cold waters of the Channel, and the harness falling about his burnt head and hands and shoulders as he knew that he was about to die.

*So I was going to die. It came to me like that—I was going to die, and I was not afraid. This realization came as a surprise. The manner of my approaching death appalled and horrified me, but the actual vision of death left me unafraid: I felt only a profound curiosity and a sense of satisfaction that within a few minutes or a few hours I was to learn the great answer. I decided that it should be in a few minutes. I had no qualms about hastening my end, and reaching up, I managed to unscrew the valve of my Mae West. The air escaped in a rush and my head went under water. It is said by people who have all but died in the sea that drowning is a pleasant death. I did not find it so. I swallowed a large quantity of water before my head came up again, but derived little satisfaction from it. I tried again, to find that I could not get my face under. I was so enmeshed in my parachute that I could not move. For the next ten minutes, I tore my hands to ribbons on the spring-release catch. It was stuck fast. I lay back exhausted, and then I started to laugh. By this time I was probably not entirely normal and I doubt it if my laughter was wholly sane, but there was something irresistibly comical in my grand gesture of suicide being so simply thwarted.*

*Goethe once wrote that no one, unless he had led the full life and realized himself completely, had the right to take his own life. Providence seemed determined that I should not incur the great man's displeasure.*

*It is often said that a dying man re-lives his whole life in one rapid kaleidoscope. I merely thought gloomily of the Squadron returning, of my mother at home, and of the few people who would miss me. Outside my family, I could count them on the fingers of one hand. What did gratify me enormously was to find that I indulged in no frantic abasements or prayers to the Almighty. It is an old jibe of God-fearing people that the irreligious always change their tune when about to die: I was pleased to think that I was proving them wrong. Because I seemed to be in for an indeterminate period of waiting. I began to feel a terrible lone-*

liness and sought for some means to take my mind off my plight. I took
it for granted that I must soon become delirious, and I attempted to
hasten the process: I encouraged my mind to wander vaguely and aimlessly, with the result that I did experience a certain peace. But when I
forced myself to think of something concrete, I found that I was still only
too lucid. I went on shuttling between the two with varying success until
I was picked up. I remember as in a dream hearing somebody shout: it
seemed so far away and quite unconnected with me. . . .

Then willing arms were dragging me over the side; my parachute
was taken off (and with such ease!); a brandy flask was pushed between
my swollen lips; a voice said, "O.K., Joe, it's one of ours and still kicking";
and I was safe. I was neither relieved nor angry: I was past caring.

It was to the Margate lifeboat that I owed my rescue. Watchers on
the coast had seen me come down, and for three hours they had been
searching for me. Owing to wrong directions, they were just giving up
and turning back for land when ironically enough one of them saw my
parachute. They were then fifteen miles east of Margate.

While in the water I had been numb and had felt very little pain.
Now that I begun to thaw out, the agony was such that I could have
cried out. The good fellows made me as comfortable as possible, put up
some sort of awning to keep the sun from my face, and phoned through
for a doctor. It seemed to me to take an eternity to reach shore. I was
put into an ambulance and driven rapidly to hospital. Through all this I
was quite conscious, though unable to see. At the hospital they cut off
my uniform, I gave the requisite information to a nurse about my next
of kin, and then, to my infinite relief, felt a hypodermic syringe pushed
into my arm.

I can't help feeling that a good epitaph for me at that moment would
have been four lines of Verlaine:

> Quoique sans patrie et sans roi,
> Et très brave ne l'étant guère,
> J'ai voulu mourir à la guerre.
> La mort n'a pas voulu de moi.

The foundations of an experience of which this crash was, if not the
climax, at least the turning point were laid in Oxford before the war.

"I mean to go on," he said, "and write about what Oxford was like
before the war."

And so I did something that I have never done before. I commissioned a book by a boy of twenty-one after hearing him read twelve pages
of it.

"If the rest is as good as that, Macmillan's will publish it. Do you
think you can keep it up?"

He said: "Of course. I've something to say, and I have to say it."

"What's that?" I asked nervously. I hoped to myself, not a message!

"Why some are taken, and others aren't. Most of my friends have been killed."

He said this without any sense of self-pity. In fact he was still smiling his sardonic smile. I felt vaguely uncomfortable and inadequate. The last thing I could have said to him was, "You've had a hard time." Physically he had, but I had a clear impression that this had not really mattered to him, that, if anything, he was getting satisfaction from his suffering, and that behind this ravaged, grinning mask was an immensely serious purpose which in some way was going to affect his life and mine. We parted a few minutes later, and I did not see him again for nearly a year.

# RICHARD HILLARY

SHOT DOWN in the Battle of Britain, Richard Hillary
was hideously injured. Here he describes his gradually
increasing awareness of what has happened to him.

■

## FROM *The Last Enemy*

### SHALL I LIVE FOR A GHOST?

I was falling. Falling slowly through a dark pit. I was dead. My body,
headless, circled in front of me. I saw it with my mind, my mind that
was the redness in front of the eye, the dully scream in the ear, the
grinning of the mouth, the skin crawling on the skull. It was death and
resurrection. Terror, moving with me, touched my cheek with hers and
I felt the flesh wince. Faster, faster. . . . I was hot now, hot, again one
with my body, on fire and screaming soundlessly. Dear God, no! No!
Not that, not again. The sickly smell of death was in my nostrils and a
confused roar of sound. Then was all quiet. I was back.

Someone was holding my arms.

"Quiet now. There's a good boy. You're going to be all right. You've
been very ill and you mustn't talk."

I tried to reach up my hand but could not.

"Is that you, nurse? What have they done to me?"

"Well, they've put something on your face and hands to stop them
hurting and you won't be able to see for a little while. But you mustn't
talk: you're not strong enough yet."

Gradually I realized what had happened. My face and hands had
been scrubbed and then sprayed with tannic acid. The acid had formed
into a hard black cement. My eyes alone had received different treatment: they were coated with a thick layer of gentian violet. My arms were
propped up in front of me, the fingers extended like witches' claws, and
my body was hung loosely on straps just clear of the bed.

I can recollect no moments of acute agony in the four days which I
spent in that hospital; only a great sea of pain in which I floated almost
with comfort. Every three hours I was injected with morphia, so while
imagining myself quite coherent, I was for the most part in a semi-stupor.
The memory of it has remained a confused blur.

Two days without eating, and then periodic doses of liquid food taken through a tube. An appalling thirst, and hundreds of bottles of ginger beer. Being blind, and not really feeling strong enough to care. Imagining myself back in my plane, unable to get out, and waking to find myself shouting and bathed in sweat. My parents coming down to see me and their wonderful self-control.

They arrived in the late afternoon of my second day in bed, having with admirable restraint done nothing the first day. On the morning of the crash my mother had been on her way to the Red Cross, when she felt a premonition that she must go home. She told the taxi-driver to turn about and arrived at the flat to hear the telephone ringing. It was our Squadron Adjutant, trying to reach my father. Embarassed by finding himself talking to my mother, he started in on a glamorized history of my exploits in the air and was bewildered by mother cutting him short to ask where I was. He managed somehow after about five minutes of incoherent stuttering to get over his news.

They arrived in the afternoon and were met by Matron. Outside my ward a twittery nurse explained that they must not expect to find me looking quite normal, and they were ushered in. The room was in darkness; I just a dim shape in one corner. Then the blinds were shot up, all the lights switched on, and there I was. As my mother remarked later, the performance lacked only the rolling of drums and a spotlight. For the sake of decorum my face had been covered with white gauze, with a slit in the middle through which protruded my lips.

We spoke little, my only coherent remark being that I had no wish to go on living if I were to look like Alice. Alice was a large country girl who had once been our maid. As a child she had been burned and disfigured by a Primus stove. I was not aware that she had made any impression on me, but now I was unable to get her out of my mind. It was not so much her looks as her smell I had continually in my nostrils and which I couldn't dissociate from the disfigurement.

They sat quietly and listened to me rambling for an hour. Then it was time for my dressings and they took their leave.

The smell of ether. Matron once doing my dressing with three orderlies holding my arms; a nurse weeping quietly at the head of the bed, and no remembered sign of a doctor. A visit from the lifeboat crew that had picked me up, and a terrible longing to make sense when talking to them. Their inarticulate sympathy and assurance of quick recovery. Their discovery that an ancestor of mine had founded the lifeboats, and my pompous and unsolicited promise of a subscription. The expectation of an American ambulance to drive me up to the Masonic Hospital (for Margate was used only as a clearing station). Believing that I was already in it and on my way and waking to the disappointment that I had not been moved. A dream that I was fighting to open my eyes and could not: waking in a sweat to realize it was a dream and then finding it to be true.

A sensation of time slowing down, of words and actions, all in slow motion. Sweat, pain, smells, cheering messages from the Squadron, and an overriding apathy.

Finally I was moved. The ambulance appeared with a cargo of two somewhat nervous ATS women who were to drive me to London, and, with my nurse in attendance, and wrapped in an old grandmother's shawl, I was carried aboard and we were off. For the first few miles I felt quite well, dictated letters to my nurse, drank bottle after bottle of ginger beer, and gossiped with the drivers. They described the countryside for me, told me they were new to the job, expressed satisfaction at having me for a consignment, asked me if I felt fine. Yes, I said, I felt fine; asked my nurse if the drivers were pretty, heard her answer yes, heard them simpering, and we were all very matey. But after about half an hour my arms began to throb from the rhythmical jolting of the road. I stopped dictating, drank no more ginger beer, and didn't care whether they were pretty or not. Then they lost their way. Wasn't it awful and shouldn't they stop and ask? No, they certainly shouldn't: they could call out the names of the streets and I would tell them where to go. By the time we arrived at Ravenscourt Park I was pretty much all-in. I was carried into the hospital and once again felt the warm September sun burning my face. I was put in a private ward and had the impression of a hundred excited ants buzzing around me. My nurse said good-bye and started to sob. For no earthly reason I found myself in tears. It had been a lousy hospital, I had never seen the nurse anyway, and I was now in very good hands; but I suppose I was in a fairly exhausted state. So there we all were, sniveling about the place and getting nowhere. Then the charge nurse came up and took my arm and asked me what my name was.

"Dick," I said.

"Ah," she said brightly. "We must call you Richard the Lion Heart."

I made an attempt at a polite laugh but all that came out was a dismal groan and I fainted away. The house surgeon took the opportunity to give me an anæsthetic and removed all the tannic acid from my left hand.

At this time tannic acid was the recognized treatment for burns. The theory was that in forming a hard cement it protected the skin from the air, and encouraged it to heal up underneath. As the tannic started to crack, it was to be chipped off gradually with a scalpel, but after a few months of experience, it was discovered that nearly all pilots with third-degree burns so treated developed secondary infection and septicæmia. This caused its use to be discontinued and gave us the dubious satisfaction of knowing that we were suffering in the cause of science. Both my hands were suppurating, and the fingers were already contracting under the tannic and curling down into the palms. The risk of shock was considered too great for them to do both hands. I must have been under the anæsthetic for about fifteen minutes and in that time I saw Peter Pease killed.

He was after another machine, a tall figure leaning slightly forward with a smile at the corner of his mouth. Suddenly from nowhere a Messerschmitt was on his tail about 150 yards away. For two seconds nothing happened. I had a terrible feeling of futility. Then at the top of my voice I shouted, "Peter, for God's sake look out behind!"

I saw the Messerschmitt open up and a burst of fire hit Peter's machine. His expression did not change, and for a moment his machine hung motionless. Then it turned slowly on its back and dived to the ground. I came to, screaming his name, with two nurses and the doctor holding me down on the bed.

"All right now. Take it easy, you're not dead yet. That must have been a very bad dream."

I said nothing. There wasn't anything to say. Two days later I had a letter from Colin. My nurse read it to me. It was very short, hoping that I was getting better and telling me that Peter was dead.

Slowly I came back to life. My morphia injections were less frequent and my mind began to clear. Though I began to feel and think again coherently I still could not see. Two VADs fainted while helping with my dressings, the first during the day and the other at night. The second time I could not sleep and was calling out for someone to stop the beetles running down my face, when I heard my nurse say fiercely, "Get outside quick: don't make a fool of yourself here!" and the sound of footsteps moving towards the door. I remember cursing the unfortunate girl and telling her to put her head between her knees. I was told later that for my first three weeks I did little but curse and blaspheme, but I remember nothing of it. The nurses were wonderfully patient and never complained. Then one day I found that I could see. My nurse was bending over me doing my dressings, and she seemed to me very beautiful. She was. I watched her for a long time, grateful that my first glimpse of the world should be anything so perfect. Finally I said:

"Sue, you never told me that your eyes were so blue."

For a moment she stared at me. Then, "Oh, Dick, how wonderful," she said. "I told you it wouldn't be long"; and she dashed out to bring in all the nurses on the block.

I felt absurdly elated and studied their faces eagerly, gradually connecting them with the voices that I knew.

# SIR HAROLD GEORGE NICOLSON

INCLUDED in this published edition of Harold Nicolson's diaries is the following letter to him from his
wife, Vita Sackville-West. It describes her visits to Vanessa Bell and Leonard Woolf, the sister and the husband of Virginia Woolf, after Virginia's suicide.

■

FROM *The Diaries and Letters of*
*Harold Nicolson*

V.S.-W. TO H.N.                                                    *8th April, 1941*

I went to see Vanessa [Bell] yesterday at Charleston. She could not
have been nicer and told me all about it. Rather to my dismay, she said
that Leonard wanted to see me. So I went to Monk's House. He was
having his tea—just one tea-cup on the table where they always had tea.
The house was full of his flowers, and all Virginia's things lying about as
usual. He said, "Let us go somewhere more comfortable," and took me
up to her sitting-room. There was her needle-work on a chair and all her
colored wools hanging over a sort of little towel-horse which she had had
made for them. Her thimble on the table. Her scribbling block with her
writing on it. The window from which one can see the river.

I said, "Leonard, I do not like your being here alone like this." He
turned those piercing blue eyes on me and said, "It is the only thing to
do." I saw then that he was right. But it must take some courage.

He talked about the whole thing perfectly calmly and in great detail,
shirking nothing. Some phrases bit. He said, "When we couldn't find her
anywhere, I went up to a derelict house which she was fond of in the
Downs, called Mad Misery, she wasn't there." I remember her telling
me about Mad Misery and saying that she would take me there one day.
They have been dragging the river, but are now giving up the search. As
the river is tidal, she has probably been carried out to sea. I hope so. I
hope they will never find her.

She could swim. I knew this because of a story she once told me
about Rupert Brooke at Cambridge, when they were both very young,
and he took off all his clothes and plunged naked into a moonlit pool,
and she thought she must do likewise; so she did, although very shy, and
they swam about together. But it appears that when she went to drown
herself, she was wearing big gum-boots (which she seldom did because

she hated them), and if those had filled with water, they would have dragged her down. Also she may have weighted her pockets with stones. The river is banked up with stones. The only thing that puzzles them is that they never found her hat floating. But Vanessa thinks it had an elastic to keep it on, so went down with her.

# EVELYN WAUGH

THE SELECTION that follows is taken from *Officers and Gentlemen,* the second volume of Waugh's brilliant World War II trilogy. The other novels in the series are *Men at Arms* and *The End of the Battle.*

■

## FROM *Officers and Gentlemen*

On the 31st of May Guy sat in a cave overhanging the beach of Sphakia where the final embarkation was shortly to begin. By his watch it was not yet ten o'clock but it seemed the dead of night. Nothing stirred in the moonlight. In the crowded ravine below the Second Halberdiers stood in column of companies, every man in full marching order, waiting for the boats. Hookforce was deployed on the ridge above, holding the perimeter against an enemy who since sunset had fallen silent. Guy had brought his section here late that afternoon. They had marched all the previous night and most of that day, up the pass, down to Imbros, down a gully to this last position. They dropped asleep where they halted. Guy had sought out and found Creforce headquarters and brought from them to the Hookforce commanders the last grim orders.

He dozed and woke for seconds at a time, barely thinking.

There were footsteps outside. Guy had not troubled to post a lookout. Ivor Claire's troop was a few hundred yards distant. He went to the mouth of the cave and in the moonlight saw a familiar figure and heard a familiar voice: "Guy? Ivor."

Ivor entered and sat beside him.

They sat together, speaking between long pauses in the listless drawl of extreme fatigue.

"This is damn fool business, Guy."

"It will all be over to-morrow."

"Just beginning. You're sure Tony Luxmore hasn't got the wrong end of the stick? I was at Dunkirk, you know. Not much fuss about priorities there. No inquiries afterwards. It doesn't make any sense, leaving the fighting troops behind and taking off the rabble. Tony's all in. I bet he muddled his orders."

"I've got them in writing from the G.O.C. Surrender at dawn. The men aren't supposed to know yet."

"They know all right."

"The General's off in a flying-boat to-night."

"No staying with the sinking ship."

"Napoleon didn't stay with his army after Moscow."

Presently Ivor said: "What does one *do* in prison?"

"I imagine a ghastly series of concert parties—perhaps for years. I've a nephew who was captured at Calais. D'you imagine one can do anything about getting posted where one wants?"

"I presume so. One usually can."

Another pause.

"There would be no sense in the G.O.C. sitting here to be captured."

"None at all. No sense in any of us staying."

Another pause.

"Poor Freda," said Ivor. "Poor Freda. She'll be an old dog by the time I see her again."

Guy briefly fell asleep. Then Ivor said: "Guy, what would you do if you were challenged to a duel?"

"Laugh."

"Yes, of course."

"What made you think of that now?"

"I was thinking about honor. It's a thing that changes, doesn't it? I mean, a hundred and fifty years ago we would have had to fight if challenged. Now we'd laugh. There must have been a time a hundred years ago when it was rather an awkward question."

"Yes. Moral theologians were never able to stop dueling—it took democracy to do that."

"And in the next war, when we are completely democratic, I expect it will be quite honorable for officers to leave their men behind. It'll be laid down in King's Regulations as their duty—to keep a *cadre* going to train new men to take the place of prisoners."

"Perhaps men wouldn't take kindly to being trained by deserters."

"Don't you think in a really modern army they'd respect them the more for being fly? I reckon our trouble is that we're at the awkward stage —like a man challenged to a duel a hundred years ago."

Guy could see him clearly in the moonlight, the austere face, haggard now but calm and recollected as he had first seen it in the Borghese gardens. It was his last sight of him. Ivor stood up saying: "Well, the path of honor lies up the hill," and he strolled away.

And Guy fell asleep.

He dreamed continuously, it seemed to him, and most prosaically. All night in the cave he marched, took down orders, passed them on, marked his map, marched again, while the moon set and the ships came into the bay and the boats went back and forth between them and the beach, and the ships sailed away leaving Hookforce and five or six thousand other men behind them. In Guy's dreams there were no exotic visitants among the shades of Creforce, no absurdity, no escape. Everything was as it had been the preceding day, the preceding night, night and day since he had landed at Suda, and when he awoke at dawn it was to the same half-world; sleeping and waking were like two airfields, identical in aspect though continents apart. He had no clear apprehension that this was a fatal morning, that he was that day to resign an immeasurable piece of his manhood. He saw himself dimly at a great distance. Weariness was all.

"They say the ships left food on the beach," said Sergeant Smiley.

"We'd better have a meal before we go to prison."

"It's true then, sir, what they're saying, that there's no more ships coming?"

"Quite true, Sergeant."

"And we're to surrender?"

"Quit true."

"It don't seem right."

The golden dawn was changing to unclouded blue. Guy led his section down the rough path to the harbor. The quay was littered with abandoned equipment and the wreckage of bombardment. Among the scrap and waste stood a pile of rations—bully beef and biscuit—and a slow-moving concourse of soldiers foraging. Sergeant Smiley pushed his way through them and passed back half a dozen tins. There was a tap of fresh water running to waste in the wall of a ruined building. Guy and his section filled their bottles, drank deep, refilled them, turned off the tap; then breakfasted. The little town was burned, battered and deserted by its inhabitants. The ghosts of an army teemed everywhere. Some were quite apathetic, too weary to eat; others were smashing their rifles on the stones, taking a fierce relish in this symbolic farewell to their arms; an officer stamped on his binoculars; a motor bicycle was burning; there was a small group under command of a sapper Captain doing something to a seedy-looking fishing-boat that lay on its side, out of the water, on the beach. One man sat on the sea-wall methodically stripping down his Bren and throwing the parts separately far into the scum. A very short man was moving from group to group saying: "Me surrender? Not bloody likely. I'm for the hills. Who's coming with me?" like a preacher exhorting a doomed congregation to flee from the wrath to come.

"Is there anything in that, sir?" asked Sergeant Smiley.

"Our orders are to surrender," said Guy. "If we go into hiding the Cretans will have to look after us. If the Germans found us we should only be marched off as prisoners of war—our friends would be shot."

"Put like that, sir, it doesn't seem right."

Nothing seemed right that morning, nothing seemed real.

"I imagine a party of senior officers have gone forward already to find the right person to surrender to."

An hour passed.

The short man filled his haversack with food, slung three water-bottles from his shoulders, changed his rifle for the pistol which an Australian gunner was about to throw away, and bowed under his load, sturdily strutted off out of their sight. Out to sea, beyond the mouth of the harbor, the open sea calmly glittered. Flies everywhere buzzed and settled. Guy had not taken off his clothes since he left the destroyer. He said: "I'll tell you what I'm going to do, Sergeant. I'm going to bathe."

"Not in *that*, sir?"

"No. There'll be clean water round the point."

Sergeant Smiley and two men went with him. There was no giving of orders that day. They found a cleft in the rocky spur that enclosed the harbor. They strolled through and came to a little cover, a rocky fore-shore, deep clear water. Guy stripped and dived and swam out in a sudden access of euphoria; he turned on his back and floated, his eyes closed to the sun, his ears sealed to every sound, oblivious of everything except physical ease, solitary and exultant. He turned and swam and floated again and swam; then he struck out for the shore, making for the opposite side. The cliffs here ran down into deep water. He stretched up and found a hand hold in a shelf of rock. It was already warm with the sun. He pulled up, rested luxuriously on his forearms with his legs dangling knee deep in water, paused, for he was feebler than a week ago, then raised his head and found himself staring into the eyes of another, a man who was seated above him on the black ledge and gazing down at him; a strangely clean and sleek man for Creforce; his eyes in the brilliant sunshine were the color of oysters.

"Can I give you a hand, sir?" asked Corporal-Major Ludovic. He stood and stooped and drew Guy out of the sea. "A smoke, sir?"

He offered a neat, highly pictorial packet of Greek cigarettes. He struck a light. Guy sat beside him, naked and wet and smoking.

"Where on earth have you been, Corporal-Major?"

"At my post, sir. With rear headquarters. With Major Hound."

"I thought you'd deserted us?"

"Did you, sir? Perhaps we both made a miscalculation."

"You mean you couldn't make the ships? Did Major Hound get away?"

"No, sir. I fear not. He miscalculated too."

"Where is he now? Why have you left him?"

"Need we go into that, sir? Wouldn't you say it was rather too early or too late for inquiries of that sort?"

"What are you doing here?"

"To be quite frank, sir, I was considering drowning myself. I am a weak swimmer and the sea is most inviting. You know something of theology, I believe, sir, I've seen some of your books. Would moralists hold it was suicide if one were just to swim out to sea, sir, in the fanciful hope of reaching Egypt? I haven't the gift of faith myself, but I have always been intrigued by theological speculation."

"You had better rejoin Sergeant Smiley and the remains of head-quarters."

"You speak as an officer, sir, or as a theologian?"

"Neither really," said Guy.

He stood up.

"If you aren't going to finish that cigarette, may I have it back?" Corporal Ludovic carefully pinched off the glowing end and returned the half to its packet. "Gold-dust," he said, relapsing into the language of the barracks. "I'll follow you round, sir."

Guy dived and swam back. By the time he was dressed, Corporal-Major Ludovic was among them. Sergeant Smiley nodded dully. Without speaking, they strolled together into Sphakia. The crowd of soldiers had grown and was growing as unsteady files shuffled from their hiding-places in the hills. Nothing remained of the ration dump. Men were sitting about with their backs against the ruined walls eating. The point of interest now was the boating party who were pushing their craft towards the water. The sapper Captain was directing them in a stronger voice than Guy had heard for some days.

"Easy . . . All together, now, heave . . . steady . . . keep her moving . . ." The men were enfeebled but the boat moved. The beach was steep and slippery with weed. ". . . Now then, once more all together . . . she's off . . . let her run . . . What ho, she floats . . ."

Guy pushed forward in the crowd.

"They're barmy," said a man next to him. "They haven't a hope in hell."

The boat was afloat. Three men, waist deep, held her; the Captain and the rest of his party climbed and began bailing out and working on the engine. Guy watched them.

"Anyone else coming?" the sapper called.

Guy waded to him.

"What are your chances?" he asked.

"One in ten, I reckon, of being picked up. One in five of making it on our own. We're not exactly well found. Coming?"

Guy made no calculation. Nothing was measurable that morning. He was aware only of the wide welcome of the open sea, of the satisfaction of finding someone else to take control of things.

"Yes. I'll just talk to my men."

The engine gave out a puff of oily smoke and a series of small explosions.

"Tell them to make up their minds. We'll be off as soon as that thing starts up."

Guy said to his section: "There's one chance in five of getting away. I'm going. Decide for yourselves."

"Not for me, sir, thank you," said Sergeant Smiley. "I'll stick to dry land."

The other men of his Intelligence section shook their heads.

"How about you, Corporal-Major? You can be confident that no moral theologian would condemn this as suicide."

Corporal-Major Ludovic turned his pale eyes out to sea and said nothing.

The sapper shouted: "Liberty boat just leaving. Anyone else want to come?"

"I'm coming," Guy shouted.

He was at the side of the boat when he noticed that Ludovic was close behind him. The engine started up, drowning the sound which Ludovic had heard. They climbed on board together. One of the watching crowd called, "Good luck, chums," and his words were taken up by a few others, but did not carry above the noise of the engine.

The sapper steered. They moved quite fast across the water, out of the oil and floating refuse. As they watched they saw the crowd on shore had all turned their faces skyward.

"Stukas again," said the sapper.

"Well, it's all over now. I supposed they've just come to have a look at their spoils."

The men on shore seemed to be of this opinion. Few of them took cover. The match was over, stumps drawn. Then the bombs began to fall among them.

"Bastards," said the sapper.

From the boat they saw havoc. One of the airplanes dipped over their heads, fired its machine-gun, missed and turned away. Nothing further was done to molest them. Guy saw more bombs burst on the now-deserted waterfront. His last thoughts were of X Commando, of Bertie and Eddie, most of all of Ivor Claire, waiting at their posts to be made prisoner. At the moment there was nothing in the boat for any of them to do. They had merely to sit still in the sunshine and the fresh breeze.

So they sailed out of the picture.

# LUDOVIC KENNEDY

LUDOVIC KENNEDY was born in Edinburgh, the son of a naval officer, and served with the Royal Navy during World War II. He is the author of several books about crime and the law, among them *10 Rillington Place* and *The Trial of Stephen Ward*. The following excerpt is from his memoir *On My Way to the Club*.

■

FROM *On My Way to the Club*

I had the first watch that May evening, a day out from the Clyde. With *Somali, Eskimo* and *Mashona* we were escorting the troopship *Britannic* and the battleship *Rodney* westwards across the Atlantic. It was, as I recall, an uneventful watch, and at about 9 p.m. while checking bearings and distance from *Rodney* for perhaps the sixth time, I heard the buzzer from the wireless office. Signalman Pearson, with whom I was sharing the watch, a barrel-shaped fellow partial to chocolate "Nutty," thrust his flabby fist into the voicepipe and hauled up the signal box.

"U-boat Disposition Report, I expect," he said.

He unraveled the signal, scanned it, then handed it to me. It was prefixed MOST IMMEDIATE, came from the cruiser *Norfolk* and went something like this: 1BS 1CR 66.40N 28.22W Co220 Sp 30.

"Pearson," I said, "does that mean what I think it means?"

"Yes, sir. One enemy battleship, one enemy cruiser, position sixty-six forty North, twenty-eight twenty-two West, course 220, speed 30 knots."

"Christ!" I said, and pressed the captain's buzzer.

In such a manner did I learn of the break-out into the Atlantic of the giant *Bismarck* together with the *Prinz Eugen*, an event followed by the most exciting week of my life. A glance at the chart showed that the German ships had been picked up in the Denmark Strait, the stretch of water that lies between Greenland and the north of Iceland. Although of intense interest the news did not then affect us personally, as we were 600 miles away and fully occupied with protecting *Rodney* and *Britannic* against U-boats. But it was the one topic of conversation throughout the ship. In the wardroom that night we discussed the likely eventualities into the early hours, and when my servant called me with tea at 7.30 next morning, I was already awake.

"Heard the news, sir?"

"No."

"*Hood*'s gone."

"*No!*"

"Yes, and *Prince of Wales* damaged."

The *Hood* gone—the most famous, most loved of British warships, the one above all others that epitomized the Navy and the country? It seemed impossible to believe. And the brand new battleship *Prince of Wales* damaged! If this is what the *Bismarck* could do in six minutes flat, what might she not achieve against the convoys from America? The question-mark that had arisen at the time of Dunkirk rose again. Loose in the Atlantic and supported by supply ships and tankers, she could prey on our shipping for months and cut the supply line on which we depended for survival.

After breakfast I went to the charthouse where Spider had put up a large scale chart of the Atlantic, and penciled on it the position of the first sighting of the German squadron, the location of the sinking of *Hood*, and the squadron's present position as received from the signals of the pursing *Norfolk*, *Suffolk* and wounded *Prince of Wales*. He had also marked the positions of the British ships closing in on *Bismarck*, and as the day passed and assuming she kept her present course and speed, it looked as though the commander-in-chief, Admiral Tovey, in his flagship *King George* V with the battlecruiser *Repulse* would be the first to engage her in the morning and (if the result was inconclusive) that we would be the second.

*Eskimo* and *Britannic* went off to the west, while we steamed south-westwards all day, the seas getting higher, the wind rising hourly. Inevitably that evening, as the gap between us gradually narrowed, one's thoughts turned to the action that lay ahead. Inevitably too one had mixed feelings, partly a desire to stop the *Bismarck* at all costs and by so doing perhaps win honor and glory, partly—and I'm not sure if it wasn't the stronger part—a reluctance to get embroiled at all. Our task, if we met, was to close in to some 6000 yards to deliver our four torpedoes. With *Rodney* soon outdistanced by the swifter enemy, we would have to undergo the full weight of his broadsides during the run-in; and we knew, without having to say it, that if we survived that, it would be a miracle.

When I came on watch again at midnight, it was blowing a gale. We had had to reduce speed to 15 knots, while *Rodney* with her long dachshund's snout pushing through the crests had lumbered past at her maximum 22 knots and was now out of sight ahead. I think that was the most uncomfortable watch I ever kept. The motion was like that of a hovercraft in a bumpy sea, greatly magnified, for we lunged at the waves rather than rode them. Throughout the watch the signals from the shadowers kept coming in, and it looked as though the commander-in-chief would make contact with the enemy at around noon. When I reached my cabin via the engine-room and boiler-room (for there was a danger of being washed overboard along the upper deck) I found the place a shambles—books, wireless and broken water carafe strewn about the deck. I left them where they were and clambered into bed.

"Sir?"

Where was I?

"Seven-thirty. Here's your tea. I've cleaned up the mess on the deck. And Jerry's done a bunk."

I thought sleepily, this man has got his priorities right.

"Lost contact, have we?"

"Not a whisper since you came off watch. Can't say I'm altogether sorry."

This is not the place to recount the changing events and fortunes of either side during the rest of the operation, for we had little knowledge of them at the time, and I have described them fully elsewhere.[1] Suffice it to say that two days later when we had begun to think that *Bismarck* had disappeared off the face of the waters, she was spotted alone (for she had detached *Prinz Eugen* for independent warfare) some 700 miles north-west of Brest. Her speed was down to 20 knots which suggested damage or a fuel problem (it was both) but which would bring her under German air cover within twenty-four hours. At that time *Rodney, Tartar* and *Mashona* (*Somali* had left us to refuel) were still bucketing around the ocean at high speed, but we were some 150 miles to the north of her, and with only a couple of knots' advantage had virtually no chance of catching up.

There was still however one British group between *Bismarck* and France, Vice-Admiral Somerville's Force H, steaming north from Gibraltar; it included the aircraft-carrier *Ark Royal*, and if one of her torpedo-planes could slow down *Bismarck* a little more, there might still be a faint chance of bringing her to book. At six that evening Admiral Tovey in *King George* V thundered over the horizon to join us, and took station in the van.

Presently a signal lamp began flashing from the flagship's bridge.

"To *Rodney*," sang out our signalman, "from C-in-C. What is your best speed?"

Then it was *Rodney*'s turn.

"To C-in-C. From *Rodney*. Twenty-two knots."

Gradually the distance between the two ships lengthened and *Rodney*'s lamp began flashing again.

"To C-in-C," shouted the signalman, "from *Rodney*. I am afraid that your twenty-two knots is faster than mine."

The flagship dropped back, and we all steamed on, less with any real hope of *Bismarck* being delivered to us than for the lack of any alterna-

---

[1] *Pursuit* (Collins, 1974), from which one or two passages are included here.

tive; if failure had to be admitted, let it not be admitted until the last possible moment. At 6.30 p.m. Tovey signaled the Admiralty that unless *Bismarck*'s speed had been reduced by midnight, *King George V* would have to return to harbor for lack of fuel; *Rodney*, with *Tartar* and *Mashona* also very short of fuel, could continue until eight the next morning. A little later came a report from Admiral Somerville that he had launched a torpedo attack with Swordfish aircraft, but they had registered no hits: if the light held, he aimed to launch another. For two hours we waited in anticipation of this, praying, hoping that it might be successful. Then came a second signal: "Attack completed. Estimate no hits."

So that was it. The long week's night was over: we had lost *Hood* and gained nothing in exchange, and *Bismarck* was freed to fight another day. In *Rodney* the captain told the crew over the public address system that their last chance of bringing the enemy to action had gone, and his commander ordered guns' crews to stand down. As for *Tartar*, it is difficult to convey the extent of the gloom in which we sat down to supper in the wardroom; nor, now that the week-long tension had been broken and the banging and buffeting were almost over, the overwhelming sense of exhaustion we all felt.

And then a most extraordinary thing happened. A signal was received from the cruiser *Sheffield*, shadowing *Bismarck* from astern: "Enemy's course 340°." Now 340° was almost due north, towards us, almost the opposite of the course of around 120° which she had been steering for Brest. On the bridge the general feeling was that the captain of the *Sheffield* must have made a mistake and thought *Bismarck* was steaming from right to left instead of left to right, understandable enough in the prevailing weather. But a few minutes later came a confirmatory signal, "Enemy's course North," and when further signals came in saying her speed was no more than a few knots, we all realized that *Bismarck* had been crippled by the last Swordfish attack (one torpedo had hit and jammed her rudder) and that she was going to be delivered to us after all.

So we made preparations for a battle which—unless *Bismarck* was able to slip away in the night—now looked inevitable; I stowed away all things breakable in my cabin, put on clean underwear and filled the brandy flask, mounted to my action station at the pom-pom, and wondered how it might be when the time came.

And then an odd thing occurred. An army officer, what the Navy calls a pongo, had come aboard when we first sailed as a wardroom guest; he had been given a week's leave, was hoping for a spot of sea breezes, had not thought to get involved in this. After dinner, not knowing the rules and having nothing to do, he had got rather tipsy, and now he appeared on the upper deck singing to the wild night his repertoire of pongo songs. When it was reported to the captain, he was ordered to go to his cabin and stay there. In former times, I suppose, he would have been clapped in irons or shot.

The weather worsened as the night wore on. The same head-wind into which *Bismarck* had involuntarily turned gave us a following sea; one in which the bows yawed sideways like a car in a skid, so that the ship leaned heavily to starboard and stayed there like a determined drunk until the quartermaster gradually eased her back to the given course. All night long we stayed at action stations while the ship slewed first one way and then the other and great rafts of spray, flung up from the bows, slapped at our oilskins and sou'westers. At first I had turned over in my mind what our role might be—perhaps a night torpedo attack—but soon anything beyond the next five or ten minutes seemed remote and irrelevant. After what felt like an eternity dawn came, with curling wave-tops, a leaden sky, wretched visibility. Presently the commander-in-chief sent a signal asking *Tartar* and *Mashona* their fuel situation. When he had been told, he sent another signal: "On receipt of executive signal, proceed as convenient to refuel at Plymouth or Londonderry." Were we not going to be allowed to be in at the kill?

During the morning watch guns' crews were allowed to go off in ones and twos for breakfast, and around 8 a.m. I went down to the wardroom for mine. Returning, I saw that *Rodney* and *King George* V had drawn well ahead of us, so popped up to the bridge for the latest news. There I found long faces and silence. I looked at the Yeoman of Signals quizzically and he handed me the signal log. "*Tartar* and *Mashona* from C-in-C," I read. "Proceed in execution of previous orders." So, thanks to our critical fuel situation (for if ordered in to a torpedo attack at speed, we would use up a great deal more), we were to be denied any part in the battle. But Tovey's original signal had said to proceed to refuel *as convenient*—"and what I'm going to find convenient," said the captain, "is to stick around for a bit and watch." I had reason for disappointment too. I had with me both my grandmother's Kodak and also a 16-millimeter Bell and Howell movie camera lent me by the father of a girlfriend; and with the pom-pom gun having no role to play, I could, had we been sent in on a torpedo attack, have obtained some unique footage.

A moment later I saw a big puff of cordite smoke above *Rodney*'s main armament and a second later heard the thud of her guns. Through my binoculars I saw in the distance, on the edge of a patch of rainfall, the dull smudge of a ship. There she was at last, the vessel that these past six days had filled our waking thoughts, been the very marrow of our lives. And, as the rain faded, what a ship! Broad in the beam, with long raked bow and formidable superstructure, two twin 15-inch gun turrets forward, two aft, symmetrical, massive, elegant, she was the largest, most handsome warship I, or any of us, had ever seen, a tribute to the skills of German shipbuilding. Now there came flashes from her guns and those of *King George* V. The final battle had begun.

In all my life I doubt if I will remember another hour as vividly as that one. It was the color contrasts I recall most, so rare in the eternal grayness of voyaging at sea. The sun appeared for the first time in days, shining from a blue sky between white, racing clouds; and the wind, still strong, was marbling and stippling the green water, creaming the tops of the short, high seas. There was the somber blackness of *Bismarck* and the gray of the British ships, the orange flashes of the guns, the brown of the cordite smoke, shell splashes tall as houses, white as shrouds.

It was a lovely sight to begin with, wild, majestic as one of our officers called it, almost too clean for the matter in hand. It seemed strange to think that within those three battleships were five thousand men; it seemed almost irrelevant, for this was a contest between ships not men. And who was going to win? None of us had any illusions about the devastating accuracy of *Bismarck*'s gunfire. She had sunk *Hood* with her fifth salvo, badly damaged *Prince of Wales*, straddled *Sheffield* and killed some of her crew the evening before, and hit an attacking destroyer in the course of the previous pitch-black night. But there were factors we had not reckoned with: the sheer exhaustion of her crew who had been at action stations for the past week, the knowledge as they waited through that long, last dreadful night that the British Navy was on its way to exact a terrible revenge, that they were virtually a sitting target.

*Rodney* was straddled with an early salvo but not hit, then with her fire divided, *Bismarck*'s gunnery sharply fell off. But that of *Rodney* and *King George* V steadily improved. As they moved in ever closer, we observed hit after hit. The hydraulic power that served the foremost turret must have been knocked out early, for the two guns were drooping downward at maximum depression, like dead flowers. The back of the next turret was blown over the side and one of its guns, like a giant finger, pointed drunkenly at the sky. A gun barrel in one of the two after turrets had burst, leaving it like the stub of a peeled banana. The main director tower had been smashed in and part of the foremost was in shreds. Through holes in the superstructure and hull we could see flames flickering in half a dozen places. But still her flag flew; still, despite that fearful punishment, she continued, though now fitfully, to fire.

It was not a pretty sight. *Bismarck* was a menace that had to be destroyed, a dragon that would have severed the arteries that kept Britain alive. And yet to see her now, this beautiful ship, surrounded by enemies on all sides, hopelessly outgunned and outmaneuvered, being slowly battered to a wreck, filled one with awe and pity. As Tovey said in his dispatch: "She put up a most gallant fight against impossible odds, worthy of the old days of the Imperial German Navy." And George Whalley, our Canadian lieutenant, wrote, "What that ship was like inside did not bear thinking of; her guns smashed, the ship full of fire, her people hurt; and surely all men are much the same when hurt." It was a thought shared by many British sailors that day,[2] yet one rarely expressed by airmen who incinerate cities or by soldiers of those they kill in tanks.

By 10 a.m. the last of *Bismarck*'s guns had fallen silent. She was still making headway through the water, though now listing heavily to port. The fires had spread, and now smoke was issuing from a hundred cracks and crevices in the deck. And then, as we looked at this silent, dead-weight shambles of a ship, we saw for the first time what had previously existed only in our imagination, the enemy in person, a little trickle of men in ones and twos, running or hobbling towards the quarterdeck to escape from the inferno that was raging forward; and as we watched they began to jump into the sea.

We had seen enough. It was time—way beyond time—to go home.

"Make to *Mashona*," said the captain, "course 045°, speed 15 knots."

We had missed taking part in one battle; but another, unsought and exclusive to us, lay just ahead.

[2] And, a few days earlier, by German ones. When the gunnery officer of the *Prinz Eugen* saw *Hood* blow up, he murmured to those around him, "Poor devils, poor devils!" No sailor of any nation enjoys watching the end of any ship.

# SIR HAROLD GEORGE NICOLSON

THE WAR comes home to Harold Nicolson, as he laments the changes he has seen. In editing Nicolson's diaries, his son Nigel here notes: "This picture of his impoverishment is endearing but fantastic. . . . His style of living never varied then, nor after the war, from what he describes here as modest."

■

FROM *The Diaries and Letters of Harold Nicolson*

DIARY                                                       *4th June, 1941*

I am rather amused, and slightly shocked, by my attitude toward my finances. I have always cherished the fantasy that I do not care about money. I made a great show of being completely independent of my wife's income. Well, now it has all crashed, and I am reduced, it seems, to £400 a year without the possibility of earning more.[1] I realize that this residue would seem to the working classes a good £8 a week. To me it appears an utter impossibility. Meanwhile I have written to Ben asking for a loan of £500.

This shows how in this dynamic age people who adjust themselves to modifications of the static are caught out. Thus I, realizing dimly that the old Edwardian world of bath-salts and ortolans[2] was doomed to disappearance, trained myself from the age of 22 to despise (and thereby not to desire) that shape of civilization which I foresaw would not last. It meant nothing whatsoever to me that Derby House and Stafford House and Chatsworth should become shabby and then dead. I achieved a different and no less self-indulgent form of elegance which seemed to me likely to survive my own lifetime. It consisted of comparatively modest establishments in the country and in London, and a gay combination of the Café Royal, Bloomsbury, rooms in the Temple, the Travellers Club, the garden at Sissinghurst, foreign travel, the purchase of books and pictures and the unthinking enjoyment of food and wine. That all seemed to us very bohemian and far more modern and self-denying than

[1] His salary as a Junior Minister was £1,500, and Income Tax was 10/- in the pound. but V.S-W's income was added to his for the purpose of assessing surtax. He had been obliged to give up all his journalistic work.

[2] A small bird, considered a delicacy.

■ 157 ■

Polesden Lacey or Londonderry House. And now this tide of self-sacrifice is lapping at our own feet. We shall have to walk and live a Woolworth life hereafter. I feel so poor. I hate the destruction of elegance. The drabness of Berlin or Moscow will creep into my lovely London streets.

We have taken Mosul.[3] But the public are in a trough of depression over Crete and acclaim victories slightly, feeling that we shall probably be turned out again. The B.E.F.[4] is being called "Back Every Fortnight."

[3] The last German base in Iraq.
[4] British Expeditionary Force.

# JULIAN BARNES

JULIAN BARNES, born in Leicester, won literary prizes in England, Italy, and France for his novel *Flaubert's Parrot.* His other novels include *Before She Met Me, A History of the World in 10½ Chapters,* and *Staring at the Sun,* from which the following excerpt was taken.

■

## FROM *Staring at the Sun*

This is what happened. On a calm, black night in June 1941 Sergeant-Pilot Thomas Prosser was poaching over Northern France. His Hurricane IIB was black in its camouflage paint. Inside the cockpit, red light from the instrument panel fell softly on Prosser's hands and face; he glowed like an avenger. He was flying with the hood back, looking towards the ground for the lights of an aerodrome, looking towards the sky for the hot color of a bomber's exhaust. Prosser was waiting, in the last half-hour before dawn, for a Heinkel or a Dornier on its way back from some English city. The bomber would have skirted anti-aircraft guns, declined the publicity of searchlights, dodged barrage balloons and night fighters; it would be steadying itself, the crew would be thinking of hot coffee fierce with chicory, the landing gear would crunch down—and then would come the poacher's crafty retribution.

There was no prey that night. At 3.46 Prosser set course for base. He crossed the French coast at 18,000 feet. Perhaps disappointment had made him delay his return longer than usual, for as he glanced up the Channel to the east he saw the sun begin to rise. The air was empty and serene as the orange sun extracted itself calmly and steadily from the sticky yellow bar of the horizon. Prosser followed its slow exposure. Out of trained instinct, his head jerked on his neck every three seconds, but it seems unlikely he would have spotted a German fighter had there been one. All he could take in was the sun rising from the sea: stately, inexorable, almost comic.

Finally, when the orange globe sat primly on the shelf of distant waves, Prosser looked away. He became aware of danger again; his black airplane in the bright morning air was now as conspicuous as some Arctic predator caught in the wrong fur by a change of season. As he banked and turned, banked and turned, he glimpsed below him a long trail of black smoke. A solitary ship, perhaps in trouble. He descended quickly towards the twinkling, miniature waves, until at last he could make out a tubby merchantman heading west. But the black smoke had stopped, and there seemed nothing wrong; probably she had just been stoking up.

At 8,000 feet Prosser flattened out and set fresh course for base. Half-way across the Channel he allowed himself, like the German bomber crews, to think about hot coffee, and the bacon sandwich he would eat after debriefing. Then something happened. The speed of his descent had driven the sun back below the horizon, and as he looked toward the east he saw it rise again: the same sun coming up from the same place across the same sea. Once more, Prosser put aside caution and just watched: the orange globe, the yellow bar, the horizon's shelf, the serene air, and the smooth, weightless lift of the sun as it rose from the waves for the second time that morning. It was an ordinary miracle he would never forget.

# GRAHAM GREENE

GRAHAM GREENE was a celebrated novelist, short story writer, and playwright. His novels include *The Power and the Glory, The End of the Affair, The Quiet American, The Honorary Consul,* and *Brighton Rock.* Among his plays are *The Potting Shed* and *The Complaisant Lover,* and he wrote the screenplay for *The Third Man,* among other notable films. His novel *The Heart of the Matter* is set in wartime West Africa, where Greene himself worked for the British government during the war.

■

## FROM *The Heart of the Matter*

They stood on the jetty next morning: the first light lay in cold strips along the eastern sky. The huts in the village were still shuttered with silver. At two that morning there had been a typhoon—a wheeling pillar of black cloud driving up from the coast, and the air was cold yet with the rain. They stood with coat collars turned up watching the French shore, and the carriers squatted on the ground behind them. Mrs. Perrot came down the path from the bungalow wiping the white sleep from her eyes, and from across the water very faintly came the bleating of a goat. "Are they late?" Mrs. Perrot asked.

"No, we are early." Scobie kept his glasses focused on the opposite shore. He said, "They are stirring."

"Those poor souls," Mrs. Perrot said, and shivered with the morning chill.

"They are alive," the doctor said.

"Yes."

"In my profession we have to consider that important."

"Does one ever get over a shock like that? Forty days in open boats."

"If you survive at all," the doctor said, "you get over it. It's failure people don't get over, and this, you see, is a kind of success."

"They are fetching them out of the huts," Scobie said. "I think I can count six stretchers. The boats are being brought in."

"We were told to prepare for nine stretcher cases, and four walking ones," the doctor said. "I suppose there've been some more deaths."

"I may have counted wrong. They are carrying them down now. I think there are seven stretchers. I can't distinguish the walking cases."

The flat cold light, too feeble to clear the morning haze, made the distance across the river longer than it would seem at noon. A native dugout canoe bearing, one supposed, the walking cases came blackly out of the haze: it was suddenly very close to them. On the other shore they were having trouble with the motor of a launch: they could hear the irregular putter, like an animal out of breath.

First of the walking cases to come on shore was an elderly man with an arm in a sling. He wore a dirty white topee, and a native cloth was draped over his shoulders: his free hand tugged and scratched at the white stubble on his face. He said in an unmistakably Scotch accent, "Ah'm Loder, chief engineer."

"Welcome home, Mr. Loder," Scobie said. "Will you step up to the bungalow and the doctor will be with you in a few minutes?"

"Ah have no need of doctors."

"Sit down and rest. I'll be with you soon."

"Ah want to make ma report to a proper official."

"Would you take him up to the house, Perrot?"

"I'm the District Commissioner," Perrot said. "You can make your report to me."

"What are we waitin' for then?" the engineer said. "It's nearly two months since the sinkin'. There's an awful lot of responsibility on me, for the captain's dead." As they moved up the hill to the bungalow, the persistent Scotch voice, as regular as the pulse of a dynamo, came back to them. "Ah'm responsible to the owners."

The other three had come on shore, and across the river the tinkering in the launch went on: the sharp crack of a chisel, the clank of metal, and then again the spasmodic putter. Two of the new arrivals were the cannon fodder of all such occasions: elderly men with the appearance of plumbers who might have been brothers if they had not been called Forbes and Newall, uncomplaining men without authority, to whom things simply happened: one had a crushed foot and walked with a crutch; the other had his hand bound up with shabby strips of tropical shirt. They stood on the jetty with as natural a lack of interest as they would have stood at a Liverpool street corner waiting for the local to open. A stalwart gray-headed woman in mosquito boots followed them out of the canoe.

"Your name, madam?" Druce asked, consulting a list. "Are you Mrs. Rolt?"

"I am not Mrs. Rolt. I am Miss Malcott."

"Will you go up to the house? The doctor . . ."

"The doctor has far more serious cases than me to attend to."

Mrs. Perrot said, "You'd like to lie down."

"It's the last thing I want to do," Miss Malcott said. "I am not in the least tired." She shut her mouth between every sentence. "I am not hungry. I am not nervous. I want to get on."

"Where to?"

"To Lagos. To the Educational Department."

"I'm afraid there will be a good many delays."

"I've been delayed two months. I can't stand delay. Work won't wait." Suddenly she lifted her face toward the sky and howled like a dog.

The doctor took her gently by the arm and said, "We'll do what we can to get you there right away. Come up to the house and do some telephoning."

"Certainly," Miss Malcott said, "there's nothing that can't be straightened on a telephone."

The doctor said to Scobie, "Send those other two chaps up after us. They are all right. If you want to do some questioning, question them."

Druce said, "I'll take them along. You stay here, Scobie, in case the launch arrives. French isn't my language."

Scobie sat down on the rail of the jetty and looked across the water. Now that the haze was lifting, the other bank came closer: he could make out now with the naked eye the details of the scene: the white warehouse, the mud huts, the brasswork of the launch glittering in the sun: he could see the red fezzes of the native troops. He thought: Just such a scene as this and I might have been waiting for Louise to appear on a stretcher—or perhaps not waiting. Somebody settled himself on the rail beside him, but Scobie didn't turn his head.

"A penny for your thoughts, sir."

"I was just thinking that Louise is safe, Wilson."

"I was thinking that too, sir."

"Why do you always call me sir, Wilson? You are not in the police force. It makes me feel very old."

"I'm sorry, Major Scobie."

"What did Louise call you?"

"Wilson. I don't think she liked my Christian name."

"I believe they've got that launch to start at last, Wilson. Be a good chap and warn the doctor."

A French officer in a stained white uniform stood in the bow: a soldier flung a rope and Scobie caught and fixed it. "Bon jour," he said, and saluted.

The French officer returned his salute—a drained-out figure with a twitch in the left eyelid. He said in English, "Good morning. I have seven stretcher cases for you here."

"My signal says nine."

"One died on the way and one last night. One from blackwater and one from—from, my English is bad, do you say fatigue?"

"Exhaustion."

"That is it."

"If you will let my laborers come on board they will get the stretchers off." Scobie said to the carriers, "Very softly. Go very softly." It was an unnecessary command: no white hospital attendants could lift and carry more gently. "Won't you stretch your legs on shore?" Scobie asked, "or come up to the house and have some coffee?"

"No. No coffee, thank you. I will just see that all is right here." He was courteous and unapproachable, but all the time his left eyelid flickered a message of doubt and distress.

"I have some English papers if you would like to see them."

"No, no thank you. I read English with difficulty."

"You speak it very well."

"That is a different thing."

"Have a cigarette?"

"Thank you, no. I do not like American tobacco."

The first stretcher came on shore—the sheets were drawn up to the man's chin and it was impossible to tell from the stiff vacant face what his age might be. The doctor came down the hill to meet the stretcher and led the carriers away to the Government rest-house where the beds had been prepared.

"I used to come over to your side," Scobie said, "to shoot with your police chief. A nice fellow called Durand—a Norman."

"He is not here any longer," the officer said.

"Gone home?"

"He's in prison at Dakar," the French officer replied, standing like a figure-head in the bows, but the eye twitching and twitching. The stretchers slowly passed Scobie and turned up the hill: a boy who couldn't have been more than ten, with a feverish face and a twiglike arm thrown out from his blanket: an old lady with gray hair falling every way who twisted and turned and whispered: a man with a bottle nose—a nob of scarlet and blue on a yellow face. One by one they turned up the hill, the carriers' feet moving with the certainty of mules. "And Père Brûle?" Scobie said. "He was a good man."

"He died last year of blackwater."

"He was out here twenty years without leave, wasn't he? He'll be hard to replace."

"He has not been replaced," the officer said. He turned and gave a short savage order to one of his men. Scobie looked at the next stretcher load and looked away again. A small girl—she couldn't have been more than six—lay on it. She was deeply and unhealthily asleep; her fair hair was tangled and wet with sweat; her open mouth was dry and cracked, and she shuddered regularly and spasmodically. "It's terrible," Scobie said.

"What is terrible?"

"A child like that."

"Yes. Both parents were lost. But it is all right. She will die."

Scobie watched the bearers go slowly up the hill, their bare feet very gently flapping the ground. He thought: It would need all Father Brûle's ingenuity to explain that. Not that the child would die: that needed no explanation. Even the pagans realized that the love of God might mean an early death, though the reason they ascribed was different; but that the child should have been allowed to survive the forty days and nights in the open boat—that was the mystery, to reconcile that with the love of God.

And yet he could believe in no God who was not human enough to love what he had created. "How on earth did she survive till now?" he wondered aloud.

The officer said gloomily, "Of course they looked after her on the boat. They gave up their own share of the water often. It was foolish, of course, but one cannot always be logical. And it gave them something to think about." It was like the hint of an explanation—too faint to be grasped. He said, "Here is another who makes one angry."

The face was ugly with exhaustion: the skin looked as though it were about to crack over the cheekbones: only the absence of lines showed that it was a young face. The French officer said, "She was just married —before she sailed. Her husband was lost. Her passport says she is nineteen. She may live. You see, she still has some strength." Her arms as thin as a child's lay outside the blanket, and her fingers clasped a book firmly. Scobie could see the wedding-ring loose on her dried-up finger.

"What is it?"

"Timbres," the French officer said. He added bitterly, "When this damned war started, she must have been still at school."

Scobie always remembered how she was carried into his life on a stretcher, grasping a stamp-album, with her eyes fast shut.

# MARIE VASSILTCHIKOV

---

MARIE VASSILTCHIKOV, a White Russian princess, found herself on her own in Berlin early in 1940. She found a minor position in the Foreign Office. Throughout the war she kept a diary in which she wrote almost every day. The entries for June 1941 through July 1943 were not available for publication, but her brother, George Vassiltchikov, who edited the diaries, drew on the letters she wrote during this period to fill the gap.

---

■

## FROM *Berlin Diaries*

*Missie in Berlin to her brother George in Rome, 1 July 1941*

Burchard of Prussia was just here, after being sent back from the Russian front because he is a "royal." He says it is absolutely beastly. Hardly any prisoners are being taken by either side. The Russians fight and torture like criminals, not soldiers, putting up their hands and then, when the Germans come up to them, shooting them *à bout portant*; they even shoot from behind the German medical orderlies who try to help their wounded. However, they are very courageous and the fighting everywhere is very heavy. All three Clary boys are now out there, which must be ghastly for their poor parents.

Met the Wrede girls, who have just heard that their brother Eddie has been killed. He was only twenty and always so bursting with beans. In general, the losses this time are incomparably greater than during the earlier campaigns. Nevertheless the German advance is progressing well, as was to be expected . . .

# GUSTAV HERLING

GUSTAV HERLING was arrested in eastern Poland while trying to cross the Lithuanian border and was sentenced to five years' forced labor in a camp near Archangel. He was freed in the amnesty that followed the signing of the pact between Poland and the Soviet Union in 1941. When Herling's labor camp memoir, *A World Apart,* was first published in England in 1951, Bertrand Russell wrote in the preface that of all the books he had read "relating the experiences of victims in Soviet prisons and labour camps, Mr. Gustav Herling's . . . is the most impressive and best written."

■

## FROM A *World Apart*

### "IN THE REAR OF THE WAR FOR THE FATHERLAND"

As for telling tales in general, it is very common. In prison the man who turns traitor is not exposed to humiliation; indignation against him is unthinkable. He is not shunned, the others make friends with him; in fact, if you were to try and point out the loathsomeness of treachery, you would not be understood.
—Dostoevsky—*The House of the Dead*

### 1. A GAME OF CHESS

The outbreak of the Russo-German war was responsible for some essential changes in my life: on June 29th, together with other foreigners and Russian political prisoners, I was taken off work at the food supply center and sent to the newly-created 57th brigade, which was to work at haymaking in the forest clearings during the summer, and in the autumn and winter to help in the saw-mills and with the loading of felled trees on to open railway trucks.

The last week which I spent at the center, however, allowed me to observe the effects of the German surprise attack, and the undisguised psychological anxiety with which the camp's garrison and administrative staff met the news of the outbreak of war. The first reaction was a mixture of astonishment and fear; only Mr. Churchill's declaration, from which we gathered that "England is with us, not against us," brought some relief. The guard attached to our brigade greeted the news with a loud "urra," throwing his fur cap and his rifle—with bayonet fixed—into the air, and began to assure us excitedly that "England has never yet lost

a war," clearly forgetting that only a few days ago England had been a
"little island" which the Germans "could cover with their hat." A similar
change of attitude, although of course in a much more intelligent form,
was noticeable in the tone of the Soviet radio. News bulletins and political commentaries, which until recently had welcomed every German
success in the West with wild acclamations, now overflowed with anti-
German propaganda and cooed gently whenever they mentioned England or the occupied countries. So, externally at least, appeared the
change of dancing partners. But actually we had already heard and recognized earlier the murmurs of the approaching storm. We did not ignore the meaning of the communiqué which Tass, the Soviet Press
agency, issued during the first days of June. It was a "categorical denial
of rumors, current in the West, that several Siberian divisions had been
moved from the Far East to the banks of the River Bug" (which was then
the boundary between Russian- and German-occupied Poland). The
agency report calmly reassured its listeners that the army movements in
question were made within the framework of normal summer maneuvers, and that the good-neighborly relations of Germany and the Soviet
Union, cemented by the pact of August 1939, could not be destroyed by
the shameful intrigues of Western warmongers. The engineer Sadovski,
once the friend of Lenin and Dierzhynski and vice-commissar for light
industry in one of the Russian post-revolutionary governments, bent
close to me and whispered in my ear that the denials of Tass are to
intelligent people in Russia what positive newspaper reports are in England or France. The outbreak of war itself did not surprise Sadovski at
all; but he would not make any prophecy as to its further course or
outcome until the first month of the fighting had elapsed.

On the day after the first German attack on Russia, we were gathered outside the wooden hut which served as an office at the food supply
center, to hear Stalin's speech on the radio. It was the speech of a broken
old man; he hesitated, his choking voice was full of melodramatic over-
emphasis and glowed with humble warmth at all patriotic catch-phrases.
We stood in silence, our eyes on the ground, but I knew that every
prisoner there was suddenly thrilled by a spasm of hope, with that bewildered blindness of slaves for whom any hand which opens the prison
gates is the hand of Providence itself. During the first few weeks of the
war we talked of the fighting rarely and surreptitiously, but always in the
same words: "They are coming!" It is a measure of the bestiality and
despair to which the new system of slavery reduces its victims that not
only the thousands of simple Russians, Ukrainians and nacmeny, for
whom the Germans were the natural ally in their struggle against the
hated labor camps, but also almost without exception all European and
Russian communists, worldly, educated and experienced men, awaited
from day to day with impatience and excitement the coming of Nazi
liberators. I think with horror and shame of a Europe divided into two

parts by the line of the Bug, on one side of which millions of Soviet slaves prayed for liberation by the armies of Hitler, and on the other millions of victims of German concentration camps awaited deliverance by the Red Army as their last hope.

The only free men whom I had an opportunity to observe, the camp guards, reacted, naturally, in quite a different fashion to the news of the German advance. For them the whole problem was summed up in the question: "Quis custodiet custodes?" They passed from the first instinctive anxiety about the fate of their "Socialist Fatherland" (which in Russians, in my opinion, has the character of an organic inferiority complex toward the Germans), to uncertainty about closer and more tangible matters, their own particular fate. Their fear was that, to meet the demands of the front, staff reduction might begin in the camp, in other words that they might be forced to give up an easy and secure job in the north to spend their time wandering about in the trenches. After the first two weeks of the war the position was made clear in the most unexpected way. There was something incredible in the arrival at Yercevo of fresh contingents of young and healthy N.K.V.D. soldiers[1] to strengthen the garrisons of camps on the shore of the White Sea, while at the same time the names of the towns mentioned in the wireless communiqués made it quite clear that the front was rapidly moving eastward. Now brigades of twenty prisoners walked out to work guarded by two armed soldiers,[2] and the first blood that the camp laid at the altar of its threatened fatherland was the declaration of total war on potential internal enemies. Thus all politicals were removed from responsible technical posts, and replaced by free officials; all German prisoners from the Volga settlements were transferred from camp offices to the forest brigades, where, however, they were treated with great respect by the Russian prisoners, who believed that they would soon rule the country; all foreign and political prisoners were taken off work at the food supply center, to prevent any danger of poisoning the food destined for co-operative stores outside the camp; the sentences of all who had been suspected of spying for the Germans were doubled, the liberation of political prisoners who were due to be released soon was postponed indefinitely, and several Polish officers, naturally suspected of pro-German sympathies, were placed in solitary confinement. The camp breathed freely again, and the wave of Russian patriotism, which had receded in the terror and fear of the first weeks, flowed back. The patriotic self-confidence of the camp garrison was doubtless greatly influenced by a certain occurrence which I witnessed during the last day of my work at the food supply center. We unloaded that day a truckful of Lithuanian pork, packed in jute wrap-

[1] The N.K.V.D. commands a powerful and quite independent army.

[2] If there were then twenty million prisoners in the camps, this must have cost the Soviet command about a million picked soldiers, who made no contribution to the war effort.

pings stamped with the German import stamp. That load evidently did not reach its original destination, and after long wanderings finally arrived at Yercevo. To commemorate the outbreak of the "War for the Fatherland" the pork was divided equally between the speclarok—the shop supplying the ten highest officers of the camp command—and the modest shop near the camp zone for the administrative staff and the garrison.

A month passed and nothing happened. Once, when we were haymaking, Sadovski was asked for his conjectures of the future. He took a few twigs, two handfuls of hay and some berries of different colors, spread them on the grass, and opened a fascinating lecture. In his opinion, the first four weeks of the fighting would be decisive. While listening to official Soviet communiqués, it was necessary to keep before one's mind the map of Russia in order to determine the speed of the German advance. If the advance was very rapid, it was a bad sign, if only moderately quick—then there was nothing to fear. The defeat of Russia could only be possible if signs of inner demoralization accompanied defeats at the front. If the Red Army retreated in such panic and at such speed that it could only be held back by the bayonets of the N.K.V.D. Army in the rear, then, finding itself between two fires, it would turn round against its own rulers and start a civil war in Russia itself. But nothing of the kind was actually happening. Soviet forces were retreating in proper order, and could retreat like that right up to the Urals, where for years a reserve center of war industry had been built up, at the cost of great technical effort and human lives from the Ural labor camps, with just such a possibility in mind. The circumstances of Russia's final victory over the Germans would depend on the military and political tactics of her Western allies.

This view of the situation appeared to me to be quite logical and accurate, and I accepted it as my own. My own position had altered greatly since the signing of the Polish-Russian pact of July 1941, and the declaration of a general amnesty for all Polish prisoners in Russia. I could now desire Russian defeat only from a feeling of revenge, not from any logical reasoning or on the basis of any particular feeling towards the Germans. I found myself among the fifteen or twenty out of the two thousand prisoners in Yercevo who in face of continuous Russian defeats had the courage to believe and say loudly that Russia would not lose the war. Later I had to pay dearly for my opinion when brought before the Third Section of the N.K.V.D.

The situation of Poles in Russia was greatly altered by the Sikorski-Maiski pact and the amnesty. Before the Russo-German war broke out we were regarded as "anti-Nazi fascists," and cowards because we had been defeated so easily by the Germans; from the beginning of the war in June, until the end of July, we were just ordinary pro-Nazi fascists and, since Russia herself was suffering heavy defeats, perhaps not such cowards after all; in August, when the pact was signed, we suddenly became fighters for freedom and allies. The guard of the 57th brigade, who, I was told, before that time had not spared Poles many insulting reproaches for their defeat in 1939, patted me on the back when the news of the amnesty came and said: "Well, my boy, now we'll fight the Germans together." This sudden reconciliation did not please me for two reasons: first, a prisoner can never forgive his warder, and second, it turned against me my fellow-prisoners, both Russian and foreign, who were not fortunate enough to have been born Poles, and to many of whom I had become attached more deeply than to any of my own compatriots. After the amnesty other prisoners became hostile towards the Poles, regarding them from that time as potential allies in the hated task of defending Soviet prisons and labor camps.

In December 1941 we heard Stalin give another and very different speech. I shall never forget that strong voice, cold and penetrating, those words hammered out as if with a fist of stone. He said that the German offensive had been arrested at the outskirts of Moscow and Leningrad, that the day of victory over German barbarism was approaching, and that the thanks for this must go not only to the heroes of the Red Army, to airmen, sailors, partisans, workers and farmers, but also to those who guarded "the rear of the war for the Fatherland." The prisoners, collected in the barracks to hear the speech, listened to it with expressions of helpless despair on their faces, while I thought of Sadovski's theory and the reinforcements of N.K.V.D. troops with which the garrisons of the Kargopol camp had been supplied just after the declaration of war. Yes, even here, we were a part of the "rear of the war for the Fatherland."

# DAVID BRINKLEY

WASHINGTON abounded with foreigners and some in-
trigue during the war. David Brinkley, now a leading
television journalist, was NBC White House correspondent for part of the war. Here he recalls a little Soviet
covert activity in the period before the USSR became
an ally.

■

FROM *Washington Goes to War*

In this period Russian undercover activities in America were about
as widespread as the Germans'. In 1941, Walter Krivitsky came to Washington trying, he said, to avoid being killed by Josef Stalin's gunmen. He
was an ex-NKVD agent and a follower of Leon Trotsky, who had been
murdered in Mexico City by a Stalin agent who split his skull with an
axe. Krivitsky had defected from the Soviet Union and had written a
book, *I Was Stalin's Agent*, which had been read with extreme displeasure in the Kremlin. Now he had been running and hiding for years. On
the night of February 10 he tried to hide in the Bellevue Hotel, a small
place near the U.S. Capitol. On the following morning he was found
dead, shot through the head. The District of Columbia police examined
the body and the hotel room and pronounced it a suicide. No one believed it, but nothing further was ever proved.

There were other nasty episodes. The State Department discovered
two blundering Soviet military attachés, one of them Major Constan-
tine Ovchinnikov, exploring aircraft plants and loudly demanding that
the plant managers hand over plans and technical drawings. They were
ordered out of the country. As soon as this got into the papers, Mrs.
Willard West of suburban Chevy Chase wrote a furious letter to the State
Department. Ovchinnikov, she said, had rented the top floor of her
house and always kept the door locked. When he left, she found he had
kept carrier pigeons in her maid's room and in the attic. "I have never
seen such filth in my life," she wrote. "It was like a barnyard." But by the
time her letter arrived, Germany had invaded the Soviet Union and the
Russians suddenly were potential allies against the Nazis. Ovchinnikov
and his colleague were pardoned while they were still in San Francisco
awaiting a ship to take them home. They both returned to the Washing-

ton embassy. As for Mrs. West's complaint about the pigeon droppings, a State Department memo from Edward Page said, "It seems rather suspicious that a military attaché should keep carrier pigeons. But perhaps it is a hobby."

# JULIA VOZNESENSKAYA

JULIA VOZNESENSKAYA, born and educated in Leningrad, was a founder of Maria, the first independent
women's group in the Soviet Union. Imprisoned in the
late 1970s and later exiled for her social and literary
activities, she was forced to emigrate to West Germany
in 1980. The following story is from *The Women's De-
cameron,* a collection of reminiscences of ordinary Soviet women, presented in their own words.

■

## Story Seven

[by the worker Olga. This story brings us back to the war, when
not only heroic exploits were performed, but crimes were committed as well.]

I actually come from the country, near Tikhvin. I didn't come to
work at the shipyard in Leningrad until I was eighteen; before that I was
just an ordinary country girl.

They say that every Russian village has its village idiot or madman.
I don't know about other villages, but ours had this old woman called
Moneybags Nyurka. Why she was given that nickname I shall tell you
right now. Her real name was Antonova.

When I knew Moneybags Nyurka she already hardly looked human
any more. She went about in rags and tatters, in winter she would find a
corner in people's huts to stay in, and in summer she just lived in the
forest near the village. She was frightening; the children were scared of
her, and they teased her and were unkind to her. This is the story they
told about her.

The evacuees from the Leningrad siege were brought through our
village. They were apparently on their way to Siberia, but the really sick
ones were taken off the train and left with us. I think the same happened
at other stations along the way, too. They were distributed round the
different huts without the owners even being asked. The order was simply given to settle the evacuees. But as for feeding them, the authorities
didn't show any concern about that, and we couldn't even get bread for
them on their cards. It was very hard.

But these people had escaped from the Germans, and they were
determined not to die now they were free. So one way or the other they
survived. The stronger ones started working on the collective farm. No-

body needed their city education, but their hands could be used, even if they were weak. Others who could hardly walk swapped their town things for bread, potatoes, and milk for their children. Our women felt very sorry for the kiddies from Leningrad. If anyone had a cow they would sit the evacuated children at the same table as their own and shove spuds and milk at them, telling them to eat it while it lasted! But there were some people who took advantage of other people's misfortune and grew rich on it. They did their best to barter the last rags out of the siege people.

When it came to grasping and greed, Nyurka Antonova took the prize. She didn't wait for the siege people to come to her to barter, oh no! She would take her basket, put eggs, lard, and a bottle of milk in it and set off round the houses.

"Have you got any foxes living with you?" she would ask. "Foxes" was her name for the siege people, because she said they had been smoked out of their holes in Leningrad, and she wanted to show she didn't care a rap for what people said about her cheating and greed. She would go into a hut where there were lodgers billeted and say to them: "Want to do some bartering? Well then, let's see what you've got!"

She wouldn't take any of the things they offered her.

"Show me everything you brought with you! I'll do the choosing!"

The people had no choice, they had to let Nyurka at their things, and she would look at them and feel them and then name her prices. She would haggle, and the people were too weak and tired to put up a fight; they would see the food and agree to anything.

Nyurka went on robbing people like that until she had a whole hut full of possessions: high-heeled fashion shoes, astrakhan coats, felt boots, fur collars. She even got herself a whole pile of hats! Our women would laugh at her: "What do you need their city hats for, Nyurka? Are you going to make a scarecrow for your vegetable patch?"

And Nyurka used to reply: "I'm going to get rich on those scum who ran away instead of defending their city, and then I'm going to apply to live in Leningrad myself. Then the hats will come in useful."

That was her plan.

Apart from the rags, Nyurka sold food for cash, too. Those poor siege people, she just ripped them off, it was daylight robbery. And then she would boast: "I've got enough money to paper my walls with, just like a city house! I've got enough to last me to the grave, and there'll be enough left over to last my son for the rest of his life, too."

Nyurka herself also had a lodger, a young woman with a child, a little girl. She had no one to turn to, so Nyurka stripped her of every copeck. They say the lodger was a clean young girl, and she got rid of all the cockroaches and bedbugs from Nyurka's hut. Only the flies were left. And then someone sent Nyurka some strips of paper soaked in fly poison.

She would put one of the bits of paper in a saucer of water, with a tiny piece of sugar on top: the flies would land on it and die. But the Leningrad girl was scared her daughter might get some sort of infection from the flies. One day the little girl happened to see the sugar in the saucer of fly poison. She ate the sugar and licked the saucer clean, and immediately started to double up with stomach pains. The mother rushed to Nyurka.

"Give me some milk for my child!" she said. "She's poisoned herself!"

But Nyurka said: "You pay me first!"

She rushed over to her trunk and pushed out everything she had left. But Nyurka already knew every piece of junk she had, and turned up her nose at it: "There's nothing worth choosing there. Just give me the whole lot for a jar of milk, or your little girl will die!"

She gave her everything, right down to the last stocking. Then she gave the child milk and water to drink and saved her life. After that incident our women said to Nyurka: "You'll pay for what you've done to the evacuees, Nyurka! If men don't punish you, God will."

And that's what did happen.

Fate tested Nyurka for a long time. First it was through her son. She wanted to save her son from going to the front, and she paid a lot of money, saying he was epileptic. But in the end they demanded such a big bribe that she decided her son wasn't worth all that money and told him to get ready to go to the front. It was the last year of the war.

"Maybe he'll be all right!" she said. "And he ought to visit Germany and get some trophies."

Her son didn't even make it to the front: his train was bombed. She was sad for a while, but it didn't make her any kinder to others, she kept trying to grab whatever she saw. Her husband didn't come back from the front either, and she took that quite calmly too: "With all my riches I'll find myself another, and I'll have a new son!"

Then the money reform finished her off. After the war they had this reform when all the money was replaced almost overnight. Nyurka couldn't exchange her hoards of money because she hadn't kept it in the savings bank, but hidden away in her cellar where no one would find it. So when her money suddenly turned into scraps of paper she just cracked. She came out of her house early the next morning, hung the fur coats and dresses on her apple trees, arranged all the shoes in a row by the gate, hung the underwear and silk stockings on the fence, and then went back into her hut. All the people gathered round and started to gossip: "Has Nyurka gone round the bend?"

They decided to go into her hut and see how she was. They went in and found her papering the walls with her money and singing songs. The woman really had gone out of her mind.

Nyurka wasn't frightening to look at, and the people would have felt sorry for her just like you felt sorry for the drunks lying under the fence and the fellows with shell-shock and the village idiots. But she would never let people forget what it was that drove her barmy. In winter and summer she was all right, but when autumn came and the leaves started falling off the trees, that's when Nyurka's madness showed itself. She would wander through the village and the forest collecting leaves and arranging them in little bundles. Then she would tie the bundles up with thread or string or anything else she could get hold of and hide them in secret places. And she would keep looking over her shoulder and repeating: "Now I've got lots of nice money again! Now I've got all my nice money back!"

But the people remembered how it used to be. That's why they gave her the nickname Moneybags Nyurka.

# LOUIS MACNEICE

THE IRISH-BORN poet Louis MacNeice was associated
with W. H. Auden, Christopher Isherwood, and Stephen
Spender in the thirties, but was never as strongly committed to Marxist doctrine. A classical scholar and lecturer in Greek and Latin, he worked for the BBC in
London for years. Among his books are *Autumn Journal,* a meditation on the course of events leading up
to Munich; *Autumn Sequel;* and *Letters from Iceland,*
which he wrote with Auden. "Swing-song" is from his
*Collected Poems.*

■

## Swing-song

I'm only a wartime working girl,
The machine shop makes me deaf,
I have no prospects after the war
And *my* young man is in the R.A.F.
    K for Kitty calling P for Prue . . .
    Bomb Doors Open . . .
    Over to You.

Night after night as he passes by
I wonder what he's gone to bomb
And I fancy in the jabber of the mad machines
That I hear him talking on the intercomm.
    K for Kitty calling P for Prue . . .
    Bomb Doors Open . . .
    Over to You.

So there's no one in the world, I sometimes think,
Such a wallflower as I
For I must talk to myself on the ground
While he is talking to his friends in the sky:
    K for Kitty calling P for Prue . . .
    Bomb Doors Open . . .
    Over to You.

# SHIRLEY HAZZARD

AUSTRALIAN-BORN Shirley Hazzard has written five novels; many of her short stories have been published in *The New Yorker*. She lives in New York with her husband, Francis Steegmuller. The following excerpt from her novel *The Transit of Venus* portrays the war-time adjustments of an Australian schoolgirl moved inland for safety.

■

## FROM *The Transit of Venus*

The following June, the greengrocer's windows were smashed because of being Italian. Manganelli's at the Junction put out a sign: WE ARE GREEKS. Once again the men set sail for history, in darkness and without streamers. France fell. There was the blitz, the RAF, and Mr. Churchill. Caro's class put aside the War of the Spanish Succession to read a book about London, the buildings standing out like heroes—the Guildhall, the Mansion House—which every night the flames consumed on the seven-o'clock news. Dora seethed under rationing, but yearned to be where bombs were falling. She took the conflict personally, frenzied by Mr. Churchill. It was Dora's war.

The neap tide of history had, as usual, left them high and dry.

Caro was becoming flesh. Her hands were assuming attitudes. In shoes dull with playground dust her feet were long and shapely. The belt of her school uniform, which at the time of Dunkirk had banded a mere child, by the siege of Tobruk delineated a cotton waist. Her body showed a delicate apprehension of other change. Caro knew the sources of the Yangtze, and words like hypotenuse. Even Grace did homework now, sitting on the floor. Dora was knitting for the merchant marine, charging this calm activity with vociferous unrest.

Greece fell, Crete fell. There was a toppling, even of history.

One hot day Caro looked up Pearl Harbor in the atlas. Buses were soon painted in swamp colors. Air-raid shelters were constructed, and a boom, useless, across the harbor mouth. You kept a bucket of sand in the kitchen with a view to incendiary bombs. Mr. Whittle was an air-raid warden, and the Kirkby boys were called up. The noble rhetoric of Downing Street scarcely applied to dark streets, austerity, and standing in the queue. Colonial families arrived from the East destitute, and

Singapore fell, fell. Orphans were numerous now; and the girls, in their civilian loss, no longer commanded special attention.

The school was moving to a country house, where the invading Japanese would hardly penetrate. Grace was too little to be saved by such methods, Caro would go alone. Caro would try out the fugitive state; if it came up to snuff, Grace might later be included.

Caro was installed one afternoon at the foot of the Blue Mountains. On the plain below, gum trees straggled back towards Sydney, bark was strewn like torn paper. The littlest children cried, but the parents would visit them in a fortnight if the petrol held up and the Japs did not arrive. There was also an ancient train as far as Penrith, but after that you were on your own. They knew about Penrith, a weatherboard town with telegraph poles and the sort of picture-house where you could hear the rain.

Grace waved out the car window: jealous, guilty, and safe.

It was Sunday. After sago pudding, they sang "Abide with Me," and Caro went out on the upstairs veranda. Fast falls the eventide. The darkness deepened in silence more desolate for the squawk of a bird they had been shown in illustrations. Incredulous response cracked in Caroline Bell's own throat. Smells of dry ground, of eucalyptus and a small herd of cows gave the sense of time suspended, or slowed to a pace in which her own acceleration must absurdly spin to no purpose. The only tremor in dim foothills was the vapor of a train on its way up to Katoomba. It was insignificance that Dora had taught them to abhor, and if ever there was to be insignificance it was here. The measure of seclusion was that Penrith had become a goal. Caro took herself in her own tender embrace, enclosing all that was left of the unknown. Caro was inland.

She had crouched into the angle formed by the balustrade and one of the high supports of the veranda. Bougainvillea was trained on the uprights; and a round plaque, cool as china, impressed her cheek. There were insects in the thorny vines, there was the scuttle of some animal in the garden below. Dora would have confirmed that death is not the worst.

In a room with six beds, all subsequently cried themselves to sleep. In the morning, Caro saw that the medallion on the balcony was blue and white, and Catholic. One of the girls told her, "Miss Holster says it's a Dellarobbier."

The house was at once seen to be peculiar. There was a lot to look at. It was owned by the Doctor, who was not a doctor at all but an architect; and Italian, even if on our side. He had withdrawn to a smaller building alongside—servants' quarters was a phrase that came readily enough to them from books, or from the old stone houses built by convicts. The Doctor wore a short white cotton jacket and a little white pointed beard and, although not lame, carried a stick. According to Miss Holster, he had seen through Mussolini from the word Go.

The house had 1928 in Roman numbers on the porch; or portico. For its construction, colored marbles and blond travertine had spent months at sea, fireplaces and ceilings had been dismantled outside Parma, where the ham and violets came from. And whole pavements of flowered tiles uprooted and rebedded. The dining-room was said to be elliptical. All the doors, even for bathrooms, were double, with panels of painted flowers, and paired handles pleasant to waggle until they dropped off. There were velvet bellpulls, intended for maids, that fell into disrepair from incessant tugging. There was also the day Joan Brinstead broke an inkpot on the white marble mantel in the music room and ammonia only made it worse. Miss Holster had a canopy over her bed; but could not say why lemon trees should be potted rather than in the ground.

These rooms enclosed loveliness—something memorable, true as literature. Events might take place, occasions, though not during the blight of their own occupancy. At evening the rooms shone, knowing and tender.

In a forbidden paddock below the house, a wire fence surrounded tents, tin buildings, and thirty or forty short men grotesquely military in uniforms dyed the color of wine. The Doctor's countrymen had come to the ends of the earth to find him, for the men who dug his fields and gathered his fruit were Italian prisoners of war. At dusk they led in the cows before being themselves led behind the wire. The Doctor could be seen in the mornings moving among them, white beard, white jacket, white panama: once more the master. They learned that, like a baby, he slept in the afternoons. They had seen, or caught, one of the prisoners kissing his hand.

From the fields, or behind the wire, the prisoners waved to the schoolgirls, who never waved back. Never. It was a point of honor.

# NATALIA GINZBURG

NATALIA GINZBURG, novelist, essayist, playwright, and politician, recalls the war years in her memoir *All Our Yesterdays*.

■

FROM *All Our Yesterdays*

One day they came to Cenzo Rena to tell him that some Jews were on the point of arriving at Borgo San Costanzo. The police authorities were distributing Jews here and there in small villages, for fear that if they remained in the towns they would harm the war in some way. There were some already at Masuri, at Scoturno, only San Costanzo seemed to have been forgotten. But now they were on the point of arriving. For a short time the people of San Costanzo had hopes of the Jews, at Masuri and the other villages very rich Jews had arrived, who spent a great deal of money. They waited for the Jews in the village square. But the Jews who arrived at San Costanzo were poor Jews, three ragged little old women from Livorno with a canary in a cage, and a Turk who was trembling with cold in a light-colored overcoat. The little old women from Livorno at once started showing the kind of shoes they were wearing, with soles worn right through to their stockings. The Secretary of the Commune took the Turk to the inn which was close by, in the village square, on the floor above the wine-shop, and the old women were taken in by the tailor, in a kind of barn that he owned. The little old women's canary died at once, La Maschiona had predicted that it would, this was no village for canaries.

Gradually the Turk and the little old women became village faces, everyone had grown accustomed to seeing them and had found out all about them, and now everyone said that Jews were just the same as other people, and why in the world did the police authorities not want them in the towns, what sort of harm could they possibly do? And these Jews were poor, too, and they had to be helped, anyone who could gave them a little bread or some beans, the little old women went round asking and came back with their aprons full. In exchange they mended clothes, they did it so well that there was nothing to be seen, they mended not with thread but with their own hair, it was a custom of the Jews. They often came up to Cenzo Rena's house and La Maschiona would make them sit down in the kitchen and would give them coffee and milk, they were old and she thought of her own mother, supposing she had had to go round begging. Only she was disgusted at the idea of the mending they did with their own hair. The little old women were three sisters, one very tall and two very short and just alike, it made a curious impression to see those two little old twin sisters that you could not tell one from the other. The Turk sat all the time in the village square, like an old monkey sick with cold, and he wore a woolen jacket with red and yellow checks which had belonged to Cenzo Rena, and he was always waiting for Cenzo Rena to come down into the square to talk Turkish with him. Winter had come all of a sudden to San Costanzo, after a long autumn, dusty and hot as summer. Winter at San Costanzo brought snow and wind and sun, a dry wind that bit at your throat and flung a cold, fine dust in your face, and whistled in the loose tiles of the roofs and shook the smoke-yellowed panes of the little windows. The paths were paved with ice and big fringes of ice hung from the fountains, and the people of San Costanzo were stupefied by all this cold, every year they were stupefied by it and complained as though they were seeing winter for the first time, and the women groaned and shivered as if taken by surprise, with bare, purple arms and fluttering little scarves round their necks. La Maschiona, too, was still wearing her torn blue summer dress, but now she wore thick black woolen stockings and men's boots, and a black scarf round her neck. Cenzo Rena had several years before given her a coat with a fur collar, but La Maschiona kept it in a cupboard and had not the courage to put it on, she went sometimes and stroked the collar and rubbed her cheeks against the sleeves and was filled with pleasure, she did not put it on because she was afraid people would laugh at her, coats were not worn in San Costanzo.

Many men from the village had gone off to the war, they had done all they could to stay at home and those who owned pigs had given the police-sergeant presents of sausages and hams, the women had gone by night to the police-station with the sausages hidden in their shawls. And some had succeeded in staying at home because of the sausages but they were few, or the amount of sausages had been small and even the police-sergeant had not been able to do anything about it. And now in almost every house there was someone who had gone to the war and a family waiting for the post. At one o'clock you could hear the radio news bulletin in the village square, but no one listened to it except the Turk, Cenzo Rena and the draper, the others did not come and listen because they could not make out from these news bulletins what was happening to the Italians, whether they were winning or losing, and they preferred to have it all explained to them by Cenzo Rena, who explained it on the map.

The Turk was very pleased that the war was not going well, in Africa the Italians were running away over the desert, in Greece there was slush and snow and mud and the Italians were unable to advance. But Cenzo Rena told him in Turkish not to delude himself too much, the war would go on for a very long time yet, the Italians were not fighting well because they had no boots and because they did not like the war, but the Germans had boots and everything, and they liked the war very much because they liked killing. The Turk trembled and grew pale at the mention of the Germans, if the Germans won the war what would happen to him, a Turkish Jew, he would never go back home again. With the Italians he had no great quarrel, all they had done to him was to send him to San Costanzo, they had spotted him in Rome selling carpets in the street and had put him in prison for a little and then had sent him here. He was getting on all right but he was very cold, even with Cenzo Rena's sweater and the coat with red and yellow checks, all they put in his room at the inn was a bowl with charcoal embers in it, which was barely enough to warm his hands. You could see he had sold carpets because he always kept his shoulders bent, as though beneath a heavy weight of carpets, you could easily picture him walking with long carpets hanging down from his shoulders.

# SIR HAROLD GEORGE NICOLSON

SIR HAROLD'S encounter with Dylan Thomas, as recorded in Nicolson's diary.

■

FROM *The Diaries and Letters*
*of Harold Nicolson*

DIARY                                                    *12th September, 1941*

Dylan Thomas comes to see me. He wants a job on the B.B.C. He is a fat little man, puffy and pinkish, dressed in very dirty trousers and a loud check coat. I tell him that if he is to be employed by the B.B.C., he must promise not to get drunk. I give him £1, as he is clearly at his wits' end for money. He does not look as if he had been cradled into poetry by wrong.[1] He looks as if he will be washed out of poetry by whisky.

[1] Most wretched men
   Are cradled into poetry by wrong:
   They learn in suffering what they teach in song.
            Shelley. *Julian and Maddalo.*

# DYLAN THOMAS

THE WELSH POET, short story writer, and playwright Dylan Thomas published his first collection of poetry, *Eighteen Poems,* when he was twenty years old. Among his other books are *The Map of Love, Portrait of the Artist as a Young Dog,* and *Adventures in the Skin Trade.* "A Refusal to Mourn the Death, by Fire, of a Child in London," one of his best-known poems, first appeared in a collection titled *Deaths and Entrances,* published in 1946.

■

## A Refusal to Mourn the Death, by Fire, of a Child in London

Never until the mankind making
Bird beast and flower
Fathering and all humbling darkness
Tells with silence the last light breaking
And the still hour
Is come of the sea tumbling in harness

And I must enter again the round
Zion of the water bead
And the synagogue of the ear of corn
Shall I let pray the shadow of a sound
Or sow my salt seed
In the last valley of sackcloth to mourn
The majesty and burning of the child's death.
I shall not murder
The mankind of her going with a grave truth
Nor blaspheme down the stations of the breath
With any further
Elegy of innocence and youth.

Deep with the first dead lies London's daughter,
Robed in the long friends,
The grains beyond age, the dark veins of her mother,
Secret by the unmourning water
Of the riding Thames.
After the first death, there is no other.

# ANATOLI KUZNETSOV

ANATOLI KUZNETSOV, born in Kiev, began writing at the age of fourteen, recording what he saw of the German occupation. When he received permission to visit London in 1969, he evaded his minders and sought asylum. Happily, Kuznetsov had brought with him microfilms of all his unpublished novels, hidden in the lining of his jacket. The following is excerpted from *Babi Yar*.

■

## FROM *Babi Yar*

### THE ORDER

On the morning of September 28th, Ivan Svinchenko from Litvinovka village turned up unexpectedly at our house. He was on his way home out of the encirclement.

He was a peasant, a decent, open-hearted, more or less illiterate man, a tremendously hard worker and the father of a large family. Before the war, whenever he came from the country to the city market, he would sleep at my grandparents'. He never forgot to bring me some simple present from the village, but I was shy of him, perhaps because he had a speech defect: sometimes as he was speaking he would seem to choke and all you could hear was a sort of indistinct mumbling—"balabala." It was a very strange defect.

Like all people who worked on the collective farms in the neighborhood, he had always turned up covered in mud and dressed in rags and tatters. But now he appeared in such rags and in such a frightful condition we could hardly recognize him. Somewhere he had managed to swap his army uniform for some old clothes.

This is what had happened to him.

Ivan Svinchenko had been defending Kiev along with his unit when the order had come to retreat, and they had crossed over on to the left bank of the Dnieper to Darnitsa. For a long time they wandered about aimlessly through the woods and along the cart-tracks, were bombed and raked with machine-gun fire from the air, and none of their officers had the slightest idea what to do. Then the officers themselves disappeared altogether and the men started shouting that they should go home. Everybody had the feeling the war was over.

But in the depths of the forest they ran into some partisans led by N.K.V.D. officers, well equipped, with transport and plenty of food; and they had a lot of weapons. The partisans warned of the dangers of falling into German hands and made Ivan join them. But he hated the N.K.V.D. and was longing to get home.

"So I hung around a bit—*bala-bala*—till it was dark, and then skipped!" he explained.

He spent several days walking through the woods and open fields and everywhere he went he came across people like himself who didn't want to fight. What were they supposed to be fighting for, they asked— for the collective farms, for the prison camps at Kolyma, to go on being poor? When all around was their native Ukraine and somewhere not far away a home, wife and children? The Ukrainians went off to their homes; the Russians, whose homes were where the Soviets were, wandered about not knowing where they were going, or else they went off in search of the Germans to give themselves up.

Ivan came across a column of a couple of hundred men who had surrendered in that way. There were just two Germans in charge of them and even they had their obviously unnecessary rifles slung over their shoulders. Ivan fell in with them, and the other men welcomed him with much shouting and whistling—they were glad that their fighting days were over and that they were going to relax as prisoners. But Ivan was unlike the others; he did not want to relax; he kept thinking about his family.

"So I went along with them for a bit—*bala-bala*—jumped into a hole and then skipped away!"

My grandmother gave the starving Ivan something to eat and sighed her sympathy. My grandfather went out on to the street for some reason, but almost at once his footsteps could be heard again on the porch and he came rushing into the room:

"I've great news for you! . . . From tomorrow there won't be a single Yid left in Kiev. It seems it's true what they said about them setting fire to the Kreshchatik. Thank the Lord for that! That'll put paid to them getting rich at our expense, the bastards. Now they can go off to their blessed Palestine, or at any rate the Germans'll deal with 'em. They're being deported! There's an order posted up."

We all dashed outside. A notice printed on cheap gray wrapping-paper, with no heading and no signature, had been stuck on the fence:

> All Yids living in the city of Kiev and its vicinity are to report by 8 o'clock on the morning of Monday, September 29th, 1941, at the corner of Melnikovsky and Dokhturov Streets (near the cemetery). They are to take with them documents, money, valuables, as well as warm clothes, underwear, etc.
>
> Any Yid not carrying out this instruction and who is found else-where will be shot.

Any civilian entering flats evacuated by Yids and stealing property will be shot.[1]

After that followed the same text in Ukrainian and then, lower
down, in very small type, the same again in German. It was a sort of
three-level poster.

I read it over twice, and for some reason it made me shudder. It was
written so very harshly, with a sort of cold hatred. What's more, it was a
cold day with a lot of wind and the street was deserted. I didn't go back
indoors but, rather disturbed, I wandered off in the direction of the
market, not quite knowing why.

Three plots away from us was the large holding belonging to the
collective vegetable farm. It was full of little mud huts, wooden sheds
and cow-stalls one on top of the other, and it was there that a great many
Jews lived, terribly poor, uneducated and in pitiful conditions. I glanced
into the yard: it was in a state of silent panic; people were rushing from
one hut to the other, carting things in and out.

The same notice had been put up in other parts of the city. I stopped
and read it through again, still not quite grasping its meaning.

In the first place, if they had really decided to deport the Jews as a
reprisal for the Kreshchatik affair, why should it affect all of them? Say a
dozen people might have been involved in the explosions, but why
should the others have to suffer? True, the explanation might be that
the Germans could not discover who were the actual incendiaries, so
they had simply decided to deport everybody. Cruel, but true, perhaps?

In the second place, there were no such streets in Kiev as Melnikov-
sky and Dokhturov, whereas Melnikov and Degtyarev Streets did exist.
The order had obviously been written by the Germans themselves with
the help of bad translators. These streets really were close to the Russian
and Jewish cemeteries in Lukyanovka, and next to it was the Lukyanovka
railway goods-yard. So they were going to put them on a train? But where
to? Were they really going to Palestine, as Gramp suggested?

But again this was very cruel: to expel thousands of people by force
from the places where they had been born and transport them to places
where they hadn't a thing to their names—how many of them would get
ill and die on the way? And all because a few of them turned out to be
incendiaries?

Did that mean that Shurka Matso would also have to go? But his
mother was a Russian and was divorced from his father, and Shurka
hadn't seen his father for ages, like me. Did it mean that Shurka would
be taken off on his own? That his mother would stay and he would go? I
began to feel sorry for him, sorry to have to part from him for ever.

Then suddenly—to my surprise, sort of spontaneously—I began to

[1] Central State Archives of the October Revolution, Moscow. Fund 7021, index 65,
item 5.

talk to myself in my grandfather's words, with that same intonation and malice: So what? Let 'em go off to their Palestine. They've grown fat enough here! This is the Ukraine; look how they've multiplied and spread out all over the place like fleas. And Shurka Matso—he's a lousy Jew too, crafty and dangerous. How many of my books has he pinched! Let 'em go away, we'll be better off without 'em—my Gramp is a clever chap, he's right.

With these thoughts in my mind I went as far as the Kurenyovka police station, where my Dad once worked. It had been taken over by the German police and had a portrait of Hitler posted up in the window. He had a stern, almost sinister look and was wearing a peaked cap with lots of braid on it. And the cap was pulled right down over his eyes.

I could not, of course, miss such a rare spectacle as the deportation of the Jews from Kiev. As soon as it was light I was out on the street.

They started arriving while it was still dark, to be in good time to get seats in the train. With their howling children, their old and sick, some of them weeping, others swearing at each other, the Jews who lived and worked on the vegetable farm emerged on to the street. There were bundles roughly tied together with string, worn-out cases made from plywood, woven baskets, boxes of carpenters' tools . . . Some elderly women were wearing strings of onions hung around their necks like gigantic necklaces—food supplies for the journey . . .

In normal times, of course, all the invalids, sick people and older folk stay indoors and are not seen. But now all of them had to turn out —and there they were.

I was struck by how many sick and unfortunate people there are in the world.

Apart from that there was another factor. The men who were fit had already been mobilized into the army and only the invalids had been left behind. Everybody who had been able to get himself evacuated, who had enough money, who had managed to go along with his office or plant or who had influence somewhere—all those had already left. (A shopkeeper from Kurenyovka by the name of Klotsman had managed to get away along with his family even after Kiev had been cut off. I don't know whether it's true, but he was said to have paid a fabulous sum to some airmen who put him and all his belongings into a plane. [When the war was over he turned up again safe and sound in Kurenyovka.])

So those who were left in the city were the really poor people, the sort of people described by Sholom Aleichem, and it was they who now came swarming out on to the street.

How can such a thing happen? I wondered, immediately dropping completely my anti-Semitism of the previous day. No, this is cruel, it's not fair, and I'm so sorry for Shurka Matso; why should he suddenly be driven out like a dog? What if he did pinch my books; that was because he forgets things. And how many times did I hit him without good reason?

Deeply affected by what I saw, I went from one group of people to the other, listening to what they were saying; and the closer I got to Podol the more people I found out on the streets. They were standing in the gateways and porches, some of them watching and sighing, others jeering and hurling insults at the Jews. At one point a wicked-looking old woman in a dirty head-scarf ran out on to the roadway, snatched a case from an elderly Jewess and rushed back inside the courtyard. The Jewess screamed after her, but some tough characters stood in the gateway and stopped her getting in. She sobbed and cursed and complained, but nobody would take her part, and the crowd went on their way, their eyes averted. I peeped through a crack and saw a whole pile of stolen things lying in the yard.

I also overheard someone say that in one place a cabby who had been specially hired to transport the luggage belonging to several families simply whipped up his horse and dashed off down a side-street, and they never saw him again.

The Glubochitsa was thick with people making their way up to Lukyanovka; it was just a sea of heads—the Jews of Podol were on the move. What a place that Podol was! (It was the most poverty-stricken part of Kiev, and you could recognize it simply by the smell—a mixture of things rotting, cheap fat and washing hung out to dry. Here from time immemorial had lived the poor of the Jewish community, the poorest of the poor—the shoemakers, tailors, the coal-merchants, the tinsmiths, porters, harness-makers, confidence tricksters and thieves . . . The court-yards were devoid of grass or greenery, with evil-smelling rubbish tips, tumble-down sheds swarming with great fat rats, lavatories which were just holes in the ground, clouds of flies, miserable streets which were either dusty or muddy, houses in a state of collapse and damp cellars—that was Podol, noisy, overcrowded and utterly dreary.)

My head was simply bursting from the noise and shouting. From all sides came the questions: Where are they taking them? What are they doing with them?

In one crowd only two words could be heard: "A ghetto, a ghetto!" A middle-aged woman came up, greatly alarmed, and interrupted: "Dear people, this is the end of us!" The old women were weeping, though it sounded almost as if they were singing. A rumor went around that some Karaites had passed through (it was the first time I had heard this name, which is apparently given to a small Semitic people)—very old men wearing robes reaching right down to the ground, who spent the whole night in their synagogue, then emerged and declared: "Children, we are going to our deaths; prepare yourselves. Let us meet it courageously, as Christ did."

This caused some indignation: fancy sowing panic in people like that! But it was already known for a fact that one woman had poisoned her children and then herself, so as not to have to go. And near the Opera a young girl had thrown herself out of a window and was still lying on the street covered with a sheet and nobody bothered to remove the body.

Suddenly there was a new cause for concern; people started saying that ahead, on Melnikov Street, a barrier had been put up, and that they were letting people in but not back out again.

At this point I myself took fright. I was tired, my head was buzzing from everything that was going on, and I was scared lest I should be unable to get back and they would cart me off. So I began to force my way back in the opposite direction to the crowd, worked my way out of it and then wandered for a long time through the deserted streets, along which a few latecomers were practically running, to the accompaniment of whistles and shouts from the doorways.

When I got home I found my grandfather standing in the middle of the courtyard, straining to hear some shooting that was going on somewhere. He raised his finger.

"Do you know what?" he said with horror in his voice. "They're not deporting 'em. They're *shooting* 'em."

Then, for the first time, I realized what was happening.

From Babi Yar came quite distinctly the sound of regular bursts of machine-gun fire: ta-ta-ta, ta-ta . . .

It was the sort of rather quiet, unexcited, measured firing you heard when they were training. Our Babi Yar lies between Kurenyovka and Lukyanovka: you have to cross it to get to the cemetery. They had driven from there, from Lukyanovka, it seemed, into our ravine.

Grandpa looked puzzled and frightened.

"Maybe it's fighting?" I suggested.

"That's not fighting!" Gramp shouted plaintively. "The whole of Kurenyovka is already talking about it. Some folk have climbed trees and seen what's going on. Victor Makedon ran all the way back; he went down with his wife, she's a Jewess, and he only just escaped being taken himself. Oh, Mother of God, Queen of Heaven, what *is* this, why do they do that to them?"

We moved indoors. but it was impossible just to sit there. The firing went on and on.

Gramp went across to Makedon to hear what had happened and found a lot of people assembled. The young man (he had been married just before the war broke out) was relating how, down there, they were simply glancing at people's identity cards and then throwing them straight on to a bonfire. But he had shouted: "I'm a Russian!" so they had dragged his wife from him and taken her off to the ravine, and the police had driven him away . . .

It was cold outside; there was a biting wind blowing, like the previous day. All the same I went outside and strained my ears. Grandma brought out my coat and hat and also stood listening and wringing her hands and muttering: "Oh God, there are women and small children there . . ." I had the impression she was crying. I turned round, and she crossed herself and, with her face to Babi Yar, she said:

"Afather, which art in heaven . . ."

At night the firing stopped, but it started up again in the morning. The word went around Kurenyovka that thirty thousand people had been shot on the first day, and that the others were sitting there waiting their turn.

My grandmother came from the neighbors with some news. A fourteen-year-old boy, the son of the collective-farm stable-man, had come running into the farmyard and was telling the most frightful stories: that they were being made to take all their clothes off; that several of them would be lined up, one behind the other, so as to kill more than one at a time; that the bodies were then piled up and earth thrown over them, and then more bodies were laid on top; that there were many who were not really dead, so that you could see the earth moving, that some had managed to crawl out, only to be knocked over the head and thrown back into the pile. They hadn't noticed him; he had managed to sneak away and had run all the way home.

"We must hide him!" my mother said. "In the trench."

"Come on, son," exclaimed Grandma. "Quickly. We'll hide him away, feed him and take care of him."

I hurried across to the farmyard.

But it was already too late. At the gate there was standing a cart drawn by a spindly horse, and a German soldier with a whip was sitting in it. Another soldier, his rifle under his arm, was leading a white-faced boy from the yard. In fact he was not even leading him; they seemed to be walking side by side.

They went to the cart and climbed on to it, one on each side, and the soldier moved the hay aside to make the boy more comfortable. He put his rifle down on the straw, and the boy lay on his side resting on his elbow. He eyed me with his big brown eyes quite calmly and indifferently.

The soldier cracked his whip, urged the horse on, and the cart moved off—all as simply and with as little excitement as though they were going off to the fields to make hay.

The women in the yard were arguing loudly with each other and I went up to listen. Some were protesting, others argued:

"She did right. Finish with the lot of 'em. That's for the Kreshcha-tik."

It was a Russian woman who lived on her own on the collective farm, working with the cows.

She had seen the boy run into his own home. She had gasped with alarm, listened to his story, put a jug of milk on the table and ordered him to sit quietly and not to go outside so that no one should see him, and then she had gone off to the police to give him away. What's more, when she got back she watched over him until the Germans came with the cart.

# NOEL COWARD

THE ENGLISH actor, dramatist, and composer Noel Coward was the son of a Teddington piano salesman. His plays include *Hay Fever, Private Lives,* and *Blithe Spirit.* He was the original author of the films *Cavalcade* and *Brief Encounter,* and wrote, directed, and starred in one of the most celebrated World War II films, *In Which We Serve.* The following selections are from his *Diaries.*

■

FROM *Diaries*

*Tuesday 7 October 1941*

Dined at Ivy. Conversation with Bobbie Helpmann[1] about how difficult it is to keep the Ballet going with people being called up all the time. Thought of Poland, Holland, Czechoslovakia, Norway, Belgium, France, etc., and felt it was indeed terrible not to be able to keep the Ballet going. To do him justice, he was very good about it, but I felt there was something intrinsically wrong with the whole subject.

*Saturday 13 December 1941*

Quiet morning. Cannot help being delighted about America being so dumbfounded at the Japanese attack [on Pearl Harbor]. This feeling is not malice but a genuine relief that (a) they have at last been forced to realize that this war is theirs as well as ours, and (b) that whatever the future brings they will never be able to say that they came in to pull our chestnuts out of the fire, as they were quite obviously caught with their trousers down.

[1] Robert Helpmann (b. 1909), Australian-born dancer, actor and director, knighted 1968; he was the leading dancer with the Sadler's Wells Ballet 1933–50.

# JAMES JONES

JAMES JONES, born in Robinson, Illinois, joined the peacetime army and wrote one of the most famous of World War II novels, *From Here to Eternity*. He was serving in Hawaii at the time of the surprise Japanese attack on December 7, 1941.

■

FROM *From Here to Eternity*

It was a typical Sunday morning breakfast, for the first weekend after payday. At least a third of the Company was not home. Another third was still in bed asleep. But the last third more than made up for the absences in the loudness of their drunken laughter and horseplay and the clashing of cutlery and halfpint milk bottles.

Warden was just going back for seconds on both hotcakes and eggs, with that voracious appetite he always had when he was drunk, when this blast shuddered by under the floor and rattled the cups on the tables and then rolled on off across the quad like a high wave at sea in a storm.

He stopped in the doorway of the KP room and looked back at the messhall. He remembered the picture the rest of his life. It had become very quiet and everybody had stopped eating and looked at each other.

"Must be doin some dynamitin down to Wheeler Field," somebody said tentatively.

"I heard they was clearin some ground for a new fighter strip," somebody else agreed.

That seemed to satisfy everybody. They went back to their eating. Warden heard a laugh ring out above the hungry gnashings of cutlery on china, as he turned back into the KP room. The tail of the chow line was still moving past the two griddles, and he made a mental note to go behind the cooks' serving table when he bucked the line this time, so as not to make it so obvious.

That was when the second blast came. He could hear it a long way off coming toward them under the ground; then it was there before he could move, rattling the cups and plates in the KP sinks and the rinsing racks; then it was gone and he could hear it going away northeast toward the 21st Infantry's football field. Both the KPs were looking at him.

He reached out to put his plate on the nearest flat surface, holding it carefully in both hands so it would not get broken while he congratulated himself on his presence of mind, and then turned back to the messhall, the KPs still watching him.

As there was nothing under the plate, it fell on the floor and crashed in the silence, but nobody heard it because the third groundswell of blast had already reached the PX and was just about to reach them. It passed under, rattling everything, just as he got it back to the NCOs' table.

"This is it," somebody said quite simply.

Warden found that his eyes and Stark's eyes were looking into each other. There was nothing on Stark's face, except the slack relaxed peaceful look of drunkenness, and Warden felt there must not be anything on his either. He pulled his mouth up and showed his teeth in a grin, and Stark's face pulled up his mouth in an identical grin. Their eyes were still looking into each other.

Warden grabbed his coffee cup in one hand and his halfpint of milk in the other and ran out through the messhall screendoor onto the porch. The far door, into the dayroom, was already so crowded he could not have pushed through. He ran down the porch and turned into the corridor that ran through to the street and beat them all outside but for one or two. When he stopped and looked back he saw Pete Karelsen and Chief Choate and Stark were all right behind him. Chief Choate had his plate of hotcakes-and-eggs in his left hand and his fork in the other. He took a big bite. Warden turned back and swallowed some coffee.

Down the street over the trees a big column of black smoke was mushrooming up into the sky. The men behind were crowding out the door and pushing those in front out into the street. Almost everybody had brought his bottle of milk to keep from getting it stolen, and a few had brought their coffee too. From the middle of the street Warden could not see any more than he had seen from the edge, just the same big column of black smoke mushrooming up into the sky from down around Wheeler Field. He took a drink of his coffee and pulled the cap off his milk bottle.

"Gimme some of that coffee," Stark said in a dead voice behind him, and held up his own cup. "Mine was empty."

He turned around to hand him the cup and when he turned back a big tall thin red-headed boy who had not been there before was running down the street toward them, his red hair flapping in his self-induced breeze, and his knees coming up to his chin with every step. He looked like he was about to fall over backwards.

"Whats up, Red?" Warden hollered at him. "Whats happening? Wait a minute! Whats going on?"

The red-headed boy went on running down the street concentratedly, his eyes glaring whitely wildly at them.

"The Japs is bombing Wheeler Field!" he hollered over his shoulder. "The Japs is bombing Wheeler Field! I seen the red circles on the wings!"

He went on running down the middle of the street, and quite suddenly right behind him came a big roaring, getting bigger and bigger; behind the roaring came an airplane, leaping out suddenly over the trees.

Warden, along with the rest of them, watched it coming with his milk bottle still at his lips and the twin red flashes winking out from the nose. It came over and down and up and away and was gone, and the stones in the asphalt pavement at his feet popped up in a long curving line that led up the curb and puffs of dust came up from the grass and a line of cement popped out of the wall to the roof, then back down the wall to the grass and off out across the street again in a big S-shaped curve.

With a belated reflex, the crowd of men swept back in a wave toward the door, after the plane was already gone, and then swept right back out again pushing the ones in front into the street again.

Above the street between the trees Warden could see other planes down near the smoke column. They flashed silver like mirrors. Some of them began suddenly to grow larger. His shin hurt where a stone out of the pavement had popped him.

"All right, you stupid fucks!" he bellowed. "Get back inside! You want to get your ass shot off?"

Down the street the red-haired boy lay sprawled out floppy-haired, wild-eyed, and silent, in the middle of the pavement. The etched line on the asphalt came up to him and continued on on the other side of him and then stopped.

"See that?" Warden bawled. "This aint jawbone, this is for record. Thems real bullets that guy was usin."

The crowd moved reluctantly back toward the dayroom door. But one man ran to the wall and started probing with his pocketknife in one of the holes and came out with a bullet. It was a .50 caliber. Then another man ran out into the street and picked up something which turned out to be three open-end metal links. The middle one still had a .50 caliber casing in it. The general movement toward the dayroom had stopped.

"Say! Thats pretty clever," somebody said. "Our planes is still usin web machinegun belts that they got to carry back home!" The two men started showing their finds to the men around them. A couple of other men ran out into the street hurriedly.

"This'll make me a good souvenir," the man with the bullet said contentedly. "A bullet from a Jap plane on the day the war started."

"Give me back my goddam coffee!" Warden hollered at Stark. "And help me shoo these dumb bastards back inside!"

"What you want me to do?" Chief Choate asked. He was still holding his plate and fork and chewing excitedly on a big bite.

"Help me get em inside," Warden hollered.

Another plane, on which they could clearly see the red discs, came skidding over the trees firing and saved him the trouble. The two men hunting for metal links in the street sprinted breathlessly. The crowd moved back in a wave to the door, and stayed there. The plane flashed past, the helmeted head with the square goggles over the slant eyes and the long scarf rippling out behind it and the grin on the face as he waved, all clearly visible for the space of a wink, like a traveltalk slide flashed on and then off of a screen.

Warden, Stark, Pete and the Chief descended on them as the crowd started to wave outward again, blocking them off and forcing the whole bunch inside the dayroom.

The crowd milled indignantly in the small dayroom, everybody talking excitedly. Stark posted himself huskily in the doorway with Pete and the Chief flanking him. Warden gulped off the rest of his coffee and set the cup on the magazine rack and pushed his way down to the other end and climbed up on the pingpong table.

"All right, all right, you men. Quiet down. Quiet down. Its only a war. Aint you ever been in a war before?"

# I. F. STONE

---

MODERN investigative journalism may well have begun with I. F. Stone, who for sixty years filled the office of America's most perspicacious radical journalist, a truly independent spirit, proprietor, editor, and sole contributor to *I. F. Stone's Weekly.*

---

■

FROM *The War Years*

WAR COMES TO WASHINGTON

*December 13, 1941*

I first heard the news from the elevator man in the National Press Building. The ticker at the Press Club, normally shut off on Sunday, carried the first flash telling of the Japanese attack on Pearl Harbor. It was a beautiful late-autumn Sunday, the sky clear and the air crisp. At the entrance to the White House a small crowd had gathered to watch Cabinet members arrive. In the reporters' room inside a group was clustered around the radio. I talked to Ambassador Hu Shih by telephone, and he said he felt "really sad" and sounded as though he meant it. The Navy Department seemed busy but calm; the War Department less so. Soldiers in helmets, carrying guns with fixed bayonets, guarded the entrance to the War Department's half of the huge old Munitions building. They looked awkward and uncomfortable.

The public-relations office of the War Department refused a request for background material on the comparative military strength of the United States and Japan on the ground that since four o'clock that afternoon all information on the composition and movement of troops abroad had been declared a secret. The Navy Department, less strict, was still giving out information already "on the record," thus saving reporters a trip to the Library of Congress. In the Navy Department reference room women employees, hastily summoned from their homes, sent out for sandwiches and coffee and joked about Japanese bombers. There as elsewhere one encountered a sense of excitement, of adventure, and of relief that a long-expected storm had finally broken. No one showed much indignation. As for the newspapermen, myself included, we all acted a little like firemen at a three-alarmer.

The first press release from the State Department spluttered. It said the Secretary of State had handed the Japanese representatives a document on November 26 stating American policy in the Far East and suggestions for a settlement. A reply had been handed the Secretary of State that afternoon. The release declared that Secretary Hull had read the reply and immediately turned to the Japanese Ambassador and with the greatest indignation said: ". . . I have never seen a document that was more crowded with infamous falsehoods and distortions—infamous falsehoods and distortions on a scale so huge that I never imagined until today that any government on this planet was capable of uttering them." I asked several other reporters at the State Department just what the Japanese had told Secretary Hull to make him so angry. Nobody seemed to know, and the release did not explain. Hull's language was later described by one reporter as being "as biting if not as deadly as his fellow-mountaineer Sergeant York's bullets." It is a long time since Secretary Hull was a mountaineer.

The Japanese memorandum, released later, made it easier to understand the Secretary's stilted indignation. One has to go back to Will Irwin's "Letters of a Japanese Schoolboy" to match this memorandum. "Ever since China Affair broke out owing to the failure in the past of China to comprehend Japan's true intentions," said one of the more humorous passages, "the Japanese government has striven for the restoration of peace, and it has consistently exerted its best efforts to prevent the extension of war-like disturbances. It was also to that end that in September last year Japan concluded the Tripartite Pact with Germany and Italy." The memorandum indicates only the vaguest shadow of any American intention to appease Japan. At one time the President seems to have offered to "introduce" peace between Japan and China and then —I suspect after the visit to the White House of Hu Shih and T. V. Soong—withdrawn it. But the kind of peace the President might have "introduced" could hardly have been to Japan's liking, though the idea may have made the Chinese uneasy. The Japanese memorandum accuses our own government of "holding fast to theories in disregard of realities," of trying to force "a utopian ideal" on the Japanese, and of "refusing to yield an inch on its impractical principles." I hope these compliments were fully deserved.

The proposals made by Secretary Hull in his letter of November 26 were so obviously unacceptable to a government like Japan's that one wonders why we negotiated at all. Japan was to withdraw all its troops from China and not to support any other government there except "the National Government . . . with capital temporarily at Chungking." Our War Department is said to have asked the White House for three more months in which to prepare, and it may be that the Japanese were also anxious to delay a crisis. It is suspected in some quarters here that the attack on Pearl Harbor was the work of a minority in Japan fearful of further "stalling." The attack came before the Emperor could reply to the President's personal appeal for peace. If it forced the hand of the

Japanese government, it also succeeded in uniting our own country behind Mr. Roosevelt. The reactions of the isolationist press and of Senators like Wheeler are indicative. If Mr. Roosevelt leaned too far in one
direction to please the anti-appeasement and pro-war faction, his tactics
served to prove to the other side that he had done all in his power to
avoid war, that war was forced upon him. Lincoln in the same way
hesitated and compromised and sought to "appease" before war came.

We are going into this war lightly, but I have a feeling that it will
weigh heavily upon us all before we are through. The vast theater on
which the struggle between this country and Japan opens makes the last
war seem a parochial conflict confined to the Atlantic and the western
cape of the Eurasian continent. This is really world war, and in my
humble opinion it was unavoidable and is better fought now when we
still have allies left. It is hoped here that the actual coming of war may
serve to speed up the pace of production and shake both capital and
labor out of a business-as-usual mood far too prevalent. There has been
a general feeling that the production problem could not be solved until
war was declared. We shall see. It is possible that a whipped-up hysteria
against labor and progressives will serve to stifle the very forces that could
be used to bring about an "all-out" effort. It is possible that the coming
of war will open the way to greater cooperation in the defense program,
to a broader role for labor in the mobilization of industry, to a lessening
of attacks on labor in Congress, and to improved morale.

My own confidence springs from a deep confidence in the President.
For all his mistakes—and perhaps some of them have only seemed mistakes—he can be counted on to turn up in the end on the democratic
and progressive side. I hate to think of what we should do without him,
and when I drive down to work early in the morning past the White
House I cannot help thinking with sympathy of the burdens that weigh
him down. On the threshold of war, and perhaps ultimately social earth-
quake, we may be grateful that our country has his leadership.

# JOHN HERSEY

JOHN HERSEY was born in China and lived there until 1925. His first novel, *A Bell for Adano,* won the Pulitzer Prize in 1945. He is also the author of *The Wall,* a novel about the uprising in the Warsaw Ghetto, and many other books. This excerpt from *The Call,* a novel about the life and times of David Treadup, a YMCA missionary in China, picks him up shortly after the Japanese attack on Pearl Harbor.

■

FROM *The Call*

## ENTERING THE CENTURY

### IN THRALL

The first days had the rough texture of surprise. Captivity was a mystery, and in its thrall Treadup did not have the energy even to think about the meaning of his new state of life.

There was plenty of room. Nineteen men of six nationalities were housed in the gymnasium. Two women, Dominican tertiary nuns recently arrived from Shensi with wilted starched wimples and dusty white habits, had the privacy of an office room. These were the only "enemies" rounded up, in or near Paoting. The boards of the gym floor, on which the men slept supperless the first night, reeked of tung oil. There was no heat. Treadup ached. "My bones were like rusty scrap iron." No less than twenty military police had been assigned to guard the foreigners; the duty men coughed and nattered all night.

Captors began padding around in stockinged feet at five o'clock on the morning of Tuesday, the ninth. They carried kerosene lanterns to cut the darkness. They fed their guests a breakfast of millet mush and pickled turnips, and green tea. They dragged in palliasses—big cotton bags stuffed with straw—for their guests thenceforth to sleep on.

After dawn a superior officer entered with a blinding smile—five chromium teeth glittered in his jaws. With the help of an arrogant Formosan interpreter, Japanese to Chinese, the officer announced that the American fleet had been turned turtle at anchor at Hawaii. He spoke as if this were a matter of course. Most of the businessmen did not understand Chinese; Treadup translated into English, which two Britishers, naturally, and two Belgians, a Dutchman, and a Swede readily grasped. The Dutchman received the details with unseemly relish.

The officer had a desk carried into the gym, and seated at it he began to interrogate his guests, one by one.

A squad of ten men went with Treadup to the Congregationalist compound. This was called an inspection. The commanding officer wanted to know who the few remaining Chinese in the compound were —the gateman, the gardener, three ministers, four doctors, a dozen nurses, charwomen, cooks, launderers, coolies, all according to their callings and functions. A consular secretary listed buildings and their uses. Treadup's only written reaction to all this was: "Their attention to exact details is breathtaking." Two men with a bucket of foul-smelling paste and a big brush affixed large paper seals, with death warnings and dire red chops on them, to all doors except those of the hospital. Round-the-clock guards were stationed at the compound gate. At this, Ting the gateman retired to his *k'ang*, ill, evidently felled by a massive and irreversible loss of face. Two men of the troop took Treadup back to the Y.

The Japanese, Treadup noted later, seemed to have been transformed by the success at Pearl Harbor. They walked straight, looked one right in the eye, sucked in less apologetic breath before speaking. They were polite. "They had stopped being caricatures of themselves," David wrote in "Search," "and had turned into real people."

On the tenth all the foreign guests were summoned to the headquarters of the military police. They were carried there in a truck which backfired through the streets, alarming the populace with sounds of yet another war. Guards stood on the running boards.

The officer with metal teeth turned out to be the commander of the MPs. His name was Matsuyama. He was very friendly. He made a speech, complete with graceful gestures of the arms—he seemed to be conducting the sweet music of war. He said pleasantly that the Japanese had a duty to protect all the peoples of Asia against the perfidy of the British and Americans. A great ship named the *Prince of Wales* had been sunk near Singapore (one of his hands sank to the bottom of the sea). The American air force in Manila had been destroyed on the ground; Japanese had landed (a hand beached itself on the Philippines). The guests, he said—giving the impression that a new measure of indulgence would follow each such Japanese triumph—were now free to return to their homes. The homeless Catholic ladies could either remain at the Y.M.C.A. or lodge with others. All door seals would be removed.

Colonel Matsuyama handed out to each guest a lengthy and intricate declaration form, with instructions to list all property at the person's home and place of business, giving the exact nature, size or quantity, and value of every item; and to return the filled form by the following Wednesday. Next he waved in the air a list of thirteen regulations governing foreigners in Paoting. These, he announced with agreeable flashes of chromium, were lenient. He read them. It was stipulated that every person must procure an identification card. Movement would be restricted. Special passes could be obtained in exceptional circumstances. All cash money would have to be surrendered. The diary: "Found it hard to concentrate on mundane matters."

The foreign guests were now dismissed to go home. On foot. It was a long walk to the American Board compound—especially for the nuns, whom Treadup had invited to inhabit the quarters of Letitia Selden and Helen Demestrie. The strong nuns carried their own sparse baggage.

They were "free" but not free. Captivity, Treadup soon found, could have relative degrees. He and the nuns were no longer confined in the Y, but Japanese guards still manned the compound gates day and night; three guards took turns at the door of the Cowley house, where Treadup was living; and three kept track of the nuns. (Too close track, those ladies quite calmly confided to Treadup after the first night. Treadup gathered that the guards, who had obtained ladders from somewhere, were vigilant at the bedroom panes perhaps to see whether there were weapons concealed beneath all those yards of white drapery. "These women have tough fiber," Treadup wrote. "No hysteria.") The foreigners' movement was indeed restricted. One had to obtain permits to go to the gate to obtain permits to go to town to obtain permits to do anything whatsoever.

In all dealings the Japanese were scrupulously polite—even, the sisters reported, while peeping, for beyond the glass they had encouragingly kept smiling and nodding. But they were, it seemed to Treadup, active to a fault. "Like mosquitoes. Always buzzing at your ear and endeavoring to land on skin." He obediently tried to draw up the required inventories, but he was interrupted again and again for what were called "routine inspections." An architect came to survey the buildings. A doctor came to look at the hospital. An army cook came to examine the kitchens. Treadup concluded that the Japanese wanted to use the compound to quarter troops.

The young lieutenant in charge of the gate guards was especially friendly. Named Koniishi, he said he had lived twelve years in California, though his accent and grammar suggested that the stay, if there had been one, had been much shorter. He remained at Treadup's shoulder all day. He knocked at the door in the evening, wanting to play parlor games. Treadup found a Crokinole set that had belonged to the boys; the pair made up rules as they went along. "I had a nice time," Treadup wrote.

> *It was my first chance to unwind into my living self. I had a companion in bewilderment. Under the layers of Greater East Asia Co-Prosperity Sphere nonsense lay a homesick and scared human being.*

The next morning Koniishi came with a summons for Treadup to appear at military police headquarters in town. In a frigid, barren office, Treadup was submitted to a fierce questioning, by metal jaws himself, about his work in the villages. Matsuyama put his questions courteously, but a Korean interpreter into Chinese, feeling the power of his necessity, snarled in the style he evidently imagined suitable for the New Order in East Asia. It seemed to be suspected that Mr. Teddy had ties to guerrillas. Many of the questions were obviously based on items Koniishi had reported from the conversation over Crokinole the previous evening. So much for soft feelings for a homesick and scared human being. At one point, Matsuyama called in a medic to take Treadup's blood pressure, to see if he was lying.

The diary: "Was having difficulty hearing, especially on the right side. Is it that I can't believe my ears half the time?"

# ▪ 1942 ▪

# HARRISON E. SALISBURY

HARRISON SALISBURY'S first assignment in the Soviet
Union was as head of the United Press bureau in Moscow in 1944. The Minneapolis native joined the *New
York Times* In 1949 and became its Moscow correspondent, filling that office for the next five years. *The 900
Days,* from which this excerpt is taken, is the definitive
account of the Siege of Leningrad. During this incredible ordeal, the longest siege ever endured by a city, it
is estimated that 800,000 people died of starvation.

■

FROM *The 900 Days*

## A NEW KIND OF CRIME

It began as winter set in, and with each week it grew—what the
pedantic clerks of the Leningrad militia or police department called "a
new kind of crime," a kind which none of the many branches of the
Soviet police had encountered before.

It was, in simplest terms, murder for food. It happened every day. A
blow from behind and an old woman in a food queue fell dead, while a
pale youth ran off with her *sumka*, or purse, and her ration card. The
quick flash of a knife and a man walking away from a bakery fell in the
snow as a dark figure vanished with the loaf of bread he had been carrying.

The Leningrad police, like all of Stalin's police, were well organized,
well staffed even in these difficult days. But the new crimes were not,
for the most part, being committed by hardened criminals (among whom
the police had an efficient network of stool pigeons). The crimes were
the acts of ordinary Soviet citizens, driven to murder and robbery by
starvation, bombardment, cold, suffering. Some had wives or children
at home, dying of dystrophy.

"It was characteristic," Militia Major A. T. Skilyagin wrote, "that
many of these crimes were committed not by inveterate criminals, not
by elements alien to our society, but simply by persons driven to desperation by hunger, bombing and shelling, persons whose psyches had been
broken by the weight of their experiences."

As the winter wore on, roving gangs of murderers appeared on the
streets of Leningrad. Sometimes they included deserters from the front,

■ 211 ■

ex-Red Army men, desperate elements of every kind. They preyed on persons standing in queues, seizing their ration cards or their food; they descended on lone pedestrians, either by day or night; they carried out bold attacks on the bread shops and even commandeered trucks and sleds, bringing supplies to the bread shops. They entered flats, rifled them of valuables, and if an occupant raised a voice (often there was no one but the dead in the apartments), they hit him on the head and set fire to the flat to cover the traces.

Not all the criminals were Soviet citizens. There were German agents in Leningrad—it was no trick to slip them through the lines in the suburbs of the city. Sometimes the agents spread rumors, stirred up trouble in the bread queues, engaged in agitation, sometimes in sabotage.

The danger from within the city had been strongly in the minds of the Leningrad leadership since the outbreak of war. It had always been a preoccupation of Stalin and his police chief, Beria. It played a significant role in the political maneuvering which handicapped Leningrad's defense in August and September. By winter Leningrad was crisscrossed with internal defense organizations, "destroyer" battalions of workers, special public order brigades of Young Communists. But as the blockade tightened, as starvation began to set in, as the "new kind of crime" appeared, none of this seemed to be enough.

On November 15 after the fall of Tikhvin confronted Zhdanov and his associates with the realization that the blockade might not quickly be lifted, that the suffering of the city might well carry beyond any parameters thus far conceived, that the spirit of Leningrad might break under the impact of these crushing blows, new steps were taken to defend the internal security of the city.

The Military Council of the Leningrad front established a special Administration for Internal Defense. This took a different form from the ill-fated effort by Zhdanov and Marshal Voroshilov to set up a Leningrad Council for Defense in August.

The new internal defense organization was to be independent and self-sufficient. It was designed to cope with any threat which might arise *within* Leningrad. It was comprised of workers battalions (often badly understrength), several brigades of Baltic Fleet sailors, the city police department, such NKVD troops as were still available within Leningrad, the fire brigades, and odds and ends of artillery and machine-gun regiments. Five workers battalions were finally organized, numbering about 16,000 men. The total command as listed on paper by December, 1941, comprised about 37,000 men. The city was divided into six sectors, with fire points in many apartment houses.

Many workers detachments continued to stand duty in the great factories of the city, although by December they were frigid morgues in which handfuls of people tried to keep alive, huddled about tiny temporary stoves. The troops were available for any emergency, including, of course, internal disturbances or uprisings. They had one other task—to guard the approaches to the city over the ice, particularly from the direction of Peterhof. There were many small engagements fought on the ice, sometimes between iceboat patrols, scudding along at sixty miles an hour, but for the most part these were just scouting skirmishes.

The precautions were by no means unjustified. The regular police had been brutally weakened by forced drafts which had sent most of the NKVD units to the front. Many functions had been taken over by women. The regular police, like everyone in Leningrad, suffered from starvation, cold and physical weakness. Some reports suggest that the police, both regular and secret, almost ceased to function in late fall and winter, because of physical debilitation. Also, some Leningrad residents assert, the police were intimidated by the plight of the city and preferred not to show themselves too readily to the civilian population.

In the dangerous days of September the police had panicked. Some commandeered planes and got out of Leningrad. Day after day they burned their files, destroying Party lists, secret documents and even house registers, lest they be used by Nazi occupation authorities for compiling execution lists. The panic was not quite so compelling as in Moscow, where, in October, the sky was clouded for days by smoke from the burning files of the secret police, and citizens sometimes found their half-burned dossiers fluttering down from the NKVD furnace chimneys into the streets. But from September onward more and more Leningraders had demonstrated less and less fear of the police. They spoke more openly among themselves, heedless of who might hear or what might be reported about them.

Official accounts lay great stress on the physical weakness of the police. In December most units had only eight or ten men on duty, and these men had to work shifts of fourteen to sixteen or even eighteen to twenty hours daily. In January 166 police in Leningrad died of starvation and 1,600 were on sick call. In February the death toll rose to 212.[1]

The criminals with whom the police had to deal were far better armed than in peacetime. Often they had military rifles, sometimes submachine guns and almost always revolvers.

As the ration was cut and then cut again and again, not all Leningraders, as one Soviet source puts it tactfully, "received the news with bravery."

One January evening with the temperature at 20 below zero Maria Razina and Peter Yakushin, political workers in a large Leningrad apartment house, went to apartment No. 5 where an evacuated family was living. The mother was dead and three small children huddled about

---

[1] The size of the Leningrad police force can only be guessed at. In the summer of 1941 the police street patrol force (exclusive of traffic police and men in stationhouses) numbered 1,200. (Skilyagin, *Dela i Lyudi*, p. 247.)

her. No ration cards could be found. Soon the owner of the flat, a man named Mark Schacht, returned and said he was making arrangements to take the youngsters to a children's home.

On a hunch Yakushin demanded that Schacht return the family's ration cards. He denied having them. Yakushin grabbed him by the throat and shouted, "Give me the cards, you bandit, or I'll kill you on the spot!"

Schacht suddenly produced the missing ration cards. Before Yakushin could summon a military tribunal (a squad of Red Army soldiers) to execute him, the landlord vanished.

Not all workers in the food distribution system could resist temptation. A grocery store director named Lokshina stole nearly 400 pounds of butter and 200 pounds of flour. She was shot. This was the fate of food criminals whenever they were uncovered. The chief of a Smolny region bread store named Akkonen and his assistant, a woman called Sredneva, cheated their customers of four or five grams of bread per ration. They sold the surplus, taking furs, objects of art and gold jewelry in exchange. They were summarily tried and shot.

As Party Secretary A. A. Kuznetsov put it bluntly in the spring of 1942, "I will tell you plainly that we shot people for stealing a loaf of bread."

In November *Leningradskaya Pravda* began to carry brief items, almost invariably on its back page, reporting the actions of military tribunals in cases of food crimes: three men shot for stealing food from a warehouse; two women shot for profiteering on the black market; five men shot for the theft of flour from a truck; six men shot for conspiring to divert food from the state system. Sometimes the defendants got twenty-five years in a labor camp. But not often. The usual penalty was shooting.

It was a rare day when *Leningradskaya Pravda* did not publish at least one such item, along with a theater listing or two (these vanished after January 10), a few notices of dissertations being defended, the daily communiqué of the Soviet Information Bureau, the press conferences of Solomon Lozovsky, the official government spokesman in Moscow, and an occasional dispatch by Vsevolod Kochetov, Nikolai Tikhonov or Vsevolod Rozhdestvensky.

The ordinary Leningrad city court was transformed, by order of the Leningrad Military Council, into a military court and the city procurator was made a military procurator. This put all persons accused of food crimes under military law. In practice it meant they went almost directly before the firing squad, with a minimum of formality and only the vaguest nod toward judicial process. A total of 3,500 Young Communists were directed into the stores and the rationing system, instructed by Party Secretary Zhdanov not to permit "even a suspicion" of dishonesty in food handling. The Young Communists carried out sudden raids on every link in food distribution and repeatedly uncovered irregularities. In one action in the Vyborg region twenty-three Young Communist units participated and exposed a whole network of food criminals. All were shot summarily.

The worst disaster which could befall a Leningrader was loss of his ration card. On June 22 Ivan Krutikov had been rowing on the lake at Pushkin when the war news broke. On December 15 he was in Leningrad, where his factory had been removed from Pushkin. He had suffered a concussion in a bombing raid and was weakened by scanty rations. On December 15 worse misfortune befell him. As he stood in a queue, a thief grabbed his ration card and fled. Krutikov gave chase but was able to run only a short distance. He saw the robber disappear and burst into tears at his helplessness. He didn't even have the breath to shout, "Stop thief!"

It was virtually impossible under the rigid rules established by Food Director D. V. Pavlov to get a substitute ration card. Prior to December a person who lost his card could apply to a regional bureau and get a new one. In October 4,800 substitute cards were issued. In November 13,000 persons got replacements. These figures seem to have been regarded as normal. But in December long lines began to form at the rationing bureaus. Before the alarmed Pavlov could halt the practice 24,000 cards had been given out. The people invariably claimed that they had lost their card during a bombardment or shelling or when their house burned down. Pavlov knew that many claims were legitimate. But he knew also that many persons must be claiming fraudulent losses in order to get a second ration. The power to issue substitute cards was withdrawn from regional offices. Hereafter new cards could be obtained only from the central office and only with irrefutable proof— testimony of eyewitnesses, supporting evidence from the building superintendent, the local Party worker, the police. For a time Zhdanov himself was the only man who was empowered to replace a lost ration card. It was impossible for the ordinary citizen to assemble the data required for issuance of a new card. Applications quickly dropped to zero for, in fact, if you lost your card you could not get another. The problem was solved, but at the cost of almost certain death for thousands of unfortunates who actually did lose their cards.

Thus Krutikov faced sixteen days without food—in other words, death. He had one hope. His factory was no longer operating due to lack of electric power, and he had applied for front-line duty in the army. On December 17 he got a notice to appear for induction and reported for medical examination. But the doctor rejected him, saying, "You have dystrophy in the full meaning of the word. We can't admit you until you have fed up a bit. Sorry not to be able to help you." At that time Krutikov weighed about eighty-four pounds, half his prewar weight. For four days he did not eat. Finally, his factory director suggested that he try to get readmission to a workers battalion in which he had formerly served.

It took Krutikov sixteen hours to walk four or five miles from his factory to the Narva Gates, where the workers battalion had its head-quarters in the Gorky House of Culture. The temperature was 25 degrees below zero. He was so weak he had to rest every fifteen or twenty paces. Krutikov's old commander put him back on the rolls, with a ration of 250 grams of bread a day plus 100 to 120 grams of cereal and a bowl of hot water for breakfast. His life was saved.

Most were by no means so fortunate.

One night a mother, a pensioner, and her sixteen-year-old daughter, Lulya, appeared at Erisman Hospital. The daughter wore a cape and carried a fur muff. Both were in a state of hysteria. A confidence woman had made the daughter's acquaintance in a bread line and promised to get her a job with good meals in Military Hospital No. 21. At the begin-ning of February, she got the mother to lend her 45 rubles (all she had), took the pair's ration cards and led them through the blackout to Eris-man Hospital for an "interview." In the complete darkness the mother and daughter heard their benefactor cry, "Follow me!" Then she van-ished.

The two wept. The mother kept saying, "Lulya, you have put me into my grave—still living." The girl looked into space and mumbled, "What a night! What a night!" Vera Inber and her husband helped them to make out a report to the police. But what good it would do no one knew. They had no ration cards and it was only February 3. Four weeks without food: a death sentence.

Vsevolod Kochetov also lost his ration card but in a different way. He had gone with his wife Vera across Lake Ladoga to the Fifty-fourth Army front in late December. About January 12 he returned to Tikhvin to find that an urgent telegram from his editor, Zolotukhin, had been waiting several days for him, ordering him back to Leningrad. A whole week passed between the arrival of the telegram and Kochetov's return to Leningrad. He got back to find that Zolotukhin—with whom he had never hit it off—had put him up on charges of violation of military discipline. He was summarily discharged from *Leningradskaya Pravda* and expelled from the Communist Party. By coincidence (or possibly not by coincidence) Kochetov's best friend and wartime companion, Mik-halev, was given similar treatment for a slightly different offense—for using the newspaper car to transport a sick colleague across Lake Ladoga.

Kochetov eventually got his expulsion from the Party reversed. But he didn't get his job back, and he didn't get his ration card back. The ration card went with the job. Regardless of cause (and the only source for what happened is Kochetov, who never paints himself in anything but heroic colors), it was no snap being caught in Leningrad in midwinter of the blockade without a ration card. At one point he was reduced to buying 900 grams of lard at one ruble a gram—900 rubles—in the black market. Finally, the radio committee gave him a job, but it was several weeks before he got a ration card. He tramped five or ten miles a day in search of food, usually going to the front, to commanders whom he knew. Sometimes they let him share a bowl of soup. Sometimes they gave him a tin of canned meat, a half-loaf of black bread or a bit of sausage. Here and there around the city he stopped to look at bulletin boards and read the announcements posted there, handwritten on bits of yellow, white or blue paper: "Will remove corpses—for bread"; "Will buy or exchange valuables for records of Vertinsky and Leshchenko"; "For Sale: Complete works of Leonid Andreyev, Edgar Poe, Knut Hamsun"; "Lost: Little girl, seven years old, in red dress and fur hood. Anyone who has seen or met her . . ."

What could have happened to the little girl in the red dress and fur hood? Had she been on the way to the food store when an air raid struck and fallen victim to a random bomb? Was she a victim of the casual shelling of German long-range guns which went on day after day at any hour, sometimes in one street, sometimes another? Had she simply collapsed of hunger and died in the street as thousands did every day? Or was there a more sinister explanation? Anything could and did happen on the streets of starving Leningrad. The possibilities of tragedy were endless. More than one child had been killed for a ration card, even though theirs were of the lowest category. As early as November mothers and fathers had begun to keep their children off the streets because of rumors of cannibalism.

Both adults and children were turned into beasts by the privations. Yclizaveta Sharypina went to a store one day on Borodinsky Street. She saw an excited woman swearing at a youngster about ten years old and hitting him again and again. The child sat on the floor, oblivious of the blows, and greedily chewed a hunk of black bread, stuffing it into his mouth as rapidly as he could work his jaws. Around the woman and the child stood a circle of silent spectators.

Sharypina grabbed the woman and tried to make her halt.

"But he's a thief, a thief, a thief," the woman cried.

She had received her day's bread ration from the clerk and had let it sit for one moment on the counter. The youngster snatched the loaf, sat down on the floor and proceeded to devour it, heedless of blows, heedless of shouts, heedless of anything that went on around him.

When Sharypina tried to calm the woman, she broke into tears and sobbed that she had taken her only child to the morgue a few weeks before. Finally, Sharypina got the people in the bread store to contribute bits of their ration to the woman who had lost hers. She then questioned the ten-year-old. His father, he thought, was at the front. His mother had died of hunger. Two children remained, he and a younger brother.

They were living in the cellar of a house which had been destroyed by a bomb. She asked why they hadn't gone to a children's home. He said they had to wait for their father. If they went to a home, they would be sent out of Leningrad and never see him again.

Even the stoutest heart began to wonder whether Leningrad could survive such a plight. Vera Inber, a woman of flaming courage who had deliberately come to Leningrad to share its fate with her physician husband, wrote in her diary for January 4:

> It seems to me that if in the course of ten days the blockade is not lifted the city will not hold out. Leningrad has taken the full brunt of this war. What is needed is that the Germans on the Leningrad front receive their due. . . . If only someone knew how Leningrad is suffering. The winter is still long. The cold is ferocious.

Three days later she wrote that everyone in Leningrad was saying that General Meretskov's troops would be in Leningrad by the tenth. "Well," she commented, "whether it is the tenth, the fifteenth or the twentieth or even the end of January, just let it happen."

The wildest rumors coursed through Leningrad. One was the legend of the "noble bandit." A young girl was attacked by a bandit gang on her way home late at night. She was compelled to hand over her fur coat, her wool dress, her new shoes. The bandits were about to leave her naked and freezing in the bitter night when one took off his leather jacket and threw it over her shoulders. The girl ran to her apartment and there, plunging her hand into the pocket of the jacket, pulled out a packet of money—5,000 rubles. Or, in another version, obviously influenced by the blockade, she put her hand in the pocket and drew out a loaf of bread and a large package of butter.

On January 12[2] Mayor Peter Popkov called a press conference at Smolny. The reporters thought he looked tired. His eyes were red and deeply shadowed, his face pale but freshly shaven. He did not rise to greet them, simply motioning to chairs at a long table covered with green baize. Without preliminaries he began to speak of the city's difficulties. His voice was hoarse, and he talked slowly without intonation. The city had been under siege for five months. There had been terrible problems with food. Now, he thought, the Ladoga road was solving them. "The enemy planned to stifle the city by hunger," he said. "This aim will be thwarted." But two things must be done. The food must be gotten into the city, and within the city a merciless struggle must be fought against robbers and "marauders," or pillagers as the officials called the organized gangs preying on Leningrad. "Robbers, speculators and marauders will be mercilessly punished by the laws of war," Popkov said.

The suffering grew worse.

[2] The date is given incorrectly as January 17 by Chakovsky (pp. 62–63). The text of Popkov's remarks was published in *Leningradskaya Pravda* January 13.

On January 25 Party Secretary Kuznetsov got an urgent telephone
call at Smolny from Power Station No. 5, the only plant still operating.
The station had been limping along on daily shipments of 500 cubic
meters of wood, delivered by the October Railroad. That day the last fuel
had been exhausted. None came in by rail.

"Try to hold out a few hours," Kuznetsov begged. But there was no
more fuel. The turbines turned slower and slower and finally halted.
That deprived Leningrad's remaining water-pumping station of power.
The pumps halted. No more water for the bread bakeries. Without water
the bakers could not bake bread.

It may have been on this day that the City Soviet telephoned Power
Station No. 2 and asked for 100 kilowatts of power. "We can't," came the
answer. "We're sitting here by an oil lamp ourselves."

Leningrad was left with a total power production of 3,000 kilowatts,
turned out by a small emergency turbine at Station No. 1.

At the Frunze regional bakery, one of eight still operating in the
city, two fire department pumpers were brought in and kept the bakery
going. In the Petrograd region the pipes quickly froze. A call was sent to
the Young Communist headquarters:

"We must have 4,000 pails of water by evening for the bakery or
there will be no bread tomorrow. We must have a minimum of 2,000
Young Communists because none of them can carry more than two
pails; they don't have the strength."

The youngsters were somehow mobilized and formed a chain from
the frozen banks of the Neva to the nearest bakery. They managed to
provide enough water and then, on children's sleds, distributed the bread
to the food shops.

By chance Vsevolod Vishnevsky made a speech before a thousand
police workers the day after the power was cut off. He spoke in a large
room at police headquarters and noted that it was in good order. There
was light, although it was being "economized." He was told that the
principal problem lay with the railroad, which was working so badly that
70,000 tons of food had piled up at Osinovets because it was impossible
to bring it into Leningrad. If Vishnevsky found anything curious in the
fact that with Leningrad bereft of light and heat the police force still was
able to assemble in lighted, heated quarters, he made no notation of the
fact. He did, however, make an oblique comment on the comparatively
well-fed appearance of the NKVD.

When Vera Inber heard the news about cessation of power, she
noted in her diary for January 25:

> 7 P.M. The situation is catastrophic. People now have fallen on
> the wooden fence around the hospital and are smashing it up for
> kindling. There is no water. If tomorrow the bakeries halt for even
> one day, what will happen? Today we hadn't even any soup—only
> cereal. There was coffee this morning, but there will be no more

liquids. Our water supply: half a teakettle (we keep it on the warm stove), half a pan for washing and a quarter-bottle for tomorrow. That's all.

The next day she wrote:

I cried for the first time from grief and bitterness. I upset the cereal in the stove. Ilya swallowed a few spoonfuls mixed with ashes. No bread yet . . .

On the twenty-seventh she learned of the bucket brigade at the Neva which had been mustered to help the bakeries. There were enormous lines at the bread shops, but bread did appear toward evening and was slowly passed out. For practical purposes, however, Leningrad's bakeries in the depth of the famine winter were closed down for about forty-eight hours.

The fuel famine worsened despite every effort of Zhdanov, Kuznetsov and the others.

Leningrad had entered the blockade in no better shape for fuel than for food. On September 1 Leningrad had gasoline and oil reserves of 18 to 20 days, coal for 75 to 80 days. The Power Trust had 18 days' supply of wood, and bread bakeries 60 days'. By September 30 fuel oil was virtually exhausted and most factories were down to their last coal. The October 1 stock of wood was 118,851 cubic meters—about two weeks' supply. It had been 370,000 cubic meters a month earlier.

By mid-October power production had fallen to one-third prewar level. Young Communist battalions were beginning to be sent out to the suburban forests to chop wood.

The city in peacetime got 120 trainloads of fuel a day. Now it had three or four trains of firewood at best.[3]

The heating of buildings virtually ceased, although it was officially supposed to be maintained at 54 degrees Fahrenheit in apartments, 50 degrees in offices and 47 degrees in factories, as of November 17. In fact, by December there was no central heating whatever. The use of electricity for lighting was limited to Smolny, the General Staff building, police stations, Party offices, AA commands, post and telegraph offices, the fire department, courts and apartment house offices. Even the military were running out of fuel. By the end of November they were down to ten to eleven days of aviation gas and seven days' supply for the trucks.

By December 15 the director of Power Station No. 1 reported he was receiving only 150 to 350 tons of coal a day against a minimum use of 700 to 800. He was compelled to exhaust his emergency supplies and closed down. In the course of December most hospitals lost all their electricity, and in the forty which were dependent on electricity for

---

[3] Pavlov, *op. cit.*, 2nd edition, p. 147. The figure is given as 36 trainloads by N. A. Manakov. (*Voprosy Istorii*, No. 5, May, 1967, p. 17.)

heating, temperatures fell to 35 to 45 degrees. Laundries ceased to operate. So did public baths.

On December 10, 2,850 persons were sent out to cut wood. On December 12 another 1,400 were mobilized, mostly Young Communists. On December 24 it was decided to demolish wooden structures for fuel. Even so, only 20 percent of the December wood quota of 130,000 cubic meters was met. The bakeries got 18,000 cubic meters of wood from the demolition of 279 houses in January. In February they got another 17,000 cubic meters.

On January 1 the city authorities estimated fuel reserves at 73,000 tons of coal, a little more than a month's supply at minimum use. There were less than 2,000 tons of anthracite left in the city. The only sources of fuel now were the small forests around the city, a little peat that lay under frozen snow and ice along the north bank of the Neva and the wooden houses and buildings of Leningrad. Andrei Zhdanov authorized the demolition of almost any structure made of wood. He promised that after the war Leningrad would be rebuilt in new grandeur. Youngsters even tore away some wooden planks around the Bronze Horseman, the heroic statue of Peter the Great. On those that remained they scrawled, "He is not cold and we will be warmed."

The principal means of heating were the *burzhuiki* set up in apartments with a chimney that went out through the *fortochka*, the small ventilating window.

The result was inevitable: hundreds upon hundreds of fires, caused by the cranky, poorly installed, poorly attended makeshift stoves. From January 1 to March 10 there were 1,578 fires in Leningrad, caused by the estimated 135,000 *burzhuiki* in the city.

When the fuel supplies ran out at Power Station No. 5, the main water-pumping station got no power for thirty-six hours, the Southern and Petrograd stations got none for four days. The temperature was 30 degrees below zero. By the time the pumps came back, Leningrad's water system had been fatally frozen. So had the sewer system.

The city began to burn down. In January there were more than 250 serious fires and an average of nearly thirty a day of all kinds. Some were caused by German bombardment but most of them by the *burzhuiki*. They burned day after day. On January 12 there was a very bad series of fires, twenty in all. One of the worst was on the Nevsky, where the Gostiny Dvor, badly battered in the September bombing, burned again.

With his usual suspiciousness Vsevolod Vishnevsky thought that Nazi diversionists must be at work, although he conceded that the fires might be due to carelessness with the *burzhuiki*.

The sight of the Leningrad fires was chilling even to an insensitive observer like Vsevolod Kochetov. It terrified him to see a fire burn in a big building and return a day or two later to find it still burning, slowly eating away apartment after apartment, often with no one making any effort to extinguish it. The pipes were frozen, there was no fuel for the fire trucks, and most of the fire fighters were too sick or too weak to answer a call even if anyone had bothered to put one in. By December only 7 percent of the fire engines were still operative. In January in a typical fire command only eight of eighty fire fighters were able to report for duty.

One night Aleksandr Chakovsky was walking back to the Astoria Hotel from Smolny. A great fire was burning in the heart of the city, the sky was ablaze and rosy shadows played on the snow. As he approached, he found a large stone apartment house afire. There were no firemen about. But several women had formed a chain and were handing possessions out of the house—a baby in a perambulator, a samovar, a kerosene stove, a couch on which a figure lay wrapped in a blanket, possibly the mother of the baby.

Fedor Grachev, a doctor in charge of a large hospital on Vasilevsky Island, was walking through Theater Square, across from the Mariinsky Theater, one evening when he saw the glow of a huge fire on Decembrists Street. He turned into the street, soot falling in his face. The flames had attacked the three upper stories of a tall building at the corner of Decembrists Street and Maklin Prospekt, a building decorated with figures and scenes from Russian fairy tales. "The House of Fairy Tales" was what the Leningraders called it.

Tongues of fire licked out of the windows, casting a lurid light over the scene, and underfoot there was a carpet of broken glass. The heat of the fire was melting snow and ice, and this had attracted a crowd of people who patiently filled their pails and buckets with the precious water. No one made any attempt to put out the fire. In fact, no one paid any heed to it, except to take advantage of the rare source of easily obtainable water.

"Has it burned a long time?" Grachev asked a woman.

"Since morning," she said.

Grachev stopped long enough to warm himself and then went on.

In an effort to prevent soldiers passing through Leningrad from deserting to the ranks of the food bandits, heavy security detachments were thrown around the suburban railroad stations. Even so, a few men managed to slip away from almost every detachment.

It was at this point that the Leningrad Military Council, the City Party Committee and the City Council began to receive letters proposing that Leningrad be declared an "open city"—that is, as the Soviet historians note, that the front be opened and the Germans be permitted to occupy the city.

There are few references to the "open city" proposal in Soviet historical works. And in each case they draw upon the same documents in the Leningrad State Archives.

The Soviet historians seem convinced that the "open city" proposals came from resident Nazi agents within Leningrad. The "open city" proposal was first advanced, they contend, at the time of the September battles. They quote a Nazi agent as saying that the German plan was to stir up revolt within Leningrad, simultaneous with the final attack on the city. Later on, the plan was changed and the Germans decided to provoke an uprising within the city, carry out a pogrom against Jews and Party commissars, and then invite the Germans into the city to restore order.[4]

Another Nazi agent (or perhaps the same one) is quoted as having said that with the deepening of the blockade the Germans hoped to touch off a "hunger revolt" in which bread shops and food stores would be attacked and women would then march out to the front lines and demand that the troops give up the siege and let the Germans enter the city.

The "agent's report" bears a striking resemblance to the events of February, 1917, when women in Petrograd, tired, angry and cold from standing day after day in the lengthening bread lines, began to demonstrate, touching off the revolution which brought down Czar Nicholas II.

The efforts of the German agents (if any) to produce in the leaden streets of Leningrad in January of 1942 a re-enactment of the events of 1917 did not succeed. But Andrei Zhdanov and the Leningrad leadership took the threat with grim seriousness despite their knowledge that Leningraders by this time hated the Germans with passion. (Desertions had long since ceased because the Russians had learned too much concerning Nazi treatment of prisoners and the occupied villages.)

The "open city" agitation obviously went a good deal further than letters to the Soviet authorities. It was a subject of conversation, if nothing more, among Soviet citizens. Special propaganda detachments were sent into many regions of the city to counteract this and other threatening or hostile moods of the populace.[5]

[4] Kochetov heard of something like this in September.

[5] There is some reason to believe that the "open city" proposals did not, as the Soviet historians insist, originate with German agents. The basic account presented by A. V. Karasev in his authoritative *Leningradtsy v Gody Blokady* is followed almost word for word in the official war history of Leningrad, a sign that security considerations are involved. Karasev cites a Leningrad propaganda work, published in 1942, to explain the "open city" agitation, another source of doubt. There is no indication from German sources that such an "open city" maneuver was undertaken in January, 1942. The Nazi line then was to starve Leningrad into oblivion and to reject any "open city" proposal that might emanate from the Soviet side. (Karasev, pp. 120, 204, 205; *Leningrad v VOV*, p. 214.) The flat assertion by D. V. Pavlov that not one of the thousands of letters received by the Party committee during the blockade expressed any despondency, bitterness or opinions differing from those of the majority of the city's defenders is obviously inexact. (Pavlov, *op. cit.*, 2nd edition, p. 142.) A letter written by a professor from his deathbed at the Astoria Hotel in late January, 1942, to Andrei Zhdanov clearly indicates that many Leningraders blamed him and the Party for the city's plight. The professor went out of his way to exempt Zhdanov of

The city became quieter as its suffering grew. There were no Nazi bombing raids, less frequent shelling.

"The Hitlerites are confident," Yelizaveta Sharypina wrote, "that hunger will break the resistance of the Leningraders. Why waste bombs and shells?"

There came to her mind a line from a poem by Nekrasov:

> In the world there is a czar
> And that czar is without mercy—
> Hunger is what they call him.

---

responsibility for the Leningrad tragedy. The implication was clear that others, in contrast, did hold Zhdanov responsible. (P. L. Korzinkin, V *Redaktsiyu Ne Vernulsya*, Moscow, 1964, p. 264.)

# LOUIS MACNEICE

THE CLASSICAL SCHOLAR and poet Louis MacNeice was born in Ireland. In the 1930s he was part of the same circle as Auden, Isherwood, and Spender, but was never as strongly committed to Marxist doctrine.

■

## The conscript

Being so young he feels the weight of history
Like clay around his boots; he would, if he could, fly
In search of a future like a sycamore seed
But is prevented by his own Necessity,
His own yet alien, which, whatever he may plead,
To every question gives the same reply.

Choiceless therefore, driven from pillar to post,
Expiating his pedigree, fulfilling
An oracle whose returns grow less and less,
Bandied from camp to camp to practice killing
He fails even so at times to remain engrossed
And is aware, at times, of life's largesse.

From camp to camp, from Eocene to chalk,
He lives a paradox, lives in a groove
That runs dead straight to an ordained disaster
So that in two dimensions he must move
Like an automaton, yet his inward stalk
Vertically aspires and makes him his own master.

Hence, though on the flat his life has no
Promise but of diminishing returns,
By feeling down and upwards he can divine
That dignity which far above him burns
In stars that yet are his and which below
Stands rooted like a dolmen in his spine.

# CLIVE JAMES

AUSTRALIAN-BORN Clive James is a regular contributor to *The Times Literary Supplement*, *The Observer*, and *The New York Review of Books*. Born in 1939, he recalls what little he knew of his father in this excerpt from *Unreliable Memoirs*.

■

FROM *Unreliable Memoirs*

### THE KID FROM KOGARAH

I was born in 1939. The other big event of that year was the outbreak of the Second World War, but for the moment that did not affect me. Sydney in those days had all of its present attractions and few of the drawbacks. You can see it glittering in the background of the few photographs in which my father and I are together. Stocky was the word for me. Handsome was the word for him. Without firing a shot, the Japanese succeeded in extricating him from my clutches. Although a man of humble birth and restricted education, he was smart enough to see that there would be war in the Pacific. Believing that Australia should be ready, he joined up. That was how he came to be in Malaya at the crucial moment. He was at Parit Sulong bridge on the day when a lot of senior officers at last found out what their troops had guessed long before—that the Japanese army was better led and better equipped than anything we had to pit against it. After the battle my father walked all the way south to Singapore and arrived just in time for the surrender. If he had waited to be conscripted, he might have been sent to the Western Desert and spent a relatively happy few months fighting the kind of Germans whose essential decency was later to be portrayed on the screen by James Mason and Marlon Brando. As it was, he drew the short straw.

# WILLIAM MANCHESTER

WILLIAM MANCHESTER has written biographies of H. L. Mencken, John F. Kennedy, Douglas MacArthur, and Winston Churchill. One day in the spring of 1942 he hitchhiked to Springfield, Massachusetts, and presented himself at the Marine Corps recruiting station. The next stop, as he wrote in *Goodbye, Darkness,* his memoir of the Pacific War, was boot camp—Parris Island.

■

FROM *Goodbye, Darkness*

## THE RAGGEDY ASS MARINES

In those days all Marine Corps recruits were assigned to one of the Corps' two boot camps. Those enlisting west of the Mississippi River were sent to San Diego; those who joined up east of the Mississippi went to Parris Island, South Carolina, an isle whose reputation was just marginally better than those of Alcatraz and Devil's Island. So I was going to see the Deep South after all. Having signed up for four years, or more if the war lasted longer; having sworn that "I will bear true faith and allegiance to the United States of America; that I will serve them honestly and faithfully against all their enemies whomsoever; and that I will obey the orders of the President of the United States, and the orders of the officers appointed over me, according to the Rules and Articles for the Government of the Army, Navy, and Marine Corps of the United States" —having, in short, put my life in hock to the most fearsome and hazardous of the country's armed forces—I boarded a special train occupied by other young men who had done the same. We had hardly begun to roll from Springfield when I made a friend in Lawrence Dudley, of Bowdoin. Dudley was heavy, flaxen-haired, and round-shouldered. He knew that once his poor posture had caught the eye of our drill instructor ("DI," we later learned, was the salty term), he would be in for a hard time. But becoming a Marine was important to him. During his college summers he had worked in the Springfield arsenal as an assistant to John Garand, who had invented the Garand, or M1, rifle, which had replaced the Springfield '03 as America's basic infantry weapon. I had fired the '03 in an ROTC course. Dudley said the M1 was better (he was wrong) and felt, as a testament to his faith, that he should carry one in combat instead of tinkering away the war years in the arsenal, which could have been easily arranged by his friends there.

In Washington we paused for three nighttime hours and were told we could go "ashore" instead of waiting in Union Station. Dudley and I repaired to a nearby nightclub. Neither of us had ever been in one before, and we were appalled. All I can remember is a drunken brunette, apparently a customer, who insisted on taking off all her clothes, and a comedian with a voice that grated like a file who kept breaking himself up by saying: "Damon went out and got Pythias drunk." It was an introduction to the kind of wartime entertainment available to American enlisted men. Back on the train we slept, and I awoke, trembling with anticipation, in the sacred soil of the old Confederacy. I rushed for the rear platform. Everything I had been told had led me to expect plantations, camellias, and darkies with banjos strumming "Old Black Joe." Instead I looked out on shabby unpainted shacks and people in rags, all of them barefoot. No Taras, no Scarletts, no Rhetts; just Tobacco Road. And this was *Virginia*, the state of Robert E. Lee. I felt cheated; disinherited; apprehensive. What awaited me on Parris Island, which was grim even by Southern standards? Despair swept me as we reached our destination, heard departing, newly graduated sea soldiers yelling, "You'll be sorreeee!" and saw noncoms in field hats carrying menacing swagger sticks. The NCOs stared at us as though we were some low and disgusting form of animal life. They spat tobacco at our feet and kept calling us "shitheads."

Astonishingly, I adored Parris Island. Boot camp is a profound shock to most recruits because the Corps begins its job of building men by destroying the identity they brought with them. Their heads are shaved. They are assigned numbers. The DI is their god. He treats them with utter contempt. I am told that corporal punishment has since been banned on the island, but in my day it was quite common to see a DI bloody a man's nose, and some boots were gravely injured, though I know of none who actually died. I recall being baffled later when Patton was reprimanded for slapping a GI. All of us had endured much more than that. The gentlest punishments were those for dropping a rifle (sleeping on eight of them) and for eating candy (carrying an oozing mass of chocolate for two days). If the boot called it "candy" he would have been punished further, the proper expression being *pogey bait*. The Corps had its own language, and boots were required to learn it, just as the inhabitants of an occupied country must learn the conqueror's tongue. A bar was a *slopchute*, a latrine a *head*; swamps were *boondocks*, and field boots, *boondockers*. A rumor was *scuttlebutt*, because that was the name for water fountains, where rumors were spread; a deception was a *snow job*, gossiping was *shooting the breeze*, information was *dope*, news was *the scoop*, confirmed information was *the word*. You said "Aye, aye, sir," not "Yes, sir." The nape of the neck was the *stacking swivel*, after a rifle part. An officer promoted from the ranks was a *mustang*. Your company commander was *the skipper*. You never went on leave; you were *granted liberty*, usually in the form of a *forty-eight* or a *seventy-two*, depending on the number of hours you could be absent. If you didn't return by then, you were *over the hill*. Coffee was *Joe*; a coffeepot, a *Joe-pot*. Battle dress was *dungarees*. A cleanup of barracks, no matter how long it lasted, was a *field day*; a necktie was a *field scarf*, drummers and trumpeters were *field musics*. Duffle bags, though indistinguishable from those used by GIs, were *seabags*. To be *under hack* meant to be under arrest. To straighten up was to *square away*; a tough fighter was a *hard-charger*; underwear was *skivvies*; manipulating people was called *working one's bolt*. *Lad* was a generic term of address for any subordinate, regardless of age. One of my people, a twenty-eight-year-old Vermont school principal, was known, because of his advanced age, as "Pop." An officer five years his junior would summon him by snapping, "Over here, lad."

Some of these terms have crept into the language since World War II, but no one outside the service knew them then. Boots had to pick them up fast. They were courting trouble if they described their combat hardware as anything but 782 *gear*, that being the number of the form you had to sign as a receipt. It was equally unwise to call a deck a "floor," a bulkhead a "wall," an overhead a "ceiling," a hatch a "door," or a ladder "stairs." Every Marine was "Mac" to every other Marine; every U.S. soldier was a "doggie" and was barked at. The Corps' patois was astonishingly varied. To "sight in" or "zero" was to determine, by trial and error, the sight setting necessary to hit a bull's-eye with a given weapon. "Snap in" could mean sighting and aiming an unloaded rifle; it could also mean breaking into, or trying out for, a new job, somewhat like the army's "bucking for." As a noun, "secure" described an outdated movement in the manual of arms; as a verb, it signified anchoring something in place or ending an activity—thus, when the Battle of Tarawa was won, the island was "secure." "Survey" was even more flexible. It could mean, not only a medical discharge from the Corps (anyone feigning combat fatigue was "snapping in for a survey"), but also retirement from the Corps, disposing of worn-out clothing or equipment, or taking a second helping of chow. There was even a word for anything which defied description. It was "gizmo."

On Parris Island these and all other customs of the boot's new way of life were flouted at great risk. You were told that there were three ways of doing things: the right way, the wrong way, and the Marine Corps way. The Corps way was uncompromising. Failure to salute your superiors—including privates first class—brought swift retribution. The worst discipline I saw came during floodlit midnight calisthenics. In one common exercise we paired off; each boot hoisted his rifle as you would hoist a battering ram and placed the butt against his buddy's forehead. The buddy would touch the butt and duck. The man with the rifle was supposed to try to strike his forehead before the other man could drop, but since you knew you were going to reverse roles, the sensible course was to let him get out of the way. Enter the vengeful noncom. *He* put a rifle butt against the offender's forehead and slugged him before there was time to dodge. The boot who merely suffered a concussion was lucky.

How could I enjoy this? Parts of it, of course, I loathed. But the basic concept fascinated me. I wanted to surrender my individuality, curbing my neck beneath the yoke of petty tyranny. Since my father's death I had yearned for stern discipline, and Parris Island, where he himself had learned discipline a quarter-century earlier, gave it to me in spades. Physically I was delicate, even fragile, but I had limitless reservoirs of energy, and I could feel myself toughening almost hourly. Everything I saw seemed exquisitely defined—every leaf, every pebble looked as sharp as a drawing in a book. I knew I was merely becoming a tiny cog in the vast machine which would confront fascism, but that was precisely why I had volunteered. Even today, despite the horrors which inevitably followed, I am haunted by memories of my weeks as a recruit. It is almost like recalling a broken marriage which, for one divorced partner, can never really end.

Our platoon was number 618, and our DI was a leathery corporal from Georgia named Coffey. The Marine Corps had always recruited a disproportionate number of men from the South, where the military traditions of the early 1860s had never died. Later I met many Raiders like that, and Coffey was typical: tall, lanky, and fair haired, with a mad grin and dancing, rain-colored eyes full of shattered light. They were born killers; in the Raider battalions, in violation of orders, they would penetrate deep behind Japanese lines at night, looking for two Nips sacked out together. Then they would cut the throat of one and leave the other to find the corpse in the morning. This was brilliant psychological warfare, but it was also, of course, extremely dangerous. In combat these Southerners would charge fearlessly with the shrill rebel yell of their great-grandfathers, and they loved the bayonet. How my father's side defeated my mother's side in the Civil War will always mystify me.

Yankee boys were just the kind of meat this Georgian Caesar fed upon. His appetite was further whetted by the fact that many of us had been university students, a fact which triggered the antiintellectual in him. He himself was illiterate and, apart from his training duties, startlingly ignorant. Even there he sometimes skidded; while specifying the rigors of our calling, he was supposed to teach us a synoptic history of the Corps, and it turned out that he thought the American Revolution had occurred in "nineteen and ten" and World War I in "nineteen and thirty-four," with the French as our enemies. After this last, a Dartmouth man unwisely laughed. Our DI flushed and declared his own war on all "wisenheimer college eight balls." He invented sobriquets, most of them scatological, for boots from New England campuses. For some reason—perhaps because I obviously felt that I had found a home in the Marine Corps—I got off lightly. I was merely "Slim," a *nom de guerre* which stuck to me throughout my forty-month cruise and was vastly preferable to my fraternity nicknames; I happened to be damned, or blessed, with outsize genitalia, so in college I had been called first "Tripod," and then "Sashweight." It embarrassed me then. Not until I joined the Marines did I learn that hefty equipment along that line was admired in some quarters. One day I found myself hip-to-hip at a trough urinal with a former Reno gigolo. He gazed down at me for a long moment and then asked thoughtfully, "Slim, what did you do in civilian life?"

As expected, Coffey's favorite target of opportunity was slope-shouldered, potbellied Larry Dudley. This was partly Dudley's fault. He couldn't help his figure, but he was remiss in other ways, too. The DI liked to say, "God gave you the face you were born with, but I'll give you the face you'll die with." That was untrue of Dudley. His expression never changed. Even when he was out of step, which was often, he looked bland, nonchalant, slightly pained. His greatest blunder, however, was a spectacular feat of tactlessness. On the evening of the day we were issued our 782 gear, Coffey stood in the doorway of a Quonset hut, facing us vassals, who ranged in a semicircle outside. The only light came from the interior of the hut, at the DI's back. He was holding an M1, fieldstripping it as he talked, naming the parts. Then he reassembled the rifle. "Now," he said triumphantly, "let's see one of you college kids do it." He thrust the weapon at the most intent member of his captive audience—Larry Dudley, lately of Garand and Dudley. *Oh, God,* I prayed; *don't let him do it.* But Dudley did it. He took that M1 apart so fast we could hardly see the blur of his moving hands; then he put it back together with the same blinding speed and handed it to the DI. There were a few stifled chuckles for the avenged shitheads of Platoon 618. Coffey turned the color of a song then popular: deep purple. His loss of face was immense, but being a DI he could strike back in many ways. He swiftly chose one. "OK, wisenheimers," he said in a pebbly voice, balancing the weapon on the palm of his hand. "If he can do it, you can all do it. Fall out here at 0500 with your pieces, ready to fieldstrip."

We were stunned. Our asses were in a sling. None of us had the faintest idea of what Dudley had been doing. We couldn't even tell the difference between the trigger-housing group and the barrel-and-receiver group. Fortunately Dudley, for all his faults, had also learned ingenuity from Garand. Though taps sounded twenty minutes after Coffey had dismissed us, and illumination of any kind was forbidden thereafter, we carried on a night-long seminar with flashlights under blankets. Dudley taught three men, each of them taught three more, and so on. By dawn we were exhausted, but we could do it. At 0450 our DI shrilled his whistle and strode down our line of bunks yelping his usual morning greeting:

"OK, shitheads! Drop your cocks and grab your socks!" When we fell out he had already adopted a tragic expression. Clearly he expected us to fail and had rehearsed one of his sinking spells, which were as memorable as the *Titanic*'s. Then, as he blinked in disbelief, each of us in turn took his rifle apart, identifying the bolt camming lug, hammer springs, sears and lugs, and the rest, put the piece back together, and smartly brought it to port arms for inspection. Cheated and smarting, Coffey put us through a grueling day: an hour of calisthentics, a second hour of close-order drill, a third hour of lunging, with fixed bayonets, at straw-stuffed dummies, a session of throwing live hand grenades and then rolling out of a fall (never creep), another session of instruction in how to use short-bladed Kabar knives in hand-to-hand combat (always ripping *up*, into the gut; a downward thrust can be blocked more easily); a cruel hundred-yard sprint wearing gas masks, suffering from inadequate oxygen; and the most idiotic drill of all, snapping in with simulated rifle fire at an imaginary enemy warplane flying overhead. Perhaps this had been practical in World War I, when Fokkers drifted lazily over no-man's-land, but since then strafing fighter planes had developed the speed to flash by before an infantryman could set his feet. Yet we were being taught to aim at the horizon, leading hypothetical Zeroes as hunters lead quail. Long before the sunset gun sounded we all knew we were being punished for Dudley's virtuoso performance. He lost a lot of popularity that day.

None of us, I think, comprehended how all this training would end on battlefields, why we were being taught monstrous things. Our thoughts and our life-style were still largely civilian. Flaked out before lights out, or standing around the lister bag, a container of pure water which resembled a seabag suspended from three tepeed poles, we whistled popular songs—the current hits were "Chattanooga Choo-Choo" and "Blues in the Night"—and shot the breeze much as we would have done at home. I remember us talking about a news item reporting America's annual consumption of seventeen billion cigarettes a year, none of us suspecting that it might be unhealthy, and what it would be like to shack up with Betty Grable or prong Hedy Lamarr. We scorned conscientious objectors and other hambos. We said inane things like, "Hello, Joe, whaddya know?" "I just got back from the vaudeville show." We laughed at pink-toothbrush ads and cartoonist Frank King's frenzied press conference, called to scotch rumors that Gasoline Alley's Skeezix Wallett would be killed in action. The more sophisticated of 618's boots yearned for a roll of moola and a seventy-two in New York, where they could wander along West Fifty-second Street and hear, at spots like the Famous Door, the Onyx Club, and Kelly's Stable, a tumultuous crash of drums heralding "In the Mood" or Harry James leading a wickedly fast "Sweet Georgia Brown," the brass section on their feet, horns swinging like cannon out across the ballroom.

Yet here, as so often, I dissented from the majority of my generation. Swing's orchestration, its utter lack of improvisation, still bored me; I preferred the brilliant riffs of Wild Bill Davidson, Muggsy Spanier, Eddie Condon, J. C. Higgenbotham, and Jack Teagarden. Neither could I share the growing nostalgia, among my fellow former undergraduates in the Quonset, for suburban New England's trellised verandas and croquet lawns. Sometimes memories of my grandmother's ancient homestead, with its wine-red sumac, its fire-red barberries, and its split silver-birch fence, tugged at my heart, but mostly I wanted to be where I was. And so, I think, did the rest, or at any rate the best, of the other boots. Without having the haziest idea of what combat would be, we wanted, in a phrase which sounds quaint today, to fight for our country. Subsequent generations have lost that blazing patriotism and speak of it, if at all, patronizingly. They cannot grasp how proud we were to be Americans.

Because of that pride, we survived jolts like our DI's torments and the sobering realization that citizen-soldiers are very different from professional soldiers. The peacetime Marine Corps assumed that enlisted men were brutes and treated them accordingly. I recall my shock the first time I saw a private being led away in chains. And I remember our collective horror when we all became suspects in a rape case. The victim was the daughter of a garrison officer. At one point in her struggle, she said, she had bitten her assailant's penis. Therefore, the commanding general decided, every man on the island must submit to a "short-arm inspection." The inspection was a massive logistic undertaking, involving thousands of loins. We stood in line hour after hour, awaiting our turn. Along the way, several oddities turned up. One exhibitionist, anticipating an inspection of his short arm sooner or later, had submitted to excruciating pain for the sake of a practical joke. He had caused the words "Hi, Doc!" to be tattooed on the inside of his foreskin. He was immediately put under hack—on what charges I neither know nor can imagine. The complex operation, as complicated in its way as an amphibious landing, produced no evidence whatever. Later I learned that the son of another officer had been arrested and charged. Still later, I met a corpsman who had served as one of the inspectors. He said it had been a shattering experience. It still haunted him. "I have these nightmares," he said hollowly. "All I can see is cocks, cocks, millions of cocks, all of them swarming around me."

My Parris Island triumph came on the rifle range. On Record Day we fired sixty-six shots, all but ten of them rapid-fire, at targets two hundred, three hundred, and five hundred yards away. Each shot was worth a maximum of five points, for a bull's-eye. Riflemen could qualify in three categories: marksman, sharpshooter, and—very rare, requiring 305 points out of a possible 330—expert rifleman. I knew I would do well. My M1 was zeroed in to perfection. I had steady hands; I could hold my breath indefinitely, steadying the muzzle; I could fold my right ankle under my buttocks for kneeling shots; and I had 20/10 vision, meaning that what was visible to a man with 20/20 vision at one hundred yards was just as sharp and clear for me at two hundred yards. I was also clever in adjusting my sling. The sling is the leather strap on a rifle, which looks useless to a civilian; it can be extended and looped around the left arm, locking the butt to the right shoulder. Record Day was clear and windless. I hardly missed anything. My score was 317. A colonel congratulated me and told me that 317 was unprecedented. Because of it, because of my adjustment to the Corps, and because of my college education, I was sent directly to the Corps' OCS in Quantico, Virginia. My world brightened a little, as though there were a rheostat on the sun and someone had turned it up a notch. Later I realized that was an illusion —that I wasn't meant to be an officer, at least not by Quantico standards, and that the attempt to make one of me was a grave error.

.

At Quantico we were quartered, rather grandly, in permanent redbrick barracks, each company with its own squad bays. The chow was excellent. Our rank was private first class, but we wore small brass insignia on our shirt collars, each reading simply "O.C." Weekends we were usually given liberty in Washington, and the departure of the Saturday noon train from Quantico to D.C. was always bedlam; it was said that the only people to wind up on board were those who had come to see their friends off. In the capital there were about six girls for every man. Saturday night a dollar admitted you to the weekly singles dance on the lowest floor of the Washington Hotel. Girls ringed the walls; a bold Marine O.C. could cruise the ballroom slowly, picking the cutest girl and, if he was really insensitive, firing questions about which had cars and apartments. Back at the base, weekday classes were conducted by decorated officers who spoke lucidly, wittily, and always to the point; a single phrase from one of them was worth more than all of poor Coffey's ramblings. There were courses in mapping, leadership, and tactics. Field exercises included forced marches, perimeter defenses, protection of platoon flanks, and how to deal with such crises as unexpected mortaring. Nobody called you a shithead. Some enlisted men on the streets even sirred you.

It was hell.

Parris Island had been an excursion into an exotic world, tolerable even at its worst because you were all in it together, and you knew that together you would all make it. But an officer candidate at Quantico had few friends. The system set each man against the others. If you could artfully make another man look like a fool, you did it; you were diminishing the competition. Everybody was on the muscle. "Shape up here or ship out" was the slogan heard most often. It meant that if you weren't commissioned here as a second lieutenant, and sent on to advanced training, you would be consigned to the serfdom of an enlisted man. But I liked enlisted men, and I wasn't at all sure that I liked these officers-to-be. I recognized their type. I had known many of them, if distantly, in college. They were upper-middle-class snobs, nakedly ambitious conservative conformists, eager to claw their way to the top. In another ten years their uniforms would be corporate gray-flannel suits. Now they yearned to wear officers' dress greens; some were already learning to fieldstrip Sam Browne belts. The thought that they might fail in their pursuit of gold bars turned them into quivering jelly. It would mean, they thought, that they had disgraced themselves in the eyes of their families and friends.

# MALCOLM MUGGERIDGE

MALCOLM MUGGERIDGE, a novelist, broadcaster, and former editor of *Punch*, wrote a two-volume autobiography titled *Chronicles of Wasted Time*.

■

## FROM *Chronicles of Wasted Time*

### ON SECRET SERVICE

But vain the Sword and vain the Bow,
They never can work War's overthrow.
—Blake

Only when a man has become so unhappy, or has grasped the misery of this existence so profoundly that he can truly say, "For me life is worthless"; only then can life have worth in the highest degree. —Kierkegaard

My instructions were to present myself at an office in Broadway, opposite St James's underground station, which I duly did. As a reader of *Ashenden* I was naturally excited at the prospect of entering the portals of the world-famous British Secret Service (or SIS as it was usually called), though I assumed that at this first preliminary encounter I should not be admitted to the actual headquarters, but only to some shadow set-up, or façade, used to try out aspirants before definitely taking them on. I may add that everyone I saw and everything that happened seemed to support such an assumption. It was only later that I came to realize I had been in contact, not with a hurriedly improvised dummy, but the real thing. While I was awaiting my own clearance at the main entrance, I was able to observe the people coming and going. A good proportion of them were in the services, with the Navy preponderating. I only saw one, as I thought, false beard—a luxuriant tangled growth, whose wearer turned out, on closer acquaintance, to be a former trade-unionist and Marxist, allegedly from the boiler-makers' union. He was responsible for providing expert guidance in industrial matters; and his beard, he assured me, was genuine, though he admitted that he had allowed it to proliferate since joining SIS, as he had also his use of strong language, and tendency to bang the table to emphasize a point. The last glimpse I had of him was towards the end of the war, in the Athenaeum Club dining-room, where he was holding forth noisily to some abashed-looking Americans, including a three-star general.

My contact, to whose office I was led, turned out to be an agreeable man named Leslie Nicholson, who had been, I learnt afterwards, a Secret Service agent himself in Riga. His manner was gentle, amiable and helpful; more in the style of a Bertie Wooster, I decided, than of a spymaster as popularly conceived. He told me that various stations were being opened up in Africa, and that the intention was to send Graham Greene to Freetown and me to Lourenço Marques in Mozambique. I said that nothing could suit me better, implying that Lourenço Marques was a place I had always been interested in and wanted to visit, though in point of fact I had never before heard of it, and had no idea where it was. My ready acquiescence, I think, pleased Nicholson, who might otherwise have had to look up where Lourenço Marques was himself, and answer questions about its climatic conditions, port facilities, population, and so on. As it was, we could agree on my departure there without either of us being unduly troubled about the whys and wherefores. When, a few days later, we dined together at Boodles, Nicholson's club, we talked, as I recall, about everything under the sun except Mozambique. I did, in point of fact, read up the entry in the *Encyclopaedia Britannica* on Mozambique, and learnt—it is the solitary fact remaining with me—that Gladstone could have bought it off the Portuguese for a million pounds, but decided the price was too high. His parsimony was ill-judged; it would have been a good buy, Delagoa Bay providing an excellent harbor, which Durban notably lacks.

My first task, as now an MI6 officer, was to get myself, notionally, transformed into a civilian. For this purpose I was handed a passport stamped to indicate that I had lately landed in the UK, and giving my address as St Ermin's Hotel. To form some idea of my place of residence I dropped in there for a drink, finding the lounge dim and quiet, suggestive of conferences to promote world governments, family planning, or the practice of eurythmics. My instructions were to go with my passport to Caxton Hall, and apply for a civilian identity card, explaining, if asked why I had not got one, that I had recently arrived at Liverpool from extensive travels abroad, and was expecting to leave the UK again at any moment for further travels. I was also instructed to memorize the number in the left-hand top corner of the form of application for an identity card, and to apply for an emergency ration card. Waiting my turn in the queue, I was seized with anxiety. Supposing they asked me the name of the ship on which I had arrived at Liverpool, what should I say? Or questioned me about the places I had been to abroad, and how long I had stayed in them? Or asked for details of my projected departure and subsequent travels. My story, as it seemed to me, was full of obvious pitfalls. And how should I ever memorize that number in the left-hand top corner when I find it impossible to remember the registration number of a car, even when I have been driving about in it for years? By the time my turn came, I was in a state of nerves which must have seemed highly suspicious in the light of my threadbare story, tremulously recounted. To my great relief, no questions were asked, the man behind the *guichet* positively winking as he handed me my identity card and emergency ration book. As for the number I was supposed to memorize—I forgot all about it, and no one ever asked me for it.

It might well be wondered—as, indeed, I wondered at the time myself—what was the point of this exercise in mystery when it would have been as easy to procure an identity card and emergency ration card for me as it had been to procure a passport. To ask such a question is to fail to understand the whole character of secret Intelligence, one of whose basic precepts is that nothing should ever be done simply if there are devious ways of doing it. With old hands it becomes second nature, for instance, to communicate in code, and to use an accommodation address, for perfectly innocuous communications; to prefer a cache in a potting-shed to a normal letter-box, and a diplomatic bag to a suitcase for carrying blameless personal effects. Kim Philby's American wife, until she got used to it, and came to regard it as a harmless eccentricity, was astonished when he sent her loving messages on tiny fragments of tissue paper, which, as he explained, could comfortably be swallowed if this should be required in the interest of security. As it happened, the address of the Broadway office and the names of most of its leading occupants had been given out on the German radio quite early on in the war following an incident when two SIS representatives at The Hague fell into enemy hands. This made no difference to security arrangements; the Chief, at the time Sir Stuart Menzies, was still known as "C" even in the internal telephone directory, and all other blown symbols and aliases were scrupulously maintained. Again, in coded messages, countries had always to be referred to by symbols—Germany, for instance, was "Twelve-land." The practice was scrupulously observed throughout the war even though, on one festive occasion at an Istanbul hotel, when the orchestra played the German national anthem, the staff of the German embassy stood to attention and sang as one man: "*Zwölfte-land, Zwölfte-land, uber alles!*" Outside "C" 's office a blue light shone, like a dispensary or a police-station; the sense of secrecy was so great that, walking by it, one instinctively tiptoed. Secrecy is as essential to Intelligence as vestments and incense to a Mass, or darkness to a Spiritualist seance, and must at all costs be maintained, quite irrespective of whether or not it serves any purpose.

The two captured Secret Service men at The Hague—both slightly parodying what they purported to be; with monocle, trimmed gray mustache, club tie, touch of the Raj, whence, in fact they came—had imagined themselves to be in touch with a group of dissident Germans, including a general, who were anxious to get rid of Hitler and call off the war in return for an honorable peace. What excitement in Broadway as the messages from The Hague came in! Passed Most Secretly from hand to hand, until they reached the Prime Minister, Neville Chamberlain himself, and his Foreign Secretary, Lord Halifax. Full approval was given to keep the contact going; finally, for a meeting face to face at Venlo, a drab little place on the Dutch-German border. There, alas, it turned out that the so prized contact was not with a dissident general at all, but with the Gestapo; and one more dream that the doom which had come upon us could be averted—the last Munich—blew up in the faces of the dreamers. One of the captured men, Payne Best, was in custody for a time with Dietrich Bonhoeffer, and went with him on the last journey, in April 1945, to the East German village of Schonberg, participating on a bright Sunday morning in the service Bonhoeffer conducted there, which concluded with the singing of *Eine Feste Burg ist unser Gott*. Almost immediately afterward, Bonhoeffer was taken away to be executed. Before leaving, he entrusted Best with a message for Dr. Bell, the Bishop of Chichester, to tell him that the "victory of our universal brotherhood, rising above all national interests, is certain." Thus, for Best, from the total fantasy of Venlo to the total reality of Schonberg; from darkness to light—the full circle.

# PHILIP ROTH

PHILIP ROTH, born and raised in Newark, New Jersey, published his first book, *Goodbye, Columbus,* in 1959. He is the author of many novels, including *Portnoy's Complaint* and *The Ghost Writer.* He published *The Facts: A Novelist's Autobiography* in 1988.

■

FROM *The Facts: A Novelist's Autobiography*

## SAFE AT HOME

The greatest menace while I was growing up came from abroad, from the Germans and the Japanese, our enemies because we were American. I still remember my terror as a nine-year-old when, running in from playing on the street after school, I saw the banner headline CORREGIDOR FALLS on the evening paper in our doorway and understood that the United States actually could lose the war it had entered only months before. At home the biggest threat came from the Americans who opposed or resisted us—or condescended to us or rigorously excluded us—because we were Jews. Though I knew that we were tolerated and accepted as well—in publicized individual cases, even specially esteemed —and though I never doubted that this country was mine (and New Jersey and Newark as well), I was not unaware of the power to intimidate that emanated from the highest and lowest reaches of gentile America.

At the top were the gentile executives who ran my father's company, the Metropolitan Life, from the home office at Number One Madison Avenue (the first Manhattan street address I ever knew). When I was a small boy, my father, then in his early thirties, was still a new Metropolitan agent, working a six-day week, including most evenings, and grateful for the steady, if modest, living this job provided, even during the Depression; a family shoe store he'd opened after marrying my mother had gone bankrupt some years before, and in between he'd had to take a variety of low-paying, unpromising jobs. He proudly explained to his sons that the Metropolitan was "the largest financial institution in the world" and that as an agent he provided Metropolitan Life policyholders with "an umbrella for a rainy day." The company put out dozens of pamphlets to educate its policyholders about health and disease; I collected a new batch off the racks in the waiting room on Saturday mornings when he took me along with him to the narrow downtown street where the Essex district office of Newark occupied nearly a whole floor of a commercial office building. I read up on "Tuberculosis," "Pregnancy," and "Diabetes," while he labored over his ledger entries and his paperwork. Sometimes at his desk, impressing myself by sitting in his swivel chair, I practiced my penmanship on Metropolitan stationery; in one corner of the paper was my father's name and in the other a picture of the home-office tower, topped with a beacon that he described to me, in the Metropolitan's own phrase, as the light that never failed.

In our apartment a framed replica of the Declaration of Independence hung above the telephone table on the hallway wall—it had been awarded by the Metropolitan to the men of my father's district for a successful year in the field, and seeing it there daily during my first school years forged an association between the venerated champions of equality who signed that cherished document and our benefactors, the corporate fathers at Number One Madison Avenue, where the reigning president was, fortuitously, a Mr. Lincoln. If that wasn't enough, the home-office executive whom my father would trek from New Jersey to see when his star began to rise slightly in the company was the superintendent of agencies, a Mr. Wright, whose good opinion my father valued inordinately all his life and whose height and imposing good looks he admired nearly as much as he did the man's easygoing diplomacy. As my father's son I felt no less respectful toward these awesomely named gentiles than he did, but I, like him, knew that they had to be the very officials who openly and guiltlessly conspired to prevent more than a few token Jews from assuming positions of anything approaching importance within the largest financial institution in the world.

One reason my father so admired the Jewish manager of his own district, Sam Peterfreund—aside, of course, from the devotion that Peterfreund inspired by recognizing my father's drive early on and making him an assistant manager—was that Peterfreund had climbed to the leadership of such a large, productive office despite the company's deep-rooted reluctance to allow a Jew to rise too high. When Mr. Peterfreund was to make one of his rare visits for dinner, the green felt protective pads came out of the hall closet and were laid by my brother and me on the dining room table, it was spread with a fresh linen cloth and linen napkins, water goblets appeared, and we ate off "the good dishes" in the dining room, where there hung a large oil painting of a floral arrangement, copied skillfully from the Louvre by my mother's brother, Mickey; on the sideboard were framed photographic portraits of the two dead men for whom I'd been named, my mother's father, Philip, and my father's youngest brother, Milton. We ate in the dining room only on religious holidays, on special family occasions, and when Mr. Peterfreund came—and we all called him Mr. Peterfreund, even when he wasn't there; my father also addressed him directly as "Boss." "Want a drink, Boss?" Before dinner we sat unnaturally, like guests in our own living room, while Mr. Peterfreund sipped his schnapps and I was encouraged to listen to his wisdom. The esteem he inspired was a tribute to a gentile-sanctioned Jew managing a big Metropolitan office as much as to an immediate supervisor whose goodwill determined my father's occupational well-being and our family fate. A large, bald-headed man with a gold chain across his vest and a slightly mysterious German accent, whose family lived (in high style, I imagined) in New York (*and* on Long Island) while (no less glamorously to me) he slept during the week in a Newark hotel, the Boss was our family's Bernard Baruch.

Opposition more frightening than corporate discrimination came from the lowest reaches of the gentile world, from the gangs of *lumpen* kids who, one summer, swarmed out of Neptune, a ramshackle little town on the Jersey shore, and stampeded along the boardwalk into Bradley Beach, hollering "Kikes! Dirty Jews!" and beating up whoever hadn't run for cover. Bradley Beach, a couple of miles south of Asbury Park on the mid-Jersey coast, was the very modest little vacation resort where we and hundreds of other lower-middle-class Jews from humid, mosquito-ridden north Jersey cities rented rooms or shared small bungalows for several weeks during the summer. It was paradise for me, even though we lived three in a room, and four when my father drove down the old Cheesequake highway to see us on weekends or to stay for his two-week vacation. In all of my intensely secure and protected childhood, I don't believe I ever felt more exuberantly snug than I did in those mildly anarchic rooming houses, where—inevitably with more strain than valor —some ten or twelve women tried to share the shelves of a single large icebox, and to cook side by side, in a crowded communal kitchen, for children, visiting husbands, and elderly parents. Meals were eaten in the unruly, kibbutzlike atmosphere—so unlike the ambiance in my own orderly home—of the underventilated dining room.

The hot, unhomelike, homey hubbub of the Bradley Beach rooming house was somberly contrasted, in the early forties, by reminders all along the shore that the country was fighting in an enormous war: bleak, barbwired Coast Guard bunkers dotted the beaches, and scores of lonely, very young sailors played the amusement machines in the arcades at Asbury Park; the lights were blacked out along the boardwalk at night and the blackout shades on the rooming-house windows made it stifling indoors after dinner; there was even tarry refuse, alleged to be from torpedoed ships, that washed up and littered the beach—I sometimes had fears of wading gleefully with my friends into the surf and bumping against the body of someone killed at sea. Also—and most peculiarly, since we were all supposed to be pulling together to beat the Axis Powers —there were these "race riots," as we children called the hostile nighttime invasions by the boys from Neptune: violence directed against the Jews by youngsters who, as everyone said, could only have learned their hatred from what they heard at home.

# ELLA LEFFLAND

ELLA LEFFLAND's short stories have appeared in *The New Yorker*, *Harper's*, and *Atlantic Monthly*. She has also published three highly praised novels. One of them, *Rumors of Peace*—from which the following is excerpted—deals with her World War II childhood in Martinez, California.

■

FROM *Rumors of Peace*

## CHAPTER 6

In March the FBI broke into the Santa Cruz home of a Nisei couple and discovered sixty-nine crates of colored flares and signal rockets.

That night I gave a prayer. I had never prayed before and was not sure how to phrase the words of a prayer. I wanted to ask that the Japs in the valley be gotten rid of before they brought the bombers in. It must be clear, direct.

"Sheriff O'Toole," I whispered, "shoot them in the morning."

One cold, blustery afternoon I saw something in the post office that kindled my hopes. Alongside the "Be Prepared" and "Back the Attack" posters was a new one, "The Mask Is Off." It showed a slimy-faced Jap with buckteeth removing a smiling mask with one hand, while clutching a dripping dagger in the other. Now even the solemn post office was in on it. Now something would happen.

On the morning of March 27 all Japanese Californians were given forty-eight hours in which to dispose of their homes and businesses. When they had done this, they were loaded onto trucks, buses, and trains and taken to detention camps.

I was outraged. They had stuffed their wireless sets in the false bottoms of suitcases and baby buggies. They would escape from the camps and spread into the countryside to work from there. It was a measly, pointless move. Those who tried to kill you should be killed.

I heard my parents talking in the living room.

"The shop went for almost nothing," My Dad said.

"It's hard to believe," Mama said, knitting on a khaki muffler. "It's disgusting."

They were referring to Mr. Nagai. I didn't want to think about Mr.

Nagai. I pushed him deeper into my storeroom and went into my bedroom, where I took my *Life* from its shelf and studied the burned head with an enravished loathing. I had never shared my burned head with anyone, but tomorrow, even if he was too scatterbrained to appreciate it on the right level, I would show the picture to Ezio. I felt a great need, tonight, to share. I felt at sea, all alone now, with the empty, silent valley.

The next morning I brought the magazine to school, but it quickly vanished from my thoughts. Ezio was yelling to a group by the swings.

"Those bastards, I'll kill 'em!"

"Who?" I asked, squeezing up to him.

"We've got to get out of any military zones! And what's military here! That bunch of crummy barracks? I'm impressed! I'm impressed."

"Get out?"

"Get out! Any Italians that don't have citizen papers, like my mother! We've got to go ten miles outside city limits! We've got to go to my uncle's in San Ramon—"

I stared at him. "How long?"

"For the whole war," answered another Italian pupil, of whom several stood listening. They only seemed bewildered. None carried on like Ezio, who struck his thigh with his fist and yanked his overseas cap down.

"What do they think, we're a bunch of Japs? I *hate* Tojo! I hate Hitler! I hate Musso—"

Miss Bonder's tall pompadour passed through the crowd. "Ezio, please don't shout. It just makes things worse."

"It doesn't either!" he yelled in her face.

"That's enough. Lower your voice." And she turned to us, thinking for a moment before she spoke. "I know it's hard to understand, but in wartime things sometimes have to be done that seem unfair. All we can do is cooperate and do our best to end this war as soon as possible."

They were a teacher's dry, empty words. It was Ezio who was real, furiously smoothing the sides of his overseas cap, standing on trembling legs as if he had just run ten miles and was ready to collapse.

It was, as Ezio said many times during the next month, the most stupid idea the government had ever had. Some of the Italians leaving town had sons in the armed services. Not only that, but those who worked in town, even at Shell, could get passes to go to their jobs. What sense did that make if the government was afraid they were going to plant a bomb by an oil tank? It was rottenness and stupidity, the whole country wasn't worth a nickle, let it rot. When Bataan fell, Ezio spoke of it with a contemptuous sneer, as if had he been consulted he might have spared us such a defeat, but at this point would have had to be begged to do so.

The day before his departure I told him I would come to his house in the morning to say good-bye.

"The hell you will. I don't want a bunch of jerks hanging around."

He must have seen the hurt look in my eyes. He said sullenly, "You can say it now."

I stood looking at him, not knowing how to phrase a farewell.

"Well. Good-bye."

"Good-bye." He crossed the street, not looking back.

But I spied on him the next morning from the big date palm down the street from his house. In blue jeans, sport jacket, and no overseas cap, his face set in an expression of aloof efficiency, he was helping his uncle load the car. Suitcases were strapped to the roof; the back seat was piled high. Mrs. Pelegrino, a brown coat over her print dress, a kerchief around her head, was trying to keep Mario by her side.

"Mario go to Port Chicago!" he yelled, twisting and pulling. "Mario go to Port Chicago!"

"Shut up, sweetheart!" she cried. "You make Mama crazy!"

"*Andiamo*," the uncle called, getting in behind the wheel. With a last glance over her shoulder, Mrs. Pelegrino climbed in and settled Mario on her lap. Ezio got in after her and slammed the door. Framed by the window, his flinty, lifted profile moved down the street, and he was gone.

Two days later the house was up for rent.

## CHAPTER 7

Behind Sheriff O'Toole's office a model air raid shelter had been completed. I went down inside and looked. It was snug and clean, but somehow seemed a worse place to die in than a cellar. By the train depot there now stood a hastily constructed USO canteen. The Native Daughters of the Golden West passed out sandwiches and coffee, and from the windows you could hear "Don't Get Around Much Anymore" and "That Old Black Magic" blaring from the jukebox. Mr. Nagai's flower shop, painted and redecorated, had reopened under a new sign: "Modern Miss Apparel." On May 6, Corregidor fell.

But the fullness of spring gathered as always. For weeks the sky had been a hard blue, and the breeze was cool. Now the sky softened, the wind vanished, the air hung hot and fragrant. Trees rustled green and heavy. Above the calm, glassy bay the hills loomed emerald green.

At school sweaters were pulled off and tied around waists. Then they were gone for good, along with pounds of hair, for everyone seemed to have had his or her hair cut, the girls' shorn straight and clean high across the neck, and the boys' clipped so close their ears stood out. Bare-necked, bare-armed, I felt a rippling freshness on my exposed skin. In the backyard, I helped Peter and Karla plant a victory garden.

All at once the Saturday matinees showed nothing but war films, ranging from *The Commandos Strike at Dawn* to *Abbott and Costello Join the Navy*. Clark Gable and Victor Mature were in uniform. Even

Elsie the cow's husband Elmer wore an overseas cap. Classmates' older brothers and cousins disappeared from soda fountains and jalopies, leaving behind blue stars in windows. Windows were filled with all sorts of information: "Block Warden" and "We Buy War Bonds!" and "Quiet, Please, War Worker Sleeping." In car windows there were pasted gas-rationing coupons and stickers saying "Give 'em a Lift!" and "Dim Lights After Dark!" At school we wrote essays on What America Means to Me. We bought defense stamps. We turned in big balls of collected tinfoil. In music class we kept to the patriotic strains of "America the Beautiful" and "My Country 'Tis of Thee," adding more raucously at recess "I'm Gonna Slap a Dirty Little Jap." Housing tracts mushroomed through the county. The stores downtown were crowded, though there was a shortage of zippers, alarm clocks, soap, fountain pens, boxed candy, even of matchbooks. Everywhere you saw people use wooden kitchen matches to light their Fleetwoods, a new and apparently dissatisfying brand that had sprung up in the absence of Camels and Chesterfields. Everyone had money to burn; but sugar, coffee, and butter were a luxury, and you stood in line at the market with your little green ration book and carried your groceries home in the same paper bag until it fell apart. Dresses were suddenly short and skimpy, with no pockets or ruffles, to conserve cloth. In place of nylon stockings, women covered their legs with tan makeup and drew in black seams with eyebrow pencil. But more often they wore pants called slacks. They worked in shipyards and defense plants. Some of them lived alone, their husbands having been drafted, and with greasy wrenches they repaired their own cars, and with hoes and mowers they cut down the lush spring grass in their backyards and planted victory gardens.

We planted beans, potatoes, and spinach. I liked working with the black pungent clods, pressing the seeds down. I envisioned the first frail shoots and then the sudden springing forth of foliage, surely a miracle. And I wondered if it was just spring that made everything seem better or if it was the fact that despite our disastrous chain of military defeats we had not yet been bombed.

It would not do to feel too sure. What the enemy banked on was our becoming relaxed, careless, as we had been before Pearl Harbor.

# JOY KOGAWA

JOY KOGAWA was born in 1935 in Vancouver, British Columbia, but like other Japanese Canadians, she and her family were persecuted and interned during World War II. *Obasan,* her first novel, was based on her own wartime experiences and on letters and documents of the time. An excerpt from *Obasan,* in the shape of letters written by Aunt Emily to her sister Nesan, follows.

A few words of explanation: Japanese immigrants born in Japan were known as Issei, or first generation. The next generation, the first to be born in Canada, were known as Nisei, and their children in turn were called Sansei.

■

FROM *Obasan*

*February 15, 1942.*

Dearest Nesan,

I thought I would write to you every day but, as you see, I haven't managed that. I felt so sad thinking about what the children are having to experience I didn't want to keep writing. But today I must tell you what's happening.

Things are changing so fast. First, all the Japanese men—the ones who were born in Japan and haven't been able to get their citizenship yet—are being rounded up, one hundred or so at a time. A few days ago, Mark told me he felt sure Sam had been carted off. I took the interurban down as soon as I could. Isamu couldn't have been gone too long because not all the plants were parched though some of the delicate ones had turned to skeletons in the front window. I tried to find the dog but she's just nowhere. I looked and called all through the woods and behind the house.

Grandma and Grandpa Nakane will be so upset and confused when they find out he's gone. You know how dependent they are on him. They went to Salt-spring Island a couple of weeks ago and haven't come back yet. I know they're with friends so they must be all right.

We know some people who have left Vancouver. Dad says we should look around and get out too, but we just don't know any other place. When we look at the map it's hard to think about all those unknown places. We were thinking of going to Kamloops, but that may be too close to the boundary of the "protected area."

It's becoming frightening here, with the agitation mounting higher. It isn't just a matter of fear of sabotage or military necessity any more, it's outright race persecution. Groups like the "Sons of Canada" are petitioning Ottawa against us and the newspapers are printing outright lies. There was a picture of a young Nisei boy with a metal lunch box and it said he was a spy with a radio transmitter. When the reporting was protested the error was admitted in a tiny line in the classified section at the back where you couldn't see it unless you looked very hard.

*March 2, 1942.*

Everyone is so distressed here, Nesan. Eiko and Fumi came over this morning, crying. All student nurses have been fired from the General.

Our beautiful radios are gone. We had to give them up or suffer the humiliation of having them taken forcibly by the RCMP. Our cameras —even Stephen's toy one that he brought out to show them when they came—all are confiscated. They can search our homes without warrant.

But the great shock is this: we are all being forced to leave. All of us. Not a single person of the Japanese race who lives in the "protected area" will escape. There is something called a Civilian Labour Corps and Mark and Dan were going to join—you know how they do everything together —but now will not go near it as it smells of a demonic roundabout way of getting rid of us. There is a very suspicious clause "within and *without*" Canada, that has all the fellows leery.

Who knows where we will be tomorrow, next week. It isn't as if we Nisei were aliens—technically or not. It breaks my heart to think of leaving this house and the little things that we've gathered through the years—all those irreplaceable mementoes—our books and paintings— the azalea plants, my white iris.

Oh Nesan, the Nisei are bitter. Too bitter for their own good or for Canada. How can cool heads like Tom's prevail, when the general feeling is to stand up and fight? He needs all his level-headedness and diplomacy, as editor of the *New Canadian*, since that's the only paper left to us now.

A curfew that applies only to us was started a few days ago. If we're caught out after sundown, we're thrown in jail. People who have been fired—and there's a scramble on to be the first to kick us out of jobs—sit at home without even being able to go out for a consoling cup of coffee. For many, home is just a bed. Kunio is working like mad with the Welfare society to look after the women and children who were left when the men were forced to "volunteer" to go to the work camps. And where are those men? Sitting in unheated bunk-cars, no latrines, no water, snow fifteen feet deep, no work, little food if any. They were shunted off with such inhuman speed that they got there before any facilities were prepared. Now other men are afraid to go because they think they'll be going to certain disaster. If the snow is that deep, there is no work. If there is no work, there is no pay. If there is no pay, no one eats. Their families suffer. The *Daily Province* reports that work on frames with tent coverings is progressing to house the 2,000 expected. Tent coverings where the snow is so deep? You should see the faces here—all pinched, gray, uncertain. Signs have been posted on all highways—"Japs Keep Out."

Mind you, you can't compare this sort of thing to anything that happens in Germany. That country is openly totalitarian. But Canada is supposed to be a democracy.

All Nisei are liable to imprisonment if we refuse to volunteer to leave. At least that is the likeliest interpretation of Ian MacKenzie's "Volunteer or else" statement. He's the Minister of Pensions and National Health. Why do they consider us to be wartime prisoners? Can you wonder that there is a deep bitterness among the Nisei who believed in democracy?

And the horrors that some of the young girls are facing—outraged by men in uniform. You wouldn't believe it, Nesan. You have to be right here in the middle of it to really know. The men are afraid to go and leave their wives behind.

How can the Hakujin not feel ashamed for their treachery? My butcher told me he knew he could trust me more than he could most whites. But kind people like him are betrayed by the outright racists and opportunists like Alderman Wilson, God damn his soul. And there are others who, although they wouldn't persecute us, are ignorant and indifferent and believe we're being very well treated for the "class" of people we are. One letter in the papers says that in order to preserve the "British way of life," they should send us all away. We're a "lower order of people." In one breath we are damned for being "inassimilable" and the next there's fear that we'll assimilate. One reporter points to those among us who are living in poverty and says "No British subject would live in such conditions." Then if we improve our lot, another says "There is danger that they will enter our better neighborhoods." If we are educated the complaint is that we will cease being the "ideal servant." It makes me choke. The diseases, the crippling, the twisting of our souls is still to come.

*March 12.*

Honest Nesan, I'm just in a daze this morning. The last ruling forbids any of us—even Nisei—to go anywhere in this wide dominion without a permit from the Minister of Justice, St. Laurent, through Austin C. Taylor of the Commission here. We go where they send us.

Nothing affects me much just now except rather detachedly. Everything is like a bad dream. I keep telling myself to wake up. There's no sadness when friends of long standing disappear overnight—either to Camp or somewhere in the Interior. No farewells—no promise at all of future meetings or correspondence—or anything. We just disperse. It's as if we never existed. We're hit so many ways at one time that if I wasn't past feeling I think I would crumble.

This curfew business is horrible. At sundown we scuttle into our holes like furtive creatures. We look in the papers for the time of next morning's sunrise when we may venture forth.

The government has requisitioned the Livestock Building at Hastings Park, and the Women's Building to house 2,000 "Japs pending removal." White men are pictured in the newspaper filling ticks with bales of straw for mattresses, putting up makeshift partitions for toilets—etc. Here the lowly Jap will be bedded down like livestock in stalls—perhaps closed around under police guard—I don't know. The Nisei will be "compelled" (news report) to volunteer in Labor Gangs. The worse the news from the Eastern Front, the more ghoulish the public becomes. We are the billygoats and nannygoats and kids—all the scapegoats to appease this blindness. Is this a Christian country? Do you know that Alderman Wilson, the man who says such damning things about us, has a father who is an Anglican clergyman?

I can't imagine how the government is going to clothe and educate our young when they can't even get started on feeding or housing 22,000 removees. Yet the deadline for clearing us out seems to be July 1st or 31st—I'm not sure which. Seems to me that either there are no fifth columnists or else the Secret Service men can't find them. If the FBI in the States have rounded up a lot of them you'd think the RCMP could too and let the innocent ones alone. I wish to goodness they'd catch them all. I don't feel safe if there are any on the loose. But I like to think there aren't any.

March 20.

Dearest Nesan,

Stephen has been developing a slight limp. Dad's not sure what's wrong with the leg. He suspects that the fall he had last year never healed properly and there's some new aggravation at the hip. Stephen spends a lot of time making up tunes on the new violin Dad got him. The old one, I told you, was broken. It's lucky our houses are so close as I can get to see the children fairly often, even with the miserable curfew.

Your friend Mina Sugimoto takes her boys to play with Stephen a fair amount but she's acting like a chicken flapping about with her head cut off since her husband left.

Last night over a hundred boys entrained for a road camp at Schreiber, Ontario. A hundred and fifty are going to another camp at Jasper. The Council (United Nisei) has been working like mad talking to the boys. The first batch of a hundred refused to go. They got arrested and imprisoned in that Immigration building. The next batch refused too and were arrested. Then on Saturday they were released on the promise that they would report back to the Pool. There was every indication they wouldn't but the Council persuaded them to keep their word. They went finally. That was a tough hurdle and the Commission cabled Ralston to come and do something.

On Thursday night, the confinees in the Hastings Park Pool came down with terrible stomach pains. Ptomaine, I gather. A wholesale company or something is contracted to feed them and there's profiteering. There are no partitions of any kind whatsoever and the people are treated worse than livestock, which at least had their own pens and special food when they were there. No plumbing of any kind. They can't take a bath. Thy don't even take their clothes off. Two weeks now. Lord! Can you imagine a better breeding ground for typhus? They're cold (Vancouver has a fuel shortage), they're undernourished, they're unwashed. One of the men who came out to buy food said it was pitiful the way the kids scramble for food and the slow ones go empty. God damn those politicians who brought this tragedy on us.

Dan has to report tomorrow and will most likely be told when to go and where. A day's notice at most. When will we see him again? Until all this happened I didn't realize how close a member of the family he had become. He's just like a brother to me. Nesan, I don't know what to do.

The Youth Congress protested at the ill treatment but since then the daily papers are not printing a word about us. One baby was born at the Park. Premature, I think.

If all this sounds like a bird's eye view to you, Nesan, it's the reportage of a caged bird. I can't really see what's happening. We're like a bunch of rabbits being chased by hounds.

You remember Mr. Morii, the man who was teaching judo to the RCMP? He receives orders from the mounties to get "a hundred to the station or else and here's a list of names." Any who are rich enough, or desperate about not going immediately because of family concerns, pay Morii hundreds of dollars and get placed conveniently on a committee. There are nearly two hundred on that "committee" now. Some people say he's distributing the money to needy families but who knows?

There's a three-way split in the community—three general camps: the Morii gang, us—the Council group—and all the rest, who don't know what to do. The Council group is just a handful. It's grueling uphill work for us. Some people want to fight. Others say our only chance is to co-operate with the government. Whichever way we decide there's a terrible feeling of underlying treachery.

*March 22, 1942.*

Dear Diary,
I don't know if Nesan will ever see any of this. I don't know anything

any more. Things are swiftly getting worse here. Vancouver—the water, the weather, the beauty, this paradise—is filled up and overflowing with hatred now. If we stick around too long we'll all be chucked into Hastings Park. Fumi and Eiko are helping the women there and they say the crowding, the noise, the confusion is chaos. Mothers are prostrate in nervous exhaustion—the babies crying endlessly—the fathers torn from them without farewell—everyone crammed into two buildings like so many pigs—children taken out of school with no provision for future education—more and more people pouring into the Park—forbidden to step outside the barbed wire gates and fence—the men can't even leave the building—police guards around them—some of them fight their way out to come to town and see what they can do about their families. Babies and motherless children totally stranded—their fathers taken to camp. It isn't as if this place had been bombed and *everyone* was suffering. *Then* our morale would be high because we'd be *together*.

Eiko says the women are going to be mental cases.

Rev. Kabayama and family got thrown in too. It's going to be an ugly fight to survive among us. They're making (they say) accommodation for 1,200–1,300 women and children in that little Park! Bureaucrats find it so simple on paper and it's translated willy-nilly into action—and the pure hell that results is kept "hush hush" from the public, who are already kicking about the "luxury" given to Japs.

I'm consulting with Dad and Mark and Aya about going to Toronto. We could all stay together if we could find someone in Toronto to sponsor us. People are stranded here and there all over the B.C. interior. I want to leave this poisoned province. But Aya wants to stay in B.C. to be closer to Sam. I'm going to write to a doctor in Toronto that Dad knows.

*March 27*

Dan's been arrested. The boys refused to go to Ontario. Both trainloads. So they're all arrested. Dan had a road map friends drew for him so they suspected him of being a "spy" and now he's in the Pool.

Nisei are called "enemy aliens." Minister of War, or Defense, or something flying here to take drastic steps.

*April 2, 1942*

Dearest Nesan,

If only you and Mother could come home! Dad's sick in bed. The long months of steady work. Since the evacuation started he's had no let-up at all. Two nights ago, one of his patients was dying. He tried to arrange to have the daughter go to the old man's bedside but couldn't. Dad stayed up all night with the man, and now he's sick himself.

I'm afraid that those kept in the Hastings Park will be held as hostages or something. Perhaps to ensure the good behavior of the men in the work camps. Dan was cleared of that idiotic spying charge and is helping at the Pool. The cop who arrested him was drunk and took a few jabs at him but Dan didn't retaliate, thank heavens. I'm applying for a pass so I can get to see him.

Dan has a lawyer working for him and his parents about their desire to stay together, especially since Dan's father is blind and his mother speaks no English at all. The lawyer went to the Security Commission's lawyers and reported back that he was told to let the matter drift because they were going to make sure the Japs suffered as much as possible. The Commission is responsible to the Federal Government through the Minister of Justice, St. Laurent. It works in conjunction with the RCMP. The Commission has three members—Austin C. Taylor, to represent the Minister of Justice, Commissioner Mead of the RCMP, John Shirras of the Provincial Police.

Only Tommy and Kunio, as active members of the Council, know what's going on and they're too busy to talk to me. The *New Canadian* comes out so seldom we have no way of knowing much and I've been so busy helping Dad I can't get to Council meetings very often. There's so much veiling and soft pedaling because everything is censored by the RCMP. We can only get information verbally. The bulletins posted on Powell Street aren't available to most people. Besides, nobody can keep up with all the things that are happening. There's a terrible distrust of federal authorities and fear of the RCMP, but mostly there's a helpless panic. Not the hysterical kind, but the kind that churns round and round going nowhere.

My twenty-sixth birthday is coming up soon and I feel fifty. I've got lines under my eyes and my back is getting stooped, I noticed in a shop window today.

Mina Sugimoto heard from her husband. Why haven't we heard from Sam? Stephen asked me the other day "Where's Uncle?" What could I say?

# J(AMES) G(ORDON) FARRELL

J. G. FARRELL won the Booker Prize in 1973 for his novel *The Siege of Krishnapur.* Born in Liverpool and educated at Oxford, he traveled widely in America, Europe, and Asia. He accidentally drowned in 1979, after moving from London to Ireland. *The Singapore Grip,* the novel from which this excerpt is taken, deals with the fall of Singapore to the Japanese on February 15, 1942, and the aftermath.

■

## FROM *The Singapore Grip*

At the Adelphi Hotel beside the cathedral someone had had the foresight to fill several baths before the water supply had failed. Although these baths had already been used by several people and the water in them had taken on a dark gray color, both Matthew and Dupigny took advantage of them and were feeling distinctly refreshed as they emerged from the hotel into the twilight and crossed the road to the cathedral grounds. Dupigny himself had decided not to try to escape. He was too old, he had explained with a shrug, and besides "*avec la Boche en France*" . . . He would stay and keep his friend the Major company during the internment which no doubt awaited them. He had agreed to drive Matthew and Vera to the boat waiting at Tanjong Rhu, however.

A great crowd had gathered round the cathedral in the dusk, and seeing it Matthew began to feel anxious again, lest they should not be able to locate Vera. A service was in progress and these people standing in devout silence several deep around the building were those who had been unable to find room inside. As Matthew and Dupigny searched the fringes of this crowd the congregation began to sing:

> *Praise, my soul, the King of Heaven,*
> *To his feet thy tribute bring,*
> *Ransomed, healed, restored, forgiven,*
> *Who like me his praise should sing?*
> *Praise him! Praise him!*
> *Praise the everlasting King!*

Suddenly a young woman detached herself from the crowd and took Matthew's arm. It was Vera. He gazed at her, smiling with relief, remembering how he had first seen her come up to him in the twilight at The Great World just like this.

"Come," said Dupigny.

It was very dark by the time they reached the aerodrome. They left the car near the entrance, having decided that in order not to attract attention it would be best to complete their journey on foot. It seemed to grow even darker, however, once they were on the airfield itself and they had to grope their way forward with the utmost caution to avoid bomb-craters and other obstacles. This wandering in the blackness seemed to take an age. Once, not far away, they saw a party of men with a powerful torch, also moving across the field. They crouched down and held their breath while the men went by, talking among themselves. It was impossible to tell what language they were speaking. The wavering light of the torch moved on for another hundred yards, then was switched off suddenly. A little later it was switched on again some distance further away and played for a moment on the shattered barrel of a spiked anti-aircraft gun. Then the torch vanished once more. Matthew, Vera and Dupigny continued their laborious journey. At last they could hear the lapping of the water and a voice spoke to them quietly from the darkness. Matthew answered. It was Major Williams.

"Glad you made it. There are some other people about so we better be quiet. They may be Japs or other escapers. You just got here in time, as a matter of fact, because we're about ready to leave. The boat's out here."

Ahead of them a shaded light appeared for a second or two on a gangplank. Matthew glimpsed the Australian corporal he had seen that morning with Williams; behind him it was just possible to make out the shadow of a boat against the water. "Come along, the sooner we shove off the better."

Matthew and Vera said goodbye to Dupigny and they wished each other luck. They shook hands. Matthew and Vera crossed the gang-plank followed by Williams. Dupigny waited to help them cast off and was just stooping to do so when a powerful beam sprang out of the darkness and played over the launch, then fastened on Dupigny. The figures on the deck froze. The Australian corporal who was holding a lamp switched it on. It illuminated a ragged party of soldiers wearing Australian hats. One of them had a revolver, another a tommy-gun. There were about a dozen of them.

"Sorry, sports, we're taking the boat," the man with the torch on Dupigny said. "Hop it."

Nobody moved or spoke. Dupigny, however, reached down for the mooring-rope to cast off. There was a shot and he began to hop about like a wounded bird, clutching his leg.

"Why don't you find your own bloody boat?" shouted the Australian corporal in a sudden rage.

"Hop it. You, too, cobber."

"There's nothing for it, I'm afraid," said Williams. One by one they came back over the gang-plank.

"Right now. Clear off and take him, too, before we do him in."

They picked up Dupigny who had now fallen over and was struggling to get up again. He said he was not badly hurt but Matthew and Williams had to take his arms over their shoulders and support him; one leg of his cotton drill trousers was already soaked in blood. Speechless with anger and frustration they made their way wearily back across the aerodrome in the darkness.

From elsewhere on the Island other parties bent on escape were also groping about in the darkness. General Gordon Bennett found himself at the docks searching for a boat in which he might sail to Malacca in search of a bigger boat which in turn might carry him to Australia and freedom; he had thought it best not to mention his departure to the G.O.C. and had left an inspiriting order for the Australian troops under his command to remain vigilantly at their posts . . . but in the meantime, where was that damn boat he needed?

As for Walter, he was making his way along a quay at Telok Ayer Basin where the *Nigel*, a handsome motor-yacht, was waiting for him and his companion, W. J. Bowser-Barrington. Poor Bowser-Barrington had fallen some way behind and was gasping under the tarpaulin-wrapped burden he carried on his shoulders. Bowser-Barrington was feeling anything but pleased, for his intention had been that Walter should carry this burden which consisted of his deceased Chairman who, though not a heavy man, was not a light one either. Walter, however, had flatly refused to have anything to do with carrying old Solomon's remains and had even gone so far as to recommend that Bowser-Barrington should simply throw his Chairman away somewhere. This, naturally, was altogether out of the question.

"Well," thought Bowser-Barrington uneasily as he struggled along the quay in Walter's wake, "once we're out at sea I'll show him who's boss." Or rather . . . wait. Perhaps that was something he should discuss with the rest of the Board. Might it not be better to wait until they had reached Australia?

"Ahhhh!" He stumbled in the darkness and, as he did so, it was almost as if his Chairman deliberately ground his sharp knee painfully into his ear. But, of course, that was out of the question. "Where are you, Walter?" he cried feebly in the darkness. "I say, old boy, please don't leave me!"

Once Dupigny, whose wound fortunately had proved none too serious, had been returned to the Mayfair, Matthew had to consider what to do next. With only a few hours left before the Japanese occupation of the city it had become urgent to find a place where Vera might be able to lie low and conceal her identity. She needed a Chinese family willing to take the risk of hiding her, but neither Vera nor Matthew knew one. The Major suggested that they should ask Mr. Wu. But Mr. Wu was nowhere to be found. Either he had managed to escape during the early part of the night or else he, too, in danger as a former officer in the Chinese Air Force, had decided to lie low. Matthew and Vera wasted two precious hours in a vain search for Mr. Wu. Such was the confusion in the city that nobody knew where anybody might be. As they made their way once again through the city center Matthew gazed with envy at the troops who had stretched out to sleep on the pavements. By now both he and Vera were too tired to think constructively: they just wandered aimlessly, hand in hand, full of bitterness and discouragement as a result of their abortive attempt to escape and longing to be at peace.

At last, in desperation, they went to visit the tenement where Vera had lived before. The building was half deserted and there was no longer anyone sleeping on the stairs or in the corridors. Evidently many of those who had lived there formerly had moved to *kampongs* outside the city to avoid the bombing and shelling. Vera's little cubicle was still as she had left it. Nothing had been touched in her absence.

"You can't stay here. Someone in the building would inform on you sooner or later."

"Where else is there to go?" Vera put a soothing hand on his shoulder. "They're simple people here. They don't know about what happened in Shanghai."

"They'll think you're suspicious. They'll have seen you with me."

"They will just think I'm a prostitute. To them all Englishmen look alike," she smiled wanly. "Really, I shall be all right. I have been in a situation like this before." She shrugged. "Besides, we have no choice." After she had rested her head against his shoulder for a little while in silence she said: "You must go now, Matthew. It would be best if we weren't seen together any more. When you have gone I shall cut my hair and take off these European clothes."

"Is there nothing else I can do for you? Let me give you some money, though it may no longer be any use once the Japanese have taken over. Perhaps it would be best to buy some things tomorrow, then exchange them later when they get rid of our currency."

Vera nodded and took the money. She began to weep quietly, saying: "I'm sorry to be like this. I feel so tired, that's all. Tomorrow when I have slept I shall be all right."

"We'll see each other again, won't we?"

"Yes, one day, certainly," she agreed.

Early on Tuesday afternoon European civilians were at last marched off to Katong on the first stage of their long journey on foot to internment

in Changi jail. They had been assembled on the *padang* all morning
under the tropical sun. Many of them were already suffering from the
heat, weariness and thirst. The Major and Matthew walked one on each
side of Dupigny who, despite his injury, insisted on walking by himself.
Matthew carried a small bundle of Dupigny's belongings as well as a
water bottle and a suitcase of his own. They walked in silence at first.
The Major, in addition to his suitcase, carried a folded stretcher they
had improvised, lest it should become necessary to carry Dupigny.

The ruined, baking streets stretched interminably ahead. In some of
the shops they passed Matthew noticed that crude Japanese flags had
already appeared. Dupigny noticed them, too, and said with a cynical
smile: "Well, Matthew, do you really believe that one day all races will
decide to abandon self-interest and live together in harmony?"

"Yes, François, one day."

They struggled on in the heat, stopping now and then to rest for a
few moments in whatever shade they could find. Once, while they were
resting, an elderly Chinese came out of a shop-house and offered them
cigarettes from a round tin of Gold Flake, nodding and smiling at them
sympathetically. They thanked him warmly and walked on, feeling encouraged.

The Chinese and Indians who had vanished from the streets after
the surrender were beginning cautiously to reappear. By a row of burned-
out shop-houses a group of young Indians had gathered to watch the
column of Europeans as they straggled by. When Dupigny, limping painfully, came abreast of them they laughed and jeered at him. Delighted,
he turned to smile ironically at Matthew.

"One day, François."

They walked on. As time passed, Dupigny found it increasingly
difficult to keep up with the others. His face was gray now and running
with sweat. The Major insisted on having a look at his leg: his wound
had opened again and his shoe was full of blood. He told the others to
go on without him; he would get a lift from one of the Japanese vehicles
which occasionally passed on the road. But the others considered this
too risky. Ignoring his protests the Major unfolded the stretcher and
made Dupigny lie down on it. Then he and Matthew picked up the
stretcher and they went forward again, leaving their suitcases to volunteers in the column behind them; meanwhile, another volunteer
searched through the column for a doctor, but presently he returned
saying none could be found: it seemed that the doctors had been de-
tained to look after the wounded in the city. They moved on once more:
Dupigny seemed hardly to have the strength to brush the flies from his
lips and eyes. They spread a handkerchief over his face to keep off the
glare of the sun.

Time passed. At last Katong was no longer very far ahead. Dupigny
lay with his eyes closed and seemed to be scarcely conscious. Again they

passed a crowd of jeering Indians. Hearing them, Dupigny opened his eyes for a moment and his mouth twisted into a smile.

In the weeks, then months, then years that followed, first in Changi, later at the Sime Road civilian camp, Matthew found that his world had suddenly shrunk. Accustomed to speculate grandly about the state and fate of nations he now found that his thoughts were limited to the smallest of matters . . . a glass of water, a pencil, a handful of rice. Hope had deserted him completely. It came as a surprise to him to realize how much he had depended on it before.

In the first weeks after his internment, news began to filter into Changi of mass executions of Chinese suspected of having helped the British. "Will all men still be brothers one day, Matthew?" asked Dupigny when he heard about these executions.

"I think so, François." And Matthew shrugged sadly.

"Ah," said Dupigny.

Many of the Chinese who were killed were towed out to sea in lighters and made to jump overboard, still bound together in twos and threes. Others were machine-gunned wholesale on the beaches. According to the rumors which reached the camp, in every part of Singapore where Chinese lived they were forced by the Japanese to leave their houses at dawn and paraded in front of hooded informers. Matthew had a chilling vision of this scene . . . the hooded man, of whose face nothing could be seen but a glitter of eyes behind the mask, moving like Death along the row of waiting people, without explanation picking out now this person, now that. What chance would Vera have? No wonder hope had deserted him and that he preferred to restrict his thoughts to simple things. A glass of water, a pencil, a handful of rice.

But then one day in his second year of captivity, while he was out with a working party on the road, a young Chinese brushed up against him and pressed something into his hand. He looked at it surreptitiously: it was a cigarette packet wrapped in a handkerchief. When he opened it he put his head in his hands: it contained a lump of sugar and two cooked white mice. And he thought: "Well, who knows? At least there's a chance. Perhaps she'll survive after all, and so will I."

# DAVID MALOUF

THE AUSTRALIAN NOVELIST David Malouf, born in
Brisbane, now lives in Sydney. Among his novels are *An
Imaginary Life, Child's Play, Harland's Half Acre,* and *The
Great World,* from which the following excerpt is taken.

■

## FROM *The Great World*

They were at a place called Hintock River Camp, one of dozens of
such work-camps that stretched for three hundred miles between the
Malay and the Burmese borders. The map of it was not clear to them,
because their knowledge of these countries was limited to the patch of
jungle that shut them in, and because the line they were on was as yet
an imaginary one.

It ran in a provisional fashion from Bangkok to Rangoon, and their
job, under the direction of a Japanese engineer and several thousand
Japanese and Korean guards, was to make it real: to bring it into existence
by laying it down, in the form of rails and sleepers, through mountain
passes, across rivers, and even, when the line met them, through walls
of rock. Eventually all the bits of it would link up. Till then, they were
concerned only with their own section, with bamboo, rock, rain and the
rivers of mud it created, the individual temperament of their guards, the
hours of work the Japs demanded of them (which kept increasing),
the length of rail the authorities decided should be laid each day or the
length of tunnel completed, and their own dwindling strength. The limits
of their world were the twenty or so attap huts that made each encamp-
ment—one of which was set apart as a hospital, or rather, a place for the
dying—and the site, off in the jungle, where their daily torment took
place.

They had come up here from the railhead at the Malayan border in
a series of night marches, since it was too hot to move by day, and had
passed many such camps, some better than the one they were in, one or
two of them a lot worse. These camps either had native names like
Nakam Patam, Kanburi, Nan Tok, or they had been given the sort of
name you might have used for a creek or a camping spot at home: Rin
Tin Tin Camp, Whalemeat Camp. One, however, was called Cholera
Camp.

The work was killing. So was the heat. So, once they started, were
the rains.

Back where they came from they had belonged, even the slowest country boy among them, to a world of machines. Learning to drive was the second goal of manhood—the first for some. Fooling about under trucks and cars, tinkering with motorbikes and boat engines, rigging up crystal sets—all this had become second nature to them, a form of dream-work in which they recognized (or their hands did) an extension of their own brains. It had created between them and the machines they cared for a kind of communion that was different from the one they shared with cattle and horses, but not significantly so. For most of them machines were as essential to the world they moved in as rocks or trees. Tractors, combine harvesters, steamrollers, cranes—even the tamest pen-pusher among them had dawdled at a street corner to look over the wire in front of a building site to see the big steamhammers at work driving piles. It had changed their vision of themselves. Once you have learned certain skills, and taken them into yourself, you are a new species. There's no way back.

Well, that was the theory.

Only they found themselves now in a place, and with a job in hand, that made nothing of all that. It might never have been. They had fallen out of that world. Muscle and bone, that was all they had to work with now. An eight-pound hammer, a length of steel, and whatever innovative technology they could come up with on the spot for breaking stone.

Some of these men had been storemen and book-keepers. Others were shearers, lawyers' clerks, wine-tasters, bootmakers, plumbers' mates, or had traveled in kitchenware or ladies' lingerie. They had had spelling drummed into them, the thirteen times table, avoirdupois and troy weight. "You'll need this one day, son. That's why I'm caning you," a lady teacher had told more than one of them, when, after getting up at four-thirty to milk a herd, they had dozed off at their desk. They were all laborers now. Someone else would do the calculations. So much for Mental! The number of inches a pair of drillers, working closely together with hammer and steel, could drive through sheer rock in ten or twelve hours a day. The amount of rubble, so many cubic feet, that could be loaded, lifted and borne by a man who had once weighed thirteen stone, now weighed eight and was two days out of a bout of malaria. All this to be balanced precisely against the smallest amount of rice a man could work on before he was no longer worth feeding and could be scrapped.

The work was killing. So was the heat. So, once they started, were the rains. But they also suffered from amoebic dysentery, malaria, including the cardiac variety, typhoid, beriberi, pellagra and cholera.

The doctors among them diagnosed these diseases, but that didn't help because they had none of the medicines they needed to cure them, and it didn't help a man to know that the disease he was dying of was pellagra, any more than it helped to know that the place he was dying *in* was called Sonkurai. The name, however exotic, in no way matched the extraordinary world his body had now entered, or the things it got up to, as if what *it* had discovered up here was a freedom to go crazy in any way it pleased.

Only one thing set them apart from the other coolies who for centuries had done this sort of work for one empire and then the next. They knew what it was they were constructing because it belonged to the world they came from: the future.

It was as if someone, in a visionary moment, had seen a machine out of the distant time to come, a steam engine, and had set out with only the most primitive tools and a hundred thousand slaves to build the line it would need to move on if it were to appear. If you could only get the line down, then the machine would follow—that was the logic. It was true, too. In this case it would happen.

So, if they could only finish the line and link up all the sectional bits of it, they would have made a way back out of here to where they had come from: the future. When the engine came steaming round the bend, its heavy wheels perfectly fitted to the track, the sleepers taking its weight, its funnels pouring out soot, they would know that time too had been linked up and was one again, and that the world they had been at home with was real, not an unattainable dream.

# RUSSELL BAKER

RUSSELL BAKER began his career in journalism in 1947 with the Baltimore *Sun*. In 1954 he joined the *New York Times,* for which he covered the White House, Congress, and national politics. He has written his "Observer" column for the *Times* since 1962, and in 1983 he won the Pulitzer Prize for his autobiography, *Growing Up,* an excerpt from which follows.

■

FROM *Growing Up*

## CHAPTER FOURTEEN

The United States had been at war seven months when I entered Johns Hopkins in the summer of 1942. Through most of my childhood there had always been war. War in Ethiopia. War in Spain. War in China. Dimly, I had been aware through all those years that worlds were burning, but they seemed far away. It wasn't my world that was on fire, nor was it ever likely to be, or so I thought. Sheltered by two great oceans, America seemed impregnable. I was like a person on a summer night seeing heat lightning far out on the horizon and murmuring, "Must be a bad storm way over there someplace." It was not my storm.

I'd just turned fourteen when Hitler and Stalin signed their non-aggression pact which cleared the European stage for World War II to start, but though I delivered the papers that told the story in gigantic headlines, I was baffled when a man bought one from me, glanced at the front page, and said, "So it's war." Wasn't there always war someplace? What was special this time?

For me, World War II began a few days later as nothing more than a mild dispute with my mother. We woke that morning to a radio blaring that the German army had marched into Poland. It was September 1, 1939, and we were still living on Lombard Street. It was one of those rare mornings when Herb was home for breakfast. "We'll be in it before long, mark my words," he said to my mother.

"This is England's war. Let England fight it," she said.

Why another German land grab in the middle of Europe should start a world war wasn't clear to me. I seldom paid attention to news of politics, dictators, and treaties. My interest centered on baseball news, comic strips, murders, and hangings. Herb was better informed.

"We're going to be in it before it's over, you just mark my words," he repeated.

This irritated my mother. She hadn't forgiven the English for denying the great lost family fortune to Papa.

"We went over there once and pulled England's chestnuts out of the fire," she said. "This time let them stew in their own juice."

Still four years shy of eighteen, I quickly calculated that the war would be over before it could take me. If it was a world war, I figured, it would last four years. The First World War had lasted four years, hadn't it? I had the idea that four years was the standard length of world wars. My mother interrupted these calculations to talk business.

"You'll be able to sell all your extras today, Buddy."

I groaned inwardly. "Extras" were the excess newspapers left over after I'd served my regular customers. The *News-Post* always sent more papers than there were customers. It was a sly way of boosting circulation, since they billed me for the extras whether I sold them on street corners or not. Usually I threw them in the trash and took the loss, for when it came to salesmanship I was no less timid than I'd been during my *Saturday Evening Post* career. My mother let me get away with wasting the extras, on grounds that it was more important to spend time on schoolbooks than hawking newspapers. Now, though, she smelled war profits.

"Today you ought to be able to sell every paper they'll send you," she said.

I decided to forget I'd heard her. After delivering the first-edition bundles that afternoon I went home as always to read until the second edition came off the truck. My mother was waiting. "Did you sell all your extras?"

I hadn't sold one, hadn't even tried.

"What kind of newspaperman are you? Take those extras up to the corner where people get off the streetcar and you can make some money."

"Nobody wants to read about this Polish stuff."

"For God's sake, Russell, show a little gumption for once in your life. This is a world war. An idiot could sell newspapers today."

School was to reopen next week after summer recess. "I think I'd better brush up on my schoolwork," I said.

"Are you going to get out there and sell those papers, or do you want me to do it for you?"

She wasn't bluffing. She had once gone out to collect overdue bills from the worst deadbeats on my route after I said it couldn't be done, and she had come back with every penny they owed. I'd felt humiliated by that. Having your mother collect the bill was bound to cost you respect among your customers.

"I'll do it," I said, and went off to badger pedestrians with quiet murmurs of, "Newspaper? Like to buy a newspaper?" In spite of my languid sales pitch I was back home in fifteen minutes with every paper sold and a pocket full of coins.

My ignorance of the world beyond schoolroom, baseball diamond, and family circle was remarkable even for a fourteen-year-old. Except for the previous year's experience at City College I had spent my childhood in the blue-collar world where there was neither money, leisure, nor stimulus to cultivate an intelligent world view. I had never been exposed to art, nor attended a concert, nor listened to a symphony even on records. A phonograph would have been an impossible luxury for my mother. The fierce political passions of the 1930s, the clash of ideas about communism, fascism, socialism, were very remote from the gray depths we inhabited. The debates that engaged the intellectual world filtered down to us in refracted and weakened distortions, like sunlight groping toward the ocean bed.

I knew about Benito Mussolini and Adolf Hitler. They were bad guys. I thought of the world in terms of bad guys and good guys, and I knew Hitler and Mussolini were bad guys, though I didn't know why. Franklin Roosevelt was a good guy of legendary proportions. All Americans were good guys, and America was invincible because it was on the good side of whatever the issue might be. Though Hitler and Mussolini were bad guys, they were also funny comic-opera figures, not only because they looked funny—Hitler with his silly mustache, Mussolini with his strut and bulbous jaw—but also because they acted as if they thought they could whip America. That was silly. Nobody could whip America.

At the movies one afternoon in 1938, my buddy John Heideman and I watched the usual newsreels of nastiness in Europe—Hitler taking the mass salute at Munich, Mussolini strutting like a rooster. In the middle of it, John nudged me and said, "America ought to go over there and clean the whole place out like a rat's nest." I had no doubt America could clean Europe out like a rat's nest if it wanted to. And even if somebody had told me the United States Army consisted of only 227,000 soldiers and had equipment for only 75,000 of those, my confidence wouldn't have fallen. By European standards our army may have looked "like a few nice boys with BB guns," as *Time* magazine put it, but that wouldn't have troubled me. For Americans, I'd have retorted, BB guns were enough to do the job.

What I knew of the world's turmoil came mostly from "War Cards" which, like baseball cards, came packed with penny bubble gum. These depicted Japanese atrocities in China, Italian atrocities in Ethiopia, and slaughters of women and children in the Spanish Civil War. From these I knew that Japan was bad and China good, that Italy was bad and Ethiopia good. The lesson on Spain was confusing. One side murdered nuns and the other bombed helpless villages, but I was uncertain which side was which, and hadn't a guess what the Spanish war was about. The passionate quarrels in intellectual circles about Nazi and Soviet intervention in Spain, and its meaning, and what decent Americans should do about it—only the slightest sense of all this seeped down to the working-class world of southwest Baltimore.

On Lombard Street and in Belleville the great menace of the 1930s was the Depression, not fascism or communism. When I entered City College, where most of my classmates came from more sophisticated families, I was surprised to find boys my own age who worried about Hitler, Stalin, and the future of Europe. Many of my classmates were Jewish, and some talked about relatives in Germany and what was happening to them under Hitler. A few had refugee relatives from Germany living in their homes. One, I was startled to discover, called himself a communist and believed communism was mankind's only hope. When he told me this I decided he was a crackpot, but went on enjoying his friendship. After all, he was a musician. I'd learned on Lombard Street that longhairs were supposed to be a little nutty.

My innocence of modern politics lasted until I went to Hopkins. As a senior in high school I was called for an interview before the Honor Society, a group composed of the school's intellectual elite. Someone had put me up for membership. The interview turned out to be a trial, with the group's president acting as prosecutor. After a few questions about my academic history, he asked, "What's your opinion about the split between Stalin and Trotsky?"

I had no opinion.

"Why not?"

"I haven't heard about it."

My interrogator stared at me. Though he was about my age, he had prematurely thinning hair, a gray complexion, and a gaunt ascetic face, which made him seem much older. He wasn't in my class and we'd never spoken before, but I'd heard of his brain-power. "You must know there was a struggle for power in Russia between the Trotskyists and Stalinists," he said.

I confessed I didn't. Eyebrows were raised in the jury box. The prosecutor looked at his colleagues and committed a little shrug, as though to say, "Need we waste more time on this clod?"

A defense attorney stood up, a boy named George Winokur. I scarcely knew him either, but for some reason he'd decided to take my case and somehow had got access to my grades. Like a lawyer leading a witness, he asked, "What was your last mark in Latin?"

It was high, very close to the top of the class. I was strong on the first century A.D.; it was the twentieth I was ignorant about. The prosecutor cut in. "Do you know who Leon Trotsky is?"

I didn't.

"Never heard of Leon Trotsky?"

I hadn't.

Winokur interrupted, trying to limit the damage. "You've also taken three years of French, haven't you?"

I had.

"Would you tell us what your mark was in French last term?"

Since the French teacher marked "on the curve" and I'd scored highest in the class, my grade was 100. Winokur smiled in triumph. He was an admirer of Clarence Darrow and felt as if he'd saved another of society's victims from the gallows.

"Very impressive," sniffed the prosecutor in a tone that conveyed how unimpressed he was. "Now tell us about Stalin. Have you ever heard of Stalin?"

"He's the dictator of communist Russia."

"Well," said the prosecutor, looking at the jury and feigning a smile, "he does know something. He's heard of Stalin." Then turning to me: "You've probably heard of Adolf Hitler, too."

The United States was now at war with Hitler. I understood what I was being told. Though ignorant, I wasn't dumb, and I refused to compound my own disgrace by dignifying his last remark with a reply. They convicted me very quickly, and not without justice, since my ignorance of the modern world hardly qualified me to join the elite.

Lombard Street society would have seemed barbaric to my prosecutor and probably to most of the boys I admired at City College. To them, 1938 was the year of Munich, when Neville Chamberlain sold Czechoslovakia to Hitler for "peace in our time." In Lombard Street, however, it was the year the dignity of the white race hung in the balance scales of history. While uptown Baltimore debated war and the future of civilization, the men of Lombard Street sat on their stoops in shirtsleeves, puffed their pipes, and pondered a cruel theological mystery. It could best be stated as a question: to wit, why had God permitted Joe Louis to become the heavyweight champion of the world?

The racial doctrine of our neighborhood was "separate and unequal." Black people were considered unworthy and inconsequential. There was "a place" for black people, and they were tolerable so long as they knew their "place" and stayed in it. Unfortunately, some became "uppity," didn't know their "place," didn't stay in it, wanted to walk right into the fancy downtown stores—Hutzler's and Hochschild, Kohn's—and try on clothes from the rack, clothes that white people might later want to try on. Most stores, of course, didn't put up with that. They didn't refuse to sell to blacks—"niggers," as everybody in my neighborhood called them—but most refused to let them try on garments before buying.

My mother had taught me contempt for bigotry. Though she still had a good bit of old Virginia la-di-dah in her attitude toward blacks, she'd taught me to look down on race baiters as "poor white trash." Blacks were to be judged just like white people, strictly on individual character and merit. On coming to Baltimore, I was shocked by the blatant racism candidly expressed daily in our new neighborhood. After a year or so there I was more shocked to hear my mother tell Uncle Harold one night, "I've got nothing against a Negro as long as he knows his place." Racism seemed to be contagious.

The blacks' place in our neighborhood was Lemmon Street, the back alley between Lombard and Pratt. There they lived in ancient brick dilapidations, tiny row houses two stories high and two windows wide with views overlooking the garbage cans of the whites. There they were tolerated so long as they didn't make an unsightly show of themselves around on Pratt or Lombard where whites presided. This social organization had been in place so long it seemed to have been divinely ordained. The superiority of the white man, the unworthiness of the black —these were assumptions at the very foundation of society. And yet, if this order had been divinely ordained, why, oh why had God permitted Joe Louis to become heavyweight champion of the world?

How could faith in the universal order be justified so long as Joe Louis, a black man, was allowed to pound white men senseless with so little exertion? Joe Louis was a living, breathing mockery of the natural order of things. He had won his title in 1937. Before then and since, he had agreeably stepped into the ring with every white hope willing to have his brains scrambled. Now at the peak of his art, Louis dispatched all comers with such finality that his challengers were called "The Bum-of-the-Month-Club." The ease with which he did the job, often in a round or two without working up a sweat, was gall in the white supremacist's soul.

Louis's exercises were broadcast on the radio and eagerly listened to by the whole community. You heard those awesome words booming out of the speaker from faraway New York: "In this corner—wearing purple trunks—weighing 197 pounds—the Brown Bomber from Detroit—" And then the monstrous roar of that faraway crowd, the gong, the crackling voice of Clem McCarthy: "—Louis measures him—a left to the jaw, a right to the body—" And then it was all over, for Louis was not a man to dawdle at his work.

And then, always, up from dismal Lemmon Street, which lay beneath our open kitchen window, I'd hear shouts, cheering, clapping, a tumult of joyous celebration issuing from the houses where the blacks lived. Out front in Lombard Street, the silence of the tomb. Once again Joe Louis had offended the white neighborhood by giving Lemmon Street a good time.

Lemmon Street people never made much fuss outside their houses. In black districts of Baltimore, celebrators poured out of houses and bars, filling the streets and whooping with pleasure each time Louis finished one of his executions, but there was none of this in white neighborhoods where blacks lived in alleys. People in Lemmon Street obviously thought too much celebration would be indiscreet. As I discovered in 1938, though, their spirit was not completely lifeless. That summer I witnessed a spectacular development in racial affairs.

For months we had been occupied with the most momentous encounter in the history of sport: Joe Louis had signed to fight Max Schmeling for a second time. Schmeling was the only man who had ever beaten Louis, and he hadn't just beaten him, he had battered him mercilessly, then knocked him out in the twelfth round. This triumph for the white cause had occured in 1936. Afterward, Schmeling published a gloating article in the *Saturday Evening Post* explaining how he had found Louis's fatal weakness. Schmeling was a white man. A German, admittedly, and officially approved by Adolf Hitler at a time when Germans were not terribly popular, but, above all, he was a white man. White pulses pounded with anticipation as the second fight approached, and black pulses, for all I know, may have pounded with dread. The white neighborhood awaited the second fight with fevered hopes. Perhaps God had raised Joe Louis so high only to humble him at the fists of the great German white hope.

At last the night of the titanic battle arrived, and I settled by my radio to attend upon the pivotal point of the modern age. What occurred was not the turning of the tide at Gettysburg nor the stand of the Spartans at Thermopylae, but hardly more than a fly-swatting. At the bell Louis left his corner, appraised Schmeling the way a butcher eyes a side of beef—we all saw it over and over again in movie newsreels later—then punched him senseless in two minutes and nine seconds. Paralyzing in its brutal suddenness, it was the ultimate anticlimax for the white race.

From Lemmon Street I heard the customary whooping and cheering rise into the sour Baltimore night. I went to the kitchen window. Doors were being flung open down there. People were streaming out into the alley, pounding each other delightedly on the back, and roaring with exultation. Then I saw someone start to move up the alley, out toward white territory, and the rest of the group, seized by an instinct to defy destiny, falling in behind him and moving en masse.

I watched them march out of the alley and turn the corner, then ran to the front of the apartment to see if they were coming into Lombard Street. They were. They seemed to have been joined by other groups pouring out of other neighborhood alleys, for there was a large throng now coming around into Lombard Street, marching right out in the middle of the street as though it was their street, too. Men in shirtsleeves, women, boys and girls, mothers carrying babies—they moved down Lombard Street almost silently except for a low murmur of conversation and an occasional laugh. Nervous laughter, most likely.

Joe Louis had given them the courage to assert their right to use a public thoroughfare, and there wasn't a white person down there to dispute it. It was the first civil rights demonstration I ever saw, and it was completely spontaneous, ignited by the finality with which Joe Louis had destroyed the theory of white superiority. The march lasted maybe five minutes, only as long as it took the entire throng to move slowly down the full length of the block. Then they turned the corner and went back into the alleys and, I guess, felt better than most of them had felt for a long time.

On Lombard Street enlightenment was hard to come by. When war began I followed the news as melodrama. Another encounter between the white hats (us) and the black hats (them). I was shocked by the speed with which the Nazis crushed Europe and occupied Paris and planted the swastika at the English Channel. That fall, carrying newspapers with gigantic headlines that told of the blitz on London, I marveled at the destruction of a civilization I'd thought eternal. Like many military thinkers, I guess, I'd expected a rerun of World War I and was surprised to find the script entirely new. Still, it never occurred to me that the Nazis could win. They were the bad guys.

I was flabbergasted when the Japanese attack at Pearl Harbor brought us into the war at the end of 1941. Though by then sixteen, I was still so innocent of the world around me that American involvement had seemed impossible. And Japan! Why in the world had Japan attacked us? I didn't know Japan had anything against us. Sitting by the small radio in the kitchen at Marydell Road that Sunday night, listening to the bulletins from Washington, I thought the Japanese attack was ridiculous. A tiny country like that, nothing more than a few specks on the map, a country whose products were synonymous with junk, a pipsqueak country on the far side of the earth—it was grotesque that such a country should take on mighty America. Settling their hash would be as easy as squashing an ant.

"It'll take about two weeks to finish them off," I told my mother.

She was less confident. "I hope it's over before you're old enough to go," she said.

I laughed. I was still two years shy of military age. In two years we would have forgotten that Japan ever existed.

By the time I entered Hopkins in the summer of 1942 I knew better. Boys I'd known in high school were already in uniform. Others were registering for the draft. Responding to the speeded-up pace of wartime America, Hopkins was operating on a year-round schedule with no summer vacation. I attended classes there the day after graduating from high school. By my seventeenth birthday that August it was obvious the war would not end in the coming year and probably not in the year after that. My mother had been right to worry. Obviously I was going to have to go. I began to look forward to it with pleasurable excitement.

# JOSEF SKVORECKY

JOSEF SKVORECKY was born in Bohemia and emigrated to Canada, where he is a professor of English
at Erindale College, University of Toronto. His novels
include *The Cowards, Miss Silver's Past, The Bass Sax-
ophone,* and *The Engineer of Human Souls,* a good
part of which deals with his wartime experiences in
Czechoslovakia and from which the following excerpt
was taken. Skvorecky won the 1980 Neustadt International Prize for Literature and the 1984 Governor General's Award for fiction in Canada.

■

## FROM *The Engineer of Human Souls*

In retrospect, it seemed to me nothing more than a rather insignifi-
cant overture to fear. A platform had been erected at one end of the
factory floor and Mr. Zimmermann, the owner, was standing at a speaker's lectern from which hung a swastika fastened to a tatty red backcloth.
He was reading out the news of the assassination in Prague of the Acting
Reichsprotektor Reinhard Heydrich. The proclamation was brief and
menacing, and the factory owner, in a green herringbone suit, read it in
a way that sounded neither sad nor threatening, and yet not so bland as
to suggest indifference to the fate of the Acting Reichsprotektor. The
menace was provided by the chief foreman, Ballon, who had come to
the obsequies stuffed into those classic dung-coloured riding breeches
that the German military favored. On the sleeve of his neatly pressed
shirt was a swastika, the kind worn by SA units. When Mr. Zimmermann
had finished, he turned the meeting over to Ballon, and Ballon began
haranguing us in German. His manner was that of all such orators—the
line of his ancestors and his descendants fades out through the dimensions of time, into the past and the future, and is lost to me in infinity.
Since most workers didn't understand German, Ballon was at a disadvantage—compared to others of his ghostly tribe—because his fiery words
had to be translated into Czech by the chief inspector, Mozol, who
although he could speak German was new to the art of interpreting. But
it didn't matter. Any language used for such purposes is internationally
comprehensible: the content, or lack of it, is interchangeable; the tone is
constant. Whether in German, Czech, Russian or the gibberish of the
Great Dictator, it always contains a threat, a threat delivered in the name

of a theoretical majority whose hard fist is about to crash down on the head of a theoretical minority.

The others on the platform stood where they always stand (or sit) on such occasions: in the background. The head accountant, Mr. Kleinenherr, the only German from Kostelec in the factory management, wore a sphinxlike expression. He was not a member of the Nazi party, perhaps because before the war there had only been three Germans in Kostelec and one of them was a Jew; they could scarcely have founded a party cell on that basis. Had Mr. Kleinenherr lived twenty kilometers away in Braunau, where the Germans were in the majority, he would likely have been a party member; not that he would have burned for the Leader— he was a reasonable and correct man—but when such parties ask you to join, it is difficult to refuse. Beside him stood the three-hundred-pound Schwarz, whom the army had rejected for obesity and because he was a specialist in Messerschmitts. He was a dumb apolitical technologist and he wore a frown because he believed the occasion demanded it. Dr. Seelich, the one-armed factory doctor, had his eyes shut. He was an old lush and was probably sound asleep. Uippelt, also in riding breeches, stood with his legs apart. He wore a huge spidery swastika in his lapel and his pince-nez made him look very severe. Beside him was Gerta Ceehova, head of the personnel department, in the uniform of the BDM, the German Girls' League, for which she was somewhat too old now. She had attended the same grammar school as I had before the war but since the Occupation she had simply stopped acknowledging my existence because I was Czech. Representing my countrymen on the platform was engineer Zavis, who was sales director for the factory. He dealt exclusively with the Germans and spent most of his time traveling in the Reich, so you could call him a collaborator, though he was not a fanatic —it was just that he was indistinguishable from the Germans. And in the far corner stood the head foreman, Jerry Vachousek, wearing the deceptive expression of a village idiot.

Nadia and I watched the antics from the drilling section, and Ballon's Great Dictator gibberish reached us over the heads of Svcstka and Hetflajs who were on the assembly line ahead of us. They were feigning intense interest but neither of them understood a word of German and at that distance Mozol's translation was incomprehensible anyway. A column of workers in blue overalls and sweaters stretched right up to the podium; most of them had apprenticed in textiles, hairdressing or the rubber industry, since there had been no heavy manufacturing in Kostelec before the Occupation.

Ballon's voice reached a climactic crescendo. He abruptly raised his arm and roared: *"Sieg!"*

The corpulent Schwarz, Uippelt and Gerta all shouted out *"Heil!"* Mr. Kleinenherr, Zimmermann and engineer Zavis said it half-heartedly. Dr. Seelich started and woke up. Jerry Vachousek didn't even open his mouth. Because there were only three to deliver the ritual antiphony with any verve it did not have the effect that Ballon desired. He stood a moment longer with his arm thrust forward and upward, evidently thought better of pressing the matter, turned red and as abruptly brought his arm down to his side. Those standing behind him followed suit. Mozol then called out in a raised voice:

"And now we will all sign the petition prepared here, stating that we condemn the assassination of the Acting Reichsprotektor, Obergruppen-führer and General of the Waffen SS and Chief of Police, Reinhard Heydrich. Would you please come forward one by one . . . and"—he wanted to finish appropriately, but he had no experience in public speaking—"and please maintain calm."

I saw the fellows up at the front of the assembly line under the podium look irresolutely at each other. "Come on now," Mozol coaxed. The gangly Siska, a weaver by profession, walked over to the table where the petition was spread out, bent over, picked up the pen and signed it while Obermeister Ballon towered over him, the wrath of the Nibelungen in his face. Automatically the workers began to form a line. I didn't want to join in, but there was nothing I could do about it. I was not illiterate, nor did I dare show open approval of the Acting Reich Protector's assassination by refusing to sign. It could be a matter of life and death. I made a move to join the line.

"Dan!" Nadia whispered urgently behind me. "I won't sign it."

"For God's sake, don't be silly," I hissed.

I won't sign it."

"Nadia, don't be crazy. It doesn't mean anything anyway."

"I can't do it, Dan."

But she got into line behind me and we began to shuffle forward.

"I really mean it. I can't sign it. My dad would turn over in his grave."

Absurdly, given the immediate danger, I recalled a verse from Jan's most recent letter. "Everything about them is steadfast; they are like the tree, born of the earth and the sun, and yet remaining what it is." It was a fairly accurate description of Nadia.

"I can't possibly do it, Dan, I just can't," she whispered into my ear. I glanced at the table. Between us and the petition there were now only Hetflajs, Svestka and two girls in sweaters, followed by Malina and Kos.

My God, what will I do if Nadia walks past the table without signing? Or does she intend to write in her *approval* of the assassination? What in the name of God will she try to pull off? Terrified thoughts raced through my mind, a tug of war between the fear that had us all signing that silly protest and my fear of looking like a coward in front of Nadia. Svestka had just signed and Hetflajs was ostentatiously preparing to do the same. I was sweating and my knees began to tremble when suddenly Nadia stumbled, gasped and then went limp, falling slightly against me so that

I managed to catch her in my arms before she fell. Her eyes were closed. She was slumped helplessly in my arms, her face like chalk—which was the way it always was anyway—her large mouth clamped shut and her arms flopping back and forth. SA Ballon took his hands off his buttocks and said with almost offended consternation, "*Was ist das los?*"

"She's taken ill," I replied in German.

Meanwhile Vachousek had already jumped off the podium and grabbed Nadia by the legs. "Lets get her to the first-aid room, quick!" he said, and we loped across the factory with our limp load, leaving the petition far behind us. And then it hit me. What magnificence! What glory! The greatness of Nadezda Jirouskova! I held the skinny girl tightly in my arms and ran with her and Vachousek the foreman along the corridor to the yard and across the yard to the first-aid room. In the yard she opened her eyes and whispered, "There's nothing wrong with me. I just did it so I wouldn't have to sign."

She didn't have to explain.

Dr. Seelich stumbled out to the first-aid room after us, unbuttoned Nadia's sweater and the blouse beneath it; a pale blue slip appeared and Dr. Seelich stuck his one arm with a stethoscope under it.

A significant gesture. But I didn't know it at the time.

It took the one-armed doctor two hours to bring Nadia around. By that time the ritual signing was long over.

# STUDS TERKEL

CHICAGOLAND's Studs Terkel, a graduate of the University of Chicago's Law School, has been a radio soap opera performer, a disc jockey, and a TV emcee. *"The Good War,"* his fifth oral history, yielded the following excerpt about the fall of Bataan and after. Bataan fell on April 9, 1942, nearly all of its 36,000 defenders killed or captured by an assault force of 200,000 Japanese. The survivors slipped off Bataan into Manila Bay and escaped to Corregidor.

■

FROM *"The Good War"*

MAURICE E. (JACK) WILSON

*Along U.S. 127, on the outskirts of Harrodsburg, Kentucky, reposes an old army tank. A white star imprinted, U.S. Army. W35. It is a replica of the tank of Company D, 192nd Tank Battalion. It is the town's hallmark: a monument to the sixty-six young men of the company, all from Harrodsburg. Twenty-nine died in the defense of Bataan and Corregidor. Thirty-seven survived. Of the survivors, twelve had died at the time of my visit. One had been killed by his wife.*

*While Wilson's wife quietly crochets in the living room, we are seated in his "war room." There is a whole shelf of books on one subject: Bataan. On the walls, as well as on the desk, are medals, ribbons, certificates; photographs of a prison camp, of a Kentucky colonel; a knife; notices of American Legion and Disabled Veterans conventions—"I'm a member of 'em all, a life member. I built this house in 1966 as a wheelchair house. See, it's made for a wheelchair all the way round."*

*The photograph on the desk of young Maurice E. (Jack) Wilson, as a tech sergeant, bears a remarkable resemblance to that of a more heavy-set Robert Mitchum in one of those World War Two films.*

*As he urges newspaper clippings, xeroxed letters, old postcards, news releases into my hand, his words tumble out, one on top of the other. He is a man possessed.*

*He is the acknowledged, though informal, historian of Company D, 192nd Tank Battalion.*

■

I joined the Kentucky National Guard with the Thirty-eighth Tank Company in 19 and 33. We went through Harlan County coal-minin' strikes, went through Kentucky floods, guarded convicts down to Frankfort. We drilled every Monday night. I got a dollar a drill. Fifteen days out of every year we went to Fort Knox on training.

In 19 and 41, we went on Louisiana maneuvers. Lieutenant General George Patton, Jr. said the 192nd Tank Battalion had showed up so good, they had selected them to go overseas.

Those was over twenty-eight years old had a chance to get out, and those that had dependents. I was around close to that. And with this eye I got hurt on the firin' range, I said, "I'll accept a discharge if you tell me are ya gonna give me a disability on it. I'm a poor boy, just an old farmer, and I don't want to pay a doctor bill all my life." So they say, "It hasn't happened long enough." I done been in the hospital eighty-nine days with it. And I said, "I won't sign a discharge that I'm well and okay." I didn't know the war was gonna start and I'd be a prisoner of war, or I'da went and signed two or three discharges. (Laughs.)

We hit Frisco and went on Angel Island. Then they loaded us, sixty-six boys from Harrodsburg, onto ships and we went over to the Hawaiian Islands. And there was a cruiser and we landed in Luzon at Manila. It was under sealed orders. It was November 20, 19 and 41. We went on to Fort Stotsenburg. It just wasn't a mile and a quarter over to Clark Field. As soon as we got there, we suspicioned somethin', but we didn't know what was goin' on. They never told us nothin' about it.

That one day, December 8, about twelve o'clock, we all went up to the chow truck and we looked up at the sky. There was fifty-four planes. I said, "Look what pretty planes we got." They was all silver-lookin'. About that time, they commenced droppin' those bombs out on the hangars. The bombers went by and here come the fighters down, shootin' them shells off toward us. It's fallin' around like hail. Of course, I run underneath the command tank.

We found one of our boys that had shrapnel from one of the bombs had cut half his head off. His name was Robert Brooks and he's from Sadieville, Kentucky. He lied about his race. We was all white, see? And he lied to get in a white outfit. He was yellow-complected, had kinda kinky hair. I called him Nig all the time and I didn't know he was a nigger, see? We found out that he was the first boy killed in the armed forces in the Philippines in World War Two. They named the parade ground at Fort Knox after Robert Brooks. They found out his mother and father in Sadieville, they was niggers and sharecroppers. So this general out there in Fort Knox said tell them people, regardless of race, creed, or color, that he was still one of the heroes of Kentucky and wanted them to be invited to the celebration.[1] But his mother and father wouldn't come. They didn't like it much because the boy had lied about his race to get in the white outfit.

We didn't know he was colored, because he came to Harrodsburg, spent the weekend sometimes with a lotta white boys. That would be somethin' unusual for a nigger. Nowadays it would be a different thing. But back in '41 . . .

*Kenneth Hourigan, another of the Harrodsburg 66, whose tales are not as oft-told as Wilson's though he shares the same experiences (in fact, some of their anecdotes are identical), remembers Brooks: "We didn't know he was colored, but we always thought he was cuttin' up and laughin' kinda like a colored guy. But you couldn't really tell by the looks of him. I mean, he was just one of the boys."*

All the airplane hangars had been destroyed. About dinnertime, that's when the Japanese came over an' caught all our airplanes down on the ground. The Japanese got to landin' just ship after ship of soldiers. Oh, they come in there by the thousands. We just couldn't fight that many, but we did the best we could.

We went an' left there and come through Manila. I said to the boys, "Listen, I had a brother in World War One. He told me if I ever come to Manila to go into the Silver Dollar Bar." So we pulled up there. All the counter was inlaid with silver pesos, one almost touchin' the other. We was in there pryin' them things out because we knew the Japanese was landin'.

So this captain found a buddy of his from his hometown and he said, "Wilson, you cain't see how to command a tank, so I'll put you here in the kitchen to be a mess sergeant." We didn't have anything to eat. Killed all the horses and mules and cut all the legs off an' skinned 'em and tried to eat the meat. Too tough to cook. We tried to grind that meat and season it up. I said, "what kinda leg is that?" Someone said it's off a Indian cow. I said, "Indian cow nothin'. I rode behind that thing the other night in Manila passin' one of them low buggies." (Laughs.) I knew it was a horse's leg 'cause the bones was too big. They finally give us three cans of salmon and two round loaves of bread to feed eighty men with.

I found this private behind the bushes and he had a whole can of salmon and bread. I said, "All these boys gotta have somethin' to eat.

[1] Major General Jacob L. Devers, Chief of Armored Force, ordered that the field be named in Brooks's honor: "For the preservation of America, the soldiers and sailors guarding our outposts are giving their lives. In death, there is no grade or rank. And in this, the greatest Democracy the world has known, neither riches nor poverty, neither creed nor race draws a line of demarcation in this hour of national crisis."

You wanna starve 'em?" And he jumped up an' give me the prettiest black eye I ever did see. He was too big. He could whip the devil outa me. So I hadda go ahead and let 'im eat the salmon and bread.

So the captain said, "Wilson, I'm gonna take your stripes away from you and reduce you down and give it to the man who can find us some food." I said, "I'm a three-grade sergeant. I've gotta be court-martialed. I've done nothin' to be court-martialed for." He said he could do any damn thing he wanted. I was reduced down to private.

He said I got dust in my eye and I couldn't see how to command a tank, and he put me in the rear echelon, and there wasn't no rear 'cause the Japanese shootin' us with shells right over our head all the time. So when I surrendered, I surrendered as a private.

We kept on afightin' in Bataan and the Japanese kept on comin' on us an' hittin' us down. Bataan Bay goes up to Manila. The boys reports they're ready to surrender. So me and about twenty-five other boys decided we wasn't gonna surrender. We was goin' down and get over to Corregidor, which was right across the water about four miles.

We see this cave an' an old man, looked like maybe seventy-eight. He was half Chinese and half Spanish an' he had a boat. But the motor won't run. We had tank mechanics an' they got it to runnin'. We went by and seen several drums of gasoline, so we loaded up and we was gonna go to Australia. Lay over in the daytime and travel at night. I had a can of sardines. Somebody else had a can of pork and beans in his shirt. We put it in one large can and said one guy eats, we all eat.

Two of the guys robbed a bank in Bataan. Pesos—they had their shirts all full. They just went in an' told the man, "Hand over the money. The Japanese are gonna get it anyhow." They put all their money in the pot an' if we need anything to buy, we'll buy.

We got ready to pull away and there's a man on another barge over there and he pulled out that sub-Thompson machine gun an' hollered over, "If you don't come by here and pick me and my men up and take us to Corregidor, I'm gonna start shootin'." So we went on to Corregidor.

We went up the bank there to a small tunnel. They had the barracks back in there. Outa concrete, real nice, but you didn't have room to squat down, you didn't have room to stand up. And we didn't have no cigarettes. Last package I bought in Bataan, I had to give twenty pesos for it. That was ten dollars.

The Japanese come and we had to surrender. We took our pistols and throwed them over in the ocean. I've seen boys light cigarettes with fifty-dollar bills and hundred-dollar bills. Some of 'em cut the threads of their clothes an' tuck bills in there.

My brother was in the navy over in Hong Kong. He had a twelve-dollar gold piece and he made me a ring out of it. It had my initial on it. The Japanese seen that ring, he pulled it and he took skin and all off. Another ol' boy I couldn't keep from laughin' at. He had a pair of Florsheim shoes, prettiest shiny things I ever did see. I had told him at Fort Drum, "You better not take 'em, that's too nice-lookin'.'" As soon's he got on that boat, the Japanese looked down an' said changee, changee. This boy's foot was bigger than this Japanese shoe. The Japanese said, "I fix it, I fix it." He cut the toe cap off and this boy's toes stuck out about that far over the end of the soles. (Laughs.) An' I got to laughin' at 'im.

Some of these boys said, "Wilson, we're gonna make an escape." I said, "You haven't got a chance. Any white man out there is enemy. And these Filipinos are getting hungry, an' if they offer 'em ten or fifteen pesos reward, they gonna squeal on you." I said, "Of course, we're over here fightin' for 'em, but they're hungry, they'll do anything for food." They said they're goin' underneath the fence that night. I said, "Don't do it, boys." They said, "Come and go with us." No, I've got dinky fever. It wasn't quite as bad as malaria, but if you don't have the quinine, it was malaria.

They was gone three or four days and the Japanese caught 'em. They tied 'em up to the fence post and made 'em squat down on their knees. Took the hat off 'em, an' blisters on their face big as goose eggs in that hot sun. They kept 'em out there for three days. Finally, the Japanese went and dug a hole up on the ridge. They took them boys up there an' they took their blindfolds off of 'em. They offered one of 'em a cigarette. That boy took a draw off it an' flipped it right in the Japanese' face. They offered another one a drink of water. He took a little taste of it and throwed it right in the Japanese' face. Then they put the blindfolds back on 'em, got back, an' commenced shootin'. All these boys went back in that hole. I coulda been one of 'em.

We went up to a sugar plantation. The Japanese lined us up to a big pile of rock. We had to pick up rock an' pass it over to the next guy. They done got mad an' took our caps off. In that ship we got real white, no sunshine on our faces. And we had them blisters come on our face, looked like eggs. They wouldn't give us no water to drink. We went for four days. Somebody said all you gotta do is pull your buttons off your shirt and suck on 'em and that would cause saliva in your mouth an' put moisture in it. I think I had done pulled every button off the shirt.

This officer, he went up to the Japanese and told 'em, "My men's gotta have water." So they said, "We'll give you a barrel, get water in the creek." On the banks of the creek were these Filipino huts. Back behind it, they had a little ol' toilet. When their droppin' fell down it went right in the creek. We had to dip water outa that. We knocked the stuff away an' dip up a bucket of water. The only way we could drink it, we had to put chlorine in it. In order to keep from takin' diphtheria an' everything else. We had it so strong, it would almost draw your mouth.

*Kenneth Hourigan, sergeant, recalls a thirst and something unexpected: "After we were captured, we hadn't had any water for two or three*

*days. We was in line and I was lucky enough to get pretty close to the
head of that line to the spigot. The line was a good half-mile long. The
guys were just thirsty, boy. Somebody bucked me like that and shoved in
front of me. I looked up. That colonel, I remembered him from giving us
such a hard time. I kinda bucked him back and he come back at me again.
I kicked him in the rear and here come a Jap. He wanted to know what
was goin' on. I said to myself I'm in trouble, him a colonel and me just a
sergeant. I told him, 'Because he's got those chickens on his shoulder, he
broke the line.' That Jap, he knocked him down with a rifle and was takin'
him to the rear of the line. The last I seen him, he was kickin' his butt.
The Jap took up for me."*

Meantime, I had a carbuncle on my back. It had eight heads. It
hurt. I tried to get an American to lance it. He said, "I don't have no
tools, the Japanese take 'em all away." I had to lay on the concrete floor
in a big wire house. If you turned over at night, you'd turn over on the
guy next to you. That much room. Go to sleep on my side and I'd turn
over an' hit that place an', boy—up I'd come. All night, same thing.

In about twelve days, they come an' picked out eighteen big broad-
shouldered buys, looked like football players. We never seen no more of
'em. Somebody tol' me last year, at Louisville when they had the defenders of Bataan an' Corregidor, what they did. They got out to drinkin'
one night an' they got their guns and just shot 'em all down.

We got these Japanese landin' barges an' we went down to Dewey
Boulevard in Manila. That's all the big fine millionaires' homes. They
made us jump out in the water way up to our neck and wade through.
We got up to the main street, front of all these homes. We marched
down through there. The Filipinos had put tubs of water and they hung
cups all the way around it. We'd reach down an' get a drink of water.
Sometimes a Filipino would throw cigarettes out on the ground, so's
we'd walk over an' pick one up. But if a Japanese caught 'em, boy, they'd
slap 'em, beat 'em up.

Then I went to Bilibid prison an' I took to diarrhea, so I messed up
my shorts. They loaded us up on boxcars, eighty and ninety men to a
boxcar. They didn't have room to squat down. It was hot in those metal
things, an' boy, when that sun was comin' down on us. They stopped to
take on water. When they did, these Filipinos come by the door an' tryin'
to sell rice cakes. I motioned to the guard that I had to take my pants
down, that I had diarrhea. He was out with a gun. So I stood right there
beside the women, squattin' down there with my pants down. I wanted
to show a little respect, see? But they thought I was fixin' to make a
getaway. Oh, it was pitiful.

They made us march. We went for about a fifteen- or twenty-mile
walk. From there out to Cabanatuan. Me an' another boy, we went out
on a detail. He got whatever he could get and divided it up with me.

Whatever I got, I divided up with him. He caught diarrhea, and my god, he died in five days' time. And he was from Mississippi. He was eatin' pony sugar. It's a mound of sugar about the size of a pound of round soap. It's got straw an' stuff in it and ol' cleanin's. We's eatin' that ol' dirty stuff.

Now they wanted twenty-five acres to put corn in. They didn't have a mule, horse, tractor and plow, or nothin'. They put a hundred of us out there with grubbin' hoes and shovels, bent over, diggin'. We come to a big anthill and down there a snake. Japanese get mad if you kill a snake. They wanted you to tell 'em. They'd put a fork over it an' caught it. He told me, "You hold it tight back here." So I held that poison snake. He said, "I'll show you how to work it." He cut that thing down through the skin, clear on down, and he brought them entrails up, level with his head, then he whacked the thing off. See, he could speak a little English. Said all the poison's right up here. None got in that meat. He took the rest of that skin off and built him a fire an' put a shovel over it like a oven and they put it on a wire and roasted that snake. They gimme a little piece of it. He said, "Good, ain't it?" I said, "Sure is good." He said, "Better than pig, ain't it?"

Several nights, an old cat kept arubbin' up against my leg when I would be eatin'. At that time we was havin' fish heads. Japanese eat the fish an' give us the heads, boiled in water. Sometimes an eye'd pop around your mouth like a grain of corn. Anyhow, I missed the cat one night. I said, "Boys, anybody seen my cat?" They says a couple of sailors killed the cat: "They over there cookin' it." See, we got a Red Cross about once ever' six months an' it weighed about twelve pounds. Two or three little cans of butter in it. These boys saved about a spoonful of it and they was fryin' that cat in butter. The limey doctor went out there to stop 'em, but got a piece of it himself. This little bitty ol' boy that lied about his age to get in the service, he says, "Boys, gimme piece o' that cat so I can go back home an' tell the folks I've eaten cat." These boys said, "Listen, you just go back home an' tell the folks you seen some guys eatin' cat. You don't get none of this damn cat." (Laughs.)

*Ken Hourigan, across the town, has his own recollections. "We caught a cat in camp. We fried it up in coconut oil. This American officer come along and he said, 'Now listen, boys, we're starvin' to death in here now. If the Japs find out you doin' that thing, we don't get nothin'.' We went and fried it up and had it on a big piece of tin layin' there. And by golly, this guy looked up and he's grinnin'. 'That does look pretty good,' he says. And damn if I thought he wasn't gonna eat it all. One little boy said, 'Gimme a piece of that cat so I can go home and tell 'em I ate a piece of cat.' I said, 'You go home, tell 'em you saw me eat a piece of cat.' (Laughs.)*

*"We had a pup there at camp, a little collie. We fed him rice. He got run over by a truck. This big old boy, he reached down, got that dog*

*by the tail, and took him out on the job. We worked in a steel mill,*
*unloadin' ships and steel. He took that dog up and when we cooked that*
*rice and things, he told me as I was goin' by, 'You want a good*
*sandwich?' Yeah, boy, I'm starvin' to death. He took the bottom out of*
*that rice cake and a slab of that dog between it. It taste pretty good, you*
*know."*

They had these cows with a big hump on 'em. They confiscated 'em
offa some Filipino and brought 'em into camp. The only time they gave
us one is when one of 'em died. We'd cut it up, had a big kettle there,
you boiled your soup in. Sometimes they give us boiled bean leaves. Boy,
they's as bitter as quinine. They'd dig the sweet potatoes an' give us the
vines. We called 'em whistle weeds. (He indicates a photograph on the
wall.) There's my picture in the Japanese prison camp. I lost ninety-five
pounds when that was taken. I weighed two hundred when they caught
me, an' when they turned me loose I weighed one hundred and five.

In September 19 and 43, they run us into Formosa. They thought
the Americans was after 'em. We had one boy with appendicitis. He was
a Spanish boy from Albuquerque. They didn't even have no operatin'
things or nothin'. They took two teaspoons, bent the handles, and put it
down in there to hold it open. An' they reached out and got that boy's
appendix an' cut it off with a razor blade. They just had enough ether to
put him to sleep. When he'd come out, they run out of ether. When they
got ready to sew him up, they hadda hold to him. The Japanese took a
likin' to that boy. He stayed around the medics an' never had to do too
much.

Finally we went on to Moji city in Japan, caught a passenger train,
had all the shades pulled down, an' we rode up to Niigata. I worked there
as a stevedore, unloadin' coal off the ships. We put it on this trestle. We
had to put a pole on our shoulder with a basket of coal swingin' in front
an' a basket swingin' in back to walk this plank an' fill up the railroad car.

In January 1944, I fell from the treslte about thirty-five feet. I broke
a joint in my back an' am paralyzed. The Japanese come every day an'
kicked me an' want me to go to work. They tried these guards at the war
crimes. They wanted me to stay over there, but I never did learn the
Japanese' names. We just nicknamed 'em, Green Eyes, White Angel,
and such. I never did try to catch none of 'em.

I tell you what got me to fall off. About four o'clock in the afternoon,
I had to urinate. I stepped over the edge of these ties. This boy back
behind me didn't see me, you couldn't see over this coal, and he knocked
me down. It wasn't two weeks before that I had seen a Japanese officer
with his uniform an' a big saber in front of me. I saw an' I just kept
pushin' an' I knocked him off. I believe that was the results I got, gettin'
knocked off, because I pushed him.

It got down to zero weather and we didn't have no heat. We had to steal coal and bring it in the pocket of our coat. If the Japanese caught us with that coal in our pocket, why, they'd beat the devil out of us. If a boy died in Japan, the Japanese wouldn't furnish the wood to burn him up with, to cremate him. We hadda go out in the woods to cut down wood to cremate him. We took the boy's ashes back to the Japanese office.

*Hourigan's remembrance: "We had to bury our own dead. There'd be a Jap undertaker ride in on a bicycle when one died, and he'd break his body up. I don't know how he done it. Had a pickle barrel about that high, he'd set 'em in that and wrap tissue paper, different colored, all around and put him on a little stand there. We never had a preacher. There was never a word said outa the Bible. They did have an old bugle there and he'd blow taps and that'd be it. There'd be a big pile of wood, and we'd set it on fire with gasoline and burn him.*

*"We'd pick up a tooth or anything we could find an put it in what looked like a shoe box and sew a white piece of silk around it and put his rank, serial number, and name and all that. When we left there, we carried every one of 'em out to the ship. Whatever remained, some ashes, we turned it over to the government and they'd put it in these urns and send 'em to the families."*

The Japanese gave us numbers, not names. I was 431. Whenever they got to my number, I didn't know what to say and they come back to where I was and they started beatin' up on me. So I said, "Boys, I gotta learn how to count in Japanese." (Laughs.) (He indicates his number on the wall) Yon Hyaku-Sanju-Ichi. 'At's me, 431.

When the Japanese left our camp, we knew it was all over. They told us the Americans were unfair, that they dropped a bomb of some kind that killed two-hundred-and-forty-some-odd-thousand people. The war was *nai*. That means finished.

The night we dropped the atomic bomb, they lined up every one of us and had us put a rope around what clothes we had. We saw our planes were flyin' around and we went on top of the roof, we found some ol' yellow paint, and we put POW K5B. They dropped two packs of cigarettes apiece, candy bars, razor blades, clothes. The Japs done left camp. *Nai.*

We found out Americans were in Tokyo, so three hundred of us went down one night and got on a Japanese train an' we didn't have no tickets or nothin'. We got there, them girls was passin' around candy bars and all. They was WACs so-and-so. I said, "WACs? What's that?" All that happened since I been in. I flew to Yokohama, stayed there ten days, and we had a chance to buy a watch and a billfold. I got on another airplane and landed on the same airstrip that I helped build when I was a prisoner. I rode a ship out to San Francisco and they put us in Letterman Hospital. Stayed there eight or ten days. They didn't give us much of a checkup.

They called out my name one day: "Here's a check for Maurice E. Wilson. It's twelve hundred dollars." I said, "What do you mean, twelve hundred dollars? For three years and five months? I'm not gonna take that check." They said, "You got to." I said, "I don't have to do nothin' !" If I hadn't got to kickin', raisin' hell—I got about five thousand dollars, the way it was.

I got one eye. My feet hangs down. I got a joint mashed in my back. I got a shoulder been broke. Feel that knot right there. But I'd go fight for my country right today.

I knew why the boys were fightin' there in Vietnam. To keep them communists from gettin' on closer to us. Why, we don't wanna let 'em get too close to us. Just like them Cubans down here, I'da never let them Cubans come in here. Now we got to feed 'em. I might be hard-hearted, but let all them Cubans come out here, I'da got me a machine gun and made 'em turn around and go back.

If it was ever to come up again and they'd need me, I'd be ready to go. I'm not a draft dodger. You're darn right. I'd go right now, boy.

# JAMES A. MICHENER

---

*TALES OF THE SOUTH PACIFIC,* James Michener's first book, published when he was forty, was followed by an endless spill of international best-sellers. Michener served in the South Pacific during World War II, after traveling throughout Europe and the United States and working as an able-bodied seaman in the British merchant marine.

---

■

FROM *Tales of the South Pacific*

## CORAL SEA

I am always astonished when an American says, "The Coral Sea? Where is that? I never heard of the Coral Sea." Believe me, Australians and New Zealanders know all about it. The battle we fought there will be in their history books for some time. Perhaps I can explain why.

In mid-April of 1942 I was one of a small group of officers who went ashore on the extreme eastern tip of Vanicoro Island, in the New Hebrides. We carried with us a broadcasting station, enough food for two months, and twelve enlisted men who knew how to repair PBY's. It was our intention to make daily reports on the weather and whatever other information we obtained. The airplane repair men were to service any flying boats forced down in our large bay.

Admiral Kester personally saw us off in the tiny tramp steamer which took us north from Noumea. "We can't go back any farther," he told us. "Take along plenty of small arms and ammunition. If the worst should come, destroy everything and head for the high hills of Vanicoro. I don't think they can track you down there. And you can depend on it, men. You can absolutely depend on it. If you can stay alive, we'll be back to get you. No matter what happens!"

Ensign Aberforce, our radio expert, hurried out from the meeting with Admiral Kester and somehow or other stole an emergency pint-sized radio transmitter. "If we go up into the hills, we'll be of some use. We'll broadcast from up there." Each of us strapped a revolver to his belt. We were a rather grim crew that boarded the rough little ship.

At Vanicoro we were thrown out upon a desolate, jungle-ridden bay where mosquitoes filled the air like incense. Of those who landed that day, all contracted malaria. No one died from it, but eleven men ultimately had to be evacuated. The rest of us shivered and burned with the racking fever. Not till later did we hear about atabrine.

We built lean-to's of bamboo and coconut fronds. A few venture-some natives came down from the hills to watch us. In silence they studied our rude efforts and then departed. Centuries ago they had learned that no one could live among the fevers of that bay. Neverthe-less, our shacks went up, and on the evening of our arrival Aberforce broadcast weather reports to the fleet.

Six times a day thereafter he would repair to the steaming shack, where jungle heat was already eating away at the radio's vitals, and send out his reports. On the eighth day he informed Noumea that we had withstood our initial Jap bombing. A Betty came over at seven thousand feet, encountered no antiaircraft fire, dropped to two thousand feet, and made four runs at us. Radio and personnel escaped damage. Two shacks were blown up. At least the Japs knew where we were. After that we were bombed several more times, and still no lives were lost. By now we had dug a considerable cave into the side of a hill. There we kept our precious radio. We felt secure. Only a landing party could wipe out the station now. The second, smaller set we buried in ten feet of earth. A direct hit might destroy it. Nothing less would.

As men do when they have been frequently bombed, we became suspicious of every plane. So we ducked for foxholes that afternoon when our lookout cried, "Betty at four thousand feet." We huddled in the sweating earth and waited for the "garummmph" of the bombs. In-stead, none fell, and the Betty slowly descended toward the bay.

Then a fine shout went up! It wasn't a Betty at all. It was a PBY! It was coming in for a water landing! It was a PBY!

The lookout who had mistaken this grand old American plane for a Betty was roundly booed. He said it was better to be safe than sorry, but none of us could believe that anyone in the American Navy had failed to recognize the ugly, wonderful PBY. Slowly the plane taxied into the lagoon formed by coral reefs. Since none of us had experience with the lagoon, we could not advise the pilot where to anchor. Soon, however, he had decided for himself, and ropes went swirling into the placid waters.

Our eager men had a rubber boat already launched and went out to pick up the crew. To our surprise, a New Zealand flying officer stepped out. We watched in silence as he was rowed ashore. He jumped from the rubber boat, walked stiffly up the beach and presented himself. "Flight Leftenant Grant," he said. Our men laughed at the way he said *leften-ant*, but he took no notice of the fact.

His crew was an amazing improvisation. One Australian, three New Zealanders, four Americans. The Allies were using what was available in those days. Our officers showed the crew to their mud-floored quarters.

"I'm reporting for patrol," Grant said briefly when he had deposited his gear. "The Jap fleet's on the move."

"We heard something about that," I said. "Are they really out?"

"We think the entire southern fleet is on the way."

"Where?" we asked in silence that was deep even for a jungle.

"Here," Grant said briefly. "Here, and New Zealand. They have eighty transports, we think."

We all breathed rather deeply. Grant betrayed no emotion, and we decided to follow his example. "I should like to speak to all of my crew and all of your ground crew, if you please." We assembled the men in a clearing by the shore.

"Men," Grant said, "I can't add anything which will explain the gravity of our situation. That PBY must be kept in the air. Every one of you take thought now. How will you repair any possible damage to that plane? Find your answers now. Have the materials ready." He returned to his quarters.

We did not see much of Grant for several days. His PBY was in the air nine and ten hours at a stretch. He searched the water constantly between the New Hebrides and Guadalcanal. One night he took off at 0200 and searched until noon the next day. He and his men came back tired, red-eyed, and stiff. They had done nothing but fly endlessly above the great waters. They had seen no Japs.

In the last few days of April, however, action started. We were heavily bombed one night, and some fragments punctured the PBY. Early the next morning men were swarming over the flying boat as she rode at anchor in the lagoon. That afternoon she went up on patrol. As luck would have it, she ran into three Jap planes. The starboard rear gunner, a fresh kid from Alabama, claimed a hit on the after Jap plane. The Japs shot up the PBY pretty badly. The radio man, a youngster from Auckland, died that night of his wounds.

Grant came to our quarters. "The Japs are out. Something big is stirring. I must go out again tomorrow. Mr. Aberforce, will you ride along as radio man?"

"Sure," our expert laughed. "I think I can figure out the system."

"I'll help you," Grant said stiffly. There was no mention of the radio man's death, but in the early morning the leftenant read the Church of England service over a dismal mound on the edge of the jungle. Some native boys who now lived near us were directed to cover the grave with flowers. There the radio man from New Zealand, a little blond fellow with bad teeth, there he rests.

That afternoon there was further action. Grant sighted a collection of Jap ships. They were about 150 miles northwest of the Canal and were coming our way. All transports and destroyers. The heavy stuff must be somewhere in The Slot, waiting for the propitious moment.

Aberforce blurted the news into his microphone. He added that Jap fighters were rising from a field on some near-by island to attack the PBY. We heard no more. There was anxiety about the bay until we heard a distant drone of motors. The PBY limped in. It had received no additional bullets, but it was a tired old lady.

Grant called the ground force to attention as soon as he landed. "It is imperative," he said in the clipped accents which annoyed our men, "that this plane be ready to fly tomorrow. And you must show no lights tonight. The Nips will be gunning for us. Hop to it, lads!" He turned and left. The men mimicked his pronunciation, his walk, his manner. All that night our men urged one another, "Hop to it, lad! Come, now, there! Hop to it!"

It was difficult to like Grant. He was the type of New Zealander who repels rather than attracts. He was a short man, about five feet eight. He was spare, wore a bushy mustache, and had rather reddish features. He affected an air of austere superiority, and among a group of excitable Americans he alone never raised his voice, never displayed emotions.

Unpleasant as he sometimes was, we had to respect him. That evening Aberforce, for example, told us three times of how Grant had insisted upon going closer, closer to the Jap vessels. "The man's an iceberg!" Aberforce insisted. "But it's grand to ride with him. You have a feeling he'll get you back." Grant, in the meantime, sat apart and studied the map. With a thin forefinger he charted the course of the gathering Jap fleet. Inevitably the lines converged on the New Hebrides . . . and on New Zealand. Saying nothing, the flight leftenant went out along the beach.

"Throw a line, there!" he called. "I'll have a look at how you're doing." It was after midnight before he returned.

Early next morning there was a droning sound in the sky, and this time our watch spotted the plane correctly as another PBY. It circled the bay and landed down wind, splashing heavily into the sea. We were accustomed to Grant's impeccable landings, in which the plane actually felt for the waves then slowly, easily let itself into the trough. We smiled at the newcomer's sloppy landing.

The plane taxied about and pulled into the lagoon. "Tell them to watch where they anchor!" Grant shouted to the men on his plane. "Not there! Not there!" He looked away in disgust and went into his quarters. A moment later, however, he was out in the early morning sunrise once more. A youthful voice was hailing him from the beach.

"I say! Grant!" A young flight officer, a New Zealander, had come ashore.

"Well, Colbourne! How are you?" The friends shook hands. We were glad to see that Colbourne was at least young and excitable. He was quite agitated as he took a drink of coffee in our mess hut.

"We won't come ashore," he said. "We must both go out at once.

There is wretched news. The entire Jap southern fleet is bearing down upon us. You and I must go out for the last minute look-see. This may be the day, Grant. We've got to find where the carriers are. I have orders here. They didn't send them by wireless. But fellows! There's a chance! There really is! I understand Fitch and Kester are on the move. I don't know with what, but we're going to fight!" The young fellow's eyes sparkled. After the long wait, we would fight. After Pearl Harbor and Manila and Macassar and the Java Sea, we would go after them. After one string of crushing defeats upon another, the American fleet, such as it was, would have a crack at the Japs!

"What is happening at home?" Grant asked, apparently not moved by the news.

Colbourne swallowed once or twice. "They are waiting," he said grimly. "It has been pretty well worked out. The old men—well, your wife's father and mine, for example. They are stationed at the beaches. They know they dare not retreat. They have taken their positions now." He paused a moment and took a drink of our warm water. We waited.

"The home guard is next. They've been digging in furiously. They occupy prepared positions near the cities and the best beaches. The regular army will be thrown in as the fighting develops. Everyone has decided to fight until the end. The cities and villages will be destroyed." He paused and tapped his fingers nervously against his cup.

"Many families have already gone to the hills. Cars are waiting to take others at the first sign of the Jap fleet. My wife and the kiddies have gone. Your wife, Grant, said to tell you that she would stay until the last." Grant nodded his head slowly and said nothing. Colbourne continued, his voice sounding strange and excited in the hot, shadowy hut. We leaned forward, thinking of Seattle, and San Diego, and Woonsocket.

"The spirit of the people is very determined," Colbourne reported. "A frightful Japanese broadcast has steeled us for the worst. It came through two nights before I left. A Japanese professor was describing New Zealand and how it would be developed by the Japs. North Island will be a commercial center where Japanese ships will call regularly. South Island will be agricultural. Wool and mutton will be sent to Japan. Maoris, as true members of the Greater East Asia Coprosperity Sphere, will be allowed special privileges. White men will be used on the farms. The professor closed with a frenzied peroration. He said that the lush fields, the wealth, the cities were in their grasp at last. The day of reckoning with insolent New Zealanders was at hand. Immortal Japanese troops would know what to do!"

No one said anything. Grant looked at his wrist watch. "It's 0630," he said. "We'll be off." He started from the hut but stopped. "Aberforce," he asked, "will you handle the radio again?"

Aberforce, somewhat subdued, left the hut. Colbourne and Grant went down to the rubber rafts and were rowed to their planes. The newcomer was first to take off. He headed directly for the Canal. Then Grant taxied into free water. His propellers roared. Slowly the plane started along the smooth water. Then it raised to the step, like a duck scudding across a still pond. It poised on the step for a moment and became airborne. It did not circle the bay, but set out directly for the vast Coral Sea.

All day we waited for news. I helped to code and transmit the weather reports Aberforce should have been sending. About noon a cryptic message came through the radio. It was apparently Grant, using a new code. Later a plain-word message came from the south. It was true. The Jap fleet was heading for our islands!

I issued the last rounds of ammunition. We dug up the tiny transmitter and drew rough maps of the region we would head for. Reluctantly we decided that there would be no defense of the beach. Each of us studied the native boys suspiciously. What would they do when the Japs came? Would they help track us down?

At about four o'clock in the afternoon Colbourne's PBY came back. His radio was gone, so he rushed to our set and relayed a plain-code message to the fleet: "The Jap fleet has apparently formed. What looked like BB's steamed from Guadalcanal. Going westward. No carriers sighted. Little air cover over the BB's. But the fleet is forming!" He then continued with a coded description of exactly what he had seen. Before he finished, Grant's plane came in. It was smoking badly. The entire rear section seemed to be aflame. At first it seemed that Grant might make his landing all right. But at the last minute the crippled plane crashed into the sea. It stayed afloat for several minutes, at the mouth of the lagoon. In that time Grant, Aberforce, and four of the men escaped. The co-pilot was already dead from Jap fire. Two men drowned in the after compartments.

We pulled the survivors from the sea. Aberforce was pale with cold and fear, cold even in the tropics. Grant was silent and walked directly in to consult with Colbourne, who stopped broadcasting. They consulted their notes, compared probabilities and started all over again. It was now dusk. When the message was finished, Grant went down to the seaside with his crew and read once more the burial service. Aberforce stood beside him, terribly white.

That night we had a wretched scene at dinner. We didn't serve the meal until late, and as soon as we sat at table, Grant announced that tomorrow he would fly Colbourne's plane. To this Colbourne would not agree. Grant insisted primly that it was his right and duty, as senior officer. In the end Colbourne told him to go to hell. Grant had crashed his damned plane and wrecked it and now, by God, he wouldn't get the other one. The younger man stamped from the room. Grant started to appeal to us for a decision but thought better of it.

In the morning Colbourne and his crew set out. We never saw them again. They submitted only one report. "Entire Jap fleet heading south."

All day we sat by the radio. There was news, but we could make nothing of it. That some kind of action was taking place, we were sure. We posted extra lookouts in the trees. In midafternoon an American plane, an SBD, lost from its carrier, went wildly past our island. It crashed into the sea and sank immediately.

Two torpedo planes, also American, flashed past. Night came on. We did not eat a regular meal. The cook brought in sandwiches and we munched them. No one was hungry, but we were terribly nervous. As night wore on, we gave up trying to work the radio. We had long since surrendered it to Grant, who sat hunched by it, his hands covering his face, listening to whatever station he could get.

Finally, he found a strong New Zealand government transmitter. We stood by silently waiting for the news period. A musical program was interrupted. "It can now be stated that a great fleet action is in progress in the Coral Sea, between forces of the American Navy and the Japanese fleet. Elements of the Royal Australian Navy are also participating. It is too early to foretell what the outcome will be. Fantastic Japanese claims must be discounted. Word of the impending action came this morning when monitors picked up a message from a New Zealand Catalina which had sighted the enemy fleet." The broadcast droned on. "The nation has been placed on full alert. Men have taken their places. In this fateful hour New Zealanders pray for victory."

At this last Grant impatiently snapped off the radio and left the hut. Soon, however, he was back, hunched up as before. He stayed there all night and most of the next day. By this time we had fabricated another receiver. A wonderfully skilled enlisted man and I sat by it throughout the day. Heat was intense, and a heavy stickiness assailed us every time we moved. Once I looked up and saw Grant down by the shore, watching the empty sky. He walked back and forth. I stopped watching him when I heard the first real news we had so far received. American fleet headquarters officially announced that the full weight of the Jap fleet had been intercepted. A battle was in progress. Our chances appeared to be satisfactory.

A wild shout from the other radio indicated that they had heard the broadcast, too. Immediately fantastic conjecture started through the camp. At the noise Grant walked calmly into my hut. "What is the news?" he asked. I told him, and he left. But in a few minutes he was back and elbowed me away from the set. For the rest of that day and night he was there. Once or twice he drowsed off, but no one else touched the radio for sixteen hours.

At about 1900, after the sun had set, we heard two pilots talking back and forth. They were over the Coral Sea. They had lost their ship. Or their ship had been sunk. They encouraged one another for many minutes, and then we heard them no more.

At 0500 the next morning a coded message came through calling on all aircraft to be on the alert for Jap ships. This message goaded Grant furiously. He stomped from the hut and walked along the beach, looking at the spot where his PBY had gone down.

By now no one could talk or think. We had been three days in this state of oppressive excitement. Three of our men lay dead in the bay; an entire plane crew was lost. And we were perched on the end of an island, in the dark. We were not even doing our minimum duty, for our planes were gone. All we could do was sit and wonder. There was much discussion as to what the cryptic message about Jap ships meant. Could it be that the Japanese fleet had broken through? In anxiety we waited, and all about the silent jungle bore down upon us with heat, flies, sickness and ominous silence.

At 1500 we intercepted a flash from Tokyo announcing our loss of the *Lexington*, two battleships, and numerous destroyers. So frantic were we for news that we believed. After all, we *had* heard those pilots. Their carrier *could* have been sunk. The news flashed through our camp and disheartened us further.

It was at 1735 that Grant finally picked up a strong New Zealand station. An organ was playing. But something in the air, some desperation of thought, kept everyone at Grant's elbow, crowding in upon him. Then came the fateful news: "Profound relief has been felt throughout New Zealand. Admiral Nimitz has announced that the Jap fleet has been met, extensively engaged, and routed." A fiery shout filled the hut. Men jumped and clapped their hands. The radio droned on: ". . . losses not authenticated. Our own losses were not negligible. Carrier aircraft played a dominant role. At a late hour today the Prime Minister announced that for the moment invasion of New Zealand has been prevented." Three Americans cheered wildly at this. The New Zealand men stood fast and listened. ". . . so we have taken the privilege of asking a chaplain of the Royal New Zealand Air Force to express our gratitude . . ." Grant was drumming on the radio with his fingers. He rose as the chaplain began to intone his prayer. Others who were seated followed his example. There, in the silence of the jungle, with heat dripping from the walls of the improvised hut, we stood at attention. ". . . and for these divine blessings our Nation and its free people . . ." One by one men left the hut. Then it began to dawn upon them that the waiting was over. Someone began to shout to a sentry up in the tree.

In disbelief he shouted back. Soon the land about the bay was echoing with wild shouts. One young officer whipped out his revolver and fired six salutes in violent order. Natives ran up, and the cook grabbed one by the shoulders. He danced up and down, and the native looked at him in wonderment. In similar bewilderment, two New Zealand enlisted men—beardless boys—who had escaped from Grant's wrecked plane, looked over the waters and wept.

Grant himself disappeared right after the broadcast. Others hung about the radio and picked up further wonderful news. Commentators were already naming it the Battle of the Coral Sea. From Australia one man threw caution far aside and claimed, "For us it will be one of the decisive battles of the world. It proves that Japan can be stopped. It proves that we shall be saved."

Grant was late coming in to chow. When he appeared, he was neatly washed and shaved. His hair was combed. In his right hand he held, half hidden behind his leg, a bottle. "Gentlemen," he said courteously, "I have been saving this for such an occasion. Will you do me the honor?" With courtly grace he presented the bottle to me and took his seat.

I looked at the label and whistled. "It's Scotch, fellows!" I reported. "It's a fine thing for a night like tonight!" I opened the bottle and passed it to the man on my right.

"After you, sir," that officer said, so I poured myself a drink. Then the bottle passed and ended up before Grant. He poured himself a stiff portion.

"I believe a toast is in order," an American officer said. We stood and he proposed, "To an allied victory." Americans and New Zealanders congratulated him on the felicity of his thought. Another American jumped to his feet immediately.

"To the men who won the victory!" he said in a voice filled with emotion. No one could censure his extremely bad taste. We knew it was unseemly to be drinking when Colbourne, Grant's fellow pilot, and so many men were missing, but we had to excuse the speaker. It was Ensign Aberforce. After that display no more toasts were given.

Instead we sat around the hut and talked about what we thought had happened, and what would happen next. It might be months before we were taken off Vanicoro. Through all our discussions Grant sat silent. He was, however, drinking vigorously. From time to time someone would report upon late radio news, but since it was favorable news, and since one doesn't get whiskey very often on Vanicoro, we stayed about the table.

At about 2300 the radio operator got a Jap broadcast which he turned up loud. "The American fleet is in utter flight. The American Navy has now been reduced to a fifth-rate naval power. Our forces are regrouping." At that last admission everyone in the room cheered.

It was then that Grant rose to his feet. He started to speak. Surprised, we stopped to listen. We knew he was drunk, but not how drunk. "Today," he began in a thick voice. "Today will undoubtedly be remembered for years to come. As the gentleman from Australia so properly observed, this was one of the decis— . . ." He stumbled badly over the word and dropped his sentence there.

"If you have not been to New Zealand," he began, and then lost that sentence, too. "If you were a New Zealander," he started over with a rush, "you would know what this means." He took a deep breath and began speaking very slowly, emphasizing each word. "We were ready to protect the land with all our energy . . ." His voice trailed off. We looked at one another uneasily. "From the oldest man to the youngest boy we would have fought. It was my humble duty to assist in preparing the defenses of Auckland. I issued several thousand picks, crowbars, and axes. There were no other weapons." He reached for his whiskey and took a long, slow drink.

"My own wife," he resumed, "was given the job of mobilizing the women. I urged her to go to the hills . . ." He fumbled with his glass. "In fact, I ordered her to go, but she said that our two children . . ." He paused. It seemed as if his voice might break. A fellow New Zealander interrupted.

"I say, Grant!"

Leftenant Grant stared at his subaltern coldly and continued: "There are some of us in New Zealand who know the Japs. We know their cold and cunning ways. We know their thirst for what they call revenge." His voice grew louder, and he beat the table. "I tell you, we know what we have escaped. A heel of tyranny worse than any English nation has known!" He shouted this and upset his glass. Two officers tried to make him sit down, but he refused. He upset another glass defending himself from his friends. We wanted to look aside but were fascinated by the scene. Grant continued his speech.

"Gentlemen!" he said with a gravity one might use in addressing Parliament. "Especially you gentlemen from our wonderful ally. I pray to God that never in your history will you have an enemy . . . will you have an enemy so near your shores!" He paused and his voice took on a solemn ring as if he were in church. His drunkenness made the combined effect ridiculous. "I pray you may never have to rely upon a shield like this." He surveyed the tiny shack and our inadequate materials. We followed his eyes about the wretched place. The radio that was pieced together. The improvised table. The thin pile of ammunition. Grant's voice raised to a shout. "A shield like this!" he cried. He exploded the word *this* and swept his right arm about to indicate all of Vanicoro. As he did so, he lost his balance. He grabbed at a fellow officer. Missing that support, he fell upon the table and slipped off onto the floor. He was unconscious. Dead drunk.

# GEORGE ORWELL

ERIC ARTHUR BLAIR, under the pen name George Orwell, wrote *1984* and *Animal Farm,* among other novels. The following is a brief entry from his *War-time
Diary.*

■

## FROM *Collected Essays, Journalism and Letters of George Orwell*

*19 May, 1942*

   Attlee reminds me of nothing so much as a recent dead fish, before it has had time to stiffen.

# JOHN COSTELLO

JOHN COSTELLO, educated at Cambridge University, worked for many years as a producer for the BBC and now divides his time between London and New York. He is the author of *The Pacific War* and *Virtue Under Fire,* a study of how World War II changed social and sexual attitudes. An excerpt follows.

■

### FROM *Virtue Under Fire*

#### COMRADES IN ARMS

Sodomy is specifically denounced as an offense under the provisions of the 93rd article of war. Administrative discharge in lieu of trial in cases of this character is not only contrary to the War Department policy, but to the express intention of Congress.
—U.S. ARMY POLICY CIRCULAR, 1941

Sex was not really an issue on the *Dido.* There was much the same atmosphere as at a fairly easy going public school.
—SEAMAN GEORGE MELLY, *Royal Navy*

"What ain't we got? We ain't got dames!" In real life on a "No women atoll" like Eniwetok, GIs had chanted less elegant choruses that advocated the so-called Pacific Prescription:

> Masturbation is the fashion
> For your unrequited passion
> If the girls can do it, why can't we?
> But out here in the Pacific,
> Purely as a soporific,
> Nothing equals simple self abuse!

What U.S. navy white-hats referred to as "the sordid imitation" was so widespread among servicemen that one British army doctor "had no hesitation" in advising the men in his unit that masturbation "was perhaps the easiest and the safest way of obtaining relief, there being no reason why they should not embellish this experience with some fantasy of their loved ones at home." But Victorian taboos died hard, even in the army. Another officer in the medical corps, however, admitted he was "shocked to learn how openly, even boastfully, masturbation was performed in some barrackrooms."

"Formerly my wife was my right hand," a World War I soldier had quipped; "in the army my right hand became my wife." In World War II many servicemen resorted to the same substitute to satisfy their sex hunger, although "masturbation guilt" was still considered a medical disorder in the psychiatric textbooks of the period. But as long as men in the armed forces kept their hands to themselves, no military regulations were broken. If their comrades, however, provided the stimulation, servicemen risked a court-martial, imprisonment—and in the case of German SS officers after 1942, the firing squad. Yet the military, because it segregated millions of young men at the height of their potency into a life devoid of female companionship, exposed many men to what was called "emergency" or "deprivation" homosexuality.

Unlike the ancient Greek armies, which had not only tolerated but exploited the amorous bond that developed between comrades in arms, modern military organizations had long proscribed homosexual activity. Not only did it offend basic Christian sexual taboos, homosexuality was perceived as a threat to the essential aggressive "manliness" of soldiers. But above all, homosexual relationships were "prejudicial to good conduct and discipline" by breaking down the divisions between military ranks. Deprivation homosexuality had long been recognized as a problem by navies. Historically it had been dealt with either by toleration and a complex hierarchical code, as in the galleons of the Spanish Armada where there was a complex pecking order for sex code, or by making it a capital offense, as in the Royal Navy when as late as Nelson's time officers had been hung from the yardarm for the offense of sodomy. "Ashore its wine, women and song, aboard its rum, bum and concertina" ran the nineteenth-century sea shanty that doubtless prompted Winston Churchill's aside during World War II: "Don't talk to me about naval tradition. It's nothing but rum, sodomy and the lash."

# PETER USTINOV

---

BORN IN LONDON of Russian, French, and German ancestry, Peter Ustinov is a playwright, actor, novelist, and short story writer. His plays include *The Love of Four Colonels* and *Romanoff and Juliet.* Ustinov's autobiography, *Dear Me,* deals largely with his wartime experiences in the British army.

---

■

FROM *Dear Me*

Not long after this incident, we were marched away from St. Margaret's to make way for elements from another regiment. We passed our successors, whistling the same silly songs of masculine loneliness, as they marched toward the pretty little village we had just left. They seemed robust and jolly chaps, as they chanted, "She'll be coming round the mountain when she comes," and I thought to myself, "There, but for the grace of God, goes a suicide battalion."

Our next duty was to try and capture the town of Maidstone from the Home Guard, that civilian task force of veterans and the infirm who were supposed to harass the Germans in case of a landing, and hold vital positions until better-armed units of the army could be deployed.

We were, on this occasion, supposed to be German. As soon as the battle began, I detached myself from my unit, and advanced alone to the center of the town by the simple expedient of knocking on people's doors. When they were opened, invariably by men in pyjamas or women in nightdresses, for it was a little before six in the morning, I would explain the vital nature of the maneuver, without ever revealing which side I was on. Flushed with patriotism, the good burghers of Maidstone forgot their annoyance at being woken so early, and let me through their houses, and into their gardens. Here I would climb into a neighboring garden, and knock on the back door of another house. These people would then let me out of their front doors. Looking both ways, I would then race across the road and knock at another front door, and the process would repeat itself. It took me over two hours to penetrate into the center of the city at right angles, as it were, to the traffic.

There, I suddenly found myself before the Home Guard headquarters. A choleric general emerged. I aimed my rifle at him, and fired. Since the rifle was empty, it only produced a click, which neither he nor the umpire, a very stout lieutenant, heard. I consequently shouted "Bang!" and then informed the general, politely, that he was dead.

Death was the farthest thing from the general's mind, and he spluttered, "Don't talk such tommyrot. Who are you, anyway?"

The umpire turned out to have a terrifying stammer. His face scarlet with effort and apology, he told the general that he was indeed d . . . , but the word simply would not come.

It was the delay in the verdict which more than anything seemed to enrage the general. "Look here," he snorted, "it's not good enough. Fellow points a gun at me and says bang. May be a bad shot for all I know. Might have come out of the encounter unscathed, what?"

"Would you have preferred me to use ammunition?" I asked.

The general lost his head. "Who asked your advice?" he blustered. "Haven't you done enough harm?"

"D . . . ead!" the umpire managed at length.

"I won't accept it. Won't accept it, d'you hear? Not from a mere lieutenant."

It was the lieutenant's turn to be annoyed. "I am the acc . . . the . . . oh . . . acc . . ."

"I don't give a damn about all that," ranted the general. "I'm off to inspect the forward positions, and I'd like to see the chap who's going to stop me."

"*Sie sind tod!*" I cried.

The general spun on me, suspicious for the first time. "What did you say?"

"*Sie sind tod, Herr General!*"

"Are you talking some foreign language, or something?" asked the general, as though he was on the trail of something big.

"*Ich bin Deutscher.*"

"German, eh?" the general asked, his eyes narrowing.

"Acc . . . redited umpire of this exc . . . exc . . . sss," the lieutenant declared.

Just then, some other Home Guards appeared out of headquarters.

"I've caught a German prisoner," cried the general. "Put him under lock and key," and then, brushing the umpire aside, he jumped into his staff car, and told the driver to leave the scene of his humiliation as quickly as possible.

The umpire was boiling with frustration.

"I'm s . . . so . . . so . . ." he hissed.

"So am I, sir," I said as I was led away.

A Home Guard major read all my correspondence, culled from my pockets, and then began a cross-examination.

I refused to answer in any language but German.

The major became very irritated. "Now look here, I'm going to report you to your unit if you don't pull up your socks and answer a few questions."

"*Dass ist mir egal*," I rasped.

"That's your final word?" he asked, evilly.

"*Heil Hitler!*" I shouted.

"That does it."

They chose to lock me in the armory.

I seized a Sten gun, broke open the door, upset the staff table, smeared ink on the maps and plans of the local high command, before I was overpowered by a cohort of old gentlemen, to whom I wished no harm, and therefore allowed myself to be locked into a disused scullery. They were all very angry indeed, and I felt that the frontier between fact and fiction had become unclear. One or two of them looked at me as though indeed I were a Nazi.

In the mid-afternoon, the colonel of my battalion arrived. He was a man whose voice rarely rose above a whisper, and whose head emerged from the front of his uniform at such an extravagant angle that from the side one could read the name of his tailor inside the jacket. He had the curious prehistoric look of a bemused turtle, and I always felt that if we ever had to face actual warfare in the company of this gentleman, he might well, in a moment of difficulty, disappear into his uniform until the storm blew over.

"Now what is all this?" he asked me almost inaudibly.

I explained, as so often, my version of the truth.

"I see," he murmured. "But was it really necessary to confuse the issue by speaking in German?"

"It's a manner in which the Germans are likely to confuse the issue, sir, if they should ever land in Maidstone," I suggested.

"See what you mean," he said, "although that's an eventuality I consider to be most unlikely, don't you?"

I was a little surprised to be consulted, but decided to suggest that if there was no likelihood of the Germans landing in Maidstone, we were all wasting our time.

"Quite, quite," he agreed absently, then smiled briefly. "Full marks."

On his way out, he hesitated a moment. "You are one of my men, are you?"

"I'm wearing the uniform sir," I pointed out.

"Yes, yes. I just thought you might belong to the Home Guard. But then, of course, there'd be absolutely no point in your talking German."

Muttering confirmations of his own opinion, he left the room, and secured my release by suggesting the Home Guard should all learn German in order to know how to deal with recalcitrant prisoners if, of course, the Germans ever had the bad taste to come to Maidstone.

# CHAIM KAPLAN

---

TWENTY YEARS after the Warsaw Ghetto was annihilated, Chaim Kaplan's diary was found intact on a farm outside of Warsaw, carefully preserved in a paraffin tin. Here he describes the actions of the local Judenrat, a council of Jewish leaders formed by the Germans to enforce their policies against the Jews. Kaplan was deported in 1942.

---

■

FROM *Scroll of Agony*

*May 23, 1942*

"Were the skies parchment, were all the reeds quills," we would be unable to count the deeds of the beloved *Judenrat*. All its ramifications and all that accompanies it (and its branches are many and its entourage vast, because its functions in the ghetto are those of a government) are ugliness and destructiveness. After the Nazi leech comes the *Judenrat* leech. There is no difference between the one and the other but that of race.

Do you wish to consider its ethical quality? Read it from the book of Isaiah: "Thy princes are rebellious, and companions of thieves; everyone loveth bribes, and followeth after rewards; they judge not the fatherless, neither doth the cause of the widow come unto them." The *Judenrat* has conducted a program of taxation which has no parallel anywhere in the world. Out of every zloty you spend on household expenses, you "contribute" about forty per cent, through fraud, for the benefit of the *Judenrat*. A tax of forty per cent has been placed on medicines, and for every zloty of the basic price, you pay one zloty and forty groszy. Even postage stamps are not free of a high tax for the benefit of the *Judenrat*, besides an additional charge for every official manipulation. All this is by law. But illegally, when you need any service from the minions of the *Judenrat*, you can never arrange your affair without behaving in accordance with the principle that one hand washes the other.

There is no end to the tales of its mischief and abominations. All along I have been careful not to write them down for fear of exaggeration and overstatement, until I saw for myself. On my honor, I do not exaggerate in the slightest.

Once an entire delegation from the *Judenrat* entered my apartment (of three rooms and a kitchen) to requisition one of the rooms for a family of refugees. The reason? I am charged with occupying an apartment in an illegal way. Instead of twelve tenants, only seven tenants are registered in my apartment. The delegation was armed with every possible kind of formality. The secretary, who had a whole portfolio of documents under his arm, presented a letter to me—a requisition signed by the august president himself. Beside him was a Jewish policeman. The third was also a representative of the *Judenrat*, but I don't know what his function was. And behind them was a fourth, the roofless refugee whom I was required by law to take into my home.

This visit occurred at a time when my wife was sick with typhus. I opposed the demand of the delegation on the ground that the room was occupied by a woman with a contagious disease who was sick to the point of death. But the delegation stuck to its demand. The sick person will be transferred to the hospital. The room will be disinfected and the requisition will take effect in accordance with law. This audacious demand infuriated me and we began a bitter, angry argument. I told them decisively that I would not allow anyone else to come into my home; that blood would be spilled; that you can't move a deathly ill patient who would die on her way to the hospital. But the quarrel didn't last long: while we were still arguing, the refugee signaled that he wanted a word with me, and in private he bared his soul. There is no one more miserable than he, for his whole family is embracing the dungheaps, but I have awakened his pity, and he agrees that a healthy family shouldn't be brought into an unclean place. But what? This whole matter cost him money. If I will reimburse him for his expenses, he will backtrack and inform the delegation that he will forgo his apartment.

When I heard his proposal my eyes lit up. But I bargained with him. The refugee demanded 100 zloty; I offered twenty. In the end he agreed to accept twenty. Right away the delegation found an excuse to make light of the whole affair. They drafted a protocol that the apartment was full and their requisition nullified. Later on I found out that I need not have been so afraid. This is the way the delegation acts with all of its creatures. They hadn't come to confiscate, but rather to receive twenty zloty. The "refugee" was hired for the occasion.

Last night was a night of watching. The Jewish police made the rounds of Jewish homes and awakened about eight hundred young men from their sleep to take them to the labor camp. Again turmoil and confusion. The police justify themselves: We are compelled by the conquerors' order to supply so many young men for labor, and we must obey orders.

The captured youths were led to the place designated for them, but half of them returned—specifically, the wealthy among them. This was a mystery. Later on, the secret was revealed; they were ordered to supply not eight hundred but four hundred. For greater security and for greater income, eight hundred were arrested, among them four hundred wealthy ones. The wealthy ones ransomed themselves and returned home; the poor ones were taken and are destined for hard labor and lingering death.

This is only an indication of what the *Judenrat* does. The rest will emerge in due time.

# GEORGE ORWELL

ERIC ARTHUR BLAIR, better known under his pen name, George Orwell, wrote *1984* and *Animal Farm,* among other novels. During the war he served as a broadcaster for the BBC. Here, in an entry from his *War-time Diary,* he records some misgivings about war reports.

■

FROM *Collected Essays, Journalism and Letters of George Orwell*

*22 August, 1942*

David Astor very damping about the Dieppe raid, which he saw at more or less close quarters and which he says was an almost complete failure except for the very heavy destruction of German fighter planes, which was not part of the plan. He says that the affair was definitely misrepresented in the press and is now being misrepresented in the reports to the PM and that the main facts were:—Something over 5000 men were engaged, of whom at least 2000 were killed or prisoners. It was not intended to stay on shore longer than was actually done (i.e. dawn till about 4 pm), but the idea was to destroy all the defenses of Dieppe, and the attempt to do this was an utter failure. In fact only comparatively trivial damage was done, a few batteries of guns knocked out etc. and only one of the 3 main parties really made its objective. The others did not get far and many were massacred on the beach by artillery fire. The defenses were formidable and would have been difficult to deal with even if there had been artillery support, as the guns were sunk in the face of the cliff or under enormous concrete coverings. More tank-landing craft were sunk than got ashore. About 20 or 30 tanks were landed but none were got off again. The newspaper photos which showed tanks apparently being brought back to England were intentionally misleading. The general impression was that the Germans knew of the raid beforehand. Almost as soon as it was begun they had a man broadcasting a spurious "eye-witness" account from somewhere further up the coast, and another man broadcasting false orders in English. On the other hand the Germans were evidently surprised by the strength of the air support. Whereas normally they have kept their fighters on the ground so as to conserve their strength, they sent them into the air as soon as they heard that tanks were landing, and lost a number of planes variously estimated, but considered by some RAF officers to have been as high as 270. Owing to the British strength in the air the destroyers were able to lie outside Dieppe all day. One was sunk, but this was by a shore battery. When a request came to attack some objective on shore, the destroyers formed in line and raced inshore firing their forward guns while the fighter planes supported them overhead.

David Astor considers that this definitely proves that an invasion of Europe is impossible. Of course we can't feel sure that he hasn't been planted to say this, considering who his parents are. I can't help feeling that to get ashore at all at such a strongly defended spot, without either bomber support, artillery support except for the guns of the destroyers (4.9 guns I suppose), or airborne troops, was a considerable achievement.

# JOHN KEEGAN

JOHN KEEGAN, Senior Lecturer for many years at the Royal Military Academy at Sandhurst, is now defense correspondent for the London *Daily Telegraph*. Among his brilliant books about men at war are *The Face of Battle* and *The Mask of Command*. A child during World War II, he was evacuated from London to the countryside. His *Six Armies in Normandy,* from which the following is excerpted, was published in 1982.

■

## FROM *Six Armies in Normandy*

### DIEPPE: THE AWFUL WARNING

Dieppe, in retrospect, looks so recklessly hare-brained an enterprise that it is difficult to reconstruct the official state of mind which gave it birth and drove it forward. Churchill himself in the planning stages expressed anxiety, and was confirmed in support for the operation only by the insistence of General Sir Alan Brooke that "if it was ever intended to invade France it was essential to launch a preliminary offensive on a divisional scale." Churchill was moved too by the need to offset in some way the recent loss of Tobruk, to say nothing of his loss of face with Roosevelt and Stalin through his opposition to Operation Roundup. And there were the raiding successes achieved by the Commandos—his "Tigers"—at Vaagso and the Lofoten Islands to lend reassurance. But a few Viking victories by the pick of the army over the small and third-rate garrisons of remote Norwegian fishing havens provided no basis at all for judging how a full-scale military operation against a defended Channel port would go. The Commandos, clinging to the edge of the sea mists of the far north, had always achieved surprise. The 2nd Canadian Division was to sally forth in high summer from ports only seventy miles from the German-occupied coastline and disembark on the esplanade of a French seaside resort. The justification for choosing an objective which the Germans were known to occupy in strength was that the feasibility of capturing a harbor by direct assault had to be tested. The risks were discounted by the argument that Commandos would disable the flanking batteries which bore on the beaches and harbor exit and that the close-in defenders would be overcome by tanks landed from the new Tank Landing Craft directly in the muzzles of their machine guns. And, to cap their case, the staff officers of Combined Operations Headquarters invoked the legendary fighting qualities of the Canadians, who had broken the Hindenburg Line in September 1918 after two years of abortive effort by the rest of the Allied armies.

But bravery was to count for nothing on the morning of August 19th, 1942. The Commandos, attacking up the high cliffs which march almost to the mouth of the little river Arques on which Dieppe stands, achieved their customary surprise and silenced the flanking batteries. But the battalions of Canadian infantry and the tanks they had brought with them were stopped almost as soon as they left their landing-craft, sometimes before.

The Royal Regiment of Canada, one of the three permanent battalions the dominion maintained in peacetime, was detailed to land in the mouth of a narrow gully which led into the cliffs at Puys, east of the harbor. It was defended by a company of the German 571st Regiment and some Luftwaffe anti-aircraft gunners. They had watched the approach of the landing-craft and, as soon as the ramps went down, directed the desperate fire of outnumbered men at the open mouths of the vessels. The Canadians, like the Irishmen on the *River Clyde* at Gallipoli, reeled momentarily before the storm and then burst through the curtain to find shelter under the sea wall. It was capped with wire. They blew a gap with their bangalore torpedoes. The first few scraped through to the cliffs beyond. The rest were barred by fire on the gap and killed by machine-guns firing "in enfilade"—that is, at an angle to the Canadians' line of advance—from under the wall. Twenty minutes later a second wave of landing-craft arrived, and soon after a third, carrying a company of the Black Watch of Canada. The landing-craft drew off behind them. Fire implacably denied their advance. By 8:30 a.m. every man on the beach was dead or captive. They had begun their landing only three hours before. The party which had crossed the sea wall was, by report of the German 302nd Division, "annihilated by assault detachment of 23 (Heavy) Aircraft Reporting Company"—a hastily assembled band of Luftwaffe technicians. Out of 554 Royal Canadians who had disembarked, 94.5 per cent had become casualties; 227 had been killed. Almost all were from the city of Toronto.

At Pourville beach, west of the town, the South Saskatchewans and Cameron Highlanders of Canada found a landing place protected from the worst of the German fusillade, fought all morning and got off with only a hundred casualties apiece. But in the center, at the harbor and along the promenade, disaster was almost as complete as at Puys, and highly spectacular. For here Combined Operations Headquarters had decided to experiment with the direct disembarkation of a new tank—the Churchill—from a new type of assault vessel, the Landing Craft Tank. Each carried three tanks. There were ten LCTs, of which the first three were to beach with the craft carrying the two assaulting infantry battalions, the Royal Hamilton Light Infantry and the Essex Scottish. In the event they arrived late, and only five of their tanks managed to get off the beach on to the promenade. The three following waves got ten of their tanks on to the promenade. But their crew, like those in the first wave, found that access to the town was blocked by large concrete obstacles, which the accompanying sappers were unable to destroy with explosives. All the tanks were therefore confined within a zone on which heavy German fire played. At first the fire was from guns too light to penetrate the thick armor of the Churchills, and the officers aboard the landing vessels offshore listened with admiration on their radios to the "cool and steady voices" of the tank crews coordinating their fire to support their infantry comrades. Gradually however the enemy brought heavier calibers to bear and, one by one, the Calgary Regiment's tanks fell silent. None was evacuated from the beach. Very few of the Hamiltons and the Essex Scottish got away; the first lost a hundred, the second two hundred dead. And, to crown the tragedy, at the last moment the force commander landed his "floating reserve," Les Fusiliers de Mont-Royal, who were bracketed by concentrated German artillery during their ten-minute run-in to the beaches, and drenched with fire as they touched ground. The French Canadians nevertheless stormed from their landing-craft. But shortly they too had lost over a hundred men killed and were pinned to the shingle, unable either to advance or retreat.

When the badly shocked survivors of that terrible morning were got home and heads counted, only 2,110 of the 4,963 Canadians who had set sail the day before could be found. It became known later that 1,874 were prisoners, but of these 568 were wounded and 72 were to die of their wounds, while 378 of the returning were also wounded. Sixty-five per cent of the Canadians engaged had therefore become casualties, almost all of them from the six assaulting infantry battalions, a toll which compared with that of July 1st, 1916, first day of the Battle of the Somme and blackest in the British army's history. The 2nd Canadian Division had, for practical purposes, been destroyed. Six months later it was still in the category of "lowest priority for employment" in the Canadian army.

Strategic as well as human criteria applied in measuring the scale of the disaster. All the tanks which had been landed had been lost, 2 by swamping between ship and shore, the other 27 by enemy action or mechanical breakdown. Lost also were 5 of the 10 precious Landing Craft Tanks. And, auguring worst of all for the future, the damage had been done not by hastily summoned reinforcements but by the forces already present; the 3 Canadian battalions which had stormed the central beach had been opposed by a single German company—at odds, that is, of 12 to 1—and the tanks and landing-craft destroyed by 28 pieces of pre-placed artillery, most of medium caliber. The gunners had worked hard —their returns showed 7,458 shells fired—but they could not be expected to work any less hard on a future occasion. And though not all these details were yet known by Combined Operations Headquarters, after-action reports and prisoner interrogation yielded enough information to point to a depressing disparity between the power of the attack and the defense. It clearly could not be overcome merely by increasing the numbers of those embarked for the assault. That would be to repeat the mistakes of the First World War, when the solution of greater numbers resulted arithmetically in greater casualties for no territorial gain. It would have to be offset by a change in technique.

It is as illuminating to say of Dieppe—as it was and is often said— that it taught important lessons about amphibious operations as to say of the *ateliers nationaux* of the 1848 revolution that they taught important lessons about state intervention in the economy, or of the *Titanic* disaster that it taught important lessons about passenger liner design. In the last case no improvements could compensate the victims, in the second none could rectify an experiment which was fundamentally misconceived. Even if Canada could not do so, it was better that the planners should forget about Dieppe. And so, in a sense, they did. The Germans concluded from the experience that the Allies, when they came for the Second Front, would still land near a port but would seek to surround it. The planners decided that they would steer as far clear of ports as possible. Fighter cover—which had worked very well at Dieppe—and the maximum radius at which it could be provided would impose the only territorial criterion they would accept. Inside that line they would look for a coastline with open beaches, low cliffs or none at all and a positive absence of harbor facilities.

But one lesson was drawn, by the man best placed to perceive it and, as luck would have it, subsequently to put it into practice. Captain (later Vice-Admiral) John Hughes-Hallett had acted both as Naval Adviser to the Chief of Combined Operations, Lord Louis Mountbatten, before the operations and as Naval Commander during it. He had come back from the raid naturally impressed by the importance of air cover—the RAF had brilliantly succeeded in sparing the Canadians the crowning agony of air attack—and concerned by the need to add to the number and types of landing-craft, to rehearse their crews in a variety of simulated beach assaults and to keep such a specialized force in permanent existence. But he was above all determined to ensure that no landing should ever again take place without covering firepower sufficient not simply to hinder the enemy from using his weapons but to shock him into inaction, stun him into insensibility or obliterate him in his positions. *"The Lesson of Greatest Importance,"* his report capitalized and italicized, *"is the need for overwhelming fire support, including close support, during the initial stages of the attack."* It should be provided by "heavy and medium Naval bombardment, by air action, by special vessels or craft" (which would have to be developed) "working close inshore, and by using the firepower

of the assaulting troops while still seaborne." He wrote while the naval
events of the operation burned fresh in his memory. It reminded him of
his four little Hunt-class destroyers, armed with four 4-inch guns, dueling with the German shore batteries, forced to use hastily laid smoke
screens for protection against the heavier metal which their thin sides
did not provide and still suffering grievous damage each time they
emerged into the sunlight. Goronwy Rees, aboard HMS *Garth*, recalled
that "the maneuver became monotonous and repetitive, and each time
harder on the nerves, especially after we had been hit twice, the second
time with considerable damage and casualties." *Garth* survived (though
HMS *Berkeley*, hit by German bombs, did not) but she and all the other
ships of the bombarding force limped home in the knowledge that, in
this latest episode of the four-century-old struggle between ship and
shore artillery, they had been clearly worsted.

# JOHN COSTELLO

EDUCATED at Cambridge University, John Costello
worked for many years as a producer for the BBC, and
now divides his time between London and New York.
His study of how World War II changed social and sexual attitudes, *Virtue Under Fire*, here discusses some
popular songs.

■

FROM *Virtue Under Fire*

"White Christmas" may have been the most popular ballad with
servicemen and their loved ones back home, but it was a German marching song that was destined to become the undisputed favorite of soldiers
in every army by the end of World War II. "Lili Marlene" was a haunting
song about a German soldier's girl that crossed the front line in North
Africa in 1942 to be adopted by the Allied troops. Her popularity sur-
passed World War I's "Mademoiselle from Armentières," and the lyrics
telling of a girl waiting in the lamplight before the barracks gate were to
be bawdified by military versifiers—and bowdlerized by the civilian
songsmiths of half-a-dozen nations. The Italians added a verse that
began "Give me a rose, and press it to my heart." The French gave it an
explicit sexuality with the line "And in the shadows our bodies entwine."
British troops of General Montgomery's Eighth Army, who had first
picked up the song from Afrika Korps radio request broadcasts and soldiers captured from Rommel's desert army, added sexually explicit stan-
zas and their own refrain: 'We're off to bomb Benghazi, we're off to
bomb BG."

The United States Office of War Information at first tried to have it
banned from American radios—on grounds that it was enemy propaganda that would harm GI morale. British WAAFs were ordered not to
whistle or sing it within earshot of German prisoners of war because it
might lead to fraternization. The BBC, concerned about the salacious
unofficial translations as much as by the infectious popularity of a German song, commissioned "official" English words. Their evocative romance and its simple marching melody made it inevitable that recordings
by Vera Lynn and Bing Crosby and later Marlene Dietrich became big
hits:

Underneath the lantern
By the barrack gate
Darling, I remember
The way you used to wait:
'Twas there that you whispered tenderly,
That you loved me,
You'd always be
My Lilli of the lamplight
My own Lilli Marlene.

The secret of "Lilli Marlene's" phenomenal success was the univer-
sality of its sentimental theme: a soldier's parting with his sweetheart.
Her remarkable international career began, according to Lilli's creator,
World War I soldier/poet Hans Leip, as a "private little love song" about
the two girls he became involved with on an officers' course in Berlin in
1917. Lilli—real name Betty—was a greengrocer's daughter at his billet.
Marleen was a part-time nurse and doctor's daughter whom he encountered in an art gallery. Dreaming of Lilli while on guard duty one rainy
evening as the lamplight flickered in the puddles, he saw Marleen pass
by waving her feather boa. It was while lying on the guardroom's iron
cot that Fusilier Leip composed his sentimental poem. "Their names
could no longer be coupled together with an 'and.' They melted into
one, not too shapely, as a single pleasure and pain."

The poem expressed the sadness of a soldier's last farewell, with its
final stanza anticipating his death in action and his ghost returning to
meet his girl again under the lamplight in front of the barrack gate.
Norbert Schultze, a struggling composer in Berlin, set the words to a
wistful march he had written. The song was first recorded by a Swedish
cabaret artist, Lale Andersen, after it had proved popular on her Radio
Cologne broadcasts in the year that war broke out. But its downbeat
theme was not considered inspiring enough to celebrate Germany's victorious conquest of Western Europe—and Lale Andersen's records were
dispatched to the basement storerooms of the Reich radio networks in
1940.

A year later an army corporal, dispatched to Vienna in 1941 to
collect a consignment of records to be played in Belgrade Radio's nightly
broadcasts to German troops in North Africa, included it in his selection.
An officer, hearing its bugle-call introduction, decided that it would
make ideal signing-off music—and that was how "Lilli Marlene" received
its first reairing on 18 August 1941. Within a week the station was flooded
with thousands of requests, and it was thenceforth played every night at
9:55 P.M. for three years on the Belgrade station—the only day it was not
heard was when Hitler banned all entertainment the day after the fall of
Stalingrad.

"Lilli Marlene's" popularity quickly spread to home audiences and although Dr. Goebbels was initially afraid that it might depress rather than boost morale, German stations were soon spinning the record up to thirty times a day. Lale Andersen became one of the most requested singers for troop broadcasts—in the course of the war she received over a million fan letters from German soldiers. What she was to call "my fateful song" saved her from the Gestapo after she failed to make good her attempt to join her long-standing Jewish boyfriend in Zurich while on a 1942 concert tour of German army camps in Italy. The security police who arrested Andersen told her that it was the end of her career. "But a BBC broadcast saved me," she was to write. "The BBC put out a report that I'd been taken to a concentration camp and died. Goebbels saw it as a golden opportunity to prove that the English radio told lies. He needed me alive."

British troops who fought in the Western Desert never forgot the important psychological contribution that the symbolic "capture" of their opponent's marching song made to their victory in the battle of El Alamein. "Look here, this is our song! This is the song we hear on our radios in the tanks in the North African desert," an Eighth Army officer claimed shortly after El Alamein. "Mouth organs strike up 'Lilli' at night. We sing it in day charges against the Germans. 'Lilli Marlene' gets us right in our guts. 'Lilli Marlene' is the theme of the Desert War and get that straight!"

Lilli marched with the British Army to Italy, where she also became a favorite with the soldiers of the American Fifth Army who added new verses that were derived from the more sentimental Italian version:

> When we are marching in the mud and cold,
> And when my pack seems more than I can hold,
> My love for you renews my might,
> I'm warm again, my pack is light.
> It's you, Lilli Marlene, it's you Lilli Marlene.

GI's "fell victim" to the "captured" German ballad because, as the celebrated cartoonist with the Fifth Army Bill Mauldin explained, "Our musical geniuses back home never did get round to a good, honest, acceptable war song, and so they forced us to share 'Lilli Marlene' with the enemy. Even if we did get it from the krauts it's a beautiful song, and the only redeeming thing is the rumor kicking around that 'Lilli' is an ancient French song, stolen by the Germans. It may not be true, but we like to believe it."

General Eisenhower did not subscribe to this commonly held belief among Allied soldiers. In 1945 he credited Schultze with being "the only German who has given pleasure to the world during the war." A reporter for the army newspaper *Stars and Stripes* succinctly summed up that it

had done "something that all Tin Pan Alley has failed to do" by giving
the GIs a song that was "good for marching, cafe singing and humming
to oneself on lonely outposts."

It was not for the want of effort that British and American songwriters failed to deliver the song that matched the universal appeal that
"Lilli Marlene" had for all servicemen. The initial war years produced
the songs of yearning for absent sweethearts like "Always in My Heart,"
"I'll Wait For You (Always)," "I'm in Love with the Girl I Left Behind
Me," and "I'm Thinking Tonight of My Blue Eyes" (and wonder whether
she's thinking of me?). These all reflected the perennial concern of soldiers over the constancy of their girls back home. "Stick to Your Knittin',
Kitten" and "Be Brave, My Beloved" became the U.S. armed forces'
favorites as the war dragged and men overseas began to doubt whether
the little lady really was waiting for her Johnny to come marching home.
"Somebody Else Is Taking My Place," was too direct an expression of
this fear to compete with the enormous success of the Andrews Sisters'
vibrant revival of the World War I song "Don't Sit Under the Apple Tree"
(with anyone else but me!).

Whatever comfort was afforded the overseas GI in 1943 by "They're
Either Too Young or Too Old" and "What's Good Is in the Army" was
undone by "You Can't Say No to a Soldier" and Sophie Tucker's gently
wicked "The Bigger the Army and Navy" (the better the loving will be).
It was not so much that the GIs worried that new stateside recruits might
seduce their girls, but "draftdodgers" and those young men who enjoyed
the benefit of a reserved occupation to stay out of uniform.

In 1944 when thirty thousand bobby-soxers rioted in New York's
Times Square before a Frank Sinatra concert, the wiry young man with
the quaff and 4-F classification that kept him out of uniform increased
the resentment many servicemen felt about the sex appeal of the young
crooner with the intense blue eyes and mellow bedtime voice. Although
Sinatra was already married and had a child, a Columbia University
psychologist surmised that "this little fella represents some kind of an
idealized hero, much like the story of Prince Charming" to explain the
new phenomenon of "mass hysteria" among his teenage female fans.
When Frank Sinatra finally made his much-publicized and often-delayed
overseas concert tour for the USO in 1945, he was greeted at first with
derisory yells until he melted the GIs' hostility with his talents as a bal-
ladeer.

In the final year of World War II the hit songs anticipated the need
to heal the wounds of separation with the passions of homecoming re-
unions. "It's Been a Long, Long Time" was followed by Perry Como's
overtly suggestive rendition of "I'm Going to Love That Gal" (like she's
never been loved before). And in Britain, "I'm Gonna Get Lit Up" (when
the lights go up in London) looked forward to a national binge on "the
day we finally exterminate the Huns," when the singer promised "we'll

all be drunk for months and months." The biggest hit of all the home-coming songs was "I'll Be Seeing You" (in all the old familiar places). Its lyrics were given a more explicit sexual reinterpretation than its composers intended by British and American servicemen. "We'll Meet Again" also offered limitless possibilities for barrack-room songwriters by changing "meet" to "mate."

If the popular songs were the sentimental bullets in the morale war, the dance bands were its heavy artillery. They sustained a romantic musical barrage throughout World War II, which an RAF serviceman evocatively recalled:

> In a smoke-hazed aeroplane hanger "somewhere in England," the floor crowded to capacity with uniformed boys and girls swaying gently or "jiving" wildly according to the dictates of that essential commodity, the dance band, the vocalist, his (or her) face almost obscured by an enormous microphone, singing of love not war. . . . The dance was on and all we were conscious of was the music (and what music it was) the exhilarating rhythm and of course, the girl in our arms. She may have been a little WAAF cook, or an ATS orderly, but as the orchestra wove its spell, she was Alice Faye, Betty Grable, Rita Hayworth or whoever our "pin-up" of that particular week may have been.

# K. S. KAROL

K. S. KAROL was a fifteen-year-old student in Lodz, Poland, when the war broke out. In accordance with an agreement between Hitler and Stalin, the Germans occupied western Poland, and the Soviets the eastern part of the country. After Hitler's invasion of Russia in June 1941, however, Karol and other young Poles joined and fought with the Red Army. The following is an excerpt from his memoir *Between Two Worlds*.

■

## FROM *Between Two Worlds*

### THE MYECHOTKA MUSKETEERS

Few people realize today that the loss of the Caucasus in 1942 would have been a catastrophe for the Allies. Even in the USSR, the history books dispatch the affair in a few lines and seem to regard this battle as one of little importance. At the time, it was otherwise. The Wehrmacht blitzkrieg in the region that yielded the greatest oil wealth in Europe, and that commanded access to Turkey—and beyond to Iran—was the subject of great concern among the general staffs of the anti-Nazi coalition. Churchill hurried to Moscow to discuss it with Stalin. It was the first and most difficult of their meetings; neither had the slightest good news to communicate. Some weeks earlier the British had abandoned Tobruk and were now fighting in Egypt, their backs to the Pyramids. For the Russians, things lurched from bad to worse after the fall of Sevastopol. They hadn't managed to stabilize the front either in the Kuban—their granary, near the Black Sea—or on the line of the Don.

From this moment forward, as it penetrated the Caucasus, the Wehrmacht seemed to be swooping down to meet its troops operating in Africa, under the command of General Rommel, the "desert fox." Such a junction of forces would have had disastrous consequences for the Allies. Conscious of the danger, Churchill asked Stalin in August 1942, omitting the diplomatic niceties, if his army was still capable of preventing the Wehrmacht from crossing the mountain passes of the Caucasus. (He is even supposed to have offered the aid of the RAF, though he doesn't mention it in his memoir-history, *The Second World War*.) Stalin then unfolded a detailed map of the region onto the table—a Georgian by birth, he was familiar with the area—studied it, and decreed, "They shall not cross the passes of the Caucasus; we will stop them in the mountains."

Churchill only half-believed him, and he reported to Roosevelt that his chief of staff, General Alan Brooke, placed even less confidence in these declarations. Reading this passage in Churchill's memoirs used to fill me with a secret joy, as if, in 1942, I had personally played a fine stroke not only against the Germans, but also against these skeptical Anglo-Saxons. Today my ex-combatant's pride is less keen, and I think that the success we eventually enjoyed was only obtained thanks to the extraordinary presumption of the Wehrmacht.

I don't propose to offer here a lengthy exposition on military strategy. A brief summary of the facts of the situation after our hasty departure from Kislovodsk will, however, allow the reader to form a better picture. What is striking is that during the Churchill-Stalin discussions in Moscow, Stalingrad was never mentioned. The two leaders reasonably inferred that the Wehrmacht would hurl the bulk of its forces on the Caucasian front—where it stood to gain everything—and not on the unrewarding steppes of the Don and the Volga. In fact, the Germans did the opposite, and drove deeper into an endless space renowned for the severity of its winters. It appears that they wanted to encircle Moscow. How, though? Imagine, if you will, an army at Lille, in the far north of France, hoping to encircle Paris by making a detour through Aix-en-Provence, almost on the Mediterranean coast. On the Russian scale the distances are even greater. Perhaps these strategists with a handle to their names—von Manstein, von Kleist (perhaps the descendant of the poet of despair?), and von Paulus—pressed forward onto the steppes of the Volga for no other reason than that they met initially with very little resistance.

Their second mistake becomes clear as soon as one considers the geography of the Caucasus. Until the discovery of the oil fields in Kuybyshev and later in Western Siberia, 90 percent of Soviet oil came from Baku and Grozny. Therefore, these two basins ought to have constituted the chief prize of the battle of 1942, such was the extent of the belligerents' dependence on petroleum for their "war of engines." Now Baku is right on the coast of the Caspian Sea and Grozny on the northern foothills of the Caucasus, not far from the littoral. To reach them, the Germans were not at all obliged to secure control of all the highest mountains, and particularly the main chain. It would have been sufficient for them to have followed the path of the Moscow-Tbilisi-Yerevan Transcaucasian railway, which, after the junction at Min. Vody, threads its way through some of the lower passes and then neatly skirts the Caspian Sea. If the Wehrmacht had concentrated its best divisions along this axis, it would certainly have arrived in Grozny and Baku. General Tyulenyev, who was responsible for the defense of this sector, recognized as much himself in his memoirs published in 1960.

The noble Prussian generals, however, tried to do everything at once: they wanted the Caucasus, but also Stalingrad; oil, but also Mount Elbrus; and all of this while simultaneously encircling the adversary in order to take large numbers of prisoners to send back to Germany. It was too much. Their appetite exceeded their means, even if, to begin with, they had possessed mastery of the air and a clear superiority in armaments. After their failure at Stalingrad they were routed from the Caucasus, narrowly avoiding becoming encircled themselves. This misguided campaign didn't yield them a single drop of oil—but only the consolation of having reached the summit of Mount Elbrus.

This aspect particularly interests me—although I have a marked aversion for climbing in general—for we in the "eleventh" school of the air force came very close to losing our lives because of it. When we abandoned Kislovodsk, our commanders had reasoned sensibly enough that the Germans were going to rush along the path of the Transcaucasian, toward the oil fields, thus leaving the road to Nalchik and Vladicaucasia more or less free. These mountain towns have strategic value only for the conquest of Georgia, and, today, more than four decades later, they are still not connected to the railway network. Such an analysis neglects to take into account, however, the Wehrmacht's tastes for mountain climbing. The main chain of the Caucasus extends to the west, close to and almost paralleling the Black Sea; it is dominated by Mount Elbrus, with its peak of 5,600 meters. The Germans were bent on planting the swastika on it at any cost. As early as mid-August their press had published a clumsy photomontage showing their *Alpenjägers* on the summit of the mountain; it had immediately provoked mocking denials from the Sovinformbureau. The Germans' self-esteem having thus been wounded, they decided, no doubt, to do whatever was necessary to take some authentic snapshots.

# OLIVIA MANNING

OLIVIA MANNING'S Balkan and Levant trilogies to-
gether form a single narrative entitled *Fortunes of War.*
"The finest fictional record of the war produced by a
British writer," wrote Anthony Burgess.

Following, an excerpt from the first novel of the
Levant trilogy, *The Danger Tree.*

■

## FROM *The Danger Tree*

Rumor came to Cairo of a battle fought inside Egypt at a railway
halt called El Alamein but, it seemed, nothing had been settled. The
Germans were still a day's tank drive away and their broadcasts claimed
they were merely awaiting fresh supplies. Any day now the advance
would begin again. Egypt would be liberated and Rommel and his men
would keep their assignation with the ladies of Alexandria.

Though the situation had not changed, the panic had died. Those
who were, or believed themselves to be, at risk, had gone. Those who
remained felt a sense of respite but were warned they might have to leave
at short notice. They were advised to keep a bag packed.

When Harriet, returning for luncheon, found a note at the pension
to say Dobson had rung her, she supposed the evacuation order had
gone out. She took out the small suitcase, the only luggage she had
brought out of Greece, and put together a few toilet articles. The suitcase
was already packed. She could leave in minutes, but she did not intend
to leave without Guy. She thought of a dozen arguments to bring down
on Dobson when he telephoned again and his voice, when she heard it,
startled her. His tone was jocular. Instead of ordering her to the station,
he invited her to meet him for drinks at Groppi's: "Come about five-
thirty."

"You sound as though you had good news?"

"Perhaps I have," he spoke teasingly. "I'll tell you when I see
you."

Back at the office, she looked through the news sheets, but they gave
no cause for rejoicing. Whatever Dobson would tell her, it could have
nothing to do with the war.

That morning she had heard that her job at the Embassy would not
last much longer. The promised team from the States was about to fly to
Egypt. Mr. Buschman, not caring to tell her himself, had sent her a

typed note. Dispirited, she went to the wall map where the black pins converged upon the Middle East.

She had taken it over during the great days of the Russian counter-offensive when everyone was saying that Russian winter would defeat Hitler as it had defeated Napoleon. Marking the Russian advances, she rejoiced as though pushing the enemy back with her own hands. Guy had picked up a new song from one of his left-wing friends and repeatedly sang it to what was, more or less, the tune of *The Lincolnshire Poacher*:

> To say that Hitler can't be beat
> Is just a lot of cock,
> For Marshal Timoshenko's men
> Are pissing through von Bock.
> The Führer makes the bloomers and his generals take the rap,
> But Joe, he smokes his pipe and wears a taxi-driver's cap.

In the desert, too, the Germans had been in retreat. The British troops, who had been making a hero of Rommel, now turned their admiration on to Stalin and the Russian generals. But that had all passed. Harriet, bringing the black pins closer to the Kuban river, thought, "A few more miles and they'll have the whole Caucasus."

Inside Egypt, the black pins stretched from the coast to a hatched-in area of the desert named on the map "Qattara Depression." When Mr. Buschman wandered over to see who was where, she asked him what this Depression was. He stood for some moments, rubbing his small, plump hand over the back of his neck, and then gave up: "All I know is, it's the end of the line."

"But why is it the end of the line? Why don't they come round that way? If they did, they could surround the whole British army."

"Too right, mem. They surely could."

Harriet asked Iqal about the Depression but he had never heard of it.

"How is your German these days?"

He smiled an arch smile, the runnels of his face quivering so he looked like coffee cream on the boil. "I brush it up now and then, but I don't know! These Germans should make more haste."

"I told you they wouldn't get here."

"That is true, Mrs. Pringle, and perhaps you spoke right. But on the other hand, perhaps not. It says in the broadcasts they regather their forces and then they come—zoom! So what is one to think? See here, Mrs. Pringle, they exhort us, 'Rise against your oppressors,' they say, 'Kill them and be free.' "

"You don't think the English are oppressors, do you?"

Iqal raised his great shoulders. "Sometimes, yes. Sometimes, no. When they break through the palace gates and tell my king what to do, what would you call them? Are they not oppressors?"

"We're fighting a war, Iqal. If the Egyptians really felt oppressed, they would turn on us, wouldn't they?"

"Ah, Mrs. Pringle, we are not fools. My friends say, 'Time enough when the Germans are at the gate—*then* we cut the English throats.' "

"Oh, come now, Iqal, you wouldn't cut my throat?"

Iqal giggled. "Believe me, Mrs. Pringle, if I would cut your throat, I do it in a kind and considerate manner."

"You wouldn't hurt me?"

"No, no, Mrs. Pringle, indeed I would not."

Harriet reach Groppi's when the sun was low in the sky. She passed through the bead curtain into the brown, chocolate-scented cake and sweet shop as the great round golden chocolate boxes were reflecting the golden sky. The garden café, surrounded by high walls, was already in shadow. It was a large café, sunk like a well among the houses, with a floor-covering of small stones and it disappointed people who saw it for the first time. A young officer had said to Harriet, "The chaps in the desert think Groppi's is the Garden of Sensual Delights—but, good grief, it isn't even a garden!"

It was, she said, a desert garden, the best anyone could hope for so far from the river. It was a garden of indulgences where the Levantine ladies came to eye the staff officers who treated it as a home from home.

The ground was planted, not with trees, but with tables and chairs and colored umbrellas. But under one wall, where there was a strip of imported earth, zinnias grew and an old, hardy creeping plant spread out and up and covered lattices and stretched as far as the enclosure that stood at one end of the café site. This creeper sometimes put out a few copper-colored, trumpet-shaped flowers that enhanced the garden idea. But this display, and there was not much of it, would have died in an hour without the water that seeped continually through the holes in a canvas hose. In spite of the water, the mat of leaves hung dry and loose, shifting and rustling in the hot wind. Only the tough, thick-petalled zinnias thrived in this heat.

When Harriet entered, the safragis were taking down the umbrellas, leaving the tables open to the evening air. At this hour people were crowding in, searching for friends or somewhere to sit. Dobson must have arrived early for Harriet found him at a vantage point, in front of the zinnias. He had seen her before she saw him and was on his feet, beckoning to her, his smile so genial she wondered if he had news of a victory.

She asked, "Has anything happened?" He did not answer but waved her to a chair. Whatever he had to tell, he was in no hurry to tell it.

A safragi, his white galabiah given distinction by a red sash and the fez that denotes the effendi's servant, wheeled over a gilded trolley laden with cream cakes. Harriet asked for a glass of white wine. Dobson urged her to choose a cake, saying, "Do join me. I think I'll have a *mille feuille*. Good for you. You've lost weight since you came here."

"I really hadn't much weight to lose."

Dobson put his fork into his *mille feuille* and said as the cream and jam oozed out, "Yum, yum," and put a large piece into his mouth then asked, as he sometimes did, about her work at the American Embassy.

"Coming to an end, I fear." Harriet gave a wry laugh. "Perhaps we're all coming to an end. Iqal was joking about cutting our throats—perhaps not just joking. He seemed to resent that occasion when the ambassador drove a tank through the palace gates."

Dobson, putting more pastry into his mouth, swayed his head knowingly, swallowed and said, "We're always having trouble with Farouk. He's a fat, spoilt baby, but he's a clever baby. The other day H.E. waited over an hour for an audience. He thought the king was with his ministers but instead he had a girl with him. She put her head out of the door and seeing H.E. there in all his regalia, she went off into screams of laughter and slammed the door on him. When he eventually got in, he found Farouk sprawled on a sofa, languid and irritable—post coitum, no doubt. He thought, with the Hun so close, he could tell us to clear out. H.E. explained why we must hold Egypt at all cost. Farouk scarcely bothered to listen and at the end, he sighed and said, 'Oh, very well. Stay if you must. But when your war's over, for God's sake, put down the white man's burden and *go*.' "

# ELIZABETH BOWEN

THE ANGLO-IRISH writer Elizabeth Bowen was considered one of the great writers about the Blitz. The following excerpt is taken from what is possibly her most famous novel, *The Heat of the Day*.

■

FROM *The Heat of the Day*

## SIXTEEN

. . . news broke. The Allied landings in North Africa. Talk was of nothing else. Nor had the quickening subsided when Montgomery's Order of the Day to the Eighth Army—"We have completely smashed the German and Italian armies"—became the order of yet another day for London. There came the Sunday set for victorious bell-ringing: throughout the country every steeple was to break silence. When at last it came, the bells' sound was not as strange or momentous as had been expected: after everything these were still the bells of the former time, climbing, striving, searching round in the air in vain for some still not to be found new note. All that stood out in cities were unreverberating lacunæ where there were churches gone. At the beginning, the invitation to rejoice brought out a few people into the sunless November morning streets, as though the peals and crashes were a spectacle to be watched passing: eyes for a moment seemed to perceive a peculiar brightness. Soon, however, even before the bells had come to a climax, people began turning away from the illusion, either because it had already begun to fade or because they knew it must. There was a movement indoors again: doors and windows shut.

# CYRIL CONNOLLY

THE IMMENSELY INFLUENTIAL English critic Cyril Connolly was the editor and founder, along with Stephen Spender, of *Horizon* (1939–1950), a legendary literary magazine that was a rare source of cultural sanity during World War II. Connolly's best-known books are *Enemies of Promise* and *The Unquiet Grave*. Here he discusses the role of literature in wartime.

■

FROM *The Selected Essays of Cyril Connolly*

It is sad on a spring evening to walk through the bombed streets of Chelsea. There are vast districts of London—Bayswater, for example, or Kensington—which seem to have been created for destruction, where squares and terraces for half a century have invited dilapidation, where fear and hypocrisy have accumulated through interminable Sunday afternoons until one feels, so evil is the atmosphere of unreality and suspense, that had it not been for the bombers, the houses would have been ignited one day of their own accord by spontaneous combustion. Behind the stucco porches and the lace curtains the half-life of decaying Victorian families guttered like marsh gas. One has no pity for the fate of such houses, and no pity for the spectacular cinemas and fun places of Leicester Square, whose architecture was a standing appeal to heaven to rain down vengeance on them. But Chelsea in the milky green evening light, where the church where Henry James lies buried is a pile of red rubble, where tall eighteenth century houses with their insides blown out gape like ruined triumphal arches, is a more tragic spectacle. For here the life that has vanished with the buildings that once housed it was of some consequence: here there existed a fine appreciation of books and pictures, and many quiet work rooms for the people who made them. Here was one of the last strongholds of the cultivated *haute bourgeoisie* in which leisure, however ill-earned, has seldom been more agreeably and intelligently made use of. Now when the sun shines on these sandy ruins and on the brown and blue men working there one expects to see goats, and a goatherd in a burnous—*"sirenes in delubris voluptatis"*— pattering among them.

Meanwhile the bombs, which have emptied so many drawing rooms, have also been blasting the reputations made in them. Our literary values are rapidly changing. War shrinks everything. It means less time, less tolerance, less imagination, less curiosity, less play. We cannot read the leisurely wasteful masterpieces of the past without being irritated by the amount they take for granted. I have lately been reading both Joyce and Proust with considerable disappointment; they both seem to me very sick men, giant invalids who, in spite of enormous talent, were crippled by the same disease, elephantiasis of the ego. They both attempted titanic tasks, and both failed for lack of that dull but healthy quality without which no masterpiece can be contrived, a sense of proportion. Proust, like Pope, hoaxed his contemporaries; he put himself over on them as a reasonable, intelligent, kind, and sensitive human being, when his personality was in fact diseased and malignant, his nature pathologically cruel and vacillating, his values snobbish and artificial, his mind (like a growth which reproduces itself at the expense of the rest of the body) a riot of alternatives and variations, where both the neurotic horror of decision and the fear of leaving anything out are lurking behind his love of truth.

For Joyce there seems almost less to be said; Proust's endless and repetitive soliloquies are at least the thoughts of an intelligent man, while those of Joyce reflect the vacuous mediocrity of his characters; both relive the past to the point of exhaustion. Both are men of genius whose work is distorted by illness, by the struggle of one to see and of the other to breathe; both seem to us to have lacked all sense of social or political responsibility.

Yet we must remember that the life which many of us are now leading is unfriendly to the appreciation of literature; we are living history, which means that we are living from hand to mouth and reading innumerable editions of the evening paper. In these philistine conditions it is as unfair to judge art as if we were seasick. It is even more unfair to blame writers for their action or inaction in the years before the war, when we still tolerate in office nearly all the old beaming second-rate faces, with their indomitable will to power, and their self-sealing tanks of complacency.

It would not be unfair to say that the England of Baldwin, MacDonald, and Chamberlain was a decadent country—"Cabbage Land," "Land of lobelias and tennis flannels," "This England where nobody is well"—its gods were wealth and sport; from any unpleasant decision it flinched in disgust; though assailed by critics from the right and left, it still wallowed supinely in a scented bath of stocks and shares, race cards and roses, while the persecuted, who believed in the great English traditions of the nineteenth century, knocked in vain at the door.

Since Dunkirk we have seen the end of the political and military decadence of England. Whatever residue of complacency, sloth, and inefficiency there may be left, England is now a great power, and able to stand for something in the world again. When the war is over we shall live in an Anglo-American world. There will be other great powers, but the sanctions on which the West reposes will be the ideas for which England and America have fought and won, and the machines behind them. We had all this in 1918 and made a failure of it. The ideas expired in the impotence of Geneva. The machines spouted Ford cars, Lucky Strike, Mary Pickford, and Coca-Cola. The new masters of the world created Le Touquet and Juan les Pins, fought each other for oil and reparations, blamed each other for the slump, and wandered blandly and ignorantly over Europe with a dark blue suit, letter of credit, set of clean teeth, and stiff white collar. Fascism arose as a religion of disappointment, a spreading nausea at the hypocrisy of the owners of the twentieth century. It is important to see that fascism is a disease, as catching as influenza; we all when tired and disillusioned have fascist moments, when belief in human nature vanishes, when we burn with anger and envy like the underdog and the sucker, when we hate the virtuous and despise the weak, when we feel as Goebbels permanently feels, that all fine sentiment is ballyhoo, that we are the dupes of our leaders, and that the masses are evil, to be resisted with the cruelty born of fear. This is the theological sin of despair, a Haw-Haw moment which quickly passes, but which fascism has made permanent, and built up into a philosophy. In every human being there is a Lear and a fool, a hero and a clown who comes on the stage and burlesques his master. He should never be censored, but neither should he be allowed to rule. In the long run all that fascism guarantees is a Way of Death; it criticizes the easy life by offering a noisy way of killing and dying. The key philosophies which the world will need after the war are, therefore, those which believe in life, which assert the goodness and sanity of man, and yet which will never again allow those virtues to run to seed and engender their opposites.

# GERMAINE GREER

GERMAINE GREER was educated at the universities of
Melbourne, Sydney, and Cambridge. Her first book, *The
Female Eunuch* (1971), was an international best-seller.
*Daddy, We Hardly Knew You* tells of her father's public
and private war.

■

## FROM *Daddy, We Hardly Knew You*

Montgomery had said that the morale of the soldier is the single
most important factor in war. He placed great stress on officers making
men feel wanted and valued, consulting them wherever possible, handling touchy issues with sensitivity. When soldiers mutinied Montgomery blamed their leaders; he would not blame the men on principle. His
position was far from democratic, for it underemphasized the soldiers'
autonomy, but against a fascist enemy it worked. Most important, Montgomery thought, was keeping the fighting man in touch with family and
friends.

The medical officers agreed. When they examined men exhibiting
signs of serious disturbance they almost invariably found the root cause
in pre-war experiences, mostly "domestic." This strengthened them in
their belief that the sick men were not first-grade material. Some had
even had breakdowns in civil life; others, astonishingly, were *homosexual*. There was no way such bounders were going to be evacuated while
better men faced the music. In Malta no psychiatric case was ever evacuated.

As an Australian intelligence officer in a British air force my father
can have had few friends. There was probably not much badinage and
bonhomie underground where everyone was either straining to unscram-
ble the cacophony in their headphones or nutting out codes. Crammed
into their damp airless shelter they were all spiritually alone. Many felt
closer to the German wireless operators than they did to the people
sitting next to them. They learned their idiosyncrasies, recognized their
styles and voices. Some of the German fighter pilots joked with the
invisible listeners to fighter traffic and some of the listeners wept when
they heard them screaming in the cockpits of their burning planes. If
Reg Greer made a single friend in Malta, he never mentioned him. To
all intents and purposes this un-Australian Australian with the super-
hush-hush job was completely alone.

I do not remember if we at home did our part to support him. Perhaps we did write, and perhaps he got our letters when he was in Egypt, but it was generally understood that mail was low on the list of priorities. I do not know that any of the letters Daddy wrote to my mother ever mentioned receiving one from her.

Letters from Australia had to cross the Indian Ocean, and then to be redistributed through rather unsteady lines of communication to the forward bases. If the Japs didn't get them it seemed the Egyptians did. None of the food parcels we sent ever arrived. During the blockade post rarely got through to Malta, but when the merchantmen began to arrive in November and December of 1942 some letters from Britain should have got through. It is not so hard to have no letters when nobody else has them, but when other men are opening theirs and you have none, then the heart may pound and the throat seize up and the nervous cough start its scratching. I know we tried to send a parcel of food. I remember its being sewn up in calico and the name, rank and serial number being lettered on it in Indian ink. And I know Daddy didn't get it.

The military proposition, that it is not war that makes men sick, but sick men that cannot fight wars, is clearly wrong, but most of the military medical corps believed it.

The experiences that make real men also reveal many who are not real men at all. Real men are a minority even among heroes. Even the flying aces occasionally flew cautious; the more sorties they had done the more cautious they flew. They began to realize that they had more in common with the men who fell past them to crash in flames than with the brass who had ordered them to stalk and kill them. As long as they could tell themselves that it was Jerry, a something not quite human, they could hunt efficiently; once they felt glad when an enemy pilot succeeded in bailing out, the end of their ruthlessness was in sight. It was as good a time to die as any.

Military mythology has to pretend that real men are in the majority; cowards can never be allowed to feel that they might be the normal ones and the heroes the insane.

The principal cause of anxiety neurosis, according to the military, is fear, not stress. Because they insisted on associating anxiety neurosis with fear, they consistently failed to identify the most likely sufferers, who were not those exposed to most danger. Real danger provokes a real response; the human organism goes into overdrive. Noradrenaline floods the heart, giving the frightened one a cocaine high, making him feel cool, detached, superhuman. And so the aces pulled off those legendary stunts; a Spitfire pilot coming in over Grand Harbour on a wing and a prayer, already shot up, one engine aflame, apparently unaware of serious injury, saw a floating bomb on course for a village on the periphery and, coming up under it, tipped it with his undamaged wing and sent it out to sea again. Cool was what the groundlings called this kind of thing.

The pilots lost their cool when they were forced to climb down to the pace of ordinary life. Then they shuddered and wept in noradrenaline withdrawal. The MOs scratched their heads. These were brave men, no mistake, so why were they gray-faced and sweating, screaming in their dreams like the worst of the shirkers and the yellow-bellies?

Sometimes the medicos took a risk and sent the men back to flying operations. Most times it paid off. The men flew and flew effectively. Many of them were killed in the clouds, still high. The most dangerous part of any flight, especially on Malta, was landing. Not too many of the aces survived to the end of the war, and those who did had a terrible time. When the excitement ebbed, soul-deep exhaustion took its place, and then they remembered the screams of their victims, the friends they had lost, the stupid mistakes, and with all the reflection that they had had no time to do came guilt, guilt that they were still alive when so many were dead. Even Monty in the last years of his life was haunted by the thought that he had led so many to their death. When he died he said that he was going to join "the men he killed" in North Africa.

RAF medical history is mostly concerned with the special health problems of the fliers; actually fliers were a small élite, served by a squad of earthbound individuals who outnumbered them five to one, not counting bods like non-flying Flying Officer Reg Greer. The fliers were the heroes of the squadrons, lionized, petted, praised. The fliers and the ack-ack gunners were the only ones who had the satisfaction of getting a crack at Jerry; everybody else had to sit tight and take it. The first bombardment caused shock and terror; when that subsided and people adapted to life under the bombardment, the health consequences were more insidious. The constant stress of irregular alerts, of months of interrupted sleep, and of appalling noise levels, sometimes for many hours at a stretch, gradually wore down men and women, military and civilians, the young and the old, all at differing rates and to different degrees. If men building aircraft dispersal pens or unloading ships in the harbor, or women plotting the box barrage or fighter control, became inattentive or began to doubt their efficiency and demand constant reassurance, the cause was not fear, after all, but the fact that, on a poor diet, in crowded conditions and with little sleep, they had run out of resilience and endurance. The authorities compounded their distress by accusing them of fear. They were actually too tired and too dispirited to feel fear.

Whoever wrote the Malta section of the official history of the Army Medical Services in World War II had deep reservations about the official attitude to anxiety neurosis.

"The official attitude in Malta during the period of the siege seems to have been based on the view that, when there is no escape from danger, there are no psychiatric casualties, or at least very few. . . . The medical specialist who had been appointed to act as the command psychiatrist suggested that an adequate survey should be made in an attempt to assess the health of the troops and that a rest center should be established where the overstrained might rest and recuperate. These suggestions were not accepted. Later he reported that as the strain of the siege increased, mental backwardness came to be more in evidence among the out-patients who were seeking escape from the intolerable in sickness and in military crime. Indeed, he came to recognize that approximately 50 per cent of all these outpatients showed evidence of some major psychiatric disorder. In his opinion at least 25 per cent of the garrison displayed a response to aerial attack in March 1942 that bordered on the pathological. By the end of April the proportion, in his considered opinion, had increased. . . .

"There was at this time in Malta, as elsewhere, a difference of opinion concerning the best methods of dealing with the progressive demoralization that comes to an individual taxed beyond his endurance . . . the "tough" school holds that the expression of fear in any form is a display of cowardice and should be treated as such. . . ."

In March 1942 a sign was put up in every gun position in Malta. It said:

- Fear is the weapon which the enemy employs to sabotage morale.
- Anxiety neurosis is the term used by the medical profession to commercialize fear.
- Anxiety neurosis is a misnomer which makes "cold feet" appear respectable.
- To give way to fear is to surrender to the enemy attack on your morale.
- To admit an anxiety neurosis is to admit a state of fear which is either unreasonable or has no origin in your conception of your duty as a soldier.
- If you are a man you will not permit your self-respect to admit an anxiety neurosis or to show fear.
- Do not confuse fear with prudence or impulsive action with bravery.
- Safety first is the worst of principles.
- In civil life "anxiety neurosis" will put you "on the club." In battle it brings you a bayonet in the bottom and a billet in a prisoner-of-war camp.

In Malta anxiety neurosis remained a dirty expression. The MO at SSQAHQ Malta who sent Reg Greer over to Imtarfa Hospital thought he might have a serious lung infection, "NYD chest C/O pain in the left side of chest anteriorly—1/52—more marked after exercise. Increasing dyspnoea past 6/12. Morning cough with expectoration and anorexia past 3/12. Loss of weight—1 and a half in 3/13 and general malaise." This time Reg Greer's bout of pleurisy had moved up from 1927–8 to "nine years ago," or 1933.

In April, Reg Greer came before the RAF medical officers at AHQ Malta; their diagnosis was that he was suffering from bronchial catarrh, not contracted in service, and "a well-developed anxiety neurosis," which was; the date and place of origin of the second was given as Malta, December 1942. The anxiety neurosis was moreover "aggravated by service in Malta under siege conditions and by unsatisfactory accommodation in which he was required to work." This time the pleurisy had retreated to seventeen years before, 1926, but the treatment had taken five months in hospital. Again they noted that he had arrived in Malta during the siege and that he had lost two stone and four pounds, his weight being nine stone and five pounds. (His enlisting weight was in fact ten stone and seven pounds.) For eight months he had been working underground. His temperature and pulse were normal. He could produce no sputum for examination. He could produce very few symptoms at all. Wing-Commander Knight and Flight-Lieutenant Dowd decided that "this Officer should be invalided from Malta and returned to Australia."

It was a month before F/O Greer got as far on his way home as Cairo. Mr. Admans came across him in the Kiwi Club. "You look terrible," he said. Reg Greer tore him off a strip.

"Been in Malta, jumping out of the signals truck into the slitty every time the bombers came over," said Mr. Admans, which was odd, because it was quite wrong. Mr. Admans felt quite sorry for Reg Greer, as everybody felt sorry for anyone who had endured the siege of Malta, which they mostly confused with the blitz. If civilians thought that he had endured the worst that the Luftwaffe could unleash, he let them think it.

How F/O Greer got from Cairo to Bombay and then to Devlali, I cannot say. In the crowded tent city of Devlali Reg Greer probably had to endure more uncomfortable conditions than he had encountered in Malta; inadequate sanitary arrangements were made worse by the mixing of men from all theaters of the war. Disease was rife, and boredom is no relief from stress. On 22 July he was admitted to No. 1 New Zealand Hospital Ship at Bombay, "in debilitated condition and showing signs of general exhaustion." After sixteen days he had "improved greatly in appearance and his general nervous stability" was "much better." The NZ Medical Corps Officer noted further that "his improvement during the last two weeks is such that the prognosis appears good and with an adequate spell should be suitable for duties in Australia in accordance with his training and ability."

At Fremantle they took another look at him and, finding him unusually fit in that he had been subjected neither to malaria nor bilharziasis nor amoebiasis, they granted him three weeks' leave and packed him off to Melbourne.

And there we met him on Spencer Street Station. My aunt asked me, "Do you know where you spent the night before you went to meet your father?"

"No," I answered, a little puzzled as to why she should ask.

"With me," she said, and waited for it to sink in.

"All night?"

"Your mother picked you up in the morning."

"I see."

When F/O Greer's three weeks were up, he was admitted to No. 6 RAAF Hospital at Heidelberg, and he stayed there for more than three weeks. There he was interviewed by Squadron-Leader Forgan, to whom he told the story of his life, in more detail than his wife and children had ever been given. Sick though he may have been Reg Greer remembered himself well enough to distort the truth, as I could see from his description of his newspaper career, which culminated in the impressive word "manager." Reg Greer was not a manager, but a rep. He continued the exaggeration of his weight loss, adding seven pounds to his enlistment weight and claiming that when he was evacuated his weight had fallen to 125 pounds. And he still allowed people to think that he had lived on Malta through the blitz.

These small lies might all be construed as permissible ploys in a bid for compassionate leave. Besides, Reg Greer was being loyal to his wife: "He had a lot of dreams last night, dreamt someone had tried to sell his wife frocks without coupons and when he got home he was very annoyed about it. His wife has always been very dependent on him and devoted to him. Suggest relationship between dream content and actual return from overseas with slightly modified home relationship." Squadron-Leader Forgan was doing well but not well enough. When Reg Greer enlisted his wife was a sheltered twenty-four; she had grown up a lot in three years and had come to some of her own conclusions about life, helped by the flattery of her dancing partners. Reg Greer's home-life was not slightly modified but completely transformed. If his marriage was to survive he was going to have to work on it. Now I know that in his description of his childhood and education there was not one word of truth, now I know that his wife and child were the only kin Reg Greer could ever call his own, I know that he was lying for me.

Lies are vile things, with a horrible life of their own. They contaminate the truth that surrounds them. Looking at the record of my father's desperate lying to Squadron-Leader Forgan, I am troubled by a nagging suspicion that the anxiety neurosis was a calculated performance. Reg Greer was not just a salesman, but a crack salesman. A salesman's chief asset is his trustability. He had learnt to use the techniques of manipulation in the desperate struggle for survival during the depression; S/L Forgan was putty in his hands. "Patient very keen to remain in RAAF," he noted. Actually the patient was very good at conveying the impression that he was keen to remain in the RAAF at the same time that he marshaled symptoms to ensure his discharge. At Heidelberg Hospital the professionals examined his urine, his feces, his sputum, auscultated his heart, lungs and abdomen, much the way that I have ferreted away in the archives for verification of his autobiography. ND. Nothing detected. No acid-fast facts to be found. Except that after three weeks of my mother's loving care and attention Reg Greer was losing the weight he had gained on the hospital ship.

On 11 October, 1943, the Central Medical Board agreed that F/O Greer should return to work, the kind of work that would allow him to live at home and sleep at nights in his own bed, but nine days later the patient was complaining that he could not carry on. "He has been at work for only three days and all his anxiety symptoms have returned," wrote S/L Forgan. "He feels that he cannot take the responsibility or stand the long hours of work. I now consider that he is unlikely to be able to carry on in the service, and recommend his discharge on medical grounds."

Reg Greer's war had lasted not quite two years. He joined the Returned Services League so that he could wear the badge and not be asked embarrassing questions about what he was doing in civvy street while Australians were dying in the Pacific. Everybody knew he had been on Malta during the siege, and that no more could be asked of any man. His marriage survived. On 5 February, 1945, my little sister was born. Seven months later the Japanese surrendered.

# SIR HAROLD GEORGE NICOLSON

---

SIR HAROLD NICOLSON reports here an incident in Parliament. A few days later he writes to his sons.

---

■

## FROM *The Diaries and Letters of Harold Nicolson*

DIARY                                                              *17th December, 1942*

Eden reads out a statement about the persecution of the Jews, and to our shame and astonishment a Labour Member[1] (having been deeply moved by a speech by Jimmy Rothschild) suggests that we should all stand up as a tribute. The Speaker says, "Such an action must be spontaneous," so everybody gets up including the Speaker and the reporters. It is rather moving in a way.

H.N. TO B.N. & N.N.                                                *20th December, 1942*
SISSINGHURST

Montgomery has assured us that he has "cut Rommel's panzer Divisions in two." It would seem that there was no truth in this. There is a certain anxiety in London regarding the boastfulness of Montgomery's communiqués. Nor do people enjoy the hunting terms which he is apt to use. People who admire him point out that Nelson and Baden-Powell were equally immodest and self-advertising.

The military arrived at Sissinghurst. It consisted of the Headquarters of a tank Brigade on exercise, heralded by a young officer of the name of Rubinstein. Recalling how but three days before I had stood in tribute to the martyred Jews of Poland, I was most polite to Captain Rubinstein. His parents, it appeared, live in Leicester. He told us that his Brigadier, plus five officers plus cook plus batmen, would appear by tea-time and wanted to stay the night. We showed him the brew-house, the oast-houses, Nigel's room, Ben's room and the loft beyond. He said that it would do nicely, and departed to inform his Headquarters what a pleasant little welcome was being prepared.

It was at that moment that Mummy remembered the onions stored on the floor of the loft. They number between two and three thousand. She said that the Army always stole onions and that we must remove them at any cost before they arrived. I said that we were only having a Brigadier and his officers and that (a) they would probably not want to steal more than three onions each, and (b) we should not miss them

---

[1] W. S. Cluse, M.P. for South Islington since 1935.

much if they did. She said that you could never tell with officers nowadays, so many of them were promoted from the ranks. So we got three
sacks and two shovels and all afternoon till darkness came we carried the
sacks across to the Priest's House and spread them on the floor of Pat's
room. We had scarcely finished with the last onion when the Brigadier
appeared. He was a nice well-behaved man and looked so little like an
onion-stealer that Mummy at once asked him to dinner.

# YAFFA ELIACH

THE HASIDIC JEWS of Eastern Europe, a pious and mystical sect dating from the eighteenth century, have traditionally illuminated the relationship of man to God with magical stories, and they continued this tradition even during the unspeakable horrors of the Holocaust. *Hasidic Tales of the Holocaust* were collected by Yaffa Eliach, who was born in Vilna and received a Ph.D. in Russian intellectual history at the Graduate Center of the City University of New York. Eliach verified the existence of the pits in this tale on a trip to Europe. The tale is based on a conversation between the Grand Rabbi of Bluzhov, Israel Spira, and Baruch Singer in January 1975.

■

## FROM *Hasidic Tales of the Holocaust*

### HOVERING ABOVE THE PIT

It was a dark, cold night in the Janowska Road Camp. Suddenly, a stentorian shout pierced the air: "You are all to evacuate the barracks immediately and report to the vacant lot. Anyone remaining inside will be shot on the spot!"

Pandemonium broke out in the barracks. People pushed their way to the doors while screaming the names of friends and relatives. In a panic-stricken stampede, the prisoners ran in the direction of the big open field.

Exhausted, trying to catch their breath, they reached the field. In the middle were two huge pits.

Suddenly, with their last drop of energy, the inmates realized where they were rushing, on that cursed dark night in Janowska.

Once more, the cold, healthy voice roared in the night: "Each of you dogs who values his miserable life and wants to cling to it must jump over one of the pits and land on the other side. Those who miss will get what they rightfully deserve—ra-ta-ta-ta-ta."

Imitating the sound of a machine gun, the voice trailed off into the night followed by a wild, coarse laughter. It was clear to the inmates that they would all end up in the pits. Even at the best of times it would have been impossible to jump over them, all the more so on that cold dark night in Janowska. The prisoners standing at the edge of the pits were skeletons, feverish from disease and starvation, exhausted from slave labor and sleepless nights. Though the challenge that had been given them was a matter of life and death, they knew that for the S.S. and the Ukrainian guards it was merely another devilish game.

Among the thousands of Jews on that field in Janowska was the Rabbi of Bluzhov, Rabbi Israel Spira. He was standing with a friend, a freethinker from a large Polish town whom the rabbi had met in the camp. A deep friendship had developed between the two.

"Spira, all of our efforts to jump over the pits are in vain. We only entertain the Germans and their collaborators, the Askaris. Let's sit down in the pits and wait for the bullets to end our wretched existence," said the friend to the rabbi.

"My friend," said the rabbi, as they were walking in the direction of the pits, "man must obey the will of God. If it was decreed from heaven that pits be dug and we be commanded to jump, pits will be dug and jump we must. And if, God forbid, we fail and fall into the pits, we will reach the World of Truth a second later, after our attempt. So, my friend, we must jump."

The rabbi and his friend were nearing the edge of the pits; the pits were rapidly filling up with bodies.

The rabbi glanced down at his feet, the swollen feet of a fifty-three-year-old Jew ridden with starvation and disease. He looked at his young friend, a skeleton with burning eyes.

As they reached the pit, the rabbi closed his eyes and commanded in a powerful whisper, "We are jumping!" When they opened their eyes, they found themselves standing on the other side of the pit.

"Spira, we are here, we are here, we are alive!" the friend repeated over and over again, while warm tears streamed from his eyes. "Spira, for your sake, I am alive; indeed, there must be a God in heaven. Tell me, Rebbe, how did you do it?"

"I was holding on to my ancestral merit. I was holding on to the coattails of my father, and my grandfather and my great-grandfather, of blessed memory," said the rabbi and his eyes searched the black skies above. "Tell me, my friend, how did you reach the other side of the pit?"

"I was holding on to you," replied the rabbi's friend.

# JOHN HORNE BURNS

JOHN HORNE BURNS, who grew up in Andover, Massachusetts, went to Harvard, and joined the army as a private in 1942. A year later he was an intelligence officer, serving in Casablanca and Algiers and then in Italy. *The Gallery,* from which the following excerpt is taken, is considered by many to be one of the most important novels to emerge from World War II.

■

FROM *The Gallery*

## FIRST PROMENADE

(CASABLANCA)

I remember the smell of the air in Casa, a potion of red clay and the dung of camels. That was the way the Ayrabs stank too.

A Liberty ship in convoy brought me to Casa from Camp Patrick Henry, Virginia. In the nineteen days of crossing the Atlantic, I remember that something happened to me inside. I didn't know what adjustment to make for where I was going, but I think I died as an American. I'd climbed the gangplank with some of that feeling of adventure with which all sodiers go overseas. All the pacifist propaganda of the twenties and thirties couldn't quite smother that dramatic mood of well-here-we-go-again-off-to-the-wars.

I remember the endless foul nights below deck, with the hatches battened, and the clunk of the depth charges, and the merchant marine eating like kings and sneering at us and our Spam-twice-a-day. We GI's were like pigs in the hold, bunks five-high to the block, latrines swilling and overflowing, and vomit or crap games on the tarpaulin-sheathed floor where we huddled. The sergeant was on the bottom tier, one inch off the floor, with his nose jutting into the rear end of the joe sleeping above him. The pfc was on the top, trying to sleep with his face against a ventilator. And everywhere a litter of barracks bags and M-1's, with every man making up deficiencies in his equipment at the expense of his neighbors. It was the first time I'd seen American soldiers stealing from one another. There were three hundred of us in that hold, looking down one another's windpipes. We lived off one another like lice. I'd believed that Americans liked to give one another elbow room, except in subways.

I remember the enforced calisthenics on the deck of the Liberty ship, the drill with the Mae Wests, the walking guard on deck lest Neptune should arise from the waves and goose the ship with his trident, the crap game that ran night and day throughout the voyage, the listening to the ship's guns spit out practice tracers. There were nurses and Red Cross girls and State Department secretaries on the boat deck, which was off limits to us. They took sun baths and dallied with the officers and screeched when the depth charges detonated. If a starboard wind blew it my way, I heard their laughter, stylized like a sound track for bobby-soxers.

I remember the harbor of Casa at 0700 hours. At first when I saw the cranes and the berths, I thought it was all a joke, and that we were really still at Hampton Roads. It took all day to disembark us replacements because the cargo security officer couldn't find a case of Coca-Cola and was worried about his date with a Casablancaise that evening. He had the one-up-on-you wisdom of one who's already been overseas, and he peddled his wisdom to us gratis:

—I tell ya, French gals can teach the American ones a trick or two.

We got two days' supply of C-rations, and we carried our M-1's and A-bags onto the soil of North Africa. The smell I'd sniffed out in the channel was now strong, like the tart sweatiness under the wing of a dying chicken. And the Ayrabs stood around our two-and-a-half-ton truck. They were wearing GI mattress covers. They held out their hands, smiling as cagily as poor relations. They had white teeth and red fezzes. We tried to buy some of those Ayrab chapeaux.

I remember the Place de France and the Boulevard de la Gare and the billboards of Publi-Maroc. There was a secret yellow bell tower I'd seen as photomontage for Humphrey Bogart. And the long cool Hôtel de Ville in the Place Lyautey, near palm trees, fountains, and an MP motor pool. However they might deal with the Ayrabs, the French had hit on a colonial architecture that seemed to grow naturally out of the pink soil of Morocco. There were stained stucco walls around the two Medinas, all of which were off limits to us.

Why is it called Casablanca? Because for all the smell there's a ghostly linen brilliance about the buildings clustered on their terraced levels. This White City is best seen at noon or sunset. I knew that I couldn't be anyplace else but in Africa. There's something festering here, something hermetically sealed. With the exception of the indigenous Ayrabs, all Caucasians here seem to be corpse intruders, animated by a squeaking desire to be somewhere else. The restlessness of Casablanca is of the damned. It's a place where all the tortures of the twentieth century meet and snicker at one another, like Ayrab women under their veils marketing in the Suk.

—What I mean to say is, I'm going to start chasing some of this French stuff tonight.

—And I'm plenty pissed off at Miss Lucy Stout, who taught third-year French at Coolidge High. Ya need more than a bong-swahr in this town.

—J'aime le jambon quand il est bon.

I think it was at Casablanca that the bottom dropped out of my personality. Americans profess to a neatness of soul because their country is Protestant, spacious, and leery of abstracts. Now I'm an American uprooted. I'm in a foreign land where I must use a ration card, where there's no relation between the money in circulation and the goods to buy with it. This was the only way I could explain to myself the looks I got from the French and the Ayrabs. That housewife who protested she was born in Lyon was thinking about the difference between my lunch and hers. That foxy old Ayrab selling leather wallets knew I was almost as rich as the Caïd. That splayfooted garçon who brought me Bière la Cigogne, tasting like straw soup, wondered whether he might have sniped at me in Fedhala on November 8, 1942. For the first time I saw the cancer of the world outside of the United States, where we put nice sterile bandages over any open sores, and signs of Men Working by sewers.

I remember that a truck carried us to a staging area outside Casa. Around this camp was barbed wire to keep us and the Ayrabs on our respective sides. But such arrangements never work, because of the x factor of human curiosity.

—Yas, ya're repple-depple boys now. Ya'll get to know these sandy tents so well. Beds made of planks and chicken wire. Ten percent pass quota. Rushes to the pro station. Details we dream up just to keepya out of mischief. . . . And don't ya dare try to write ya mom about ya sorrows. That's what the army has censorship for. . . . The slip of a lip may sink a ship, but the slip of ya pen may upset the Congress of the United States.

I remember the Old Man of repple-depple. He was a major. Once he'd been a lieutenant colonel. We heard that at Salerno he got the idea of marching his battalion in parade formation up the beach. The battalion didn't exist any more, and neither did his lieutenant-colonelcy. So now he toughened up infantry replacements. He used to walk all over camp waving his stock and wearing his campaign ribbons. He loved to make inspections. He always wore leggins. Sometimes he carried a bull's pizzle to beat the Ayrabs with. And at all hours his voice came over his personal public-address system, through the whirling sand and the flapping lonely tents:

—Men, I know what war is . . . you don't . . . yet. . . .

Evenings he might be seen at the Automobile Club in Casa with a French WAC officer built like Danielle Darrieux. But he had trouble with the parachutists in our repple-depple. They'd shoot holes in their tents when they couldn't get out on pass. Then our major would drive through the areas in a jeep, with a tommy gun pointed out of his sound truck.

At midnight the parachutists would take off under the barbed wire for Casa, for at reveille everybody answered to everybody else's name. In repple-depples the noncoms were only acting, with brassards pinned sheepishly to their arms. Even our first sergeants were only casuals themselves—privates. So they couldn't chew us out too much because we'd get them later at the Bar Montmartre or at the Select or at Pepita's, and we'd fix them up with Marie the Pig, who was malade.

I remember that at Casablanca it dawned on me that maybe I'd come overseas to die. Thus I was put for the first time in my life against a wall that I couldn't explain away by the logic of Main Street or the Weltanschauuing of Samuel Goldwyn. I'd read of the sickness of Europe and shrugged my shoulders—Oh those furreners. It didn't occur to me that they were members of the human race. Only Americans were.

And I remember finding myself potentially expendable according to the Rules of Land Warfare, trapped in a war which (I said) was none of my making. So I began to think of my Life with the tenderness of a great artist. I clasped myself fondly to myself. I retreated into my own private world with the scream of a spinster when she sees a mouse. And I remember that I saw the preciousness of the gift of my Life, a crystal of green lymph, fragile and ephemereal. That's all I am, but how no-accounting everything else is, in juxtaposition to the idea of Me! What does anything else matter? The world ceases to exist when I go out of it, and I have no one's assurance but my own for the reality of anything. Those who were machine-gunned in 1918—it's the same as though they had never been.

I remember that I began to think these things in Casablanca, though I didn't utter them. Therefore in a sense I went mad. Those who brood on death in wartime find that every pattern of life shrivels up. Decency becomes simply a window-shade game to fool the neighbors, honor a tremolo stop on a Hammond organ, and courage simply your last hypocrisy with yourself—a keeping up with the Joneses, even in a foxhole.

Oh my sweet Life, my lovely Life, my youth—all destined for a bullet. . . . Perhaps it were better if my mother hadn't borne me. I wondered whether my father really wanted children, or was feeling sorry for himself after a rough day at the office.

I remember in Casa going to the Gare on MP duty from the reppledepple to see that some of our joes got loaded on the forty-by-eights—forty hommes and eight chevaux. They were going to Oran, then to Algiers, then to Italy. We'd heard that General Patton had GI's walking about in the Algiers summer in OD's and neckties. Even the French could tell what was cooking.

—Forty American men in a boxcar like cattle. Wish I had my camera. The American people ought to know about this. Wish I could write my congressman.

    —They look like the French Foreign Legion.

    —Are your canteens full, men?

    —The Ayrabs sell vin rouge all along the route.

    —And buy the shirt offn your back.

    —This is an outrage to American manhood.

    —Americans are dying in Italy right now. The American people know that, don't they?

    —Yes, but do they care as long as we preserve their standard of living for a few more years? D'ya think they give one healthy you-know-what when they get up in the morning?

    —See the chaplain. . . .

O my Life, my green ignorant dreaming Life! I said so long to them as the forty-by-eights left the Gare at Casa.

And when I remembered that soon it would be my turn to go to Oran, I didn't go back to the repple-depple, even though my pass said I should. We kept on our MP brassards, and bigtimed it through Casablanca in our leggins. The bars didn't open till 1700 hours. So we went to the Vox Theater, which the Red Cross was operating, and saw a movie in technicolor. It was all about the glory of the Army Air Forces, those same ones who at the repple-depple bitched about the calisthenics and the sleeping on chicken wire.

I remember waiting for it to get dark in Casa because as an American I'd all sorts of ideas about the Romance of Evening. I wanted a girl, but it was the American code to pick them up in twos, with your buddy. From high school on I'd doubledated. Going steady and gettin a little lovin weren't private affairs, because they were done in parked cars. I couldn't understand how a French sailor, and cold sober too, could walk up to a girl by herself, talk to her, and take her arm. No sense of shame at all. French love and all that. I thought that love, till you got married, was a business of foursomes. Otherwise it seemed something rather sneaky. You were expected to kid back and forth at some bathing beach or rollerdrome. Eventually you reached over somewhat sheepishly and the foursome broke up into two twosomes.

    —Nossir, nothin in the world like American wimmin. Maybe a little independent, but then ya can't spend all ya time in bed.

    —I never did understand those Lysol ads and all that talk about keepin yaself dainty.

    —I knew a Polish beast once. She loved it.

    —French girls do things that no decent American woman would.

    —A chaplain once explained to me the difference between love and lust. But I can't remember exactly what he told me.

    —All I know is, boy, when you're in love, everything you do together seems beautiful. . . .

Those Casablancaises—it wasn't hard to get myself invited to their homes if I came armed with half my PX rations. Maman always claimed she wasn't born in North Africa, but of course France after June, 1940, wasn't fit to live in. Her girls went to the cinéma and to bicycle club and to dancing school. They loved to be taught American songs by rote. That was one way to kill an afternoon. They liked to be called Jackie.

But I remember that the surer bets were in the bars. There the widows of French officers sipped crème de menthe. Not a one that didn't claim mon mari had been killed in Tunisie; not a one whose rank had ever been lower than commandant.

—Je suis seule ce soir avec mes rêves. . . .

I remember how the fetid fragrance of Casablanca let up in the evenings. The oleanders came out with the bats. There was a hum and clatter from the New and Old Medinas. Little Ayrabs ceased their operating and promoting. The sound of donkeys wheezing and snorting and stalling died with their clopclopping in the streets. Then I knew that I was far, far from the States, and that nothing I had brought with me of my own personal universe would make Casa anything other than Casablanca, a hinterland of secrecy, where German submarine captains came ashore in civvies and drank by my elbow in bars.

I remember that I first knew loneliness in Casablanca, the loneliness that engenders quietism. I was stripped of distractions and competitions since I no longer was a citizen of my own hermetical country, with ideas on progress, better homes, and sanitation. These thoughts often assailed me on the benches in the Parc Lyautey after sunset. My loneliness was that of a drunken old man sitting in a grotto and looking out on an icy sea at world's end. Then, sinking away under the weight of time, I'd be constrained to draw down the head of her on the bench beside me. I'd kiss her in an attempt to focus all my longing and my uneasiness.

—Demain sans doute il fera beau, et après-demain, et la semaine prochaine.

—L'ombre s'enfuit. . . .

Through her hair I counted the spines of barbed wire in the enclosure of the tank park. There the French kept old tanks lined up for a surprise review by General de Gaulle.

Along with the barren names of Cazes and Mogador and Mazagan I remember birdlike ones, Henriette and Marie and Suzanne and a chorus of others who rode their bicycles by me on Saturday afternoons and made me teach them to jitterbug. They were almost like pretty boys, those Casablancaises. They had the pinched brilliance of old paupers' garments, lovingly mended and darned.

—Darling, they said, il faut gémir quand nous faisons l'amour. Et la prochaine fois je te prie de m'apporter un peu de chewing gum.

I remember Casa. . . .

■ **1943** ■

# DAN DAVIN

IN WORLD WAR II the New Zealand novelist and short story writer Dan Davin saw active service in Greece and Crete, served at GHQ in Cairo, and was an intelligence officer with the Second New Zealand Division in the Western Desert and Italy.

■

## FROM *East Is West*

It was the first day he had been able to get around without his crutch and so the sergeant was rather pleased with himself. In fact, although it was still an hour to midday, he thought he deserved a beer. The Sudanese barman gave him a bottle of Stella and a glass and he hobbled back to the table where he had left his writing things. He put down the bottle and glass and then, supporting himself with his left hand on the chair, swung his left leg under the table. He lowered himself carefully on to the seat, with his weight on his good leg. The other one stuck out under the table and the heavy plaster rested on the iron bar that did duty for a heel.

It was still winter; so, though the sun outside was hot on the empty parade-ground, in here it was cool and there was no need to shut the windows or draw the blinds. As he looked out to the desert beyond the barrack huts he smiled. It wasn't so bad. This was one rest camp where they really did leave you alone. If only he didn't have this letter to write.

He poured the beer out slowly and watched the bubbles spring to the surface in a fine froth.

Two other chaps came in and began to play ping-pong in the far corner. Before long they had their shirts off and were playing only in their shorts. They still hadn't quite got rid of the yellow stage of jaundice.

The sergeant sipped his beer, then lit a cigarette and took a couple of draws, rather fast. A fly flicked at his mouth, thirsty, came back and flicked again. He brushed it away every time it came till it gave up and settled on his writing pad. It crawled till it found the place where the sweat of his hand had moistened the paper. Fingers spread so as not to give it the advantage of the draught, his hand smacked down. He brushed the squashed body aside and tore off that sheet. But there was another sheet beneath, just as blank. He picked up his pen, suddenly.

"Dear Mrs. Curtis," he wrote. Then he put the pen down again. What the hell was he going to say? He'd written these letters before and it hadn't been easy. But this one seemed to be impossible altogether. What could he say? He could feel sorry for Curtis all right, poor sod. He was dead now, anyway, and it didn't matter much what sort of bloke he'd been. But that was no good. You couldn't very well say that to his mother. Was there anything in the whole rotten business you could say to her?

What did it have to happen for anyway? Why should he have to write the bloody letter? It was only a bit of bad luck he'd come across Curtis at all.

Only it had looked like good luck then. Or it would have if he hadn't been so bomb-happy at the time that he took everything for granted. You took everything for granted at a time like that, when you'd just had your tank brew up under you and seen the only other bloke who managed to get out take a burst of Spandau in the chest and face before he even hit the ground.

He'd dragged George Black for a few yards until he saw there was no future in it. George was dead. The bullets were flying and the ammo in the tank would go up any minute. George slumped back when he let go. His shirt had ridden up the back and you could see where the bullets had come out.

Smoke, very dense and black, was pouring out of the tank. There was a terrific stink of oil and petrol and explosive. It wasn't the only tank either. You could see others of them going up in the same way all over the ridge.

He'd got his breath and his nerve back now. Without looking at George he jumped to his feet and bolted into the smoke, going down wind with it. Anything to get away before she went up for good.

So it didn't seem surprising when he found himself being hauled into the cab of a Dodge pick-up. Or even when he saw it was Curtis and him with a captain's pips up, though the last time he'd seen him was in camp when they were Territorials and Curtis had only one stripe.

Curtis leaned across him and slammed the door to. The driver got back into gear and the truck went on, hell for leather.

"What happened, Sergeant? You all right?"

That brought him to a bit. Sergeant. It used to be Bob in the old days.

"OK, thanks. Tank went up. Only me and George got out. And they got George."

He felt dopey and at the same time he wanted to talk. But he couldn't bring himself to call Curtis "sir." And he wasn't the sort of chap you could talk to about old George.

After a while he pulled himself together. "Where are we off to?"

"B Ech HQ at Brigade," Curtis said.

As good as anywhere else. It'd been a good tank. You'd never get a pal like old George again.

But B Ech was pulling out when they got there. There was a fat major stamping round, giving all sorts of orders. A bit of a flap on.

"Get your truck into the convoy, Curtis," said the major. "There's a column of Jerry armor coming along Trigh Capuzzo. We'll all be overrun and in the bag, if we don't get out of this a bit more smartly. Haven't you got that kit aboard yet, Rumbold?" He had turned toward a little fellow who was trying to shoulder a valise as big as himself into the back of a staff-car.

The sergeant couldn't see any sign of a Jerry column. But he didn't care. It was their show now. They were officers. Let them handle it. None of his business. He'd had enough for just now.

"Come on, Grace, get a move on," said Curtis.

The driver took the Dodge into the column. It was in desert formation but pretty ragged. The front vehicles began to move off without waiting. Those behind started off as best they could and began to find their places. The staff-car was the last to get away, the major even helping Rumbold with the camp-bed he was in such a hurry. He cut across the Dodge's bows as he went up to the front. The sand behind him swirled in their open window.

"Put up that window, will you, Sergeant?" said Curtis.

"It looks as if we're going east," said the sergeant.

"Where else? The show's a wash-out. You tankies have let him run all over you."

The sergeant flushed This from a man who wore the black beret, even if he was in B Ech. But he said nothing.

Behind them, half left, on the ridge, they saw the flying sand of a column. Curtis opened the trap in the roof and looked through his glasses.

"Jerry," he said, bending his knees and coming down. "Put your foot on it, Grace."

The driver went on at the same pace. He had to keep in formation.

A black gusher of smoke came up between two of the trucks in front. The convoy kept on. Another and another. One of the leading trucks, apparently unhit, began to blaze all the same. Men spilled over the tailboard on to the sand.

"Shall we pick some of them up, sir?" said Grace.

"No time. Let one of the three-tonners do it. They've got more room."

But he felt the sergeant's stare. "All right. Stop."

"Only three of you. In the back. Hurry."

Another truck, fifteen-hundredweight, pulled up. A young lieutenant got out of the cab.

"Pile in with my blokes, the rest of you," he said. "Come on, you're not out blackberrying." He watched them aboard, smiling. The sergeant began to feel better.

"They're all aboard, Grace," Curtis said. "What are you waiting for? They're bound to get us if we hang round any longer."

As they moved off there was a crash behind them.

The sergeant looked back. At first there was nothing but smoke. When it cleared he saw the other truck coming on. The officer was standing with his head and shoulders halfway out of the trap, his binoculars resting on the roof of the cab in front. He waved. The sergeant waved back. A good bloke.

The convoy had become a single column now with wide intervals between trucks. You could feel all they had in common was that they wanted to go fast and in the same direction.

B Ech bastards, the sergeant thought. He was already homesick for his squadron. What had happened to them all? Were things really as bad as this?

"Step on it, Grace."

"Yes, sir," said the driver. He drove at the same steady pace. He's all right, that chap, the sergeant thought.

"Any idea where we are?" he asked.

"El Gubbi is on the right somewhere," said Curtis. "We should get to the wire soon."

The way he said it didn't sound as if he had much idea. They seemed to be going south-east now. So they'd probably strike the wire all right. Anyhow, it was Curtis's business. He was the officer. And didn't he know it? But he was the officer all the same. You couldn't get past that. But the sergeant couldn't help remembering they used to call him Blanco in the Terries.

Curtis took out a packet of Players. The sergeant hadn't had a smoke since the battle began that morning. But he was damned if he was going to ask for one. He looked straight ahead through the windscreen. The sand from the truck in front uncoiled and expanded toward them, like a spring. Curtis was tapping a cigarette against the packet.

"Have one?"

"Thanks," said the sergeant and took it. There were tears of relief in his eyes. The driver's face looked very set.

"What about the driver?" the sergeant said.

"Have one, Grace?" said Curtis, quite amiably.

"Thanks very much, sir," said the driver.'

It was getting on towards four when they came to the gap in the wire. There were no MPs there. Trucks had converged on it from all directions. You could see from all the different unit signs mixed up together, odds and sods of all sorts, that there'd been a pretty fair MFU, a real balls-up. Even if everyone hadn't been going the wrong way.

"We'll be hours getting through at this rate," said Curtis.

"The sergeant got out of the truck.

"I'll have one too," Curtis said. He got out and began to unbutton his fly. But the sergeant was walking towards the gap.

"Where are you off to?" called Curtis.

"Must try and help straighten this out," said the sergeant.

All it needed was someone to see that too many didn't try to get through at once. Soon he had the traffic going in a steady stream. Luckily no Jerry planes had turned up in time.

The Dodge came up. "No point in staying there all night," Curtis said. "You might as well jump aboard. Let some other mug take a turn."

On the other side the trucks had streamed away as fast as they got through. No one had any notion where the leading truck had got to. The convoy was well scattered, disorganized.

After a while the sergeant saw they might as well give up trying to keep in convoy. "Let's pull out and have something to eat," he said. "If you've got any grub, that is."

"There's plenty in the back," Curtis said. "But do you think it's all right? He might be pretty close behind us." He seemed rather subdued.

"Might as well take a chance. We can always bolt for it."

They got out and went round to the back of the truck. Curtis undid the flap. The three men who'd got aboard and his batman were sitting there, with knees drawn up. Their faces were caked with the fine sand that had got through the flap. They climbed out stiffly. One of them was a corporal.

The batman got some biscuits and bully and a tin of cheese. "Here you are, sir." Curtis took some.

"Have some, Sergeant?" said the batman.

"Thanks, chum."

"There you are now, Corp." The batman passed what was left to the corporal and he began to share it out.

"Think I should brew up and make a cup of char, sir?" said the batman.

"Christ, no. No time."

The others all looked glum.

"What's the next move?" said the sergeant.

"There's nothing to stop the Jerries between here and Mersa. We'll have to go south-east a good bit before we turn up to join the reserves there."

"Nothing between us and Mersa?" said the sergeant.

"I know what I'm talking about."

The sergeant shrugged. Perhaps he did know. His own unit had been fighting off and on for three days. He had no idea what had been happening anywhere beyond what you could see from the tank. And not much about that either. But if Curtis was right things were pretty bad.

"Planes," said one of the men.

There were three of them, coming out of the sun.

The sergeant had noticed a Bren in the back of the truck. He grabbed it and fitted a magazine.

"Put her on my shoulder," said the corporal, running round to his front.

"OK, Corp." He rested the barrel on the corporal's shoulder and waited.

"What's your unit?" he asked.

"I was order room corporal at B Ech HQ."

"Good for you." He wasn't sure what he meant. But he liked the corporal.

"Just as well the traffic's mostly through the gap," the corporal said. "What a target it was."

The planes curved away and down towards a column of transport that had followed them through the gap and was now dispersed on the ridge opposite. They peeled off and dived, machine-gunning and bombing. There was some scattered AA fire.

When the planes had dropped their stuff and wheeled off west again, the sergeant and the corporal walked back to the truck.

"That sounded like Jerry AA to me," said the sergeant.

"Rubbish, Sergeant," Curtis said. He got up and brushed the sand from his battledress. "It can't be. They can't have got here already."

"The planes did look a bit like Tomahawks," said the corporal.

"Nonsense." Contradicting them made Curtis feel more confident. "We'll drive over and see what the news is."

This time the sergeant kept a look out from the trap.

"Could I borrow your glasses?" he called down.

Curtis got them out of their case. But already the truck was close enough.

"Jerries," the sergeant said as he shot down through the trap. "Quick, driver, left hand down." They were no more than a couple of hundred yards away.

"We'll have to turn it in," Curtis said.

The sergeant stared at him. His mouth was slightly open, face pale. He did not meet the sergeant's eye.

"Flat out," said the sergeant across Curtis to the driver. There was a slight flush on the driver's cheekbone and a little ridge of cartilage riding up and down where the jaws joined. The truck righted itself as it came out of the swerve, the driver's foot hard on the accelerator.

They were running across the enemy's front now, a good target. The sergeant could see Jerries at the turrets of a few tanks which had been hidden behind the ridge. Resting up or getting ready to laager for the night.

A rip of bullets smashed through glass.

"It's no go," said Curtis. "We'd better turn it in."

The bullets had smashed diagonally through the right-hand window, above the driver's head. The sergeant stared through the windscreen to the front, watching the desert come flying to meet them and waiting for the finishing burst. If he were driving he would hardly have had the spare energy to feel like this. He did not want to look at Curtis.

He got up and peered over the edge of the trap, looking back. The enemy trucks were well behind, perhaps already out of effective range. He came down into the cab again.

"I knew we shouldn't have stopped there," Curtis said.

They drove on and didn't stop till it was safe to take a bearing.

"Don't you think we should head up towards the coast?" the sergeant said.

"They're probably all along the coast road by now," Curtis said. "They'll have come down Halfaya Pass, I'll bet."

He had the compass and the sergeant was too tired to argue. But he suspected the navigation was very much by guess and by God. It would have been more comfortable if they'd had the coast road to guide them.

Last light came.

"I think it's safe to turn more to the north now," Curtis said.

"Or perhaps brew up and bed down for the night?" suggested the sergeant. There didn't seem much sense in just plunging on through the night. And it was risky, too.

"We must try and join up with the rest at Mersa as soon as we can."

But he told the driver to stop all the same and they had some more bully and biscuits. The men were getting a bit jittery. They'd obviously got Curtis pretty well summed up already. They sat off in a group by themselves in the sand and talked in low voices. The driver was evidently telling them how close they'd been to the bag. The batman skipped about, putting things away. The sergeant was left with Curtis. Curtis didn't talk much. He had become more and more the officer as he felt his prestige going down.

"Come on men," he said at last. "No time to waste. All aboard."

The sergeant drove for a while. Then Curtis took over. The driver was supposed to be having a sleep. But it was his truck and, though both Curtis and the sergeant drove well, he was uneasy till it was his turn again. The sergeant dozed, waking at heavier jolts, then going off again. Once he was back in his tank just after it caught fire. Only this time the hatch had jammed. After that he didn't sleep for quite a while and even managed to ask Curtis for a cigarette. When it was finished he slept again.

A shell had smashed the tank track. Yet it seemed to be going on clanking.

"Sounds like a bit of wire or something caught in the mudguard," he woke to hear the driver saying. "We'd better stop and have a look."

They got out and had a look. The truck had hit a single strand of wire and dragged it along.

"A minefield," said the sergeant.

"It can't be," Curtis said. "They've never got as far as this."

"It might be one of ours. We'd be wiser to stop where we are till first light. There's not even a moon."

"Look," said the driver. "Flares."

They turned round. Back the way they had come the flares were shooting up into the sky, lingering, then dropping slowly to a darkness that closed on them before they reached the ground.

"Jerries," said Curtis.

"Might be our chaps."

"I tell you, Sergeant, there's nothing to stop them between where they are and Mersa. We've got to get on."

"I think we should stop where are till first light. We'll be able to see then whether we're in a minefield or not."

"And get picked up by the Jerries in the morning just for fear of a few imaginary mines? I thought you had more guts than that, Sergeant." This was his revenge for the afternoon.

"I still think it's crazy."

"It doesn't matter what you think. I'm the superior officer here and I say we're going on." There had been a fresh outbreak of flares.

The driver had unwound the wire from the axle. They went back to the cab.

"I'll tell you what," Curtis said, amiable again. "You take a spell at the wheel and I'll get out on the mudguard, just to please you."

The sergeant took her along slowly. The driver sat beside him, very uneasy, and then after a bit climbed out on the left. The sergeant's eyes strained out through the windscreen to the moving glimmer of desert in front. He thought how thin the flooring was that separated him from the upward blast that might come at any moment.

When it came it flung him through the door and out on his face. The flash left his eyes and he was staring at the sand, his ears singing on this side of a wall of deafness. He got up still stupid and staggered out of the black fumes. He found himself at the back of the truck.

"Mines," he said to the faces that stared out at him.

Then he remembered Curtis and the driver. He came round to the front again. Curtis seemed to be trying to raise himself on his hands and each time falling on his face, half-sideways. The driver was coming round the bonnet from the other side. He seemed all right.

Curtis was lying on his face when they got to him, no longer trying to get up. The sergeant turned him on his back. His right leg was gone,

from the thigh. The left fioot was hanging from the shinbone by a few
ragged strands.

"Get out your field-dressings," the sergeant said to the others who
had all come up. He got out his own as well.

Curtis was beginning to struggle again. "Sit on him," said the sergeant to the driver. "He mustn't see his legs."

The driver sat on Curtis and lit him a cigarette. The corporal knelt
and kept his fingers pressed down on the artery just below where it joined
the groin. The sergeant from the other side tried to find enough thigh to
get a purchase for the tourniquet. Curtis had begun to scream now and
heaved from time to time. Each time the blood gulped out more swiftly
than ever. The dressings were soaking already. The sergeant did his best
with the tourniquet and then turned to the left leg. The ragged trouser
was in the way.

"Anyone got a knife?"

Nobody had, but the sergeant remembered seeing one in the cab.
Quicker to find it himself. His own foot was giving trouble now but he
got to the cab, fumbled for the jack-knife which had slipped down behind
the seat, got it and came back. He got on a second tourniquet and
dressings.

Suddenly the corporal flopped. He had fainted. Curtis gave a sort of
final heave and sat up. He saw what had happened to his legs.

"My legs," he said, "Jesus Christ, my legs."

The blood was still coming from the right thigh, in spite of the
tourniquet. Curtis got weaker and his voice quieter. "Why did it have to
be me?" he kept moaning. "Oh, sweet Jesus Christ, why did it have to be
me?"

The corporal came up and tried to stop the bleeding with his fingers
on the artery again.

"Shall I make a cup of char on the Primus, Sergeant?" said the
batman.

"OK. Here, corporal, give us a strain on this, will you?"

But it was no good. The blood kept getting away, soaking the dressings, the sand. And the pain was getting worse as the shock passed off.
Curtis seemed to be going out of his mind with it. Sometimes he cried
like a baby and called out for his mother.

Then he seemed to get himself under control again. He recognized
the sergeant.

"Bob," he said, "shoot me, Bob, for Christ's sake. I can't stand it.
Shoot me."

The sergeant crouched beside him.

He did not know whether it was a long time or a short time before
Curtis died.

He had to cut away the boot from his own foot then. Its aching did not let him sleep and he kept hearing Curtis and seeing Curtis, though Curtis was silent now under his last blanket. He was glad when first light came.

The corporal and he stabbed about with bayonets till they found a spot where there were no mines. They dug a grave and buried Curtis. His body was the color of skimmed milk.

The batman made tea and they had breakfast, bully and biscuit. The driver stood with his mug in his hand, looking at the wrecked wheel and mudguard and shaking his head. The sergeant's foot was too swollen now for him to walk.

When the column of Indians who had leaguered a mile away that night rescued them from the minefield the sergeant had to be carried.

If it had been poor old George that had asked me I'd have done it for him, the sergeant was thinking now. I'd have known it was all right if it'd been a pal like George.

He hobbled up to the bat to get another beer. "Dear Mrs. Curtis," was as far as he'd got. It was as far as he'd got yesterday, and the day before.

# GEOFFREY WOLFF

---

THE CRITIC AND NOVELIST Geoffrey Wolff was born in Los Angeles. He has written a biography of Harry Crosby, *Black Sun,* and four novels, among them *Bad Debts* and *Providence.* The following excerpt comes from an autobiographical work, *The Duke of Deception: Memories of My Father.*

---

■

## FROM *The Duke of Deception: Memories of My Father*

A few days before Pearl Harbor my father flew to London by way of the Azores and neutral Lisbon, where he dropped a few hundred dollars of expense money betting against a Luftwaffe officer shooting craps at the Estoril Casino. His plane was shot at when it crossed France, and the night my father landed in England bombs fell on the East London docks, raising huge columns of fire into the searchlight-crossed sky. He was afraid, he confessed, but not enough afraid to want to be any place other than where he was.

North American had given my father the title of Assistant Chief Designer, and the responsibility to work gremlins out of the RAF's new Mustangs. He was installed in a four-room flat on Park Lane, a block from the Dorchester and overlooking Hyde Park. Officers of the American embassy had dubbed my father an Air Corps major, a common practice that protected him with military privileges under the Geneva Convention were England invaded and occupied. The honorary rank mattered to him, crucially, for the rest of his life.

When Father left us in New York Mother drove the cream Packard with its red interior aimlessly around America, and settled finally into a California shorefront apartment at Hermosa Beach. Shortly after Pearl Harbor a midget Japanese sub had lobbed a few rounds at the Santa Barbara Biltmore, missing it but depressing waterfront rents. There were soldiers and heavy artillery pieces set beneath the boardwalk on the beach in front of our place, ready to blow away the Nips when they waded ashore, any minute now. The soldiers were friendly; they teased me and gave me candy and chevrons, which Mother sewed on my T-shirts. They flirted with her, innocent kid stuff, and Mother was friendly to them, and let the soldiers buy her a beer or a coke while I filled a beachside jukebox with their nickels, playing "Pistol-Packin' Mama" and "Deep in the Heart of Texas" till I ran them out of coins.

My father stayed fourteen months in London, until early 1943. Duke liked being part of those nights of Blitz and days of Churchill. He was proud that his father had been born in London, and in short order he found Mullins of Bond Street, a genealogical boutique where he bought a book bound in soft red calf, *A History of the Name Ansell*, tracing the family of his grandmother Sarah Ansell back to the *Domesday Book*, and from it he chose a coat of arms for the "Ansell Wolff" line.

He liked British manners and the mumbly, marble-chewing accent of the upper class. He couldn't get enough of understatement, the self-deprecation of the squadron leader who had just returned from his ninth flight of the day with his Spitfire shot full of holes and three ME-109s confirmed killed, *Fox gave us rather of a chase, never mind, rum job for him.*

I wonder how much he tried to sneak past them. Americans, socially insecure, will believe anything. Hints about "Sent Pawl's" and "Bones" register without challenge; I heard my father tell a Yale man that they were together in the same class at Yale, in the same entry of the same college, and the man was ashamed of his memory lapse rather than suspicious. The English work differently: *Duke, is it? Duke of what, old man? Oh quite, I see, Duke of nothing then, rilly. At Eton were you? What years? Then you know Bamber Lushington? No? Then you weren't at Eton, were you?*

If Arthur III stepped delicately through the minefields of British social complication, he ran amok with easy credit. Field boots from Lobb, lighters and pipes from Dunhill, tobacco from Fribourg & Treyer, a collapsible silver drinking cup from Garrard. Hawes & Curtis made his shirts, Huntsman his hacking jacket. Holland and Holland contributed a matched pair of guns, Foyle's threw in a few first editions, and North American Aviation—advised that their Duke was blitzing Mayfair and Belgravia—brought my father home and fired him.

When he came home in disgrace, with a steamer trunk filled with booty and no end of entertaining routines about life under the bombs, he tried at once to enlist in the Air Corps. Everything went against him: his eyes were weak, he stammered, he had a bad back, his teeth were unsatisfactory. The Navy wouldn't have him either, but the Army said his teeth made the worst case against him, so he had all his uppers pulled, and after he got a plate Mother and I drove him to Fort Ord, where he tried one last time to enlist, and was turned away. I remember his blank silence, and for the first time he frightened me. He drove us home to Hermosa Beach and disappeared into Mexico. Mother bailed him out of jail three days later in Tijuana. The charge was drunk and disorderly.

He got a job soon enough with Rohr Aircraft. Jobs were easy then, and no one took time to meditate on the character of prospective employees; if men were sane, American, and exempt from military service, they were just fine.

My parents bought a new-built tract house in Chula Vista as soon as Rohr signed Duke on. The house hadn't been painted, the front lawn hadn't been seeded, when he was offered a better job as chief engineer of a B-24 and B-29 modification center in Birmingham, Alabama. We had owned and lived in that little house less than three weeks when my father sold it, and our last night there my mother read me the fable of Pandora's box, and I lay awake staring at my father's locked steamer trunk.

My father was paid more than a thousand a month in Birmingham, a lot of money then. The plant where he worked was run by an engineering firm called Bechtel, McCone and Parsons, and my father's principal superiors were Ralph Parsons and John McCone, neither of whom approved of Duke's character, both of whom recognized his energy and resourcefulness.

The plant Duke supervised was a huge network of hangars beside the airport to which bombers fresh off assembly lines were flown by ferry pilots to Birmingham for changes or additions to their bombsights, armaments, navigational gear, or interiors. As soon as they were modified, other ferry pilots flew them to Guam or England or India. The pace of work was hectic, the pressure to perform extreme, the cost of error mortal.

It was among Duke's inspirations in Birmingham to hire midgets to work the tight places inside wings and fuselages, to rivet joints and lead wires through places inaccessible to grosser persons. To round them up, my father sent hiring scouts with contracts and pockets filled with money to cities across America, where they hung around race tracks and booking agencies and penny arcades and carnivals, and within a few weeks a new labor force was on the case. (Later, when the war was winding down, just before my father was fired, his midgets were laid off, and I saw them protesting, milling in their city clothes with signs and sandwich boards outside the locked chain-link gate of the dismal plant, protesting how things were with a single word: UNFAIR!)

At the beginning in Birmingham my father rode high, and so did Rosemary: "I was drunk with all that money." We spent a few weeks in a suite at the Tutweiler Hotel, looking for suitable quarters for a chief engineer, and then moved into a showplace on Beechwood Road, directly across the street from the entrance to the Mountain Brook Club.

The house was white, with a columned slate terrace surrounded by lilac and magnolia trees. Live oaks grew from an acre and more of lawn that sloped down to a boxwood hedge, and there was a formal garden out back, and a Victory Garden for vegetables, and to tend these growing things a gardener was employed, an old black man with one arm who

ingratiated himself to Duke by holding open the Packard's door when my
father left for work, saying "Mornin', Cunnel Woof." The rest of the day
the gardener napped under a shadetree, with a Mason jar of my mother's
lemonade beside him, watching the grass grow, and sometimes shooing
away flies with his good arm.

I remembered this house as about the size of Mount Vernon, with
race horses gamboling along a mile-long split-rail fence. When I saw it
recently it had shrunk, in beauty as well as scale, but it drove my mother
and father into the poorhouse. Although the rent was only two hundred
per month (my parents had never before paid half as much) and the
gardener and fulltime maid together cost fifteen dollars a week, the house
was unfurnished, and its many rooms were a challenge to the Wolffs'
extravagance.

My mother and father had fun. There were many friends, a rootless
assortment such as war and natural calamity can throw together: artists
who drew the modifications my father required, pilots, inventors, mechanics, gunsmiths, mathematicians. These people came together without histories, and were peculiarly alive to the present. The house on
Beechwood Road was open to anyone passing through Birmingham who
had anything to do with airplanes.

A pilot stayed with us. He had been shot down over Rabal, and was
horribly burned. Natives brought him back to life and hid him from the
Japanese, and he escaped on a raft. The pilot gave me a Japanese bayonet, and told me never to call Japanese people Japs. He also told me my
dad was "one hell of a man." He set up his dozen or so electric trains in
our basement, with an insane network of HO gauge tracks, Gordian
crossovers and model alpine villages and engines that whistled and blew
steam. Where this pilot went his trains went, and when he prepared to
fly his Dukefied B-29 to Guam, I saw the trains, packed in wooden crates,
loaded into the plane's bomb bay. He wore dark glasses and a flight hat
with sheepskin earmuffs, and gave me the thumbs-up just before he
revved his engines and rolled away.

# PHILIP LARKIN

PHILIP LARKIN was born in Coventry and educated at St. John's College, Oxford. He wrote two novels: *Jill,* set in wartime London, and *A Girl in Winter.* His early poems appeared in an anthology, *Poetry from Oxford in Wartime.*

■

## A Stone Church Damaged by a Bomb

Planted deeper than roots,
This chiselled, flung-up faith
Runs and leaps against the sky,
A prayer killed into stone
Among the always-dying trees;
Windows throw back the sun
And hands are folded in their work at peace,
Though where they lie
The dead are shapeless in the shapeless earth.

Because, though taller the elms,
It forever rejects the soil,
Because its suspended bells
Beat when the birds are dumb,
And men are buried, and leaves burnt
Every indifferent autumn,
I have looked on that proud front
And the calm locked into walls,
I have worshipped that whispering shell.

Yet the wound, O see the wound
This petrified heart has taken,
Because, created deathless,
Nothing but death remained
To scatter magnificence;
And now what scaffolded mind
Can rebuild experience
As coral is set budding under seas,
Though none, O none sees what patterns it is making?

# ANDRÉ GIDE

ANDRÉ GIDE, the author of more than eighty books, is considered one of the most distinguished French writers of the twentieth century. He spent the war years in North Africa. Following are two wartime entries from *The Journals of André Gide*.

■

FROM *The Journals of André Gide*

3 *January, 1943*

No, according to other information that seems more trustworthy, the harbor of Tunis is apparently not sheltering any Italian ship at the moment. Easy to verify, moreover.[1] It is less easy to estimate the number of bombs dropped on La Goulette at noon the day before yesterday. A French officer, trustworthy and well informed, claims to have counted seventy-seven, with seven of them on the electric power-house (the damage caused to it can be readily repaired, it is said; but meanwhile we are without light and without radio). From the R.s' living-room windows I could see the wreaths of smoke from the explosions: a broad fringe above the horizon line. The raid was very short and had ended before the A.A. had begun to react.

But I cannot set down here the echo of all the current rumors. It is repeated above all that last Sunday the Americans were on the point of entering Tunis. A very considerable spearhead of tanks is said to have been routed by a handful of German motorcyclists who had set out to meet them and whom they took to be the forerunners of considerable resistance forces. If only those tanks had continued their advance, they would easily have mastered the city. Reported as they are here, such stories seem childish; but many examples are given of the incompetence and lack of dash of the American army, turning tail at the slightest threat and refusing combat so long as they are not sure of being twenty to one. At another point (Tebourba?) a column of tanks, attacked by enemy aviation, is said to have been routed, the men forsaking their wonderful and costly machines intact in order to flee under the olive trees, so that the German army, having seized the tanks, brought them in triumph into town, where everyone could see them. The Americans' equipment is supposedly marvelous, excellent even in its smallest details, but the

---

[1] Yes, asserts a dock-hand: since yesterday a German warship and two Italian warships.

combat value of the men almost non-existent; in any case, they are altogether inexperienced, incapable of measuring up to the quality of the Germans, who are sending their best to Tunisia. I fear that there may be much truth in this; and in any case the Allies have to deal with serious opponents, resolute, convinced men, long prepared and disindividualized to the point of ceasing to exist except in terms of fighting.

We are wallowing in suppositions; but one certainty is that a dozen eggs cost a hundred and twenty francs.

# JAMES JONES

JAMES JONES' vast novel *From Here to Eternity* is one of the epics of the war. A peacetime soldier, Jones abruptly found himself in the middle of the war after Pearl Harbor. The following letter to his brother tells all the censor would allow.

■

FROM *Selected Letters*

GUADALCANAL

*January 28, 1943*

*Dear Jeff* [James's brother],

I'm writing this more or less to set your mind at ease concerning me. I've inquired around here as to what a guy is able to write, and—as per usual—I've found that there's not a helluva lot to say that won't be censored.

It's apparently OK for me to tell you that I've been wounded and have just been released from a Base Hospital in the South Pacific. I'll elaborate that statement before moving on to something else. I wasn't hit very badly—a piece of shrapnel went thru my helmet and cut a nice little hole in the back of my head. It didn't fracture the skull and is healed up nicely now. I don't know what happened to my helmet; the shell landed close to me and when I came to, the helmet was gone. The concussion together with the fragment that hit me must have broken the chinstrap and torn it off my head. It also blew my glasses off my face. I never saw them again, either, but I imagine they are smashed to hell. If I hadn't been lying in a hole I'd dug with my hands and helmet, that shell would probably have finished me off. The hole was only six or eight inches deep, but that makes an awful lot of difference, and it looked like a canyon. I'm not much good without glasses; it bothers you a lot to know you can't see well and that any minute some sniper you should have seen but couldn't is liable to cut you down. The glasses don't help a lot either; you have to keep wiping sweat off of them every five minutes, and after a couple of days you don't have any rags or handkerchiefs clean enuf to wipe them without leaving them badly smeared. That surprised me quite a bit, because before I hadn't thot wearing glasses would make much difference. But it does, a helluva lot: the knowledge that you can't see well bothers the shit out of you—especially when you can't make more than one misstep. I learned a lot of other things, too.

I found that reading books about other people fighting wars is adventurous, but when you are doing the fighting, it's a helluva lot different. When you read a book like *All Quiet* [*on the Western Front* by Erich Maria Remarque] you understand what the hero is going thru and sympathize with him. Even when he gets killed at the end of the book you sympathize, and in sympathizing, you feel a sadness you enjoy. But all that time while you are putting yourself into the hero's place you still have the knowledge that after the hero dies you still will be around to feel sad about it. When at any second you may die, there is no adventure; all you want is to get the fighting over with. You don't spend any time in consoling yourself that if you die, you will be dying for your country and Liberty and Democracy and Freedom, because after you are dead, there is no such thing as Liberty or Democracy or Freedom. It's impossible to look at things thru the viewpoint of the group rather than your individual eyes. The group means nothing to you if you cannot remain a part of it. But in spite of all this, you keep on fighting because you know that there is nothing else for you to do.

I also learned that in spite of all the training you get and precautions you take to keep yourself alive, it's largely a matter of luck that decided whether or not you get killed. It doesn't make any difference who you are, how tough you are, how nice a guy you might be, or how much you may know, if you happen to be at a certain spot at a certain time, you get it. I've seen guys [move] out of one hole to a better one and get it the next minute, whereas if they'd stayed still they wouldn't have been touched. I've seen guys decide to stay in a hole instead of moving and get it. I've seen guys move and watch the hole they were in get blown up a minute later. And I've seen guys stay and watch the place to which they had intended to move get blown up. It's all luck.

The guys who are fighting now will have less of a chance of being alive when the war is over than the guys who haven't started fighting yet. Of course, some of us will live thru it, but that doesn't help one guy any, because if he doesn't live thru it, what happens to the rest doesn't make any difference. I've sort of got a hunch that I'm not going to make it. Partially that comes from having seen how much luck has to do with it and because from now on until the war ends I'll probably be in and out of action all the time. Then, part of it comes from being hit. Until you get hit, there's a sort of egotism in your subconscious mind that, even while your conscious mind is tearing itself apart with fear and anxiety, gives you confidence in the fact that this might happen to other guys but not to you; you can't conceive yourself getting hit. After you've been hit, you lose that confidence. The more fights you go thru without being hit, the stronger it gets. But once you're hit, you realize as an individual you'll have to be God damned lucky to get out alive.

I'm going to ask you something. If I do get killed, and I honestly don't see how I can help it, I want you to write that book we were thinking about when I enlisted. If I get it, it's a cinch I won't be able to do it, and it would make me feel a whole lot better to know that if not my name and hand, at least, the thot of me would be passed on and not forgotten entirely. You know, sort of put into the book the promise that I had and the things I might have written so at least the knowledge of talent wasted won't be lost. This girl, Peggy, I told you about told me once that the day after my last pass, Dr. Schwartz, during her lecture to Peggy's class, said something about how much talent would be lost without anyone having guessed it existed because of this war. Peggy told me that she thot Schwartz had me in mind when she said that. If I get it, no one will ever know to what heights I might have gone as a writer. Maybe if you wrote about the promise that was there, all wouldn't be lost.

Give my love to Sally and the boys and to Tink. You might tell Dave if I ever get the Purple Heart I got coming, I'll send it to him. It probably wouldn't bring six bits in a hock shop.

*Jim*

# WILLIAM MANCHESTER

TODAY William Manchester is known as the biographer
of H. L. Mencken, John F. Kennedy, Douglas Mac-
Arthur, and Winston Churchill. In 1943 he was a Marine
sergeant on a Pacific island, facing savage fighting and a freshly arrived officer, as recalled in *Goodbye,
Darkness,* a memoir of his wartime experiences.

■

FROM *Goodbye, Darkness*

Seawalls are to beachheads what sunken roads—as at Waterloo and
Antietam—are to great land battles. They provide inexpressible relief to
assault troops who can crouch in their shadows, shielded for the moment
from flat-trajectory fire, and they are exasperating to the troops' commanders because they bring the momentum of an attack to a shattering
halt. On Tarawa the survival of the American force depended upon
individual decisions to risk death. Wellington said, "The whole art of war
consists of getting at what is on the other side of the hill." If no one
vaulted over the wall, no Marine would leave Betio alive. Naturally
everyone wanted others to take the chance. In the end, some did—not
many, but a few—and they were responsible for the breakthrough. In
defense of those who chose to remain until the odds were shorter it
should be said that Tarawa was exceptional. In most instances frontal
attacks are unnecessary. Cunning is more effective than daring. Even
on Betio, even after the reef blunder and the failure to bombard the
enemy until the last possible moment, permitting the shift of defenders
to prepared positions on the lagoon side, there was a way out. Ryan
provided it. He had turned the Jap flank. If Shoup's radio had worked he
would have known that and could have strengthened Ryan, rolling up
the Nip defenses from the rear. So the instincts of the rifleman who
hides behind the wall are usually sound. At least that is what I tell myself
whenever I think of Tubby Morris.

My seawall was on Oroku. There was no reef to speak of, and though
enemy fire was heavy as the Higgins boats brought us in—we were
soaked with splashes from near misses, and we could hear the small-arms
lead pinging on our hulls—we lost very few men in the landing. Then
we saw the seawall and thanked God for it. It was built of sturdy logs and
stood over five feet high. Incongruously, an enormous scarlet vine rioted

over the lower half of it. Between there and the surf line the beach was about ten feet deep. It looked wonderful. I was prepared to spend the rest of my life on those ten feet. A braver man, I knew, would try to skirt the wall and find Jap targets. But enemy machine gunners knew where we were. Nambus were chipping at the top of the wall; you could see the splinters. Even if I hadn't been determined to save my own skin, which I certainly was, there were other reasons for staying put. I was surrounded by the Raggedy Ass Marines, the least subordinate of fighters. I knew that if I went up I would be alone. Furthermore, it seemed possible, even probable, that the First Battalion, on our extreme right, could envelop the Nips. The seawall tapered off in that direction, and the map showed an inlet where our men had room to move around. Anyhow, I was going to give them their chance and all the time they wanted.

That was when Tubby arrived in the third wave. He had been in my officer candidate class at Quantico, and unlike me he had been commissioned. Now he was a second lieutenant, a replacement officer making his debut as a leader, or presumed leader, of seasoned troops. If there is a more pitiful role in war, I don't know it. Troops are wary of untested officers, and the Raggedy Ass Marines were contemptuous of them. Some of them, like me, remembered him from Quantico. He hadn't changed since we had last seen him; he was a stubby, brisk youth, in his early twenties but already running to fat around the jowls and belly. He had the sleek peach complexion of a baby and a perpetual frown, not of petulance but of concentration. I hadn't known him well. He had the megalomania of undersized men. He was like one of those boys who always do their homework at school and never let you copy. He had been an overachiever, determined to please his superiors, but there had been many like him at Quantico. Here, however, he was unique. Among men who prided themselves on the saltiness—shabbiness—of their uniforms, his was right off the quartermaster's shelf. I wondered whether he had been disappointed when they told him not to wear his bars in combat, for whatever his other failings he was, and was soon to prove, courageous.

He caught his breath, looked around, and said, "I'm your new officer." I grinned, held out my hand, and said, "Hi, Tubby." That was stupid of me. He glared and kept his own hand on his trouser seam. Standing cockily like a bantam rooster—the wall was just high enough to let him stand—he crisply asked, "Sergeant, are these your men?" The Raggedy Asses grinned at one another. The very thought of belonging to *anyone* amused them. I felt cold. This wasn't the good-natured Tubby I had known. This was trouble. I said, "Tubby—" and he cut me off: "Slim, I am an officer and I expect to be treated with proper military courtesy." That broke the men up. He heard their stifled chuckles and looked around furiously. It was an insane situation. Here we were, in the middle of a battle, and Tubby seemed to expect a salute, if not homage, from me. There wasn't much room, but I said in a low voice, "Let's talk this over," moved away a few feet, and knelt. He bridled, but came over and squatted beside me. I told him that I didn't want to undermine him, that I hadn't meant to sound familiar, and that I was sorry. His jaw muscles were working. He said, "You should be." Anger stirred in me. Looking back, I see that my motives were less selfless than I thought then. My sympathy for his position, though genuine, was tainted by resentment at taking orders from this little man whose background was no different from mine, by irrational scorn of junior officers who hadn't yet proved themselves, and by the arrogance which combat veterans feel toward all green replacements, especially platoon leaders. At that moment, however, all I saw was that there was bound to be a certain stiffness between us which we would probably work around in time. Then I learned that for Tubby there wasn't much time. He said, "Don't tell me. Show me. I'm going to lead these people over the top, and I want you with me."

He actually said "over the top." We didn't talk like that. He must have heard it from his father. World War I soldiers left their trenches to go over the top, over the parapet, into no-man's-land. Then the implication of what he had said hit me. I whispered, "You mean over this wall?" He nodded once, a quick little jerk of his head. He said, "That's where the Japs are. You can't kill them if you can't see them." I felt numb. I said, "Look, Tubby—Lieutenant—I think—" He snapped, "You're not paid to think. You're paid to take orders." I considered saying the hell with it. But this was literally a matter of life or imminent death. I tried again, earnestly: "Going up there would be suicide. The First Bat's down there," I said, pointing. "Give them a chance to turn the Nips' flank and roll up those machine-gun nests." He growled, "What's the matter with *this* battalion?" I said, "We're pinned down, so the action is on the flanks." I could see I wasn't convincing him, and I said hoarsely, "Tubby, I know they didn't teach you that at Quantico, but that's how we do it here. You're not on some fucking parade ground. You can't just pump your fist up and down and expect the men to spring up. They won't do it. *They won't do it.* I've been out here a long time, Tubby. I *know.*"

He stared at me for a long time, as though waiting for me to blink first. I blinked and blinked again. Letting his voice rise, he said, "You're scared shitless, aren't you?" I nodded emphatically. His voice rose higher. All the guys could hear him now. He said, "That's why I put up bars and you're just an NCO. They could tell the difference between us in O.C. I've got balls and you haven't." There was just a tremor in his voice, and it dawned on me that he himself was petrified—he was masking his fear with his rudeness to me. But what he said next smothered my compassion. He sneered, and keeping his voice in the same register, he said: "I know your kind, Bub. You think we couldn't hear you back there in the squad bay, masturbating every night? Did you think they'd give a Marine Corps commission to a masturbator? Only thing I couldn't make out was how you dried the come. I figured you had a handkerchief." I heard a titter from Bubba. I'm sure Bubba had never masturbated. His father, the Alabama preacher in whose steps he hoped to follow, had shown him the way to what he called "Nigra poontang" when he reached adolescence. But I wasn't interested in Bubba's good opinion. What Tubby had done, and it was unforgivable, was make me look ridiculous in the eyes of all my men. He knew that was wrong. They *had* taught *that* at Quantico. By mocking me he had contaminated both of us. I thought: *Since I am a dog, beware my fangs.* He and I were through. He was past saving now. His longevity would be less than a Jap's. No one could lengthen it for him. I've kept telling myself that all these years, but there will always be a tug of guilt.

Rising in one swift motion, he wiped his hands on his sturdy thighs, stood with arms akimbo, and barked: "Men, I know you'd like to stay here. I would myself. But those yellow bastards down the beach are killing your buddies." He didn't even realize that a combat man's loyalty is confined to those around him, that as far as the Raggedy Ass Marines were concerned the First Battalion might as well have belonged to a separate race. He said, "Our duty lies up there." He pointed. He went on: "That's what we call a target of opportunity, lads." He paused, and his pouter-pigeon breast swelled. I wondered if he was trying to imitate Chesty Puller, that legendary Marine hero who is said to have boasted that he would win a Medal of Honor if he had to bring home a seabag full of dog tags. Tubby said, "I'm not going to ask any of you people to do what I don't do. I'm going up first. Your sergeant will—" He checked himself. "It's your sergeant's job to see that every man follows me." I was still down on one knee, eyes averted, running sand through my fingers. I wanted no part of this. He asked, "Any questions?"

They looked up at him glassily. He hesitated, probably wondering whether he should threaten them with courts-martial. Then he turned and sprang at the seawall. He was too short. He couldn't get a footing. He tried to stick one boondocker in a vine crotch, but the V was too tight. He could only wedge his toe in sideways, and that didn't give him the right leverage. Panting, he tried again and again. He turned to me, his face flushed. He said, "Help me." He must have hated to ask. I certainly hated his asking. I felt an insane urge to laugh, which I knew would turn into weeping. I looked into his wide eyes and said, "My legs are too shaky." It was true. He said between his teeth, "I'll take care of you later." He turned, pointed to Bubba, and said, "You, over here." Bubba came over and linked his hands. Tubby put in a foot, as if into a stirrup, swung up, rolled atop the wall, and rose till he stood sideways. Both his hands were pointing. His left forefinger was pointed down at us, his right forefinger at the Japs. It was a Frederic Remington painting. He breathed deeply and yelled, *"Follow me!"*

The men's faces still were turned up, expressionless. Nobody moved. I stood beneath the wall, my arms outstretched, waiting to catch what would be left. At that moment the slugs hit him. It was a Nambu; it stitched him vertically, from forehead to crotch. One moment he was looming above us in that heroic pose; in the next moment red pits blossomed down him, four on his face alone, and a dozen others down his uniform. One was off center; it slammed into the Marine Corps emblem over his heart; the gunner knew his job. Blood had just begun to stream from there, from his face, from his belly, and from his groin, when he collapsed, tottering on the edge and falling and whumping in my arms face up. His features were disappearing beneath a spreading stain, and he was trying to blink the blood out of his eyes. But he could see. He saw me. He choked faintly: "You . . . you . . . you . . ." Then he gagged and was gone.

I looked away, feeling queasy. My blouse was wet with gore. Mo Crocker and Dusty Rhodes took Tubby from me and gently laid him out. There was no malice in the section. They mourned him as they would have mourned any casualty. They—and I above all—had merely been unwilling to share his folly. It was followed by savage irony. We had scarcely finished trussing him up in a poncho when we heard the sound of cheering to our right. The First Bat had turned the Jap flank. You could just see the bobbing of the camouflaged helmet covers and the moving line of smoke, and you could hear the snuffling of the tanks as their drivers shifted gears. I raged as I had raged over the death of Zepp. It was the sheer futility of it which was unbearable. Then I was diverted, as death in its grisly mercy diverts you, by the necessity of disposing of the corpse. I said to Knocko, "Pass the word to Buck Rogers—" Suddenly I realized that Buck might not still be alive, and that because Tubby had arrived so recently, his name might be unknown at the CP anyhow. Instead, I said, "The new lieutenant is dead. Pass the word to the nearest officer."

# JOHN COSTELLO

U.S. ARMY Chief of Staff General George Marshall was a strong supporter of the enlistment of women in the armed services, and on July 1, 1943, President Franklin Roosevelt signed the Women's Army Corps into being. In *Virtue Under Fire,* John Costello, a producer for many years for the BBC, reports how women won their way into World War II.

■

## FROM *Virtue Under Fire*

### "YOU'RE IN THE ARMY NOW, MISS JONES!"

Women made, in my opinion, the best soldiers in the war.
—GENERAL IRA C. EAKER, USAAF, 1945

We want to help make the world free—and get a thrill out of doing it. —WAC PRIVATE, 1943

The military services are so conspicuously a man's world that the appearance of women therein was startling. Women who joined to do a job found themselves objects of great curiosity. Suddenly they were representatives of "womanhood." . . . The surprise of men at the accomplishment of women was not flattering, but it was fun.
—CAPTAIN MILDRED MACAFFEE HORTON, U.S. WAVES

Long before the Japanese attack on Pearl Harbor, the fascination of Americans with the role that women were playing in the war in Europe was evident from popular magazines like *Life* and *Saturday Evening Post*, which found Russian female fighters and British girls in tin helmets operating searchlights, dousing blitzed buildings, and marching with snappy precision irresistible subjects for photo spreads and articles. Yet surprisingly, for a nation where women already played a more prominent role than in any European society, it was to take nearly five months of intensive public debate and lobbying by the administration on Capitol Hill before the House of Representatives and Senate passed the bill that allowed American women to serve their country in uniform.

A similar uneasiness over the establishment of a female militia had surfaced in World War I. In 1917 the secretary of war had refused a petition from the New York Women's Self Defense League Auxiliary to be sent to France after diligently drilling at the 66th Street Armory with puttees and rifles. With the same finality he rejected a proposal from the chiefs of staff for congressional approval of a women's army auxiliary that would parade in "soft brown" uniforms—"no furs shall be worn"— because "the action provided for in this bill is not only unwise, but exceedingly ill-advised."

The War Department held firm to its policy even after receiving repeated requests from the commander in chief of the American Expeditionary Force in France for five thousand female auxiliaries. General John ("Black Jack") Pershing had been so impressed with the WAAC telephonists that he had arranged to "borrow" a hundred for his headquarters, but the contingent of American volunteer civilian telegraphists that he was sent never matched the efficiency of the British army auxiliaries because they were not subject to military discipline.

The Navy Department, however, had already enlisted 12,500 women clerical assistants as "Yeoman F"—popularly known as "yeomanettes"—bypassing the need for obtaining the necessary congressional approval by the ingenious device of assigning them as crew members to abandoned navy tugs. The Marine Corps had also appointed three hundred "marinettes" and the original estimate that three women could replace two marines engaged in clerical duties, proved to be a ratio that was reversed in actual practice.

The American generals proved to have a far greater aversion to women in uniform than the admirals, and not until 1917 were female civilians permitted to be employed in military camps, and then only under "careful supervision" to prevent "moral injury either to themselves or to the soldiers." Proposals for a women's auxiliary were still being shuffled around the War Department when the end of the war enabled the secretary of war to shelve the controversial plans. The yeomanettes and marinettes left off their uniforms and were rehired back at their old jobs.

During the interwar years, the U.S. army's plans for a female auxiliary service were intermittently dusted off and revised by ranking officers who did not share the traditional antipathy to the idea of women in uniform. But it was not until Hitler went to war on the other side of the Atlantic that the patriotic fervor of women's organizations in the United States once again became a voice that dimly penetrated the offices of the War Department.

The indefinite extension of the Selective Service Act for men that followed President Roosevelt's declaration of a National Emergency in 1941 prompted groups like the Women's Self Defense League to enroll seventeen thousand members "who can do anything helpful to replace a man in the event of war." From Los Angeles to Pittsburgh and Washington to Toledo, the War Department was bombarded with pleas from similar groups "to include women in the national defense plan in some capacity." In May 1941 Congresswoman Edith Nourse Rogers, who had herself served in France as one of Pershing's civilian auxiliaries in World War I, launched a bill in the House that would establish a twenty-five-thousand-strong noncombatant Women's Auxiliary Army Corps.

The majority of the U.S. army staff were still nursing their World War I distaste for anything that smacked of a "petticoat army." With little encouragement from the War Department, the Rogers bill quickly sank under the weight of male congressional opposition. Only in the crisis weeks of November 1941, when it became clear in Washington that the United States was sliding toward war with Germany and Japan, did the army change its tune. An aide to the U.S. army chief of staff, who had been one of the few supporters of the idea of a female auxiliary, remembered how "General Marshall shook his finger at me and said, 'I want a woman's corps right away and I don't want any excuses!' At that, I displayed considerable energy."

More energy and considerably greater initiative was to be shown by a handful of enterprising American women who set out to enlist in the British armed forces as soon as the Japanese attack on 7 December 1941 had plunged the United States into the global war. One of them was Maria Elizabeth Ferguson, who showed her bravery soon after sailing from New York when her ship, the ill-fated *Avila Star*, was torpedoed in a U-boat attack. The nineteen-year-old girl was awarded the British Empire Medal for "magnificent" courage during the grueling twenty-one days that she spent in an open boat nursing twenty-seven male survivors, eleven of whom perished in the three-week ordeal before rescue finally came. Another who risked the U-boat-infested Atlantic and reached the shores of England safely early in 1942 was Emily Chapin, a secretary and spare-time pilot from New Jersey who joined the select band of women flyers in Britain's Air Transport Auxiliary ferrying fighters and bombers to RAF bases.

American women wearing British uniforms were already helping to defeat Hitler while Congress debated the pros and cons of authorizing the U.S. army to set up its own female auxiliary. Congresswoman Rogers had by now won official War Department and White House backing for a relatively small female auxiliary force of twenty-five thousand, but the arguments continued to delay the passages of her bill through Congress. In Britain, however, there was little opposition at the end of April 1942 when Parliament approved the conscription of all able-bodied women between the ages of nineteen and twenty-five not already in essential work. The only exceptions were mothers of children under twelve.

Like the British government, military authorities in the United States insisted women must never be allowed actually to fire guns or engage in combat. Opponents of the bill for establishing a female army auxiliary argued that this violated the historic right of men to fight in defense of their womenfolk and homes. If women were once allowed to bear arms and female generals conduct battles, it would undermine the central male rationale for war. The traditionally conservative military mind subconsciously resisted the idea of women in uniform because it directly challenged an exclusive male preserve.

"I think it is a reflection upon the courageous manhood of the country to pass a law inviting women to join the armed forces in order to win a battle," thundered one member of the House of Representatives. "Take the women into the armed service, who will then do the cooking, the washing, the mending, the humble homey tasks to which every woman has devoted herself? Think of the humiliation! What has become of the manhood of America?"

The belief that women in uniform were an insult to the collective machismo of the American male was a theme repeated in many of the letters that flooded in from soldiers already locked in battle with the Japanese enemy in the Pacific. Typical of them was the GI who protested that "we would throw away our own self-respect—our right to pledge in earnestness to 'Love, Honor, and Protect' the girls we want to marry when we get back."

That this was not a view shared by the majority of women was evident from the even greater volume of mail that the War Department received from wives and relations of draftees, who begged to be given the chance to serve their country in uniform. At last, on 14 May 1942, the WAAC Bill for establishing the Women's Auxiliary Army Corps was squeezed out of the Senate by an insubstantial margin of just eleven votes. The navy, which had calculatedly resisted all efforts to win its support for a joint bill, had already initiated its own separate legislative authority—but only after Mrs. Roosevelt had interceded with the president to obtain the secretary's support. The navy bill was passed by Congress ten weeks later for a women's auxiliary, which would become known as the WAVES, a contrived acronym for "Women Appointed for Voluntary Emergency Service" that was soon jokingly interpreted as "Women Are Very Essential Sometimes."

The navy bill also authorized a woman's reserve for the marines, in which its commandant, in the best tradition of the corps, refused to make any sexual distinction between male or females—they were all called "marines." The members of the corps out in the Pacific took a somewhat more jaundiced view of this egalitarianism. "Female Marines? They'll be sending us dogs next!" spat one hardened old Leatherneck. The U.S. coast guard, which had also come under direct navy control on the outbreak of the war, decided to call its female corps the SPARS, a contraction of its motto " 'Semper Paratus,' Always Prepared."

The final passage of the WAAC Bill had been assisted by the increasing sense of national emergency fostered by Allied defeat and reverse on every global battlefront. In the week before the crucial Senate vote, Japan had stormed the Philippine fortress island of Corregidor, the British army in Burma was retreating toward the frontier of India, and the

Japanese fleet was threatening Australia from the Coral Sea. German panzer divisions in Russia were pounding their way toward Stalingrad and advancing unchecked in the Crimea. In North Africa, Rommel's Afrika Korps appeared poised to drive through Egypt and on to the Middle East. With fewer than two million American men under arms, the female auxiliaries offered the opportunity for a quick increase in the frontline strength of the army if the nightmare of final Axis victory in Russia, the Mediterranean, and Far East became a reality.

Even as Mrs. Oveta Culp Hobby was being sworn in by General Marshall as the first WAAC and the new corps' "director," the War Department doubled its intended strength to fifty thousand. This presented a formidable task for the wife of the former Texas governor, an ex-newspaper executive and thirty-seven-year-old mother of two who was chosen for the post that she had helped to bring into being from her work in the War Department liaison office. Mrs. Hobby was short in stature but long on legal training and had been in Washington long enough to have learned how to cut through bureaucratic tangles with a determination that earned her the nickname "Spark-Plugs."

At her first press conference questions focused on such burning issues as whether WAACs would be permitted to wear makeup, if they would be allowed to date enlisted men, and what would happen to them if they became pregnant. The next day her careful answers were sensationalized under headlines such as "Doughgirl Generalissimo" and "Petticoat Army," which suggested that opposition to the whole idea of women auxiliaries was not yet dead. The press proved unable or unwilling to resist the temptation of running pictures under such captions as "Whackies," "Powder Magazines," and "Fort Lipstick." One columnist compared the WAACs with "the naked Amazons . . . and the queer damozels of the Isle of Lesbos." Another demanded with ill-concealed prejudice: "Give the rejected 4F men a chance to be in the Army and give the girls a chance to be mothers."

The U.S. army's determination to make no concessions to "feminine vanity and civilian frippery" soon resulted in a wrangle over women's uniforms. Director Hobby argued for a stylish martial cut patterned on uniforms of regular soldiers. Army brass, determined to put as much distance as possible between men and women, argued for blue uniforms —and only conceded to olive drab because the use of existing army cloth was an economy measure. The final design was a committee compromise; the skimped, unpleated skirt with belted jacket and the kepi-style cap had none of the smartness or practicality the navy achieved with no acrimony by commissioning its ensemble from the New York fashion house of Mainbocher, the couturier patronized by the Duchess of Windsor and Hollywood stars.

The U.S. army was also to deny its female auxiliary the coveted eagle badge, and WAAC officers wore a hybrid in their caps that some said was a buzzard. Director Hobby rejected the proposed "Busy Bee" shoulder insignia because it looked like a "bug." The head of Pallas Athene, the Greek goddess of wisdom, was finally deemed appropriate.

"It will be no picnic for glamour girls" was how the camp commandant welcomed the press, inquisitive to look over Fort Des Moines, in the heart of Iowa, where the first four hundred white and forty black WAAC recruits, selected from thirty thousand applicants, were due to arrive for basic training in August 1942. Female reporters were shocked by the spartan conditions of an old cavalry barracks, which lacked partitioned showers and toilets. The first intake of WAACs, however, were most perturbed by the disconcerting mud-brown slips and foundation garments.

"You're in the Army Now, Miss Jones," was the popular adaptation of the previous year's hit song about the rigors facing male recruits. Women knew they were entering hostile territory when they faced the wolf-whistles of the draftees at the army recruiting offices. "The recruiting station was the dirtiest place I ever saw," complained one recruit. "It was in the post office next to the men's toilets," recalled another, and many would-be WAACs had second thoughts, particularly one girl at whom a captain bawled out, "Are you one of them Wackies?"

Much of this ill-concealed resentment by male enlistees was because the women could choose whether to volunteer for military service, whereas the men were drafted. The female intake was also of a much higher standard. Nine out of ten were college graduates and the others were chosen because they had made successful civilian careers before they had stepped forward to serve their country "for the duration plus six months."

"You have just made the change from peacetime pursuits to wartime tasks—from the individualism of civilian life to the anonymity of military life," said Director Hobby addressing the first intake. "You have taken off silk and put on khaki. All for essentially the same reason—you have a debt and a date. A debt to democracy, a date with destiny." These inspiring words were perhaps the reason that none of the new WAACs had need of the smelling salts proffered awkwardly by an embarrassed male medical orderly as the girls received their inoculation shots.

Most women were already earmarked for the first officer class and most surprised their male instructors—just as the British ATS had done —by their aptitude and affection for precision drill routines. "They learn more in a day than my squads of men used to learn in a week," a sergeant confessed. But on the eve of the parade three weeks later, when they were due to muster out as full-fledged WAACs, it was found that their young male instructors had given the highest marks to the youngest and prettiest WAACs. Since the average age of the female intake was significantly higher than that of the men who trained them, the younger women had been unfairly upgraded by ex-college soldiers of nineteen, to whom any woman over thirty was already an antique. Yet the mature judgment and stability of the adult women volunteers was soon to prove one of the corps' most valuable assets.

U.S. Army Chief of Staff General Marshall, a fervent supporter of employing women to release men for active duty, encouraged the War Department to increase the planned strength of the WAACs after initial surveys showed that women might eventually replace two out of three men in clerical and administrative jobs, in motor transport, and the supply corps as well as in radio communications. The only duties now considered "improper for women" were those that might expose them to enemy fire—or supervisory positions in which they could decide which men went into combat!

Accordingly, it was decided that by recruiting 1.5 million women, an equivalent number of men could be released for frontline duty. On paper, a woman's auxiliary on this scale translated into a hundred infantry divisions at the front. This was on the bold assumption that the WAACs could recruit nearly 10 percent of the estimated 13 million American women of service age. Director Hobby appealed for caution, since her advisers were strongly of the opinion that even reaching the new targeted strength (150,000) for the corps in little over two years would not be practical without British-style conscription.

Soundings taken on Capitol Hill, however, quickly revealed that the chances of getting Congress to pass a female draft act were nil. Moreover, as American production geared up, the War Manpower Directorate argued that industry must be given priority for recruiting able-bodied women, who, they insisted, would make a more effective contribution to the so-called Victory Plan in the shipyards and factories rather than by unproductive drilling in military uniform.

The services could not offer the same economic incentives as the production line, and a powerful disincentive to military service was what WAVE director Mildred MacAffee Horton termed "a threat to their individuality." Moreover, since the WAACs like the WAVES were volunteers, nothing could be done to keep those women who grew unhappy with military routine and discipline. After a year, military service had lost much of its glamour for many of the original enlistees. Desertion and AWOL rates began rising sharply after two sisters established a unique military precedent ordering their own discharge by cable to their commanding officer:

HAVE BEEN IN WAACS 3½ MONTHS. NOW AT HOME ON EMERGENCY FURLOUGH. HAVE NO INTENTION TO RETURN. CANNOT TAKE BEING IN CORPS. NERVOUS WRECK AND WILL LOSE OUR MIND IF NOT RELEASED. MA NEEDS US BOTH AT HOME AND CANNOT UNDER ANY CIRCUMSTANCES STAY. PLEASE TAKE IMMEDIATE ACTION AND REPLY.

New recruits vented their frustrations in songs that nevertheless expressed a "grin and bear it" determination, such as one of the many choruses that became popular at the Des Moines training camp in 1943:

> Hats and shoes and skirts don't fit,
> Your girdle bunches when you sit,
> Come on, rookie, you can't quit—
> Just heave a sigh, and be G.I.

To check desertions while boosting the prestige and flagging recruiting drive, the War Department asked Congress to pass legislation changing the status of the corps from an auxiliary to an integral part of the U.S. army—a step the British government had taken a year earlier with the ATS. After months of renewed political wrangling over the desirability of having women in uniform at all, the WAC (Womens Army Corps) was given its birth by a stroke of President Roosevelt's pen on 1 July 1943.

# DAVID BRINKLEY

A UNITED PRESS and White House correspondent during World War II, David Brinkley here reports on the
home front—and the difficulty of finding a home.

■

## FROM *Washington Goes to War*

In 1943, a young reporter, new to Washington, answered an ad offering a room for rent in a house on Windom Place. He found it to be one of Washington's typical 1930s houses—pink brick, two-story "colonial" with a patch of grass in front, a concrete walk leading up to a white doorway and two pointy cedars standing symmetrically beside the steps.

Answering the door was an attractive woman in her thirties, redhaired, green-eyed, and hesitant to open the door to a man she did not know. The room offered for rent was upstairs in the back. Her own bedroom adjoined it, a double-width sliding door between them. The door was standing open. While he examined the room she examined him.

"My husband's a major in the army. When I'm here alone I keep that sliding door open. Better air circulation on hot nights."

"It's very nice. How much is the room?"

"Well, I haven't decided exactly. Do you like it?"

As Washington rentals went in the 1940s, it was far better than most. A walnut four-poster double bed, a white candlewick bedspread, a couple of chairs, lamps and a dresser. It had a separate bathroom with no handlettered signs in it. Its windows looked out into maple trees. In the background were the sounds of traffic out on Massachusetts Avenue. On the walls were framed and matted arrangements of dried wildflowers. Pretty.

"I made those myself. Sort of a hobby. I grow the flowers out back —gives you something to do when you're alone. My husband's been away two years now, in Europe. My mother had this room until a year ago. She hated Washington. Moved back home to Florida."

She wanted to talk, a lonely woman in a lonely city crowded with new people who did not know each other and would never know each other. She was tense, pacing the room, straightening her wildflower pictures, pulling a corner to straighten a bedspread already straight, turning a lamp on and off and asking who he was and where he came from and what he did. His answers seemed to please her.

"The room is very nice. How much?"

"You know, I don't need the money, really. I've thought a long time about doing this. These classified ads, it's a gamble. You could wind up with some bum in the house. Some slob."

"Then why are you doing it?"

"Roosevelt says it's our patriotic duty," she said with a little smirk. "But, really, it would be nice to have somebody around to talk to, I guess. Soon as we bought this house they sent him overseas and left me stuck here alone. He's been gone two years and he never writes. I don't know anybody in Washington but a few women, all army. Their husbands are away, too. We play bridge, four women, somebody makes a casserole and a salad and I come home and go to bed alone. You understand, don't you?"

"Yes. I can see you don't like to talk about money but if you want to rent the room you have to tell me what the deal is."

She paused, fluffed a pillow, hesitated again, looking out the window. There was no sound but the L4 bus groaning up the Massachusetts Avenue hill toward American University. It was late, half-dark now, the sun descending into Virginia across the Potomac. She had to force herself to say it. "The room is fifty dollars a month if you want total privacy, if you want to keep the sliding door closed and stay to yourself. If you want to leave it open and be sociable, talk to me, it's twenty-five dollars and the whole house is yours and I'll give you breakfast."

She looked almost frightened, as if she had stripped herself naked before a stranger. Her hands shook. She fluffed the same pillow again.

Nobody said anything. He pretended to examine the framed wild violets and yellow asters.

"Suppose your husband comes home?"

"He never comes. Maybe when the war's over. By then you'll have your own apartment. But he won't come. He won't even write. It's not one of your great marriages."

He wondered how many women like this there were in Washington. Was it true, all those cute stories he'd read? All that stuff in *Newsweek* and so on about Washington having ten women to every man? True or not, what if the major did come home on leave and find him alone in the house with his wife? Suppose he arrived, full military zeal and bravado, carrying in his bag the .45 Browning automatic issued to all officers? Suppose on his way home he stopped at the flower stand in Union Station and bought her a few roses? He considered the possibility of hearing (or even worse, not hearing) a taxi door slam at 2 a.m. out on Windom Place and the major, bearing roses for his wife, striding purposefully up the stairs and into the bedroom. No.

"You are very nice and the room is very nice, but I have another place to look at and I'll let you know."

She knew it was a lie. "My husband will not come until the war is over. He may not even come then. If you like the room you ought to take it."

"Thank you. I'll let you know."

# JULIAN MACLAREN-ROSS

IN *Memoirs of the Forties,* Julian Maclaren-Ross remembers a poet and editor whom he met after his discharge from the army. A short story writer, novelist,
and critic, Julian Maclaren-Ross was a regular in London's Soho.

■

FROM *Memoirs of the Forties*

## TAMBIMUTTU AND THE PROGRESS OF
## POETRY LONDON

J. Meary Tambimuttu, poet and founder-editor of *Poetry London,*
was according to himself a Prince in his own country. He was an Indian
like his friend the short-story writer Alagu Subramaniam, but both of
them came from Ceylon: the nearest parallel being perhaps the Glasgow
Irish, Subra was a Hindu, Tambi a Christian, and some said that the
initial preceding his name stood for Jesus. I never found out what it
actually stood for.

A girl known as Kitty of Bloomsbury told me that Tambi's family
seat was called Tambimuttu Towers. She said that at one time he used
special crested writing paper, with a picture of the Towers embossed in
the top left-hand corner. This was when he first came to London, abdi-
cating his territory to become a literary pundit and famous figure of the
Forties.

"A poet," he would say, "is a citizen of the world. All mankind is his
country," or "My principality is everywhere. The Principality of the
Mind."

When Kitty came down from Oxford and was looking for a job, he
took her to a bare basement room containing a half-collapsed camp bed,
a kitchen chair and a wooden table on which were a bottle of blue-black
ink, a chewed post office pen-holder, and stocks of the embossed crested
paper.

"This was my office," he said. "Now it is yours. I engage you as my
secretary and poetry-reader." Squashing a cockroach on the sweating
wall with a rolled-up copy of *Poetry London*, he waved this at a chaos of
accumulated MSS in a corner.

"Poems," he said. "Contributions. You know? I have not time to
read them. If they're no good perhaps they should be returned. They

■ 383 ■

have been here a long time, the rats have eaten some. We have no typewriter yet but there is ink and paper to write the authors. You will be paid fortnightly, on Fridays. Do you have any money?"

"Yes thank you. I've got £5."

"That is good," Tambimuttu said. "I am a Prince in my country and princes don't carry money, you know. Give me the fiver and later the firm will refund you. I am going to lunch with T.S. Eliot. You know who is T.S. Eliot?"

"Yes indeed."

Tambi stowed away the fiver. "He takes interest in me and in the quarterly," he said.

This was true. On arrival in England (completely penniless according to legend: there was garbled talk of privation and an open boat) he secured an introduction to Eliot, who had been impressed by him and helped in the starting of *Poetry London*. The great grandson of a great Victorian novelist helped the most, and Tambi was no longer penniless though the grandson as a result became relatively so; but the tale has many versions and there are many more competent to tell it than I. The grandson had enlisted in the army and gone overseas during the war, and I only saw him once, in the uniform of a captain and looking ineluctably sad: as well he might if the stories are true.

Kitty's £5 was supposed to last her a week. She slept on the camp bed in the basement, living on bread and cheese: not an ideal food as it attracted the rats who'd got bored with gnawing a way through the poetry contributions and needed a change of diet. But Kitty survived without being eaten and when after ten days Tambi returned, he surveyed with approval the pile of stamped addressed envelopes that almost hid his secretary from sight.

"But the stamps?" he said. "Where did you get them? I did not think that there were any."

"I bought them."

"Then you still have some money?"

"An aunt sent me £3."

"That is good. Give me what remains, I am tonight entertaining Edith Sitwell. You know about Edith Sitwell?" He added, dropping the money into his pocket: "Remember, next Friday is settlement day. Payment every fortnight."

But when he did look in, after a further fortnight, he found a polite note of resignation written on the embossed stationery and the basement floor deep in peevish letters from rejected contributors addressed to K. Banks, Esq, Banks being Kitty of Bloomsbury's surname. She hadn't been able to send back all the poems, having no more money left to buy stamps, so she'd gone and got herself a job in the foreign office.

"All the same," Kitty concluded, telling me this in 1943, "he's a great editor. No, stop laughing, he is. He has such *flair*."

# JANINA BAUMAN

---

JANINA BAUMAN, a survivor of the Warsaw Ghetto, left Poland in 1968. While hiding in the ghetto, she met Mr. Lusternik, who spent his days writing stories about the tragedies of the war and encouraged her to record everything she had seen or heard. This is an abbreviated version of a story she wrote about an incident told to her by someone who witnessed it.

---

■

## FROM *Winter in the Morning*

A lonely teenage boy was caught in a roundup and dragged to the *Umschlagplatz* together with a crowd of screaming, lamenting people. The boy did not scream but walked silent, aloof, holding his only property: a violin. In the *Platz*, swollen with human misery, resounding with cries, shots and hoots of the train leaving for the gas chambers of Treblinka, he was noticed by Commandant Brandt, the chief of the *Umschlagplatz*, well known for his cruelty as well as for his occasional fits of benevolence that sometimes saved someone's life. This time Brandt was in just such a mood. He stopped the boy and ordered him to play. An uncanny silence at once superseded the uproar. People huddled together to make room for the field-gray uniforms that pushed their way through the crowd, eager for entertainment. In the middle of the little clearing, the slim, pale boy with the violin shivered from fear in front of the bulky Nazi. For a while he could not bring himself to start, his fingers trembled. Then, suddenly, he played. It was a subtle, inspired music which sounded like a prayer, like a mighty call for help to God himself. The condemned and the butchers held their breath. They all believed the life of the gifted child was going to be saved. The boy knew it, too, and smiled. He finished with rich powerful chords of thanksgiving. There was silence again. The boy waited. The listeners waited, too. Commandant Brandt stood numb, spellbound. Raising himself, he glanced at his watch and pointed at the boy: "Same time tomorrow," he said with a spark of amusement. "He'll play in Treblinka." And, as if to himself, he added, "Pity!"

# NORMAN MAILER

NORMAN MAILER, born in Brooklyn and educated at Harvard, served in the Pacific during World War II. At the age of twenty-five he won instant fame with the publication of *The Naked and the Dead*, one of the most celebrated novels about the war. His other novels include *Barbary Shore* and *The Deer Park*, and there have also been many works of nonfiction, among them *Advertisements for Myself*, *The Armies of the Night*, and *The Executioner's Song*.

■

FROM *The Naked and the Dead*

## CHAPTER 7

After the night when the Japanese failed to cross the river, the first squad remained in its position for three days. On the fourth day, 1st Battalion advanced a half mile and recon moved up with A Company. Their new outpost was on the crest of a hill which looked down into a tiny valley of kunai grass; they spent the rest of the week digging new holes, stringing barbed wire, and making routine patrols. The front had become quiet. Nothing happened to the platoon, and they seldom saw any other men except for the platoon of A Company whose positions were on an adjoining hill a few hundred yards away. The bluffs of Watamai Range were still on their right, quite close, and in the late afternoon the cliffs hung over them like a wave of surf about to break.

The men in recon spent their days sitting in the sun on top of the hill. There was nothing to do except eat their rations and sleep and write letters and stand guard in their foxholes. The mornings were pleasant and new, but by afternoon the men were sullen and drowsy, and at night they found it hard to sleep, for the wind moved the grass in the valley beneath them and it looked like a column of men moving toward their hill. At least once or twice every night, a man on guard would awaken the entire squad and they would sit in their holes for almost an hour searching the field beneath them in the silver uncertain moonlight.

Occasionally, they would hear the crackling of some rifles in the distance sounding like a bonfire of dry twigs on an autumn day, and often a shell or two would arch lazily overhead, sighing and murmuring before it crashed into the jungle beyond their lines. At night the machine

guns would be hollow and deep, and would hold the mournful boding
note of primitive drums. Almost always, they could hear some noise like
a grenade or a mortar or the insistent shrill tatting of a sub-machine gun,
but the sounds were so far away and so muffled that in time they disregarded them. The week went by in an uncomfortable suspended tension
which they felt only in their unvoiced fear of the towering mute walls of
Watamai Range on their right.

Every day a ration detail of three men would trudge over to the hill
on which the adjacent platoon of A Company was bivouacked, and return with a box of 10-in-1 rations and two five-gallon jerricans of water.
The trip was always uneventful and the men did not dislike it, for the
monotony of the morning was broken and it gave them a chance to talk
to someone other than the men in their squad.

On the last day of the week, Croft and Red and Gallagher filed down
their hill, wove through the six-foot kunai grass in the valley beneath
them, emerged into a bamboo grove, and from there followed the trail
that led to A Company. They filled their empty water cans, strapped
them to pack boards, and talked for a few minutes with some of the men
in A Company before starting back. Croft was leading them, and when
he reached the beginning of the trail he halted, and motioned to Red
and Gallagher to come forward.

"Listen," he whispered. "You men were making too goddam much
noise coming down the hill. Just 'cause this is a short distance and you
got a little weight on your back don' mean you're supposed to wallow
round like a bunch of goddam pigs."

"Okay," Gallagher muttered sullenly.

"C'mon, let's go," Red muttered. He and Croft had hardly spoken
to each other all week.

The three men filed slowly down the trail keeping a distance of ten
yards between them. Red found himself treading warily, and he realized
with a trace of anger that Croft's command was influencing him. He
walked along for many yards trying to determine whether he was afraid
of Croft's anger or his caution came from habit. He was still debating
this when he saw Croft stop abruptly, and creep through some bushes
on the side of the trail. Croft turned around and looked at Gallagher and
him, and then waved his arm forward in a slow silent motion. Red looked
at his face; Croft's mouth and eyes were expressionless but there was a
poise and tension about his entire body which was imperative. Red
crouched and moved up beside him. When the three of them were
together, Croft held his finger to his mouth, and then pointed through a
break in the foliage beside the trail. About twenty-five yards away there
was a tiny hollow. It was actually no more than a small clearing, encircled by jungle, but in the middle of it three Japanese soldiers were
sprawled on the ground, resting with their heads on their packs, and a

fourth soldier was sitting beside them with his rifle across his lap, his chin resting on his hand. Croft looked at them for a long tense second, and then stared fiercely at Red and Gallagher. His jaw had tightened, and a small lump of cartilage beneath his ear quivered once or twice. Very carefully, he slipped off his pack board and laid it noiselessly on the ground.

"We can't get through that brush without making a noise, he whispered almost soundlessly. "Ah'm gonna throw a grenade, and then we all rush together. Y'understand?"

They nodded dumbly, stripping their packs. Then Red peered through the yards of brush that separated them from the draw. If the grenade failed to kill the Japs, all three of them would be exposed as they went charging through the brush. Actually he hardly thought of this; he rebelled against everything in the situation. It was unbelievable. He always had a similar reaction when he knew he would be in combat in a few seconds. It always seemed impossible he would move or fire his gun, expose his life, and yet he always advanced. Red was feeling now the anger that always followed this, a rage at his desire to avoid the moment to come. I'm as good as any man jack, he told himself numbly. He looked at Gallagher, whose face was white, and Red felt a surprising contempt although he knew that he was himself equally frightened. Croft's nostrils had dilated, and the pupils of his eyes looked cold and very black; Red hated him because Croft could enjoy this.

Croft slipped a grenade out of his belt, and pulled the safety pin. Red looked through the foliage again and stared at the backs of the Japanese soldiers. He could see the face of the man who was sitting up, and it added to the unreality; he felt as though something were choking him. The Japanese soldier had a pleasant bland face with wide temples and a heavy jaw; he looked cow-like and his thick hands appeared sturdy and callused. Red had for a moment an odd detached pleasure, quite incongruous, which stemmed from the knowledge that he was unobserved. And yet all of this was mixed with dread, and the certainty that none of it was real. He could not believe that in a few seconds the soldier with the broad pleasant face was going to die.

Croft opened his fingers, and the handle of the grenade snapped off and spun a few feet away. The fuse in the grenade popped, and a sputtering noise destroyed the silence. The Japanese heard it, sprang to their feet with sudden cries, and moved a few steps uncertainly back and forth in the tiny circle of the draw. Red watched the expression of terror on one soldier's face, heard the sizzling of the grenade, the sound mixing with the ringing in his ears and the pounding of his heart, and then dropped to the ground as Croft lofted the grenade into the draw. Red grasped his tommy gun and stared intently at a blade of grass. He had time before the grenade exploded to wish he had cleaned his gun that morning. He heard a terrifying shriek, thought once of the soldier with the broad face, and then found himself afoot, crashing and stumbling through the brush.

The three of them halted on the edge of the draw and looked down. All four of the Japanese soldiers were lying motionless in the trampled kunai grass. Croft gazed at them and spat softly. "Go down and take a look," he told Red.

Red slid down the bank to the gully where the bodies lay sprawled. He could tell at a glance that two of the men were certainly dead; one of them reposed on his back with his hands clawed over the bloody mash of what had once been his face, and the other was crumpled on his side with a great rent in his chest. The other two men had fallen on their stomachs and he could see no wounds.

"Finish them off," Croft shouted down to him.

"They're dead."

"Finish them off."

Red felt a pulse of anger. If it'd been anyone else but me, the bastard would have done it himself, he thought. He stood over one of the motionless bodies, and brought the sights of his tommy gun to bear on the back of the soldier's head. He took a little breath, and then fired a burst. He felt nothing except the rising quivering motion of the gun in his hands. After he had fired, he noticed that it was the soldier who had been sitting with his rifle across his thighs. There was an instant in which he hovered on the lip of an intense anxiety, but he repressed it and strode over to the last soldier.

As he looked down upon him, Red felt a wash of many transient subtle emotions. If he had been asked, he might have said, "I didn't feel a goddam thing," but the back of his neck was numb, and his heart was beating rapidly. He had an intense distaste for what he was about to do, and yet as he stared at the body and pointed his sights at the man's neck, he was feeling a pleasurable anticipation. He tightened his finger on the trigger, taking up the slack, tensing himself for the moment when he would fire and the slugs would make round little holes in a cluster, and the corpse would twitch and shake under the force of the bullets. He pictured all those sensations, pulled the trigger . . . and nothing happened. His gun had jammed. He started to work the bolt when the body underneath him suddenly rolled over. It took Red almost a second to realize that the Jap was alive. The two men stared at each other with blank twitching faces, and then the Jap sprang to his feet. There was a fraction of a second in which Red could have knocked him down with the stock of his gun, but the frustration he had felt when the gun jammed, added to the shock he experienced when he realized the soldier was alive, combined to paralyze him completely. He watched the soldier stand up, move a step toward him, and then Red's muscles worked suddenly, and he hurled his gun at the Jap. It missed, and the two soldiers continued to stare at each other, not three yards apart.

Red could never forget the Jap's face. It was gaunt and the skin was drawn tightly over the eyes and cheeks and nostrils so that he had a hungry searching look. He had never seen a man's face so intensely; his gaze concentrated until he could detect every imperfection in the man's skin. He saw blackheads on the Jap's forehead, and a tiny pustule on the side of his nose, and drops of sweat in the deep hollows under his eyes. Perhaps they stared at each other for half a second, and then the Jap unsheathed his bayonet, and Red turned and ran. He saw the other man lunging toward him, and Red thought inanely, Horror movie. With a great effort he shrieked over his shoulder, "Get him, GET HIM, CROFT!"

Then Red tripped, and lay motionless on the ground, half stunned. He was trying to ready himself for the flash of pain the knife would cause as it pierced his back, and he held his breath. He heard his heart beat once, and then once more. His alertness was returning, and he poised his body. His heart beat again, and again, and again. Abruptly, he realized that nothing was going to happen.

Croft's clear cold voice grated in his ear. "Goddam, Red, how long you gonna lay on the ground?"

Red rolled over and sat up. He repressed a groan with difficulty, but the effort made him shudder. "Jesus," he said.

"What do you think of your boy friend?" Croft asked softly.

The Jap was standing several yards away with his hands in the air. He had dropped the bayonet, and it lay at his feet. Croft walked over and kicked it away.

Red looked at the Japanese soldier, and for an instant their eyes met. Both men looked away, as if they had each been caught in something shameful. Red realized suddenly how weak he felt.

Yet even now he could not admit any weakness to Croft. "What took you guys so goddam long?" he asked.

"Got down as fast as we could," Croft said.

Gallagher spoke up abruptly. His face was white and his mouth trembled. "I was gonna shoot the mother-fugger but you were in the way."

Croft laughed quietly, and then said, "Ah' guess we frightened him more than you, Red. He damn sure stopped running after you when he saw us."

Red found himself shuddering again. He felt a grudged admiration for Croft, and with it a great deal of resentment at being in his debt. For a second or two he tried to find some way to thank him, but he could not utter the words.

"I guess we might as well head back," Red said.

Croft's expression seemed to change. A glint of excitement formed in his eyes. "Why don't you head on back, Red?" he suggested. "Gallagher and me'll follow you in a couple of minutes."

Red forced himself to say, "Want me to take the Jap?" There was nothing he wanted less. He found himself still unable to look at the soldier.

"No," Croft said. "Gallagher and me'll take care of him."

Red realized there was something odd about Croft at this moment. "I can take him okay," he said.

"No, we'll take care of him."

Red looked once at the bodies lying limp in the green draw. Already a few insects were buzzing over the corpse who had lost his face. Everything that had happened to him seemed unreal again. He looked at the soldier from whom he had fled, and already his face seemed anonymous and small. A part of him wondered why he had not been able to meet his eyes. Jesus, I feel pooped, he thought. His legs quivered a little as he picked up his tommy gun. He felt too tired to say anything more. "Okay, see you up on the hill," he muttered.

For some obscure reason, he knew he should not leave, and as he walked away down the trail he felt again the curious shame and guilt the Japanese soldier had caused him. That Croft's a bastard, he told himself. Red felt leaden, in fever.

When he had gone, Croft sat down on the ground and lit a cigarette. He smoked intently without saying anything. Gallagher sat beside him, looking at the prisoner. "Let's get rid of him and get back," he blurted suddenly.

"Hold your water," Croft told him softly.

"What's the use of torturin' the poor bastard?" Gallagher asked.

"He ain't complainin'," Croft said.

But then, as if he had understood them, the prisoner crumpled suddenly to his knees and began to sob in a high-pitched voice. Every few seconds he would turn to them, and extend his hands with pleading motions, and then he would beat his arms on the ground as if he despaired of making them understand. Out of the spate of words, Gallagher could distinguish something that sounded like "kood-sigh, kood-sigh."

Gallagher was a little hysterical from the abruptness with which the combat had begun and ended. His momentary compassion for the prisoner lapsed and was replaced by an intense irritation. "Let's cut out that 'kood-sigh' shit," he roared at the Jap.

The soldier was silent for a moment, and then began to plead again. His voice had a desperate urgency which rasped Gallagher's senses. "You look like a fuggin Yid with all that handwaving," he shouted.

"Let's keep it down," Croft said.

The soldier approached them, and Gallagher looked uncomfortably into his black pleading eyes. A powerful fishy stench arose from his clothing. "They sure can stink," Gallagher said.

Croft kept staring at the Jap. An emotion was obviously working through his mind, for the lump of cartilage under his ear kept pulsing. Croft actually was not thinking at all; he was bothered by an intense sense of incompletion. He was still expecting the burst that Red's gun had never fired. Even more than Red, he had been anticipating the quick lurching spasms of the body when the bullets would crash into it, and now he felt an intense dissatisfaction.

He looked at his cigarette, and on an impulse he handed it to the Japanese soldier. "What're you doing that for?" Gallagher asked.

"Let him smoke."

The prisoner puffed at it eagerly, and yet self-consciously. His eyes kept darting suspiciously at Croft and Gallagher, and the sweat glistened on his cheeks.

"Hey, you," Croft said, "sit down."

The Jap looked at him with uncomprehending eyes. "Sit down." Croft made some motions with his hands, and the prisoner squatted with his back against a tree. "You got anything to eat?" Croft asked Gallagher.

"I got a chocolate bar from the ration."

"Let's have it," Croft said. He took the bar from Gallagher and handed it to the soldier, who looked at him with dull eyes. Croft made eating motions with his hands, and the prisoner, comprehending, ripped the paper away, and wolfed down the chocolate. "Goddam, he sure is hungry," Croft said.

"What the fug are you doin' it for?" Gallagher asked. He felt exasperated to the point of tears. He had been saving the candy for over a day, and its loss pained him; moreover, he was vacillating between irritability at the prisoner and a grudged compassion. "The dumb bastard sure is skinny," he said with the superior affection he might have used if he saw a mongrel dog shivering in the rain. But then immediately afterward he watched the last piece of chocolate disappear in the Jap's mouth, and he muttered angrily, "What a goddam pig he is."

Croft thought of the night the Japanese had tried to cross the river. He felt a shiver work its way through him, and he stared for a long time at the prisoner. He felt an intense emotion toward him which made him clench his teeth. But what it was, he could not have said. He removed his canteen and took a drink. He saw the prisoner watching him as he gulped down the water, and on an impulse he handed him the canteen. "Go ahead, drink," he said. Croft gazed at him as he swallowed with long eager draughts.

"I'm a sonofabitch," Gallagher said. "What got in ya?"

Croft did not answer. He was staring at the prisoner, who had finished drinking. There were a few tears of joy in the Jap's face and he smiled suddenly and pointed to his breast pocket. Croft extracted a wallet, and opened it. There was a picture of the Japanese soldier in civilian dress and beside him was his wife and two children with round doll faces.

The Japanese soldier pointed to himself and then made two gestures with his hands above the ground to indicate how tall his children had grown.

Gallagher looked at the picture, and felt a pang. For an instant he remembered his wife and wondered what his child would look like when it was born. With a shock he realized that his wife might be in labor now. For some reason which he did not understand he said suddenly to the Jap, "I'm gonna have a kid in a couple of days."

The prisoner smiled politely, and Gallagher pointed angrily to himself and then held his hands extended and about nine inches apart. "Me," he said, "me."

"Ahhhhhh," the prisoner said. "Chiisai!"

"Yeah, cheez-igh," Gallagher said.

The prisoner shook his head slowly, and smiled again.

Croft came up to him, and gave him another cigarette. The Japanese soldier bowed low, and accepted the match. "Arigato, arigato, domo arigato," he said.

Croft felt his head pulsing with an intense excitement. There were tears in the prisoner's eyes again, and Croft looked at them dispassionately. He gazed once about the little draw, and watched a fly crawl over the mouth of one of the corpses.

The prisoner had taken a deep puff and was leaning back now against the trunk of the tree. His eyes had closed, and for the first time there was a dreamy expression on his face. Croft felt a tension work itself into his throat and leave his mouth dry and bitter and demanding. His mind had been entirely empty until now, but abruptly he brought up his rifle and pointed it at the prisoner's head. Gallagher started to protest as the Jap opened his eyes.

The prisoner did not have time to change his expression before the shot crashed into his skull. He slumped forward, and then rolled on his side. He was still smiling but he looked silly now.

Gallagher tried to speak again but was incapable of it. He felt an awful fear and for an instant he thought of his wife again. Oh, God save Mary, God save Mary, he repeated to himself without thinking of the meaning of the words.

Croft stared for almost a minute at the Jap. His pulse was slowing down and he felt the tension ease in his throat and mouth. He realized suddenly that a part of his mind, very deeply buried, had known he was going to kill the prisoner from the moment he had sent Red on ahead. He felt quite blank now. The smile on the dead man's face amused him, and a trivial rill of laughter emitted from his lips. "Goddam," he said. He thought once again of the Japanese crossing the river, and he prodded the body with his foot. "Goddam," he said, "that Jap sure died happy." The laughter swelled more strongly inside him.

# THOMAS BERNHARD

THE NOVELIST, playwright, and poet Thomas Bernhard, one of the most admired writers in German of his generation, was born in the Netherlands and grew up in Salzburg during World War II. What follows is an excerpt from his memoir of his childhood and youth, *Gathering Evidence*.

■

FROM *Gathering Evidence*

There was an air-raid warning almost every night, and later we had them in the daytime too. The flights of bombers, often well over a hundred of them, grouped above our heads and turned toward Munich to drop their deadly loads there. All the interesting things were now taking place in the air, in all weathers. We saw and heard them and were scared. One glorious day around noon, when my grandmother was sitting at the sewing machine in our apartment in the Schaumburgerstrasse, the roar of a bomber formation made us look out of the window. The American planes, in formations of six, gleamed in the sky on their rigid course towards Munich. Suddenly, from a still greater height, a German plane, a Messerschmitt 109, appeared and in no time shot down one of the silver giants. My grandmother and I saw the bomber drop out of formation and finally, with tremendous force, break into three parts which landed at widely separated spots. At the same time there were several white points indicating the members of the crew who had bailed out by parachute. It was a spectacle of unrelieved tragedy. Our stark noonday picture showed several parachutes which failed to open: we could see the black dots falling to earth faster than the parts of the plane. Other parachutes opened but caught fire for some reason and burnt out in no time, falling to earth with the crew-members attached to them. All this had no effect whatever on the bomber formation as a whole. It flew on to Munich. The town was too far away for us to hear the detonation. My grandmother, sensing excitement, got hold of me and ran with me to catch the next train to Waging, where she suspected the parts of the destroyed plane would have landed. She was right. At Otting, a place of pilgrimage situated on a hill, one stop before Waging, the remains were still smoking. One of the bomber's two enormous wings, about a hundred feet long, had fallen directly onto a pigsty, setting it on fire and killing about a hundred pigs. There was an unimaginable stench in the air when we at last arrived, out of breath, at the top of the hill. It was winter, and the air was icy. We had had to trudge through deep snow from the station up to the village. The inhabitants of Otting stood looking at the wreckage and finding fresh fragments of it. Great holes were to be seen in the snow, where the bodies of the Canadians (as they turned out to be) lay shattered after falling from the sky. I was horrified. Everywhere the snow was spattered with blood. There's an arm! I said, and on the arm was a watch. I no longer enjoyed the sight of war. What had been merely a sensation I now saw from a different angle. I wanted to see nothing more of war, which had now shown its horrible face to us, having until now been known only from a distance. We went back to Traunstein. I sought comfort from my grandfather. He had nothing to say. In the evening he and my grandmother sat in a corner of the room listening to a Swiss radio station. At the end of February and the beginning of March Schorschi and I spent our afternoons dragging the dead deer and their young out of their last retreats. We dug ditches and buried the frozen carcasses in them. I spent whatever time I could in Ettendorf. When my great-aunt Rosina died, my grandfather, her brother, went to Henndorf to attend the funeral. He had kept away from his birthplace in recent years. After the so-called funeral feast, which the mourners ate in the large assembly room of the family hotel, Rosina's younger sister, the much-traveled artist's widow, is said to have launched into a speech in which she repeatedly referred to herself as a *German woman. She referred to herself nonstop as a German woman, inspired by her new ideal, National Socialism. That was too much for me in the end, so I jumped up and said, Do you know what you are? You're not a German woman, you're a German sow!* They never saw each other again. They broke with each other over National Socialism.

# MARIE VASSILTCHIKOV

MARIE VASSILTCHIKOV's diaries provide a detailed picture of life in wartime Berlin. Marie was stranded with
one of her sisters in Germany in 1939, having spent
the summer in Silesia. She held a minor position in
the Foreign Ministry. Many of her friends were involved
in the July 20, 1944, plot to assassinate Hitler. Her
brother, George Vassiltchikov, who edited her journals
for publication, calls her "a compulsive diarist." Her
compulsion has yielded a remarkable account.

■

FROM *Berlin Diaries*

In front of another wrecked building a crowd was watching a young
girl aged about sixteen. She was standing atop a pile of rubble, picking
up bricks one by one, dusting them carefully and throwing them away
again. Apparently her entire family was dead, buried underneath, and
she had gone mad. This part of the town looked truly ghastly. In some
places one could not even tell where the streets had been and we no
longer knew where we were. But eventually we reached Rauchstrasse
and our own office.

Miraculously, it had survived. Downstairs I ran into one of our
personnel officers. I told him that I had an aged father, whom I had an
opportunity to take to the country. At first he was reluctant, but on
hearing that we were *Bombengeschädigte* [bomb victims]—a life-saving
word in times like these!—he agreed. I assured him that I would return
as soon as I was needed again and, giving him Tatiana's address and
telephone number, I took off before he could change his mind.

After some hot soup at the Gersdorffs' just around the corner, Loremarie and I continued on our round, combing the town street by street
in search of lost friends.

These last days innumerable inscriptions in chalk have appeared on
the blackened walls of wrecked houses: "Liebste Frau B., wo sind Sie?
Ich suche Sie überall. Kommen Sie zu mir. Ich habe Platz fur Sie"
[Dearest Frau B., where are you? I have been looking for you every-
where. Come and stay with me. I have room for you"] or "Alle aus
diesem Keller gerettet!" ["Everyone from this cellar has been saved!"] or
"Mein Engelein, wo bleibst Du? Ich bin in grosser Sorge. Dein Fritz"
["My little angel, where are you? I worry greatly. Your Fritz"], etc.

Gradually, as people return to their homes and read these messages, answers start to appear, chalked underneath. We discovered the whereabouts of several of our friends this way and on reaching the ruins of our own office we, too, picked up some chalk in the rubble and wrote in large square letters on the pillar next to the entrance: "Missie und Loremarie gesund, befinden sich in Potsdam bei B." ["Missie and Loremarie are well, staying in Potsdam at the B(ismarcks)."] Our top boss doubtless would have disapproved, but we were thinking above all of our various beaux, who are in the habit of telephoning at all hours of the day and who might come by to look for us.

# ANDRE SCHWARZ-BART

ANDRE SCHWARZ-BART, a Hungarian Jew, joined the French Resistance at the age of fifteen. In 1960 he won the Prix Goncourt for his novel *The Last of the Just,* from which the following extract is taken. Largely self-educated, he was, at the time, working as a porter in the great vegetable market of Les Halles in Paris.

■

FROM *The Last of the Just*

Ernie was amazed that the men of the Marais never tired of God. In a tiny block of houses condemned to disappear shortly in the great flood of death, they went on waving their arms to heaven, clinging to it in all their fervor, in all their torment, in all their pious despair. Every day a new raid netted friends or relatives, next-door neighbors, flesh and blood beings with whom only yesterday words had been exchanged; but the little synagogues in the rue du Roi-de-Sicile, in the Rue des Rosiers or in the rue Pavée were never empty. The four little old men dragged their guest there regularly, so that he should participate in their fiery prayers. Sometimes young people adorned with fleurs de lys were waiting for them when they came out, bludgeons in hand, elegant sarcasms on their lips. "It's like that every day now," the little old men moaned, trotting along close to the wall. "And yet we can't miss the Office. That's what they want, you know."

Between raids a swarming fish-pond of an existence continued in the branded alleyways and cul-de-sacs. Communal cauldrons of soup appeared; no one knew how. In those springtime days of 1943 even the starred scum of the earth enjoyed the privilege of the pale sun that shone dimly through the gray, medieval waters of the Marais. Ernie had found work, with a furrier who had a green identity card. People were already passing word along that it was the turn of the white cards next; but it was the red ones. Thus the anglers on the bank confused their prey with the painful bait of survival.

# GEORGE ORWELL

DURING THE WAR, Orwell wrote a regular "London Letter" for *Partisan Review*. An excerpt from his letter of July–August 1943 discusses British antisemitism.

■

## "London Letter" to *Partisan Review*

Finally a word about antisemitism, which could now be said to have reached the stature of a "problem." I said in my last letter that it was not increasing, but I now think it is. The danger signal, which is also a safeguard, is that everyone is very conscious of it and it is discussed interminably in the press.

Although Jews in England have always been socially looked down on and debarred from a few professions (I doubt whether a Jew would be accepted as an officer in the navy, for instance), antisemitism is primarily a working-class thing, and strongest among Irish laborers. I have had some glimpses of working-class antisemitism through being three years in the Home Guard—which gives a good cross-section of society—in a district where there are a lot of Jews. My experience is that middle-class people will laugh at Jews and discriminate against them to some extent, but only among working people do you find the full-blown belief in the Jews as a cunning and sinister race who live by exploiting the Gentiles. After all that has happened in the last ten years it is a fearful thing to hear a working man saying, "Well, I reckon 'Itler done a good job when 'e turned 'em all out," but I have heard just that, and more than once. These people never seem to be aware that Hitler has done anything to the Jews except "turned 'em all out"; the pogroms, the deportations, etc. have simply escaped their notice. It is questionable, however, whether the Jew is objected to as a Jew or simply as a foreigner. No religious consideration enters. The English Jew, who is often strictly orthodox but entirely anglicized in his habits, is less disliked than the European refugee who has probably not been near a synagogue for thirty years. Some people actually object to the Jews on the ground that Jews are Germans!

But in somewhat different forms antisemitism is now spreading among the middle class as well. The usual formula is "Of course I don't want you to think I'm antisemitic, but—" —and here follows a catalogue of Jewish misdeeds. Jews are accused of evading military service, infringing the food laws, pushing their way to the front of queues, etc. etc. More thoughtful people point out that the Jewish refugees use this country as a temporary asylum but show no loyalty towards it. Objectively this is true, and the tactlessness of some of the refugees is almost incredible. (For example, a remark by a German Jewess overheard during the Battle of France: "These English police are not nearly so smart as our SS men.") But arguments of this kind are obviously rationalizations of prejudice. People dislike the Jews so much that they do not want to remember their sufferings, and when you mention the horrors that are happening in Germany or Poland, the answer is always "Oh yes, of course that's dreadful, but—" —and out comes the familiar list of grievances. Not all of the intelligentsia are immune from this kind of thing. Here the get-out is usually that the refugees are all "petty bourgeois"; and so the abuse of Jews can proceed under a respectable disguise. Pacifists and others who are anti-war sometimes find themselves forced into antisemitism.

One should not exaggerate the danger of this kind of thing. To begin with, there is probably less antisemitism in England now than there was thirty years ago. In the minor novels of that date you find it taken for granted far oftener than you would nowadays that a Jew is an inferior or a figure of fun. The "Jew joke" has disappeared from the stage, the radio and the comic papers since 1934. Secondly, there is a great awareness of the prevalence of antisemitism and a conscious effort to struggle against it. But the thing remains, and perhaps it is one of the inevitable neuroses of war. I am not particularly impressed by the fact that it does not take violent forms. It is true that no one wants to have pogroms and throw elderly Jewish professors into cesspools, but then there is very little crime or violence in England anyway. The milder form of antisemitism prevailing here can be just as cruel in an indirect way, because it causes people to avert their eyes from the whole refugee problem and remain uninterested in the fate of the surviving Jews of Europe. Because two days ago a fat Jewess grabbed your place on the bus, you switch off the wireless when the announcer begins talking about the ghettoes of Warsaw; that is how people's minds work nowadays.

That is all the political news I have. Life goes on much as before. I don't notice that our food is any different, but the food situation is generally considered to be worse. The war hits one a succession of blows in unexpected places. For a long time razor blades were unobtainable, now it is boot polish. Books are being printed on the most villainous paper and in tiny print, very trying to the eyes. A few people are wearing wooden-soled shoes. There is an alarming amount of drunkenness in London. The American soldiers seem to be getting on better terms with the locals, perhaps having become more resigned to the climate etc. Air raids continue, but on a pitiful scale. I notice that many people feel sympathy for the Germans now that it is they who are being bombed—a change from 1940, when people saw their houses tumbling about them and wanted to see Berlin scraped off the map.

# WILLIAM STYRON

WILLIAM STYRON, born and raised in Virginia, pub-
lished his first novel, *Lie Down in Darkness*, in 1951.
His other novels include *Set This House on Fire; The
Confessions of Nat Turner,* which won the Pulitzer
Prize; and *Sophie's Choice,* from which the following
is excerpted.

■

FROM *Sophie's Choice*

She had been thumbing through a copy of *Look* magazine several
weeks old, when the image of Höss burst out from the page, causing her
such shock that the strangled noise which came from her throat made
the woman sitting next to her give a quick reflexive shudder. Höss was
within seconds of a final reckoning. His face set in an expressionless
mask, manacled, gaunt and unshaven as he stood in disheveled prison
fatigues, the ex-Commandant was clearly at the edge of embarking upon
a momentous journey. Entwined around his neck was a rope, depending
from a stark metal gallows tree around which a clutch of Polish soldiers
was making last preparations for his passage into the beyond. Gazing
past the shabby figure, with its already dead and vacant face like that of
an actor playing a zombie at the center of a stage, Sophie's eyes sought,
found, then identified the blurred but unspeakably familiar backdrop:
the squat begrimed shape of the original crematorium at Auschwitz. She
threw the magazine down and got off at the next stop, so disturbed by
this obscene encroachment on her memory that she aimlessly paced the
sunlit walks around the museum and the botanic gardens for several
hours before showing up at the office, where Dr. Blackstock commented
on her haggard look: "Some ghost you've seen?" After a day or two,
however, she was able to banish the picture from her mind.

Unknown then to Sophie or to the world in general, Rudolf Höss,
in the months preceding his trial and execution, had been composing a
document which in its relatively brief compass tells as much as any single
work about a mind swept away in the rapture of totalitarianism. Years
were to pass before its translation into English (done excellently by Con-
stantine FitzGibbon). Now bound into a volume called *KL Auschwitz
Seen by the SS*—published by the Polish state museum maintained today
at the camp—this anatomy of Höss's psyche is available for examination
by all those who might thirst for knowledge about the true nature of evil.

Certainly it should be read throughout the world by professors of philosophy, ministers of the Gospel, rabbis, shamans, all historians, writers, politicians and diplomats, liberationists of whatever sex and persuasion, lawyers, judges, penologists, stand-up comedians, film directors, journalists, in short, anyone concerned remotely with affecting the consciousness of his fellow-man—and this would include our own beloved children, those incipient American leaders at the eighth-grade level, who should be required to study it along with *The Catcher in the Rye, The Hobbit* and the Constitution. For within these confessions it will be discovered that we really have no acquaintance with true evil; the evil portrayed in most novels and plays and movies is mediocre if not spurious, a shoddy concoction generally made up of violence, fantasy, neurotic terror and melodrama.

This "imaginary evil"—again to quote Simone Weil—"is romantic and varied, while real evil is gloomy, monotonous, barren, boring." Beyond doubt those words characterize Rudolf Höss and the workings of his mind, an organism so crushingly banal as to be a paradigm of the thesis eloquently stated by Hannah Arendt some years after his hanging. Höss was hardly a sadist, nor was he a violent man or even particularly menacing. He might even be said to have possessed a serviceable decency. Indeed, Jerzy Rawicz, the Polish editor of Höss's autobiography, himself a survivor of Auschwitz, has the wisdom to rebuke his fellow prisoners for the depositions they had made charging Höss with beatings and torture. "Höss would never stoop to do such things," Rawicz insists. "He had more important duties to perform." The Commandant was a homebody, as we shall observe, but one dedicated blindly to duty and a cause; thus he became a mere servomechanism in which a moral vacuum had been so successfully sucked clean of every molecule of real qualm or scruple that his own descriptions of the unutterable crimes he perpetrated daily seem often to float outside and apart from evil, phantasms of cretinous innocence. Yet even this automaton was made of flesh, as you or I; he was brought up a Christian, nearly became a Catholic priest; twinges of conscience, even of remorse, attack him from time to time like the onset of some bizarre disease, and it is this frailty, the human response that stirs within the implacable and obedient robot, that helps make his memoirs so fascinating, so terrifying and educative.

A word about his early life will suffice. Born in 1900, in the same year and under the same sign as Thomas Wolfe ("Oh lost, and by the wind, grieved, Ghost . . ."), Höss was the son of a retired colonel in the German army. His father wanted him to be a seminarian, but the First World War broke out and when Höss was but a stripling of sixteen he joined the army. He participated in the fighting in the Near East—Turkey and Palestine—and at seventeen became the youngest noncommissioned officer in the German armed forces. After the war he joined a militant nationalist group and in 1922 met the man who would hold him in thrall for the rest of his life—Adolf Hitler. So instantly smitten was Höss by the ideals of National Socialism and by its leader that he became one of the earliest bona-fide card-carrying members of the Nazi party. It is perhaps not odd that he committed his first murder soon, and was convicted and sent to jail. He early learned that murder was his duty in life. The victim was a teacher named Kadow, head of a liberal political faction which the Nazis considered inimical to their interests. After serving six years of a life sentence, Höss drifted into a career of farming in Mecklenburg, got married, and in time sired five children. The years appear to have hung heavy on Höss's hands there near the stormy Baltic, amid the ripening barley and wheat. His need for a more challenging vocation was fulfilled when in the mid-1930s he met an old friend from the early days in the *Bruderschaft*, Heinrich Himmler, who easily persuaded Höss to abandon the plow and the hoe and to sample those gratifications that the SS might offer. Himmler, whose own biography reveals him to be (whatever else) a superlative judge of assassins, surely divined in Höss a man cut out for the important line of work he had in mind, for the next sixteen years of Höss's life were spent either directly as Commandant of concentration camps or in upper-echelon jobs connected with their administration. Before Auschwitz his most important post was at Dachau.

Höss eventually developed what might be called a fruitful—or at least symbiotic—relationship with the man who was to remain his immediate superior: Adolf Eichmann. Eichmann nurtured Höss's gifts, which led to some of the more distinguished advances in *die Todentechnologie*. In 1941, for example, Eichmann began to find the Jewish problem a source of intolerable vexation not only because of the obvious immensity of the approaching task but because of the sheer practical difficulties involved in the "final solution." Until that time mass extermination—then conducted by the SS on a relatively modest scale—had been carried out either by shooting, which posed problems having to do with simple bloody mess, unhandiness and inefficiency, or by the introduction of carbon monoxide into an enclosed sealed space, a method which was also inefficient and prohibitively time-consuming. It was Höss who, having observed the effectiveness of a crystalized hydrocyanic compound called Zyklon B when used as a vapor on the rats and the other verminous creatures that infested Auschwitz, suggested this means of liquidation to Eichmann, who, according to Höss, jumped at the idea, though he later denied it. (Why *any* experimenter was so backward is hard to understand. Cyanide gas had been used in certain American execution chambers for over fifteen years.) Turning nine hundred Russian prisoners of war into guinea pigs, Höss found the gas splendidly suited to the quick dispatch of human beings and it was employed thereafter extensively on countless inmates and arrivals of whatever origin, although after early April, 1943, exclusively on Jews and Gypsies. Höss

was also an innovator in the use of such techniques as miniature minefields to blow up wayward or escaping prisoners, high-voltage fences to
electrocute them and—his capricious pride—a pack of ferocious Alsa-
tians and Doberman pinschers known as the *Hundestaffel* that gave Höss
mingled joy and dissatisfaction (in a fussy concern that runs persistently
through his memoirs), since the dogs, though hounds of hell in savagery
by which they had been trained to chew inmates to shreds, did become
torpid and ungovernable at moments and were all too skilled at finding
out-of-the-way corners to go to sleep. In a large measure, however, his
fertile and inventive ideas were successful enough that it may be said
that Höss—in consummate travesty of the way that Koch and Ehrlich
and Roentgen and others altered the face of medical science during the
great German efflorescence of the last half of the previous century—
worked upon the entire concept of mass murder a lasting meta-
morphosis.

For the sake of its historical and sociological significance it has to be
pointed out that of all Höss's co-defendants at the postwar trials in Poland
and Germany—those satraps and second-string butchers who made up
the SS ranks at Auschwitz and other camps—only a handful had a military background. However, this should not be particularly surprising.
Military men are capable of abominable crimes; witness, in our recent
time alone, Chile, My Lai, Greece. But it is a "liberal" fallacy that
equates the military mind with real evil and makes it the exclusive province of lieutenants or generals; the secondary evil of which the military
is frequently capable is aggressive, romantic, melodramatic, thrilling,
orgasmic. Real evil, the suffocating evil of Auschwitz—gloomy, monotonous, barren, boring—was perpetrated almost exclusively by civilians.
Thus we find that the rolls of the SS at Auschwitz-Birkenau contained
almost no professional soldiers but were instead composed of a cross
section of German society. They included waiters, bakers, carpenters,
restaurant owners, physicians, a bookkeeper, a post office clerk, a waitress, a bank clerk, a nurse, a locksmith, a fireman, a customs officer, a
legal advisor, a manufacturer of musical instruments, a specialist in machine construction, a laboratory assistant, the owner of a trucking firm
. . . the list goes on and on with these commonplace and familiar citizens' pursuits. There needs only to be added the observation that history's greatest liquidator of Jews, the thick-witted Heinrich Himmler, was
a chicken farmer.

No real revelation in all this: in modern times most of the mischief
ascribed to the military has been wrought with the advice and consent of
civil authority. As for Höss, he seems to be something of an anomaly,
inasmuch as his pre-Auschwitz career straddled agriculture and the military. The evidence shows that he had been exceptionally dedicated, and
it is precisely that rigorous and unbending attitude of spirit—the concept
of duty and obedience above all which dwells unshakably in the mind of

every good soldier—that gives his memoirs a desolating convincingness. Reading the sickening chronicle, one becomes persuaded that Höss is sincere when he expresses his misgivings, even his secret revulsion, at this or that gassing or cremation or "selection," and that dark doubts attend the acts he is required to commit. Lurking behind Höss as he writes, one feels, is the spectral presence of the seventeen-year-old boy, the brilliantly promising young Unterfeldwebel of the army of another era, when distinct notions of honor and pride and rectitude were woven into the fabric of the Prussian code, and that the boy is stricken dumb at the unmentionable depravity in which the grown man is mired. But that is of another time and place, another Reich, and the boy is banished into the farthest shadows, the horror receding and fading with him as the doomed ex-Obersturmbannführer scribbles indefatigably away, justifying his bestial deeds in the name of insensate authority, call of duty, blind obedience

One is somehow convinced by the equanimity of this statement: "I must emphasize that I have never personally hated the Jews. It is true that I looked upon them as the enemies of our people. But just because of this I saw no difference between them and the other prisoners, and I treated them all in the same way. I never drew any distinctions. In any event, the emotion of hatred is foreign to my nature." In the world of the crematoriums hatred is a reckless and incontinent passion, incompatible with the humdrum nature of the quotidian task. Especially if a man has allowed himself to become depleted of all such distracting emotions, the matter of questioning or mistrusting an order becomes academic; he immediately obeys: "When in the summer of 1941 the Reichsführer SS [Himmler] himself gave me the order to prepare installations at Auschwitz where mass exterminations could take place, and personally carry out these exterminations, I did not have the slightest idea of their scale or consequences. It was certainly an extraordinary and monstrous order. Nevertheless, the reasons behind the extermination program seemed to me right. I did not reflect on it at the time: I had been given an order and I had to carry it out. Whether this mass extermination of the Jews was necessary or not was something on which I could not allow myself to form an opinion, for I lacked the necessary breadth of view."

And so the carnage begins, beneath Höss's narrow, watchful and impassive eye: "I had to appear cold and indifferent to events that must have wrung the heart of anyone possessed of human feelings. I might not even look away when afraid lest my natural emotions get the upper hand. I had to watch coldly, while the mothers with laughing or crying children went into the gas chambers. . . .

"On one occasion two small children were so absorbed in some game that they refused to let their mother tear them away from it. Even the Jews of the Special Detachment were reluctant to pick the children up.

The imploring look in the eyes of the mother, who certainly knew what was happening, is something I shall never forget. The people were already in the gas chamber and becoming restive, and I had to act. Everyone was looking at me. I nodded to the junior noncommissioned officer on duty and he picked up the screaming, struggling children in his arms and carried them into the gas chamber, accompanied by their mother, who was weeping in the most heartrending fashion. My pity was so great that I longed to vanish from the scene: yet I might not show the slightest trace of emotion. [Arendt writes: "The problem was how to overcome not so much their conscience as the animal pity by which all normal men are affected in the presence of physical suffering. The trick used . . . was very simple and probably very effective; it consisted in turning those instincts around, as it were, in directing them toward the self. So that instead of saying: What horrible things I did to people!, the murderers would be able to say: What horrible things I had to watch in the pursuance of my duties, how heavily the task weighed upon my shoulders!"] I had to see everything. I had to watch hour after hour, by day and by night, the removal and burning of the bodies, the extraction of the teeth, the cutting of the hair, the whole grisly, interminable business. I had to stand for hours on end in the ghastly stench, while the mass graves were being opened and the bodies dragged out and burned.

"I had to look through the peephole of the gas chambers and watch the process of death itself, because the doctors wanted me to see it. . . . The Reichsführer SS sent various high-ranking party leaders and SS officers to Auschwitz so that they might see for themselves the process of extermination of the Jews. . . . I was repeatedly asked by them how I and my men could go on watching these operations and how we were able to stand it. My invariable answer was that the iron determination with which we must carry out Hitler's orders could only be obtained by a stifling of all human emotions."

But granite would be tormented by such scenes. A convulsive despondency, megrims, anxiety, freezing doubt, inward shudders, *Weltschmerz* that passes understanding—all overwhelm Höss as the process of murder achieves its runaway momentum. He is plunged into realms that transcend reason, belief, sanity, Satan. Yet his tone is rueful, elegiac: "I was no longer happy in Auschwitz once the mass exterminations had begun. . . . If I was deeply affected by some incident, I found it impossible to go back to my house and my family. I would mount my horse and ride until I had chased the terrible picture away. Often at night I would walk through the stables and seek relief among my beloved animals. When I saw my children happily playing or observed my wife's delight over our youngest, the thought would often come to me: How long will our happiness last? My wife could never understand these gloomy moods of mine and ascribed them to some annoyance connected with my work. My family, to be sure, were well provided for in Auschwitz. Every wish that my wife or children expressed was granted them. The children could live a free and untrammeled life. My wife's garden was a paradise of flowers. The prisoners never missed an opportunity for doing some little act of kindness to my wife or children, and thus attracting their attention. No former prisoner can ever say that he was in any way or at any time badly treated in our house. My wife's greatest pleasure would have been to give a present to every prisoner who was in any way connected with our household. The children were perpetually begging me for cigarettes for the prisoners. They were particularly fond of the ones who worked in the garden. My whole family displayed an intense love of agriculture and particularly for animals of all sorts. Every Sunday I had to walk them all across the fields and visit the stables, and we must never overlook the kennels where the dogs were kept. Our two horses and the foal were especially beloved. The children always kept animals in the garden, creatures the prisoners were forever bringing them. Tortoises, martens, cats, lizards: there was always something new and interesting to be seen there. In the summer they splashed in the paddling pool in the garden, or in the Sola River. But their greatest joy was when Daddy bathed with them. He had, however, so little time for these childish pleasures. . . ."

It was into this enchanted bower that Sophie was to stray during the early fall of 1943, at a time when by night the billowing flames from the Birkenau crematoriums blazed so intensely that the regional German military command, situated one hundred kilometers away near Cracow, grew apprehensive lest the fires attract enemy air forays, and when by day a bluish veil of burning human flesh beclouded the golden autumnal sunlight, sifting out over garden and paddling pool and orchard and stable and hedgerow its sickish sweet, inescapably pervasive charnel-house mist. I do not recall Sophie's telling me about ever being the recipient of a present from Frau Höss, but it confirms one's belief in the basic truthfulness of Höss's account to know that during Sophie's brief stay under the Commandant's roof she, like the other prisoners, just as he claimed, was never in any way or at any time badly treated. Although even this in the end, as it turned out, was not so much really to be thankful for.

# NORMAN LEWIS

THE ENGLISH NOVELIST and travel writer Norman Lewis served as an intelligence officer during the war. On September 1, 1943, he was temporarily attached to HQ staff of the American Fifth Army and four days later joined the invasion fleet bound for Salerno. *Naples '44,* a superb account of his experiences in the Italian campaign, was written in the form of a diary.

■

FROM *Naples '44*

*September 10 [1943]*

A warm, calm, morning. We set out to explore a little of our immediate environment and were admiring the splendid husk of the Temple of Neptune when the war came to us in the shape of a single attacking plane. Hearing its approach, we crouched under a lintel. The plane swooped, opened up with its machine-guns, and then passed on to drop a single bomb on the beach before heading off northward. One of my friends felt a light tap on a pack he was wearing, caused by a spent machine-gun bullet which fell harmlessly to the ground. The experience was on the whole an exhilarating one. We appreciated the contrasts involved and no one experienced alarm.

In our small way we have become seasoned to the hazards of war. Some delicate inbuilt mechanism of the nerves has accepted and acclimatized itself to a relative loss of security, and minor dangers. This happy situation did not apply in the case of some of the American HQ troops we encountered, who were utterly raw and had been shipped out here straight from the eternal peace of places like Kansas and Wisconsin. The state of their nerves constituted a much greater threat than the FW 190 which paid us a visit about once an hour. Armed hill-billies were constantly jumping out from behind a hedge to point their rifles at us and scream a demand for an answer to a password that nobody had bothered to give us.

Our isolation continues. Battles must be going on somewhere, but all we know of them are the rumors picked up when we join the chow-line. At meal times, when the Sergeant-Major tries to talk to any of the HQ staff, he is waved away, so we are free to come and go exactly as we please, and occupy ourselves as we think fit. My own personal isolation is of a more absolute order—an isolation within isolation—for as a new-

comer to the section I am unavoidably something of an outsider. These
men I have known little more than one week have been through the
North Africa campaign together, and whatever their original incompat-
abilities, they have long since shaken down to form their own little closed
society. When trouble comes they lock their shields together, and keep
their heads down. For the moment I am very much of a stranger. . . .

*September 12*

Suddenly, today, the war arrived with a vengeance. We were sitting
outside our farmhouse, reading, sunning ourselves and trying to come
to terms with the acrid-tasting wine, when we noticed that a rumble of
distant cannonades, present from early morning, seemed suddenly to
have come closer. Soon after, a line of American tanks went by, making
for the battle, and hardly any time passed before they were back, but
now there were fewer of them, and the wild and erratic manner in which
they were driven suggested panic. One stopped nearby, and the crew
clambered out and fell into one another's arms, weeping. Shortly afterwards there were cries of "gas," and we saw frantic figures wearing gas-
masks running in all directions.

Chaos and confusion broke out on all sides. The story was that there
had been a breakthrough by the 16th Panzer Grenadier Division, which
struck suddenly in our direction down the Battipaglia road, with the clear
intention of reaching the sea at Paestum, wiping out the Fifth Army HQ,
and cutting the beach-head in half.

Rumors began to come in thick and fast, the most damaging one
being that General Mark Clark was proposing to abandon the beach-
head and had asked the Navy for the Fifth Army to be re-embarked. No
one we spoke to believed that this operation was feasible, the feeling
being that at the first signs of a withdrawal the Germans would simply
roll forward and drive us into the sea.

In view of the general confusion, and the absence of precise information of any kind, Sergeant-Major Dashwood decided to send four
members of the Section on their motorcycles to Salerno tomorrow, using
a narrow track running along the shore. The hope was that the Field
Security Officer might have arrived there by now, and be able to issue
the order releasing us from this absurd predicament. It sounded a hazardous adventure for the people concerned, as no one was even quite
certain whether or not the Germans had reached the sea at any point
between us and the city. They are certainly in solid possession of the
main road running parallel with the track.

This afternoon distraught American ack-ack gunners brought down
their third Spitfire. This had just flown in from Sicily and, taking off in
pursuit of FW 190s, was immediately shot down, while flying at about
300 feet.

# ALAN ROSS

POET ALAN ROSS served with the Royal Navy during World War II. He succeeded John Lehmann as editor of *The London Magazine* in 1961.

■

## Night Patrol

We sail at dusk, the red moon
Like a paper lantern setting fire
To our wake. Headlands disappear,
Muffled in their own velvet.

Docks dwindle, rubbed out by mists,
Their cranes, like drunks, askew
Over jetties. Coal is unloaded
Under blue arc-lights.

Turning south, the mapped moon
Swings between masts, our aerials
Swollen and lurching. The bag
Of sea squirts black and sooty.

Flashes of gunfire, perhaps lightning,
Straddle our progress, a convoy
Of hearses. The bow-waves of gunboats
Sew us together, helplessly idling.

The watch changes, and changes
Again. We edge through a minefield,
Real or imaginary. The speed of a convoy
Is the speed of the slowest ship.

No one speaks, it might be a funeral.
Altering course, the moon congeals
On a new bearing. The telegraph rings,
And, at speed now, clouds grow visible.

We're on our own, making for harbor.
In tangerine light we sniff greenness,
Tremble like racehorses. Soon minesweepers
Pass us, continuing our business.

# NICHOLAS MONSARRAT

NICHOLAS MONSARRAT, author of the novel *The Cruel Sea,* served with the Royal Navy during World War II. He spent most of his time on convoy duty, ending up as commander of a frigate.

■

FROM *The Cruel Sea*

Another ship, on the opposite wing, went down at four o'clock, just before dawn; and then, as daylight strengthened and the rags of the convoy drew together again, they witnessed the last cruel item of the voyage.

Lagging behind with some engine defect, a third ship was hit, and began to settle down on her way to the bottom. She sank slowly, but owing to bad organization, or the villainous list which the torpedoing gave her, no boats got away; for her crew it was a time for swimming, for jumping into the water, and striking out away from the fatal downward suction, and trusting to luck. *Compass Rose*, dropping back to come to her aid, circled round as the ship began to disappear; and then, as she dipped below the level of the sea and the swirling ripples began to spread outwards from a central point which was no longer there, Ericson turned his ship's bows towards the center of disaster, and the bobbing heads which dotted the surface of the water. But it was not to be a straightforward rescue; for just as he was opening his mouth to give the order for lowering a boat, the asdic-set picked up a contact, an under-sea echo so crisp and well-defined that it could only be a U-boat.

Lockhart, at his Action Station in the asdic-compartment, felt his heart miss a beat as he heard that echo. At last. . . . He called through the open window: "Echo bearing two-two-five—moving left!" and bent over the asdic-set in acute concentration. Ericson increased the revolutions again, and turned away from the indicated bearing, meaning to increase the range: if they were to drop depth-charges, they would need a longer run-in to get up speed. In his turn, he called out: "What's it look like, Number One?" and Lockhart, hearing the harsh pinging noise and watching the mark on the recording set, said: "Submarine, sir—can't be anything else." He continued to call out the bearing and the range of the contact: Ericson prepared to take the ship in, at attacking speed, and to drop a pattern of depth-charges on the way; and then, as *Compass Rose* turned inwards towards the target, gathering speed for the onslaught, they all noticed something which had escaped their attention before. The place where the U-boat lay, the point where they must drop their charges, was alive with swimming survivors.

The Captain drew in his breath sharply at the sight. There were about forty men in the water, concentrated in a small space: if he went ahead with the attack he must, for certain, kill them all. He knew well enough, as did everyone on board, the effect of depth-charges exploding under water—the splitting crash which made the sea jump and boil and spout skyward, the aftermath of torn seaweed and dead fish which always littered the surface after the explosion. Now there were men instead of fish and seaweed, men swimming toward him in confidence and hope. . . . And yet the U-boat was there, one of the pack which had been harassing and bleeding them for days on end, the destroying menace which *must* have priority, because of what it might do to other ships and other convoys in the future: he could hear the echo on the relay-loud-speaker, he acknowledged Lockhart's developed judgement where the asdic-set was concerned. As the seconds sped by, and the range closed, he fought against his doubts, and against the softening instinct of mercy: the book said: "Attack at all costs," and this was a page out of the book, and the men swimming in the water did not matter at all, when it was a question of bringing one of the killers to account.

But for a few moments longer he tried to gain support and confidence for what he had to do.

"What's it look like now, Number One?"

"The same, sir—solid echo—exactly the right size—*must* be a U-boat."

"Is it moving?"

"Very slowly."

"There are some men in the water, just about there."

There was no answer. The range decreased as *Compass Rose* ran in: they were now within six hundred yards of the swimmers and the U-boat, the fatal coincidence which had to be ignored.

"What's it look like now?" Ericson repeated.

"Just the same—seems to be stationary—it's the strongest contact we've ever had."

"There are some chaps in the water."

"Well, there's a U-boat just underneath them."

All right, then, thought Ericson, with a new unlooked-for access of brutality to help him: all right, we'll go for the U-boat. With no more hesitation he gave the order: "Attacking—stand by!" to the depth-charge positions aft: and having made this sickening choice he swept in to the attack with a deadened mind, intent only on one kind of kill, pretending there was no other.

Many of the men in the water waved wildly as they saw what was happening: some of them screamed, some threw themselves out of the ship's path and thrashed furiously in the hope of reaching safety: others, slower-witted or nearer to exhaustion, still thought that *Compass Rose* was speeding to their rescue, and continued to wave and smile almost to their last moment. . . . The ship came in like an avenging angel, cleaving the very center of the knots of swimmers: the amazement and horror on their faces was reflected aboard *Compass Rose*, where many of the crew, particularly among the depth-charge parties aft, could not believe what they were being called upon to do. Only two men did not share this horror: Ericson, who had shut and battened down his mind except to a single thought—the U-boat they must kill: and Ferraby, whose privilege it was to drop the depth-charges. "Serve you bloody well right!" thought Ferraby as *Compass Rose* swept in among the swimmers, catching some of them in her screw, while the firing-bell sounded and the charges rolled over the stern or were rocketed outwards from the throwers: "Serve you right—you nearly killed us last night, making us stop next door to that fire—now it's our turn."

There was a deadly pause, while for a few moments the men aboard *Compass Rose* and the men left behind in her wake stared at each other, in pity and fear and a kind of basic disbelief; and then with a huge hammer-crack the depth-charges exploded.

Mercifully the details were hidden in the flurry and roar of the explosion; and the men must all have died instantly, shocked out of life by the tremendous pressure of the sea thrown up upon their bodies. But one freak item of the horror impressed itself on the memory. As the tormented water leapt upwards in a solid gray cloud, the single figure of a man was tossed high on the very plume of the fountain, a puppet figure of whirling arms and legs seeming to make, in death, wild gestures of anger and reproach. It appeared to hang a long time in the air, cursing them all, before falling back into the boiling sea.

When they ran back to the explosion area, with the asdic silent and the contact not regained, it was as if to some aquarium where poisoned water had killed every living thing. Men floated high on the surface like dead goldfish in a film of blood. Most of them were disintegrated, or pulped out of human shape. But half a dozen of them, who must have been on the edge of the explosion, had come to a tidier end: split open from chin to crutch, they had been as neatly gutted as any herring. Some seagulls were already busy on the scene, screaming with excitement and delight. Nothing else stirred.

No one looked at Ericson as they left that place: if they had done so, they might have been shocked by his expression and his extraordinary pallor. Now deep in self-torture, and appalled by what he had done, he had already decided that there had been no U-boat there in the first place: the contact was probably the torpedoed ship, sliding slowly to the bottom, or the disturbed water of her sinking. Either way, the slaughter which he had inflicted was something extra, a large entirely British-made contribution to the success of the voyage.

# LOTHAR-GÜNTHER BUCHHEIM

LOTHAR-GÜNTHER BUCHHEIM, born in Weimar, joined the German navy when war broke out and served on minesweepers, destroyers, and submarines. An excerpt follows from *The Boat*, Buchheim's autobiographical account of life aboard a U-boat in the Atlantic.

■

FROM *The Boat*

The weather has grown even worse. Low-hanging squalls of rain darken the sky around us. All the daylight is gone: It might as well be evening. Wind-driven spray covers the watery landscape with a pale mist.

The boat's rolling heavily. Waves coming from the port beam. Water spurts through the open hatch, but we have to keep this open because the enemy may surprise the boat at any moment.

The propellers race, the diesels are running flat out. The Commander is rooted to the bridge. Under the rain-slicked, downturned brim of his sou'wester he searches the sea. He stands motionless; only his head pivots slowly from side to side.

After a quarter of an hour I climb down to inspect developments on the chart table. The navigator is hard at work calculating. Without lifting his eyes he says, "Here we are—and here's where we can expect the convoy. Unless it's tacked again."

Standing around aimlessly embarrasses me. I already have my left hand on the aluminum ladder when I tell myself that all this climbing up and down makes me look nervous. Just take it easy: relax. Whatever's happening, I'll find out in good time. How late is it really? Past twelve? Well, I just have to act as though none of this is out of the ordinary, so I peel off my wet things.

I sit in the mess, trying to read a book, until the steward finally brings in plates and cups for lunch. The Commander doesn't appear.

We've scarcely sat down at the table—the Chief, the Second Engineer, and I—when there's a roar from the control room. The Chief looks up quickly. A report comes down from the bridge. "Masthead off the port bow!"

Almost without thinking, I'm halfway to the control room: the convoy.

I'm ahead of the Chief to the bridge. The rain is worse. My sweater is immediately soaked from spray and the downpour. I was in such a hurry, I forgot to grab my oilskin from its hook.

I hear the Commander. "Hard to starboard. Steer one hundred eighty degrees!"

A bridge guard hands me his binoculars unasked. I start searching the same area as the Commander. Gray streamers of rain. Nothing else. Holding my breath, I force myself to stay calm, search the righthand edge of this banner of water and then swing my glasses very slowly across it to the left. There—in the streaks of gray—a hair-breadth line that immediately disappears again. An illusion? Imagination? I take a deep breath, relax my knees, give myself a gentle shake, balance the glasses on my fingertips. The boat heaves under me. I lose my bearings, then reorient myself by the Commander. There it is again.

It trembles and dances in the glasses. A mast! No doubt of it. But— a mast and no accompanying plume of smoke? Only this single hairline? Hard as I look, I can find nothing else; it seems to be pushing its way slowly over the horizon.

Every steamer is supposed to have a plume of smoke that betrays it long before its radio masts appear. So this can't be a steamer.

Hell and damnation—where is it? Now I have it again. I should be able to see it with the naked eye. I put down my glasses and search— there it is all right!

The Commander is chewing his lower lip. He takes up the binoculars again, muttering half to himself—"Shit! Destroyer!"

A minute goes by. My eyes are glued to the thin line above the horizon. I'm choking with excitement.

No more doubt about it: It's a radio mast, so the destroyer is coming directly at us. Without slow engines there's no chance we can get away on the surface.

"They must have seen us. Goddammit!" The Commander's voice hardly changes at all as he gives the alarm.

One bound and I'm down the tower hatch. Boots ringing on the floor plates. The Commander is the last in. He pulls the hatch shut. Even before it's completely sealed he orders, "Flood!"

He stays in the tower. In a steady voice he calls instructions down to the control tower. "Proceed at periscope depth!" The Chief balances the boat. The needle of the depth manometer stops, then slowly moves backward over the scale. Dufte is beside me, breathing heavily in his wet oilskins. Zeitler and Bockstiegel are sitting in front of the buttons of the hydroplane controls, their eyes glued to the water column in the Papenberg. The First Watch Officer bends forward to let the rainwater run off the brim of his sou'wester.

No one says a word. Only the electric hum of the motors can be heard, as if through padded doors, coming from the stern.

From above us, the voice of the Commander finally breaks the silence. "Report depth."

"Seventy feet!" from the Chief.

The water column in the Papenberg sinks slowly: the boat is rising. The lens of the periscope soon comes clear.

The boat is not yet on an even keel, so the Chief orders water pumped from the forward trim tank toward the stern. Slowly the boat attains the horizontal. But it doesn't stay there. The waves roll us in all directions. Sucking, dragging, pushing. Periscope observation is going to be damned difficult.

I listen intently, waiting to hear from the Commander, when the hydrophone operator reports, "Destroyer hard on the starboard beam!"

I pass the report up.

"Acknowledged." Then, just as dryly, "Man battle stations!"

The operator is bent out of the sound room into the passageway, his eyes wide and blank. The direct lighting makes his face a flat mask, the nose simply two holes.

Along with the Commander, the operator is now the only one in contact with the world outside our steel tube. The Commander can see the enemy, the operator hears him. The rest of us are blind and deaf. "Auditory contact stronger—moving slowly astern!"

The Commander's voice sounds choked. "Flood tubes one to four!"

Just as I thought: The Old Man is going to take on the destroyer. He wants a red pennant. The only thing still missing from his collection. When he ordered periscope after the alarm, I knew for sure.

His voice comes down again. "To control room—Chief—hold our exact depth!"

How can he possibly do it, I ask myself, in this rough sea? The muscles in the Chief's gaunt face tense and relax rhythmically. He looks as if he's chewing gum. If the boat rises too far, and the upper part of the hull breaks the surface—disaster: it will betray us to the enemy.

The Commander is astride the periscope saddle in the narrow space between the periscope shaft and the tower wall, his face pressed against the rubber shell, his thighs spread wide to grip the huge shaft. His feet are on the pedals that enable him to spin the great column and his saddle through 360 degrees without making a sound; his right hand rests on the lever that raises and lowers it. The periscope motor hums. He's lowering it a little, keeping its head as close to the surface of the water as he possibly can.

The Chief is standing immobile behind the two men of the bridge watch who are now operating the hydroplanes. His eyes are glued to the Papenberg and its slowly rising and falling column of water. Each change in it means the boat is doing the same.

Not a word from anyone. The humming of the periscope motor

sounds as if it's coming through a fine filter; the motor starts, stops, starts again, and the humming resumes. The Commander ups periscope for fractions of a second and immediately lets it sink below the surface again. The destroyer must be very close.

"Flood tube five." The order is a whisper.

It's passed on softly to the main motor room. We're in the midst of battle.

I sink down onto the frame of the circular door. The whispered report comes back from astern, "Tube five ready to fire when torpedo door opened."

So—all tubes are flooded. All that's needed is to open the doors and release a blast of compressed air to send them on their way. The Commander wants to know the position of the helm.

Suddenly I notice that I still have a half-chewed bit of bread in my mouth. Mushy bread and sausage fat. It's beginning to taste sour.

I have the feeling that I've lived all this somewhere before. Images shift about in my mind, jostling, overlaying one another, merging into new combinations. My immediate impressions seem to be being transmitted by a complicated circuit to my brain center from which they re-emerge into my consciousness as memories.

The Old Man's mad—attacking a destroyer in this sea.

But it has its advantages too. Our periscope can't be all that visible. The streamer of foam that would betray it must be hard to distinguish among the cresting waves.

The drip in the bilge is deafening. Sounds as if it's coming over a loudspeaker. Lucky that everything's worked so far: no problem maintaining depth. The Chief was well prepared, had it all figured out.

If the Old Man decides to fire, the Chief must flood at once to make up for the weight of the torpedo. Otherwise the boat will rise. A torpedo weighs three thousand pounds—so an equivalent weight of water has to be taken on for each one launched. Multiplied by the number of torpedoes fired—it's a lot.

Not a word from the Commander.

It's very difficult to hit a destroyer. Shallow draft. Easily maneuverable. But score a hit, and it's gone in a flash, blown away. The explosion of the torpedo, a geyser of water and torn steel, then nothing.

The Commander's steady voice comes down. "Open torpedo doors. Switch on tubes one and two! enemy course fifteen. Bow left. Direction sixty. Range one thousand!"

The Second Watch officer puts the figures in the calculator. The bow compartment reports torpedo doors opened. The First Watch Officer relays the message softly but distinctly. "Tubes one and two ready to fire!"

The Commander has his hand on the firing lever and is waiting for the enemy to move into the crosshairs.

If only we were able to see!

Imagination runs riot in this silence. Visions of catastrophe: a destroyer swinging until it's at angle zero. The foaming bow, the white bone in its teeth, towering over us, ready to ram. Staring eyes, the sharp rending of metal, jagged edges of steel, green surge of water through fissures like opened stopcocks.

The voice of the Commander, as sharp as a descending whiplash. "Close torpedo doors. Dive to two hundred feet. Fast!"

The Chief is only a fraction of a second behind him. "Hard down both—both engines full ahead! All hands forward!"

Loud confusion of voices. I flinch, press myself to one side, have trouble staying on my feet. The first man is already forcing his way through the circular door aft, staggers, recovers his balance and rushes, half crouched, past the sound room toward the bow.

Wide-open questioning eyes fixed on me. Chaos: slipping, stumbling, hurrying, staggering. Two bottles of lemonade come tumbling in from the petty officers' mess and smash noisily against the wall of the control room.

Both hydroplanes are hard down. The boat is already distinctly bow heavy, but the men keep coming from astern. They slide through the tilted control room as if it's a chute; one falls full length, cursing.

Only the engine room personnel are left in the after part of the ship. The floor slips away beneath me. Fortunately I manage to grab the periscope stanchion. The sausages swing out at an angle from the wall. I hear the Old Man's voice from above us, cutting through the scuffling and stamping of boots. "Depth charges next!" He sounds perfectly calm, as though passing on a piece of casual information.

He climbs down with exaggerated deliberation, as if it's an exercise. Traverses the slope, hanging on to both sides, and props one buttock on the chart chest. His right hand grasps a water pipe for support.

The chief slowly levels the boat out and orders, "Man diving stations!" The seamen who rushed forward now work their way back hand over hand up the slope. The sausages act like a scale: we're still a good thirty degrees bow heavy.

*Rrabaum!—Rrum!—Rrum!*

Three crashing sledgehammer blows spin me around. Half stunned, I hear a dull roar. What is it? Fear claws at my heart: that roaring! Finally I identify it: it's water pouring back into the vacuum created in the sea by the explosion.

Two more monstrous explosions.

The control-room mate has hunched his head into his shoulders. The new control-room assistant, the Bible Scholar, staggers and seizes hold of the chart table.

Another explosion, louder than the rest.

The lights go out. Darkness!

"Auxiliary lighting gone," someone calls.

The orders from the Chief seem to come from a distance. Pocket flashlights cut whitish cones in the darkness. Someone calls for a damage report. The section leaders' replies come through the speaking tubes. "Bow compartment in order!"—"Main motor room in order!"—"Engine room in order!"

"No leakage," says the navigator. His voice is as matter-of-fact as the Commander's.

Before long, two double explosions make the floor plates dance.

"Pump out torpedo cell one!" With a sharp hum the bilge pump springs into action. As soon as the roar of the detonations has subsided, the pump will be stopped again. Otherwise it could supply a bearing to the enemy's hydrophones.

"Raise bow!" The Chief to the hydroplane operators. "Boat's in balance," he reports to the Commander.

"There'll be more," says the Old Man. "They actually saw our periscope. Amazing—with the sea running this high."

He looks around. No trace of fear on his face. There's even an undertone of scorn in his voice. "Now it's psychological warfare, gentlemen."

Ten minutes pass; nothing happens. Suddenly a violent explosion shakes the whole boat. Then another and another. It quivers and groans.

"Fifteen!" counts the navigator. "Sixteen, seventeen, eighteen!"

The Chief stares at the needle of the depth manometer, which jumps a couple of points at each detonation. His eyes are huge and dark. The Commander's are closed to obliterate his surroundings and concentrate on his calculations: our own course, enemy course, ways of escape. He must react with lightning speed. He's the only one among the lot of us who's actually fighting. Our lives hang on the correctness of his orders.

"Hard a-port!"

"Helm hard a-port!"

"Hold zero bearing!"

The Commander never stops calculating. The basic factors in his reckoning change with each report; he must determine an escape route according to the strength of the sound of propellers and the approach angle of the destroyer. His senses no longer supply him with any immediate information: he must guide the boat like a pilot flying blind, his decisions based on indications given him by the instruments.

Against closed eyelids I see the gray-black cans twisting heavily as they shoot downward from the launchers, plunge into the water, spin lazily into the depths leaving bubbling trails, and then explode in the darkness—blazing fireballs of magnesium, incandescent suns.

Water transmits pressure much more strongly than air. If an intense pressure wave hits a boat it rips it apart at the seams. To destroy a submerged U-boat, depth charges don't have to hit it; they need only explode within the so-called lethal radius. The small depth charges dropped by airplanes weigh about 150 pounds, the destroyer bombs about 500 pounds. At a depth of 350 feet, the lethal radius extends about 275 to 350 feet. Once you've learned something, it sticks. I feel a kind of satisfaction that I now know this kind of thing by heart.

For a while all is quiet. I strain my ears. No propeller noise, no splashing of bombs. Only the thin humming of our electric motors. Not even the sound of breathing. The Commander suddenly seems to remember that we're here. He doesn't move, but he glances around and whispers, "I could see them clearly. They were standing on the bridge, gaping straight at us. There were three men in the crow's nest. A corvette!"

He bends forward and whispers through the circular door to the sound man, "See if they're going away." Still bending forward a minute later, his question becomes more urgent: "Louder or weaker?"

The operator answers immediately. "No change." It's Herrmann: face like a Noh-mask—colorless, eyes and mouth thin lines. The Old Man orders us down farther.

Our pressure hull can withstand a good deal. But the flanges, all those damned pierced sections, are our Achilles' heel. And there are too many of them.

The most dangerous bombs for the boat are those that explode diagonally under the keel, because the underside has the largest number of flanges and outboard plugs. The deeper you go, the smaller the lethal radius: the water pressure, which is itself a threat at such depths because of the overloading on the seams, also limits the effective radius of the bombs—at 130, it's perhaps 160 feet.

"Suddenly a handful of pebbles rattles against the boat.

"Asdic!" I hear a voice from the stern end of the control room. The jagged word suddenly stands out in my head in glaring capitals.

A shudder runs down my spine: *Anti-Submarine Development Investigation Committee*; the supersonic detection system!

It's the impact of the directional beam against our side that produces this low tinkling, chirping sound. In the absolute silence it has all the force of a siren. Time between impulses: about thirty seconds.

"Turn it off!" I want to shout. The chirping grates on my nerves. No one dares so much as lift his head or speak, even though it will find us even if we remain as silent as the grave. Against it, silence is useless. So is stopping the E-motors. Normal hydrophones are outclassed by the E-motors, but the Asdic isn't dependent on sound, it reacts to our mass. Depth no longer affords any protection.

The nervous tension is infectious. My hands are shaking. I'm glad I don't have to stand up; instead I'm able to sit in the frame of the circular doorway. I try out actions that require no major bodily movement: swallowing, blinking, grinding my teeth, making faces—a crease to the right, a crease to the left, forcing saliva between my teeth.

The operator whispers, "Getting louder!"

The Commander frees himself from the periscope shaft, makes his way past me almost on tiptoe. "Any change in direction?"

"Bearing still two hundred ninety-five degrees."

Four detonations in quick succession. The roaring, gurgling surge of the explosions has barely subsided when the Commander says in a low voice, "She was well camouflaged, a fairly old ship, rather squat."

A hard blow against my feet jolts me badly. The floor plates rattle.

"Twenty-seven—twenty-eight!" the navigator counts, trying to imitate the Old Man's elaborate casualness.

A pail goes rattling partway across the floor plates.

"Hell and damnation—quiet!"

Now it sounds as if the pebbles are in a tin can, being shaken this way and that; in between is a louder, singing sound, with an underlying quick, sharp chirping, like crickets—the whirling propeller blades of the corvette. I stand rigid, frozen. I don't dare make the slightest movement; it's as if any motion, even the smallest slithering sound, would bring the beating propellers closer. Not a flicker of an eyelash, a twitch of the eye, not a breath, not a quiver of a nerve, not a ripple of the muscles, not even a goose pimple.

Another five bombs! the navigator adds them to the total. My expression doesn't change. The Commander raises his head. Clearly emphasizing each word, he speaks into the echo of the crashing water. "Keep calm —calm, gentlemen. This is nothing at all."

His quiet voice does us good, eases our jangled nerves.

Now we are struck by a single ringing blow, like a giant cudgel on a sheet of steel. Two or three men begin to stagger.

The air is hazy, hanging in blue layers. And again the heavy explosions.

"Thirty-four—thirty-five—thirty-six!" This time the counting comes in a whisper.

The Commander remains firm. "What in the world—is bothering you?" He withdraws into himself once more, calculating courses. It's deathly still in the boat. After a while the whispering voice comes again. "What's his bearing now?"

"Two hundred sixty degrees—getting louder!"

The Commander raises his head. He's reached a decision.

"Hard a-starboard!" And immediately afterward, "Sound room— we're turning to starboard!"

A wrench has to be passed through to the stern. I reach for it eagerly and hand it on. Dear god, to be able to *do* something—turn handwheels, adjust levers, man the pumps . . .

The operator leans out into the passageway again. His eyes are open but he's staring into infinity. He sounds like a medium speaking. "Sounds growing louder—two hundred thirty—two hundred twenty."

"Nonessential lights out," the Old Man orders. "Who the hell knows how long we may need the current!"

The operator reports again, "Attacking again—sounds bearing two hundred ten degrees—getting louder fast! Quite close!" The excitement has upset his delivery.

The Commander orders: "Both engines full ahead!"

The seconds stretch out. Nothing. No one moves.

"Let's hope they don't get their friends in on it!" The Old Man voices a fear that's been in my bones for a long time: the sweepers, the killers . . . a pack of dogs is death to the hare.

Whoever has us on the hook now is no beginner, and we're defenseless in spite of the five torpedoes in our tubes. We can't surface, we can't come speeding from behind cover and throw ourselves on the enemy. We haven't even the grim assurance to be had from simply holding a weapon in your hand. We can't so much as shout at them. Just creep away. Keep going deeper. How deep are we now? I can't believe my eyes: the pointer of the manometer stands at 465. "Shipyard guarantee three hundred" flashes through my mind.

Ten minutes pass and nothing happens.

Another handful of pebbles hits the boat high up on the port buoyancy tank. I can see from the operator's face that more depth charges are coming. He's moving his lips, counting the seconds before detonation.

The first is so well aimed that I feel the shock all the way up my spine. We're in a huge drum with a steel plate for a drum head. I see the navigator's lips moving but I hear nothing. Have I gone deaf?

But now I can hear the Commander. He's ordering higher speed again. He raises his voice to be heard over the pandemonium. "All right! Carry on just as you are, gentlemen, pay no attention to this nonsense! At home there are . . ."

He breaks off in mid-sentence. Suddenly there's a humming stillness. Only the occasional swish and slap from the bilge.

"Bow up! Steady!" the Chief orders the hydroplane men. His whisper sounds too loud in the silence. Once again the E-motors have been reduced to crawling speed. Bilge water gurgles toward the stern. Just where does it all come from? Wasn't it properly bailed in advance?

"Thirty-eight . . . forty-one!" the navigator counts.

With the roaring and bursting of the bombs still in my ears the silence that follows seems like a bizarre acoustical black hole, bottomless. Probably just to keep the silence from becoming too painful, the Commander whispers, "I'm not sure whether those characters up there are in contact!" At the same moment new detonations shake the depths: the answer is plain.

Once more my ears can't distinguish one explosion from the next. Nor have I any impression of whether the bombs are exploding right or left, above or below the boat. But the Old Man can obviously locate them. He's probably the only one who knows our position relative to our tormentor. Or is the navigator calculating too? In any case I no longer have the slightest clue. I see only the needle of the depth manometer moving slowly forward over the dial. We're going deeper again.

The Chief is bending forward toward the hydroplane operators. His face is thrown into unnatural relief against the dark background, like that of an actor lit only by the footlights, every bone emphasized by dark lines or shadow. His hand looks waxen. There's a black streak across his right cheek. He's narrowed his eyes as if dazzled by the light.

The two hydroplane operators crouch motionless in front of their control buttons. Even when they change the hydroplane settings one sees no movement. The slight pressure of a finger requires no shift of their limbs. Our hydroplanes are power-operated. What more could we possibly want? Except for some piece of equipment that would allow us to observe the enemy from way down here.

A breathing space? I try to settle myself more firmly. The corvette certainly won't keep us waiting long. It's simply circling again; even when it's moving away from us, the goddam Asdic keeps us cornered. The people up there have got every man they can spare on the bridge, peering at the choppy sea, searching the marbled foam for some sign of us. Nothing—zebra patterns drawn in green; green and white oxgall paper streaked with black . . . but it's the iridescent sheen of oil they're really after.

Still no move from the hydrophone operator: no sounds to report.

A strange clicking noise. A new device to locate us? Minutes pass. No one moves a muscle. The clicking stops; in its place another handful of pebbles strikes the boat, small gravel stones this time. Abruptly the Commander raises his head. "D'you think we'll get them—again?"

Get them again? Does he mean the convoy, or the corvette?

He leans forward and speaks softly to the hydrophone man. "Find out if she's going away." Seconds later he asks impatiently, "Louder or weaker?"

"Staying the same," replies the operator, and after a while, "Getting louder."

"Any deviation?"

"Bearing still two hundred twenty degrees."

The Commander immediately has the rudder put hard to starboard. So we're going to double back again.

And now he orders both motors slow ahead.

Drops of condensation punctuate the tense silence at regular intervals: *Pit-pat—tick-tack—pitch-patch.*

A hard blow makes the floor plates jump and rattle. "Forty-seven—forty-eight." And then, "Forty-nine—fifty—fifty-one."

A glance at my wristwatch: 14:30. When was the alarm? Must have been shortly after twelve. We've been under pursuit for two hours!

My watch has a red second hand on the same pin as the two main hands, so that it's constantly circling the dial in a series of jerky movements. I concentrate on this hand, measuring the interval between the individual detonations: two minutes, thirty seconds—another one; thirty seconds—the next; then twenty seconds.

I'm happy to have something to do. Nothing else exists. I take a tighter grip with my right hand as though to focus my concentration. It has to come to an end. *Has to.*

Another hard, sharp blow: forty-four seconds this time. Up to this point I've been mouthing syllables noiselessly, but now I can clearly feel my lips spread into a flattened oval, baring my teeth. Now I need my left hand to hang on with too.

The Commander orders us down another seventy feet.

Almost seven hundred now. A loud crackling and snapping runs through the boat. The new control-room assistant glances at me in fear.

"Only the woodwork," whispers the Commander.

"It's the wooden paneling that creaks and snaps so loudly. The interior structure can't stand the compression. Seven hundred feet. Every square inch of steel skin now has to withstand a weight of 284 pounds, which means over twenty tons per square foot. All this on a hull less than an inch thick.

The crackling's getting sharper.

"Unpleasant," murmurs the Chief.

The excruciating tension exerted on the steel skin is torture to me: I feel as if my own skin were being stretched. Another crack resounds, as loud as a rifle shot, and my scalp twitches. Under this insane pressure our hull is as fragile as an eggshell.

The ship's fly appears less than two feet away. I wonder how she likes this infernal drum solo. Each of us chooses his own fate: it's as true for the fly as it is for me. We both embarked on this undertaking of our own free will.

A double blow, then a third, not much weaker than its predecessors. The people up there are fishing for us with an even tighter net.

Renewed clattering of floor plates and deafening after-roar.

Peace lasts only a couple of heartbeats. Then two shattering blows and the glass plates of the depth manometers fall tinkling to the floor. The light goes out.

The cone of a pocket flashlight wavers across the walls and comes to rest on the dial of the depth manometer. I make a terrifying discovery: the hands of both manometers are gone. The water gauge between the two hydroplane operators has cracked and is shooting a hissing stream of water straight across the room.

"Leak through the water gauge," I hear a shaky voice report.

The Commander snarls, "Nonsense, cut the dramatics!"

The empty dials stare like the eyes of a corpse. We can no longer tell whether the boat is sinking or rising.

My scalp crawls again. If the instruments have failed us, we have no way of telling our position.

I stare intently at the black ends of the shafts, but without a pointer they are meaningless.

The control-room mate fumbles about among the pipelines by flash-light. Apparently trying to reach some valve that will close off the spurting stream of water. He's soaked to the skin before he finds it. Although the flow is choked off, he continues to feel about on the floor. Suddenly he's holding a pointer. Cautiously he lifts his precious find and places it on the square shaft of the small manometer, the one that registers the lowest depths.

It feels as if all our lives depend on whether the thin strip of metal will move or not.

The man takes his hand away. The needle quivers and slowly begins to turn. Silently the Commander nods approbation.

The manometer shows six hundred feet.

The hydrophone man reports, "Sounds getting louder—two hundred thirty degrees—two hundred twenty degrees!"

The Commander takes his cap off and lays it on the chart chest. His hair is matted with sweat. He takes a deep breath and says, "Keep it up!"

For once his voice isn't entirely under control. There is an unmistakable undertone of resignation in it.

"Noises bearing two hundred ten degrees! Growing louder—attack beginning again!"

The Commander immediately orders full speed ahead. A sharp jolt runs through the boat as it leaps forward. The Commander leans against the shining oily column of the sky periscope, resting the back of his head on it.

Long-forgotten images rise in my mind: two cardboard disks painted in spirals and spinning in opposite directions on the ice cream machines at country fairs. The tangle of red and white completely fills my head and becomes the trail of two depth charges, flaring comets that consume everything in a blaze of white.

The hydrophone operator startles me. Another report. I stare at his mouth, but his words don't penetrate.

More waiting, more holding my breath. Even the smallest sound is painful, a touch on a raw wound. As if my nerves had escaped the outer layer of skin and were now exposed. I have only one thought: they're up there. Right overhead. I forget to breathe. I'm stifling before I slowly, cautiously, fill my lungs with oxygen. Against closed eyelids I see bombs tumbling perpendicularly into the depths trailing sparkling air bubbles, exploding into fire. Around their incandescent cores all the colors of the spectrum flare up in mad combinations, leaping and dying again but growing steadily more intense until the whole interior of the sea glows like a blast furnace.

The control-room mate breaks the spell. Gesturing and whispering, he calls the Chief's attention to a corner of the control room where a can of lubricating oil is overflowing. This is about the most trivial problem imaginable right now, but it upsets him.

The chief nods permission for him to do something about it. The pipe that is dripping oil reaches straight into the can. He can't simply take the can away from under it, but has to tilt it to get it out. As a result, more oil spills onto the floor plates and forms an ugly black puddle.

The navigator shakes his head in disgust. The control-room mate withdraws the overfilled can as cautiously as a thief trying to avoid setting off a burglar alarm.

"Corvette noises receding astern!" reports the operator. Almost simultaneously, two more bombs explode. But the roar of the detonations is weaker and duller than before.

"Way off," says the Commander.

*Rwumm—tjummwumm!*

Even fainter. The Commander seizes his cap. "Practice maneuvers! That's the sort of thing they ought to work on at home!"

The control-room mate is already busy fitting new glass tubes into the broken water gauges; he seems to know that the mere sight of the breakage effects us like poison.

When I stand up, I'm stiff all over. No feeling in my legs. I try to put one foot in front of the other—feels like stepping into the void. I hold fast to the table and look at the chart.

There is the pencil line showing the boat's course, and the pencil cross indicating its last position. And here the line suddenly stops—I'm going to make a note of the latitude and longitude of the place if we get out of this.

The operator sweeps the whole circumference of his dial.

"Well?" asks the Commander. He acts bored, pushing his tongue into his left cheek till it bulges.

"Going away!" the operator replies.

The Commander looks around. Satisfaction personified. He even grins. "As far as I can see, gentlemen, the incident is over."

# MARIE VASSILTCHIKOV

DIARIST Marie Vassiltchikov found herself, early in 1940, a stateless person in Berlin. Her language skills won her a minor position in the Foreign Office. Later that year she was joined by her father, Prince Lilarion Vassiltchikov, who was smuggled out of Lithuania into Germany. In Berlin he gave Russian lessons. Many of Marie's friends were involved in the July 10, 1944, plot to assassinate Hitler. After her death in 1978, her brother, George Vassiltchikov, prepared her Berlin diaries for publication.

■

FROM *Berlin Diaries*

*Tuesday, 23 November*

Last night the greater part of central Berlin was destroyed.

In the afternoon there was heavy rain. I had been sent out to fetch a document that was needed for the conference. Our new boss Büttner has a mania for such conferences; they take place almost daily. He probably just likes to "review his troops." I find them a complete waste of time. I got drenched on the way and arrived late at the meeting, which went on until shortly after 7 P.M. I was rushing down the stairs to go home when the hall porter intercepted me with the ominous words "Luftgefahr 15" ["air-raid danger 15"]. This meant that large enemy air formations were on their way. I took the stairs back two at a time to warn those of my colleagues who lived far away to stay put, since they might otherwise be caught out in the open. The sirens sounded just as I was leaving the building. It was still raining hard and since the buses would be stopping shortly, I decided to walk home. On the way I popped a long letter I had just written to Tatiana into the mail box on the corner.

The streets were full of people. Many just stood around, for the visibility was so poor on account of the rain that nobody expected the raid to last long or cause much damage. At home I was met by Maria Gersdorff, who told me that her husband Heinz had just telephoned from his office at the Stadt-Kommandantur [H.Q. of Berlin's garrison] to warn her that the enemy air formations were larger than usual, that the raid might therefore be serious and that he was staying on at the office for the night. Having had no time for lunch, I was ravenous. Maria asked old Martha the cook to warm up some soup while I went upstairs to change into slacks and a sweater. As one does now in such cases, I also packed a few things into a small suitcase. Papa was in his room, giving a language lesson to two young men. He told me that he did not wish to be disturbed.

I had just finished packing when the *flak* opened up. It was immediately very violent. Papa emerged with his pupils and we all hurried down to the half-basement behind the kitchen, where we usually sit out air-raids. We had hardly got there when we heard the first approaching planes. They flew very low and the barking of the *flak* was suddenly drowned by a very different sound—that of exploding bombs, first far away and then closer and closer, until it seemed as if they were falling literally on top of us. At every crash the house shook. The air pressure was dreadful and the noise deafening. For the first time I understood what the expression *Bombenteppich* ["bomb carpet"] means—the Allies call it "saturation" bombing. At one point there was a shower of broken glass and all three doors of the basement flew into the room, torn off their hinges. We pressed them back into place and leant against them to try to keep them shut. I had left my coat outside but didn't dare go out to get it. An incendiary flare fell hissing into our entrance and the men crept out to extinguish it. Suddenly we realized that we had no water on hand to put out a possible fire and hastily opened all the taps in the kitchen. This dampened the noise for a few minutes, but not for long . . . The planes did not come in waves, as they do usually, but kept on droning ceaselessly overhead for more than an hour.

In the middle of it all the cook produced my soup. I thought that if I ate it I would throw up. I found it even impossible to sit quietly and kept jumping to my feet at every crash. Papa, imperturbable as always, remained seated in a wicker armchair throughout. Once, when I leapt up after a particularly deafening explosion, he calmly remarked: "Sit down! That way, if the ceiling collapses, you will be farther away from it . . ." But the crashes followed one another so closely and were so ear-splitting that at the worst moments I stood behind him, holding on to his shoulders by way of self-protection. What a family *bouillabaisse* we would have made! His pupils cowered in a corner while Maria stood propped against a wall, praying for her husband and looking desperate. She kept advising me to keep away from the furniture, as it might splinter. The bombs continued to rain down and when a house next to ours collapsed, Papa muttered in Russian: "Volia Bozhia!" ["Let God's will be done!"]. It seemed indeed as if nothing could save us. After an hour or so it became quieter, Papa produced a bottle of schnapps and we all took large gulps. But then it started all over again . . . Only around 9:30 P.M. did the droning of planes overhead cease. There must have been several hundreds of them.

Just then, marvel of marvels, the kitchen telephone rang. It was Gottfried Bismarck, from Potsdam, inquiring whether we were all right.

They had heard hundreds of planes flying very low over their heads, but because of the poor visibility they could not tell how much damage had been done. When I said: "It was awful!" he volunteered to come over and fetch me, but I told him that it was not worth it, as the worst seemed over. He promised to find out where Loremarie Schönburg was and ring back.

The all-clear came only half an hour after the last planes had departed, but long before that we were called out of the house by an unknown naval officer. The wind, he told us, thus far non-existent, had suddenly risen and the fires, therefore, were spreading. We all went out into our little square and, sure enough, the sky on three sides was blood-red. This, the officer explained, was only the beginning; the greatest danger would come in a few hours' time, when the fire storm really got going. Maria had given each of us a wet towel with which to smother our faces before leaving the house—a wise precaution, for our square was already filled with smoke and one could hardly breathe.

We went back into the house and Papa's pupils climbed up on the roof to keep an eye on the surrounding fires. Then the Danish chargé d'affaires Steenson (who lives next door) appeared, hugging a bottle of brandy. While we stood in the drawing-room, talking and taking an occasional gulp, the telephone rang once more. It was again Gottfried and he sounded desperately worried. He had called up Berndt Mumm's flat, where Loremarie had been dining with Aga Fürstenberg, only to be told that Loremarie had disappeared immediately after the all-clear and no one knew where she had gone. Gottfried thought that she might be trying to rejoin me, but as we were inside a ring of fire, I doubted whether she would get through.

Strangely, as soon as he hung up our telephone broke down; that is, people could still call *us*, but *we* could not get through to anyone. Also the electricity, gas and water no longer worked and we had to grope our way around with electric torches and candles. Luckily we had had time to fill every available bath tub, wash basin, kitchen sink and pail. By now the wind had increased alarmingly, roaring like a gale at sea. When we looked out of the window we could see a steady shower of sparks raining down on our and the neighboring houses and all the time the air was getting thicker and hotter, while the smoke billowed in through the gaping window frames. We went through the house and found to our relief that apart from the broken windows and the unhinged doors, it had not suffered any real damage.

Just as we were swallowing some sandwiches, the sirens came on once more. We stood at the windows for about half an hour, in total silence. We were convinced it would start all over again. Then the all-clear sounded again. Apparently enemy reconnaissance planes had been surveying the damage. Maria, who had until then been a brick, now burst into tears, for her husband had given her as yet no sign of life.

Though by now I was terribly sleepy, we decided that I would keep vigil near the phone. Putting it on the floor near me, I rolled myself up in a blanket on a sofa. About 1 A.M. Gottfried and Loremarie called from Potsdam. We were cut off almost immediately, but at least we were spared further anxiety on her account.

Towards 2 A.M. I decided to sleep for a while. Papa came and held his torch over me as I took off my shoes and tried to wash. Toward three, Maria also lay down. Presently I heard the telephone ring and then her ecstatic "Liebling!," which meant that Heinz was all right. Soon she, too, fell asleep. Every now and then a crashing building or a delayed time bomb would tear one awake and I would sit up with a pounding heart. By now the fire storm had reached its peak and the roar outside was like a train going through a tunnel.

# JAMES JONES

THE NOVELIST James Jones was a peacetime soldier when the war started. In 1975 he wrote a personal account of the war, *World War II,* from which the following excerpt is taken.

■

FROM *World War II*

## HOSPITAL

In the Army General Hospital in Memphis, where I was sent from San Francisco, we had two full wards of foot and lower-leg amputations from frozen feet in the invasion of Attu in the Aleutians, where some forgetful planner had sent the troops in in leather boots. This was in full accord with the general grim air and iron-cold mood the hospital had. Men there did not laugh and smile about their wounds, as they always seemed to do in the pictures in *Yank* and the civilian magazines.

Of course, not everybody there came from overseas. The others, broken legs, broken heads, service-connected Stateside illnesses, were still in the majority. We overseas returnees comprised about one quarter of the patients in mid-1943. The percentages would rise later as the war broadened abroad. We were among the first big influx.

There was a noticeable difference between the overseas combat men and the others. The combat men were clannish, and stayed pretty much by themselves, and there was this grim sort of iron-cold silence about them, except when they were in town and had a bottle in their hand. They made everybody else uncomfortable, and did not seem to care if they did or not. Almost without exception, they were uncheerful about their wounds. Alongside them, the others seemed much younger, and very much more cheerful about everything.

I myself was somewhere in the middle of all this. I wasn't there because of a wound—but I had been wounded, and had been overseas, and so was automatically a member of the clan, and I tended to associate mentally with the overseas men, and could understand what they were feeling, because I was feeling it myself. I suppose the best way to describe it—or the kindest way to describe it—is that they felt a certain well-controlled angry irascibility because everyone but themselves took everything so much for granted.

Whenever I looked at them I was reminded of a little scene I'd witnessed the day I was hit. I had arrived at the regimental aid station with my face all covered in blood from what turned out to be a minor head wound, no doubt looking very dramatic, and the first person I saw was our old regimental surgeon with a cigar butt in his teeth, cutting strips of skin and flesh out of a wound in the back of a boy sitting on the table. I had known old Doc, at least to speak to, for at least two years and when he quit working on the other boy and examined me, he said, "Hello, Jonesie. Getting more material for that book of yours you're gonna write?"

I laughed, a little hysterically probably. "More than I want, Doc." Though he was a light colonel, we always called him Doc. When he found I had no hole in my head, only an unseparated crack, he went back to working on the boy. The wound in his back was inside and down from the shoulder-blade and about the size of three silver dollars laid edge to edge, and was just a hole, a red angry wet hole, from which blood kept welling up and spilling in a red rill down his back, which Doc had to keep wiping up. That little rill of blood that wouldn't quit kept fascinating me. "How bad is he?" I asked. "He going to be all right?"

"I think so. Too soon to tell for sure. Doesn't seem to have internal bleeding," Doc said, and picked out another shred with his tweezers and cut it off with his scalpel. "But there may be some small pieces down in there." I nodded, not knowing what else to say. The boy, whom I didn't know, turned his head, favoring his bad side, and gave us both such a silent cold unforgiving look that I have never forgotten it. "There you are, son," old Doc said around his cigar butt, and patted his good shoulder. "No, don't get up. Lie down here and they'll come get you."

That look the wounded boy gave Doc and me was the same cold silent unforgiving stare the overseas men at the hospital gave to everybody who was not one of them. It was not so much that they were specifically blaming anyone for anything, as that everybody remained unforgiven. I felt the same way myself.

They had other peculiarities. For some reason I could never find the source of, none of the combat men at the hospital would ever wear their decoration ribbons or campaign ribbons when they went into town in uniform on pass. The only decoration they would allow themselves to wear, at least for the infantrymen, was the blue and silver Combat Infantryman's Badge, with the silver wreath around it. There was an awards ceremony at the hospital about every two or three weeks, and after I had been there about a month I was awarded my Purple Heart and my mysterious Bronze Star. But I never wore either of the ribbons. I knew without being told by anyone that we just didn't wear them. So instead I bought myself a Combat Infantryman's Badge (which I had not been officially awarded yet) and wore that.

Nobody ever mentioned aloud that you shouldn't wear your decorations. It was not some kind of private conspiracy. But everybody got the message just the same. As far as I know, no one ever asked if they were *not* supposed to wear their ribbons. Once a couple of men I knew, as a sort of ironic joke, started wearing the Good Conduct ribbon—a decoration which just about every man in the army received who had not been convicted of murder. Nobody ever said to them that they should not wear it, but at the same time nobody laughed, either. After a few days they stopped.

Our hangout in Memphis was a hotel called the Peabody in downtown Memphis on Union Street. It was just about everybody else's hangout, too. In addition to flocks of ground troops and administrative troops in the area, there was a Naval Air Training Station in Memphis, as well as an Army Air Force field. It was a regular stop and center for the Air Transport Command also. Apparently before the war the Peabody had been the chic place in Memphis, and it sported a Starlight Roof with dancing music and dinner. But the great influx of servicemen had taken it over from the local gentry, and at just about any time of day or night there were always between half a dozen and a dozen wide-open drinking parties going in the rooms and suites, where it was easy to get invited simply by walking down the corridors on the various floors until you heard the noise.

Money was not much of a problem. Nor were women. There was always plenty of booze from somebody, and there were also unattached women at the hotel floor parties. You could always go up to the Starlight Roof and find yourself a nice girl and dance with her a while and bring her down. Everybody screwed. Sometimes, it did not even matter if there were other people in the room or not, at the swirling kaleidoscopic parties. Couples would ensconce themselves in the bathrooms of the suites and lock the door.

Most of the overseas men received pretty substantial payments in back pay. I received, in one lovely lump sum, eleven months' back pay at a corporal's rate, when I finally got paid. This plus an allotment I'd been sending home to a bank for years to go to college on when I got out, gave me something over four thousand dollars. Two other overseas men and I kept a living room, two-bedroom suite, paying daily rates, for something like just under two months. If none of us happened to be going to town from the hospital on any given day, we would loan one of the keys to someone else. Our suite became one of the chief centers of what passed for gaiety at the Peabody Hotel in 1943. And we liked that.

No nation in history ever laid out such enormous sums and went to such great lengths to patch up, repair and take care of its wounded and its injured as the United States did in World War II. Other nations watched and wondered at the United States's richness and largesse to its damaged. It was only in the functioning and in the administration of it that there was slippage, and graft. But the government couldn't be blamed for that. Any more than the government could be blamed for the grafting congressmen and senators the people chose to elect to office. Most of us overseas men knew that we would probably be returned to duty in some limited form or other, and that would probably mean heading out for General Eisenhower's Europe.

Except for a lucky few who were too crippled up to be of even partial use, we were essentially in the same boat as the others who had never been over and were finishing up their training and heading out every few days. Except for the sole fact that we had already been there, and knew what to expect. It was a pretty big sole fact.

There is a regulation in army hospitals that no man can be sent back into duty until he is physically fully ready for Full Duty, or physically fully ready for Limited Duty. There are only the two categories. And it could be no other way, since in the army there is no convalescent period at home. All told, I spent the last seven months of 1943 in the Memphis hospital. I was in love at least six times. I learned a lot about living on the home front. When I was shipped back out marked fit for Limited Duty, my four thousand dollars was gone and all I had to show for it were two tailored tropical worsted officer's uniforms with shoulder straps that I couldn't wear on the post. That, and a lot of memories. Memories I didn't want, particularly. It was during a period when nobody wanted to remember things.

I was shipped to what was then Camp Campbell (now Fort Campbell), Kentucky, in late December, 1943, a Limited Duty soldier.

## THE HOME FRONT

The *New York Times* on Christmas Day, 1943, a Saturday, carried headlines that Gen. Dwight D. Eisenhower had been named as Commander for the European invasion, and from that time on, every American began to wait for it to start.

We Americans had always known we were going to win the war for the Europeans. Now there wasn't any question. If there had ever been any doubts (and no one believed now that there ever had been) these were dispelled by the news that the invasion was on the way. American production was winning—had already won—the war. (Encased in its gold wreath, the coveted army-navy "E" for Efficiency proved that, didn't it?) Hadn't old Joe Stalin himself toasted American production at Teheran as the winner?

To the overseas men who returned—the wounded, injured, sick— perhaps nothing was quite the slap in the face as the vast and sanguine confidence of the home "front" after mid-1943. It was a little like the battered dogface, who, hearing "Blood & Guts" Georgie Patton being extolled muttered into his beer: "Yeah, his guts and our blood." It was a little like that with the "E" award: "Yeah. Their 'E' and our 'B.' " It did not give him any great charge to see large color photos of pretty but unfuckable-looking young ladies sewing up huge flags and recruitment posters at the Quartermaster Depot in Philadelphia.

Another thing that shocked, and even rankled, was the richness of everybody. True, we overseas men had read all about it in the home papers that got up to us, but even the hyperbole of newsprint had not done it justice. True that the thirties had been lean years, and that everybody was happy to be back at work full swing, and that everybody was belaboring it for all they were worth. Who could blame anybody for making everything he could out of such a good thing? (After all, who knew how long it would last?) But the sheer magnitude of it shocked. And there were moments when it seemed they were truly making it off our red meat and bone. Rankled or not, the old crippled veteran was not above taking advantage of it every chance he got. But in the end, about all he could do was to cadge free drinks by telling gory made-up war stories to businessmen and their mistresses in bars, and that soon palled.

We retreads upset everybody. Retread was one of those words and phrases like Kilroy which swept like wildfire across the globe into every theater. It was a term originally coined by some soldier in World War II, when retread auto tires came into usage, to designate the used-up combat soldier who was sent back through the mill again. Later, in the Korean war, it came to mean reservists called back to service. But we had it first. And at home, the retread was like a man who has survived some epidemic, and been shipped out of the disaster area to a care center. People treated him nicely, and cared for him tenderly, and then hurried to wash their hands after touching him. They did not want what he had caught to rub off, and they did not like it that he made them think of disaster.

Another thing that irritated the retread was the movies. They didn't understand anything about the war. And they didn't try to understand. Instead of trying to show the distressing complexity and puzzling diffusion of war, they pulled everything down to the level of good guy against bad guy. Instead of showing the terrifying impersonality of modern war, they invariably pulled it down to a one-on-one situation, a man-against-man, like a tennis match. At best they made it like a football game. But modern war was not a football game. And modern war was not man against man—if it ever had been. It was machine against machine. It was industry against industry. And we had the best machine. Our industry was better than their industry. But men had to die or be maimed to prove it. Men had to die at the wheels or triggers of the machines.

It could even be worked out mathematically: $n$ number of men had to be invested, and $x$ number had to die, in order for objective $y$ to be reached, and finale $z$ achieved. That was the horrible, true meaning of anonymity to the soldier.

But the movies never showed this, except only very occasionally, and probably the movie-makers never did understand the tragedy or even the problem. And by extension, the great home public apparently never understood it either. They went religiously to see the man-against-man war movies, and thought they were seeing the real war, and then went back to the factory to make more machines.

Take hand grenades. In the movies young sailors (caught on shore in Bataan) or old soldiers everywhere were perpetually wearing hand grenades dangling by the rings from their pocket flaps, pulling the pins with their teeth, tossing grenades on the other side of a coconut log three feet away, or letting the spoons fly off and counting three before tossing the grenade. Now, grenades were one of the most fearfully respected and accident-prone tricky instruments an infantryman had to deal with. They were as often likely to hurt your own people or yourself as the enemy. Usually we spread the cotter pins so wide it took a strong arm to pull the pin at all; teeth wouldn't do it. And if we wore them hanging by their rings under our pocket flaps, we made damn sure the spoon levers were taped to the grenade body with the tape from the cylinders the grenades came in. You didn't let the spoon fly off and ignite the fuse in your hand, because many grenades, though they were supposed to have three-second fuses, had fuses of two seconds, one second, and a lethal few had half-second fuses. A lady fuse-cutter at the grenade factory defense plant with a hangover could wreak real havoc with a box of grenades.

But none of the movie-makers took any of those "industrial" problems into account, and neither did the folks back home who went to see the films. The retread coming back soon realized the home front didn't understand the war, and probably never would understand it. True, they were winning the war with their industrial production, but on the other hand, they got very well paid for it. A lot better than the combat soldier who had to maneuver their machines and pull their triggers.

## LOVE AMONG THE RIVETERS

They weren't all of them easy lays, by any means. Not half easy enough, by most of the retreads. Yet it was clear enough to any eye that had been away abroad that the mores and morals of the nation's middle class were swiftly undergoing a sea change. The wild gaiety and rollicking despair that characterized the towns and cities near the camps certainly helped this. At least half of the girls who used to visit the drinking parties of our Peabody suite were defense plant workers or in some defense-connected industry. Many of them were country girls or small town girls who had come into Memphis to help the nation's war effort by working and, incidentally, get at the same time some excitement into their lives. I often shuddered to think what their trembling fingers might do next day to some piece of armament destined for some poor dogface in the mud of Italy or the Pacific. But in a mass war as mass as our war was mass, one man couldn't take account of everything. Besides, if they were cautioned to go home and sober up and get some sleep before going to work at the plant, they would only leave us and go down the hall to the next suite's party on the floor below. And we would be out a girl, and the poor Government Issue in Italy would be no better off.

We had a lieutenant in my outfit who had his hand blown nearly off by a half-second grenade. The thing hardly left his hand before it exploded in mid-air above his head. Fortunately he was not up on the line when it happened, but was using the grenade to go fishing in the Matanikau River. So they were able to get him and what was left of his hand back to the hospital quickly. The principle, of course, of grenade fishing was that the concussion of the grenade going off underwater would kill all the fish nearby, where they would float belly up with their air bladders ruptured to be picked up by the fisherman.

I ran into him later in the hospital, where he had his various fingers stretched out and pinned to a big wire frame the size of a large baseball glove. When they finally let him out on pass, I went out with him drinking a couple of times. He certainly had a way with women. He was a cheerful, rapacious, malevolent type of a guy, and claimed that because of what the bad grenade had done to his hand, it was his project to screw every riveter, welder, lathe-operator and fuse-cutter that he could get his one good hand on for the rest of the war. That was to be his revenge. The little I saw of him, it appeared he might realize his ambition, if they would only transfer him around to enough different hospitals in different cities.

For a while I went with a little girl who worked in a defense plant and lived at home in Memphis. This little girl's parents and two older sisters worked in defense plants, too. This family's morals had changed sufficiently that nobody in the household cared if I came home and slept with her there in her little thin-walled room, as long as I did not keep her from getting to her plant in time for work on whatever shift it was she happened to be working at the time.

But of course we lost out on all that sport when we were returned to Limited Duty at Camp Campbell, Kentucky.

▪ **1944** ▪

# JOHN O'HARA

THE AMERICAN short story writer and novelist John O'Hara was born in Pottsville, Pennsylvania. He established his reputation with his famous first novel, *Appointment in Samarra,* published before he was thirty. Among his other well-known works are *Butterfield Eight, Pal Joey,* and *A Rage to Live. The Collected Stories of John O'Hara* was published in 1984.

■

## Graven Image

The car turned in at the brief, crescent-shaped drive and waited until the two cabs ahead had pulled away. The car pulled up, the doorman opened the rear door, a little man got out. The little man nodded pleasantly enough to the doorman and said "Wait" to the chauffeur. "Will the Under Secretary be here long?" asked the doorman.

"Why?" said the little man.

"Because if you were going to be here, sir, only a short while, I'd let your man leave the car here, at the head of the rank."

"Leave it there *anyway*," said the Under Secretary.

"Very good, sir," said the doorman. He saluted and frowned only a little as he watched the Under Secretary enter the hotel. "Well," the doorman said to himself, "it was a long time coming. It took him longer than most, but sooner or later all of them—" He opened the door of the next car, addressed a colonel and a major by their titles, and never did anything about the Under Secretary's car, which pulled ahead and parked in the drive.

The Under Secretary was spoken to many times in his progress to the main dining room. One man said, "What's your hurry, Joe?" to which the Under Secretary smiled and nodded. He was called Mr. Secretary most often, in some cases easily, by the old Washington hands, but more frequently with that embarrassment which Americans feel in using titles. As he passed through the lobby, the Under Secretary himself addressed by their White House nicknames two gentlemen whom he had to acknowledge to be closer to The Boss. And, bustling all the while, he made his way to the dining room, which was already packed. At the entrance he stopped short and frowned. The man he was to meet, Charles Browning, was chatting, in French, very amiably with the maître d'hôtel. Browning and the Under Secretary had been at Harvard at the same time.

The Under Secretary went up to him. "Sorry if I'm a little late," he said, and held out his hand, at the same time looking at his pocket watch. "Not so very, though. How are you, Charles? Fred, you got my message?"

"Yes, sir," said the maître d'hôtel. "I put you at a nice table all the way back to the right." He meanwhile had wigwagged a captain, who stood by to lead the Under Secretary and his guest to Table 12. "Nice to have seen you again, Mr. Browning. Hope you come see us again while you are in Washington. Always a pleasure, sir."

"Always a pleasure, Fred," said Browning. He turned to the Under Secretary. "Well, shall we?"

"Yeah, let's sit down," said the Under Secretary.

The captain led the way, followed by the Under Secretary, walking slightly sideways. Browning, making one step to two of the Under Secretary's, brought up the rear. When they were seated, the Under Secretary took the menu out of the captain's hands. "Let's order right away so I don't have to look up and talk to those two son of a bitches. I guess you know which two I mean." Browning looked from right to left, as anyone does on just sitting down in a restaurant. He nodded and said, "Yes, I think I know. You mean the senators."

"That's right," said the Under Secretary. "I'm not gonna have a cocktail, but you can. . . . You want a cocktail?"

"I don't think so. I'll take whatever you're having."

"O.K., waiter?" said the Under Secretary.

"Yes, sir," said the captain, and went away.

"Well, Charles, I was pretty surprised to hear from you."

"Yes," Browning said, "I should imagine so, and by the way, I want to thank you for answering my letter so promptly. I know how rushed you fellows must be, and I thought, as I said in my letter, at your convenience."

"Mm. Well, frankly, there wasn't any use in putting you off. I mean till next week or two weeks from now or anything like that. I could just as easily see you today as a month from now. Maybe easier. I don't know where I'll be likely to be a month from now. In more ways than one. I may be taking the Clipper to London, and then of course I may be out on my can! Coming to New York and asking *you* for a job. I take it that's what you wanted to see me about."

"Yes, and with hat in hand."

"Oh, no. I can't see you waiting with hat in hand, not for anybody. Not even for The Boss."

Browning laughed.

"What are you laughing at?" asked the Under Secretary.

"Well, you know how I feel about him, so I'd say least of all The Boss."

"Well, you've got plenty of company in this goddam town. But why'd you come to me, then? Why didn't you go to one of your Union League or Junior League or whatever-the-hell-it-is pals? There, that big jerk over there with the blue suit and the striped tie, for instance?"

Browning looked over at the big jerk with the blue suit and striped tie, and at that moment their eyes met and the two men nodded.

"You *know* him?" said the Under Secretary.

"Sure, I know him, but that doesn't say I *approve* of him."

"Well, at least that's something. And I notice he knows you."

"I've been to his house. I think he's been to our house when my father was alive and naturally I've seen him around New York all my life."

"Naturally. Naturally. Then why didn't you go to *him?*"

"That's easy. I wouldn't like to ask him for anything. I don't approve of the man, at least as a politician, so I couldn't go to him and ask him a favor."

"But, on the other hand, you're not one of our team, but yet you'd ask me a favor. I don't get it."

"Oh, yes you do, Joe. You didn't get where you are by not being able to understand a simple thing like that."

Reluctantly—and quite obviously it was reluctantly—the Under Secretary grinned. "All right. I was baiting you."

"I know you were, but I expected it. I have it coming to me. I've always been against you fellows. I wasn't even for you in 1932, that's a hell of an admission, but it's the truth. But that's water under the bridge —or isn't it?" The waiter interrupted with the food, and they did not speak until he had gone away.

"You were asking me if it isn't water under the bridge. Why should it be?"

"The obvious reason," said Browning.

" 'My country, 'tis of thee'?"

"Exactly. Isn't that enough?"

"It isn't for your Racquet Club pal over there."

"You keep track of things like that?"

"Certainly," said the Under Secretary. "I know every goddam club in this country, beginning back about twenty-three years ago. I had ample time to study them all then, you recall, objectively, from the outside. By the way, I notice you wear a wristwatch. What happens to the little animal?"

Browning put his hand in his pocket and brought out a small bunch of keys. He held the chain so that the Under Secretary could see, suspended from it, a small golden pig. "I still carry it," he said.

"They tell me a lot of you fellows put them back in your pockets about five years ago, when one of the illustrious brethren closed his downtown office and moved up to Ossining."

"Oh, probably," Browning said, "but quite a few fellows, I believe, that hadn't been wearing them took to wearing them again out of simple loyalty. Listen, Joe, are we talking like grown men? Are you sore at the Pork? Do you think you'd have enjoyed being a member of it? If being sore at it was even partly responsible for getting you where you are, then I think you ought to be a little grateful to it. You'd show the bastards. O.K. You showed them. Us. If you hadn't been so sore at the Porcellian so-and-so's, you might have turned into just another lawyer."

"My wife gives me that sometimes."

"There, do you see?" Browning said. "Now then, how about the job?"

The Under Secretary smiled. "There's no getting away from it, you guys have got something. O.K., what are you interested in? Of course, I make no promises, and I don't even know if what you're interested in is something I can help you with."

"That's a chance I'll take. That's why I came to Washington, on just that chance, but it's my guess you can help me." Browning went on to tell the Under Secretary about the job he wanted. He told him why he thought he was qualified for it, and the Under Secretary nodded. Browning told him everything he knew about the job, and the Under Secretary continued to nod silently. By the end of Browning's recital the Under Secretary had become thoughtful. He told Browning that he thought there might be some little trouble with a certain character but that that character could be handled, because the real say-so, the green light, was controlled by a man who was a friend of the Under Secretary's, and the Under Secretary could almost say at this moment that the matter could be arranged.

At this, Browning grinned. "By God, Joe, we've got to have a drink on this. This is the best news since—" He summoned the waiter. The Under Secretary yielded and ordered a cordial. Browning ordered a Scotch. The drinks were brought. Browning said, "About the job. I'm not going to say another word but just keep my fingers crossed. But as to you, Joe, you're the best. I drink to you." The two men drank, the Under Secretary sipping at his, Browning taking half of his. Browning looked at the drink in his hand. "You know, I was a little afraid. That other stuff, the club stuff."

"Yes," said the Under Secretary.

"I don't know why fellows like you—you never would have made it in a thousand years, but"—then, without looking up, he knew everything had collapsed—"but I've said exactly the wrong thing, haven't I?"

"That's right, Browning," said the Under Secretary. "You've said exactly the wrong thing. I've got to be going." He stood up and turned and went out, all dignity.

# ELIE WIESEL

THE WINNER of the Nobel Peace Prize in 1986, Romanian-born Elie Wiesel is a survivor of both Auschwitz and Buchenwald. He wrote *Night*, his memoir of life in the camps, at the urging of François Mauriac.

■

## FROM *Night*

Lying down was out of the question, and we were only able to sit by deciding to take turns. There was very little air. The lucky ones who happened to be near a window could see the blossoming countryside roll by.

After two days of traveling, we began to be tortured by thirst. Then the heat became unbearable.

Free from all social constraint, the young people gave way openly to instinct, taking advantage of the darkness to copulate in our midst, without caring about anyone else, as though they were alone in the world. The rest pretended not to notice anything.

We still had a few provisions left. But we never ate enough to satisfy our hunger. To save was our rule; to save up for tomorrow. Tomorrow might be worse.

The train stopped at Kaschau, a little town on the Czechoslovak frontier. We realized then that we were not going to stay in Hungary. Our eyes were opened, but too late.

The door of the car slid open. A German officer, accompanied by a Hungarian lieutenant-interpreter, came up and introduced himself.

"From this moment, you come under the authority of the German army. Those of you who still have gold, silver or watches in your possession must give them up now. Anyone who is later found to have kept anything will be shot on the spot. Secondly, anyone who feels ill may go to the hospital car. That's all."

The Hungarian lieutenant went among us with a basket and collected the last possessions from those who no longer wished to taste the bitterness of terror.

"There are eighty of you in the wagon," added the German officer. "If anyone is missing, you'll all be shot, like dogs. . . ."

They disappeared. The doors were closed. We were caught in a trap, right up to our necks. The doors were nailed up; the way back was finally cut off. The world was a cattle wagon, hermetically sealed.

# EVELYN WAUGH

EVELYN WAUGH, one of this century's major novelists, wrote a trilogy about the war. Following is an excerpt from the last volume of that trilogy, which was titled *Unconditional Surrender* in the United Kingdom and *The End of the Battle* in the United States.

■

## FROM *The End of the Battle*

Few foreigners visited Bari from the time of the Crusades until the fall of Mussolini. Few tourists, even the most assiduous, explored the Apulian coast. Bari contains much that should have attracted them—the old town full of Norman building, the bones of St. Nicholas enshrined in silver; the new town spacious and commodious. But for centuries it lay neglected by all save native businessmen. Guy had never before set foot there.

Lately the place had achieved the unique, unsought distinction of being the only place in the Second World War to suffer from gas. In the first days of its occupation a ship full of "mustard" blew up in the harbor, scattering its venom about the docks. Many of the inhabitants complained of sore throats, sore eyes and blisters. They were told it was an unfamiliar, mild, epidemic disease of short duration. The people of Apulia are inured to such afflictions.

Now, early in 1944, the city had recovered the cosmopolitan, martial stir it enjoyed in the Middle Ages. Allied soldiers on short leave—some wearing, ironically enough, the woven badge of the crusader's sword—teemed in its streets; wounded filled its hospitals; the staffs of numberless services took over the new, battered office-buildings which had risen as monuments to the Corporative State. Small naval craft adorned the shabby harbor. Bari could not rival the importance of Naples, that prodigious, improvised factory of war. Its agile and ingenious criminal class consisted chiefly of small boys. Few cars flew the pennons of high authority. Few officers over the rank of brigadier inhabited the outlying villas. Foggia drew the *magistras* of the Air Force. Nothing very august flourished in Bari, but there were dingy buildings occupied by Balkan and Zionist emissaries; by a melancholic English officer who performed a part not then known as "disc jockey," providing the troops with the tunes it was thought they wished to hear; by a euphoric Scotch officer surrounded by books with which he hoped to inculcate a respect for

English culture among those who could read that language; by the editors of little papers, more directly propagandist and printed in a variety of languages; by the agents of competing intelligence systems; by a group of Russians whose task was to relabel tins of American rations in bold Cyrillic characters, proclaiming them the produce of the U.S.S.R., before they were dropped from American airplanes over beleaguered gangs of Communists; by Italians, even, who were being coached in the arts of local democratic government. The allies had lately much impeded their advance by the destruction of Monte Cassino, but the price of this sacrilege was being paid by the infantry of the front line. It did not trouble the peace-loving and unambitious officers who were glad to settle in Bari.

They constituted a little world of officers—some young and seedy, some old and spruce—sequestered from the responsibilities and vexations of command. Such men of other rank as were sometimes seen in the arcaded streets were drivers, orderlies, policemen, clerks, servants and sentries.

In this limbo Guy fretted for more than a week while February blossomed into March. He had left Italy four and a half years ago. He had then taken leave of the crusader whom the people called "il santo inglese." He had laid his hand on the sword that had never struck the infidel. He wore the medal which had hung round the neck of his brother Gervase when the sniper had picked him off on his way up to the line in Flanders. In his heart he felt stirring the despair in which his brother Ivo had starved himself to death. Half an hour's scramble on the beach near Dakar; an ignominious rout in Crete. That had been his war.

Every day he reported to headquarters. "No news yet," they said. "Communications have not been satisfactory for the last few days. The Air Force aren't playing until they know what's going on over there."

"Enjoy yourself," Brigadier Cape had said. That would not have been the order of Ritchie-Hook. There was no biffing in Bari.

Guy wandered as a tourist about the streets of the old town. He sat in the club and the hotel. He met old acquaintances and made new ones. Leisure, bonhomie and futility had him in thrall.

After a brief absence Lieutenant Padfield reappeared in the company of a large and celebrated English composer whom U.N.R.R.A. had mysteriously imported. On the Sunday they drove Guy out to the road south to visit the beehive dwellings where the descendants of Athenian colonists still lived their independent lives. Nearby was a small, ancient town where an Italian family had set up an illicit restaurant. They did not deal in paper currency but accepted petrol, cigarettes and medical supplies in exchange for dishes of fresh fish cooked with olive oil and white truffles and garlic.

The Lieutenant left his car in the piazza before the locked church. There were other service vehicles there and, when they reached the house on the water front, they found it full of English and Americans; among them Brigadier Cape and his homely hospital nurse.

"I haven't seen you," said the Brigadier, "and you haven't seen me," but the nurse knew all about the musician and after luncheon insisted on being introduced. They all walked together along the quay, Guy and the Brigadier a pace behind the other three. This place had been left untouched by the advancing and retreating armies. The inhabitants were taking their siestas. To seaward the calm Adriatic lapped against the old stones; in the harbor the boats lay motionless. Guy remarked, tritely enough, that the war seemed far away.

The Brigadier was in a ruminative mood. He had eaten largely; other pleasures lay ahead. "War," he said. "When I was at Sandhurst no one talked about war. We learned about it, of course—a school subject like Latin or geography; something to write exam papers about. No bearing on life. I went into the army because I liked horses, and I've spent four years in and out of a stinking, noisy tank. Now I've got a couple of gongs and a game leg and all I want is quiet. Not *peace*, mind. There's nothing wrong with war except the fighting. I don't mind betting that after five years of peace we shall all look back on Bari as the best days of our life."

Suddenly the musician turned and said: "Crouchback has the death wish."

"Have you?" asked the Brigadier with a show of disapproval.

"Have I?" said Guy.

"I recognized it the moment we met," said the musician. "I should not mention it now except that Padfield was so liberal with the wine."

"Death wish?" said the Brigadier. "I don't like the sound of that. Time we were off, Bettie."

He took his nurse's arm and limped back towards the piazza. Guy saluted as Halberdiers did. The Lieutenant tipped his cap in a gesture that was part benediction, part a wave of farewell. The musician bowed to the nurse.

Then he turned towards the open sea and performed a little parody of himself conducting an orchestra, saying: "The death wish. The death wish. On a day like this."

# ELIE WIESEL

BORN IN Romania in 1928, Wiesel as a teenager survived both Auschwitz and Buchenwald. He has served
as witness to the Holocaust in numerous books and
lectures and has been decorated by the French and
U.S. governments. The recipient of many major literary
awards, he was honored with the Nobel Peace Prize in
1986.

■

## FROM *Night*

We had reached a station. Those who were next to the windows told
us its name:

"Auschwitz."

No one had ever heard that name.

The train did not start up again. The afternoon passed slowly. Then
the wagon doors slid open. Two men were allowed to get down to fetch
water.

When they came back, they told us that in exchange for a gold
watch, they had discovered that this was the last stop. We would be
getting out here. There was a labor camp. Conditions were good. Families would not be split up. Only the young people would go to work in
the factories. The old men and invalids would be kept occupied in the
fields.

The barometer of confidence soared. Here was a sudden release
from the terrors of the previous nights. We gave thanks to God.

Madame Schächter stayed in her corner, wilted, dumb, indifferent
to the general confidence. Her little boy stroked her hand.

As dusk fell, darkness gathered inside the wagon. We started to eat
our last provisions. At ten in the evening, everyone was looking for a
convenient position in which to sleep for a while, and soon we were all
asleep. Suddenly:

"The fire! The furnace! Look, over there! . . ."

Waking with a start, we rushed to the window. Yet again we had
believed her, even if only for a moment. But there was nothing outside
save the darkness of night. With shame in our souls, we went back to our
places, gnawed by fear, in spite of ourselves. As she continued to scream,
they began to hit her again, and it was with the greatest difficulty that
they silenced her.

The man in charge of our wagon called a German officer who was walking about on the platform, and asked him if Madame Schächter could be taken to the hospital car.

"You must be patient," the German replied. "She'll be taken there soon."

Towards eleven o'clock, the train began to move. We pressed against the windows. The convoy was moving slowly. A quarter of an hour later, it slowed down again. Through the windows we could see barbed wire; we realized that this must be the camp.

We had forgotten the existence of Madame Schächter. Suddenly, we heard terrible screams:

"Jews, look! Look through the window! Flames! Look!"

And as the train stopped, we saw this time that flames were gushing out of a tall chimney, into the black sky.

Madame Schächter was silent herself. Once more she had become dumb, indifferent, absent, and had gone back to her corner.

We looked at the flames in the darkness. There was an abominable odor floating in the air. Suddenly, our doors opened. Some odd-looking characters, dressed in striped shirts and black trousers leapt into the wagon. They held electric torches and truncheons. They began to strike out to right and left, shouting:

"Everybody get out! Everyone out of the wagon! Quickly!"

We jumped out. I threw a last glance towards Madame Schächter. Her little boy was holding her hand.

In front of us, flames. In the air that smell of burning flesh. It must have been about midnight. We had arrived. At Birkenau reception center for Auschwitz.

# HEINRICH BÖLL

HEINRICH BÖLL, winner of the Nobel Prize for Literature in 1972, was an infantryman during the war. His
novels include *The Clown, Billiards at Half-Past Nine,*
and *Group Portrait with Lady.* An excerpt from one of
his short stories, "The Casualty," follows.

■

# The Casualty

At the point where, half an hour earlier, the dust cloud of the at-
tackers had been, there was now the dust cloud of fleeing men. The
dusty haze was drifting over the shimmering steppe toward the military
police, confusing them and increasing their fury. Raising their machine
pistols they roared: "Stop, you bastards—stop—back to your positions!"

The air was filled with the screams of wounded men left lying on the
ground, the shouts of the Russians—a hoarse, frightened barking, and
the cries of fleeing men: like a herd of wild horses scenting an obstruc-
tion, they halted when confronted by the barrels of the machine pistols,
then turned in weary submission and went back.

From behind me I could hear the shouts of the officers as they
grouped their men for a new thrust. I could hear the rumbling of tanks,
the howling of shells, and still the screams of the badly wounded. Slowly
and with a feeling of extraordinary happiness I walked toward the line of
military police. They couldn't touch me, I'd been wounded, although
there was nothing to show for it in front.

"Stop!" they shouted. "Get back there, you bastard!"

"I've been wounded!" I yelled at them. With suspicious looks they
let me approach. I went up to a tense, infuriated lieutenant, turned
round and showed him my back. It must have been a pretty big hole, I'd
run my hand over it once: damp, sticky blood and shreds of cloth. But I
could feel nothing, it was a superb wound, a wound made to order, they
couldn't touch me. Actually it must have looked worse than it was. The
lieutenant growled something, then said more calmly: "There's a doctor
over there."

The valley was empty and silent: half an hour earlier it had contained tanks, artillery, staff officers in their vehicles, the whole hysterical
uproar that precedes an attack. Now it was quiet. The doctor was sitting
under a tree. Behind me, more wounded men were slowly arriving. I was
the first patient of this attack.

"Over here, my friend," said the doctor. He lifted the shreds of cloth. It tickled a bit; then he clucked his tongue and said: "Spit, please." I gagged, my throat was all dry, but I managed to produce a blob.

"Nothing," said the doctor. "You've been lucky, doesn't seem to be anything in your lungs. But, Jesus, that could've been a bad one!" He gave me a tetanus shot. I asked for some water, and he pulled out a flask. I reached out for it, but he held it to my mouth and allowed me only a brief swallow. "Take it easy, lad—d'you have any pain?"

"Yes."

He gave me a pill. I swallowed it. I didn't feel a thing, it was a marvelous wound, made to order, it would take at least four months for the hole to heal, and by that time the war would be over.

"There, you can go now," said the doctor. Next in line stood a man who had been shot in the calf; he was groaning with pain, but he had walked all the way here, using his rifle as a stick.

The valley was magnificent, the loveliest valley I had ever seen. Just bare slopes covered with steppe grass sweltering in the sun. A hazy sky above, nothing else. But it was the most magnificent valley, as glorious as my wound that didn't hurt me and yet was serious. I walked slowly, no longer thirsty and with no back-pack—I'd left that at the front. And I was alone. I sat down somewhere and had a smoke. All this takes time off the war, I thought, they can't touch you, you've been wounded and you're entitled to a bit of a rest. From my vantage point I could look down on the place where the doctor was. There were a lot of men down there, some of them walking along the valley and looking in that barren scene like strollers in the desert. A car was parked there too, right beside the doctor, but I didn't feel like being driven in it, I had plenty of time, they couldn't touch me.

Slowly I walked on. Only now did I realize what a long way we had advanced from Jassy. No matter how often I reached the top of a ridge, there was nothing of the town's white walls to be seen. It was very quiet, apart from a few desultory shots in the distance. Then I saw a forest, and out of the forest came a big, furious car raising a cloud of dust. It was really angry, that car, impatient, irritable, annoyed. It stopped right in front of me. In it sat our general, wearing his steel helmet, and when generals wear their steel helmets something has gone wrong. There was also a colonel, wearing a Knight's Cross, no other decoration. It looked very chic and elegant. The general stood up in the car and yelled at me: "What d'you suppose you're doing?"

"I've been wounded, sir," I replied, and turned round. I almost had to laugh, it was so funny the way I turned my backside to the general.

"It's all right, son." I turned again. His round, red face was still furious, as furious as the car, even though he'd said "son." Generals always say "son"; they don't show much imagination when they speak to you.

"How are things up front?" he asked.

"First they went back, then forward again, I don't really know."

"Where's your rifle, son?"

"Smashed, sir. It was a hand grenade, fell right beside me. My rifle lay on that side and got smashed to pieces."

"Here, have a smoke," he said, handing me a whole packet of cigarettes. Generals usually hand out cigarettes. I thanked him by standing to attention, and off they drove. The colonol touched his cap, which I found quite something considering he had the Knight's Cross and I had nothing on my chest.

On coming out of the forest I saw the town lying all white on its hills and looking magnificent. I felt very happy, they couldn't touch me, I'd been wounded right at the front, ten meters away from the Russians, and maybe I was a hero. They couldn't touch me. I was carrying my haversack, it contained two pairs of socks, and for that I would drink some wine in town, maybe get something to eat, but the idea of eating made me feel quite sick; I'd had nothing to eat or drink for a day and a half. Yet at the thought of wine I walked faster. I crossed a heath that was all torn up by tank tracks and bombs; a few corpses were lying around, and some dead horses. Beyond this bit of heath the path rose steeply past some houses: I was in town. A tram was waiting in a square. I ran to catch it, like at home. I just made it, and we moved off at once. Maybe the driver had seen me, I thought, and waited for me. The tram was empty. It must have been about noon. It was hot; to right and left the houses slept in the sun. There were only a few dogs running round, and some chickens.

The conductress came toward me with her pouch, wanting money. That's right, I thought, the Romanians are our allies, we're supposed to pay. I shrugged and laughed. But she was quite serious. "Nix," she said firmly. Turning my wound toward her I said: "Kaputt, see?" but that didn't move her. She shrugged her shoulders and rubbed thumb and forefinger. "Nix," she repeated. Digging into my haversack I found some writing paper, a few crushed cigarettes that I intended to smoke in my pipe, the socks, and a pair of nail scissors. I showed her the nail scissors. The driver raced along at breakneck speed. Some other people had got on. The conductress attended to them, then came back. I showed her the scissors. "How many lei?" I asked. She wrinkled her nose. She was quite pretty, and I could see that the scissors appealed to her. She snipped her nails with them, smiled at me and indicated "twenty" with her fingers. I nodded. I was so happy, for they couldn't touch me, maybe I was a hero, I'd been wounded right at the front, ten meters away from the Russians. The conductress gave me a ten-*lei* bill and the ticket for five *lei*. That was all. But I didn't mind. I was happy, they couldn't touch me.

I turned to look out at my surroundings. We passed a café, and I remembered I hadn't had anything to drink for two days and had a raging thirst. The tram stopped at a big square where there was a cinema for the military and some cafés and department stores. It was a busy scene, with soldiers milling round, and whores, and peddlers with their barrows. The whores were fantastically beautiful, with almond eyes and scarlet mouths, but they looked pretty pricey to me.

I got off and went into a café; no one paid any attention to me, no one saw the wound in my back, a superb wound, all bloody, with shreds of cloth and needing at least four months to heal. There was just one soldier in the café, sitting at the back, a corporal, and I could tell at once that he was drunk. To the left sat a man with black hair, coal black, and a fat, pale face, eating a pickled cucumber and smoking a black cigar. To the right sat a woman who smiled at me. She was smoking a cigarette, puffing fiendish smoke rings.

"Loverboy!" she called out, but I didn't like the looks of her, and I was sure she would be very pricey. The corporal at the back called out: "Hey, there!" I walked toward him. His eyes were dim and unfocused. His chest was covered with medals, and he had a large carafe of wine in front of him.

"Help yourself!" he said. My God, how glorious it was to drink! I drank straight from the carafe. My God, how wonderful it was to drink! I could physically feel how parched I was, and it was a cool wine, on the dry side.

"Help yourself!" said the corporal, but the carafe was empty. "Hey, pal!" he called out, and a greasy-looking fellow immediately came from behind a curtain, snatched up the carafe, and carried it off. The black-haired man was now sitting with the woman, who was as blonde as he was dark. He let her take a bite of his pickle and a puff of his cigar; then they both laughed, and the black-haired man called out toward the cur-tain something that sounded like Latin, a slushy kind of Latin.

The greasy youth arrived with the carafe, a bigger one than the last, and he also brought along another glass.

"Help yourself!" said the corporal.

He poured, and we drank. I drank, I drank, it was glorious, it was wonderful.

"Have a smoke," said the corporal, but I hauled out my general's packet and slapped it onto the table. The blonde woman was laughing with the black-haired man; now they were drinking wine. Wine on top of pickles, I thought, that's asking for trouble, but they seemed to be enjoy-ing it as they blew their fiendish smoke rings in the air.

"Drink away," said the corporal. "I have to go back to the front tonight, for the fifth time, goddammit!"

"Take the tram," I said, "I've just come from there, for the third time."

"Where've you come from?"

"From the front."

"Did you skedaddle?"

"No, I was wounded."

"Oh, come on!"

I showed him my back.

"Goddammit," he exclaimed, "aren't you the lucky one! That's fantastic. Sell it to me!"

"Sell what?"

"That thing there, that red mess on your back—sell it to me!"

He slapped a whole pile of bills on the table, picked up the carafe, and lifted it to his mouth. Then I drank, then he, then I . . .

"Hey, pal!" he called.

The greasy youth reappeared and brought another carafe, and we drank.

"Sell it to me, you coward," shouted the corporal. "I'll give you a thousand *lei*, two thousand, three thousand, you can buy yourself the best-looking whores, and tobacco, and wine, and you . . ."

"But you can buy wounds right here, they made me an offer at the station."

The corporal suddenly turned sober and grabbed my arm.

"Where?" he asked hoarsely.

"At the station," I said, "they made me an offer right there."

"Hey pal!" shouted the corporal. "How much?" He slapped some money on the table, grabbed my arm, and said: "Wait here."

He put on his cap, tightened his belt and left.

The greasy youth brought another carafe. "It's paid for," he said with a grin. And I drank. The blonde woman was sitting on the black-haired man's knee, shrieking away. She had a cigar in her mouth and a cold pork chop in her hand. The black-haired man was already quite drunk. I drank and smoked. It was glorious, I was drunk, wonderfully drunk, and I'd been wounded, and they couldn't touch me, maybe I was a hero. Wounded for the third time. The wine was glorious, glorious . . .

"Hey, pal!" I called out. The greasy youth came and stood grinning in front of me. I pulled the socks out of my haversack and held them out: "How much wine?" He shrugged and wrinkled his nose, then took the socks and held them up to his face. "Not new," he said, sniffing with his long nose.

"How much?" I asked.

"Give you wine, two like that." He pointed at the carafe.

"Bring it," I said, "bring it here, the wine."

He brought it. Both carafes at once. I drank, I drank, it was glorious, it was wonderful, I was completely drunk, but as sober as only a happy man can be. It was indescribable how cool and dry the wine was, and I paid for it with two pairs of socks. The woman ate a second pork chop as she smoked a cigarette. She was a thin little creature and shrieked like crazy as she sat on the black-haired man's knee. I saw everything clear as clear, drunk though I was. I could see she wasn't wearing either a slip or underpants, and the black-haired man kept pinching her behind; that made her shriek, she shrieked because of that too. Then the black-haired man started yelling his head off, lifted the woman high in the air, and carried her out through the door.

At that moment the corporal walked in again.

"Help yourself!" I called out to him.

"Hey, pal!" shouted the corporal, whereupon the greasy youth appeared at once.

"Wine!" shouted the corporal. "A whole barrel of wine!" and I knew that it had worked. He picked up my second carafe, drank it down at one go, and smashed it against the wall.

"Those fellows," said the corporal, "do a great job. Pistol with silencer. You stand round a corner and stick out your paw, and plop— take a look."

He pulled up his sleeve. They had put a nice clean hole through his forearm, bandaged it, and even supplied him with a casualty certificate.

The greasy youth brought a large carafe. The corporal was beside himself, shouting and drinking, shouting and drinking. And said: "My name's Hubert."

And I drank; it was wonderful.

Then we went off to the first-aid station. Hubert knew all the ropes. As we arrived, a few freight cars were just being loaded with minor casualties. There were two doctors, and in front of each stood a long queue of walking wounded. Since we were drunk, we wanted to come last. We joined the second queue because that doctor looked kinder than the other one. A corporal stood beside him calling out "Next!" Some cases took a long time, and those who had been treated walked through a long corridor leading to a courtyard.

We sat down on a bench, since we were drunk and rather unsteady on our legs. Next to me sat a man who'd had a bullet through the palm of his hand, clear through it, and he was bleeding like a pig onto the bench. He was quite gray in the face.

The doctors were working with the door open, cigarettes between their lips, and sometimes they would take a pull from a bottle. They were slaving away like crazy, and the one I was queueing up for had a nice face, an intelligent face, and I noticed he had skillful, quiet hands. A vehicle arrived with some serious casualties, and we had to wait. The corporal shut the door, and we could hear screams, and there was an even stronger smell of blood and ether. The man with the injured hand had fallen asleep and had stopped bleeding. The blood from his hand had gone all over me, and when I took my paybook out of my left pocket I found it soaked in blood; the first few pages were no longer legible. I was drunk, I didn't care, and they couldn't, they couldn't touch me, they couldn't get at me, I'd been wounded, I'd been wounded right at the front, and maybe I was even a hero.

So now I was the unknown soldier.

I said aloud to myself, "I am the unknown soldier," but the others, sitting on the ground or on the bench, called out "Shut up!" I shut up and looked out onto the street. Hubert had fallen asleep, with his arm stuck out stiffly; it looked very impressive, like a genuine battle injury. They had done a good job; I must be sure and ask him how much it cost. And if the war wasn't over in four months, I'd get them to shoot me through the arm, too, then I'd get the gold badge, then I'd be a proper official hero, and they wouldn't be able to touch me at all. But now he was asleep, they still hadn't finished with the six stretcher cases, and all we could hear was their screaming. I wasn't all that drunk any more. Someone in the queue suddenly asked quietly: "Got a smoke, anyone?" I recognized the man with the leg who had supported himself on his rifle. But he didn't recognize me. He still had his rifle, and his face was the face of a real hero. He was proud. I gave him a few of the general's cigarettes. Hubert was sound asleep and snoring; now his face was quite happy. Then the door opened, and the corporal called out again, "Next!"

After that everything went very fast, and no more vehicles arrived. I was still drunk after all, but I felt fine, with no pain to speak of.

"Hey, next, it's your turn!" the corporal shouted.

I stepped into a classroom where the benches had been piled up and Marshal Antonescu looked down from the wall, together with Crown Prince Michael. There was a disgusting smell of blood and ether. I took off my tunic and shirt, unaided; I was still drunk. "Hurry up!" said the corporal. Crown Prince Michael had a really stupid Hohenzollern face and he was boss over the black-haired people and the whores and the greasy youths, the onions and the pickles and the wine. But Romania was a real mess, and he'd never bring it off, nor would Antonescu.

At that moment I became perfectly sober, for the doctor was snipping away in my back. I could feel nothing as he had given me a local anaesthetic, but it is a very queer sensation when they snip away in you like that. I could see it all quite clearly: in front of me was a big glass-doored cupboard and behind me a glass instrument-case. And I could see my smooth back and the big hole in it, and the doctor snipping the edges nice and smooth and picking something out of the hole. I felt like a frozen carcass being divided up between two butchers. His snipping was quick and deft; then he dabbed something onto the wound, and I saw that the hole had become much bigger. Go on, make it a little bigger, I thought, then it'll take six months. Maybe the doctor was thinking the same thing. Once again he started snipping and probing. Then came more dabbing, and the corporal, who had been holding me as a matter of routine, went to the door and called out, "Next!"

"Hand grenade, was it, my boy?" the doctor asked as he placed a large wad of cotton wool on the hole in my back.

"I think so," I replied.

"Quite a nice long piece, want to keep it?" He held out a crumpled, bloodied strip of metal.

"No, thanks," I said. He tossed it in the garbage can, and I could see a leg lying there, a real, perfectly good, splendid leg. I was cold sober.

"I'm sure there's a bit of wood in there still, and some shreds of cloth, they'll all have to come out with the pus—just make certain nothing stays behind." He laughed. The corporal bandaged me up, winding all sorts of stuff round me, and now dammit I really did feel like a hero, goddammit, wounded by a hand grenade, right at the front.

The doctor looked at Hubert's clean hole, then at the corporal, and his expression became serious. "Made to order, my friend, just made to order."

I felt hot all over, but Hubert remained cool.

"A really magnificent home-leave shot, that's the fifth today," said the corporal.

"Magnificent," said the doctor, but he didn't touch it, merely glanced at the corporal, and the corporal, who was still bandaging me, went across to have a good look at it; then he too looked at Hubert. "Magnificent," he said.

# NORMAN LEWIS

*NAPLES '44* is a splendid account of Norman Lewis's experiences in the Italian campaign, written as a diary. Lewis, an English novelist and travel-writer, was an intelligence officer during the war. In September 1943, temporarily attached to HQ staff of the American Fifth Army, he joined the invasion fleet bound for Salerno.

■

FROM *Naples '44*

*March 3*

A story has come to light of yet another almost incredible scheme dreamed up by A-Force—operating in enemy-occupied territory—which has ended in typical catastrophe. It seems likely that the germ of this macabre idea originated as a result of a circular sent to all units at about Christmas, worded in part as follows:

> From reports that have been received it is apparent that prostitution in occupied Italy, and Naples in particular, has reached a pitch greater than has ever been witnessed in Italy before. So much is this so that it has led to a suggestion that the encouragement of prostitution is part of a formulated plan arranged by pro-Axis elements, primarily to spread venereal disease among Allied troops.

A-Force, mulling over this, would have known that the incidence of VD in German-occupied areas is very low indeed. This is partly because it is a criminal offence under Italian law, punishable by one year in prison, to communicate syphilis to a second person, and partly because the Germans have maintained the strictest of medical supervision over brothels. Thus, for one reason or another, the German-occupied North is virtually clear of streptococci and gonococci which to all intents and purposes were reintroduced into Italy with the arrival of the American troops. A-Force's plan was to arrange for the spread of these infections, which have reached epidemic levels in the South, across the lines into the uninfected North, and thus diminish the fighting efficiency of the German Army, while turning their backs on all such considerations as the suffering likely to be endured by the civilian population, and the many babies doomed to be born blind.

By the first week in January, a number of attractive young Neapolitan prostitutes had been rounded up, and of these twenty were selected, who, while showing no outward sign of infection, were believed by the medical men called in to co-operate with the A-Force scheme to be suffering from an exceptionally virulent and virtually ineradicable form of syphilis.

They were removed to a guarded villa in the Vomero, pampered in every way, given all the army white bread and spaghetti they could eat, taken on a day-trip to Capri—although of necessity denied any form of medical attention, apart from regular inspections to see that no unsightly chancres had developed. The news was then broken to them what was expected of them, and the trouble began. However many inducements were offered, they were naturally terrified at the idea of crossing the lines in the care of A-Force agents. Payment was to be made in the form of gold coins to be carried in the rectum, as well as original lira notes; but handsome as it was, the girls knew only too well how harsh was the economic climate of the North by comparison with Naples, and how hard and how risky it would be to make a living once the original bonuses were spent. One girl recruited from a staff of twelve resident prostitutes employed by the Albergo Vittoria, Sorrento, taken over as a rest hotel for American personnel, was accustomed to receive 1000 lire a night. In Rome she knew she would be lucky to earn 100 lire, and could not be convinced that her condition would long escape discovery by the German doctors.

But the main obstacle to the enterprise appears to have been an emotional one. All these girls had pimps from whom they could not bear to be parted. Some of the pimps were big enough in the scale of their professions, too, to be able to buy favors, and they were beginning to make trouble through AMGOT. Finally, like so many wild A-Force schemes, the thing was dropped, and the girls were then simply turned loose on the streets of Naples. The situation now is that as many hospital beds in the Naples area are occupied by sufferers from the pox as from wounds and all the other sicknesses put together.

# ALUN LEWIS

ALUN LEWIS was killed in Burma in 1944. Born in a
Welsh mining village, he joined the army in 1940. In
his brief life he composed a volume of poems, *Raiders'
Dawn,* published in 1942, and a year later a volume of
short stories, *The Last Inspection,* from which the following story is taken.

■

## The Earth Is a Syllable

"What I say is, if you're in trouble, take it easy," the ambulance
driver said. "Always have done. Once I got a girl in trouble and I wasn't
going to get gray hairs over that. And now I've bust the gasket and she
won't budge and maybe the Jap is nearer than our own boys, but there
you are, you're no better off if your nose bleeds, are you now?"

He'd often thought he'd die; it was a familiar idea; why shouldn't it
be, if there's a war on and you're young and you try to be in it, somewhere? It had taken him a long time to succeed. He'd got into the army
easy enough, but the war seemed to elude him all the time. If he was in
England it would be in France in hot summer weather and he'd be eating
Wall's ice-cream outside the barracks. If he was in India it would be in
Egypt and he'd think of the Eighth Army glowing in the desert, attracting
him like a moth to its fiery circle. He used to fancy himself flying there
like a queen ant on her nuptial flight, and shedding his wings when he
lighted, and going to ground there. And now that he had caught up with
it, here in Burma, well, it hadn't been much of a show. But he'd never
liked the idea of Burma. He'd always known he'd die if he caught up with
it in Burma. "Can't you stop tossing and kicking them blankets?" the
ambulance driver said. "Wear yourself out quicker like that. Take it easy,
I say. I been in some bad spots off and on. Narvik for a kick-off, and
Crete for a birthday, and a bloody narrow escape from going into Libya
with Ritchie; thought I was lucky once being sent out here instead. But
I reckon it's all the same where I go. There's sure to be a war there." He
spoke very mournfully, a sort of thoughtful incantation. "I've had more
crump than crumpet this war. That's why I take it easy, mate. You got
to last a long time, you know. A long time."

The driver had given up trying to repair the damage to the cylinder
head of his 15-cwt. Bedford; the tropical heat and the dust of the bumpy
track that cavorted through the misleading jungle had dried up his water

and blown the gasket. It was useless. They were on their way to the rendezvous where the wounded from the advanced dressing stations were handed over to the main dressing station ambulances. To-morrow they'd have to find out where the new rendezvous was; it changed daily, same as everything else changed daily; the situation was very confused, the Japs were said to have worked right round their left flank somewhere up the Sittang, and to have landed above Rangoon. To-morrow they'd have to find out where the new rendezvous was, if it still mattered.

He was lying on a stretcher in the back of the truck and it was a bit awkward because the truck was tilted steeply, one side in the ditch so as to let the traffic pass up the track to the front, what front there was. The rear flaps were strapped up to give him some air and he could see the darkness of the jungle encircling them. It was dark and soft like a mass of congealed blood. If the Japs were there they'd be sleeping. They had to sleep. Or a snake or a tiger would get them, they weren't all that clever. Any case you could hear them if they were there, calling each other like owls, because they were lonely, maybe. And the jungle was utterly silent, dark and shimmering with darkness like ebony, and malevolent. And he was quite at peace. He'd been more nervous in India than he was here. It was lonely in India, no friendship there, nor any active hostility to brace you. Just loneliness and strangeness. It wasn't dangerous there; just nerves, that's all. You couldn't walk into a native village and have a good time like you wanted to. QUIT INDIA they painted on the walls, Quit India. The silly fools. How can we? India is part of the world. It's the world we can't quit. No, it was just nerves in India. Riding back to camp after the pictures in a trotting tonga with the bells tinkling on the skinny mare's back, it was so dark it was like riding to your death. Just nerves. Here he was quite peaceful.

There was a sudden murmur in the jungle, a sigh, a growing perturbance. Dust. The wind puffed up with a hot dry sigh and the dust came riding in on them in a thick irritating column, into their eyes and mouths, making them swear and spit and blink, and extinguishing the petrol cooker on which the driver was brewing some char. His own lamp spat a high flame and cracked the glass and then subsided. He didn't move. He liked the dust storms by day, the whirling cylinder of tall red dust moving across the plain, the moving red towers that touched the blue sky. He didn't like it at night so much; now when he put his hand over his face his skin was dry and dusty like a statue in a dilapidated museum, like an embalming. The blanket was filthy, it set the skin of his fingers on edge, and he saw with sudden distaste that it was covered with hairs and dandruff under his cheek. It made him think of his wife, she'd written to say he'd left some hairs on his pillow the time he was on embarkation leave, and she'd felt terribly cruel to shake them off, she said. But she was so beautiful and fresh always, and the house always so clean and simple, with the sun or the snow always lighting it. She wouldn't like this dust.

"Well, we'll have to go without a cup of you an' me," the driver said, grinning and sweating as he leaned over the tailboard to stow the cooker away. " 'Tisn't the first thing I've gone without by a long chalk. Christ, I've been without work before now. That's a real nasty thing, being without work. I don't suppose you've been without work, chum, being an officer?"

His mouth was bitter and dry and it hurt him when he smiled. It was the lump the shrapnel had taken out of his throat was hurting now when he smiled. Life had been pretty heartless off and on, but you usually got a laugh out of it. When he'd written three novels one after the other and failed to sell any of them, and gone round to an agency for a job and the old clerk asked him if he could type and he said two fingers only and the clerk said No Good, and he went to sea then as a trimmer. He'd never thought of dying in those days, though, it didn't seem a physical fact at all. Just something you wrote and theorized about. Not like *this*.

"Speaking for myself," said the driver, "I've found it a bloody sight easier with a war on. You don't have to bother now. It's all buttoned up Food and clothes and dentists, trucks to drive, loads to carry, allowances for the missus. It's all laid on for you now. You don't have to bother."

Yes, he thought, it's been pretty easy. You sink your scruples in conscription, and then there's always something interesting if you take the trouble of finding it. Infantry schemes, sleeping under hedges, swimming a river in full kit, being hungry, talking to a stranger. And since his regiment had been mechanized the tanks had him by the hair—the iron maidens—he'd never tire of pulling on the Tiller bars and stamping on the clutch and pulling like hell on the gear lever and the thrill as she surged softly forward, grunting peacefully and bellying over a slope so sweet and easy. And the big 75 mm. gun and the voices of your friends in your headsets coming over the air. And the queer consolation of the other things he'd tried and written off as failures and now recalled—the little meetings he'd tried to run, debates round a hurricane lamp on the FUTURE, talks he'd carefully put together on RECONSTRUCTION, gramophone records he'd borrowed and played for the lads, the choir he'd tried to make something good of; naturally it was no good for a few odd men to sit round and discuss how to prevent another war, naturally they couldn't "succeed." Still, it was all right to remember it.

No. The terrible struggles had been quieter and less obvious than voyages and armored regiments. They were just something inside you— simply whether to say Yes or No to a thing—to chastity or pity or love or a drink with another man's wife. Maybe if you could avoid saying Yes or No to life, and yet be free, you'd be stronger, better? Would you? How did the dust columns form? What did the Upanishads say? The earth is a syllable. "I'm turning in, mate," said the driver. "There ain't nothing I can do till a truck comes along. Get you back then, if a truck comes along. It's so bleeding quiet in these parts, that's what I don't like. Makes you think we missed the road back somewhere, or missed the war or sommat. I never did like the quiet. Give me a pub that can sell its liquor, not keep it. Give me a call if your pains come back, chum, though there ain't nothing I can do. Jesus, I'm tired. Good-night, cocky."

He stumped up the road a few yards to where he'd slung his mosquito net among the bushes. He sighed aloud as he pulled each boot off.

Now he was left alone and whatever he had he was alone with it. It was all right as long as he was alone. Whatever he had he could manage it now. His lamp still burned calmly and it might last an hour yet. He didn't want the dark to come any nearer. He could see exactly where it started, just this side of his feet. And then it went on and on. The dawn is the head of a horse. He lay quietly among the crickets and the darkness and the moths came suddenly tilting head-on against this lamp and righted themselves on his face and flew on again. It was very still, except for the pain. There was a translucent golden influence at the core of his being. He could see his wife. She'd wanted a child before he left England but it hadn't turned out that way. And now in a way he was glad. There was only her left, besides himself. She would understand. He'd tried bloody hard; he'd roughed it now and he was cut up a lot and he could smell the poison where the left shoulder and arm had been. But he was still her little house. That was all. He didn't want to go to Burma; he knew it would be a bad place for him. But all striving is a blind guess, and he wasn't in Burma now, he was in the night in the common ground of humanity, and he wasn't alone now.

He wanted to get up and enter the darkness and enter the silent village under the hill and enter it with his wife alone. Not in a tank, for that was a schoolboy's thrill, nor in Burma, because it was a bad place for him. So he pushed himself up on his spare arm and sweated all over; Judas! it hurt. But he hated the dirt and hair of his blanket, and being hot in bed, and he wanted to have his little walk. So he went across the plain in the night and the darkness was hot and tepid and after a while he didn't know where the hell he was, but he knew he was all right, and he loved her so much that he knew he could throw the darkness over the hill.

The driver found him five yards away from the truck.

# NATALIA GINZBURG

NOVELIST, essayist, and playwright, Natalia Ginzburg is also a member of the Italian parliament. *All Our Yesterdays* is her memoir of World War II.

■

FROM *All Our Yesterdays*

When Anna came back to San Costanzo the Germans were no longer there but instead there were the English, and the American and English and Italian flags were fluttering from the balcony of the municipal office. The walls of the village hall and the walls of the police station and of a few other houses along the road were full of round holes from the English shells that had been fired.

The Germans had freed the hostages they had taken that day but then during the night they had come back and taken some more, two sons of the dressmaker's and a sister of La Maschiona's seducer and a shepherd boy of fourteen years old, and they had taken them into the mayor's stable and had poured tins of petrol over the stable and set fire to it. They had searched for the farrier and for La Maschiona's brother too, but they had escaped into the fields.

The mayor's stable was now a heap of ashes, and you still seemed to hear the lowing of the cows and the shrieks of the shepherd boy calling to his mother. No one could understand why the Germans should have burnt down the stable with the cows and the people inside, but perhaps it was only because they had some petrol to throw away. In any case tales were coming in from all directions of the things the Germans had done before they went away, at Masuri they had driven fifteen people into a farmhouse, children and women, and had fired into the windows. The Germans were far away now, beyond Borgoreale, but there were times when the *contadini* were frightened that they would come back. The *contadini* stood looking at the English as they sat smoking on the low garden walls, they stood spell-bound looking at these soldiers dressed like the Germans in yellowish cloth with short trousers and blond, hairy knees. And they asked if the Germans would come back and the English shook their heads to say no. And the *contadini* were very pleased indeed with these new soldiers who did not kill them, and they were very pleased to eat the insipid bread made of rice flour which they threw away.

# NORMAN LEWIS

NAPLES in 1944 seethed with a struggle for survival among the poor and desperate—a struggle captured by the English novelist and travel-writer Norman Lewis in *Naples '44,* an account in the form of a diary of his experiences in the Italian campaign. An excerpt follows.

■

FROM *Naples '44*

*March 26*

The streets of Naples are full of people hawking personal possessions of all kinds: pieces of jewelry, old books, pictures, clothing, etc. Many of them are members of the middle class, and the approach is made in a shamefaced and surreptitious way. One and all, they are in a state of desperate need.

Today at the top of the Via Roma near the Piazza Dante I was stopped by a pleasant-faced old lady, who had nothing for sale but who implored me to go with her to her house in a side-street nearby. She had something to show me, and was so insistent that I followed her to the typical *basso* in a side-street, where she lived. The single, windowless room was lit by a minute electric bulb over the usual shrine, and I saw a thin girl standing in a corner. The reason for the appeal now became clear. This, said the woman, was her child, aged thirteen, and she wished to prostitute her. Many soldiers, it seems, will pay for sexual activity less than full intercourse, and she had a revolting scale of fees for these services. For example, the girl would strip and display her pubescent organs for twenty lire.

I told the woman that I would report her to the police, and she pretended to weep, but it was an empty threat, and she knew it. Nothing can be done. There are no police to deal with the thousands of squalid little crimes like this committed every day in the city.

On my way back I was stopped and drawn into a corner by a priest, white-lipped and smiling. He opened a bag full of umbrella handles, candlesticks and small ornaments of all kinds carved out of the bones of the saints, i.e. from bones filched from one of the catacombs. He, too, had to live.

# SIR HAROLD GEORGE NICOLSON

THE DIPLOMAT Sir Harold Nicolson kept a diary from the moment he resigned from the Foreign Office in 1929 until October 1964. His son Nigel edited the three volumes covering the years 1930 to 1962. The following excerpt deals with wartime London social life.

■

*1st March, 1944*

I pick up Viti [Nicolson's wife, Victoria Sackville-West] and go to Buckingham Palace for a tea-party. It takes place in the hall. The company is divided into two groups each side of the Propylaea, and the King and Queen stand in the middle. There are many foreign diplomatists whom they greet. I am taken to talk to the Princesses. Princess Elizabeth is a clear, nice girl. I talk to her about the Grenadiers.[1]

I dine with James [Pope-Hennessy, literary critic and art historian] at Rules and we go on to Pratts. James cannot understand how it comes that I am so interested in politics. Pratts is a political kitchen. During the raid last Wednesday there was a committee meeting on. Suddenly there was a crash, all the lights went out, and the building rocked. Then the lights went on again. "Well, gentlemen," said Eddy Devonshire, "I am not quite clear whether we elected that fellow or not."

It is sad on my return to see so many people sleeping on the tube platforms. It is more disgraceful than ever to see the Americans with the East End Jewish girls, shouting among those unhappy and recumbent forms. I hate it.

[1] Princess Elizabeth, who was then nearly 18, had been appointed Colonel of the Grenadier Guards in February 1942.

# YAFFA ELIACH

THE HASIDIM, a pious and mystical sect of East European Jews dating from the eighteenth century, uphold a tradition of storytelling to illumine their belief in God and man's goodness. Even as the Germans were ruthlessly destroying European Jewry during the war, the Hasidim continued their tradition. These tales were collected by Yaffa Eliach and her students at Brooklyn College and published in 1982. The following story is based on a conversation of the Grand Rabbi of Bluzhov, Israel Spira, with Aaron Frankel in January 1974.

■

## Two Capsules of Cyanide (I)

Among the many devilish torments devised by the S.S. men at the Janowska Road Camp was a ceremony at dusk at the camp's gate. The S.S. men formed two lines at the entrance to "welcome" the inmates upon their return from a day's slave labor. The pageantry at hell's gate began to unfold when the first working detachment reached the gate, pageantry which might aptly have been called Conquerors and Vanquished at Twilight. The Germans would shout gleefully: "Who is the most respected race on the face of the earth?" The inmates, exhausted from their labor, would respond hoarsely: "The Third Reich!"

"And who is the most accursed race on earth?" the S.S. men would continue the diabolic dialogue. Prisoner's caps would fly in the air and above them once more the Jewish voices would rise in unison: "The Jewish people!"

"Louder!" the German command would roar and the Jews would respond again and again: "The Jews are the most accursed race on the face of the earth." This they would repeat while filing through the gate, trying to protect their bodies from the blows of rubber truncheons swinging at them from all directions.

In those days Rabbi Israel Spira, the Rabbi of Bluzhov, worked side by side with a distinguished lawyer from Borislav by the name of Hurowitz. One day the lawyer said to the rabbi, "Mr. Spira, I think that during the short time that we have worked together, I have come to know you quite well. How can you join in the diabolic choir and announce publicly that they are the chosen people and we are the accursed race?" He did not wait for the rabbi's response and continued, "I had two thousand dollars sewn into the lapel of my concentration-camp jacket so that when an opportunity came to redeem my life, I would have something with which to pay, or at least to bargain. Last night, I was a lucky man. For the two thousand dollars, I was able to buy two capsules of cyanide at a thousand dollars apiece—one for you and one for me."

The Rabbi of Bluzhov touched his friend's shoulder with gratitude. "I envy you that you are able to do it, but I cannot. My father was a rebbe, my grandfather was a rebbe, and my great-grandfather was a rebbe. When my time is up, I will join them in the World of Truth. I will come then with the rest of the Jews. But I will not be able to enter the World of Truth and face my illustrious ancestors as a murderer, as one who has taken a life—even his own life. Thank you, my friend, for your friendship."

That day, at dusk, when the inmates returned to camp, the S.S. men were lined up in their usual manner at the entrance. On their well-fed faces were malicious smiles of anticipation as they awaited their regular evening entertainment. As the prisoners neared the gate, some of the Germans cleared their throats so that their evening performance would be worthy of their superior racial status.

The anonymous, faceless, gray column was at the gate.

"Who is the most respected race on earth?" thundered the S.S. men in their strong, clear-throated voices.

"The Jews!" proclaimed one voice that overpowered all the others. The German commander ordered the question to be repeated.

"The Jewish people are the most respected race on the face of the earth!" proclaimed the same single powerful voice, and the echoes from what seemed like thousands of voices resounded from the surrounding hills: "The Jews, the Jews, the Jews."

The S.S. men rushed in the direction of the dissident voice. On the ground lay stretched out the body of Hurowitz, the Borislav lawyer. On his lifeless face was frozen a smile of victory, and his gaping mouth continued silently to proclaim the eternity and greatness of the Jewish people.

# JOHN COSTELLO

---

U.S. SERVICEMEN arrive in Britain and their reputation meets the British head on. In *Virtue Under Fire,* John Costello, a producer for the BBC, has studied the effect of World War II on social and sexual attitudes.

---

■

FROM *Virtue Under Fire*

### OVERSEXED, OVERPAID, AND OVER HERE!

Americans were "cheeky" compared to our usual "Mr. Frigidaire Englishman," but what a boost to the ego when one is greeted with "Hello, Duchess" (and you were treated like one!) or "Hi, Beautiful!" That was so GOOD! As we got to know these boys, how generous they were; we never lacked for chocolate or cigarettes and even precious luxuries like nylons they could get for us.

—BRITISH GIRL

The million and a half GIs who "invaded" Britain before D-Day faced neither the hazards of language nor the army of prostitutes encountered in Italy. Instead the American command had to overcome traditional reserve and downright prudery. "The British consider sex behavior as entirely a personal matter not subject to legislation and regulation," reported the U.S. army's chief of preventative medicine. "Public opinion frowns on brothels and so very few are known to exist, and outside London there was very little commercialized prostitution."

But the average GI had very little difficulty in satisfying a hunger for female companionship.

To British women, the arrival of the Americans was a bright flash of excitement after nearly three years of blackouts and Blitz. It seemed to many that these strapping, well-fed, and confident young men had stepped straight out of a Hollywood movie. "Suddenly the GIs were there," recalled a Derby woman. "If they'd dropped from Mars we couldn't have been more surprised." A shy Preston girl remembered blushing when a smiling-faced GI told her, "Gee, you've got lovely eyes," and his partner called out, "She's just like a baby Betty Grable!" Another woman from Birmingham, who was a teenager at the time and described herself as "fancy free," was more explicit about the instant sexual attraction that drew British women to American soldiers:

We were half starved and drably clothed, but the GIs said we looked good anyway. A lot was said about them being oversexed, overpaid and over here; maybe it applied to a few, but it was mainly a myth which was put over by Lord Haw Haw in his Nazi propaganda broadcasts from Germany to upset British soldiers overseas and try to split the Allies. That's my story anyway—and I'm sticking to it! It was just the case that the British women and the American GIs were in the same place at the same time—it was rather pleasant, really!

Myth or not, the glamor of the American serviceman presented an implicit sexual rivalry to British husbands and older brothers, who resented the fascination that the "Yanks" held for their wives and girlfriends. It was the British male who coined and gave lip service to the wartime anti-American epithet that the only thing wrong with their Allies was that they were "overpaid, oversexed, and over here!" The reputation of "Yanks" was encouraged by wild press reports and letters from reactionary matrons like (MRS. SPECTATOR) who expressed outrage that "girls of thirteen and fourteen have attached themselves to colored soldiers and others and been able to see films that only have the effect of arousing in them instincts that ought to be unknown to them for many years."

It was not just the physical exuberance of the smartly turned-out American serviceman, touched with the aura of Hollywood extra, that provoked suspicion and hostility in the native male population. It was also a question of hard cash. British soldiers found themselves at a huge financial disadvantage when it came to competing for the entertainment of their own womenfolk. Even a lowly American private with his $3,000 average annual paycheck was a big spender by comparison with the 100 pounds received by his British ally. With 50 percent extra pay for flying duty and 20 percent extra for overseas and sea duty, nine out of ten GIs were above the $50 a month averaged in civilian life, and those who were single never had as much money in their lives—and the only thing to spend it on was entertaining British girls! They were also prodigal with gifts of luxury foods passed on from their military supplies.

Even the way the Americans spoke marked them out as different and glamorous, often provoking naughty giggles from English girls when they used the GI slang expressions such as "bum" for a layabout and "rubbers"—the native word for erasers—when they referred to contraceptive sheaths. The prudish Hollywood Hays office censors had unwittingly protected movie audiences from many of the coarse expressions that were common parlance among American soldiers. "Holy Cow!" "Jeez!" and "Goddamn!" upset the girls who operated the telephone exchanges, who complained about the "blasphemous language" used by GIs. British teenagers, however, relished the new oaths that so upset their parents' sensibilities. A boy recalled the adolescent enthusiasm with which he and his friends bandied about their favorite GI expletives: "And I ain't a-shitting, boy!" or "You ain't a-tooting, boy!"

The British miltary authorities soon found it necessary to prepare a pamphlet for the female staff of the NAAFI military canteens advising them that the language and apparent freshness of the GIs should not always be taken at face value:

> The first time that an American soldier approaches the counter and says, "Hiya, Baby!" you will probably think he is being impudent. By the time several dozen men have said it, you may have come to the conclusion that all Americans are "fresh." Yet to them it will be merely the normal conversational opening, just as you might say, "Lovely day, isn't it?" Remember that most Americans think that English people are "standoffish." If you snub them you will merely confirm this impression.

Eisenhower's headquarters had also prepared a handbook that advised American soldiers of the more staid British customs and habits. At the same time the U.S. provost marshal had issued a leaflet "How to Stay Out of Trouble," which contained stern warnings about the "females of questionable character" who were eagerly awaiting them to get Yankee dollars. These were the very women that many GIs were hoping to encounter, of course—and they were not to be disappointed. "Their main aim in life," recalled a British wartime taxi driver, quoting the American vernacular, "seemed to be to get something to drink and 'a cute piece of ass.' "

Too young to be called up himself, John Lazenby spent the year before D-Day driving carloads of offduty GIs through picturesque Cotswold villages in pursuit of drink and girls. He learned all about their "camp-followers secreted in cottage attics" and "illicit trysts with local ladies." Their sexual banter and adventures with women resulted in his "rapid education in varied directions," like his "dreadfully innocent consternation one evening hearing a bunch of them yelling 'Just you look at Red's broad's tits like two goddamn milk bottles!' "

American servicemen deserved their reputation of being "wolves in wolves' clothing" when it came to making passes, but not all the English girls surrendered to their assualts. One ATS corporal recalled the evening she and two companions were trudging in pouring rain back to their barracks along a lonely road:

> Along came a jeep with four Yanks in it. They stopped and offered us a ride. Although there were three of us, we just didn't trust them and turned the offer down. When I tell you that we had to walk the whole five miles back to camp, and preferred this to the lift, you will appreciate just how strongly we felt. I knew quite a few civvy girls who were "loved and left"—literally holding the baby.

The refusal of many predatory American soldiers to take no for an answer from a pretty girl, led to frequent complaints of sexual molestation. According to Mrs. Anne F., the mothers on a Birmingham housing estate near a U.S. army base protested that they had to use physical force to fend off the GIs. She soon developed her own technique of repulsing unwanted advances:

> Almost every evening, I among others, would hear a knock on the front door and on opening it would find a GI who stated that a Greg So-and-So had sent him. When one flatly denied knowing his friend, he would calmly say, "Come on, baby, I know your husband is away in the forces." One would have to slam the door in their faces to keep them out. I remember one afternoon and evening the local camp was invaded by teenage girls and women from miles around. There were hundreds of them looking for Yanks. Next day the woods behind our estate were put "Out of Bounds" to the GIs. But the things we found in our front gardens were unbelievable! Some of the women had a "good time" with Americans, others just did their washing for them, while others completely ignored them. The pubs made a packet out of them and the kids went a bundle on them as they were very generous with chocolate and sweets.

In London, the assault was more likely to be made first by the freelance prostitutes known as "Piccadilly Commandos." These most brazen of wartime British tarts swarmed around the entrance of the Rainbow Club that was opened for Americans in 1942 in the old Del Monico's on the corner of Shaftesbury Avenue. The sign over the reception desk indicated "New York—3,271 Miles," but the club promised a taste of home with its canteens, jukeboxes, and pool tables. "Rainbow Corner" became a magnet not only for homesick GIs in the London blackout, but also the regiments of streetwalkers whose opening "Hello, Yank, looking for a good time?" became a much parodied wartime joke.

Piccadilly *was* wartime London for American servicemen. Former Staff Sergeant Robert Arib recalled the standing joke in the Rainbow Club that it was "suicide" for a GI to go out into the blacked-out streets without his buddy:

> The girls were there—everywhere. They walked along Shaftesbury Avenue and past the Rainbow Club, pausing only when there was no policeman watching. Down at the Lyons Corner House on Coventry Street they came up to soldiers waiting in the doorways and whispered the age-old questions. At the underground entrance they were thickest, and as the evening grew dark, they shone torches on their ankles as they walked and bumped into the soldiers murmuring "Hello, Yank," "Hello, soldier," "Hello, dearie!" Around the dark estuaries of the Circus the more elegantly clad of them would stand quietly and wait—expensive and aloof. No privates or corporals for these haughty demoiselles. They had furs and silks to pay for.

Betty Knox, a former dance-hall singer turned breezy columnist for the *London Evening Standard*, related a story that was supposedly typical of the GIs' attitude to London: "One night, as Ambassador John G. Winant left the American embassy he met two soldiers. Could he do anything for them, Winant inquired. 'Are there any dames in this joint?' one soldier asked. 'This is the American embassy, and I am the Ambassador,' Winant replied. 'Say, those Limies must have been pulling our legs,' the soldier stammered, backing off into the blackout."

# DAVID RUSSELL WAGONER

DAVID WAGONER has won numerous awards for his poetry, among them the English-speaking Union Prize and the Sherwood Anderson award. A fellow of both the Guggenheim and Ford Foundations, he published his *Collected Poems* in 1976; his novels include *The Man in the Middle* and *The Escape Artist*. The two poems that follow are taken from the collection *Through the Forest*.

■

## To the Last Man

At the point of farthest advance in the misfortunes
Of war, in the pitch and tossing-away of battle
When your sense of direction turns
Against you and it doesn't matter where
You align your sights or level your blank face
To know the enemy—that source of crossfire
And enfilading fire, that withering
Of overhead fragmentation and blazing flares,
That upheaval of landmines—when the chain of command
No longer connects you to superiors
But ends at its weakest link, you may find yourself
Alone at the break of morning, a one-man force
In a land whose landmarks blur your memories
Of maps and numbers, and all you see around you
Is wreckage and mud, the decay of comrades
At peace now in their newly disarmed divisions.
Yet if you seem to have nothing left worth doing
But joining that darker effort, that quieter chaos,
All may not be lost. For all you know,
You are the single unpredictable crucial
Element at a point of counterattack,
A voice come back from a body count of the dead
For a reckoning over bones that now depend
On you to make the most of what's left around them,
Not carcasses of the truth but the whole truth
Breathing and insane, of which you are the insane
Defender, your story as magically royally blooded,

As circled by fire, as holy, as otherworldly,
As dreadful as the world that dreamed it among
Ancestral voices prophesying you.
Even with no one listening, you must tell it.

## Victory

From the exhausted hoofbeats of the drums in the earth softly
At first to the bugles of engines coming the faint far-off
Screaming then bright at the parapet of your mouth your breath
Your fingers catching your opening eyes the whole blood
Rushing from heart to face to fulfill to overflow
Your stiffening body to leap your arms rising your hands
Held high you knew at last it was here it was all yours now.

# NORMAN LEWIS

EVERYTHING was for sale in Naples in 1944, much of it stolen. The English novelist and travel-writer Norman Lewis saw it as an intelligence officer temporarily attached to HQ staff of the American Fifth Army. *Naples '44* is his account of his experiences in the Italian campaign.

■

FROM *Naples '44*

*May 9*

The impudence of the black market takes one's breath away. For months now official sources have assured us that the equivalent of the cargo of one Allied ship in three unloaded in the Port of Naples is stolen. The latest story going the rounds is that when a really big-scale coup is planned and it is necessary to clear the port to handle bulky goods, someone arranges for the air-raid sirens to sound and for the mobile smoke-screens to provide their fog, under the cover of which the shock-troops of the black market move in to do their work.

Stolen equipment sold on the Via Forcella, and round the law courts —where one-man-business thieves without protection are tried and sentenced by the dozen every day for possession of Allied goods—is now on blatant display, tastefully arranged with colored ribbon, a vase of flowers, neatly-written showcards advertising the quality of the looted goods. COMPARE OUR PRICES . . . WARRANTED PURE AUSTRALIAN WOOL . . . MONEY BACK IF FOUND TO SHRINK . . . YOU CAN MARCH TO KINGDOM COME ON THESE BEAUTIFUL IMPORTED BOOTS . . . IF YOU DON'T SEE THE OVER-SEAS ARTICLE YOU'RE LOOKING FOR, JUST ASK US AND WE'LL GET IT. Tailors all over Naples are taking uniforms to pieces, dying the material, and turning them into smart new outfits for civilian wear. I hear that even British Army long-coms, which despite the climate still find their way over here, are accepted with delight, dyed red, and turned into the latest thing in track suits.

In the first days the MPs carried out a few half-hearted raids on the people specializing in these adaptations, but they found too many smart new overcoats made from Canadian blankets awaiting collection by Italian friends of General this and Colonel that to be able to put a stop to the thing. Last week the Papal Legate's car, held up by pure accident in some routine road-check, was found to be fitted with a set of stolen tires.

Many apologies and smiles and His Reverence was waved on. Other than commando daggers and bayonets, they don't display looted weapons in the stalls, but the advice from my contacts is that there is no problem except the cash in arranging to buy anything from a machine-gun to a light tank.

The trouble now is that certain items which can be freely and easily bought on the black market are in short supply in the Army itself. This applies currently to photographic equipment and materials, practically all of which has been stolen to be sold under the counter in shops in the Via Roma, and to certain medical supplies, in particular penicillin. Every sick civilian can go to a pharmacist and get a course of penicillin injections at a time when supplies in the military hospitals are about to run out. At last the time has come when the effect of the black market on the war effort has become evident. It could have been wiped out, but because of the secret involvement in it through their Italian connections of some of our high authorities, it was not. Now, the decision has been reached that something will have to be done. It is too late now to abolish the black market, but at least an attempt will be made to tidy it up. Probably for this reason I was called on today by the FSO and ordered to investigate the penicillin racket.

The first move was to visit the pharmacist Casana with whom we have been on excellent terms, and to ask him in the strictest confidence where his penicillin came from. Casana a little shocked, but resigned, supplied the name Vittorio Fortuna, living in the Via dei Mille, but warned me that if he was called as a witness against this man he would probably lose his life. I checked this name with other pharmacists, all of whom knew of Fortuna and agreed that he was known to deal in penicillin, although they all denied any connection with him. Fortuna, they agreed, was under the protection of someone in Allied Military Government. Having heard this, I decided that my best course was to go to the American Counter-Intelligence Corps, who are well in with AMG, whereas we are not.

Although we and the CIC perform roughly the same function in Naples, and they have recently moved into the floor above us in the same building, there has never been any official contact between us. Currently their strength is about 25 agents and one officer. Those who have been lucky enough to glimpse it say they have the finest filing system in all Italy, but they are handicapped by the fact that not a single one of them speaks a word of Italian, which makes them wholly dependent upon an interpreter who once featured on our list of suspects. The organizations, often working separately and without any exchange of information on the same cases, constantly overlap and sometimes come into conflict, so that with fair frequency we lock up each other's friends, and spring each other's suspects, treading on each other's toes with what might be described as good-humored tolerance.

Our only collaboration with the CIC has been the agreement by which we borrow their jeeps for holiday jaunts in return for a bottle of whisky, which inexplicably is the only thing any American soldier could possibly desire for his pleasure or comfort that the PX does not supply. My whisky-for-jeep arrangement is with Special Agent Frank Edwards, and I discussed the matter of Fortuna with him.

Edwards said that it was well known in the CIC that Fortuna was a lieutenant of Vito Genovese, and he gave me a thumbnail sketch of Genovese's history. Genovese, according to Edwards, was not, as described on our files, ex-secretary to Al Capone, nor was he even a Sicilian, but had been born in the village of Ricigliano, near Potenza. He had been second-in-command of a New York Mafia "family" headed by Lucky Luciano, Edwards said, and had succeeded to its leadership when Luciano was jailed, after which he had been acknowledged as the head of all the American Mafia. Shortly before the outbreak of war Genovese had returned to Italy to escape a murder indictment in the US, had become a friend of Mussolini's, and then, with the Duce's fall, transferred his allegiance to Allied Military Government, where he was now seen as the power behind the scenes. Genovese controlled the sindacos in most towns within fifty miles of Naples. He leased out rackets to his followers, took a toll of everything, threw crumbs of favor to those who kept in step with him, and found a way of punishing opposition.

What was to be done? Nothing, Edwards said. The CIC had soon learned to steer clear of any racket in which Genovese had a finger—and his finger was in most. Too many American officers had been chosen to go on the Italian campaign because they were of Italian descent. For this reason it was hoped they might easily adapt to the environment, and this they had done all too well. The American-Italians in AMG reigned supreme and knew how to close their ranks when threatened from without. An American CID agent who had cottoned on to the fact that the notorious Genovese was in virtual control in Naples and set out to investigate his present activities, soon found himself isolated and powerless, and all the reward he had had for his pains was loss of promotion. And would this situation apply in his opinion in the case of any Briton who threatened Genovese's interests? Edwards didn't know, and suggested I might go ahead and try. He would be most interested to see what happened.

The Allied Military Proclamation, in one or another of its many clauses, seems to authorize one to do almost anything to anybody who, to use the proclamation's own words, "does any act to the prejudice of the good order, safety or security of the Allied Forces," and I put a copy of the proclamation into my pocket before going to see Fortuna. He was a calm, handsome man, with a religious medal dangling in the opening of his shirt, a controlled but charming smile, and a strange primness of manner, which came out in the exclamation "*Mamma mia!*" when I explained the reason for my call. He irritated me by addressing me as if

I were a child, using verbs in the infinitive and speaking with exaggerated slowness and clarity. I showed him the proclamation and told him I was going to search his flat, and he smiled and shrugged his shoulders and invited me to go ahead. The search took a full hour. I worked my way methodically through the rooms, and in doing so discovered nothing more than the normal range of black-market goods that one would expect to find in any flat of this kind. I probed and poked into every corner, examined floorboards, tapped on walls, checked the cistern, dismantled a big old-fashioned gas-heater, and at last in a waste-paper basket under the kitchen sink, found an empty carton that had contained penicillin and with it one damaged phial.

Showing Fortuna the penicillin I told him I was going to arrest him and, still perfectly relaxed and agreeable, he said, "This will do you no good. Who are you? You are no one. I was dining with a certain colonel last night. If you are tired of life in Naples, I can have you sent away."

On the way to Poggio Reale his mood never changed, and he became chatty and affable. Would they cut his hair off and make him wear prison uniform? I told him they wouldn't until he'd been tried, found guilty and sentenced. When was I going to question him? To this I replied, as soon as I could find the time, but that there might be some little delay, owing to pressure of work. And in the meanwhile? he asked. In the meanwhile, I told him, he'd stay in Poggio Reale where he'd be out of harm's way. I handed him over to the half-crazy turnkeys, who fingerprinted him and signed him in, and told him I'd see him in two or three days. He laughed, and said, "You won't find me here when you come back."

*May 28*

The French colonial troops are on the rampage again. Whenever they take a town or a village, a wholesale rape of the population takes place. Recently all females in the villages of Patricia, Pofi, Isoletta, Supino, and Morolo were violated. In Lenola, which fell to the Allies on May 21, fifty women were raped, but—as these were not enough to go round—children and even old men were violated. It is reported to be normal for two Moroccans to assault a woman simultaneously, one having normal intercourse while the other commits sodomy. In many cases severe damage to the genitals, rectum and uterus has been caused. In Castro di Volsci doctors treated 300 victims of rape, and at Ceccano the British have been forced to build a guarded camp to protect the Italian women. Many Moors have deserted, and are attacking villages far behind the lines, and now they are reported to have appeared in the vicinity of Afragola to add a new dimension of terror to that already produced by the presence of so many marauders.

Today I went to Santa Maria a Vico to see a girl said to have been driven insane as the result of an attack by a large party of Moors. I found her living alone with her mother (who had also been raped a number of times), and in total poverty. Her condition had improved, and she behaved rationally and with a good deal of charm, although she was unable to walk as the result of physical injuries. The Carabinieri and the PS said that she had been certified as insane, and would have been committed to an asylum had a bed been available. She would be unlikely in the circumstances ever to find a husband.

At last one had faced the flesh-and-blood reality of the kind of horror that drove the whole female population of Macedonian villages to throw themselves from cliffs rather than fall into the hands of the advancing Turks. A fate worse than death: it was in fact just that.

Back at the Municipio I was confronted by a group of sindacos from neighboring towns, and an ultimatum was presented: "Either clear the Moroccans out, or we will deal with them in our own way." All these men looked like the toughest of movie gangsters, and I was convinced they would carry out their threat.

# YUKIO MISHIMA

THE NOVELIST, playwright, and essayist Kimitake Hi-
raoka, who wrote under the pen name Yukio Mishima,
committed ritual suicide in the traditional samurai manner in 1970. His novels include *Confessions of a Mask*
(from which this excerpt comes), *The Sound of Waves,
The Temple of the Golden Pavilion,* and a tetralogy,
*The Sea of Fertility.*

■

## FROM *Confessions of a Mask*

Sonoko and I exchanged photographs like any boy and girl in their
first love affair. She wrote saying she had put mine in a locket and hung
it over her breast. But the photograph she sent me was so large that it
would only barely have fitted into a brief case. As I could not get it in my
pocket, I carried it wrapped in a carrying-cloth. Fearing the factory might
burn down with the picture in it, I took it with me whenever I went
home.

One night I was on the train returning to the arsenal when the sirens
suddenly sounded and the lights were put out. In a few minutes there
came the signal to take shelter. I searched in the luggage-rack with groping hands, but the large bundle that I had put there had been stolen, and
with it went the carrying-cloth containing Sonoko's picture. Being inher-
ently given to superstition, from that moment I became obsessed with
the idea that I must go to see Sonoko quickly.

That air raid of the night of May the twenty-fourth, as destructive
as the midnight raid of March the ninth had been, brought me to a final
decision. Perhaps my relationship with Sonoko required the miasmal air
exhaled by this accumulation of calamities; perhaps that relationship was
a sort of chemical compound that could be produced only through the
agency of sulfuric acid.

We left the train and took shelter in the many caves that had been
dug along a line where the foothills opened onto the plain, and from our
shelter we watched the sky over Tokyo turn crimson. From time to time
something would explode, throwing a reflection against the sky, and
suddenly between the clouds we could see an eerie blue sky, as though
it were midday. It was a sliver of blue sky appearing for an instant in the
dead of night.

The futile searchlights seemed more like beacons welcoming the enemy planes. They would catch the glittering wings of an enemy plane exactly in the middle of two beams that had crossed momentarily and would then beckon the plane courteously, handing it on from one baton of light to the next, each time nearer Tokyo. Nor was the antiaircraft fire very heavy in those days. The B-29's reached the skies over Tokyo in comfort.

From where we were it was unlikely that anyone could actually distinguish friend from foe in the air battles that were taking place above Tokyo. And yet a chorus of cheers would rise from the crowd of watchers whenever they spotted, against the crimson backdrop, the shadow of a plane that had been hit and was falling. The young workmen were particularly vociferous. The sound of hand-clapping and cheering rang out from the mouths of the scattered tunnels as though in a theater. So far as the spectacle seen from this distance was concerned, it seemed to make no essential difference whether the falling plane was ours or the enemy's. Such is the nature of war. . . .

# A. J. LIEBLING

A. J. LIEBLING, reporter and war correspondent, joined the staff of *The New Yorker* in 1935. From 1945 until his death in 1963 he wrote that magazine's "The Wayward Press" column. His books include *The Earl of Louisiana* and *The Wayward Pressman*. The following piece was part of his wartime reportage for *The New Yorker*.

■

## Cross-Channel Trip

Three days after the first Allied landing in France, I was in the wardroom of an LCIL (Landing Craft, Infantry, Large) that was bobbing in the lee of the French cruiser Montcalm off the Normandy coast. The word "large" in landing-craft designation is purely relative; the wardroom of the one I was on is seven by seven feet and contains two officers' bunks and a table with four places at it. She carries a complement of four officers, but since one of them must always be on watch there is room for a guest at the wardroom table, which is how I fitted in. The Montcalm was loosing salvos, each of which rocked our ship; she was firing at a German pocket of resistance a couple of miles from the shoreline. The suave voice of a B.B.C. announcer came over the wardroom radio: "Next in our series of impressions from the front will be a recording of an artillery barrage." The French ship loosed off again, drowning out the recording. It was this same announcer, I think—I'm not sure, because all B.B.C. announcers sound alike—who said, a little while later, "We are now in a position to say the landings came off with surprising ease. The Air Force and the big guns of the Navy smashed coastal defenses, and the Army occupied them." Lieutenant Henry Rigg, United States Coast Guard Reserve, the skipper of our landing craft, looked at Long, her engineering officer, and they both began to laugh. Kavanaugh, the ship's communication officer, said, "Now, what do you think of that?" I called briefly upon God. Aboard the LCIL, D Day hadn't seemed like that to us. There is nothing like a broadcasting studio in London to give a chap perspective.

I went aboard our LCIL on Thursday evening, June 1st. The little ship was one of a long double file that lay along the dock in a certain British port. She was fast to the dock, with another LCIL lashed to her on the other side. An LCIL is a hundred and fifty-five feet long and about three hundred dead-weight tons. A destroyer is a big ship indeed by comparison; even an LST (Landing Ship, Tanks) looms over an LCIL like a monster. The LCIL has a flat bottom and draws only five feet of water, so she can go right up on a beach. Her hull is a box for carrying men; she can sleep two hundred soldiers belowdecks or can carry five hundred on a short ferrying trip, when men stand both below and topside. An LCIL has a stern anchor that she drops just before she goes aground and two forward ramps that she runs out as she touches bottom. As troops go down the ramps, the ship naturally lightens, and she rises a few inches in the water; she then winches herself off by the stern anchor, in much the same way a monkey pulls himself back on a limb by his tail. Troop space is about all there is to an LCIL, except for a compact engine room and a few indispensable sundries like navigation instruments and anti-aircraft guns. LCILs are the smallest ocean-crossing landing craft, and all those now in the European theater arrived under their own power. The crews probably would have found it more comfortable sailing on the Santa María. Most LCILs are operated by the Navy, but several score of them have Coast Guard crews. Ours was one of the latter. The name "Coast Guard" has always reminded me of the little cutters plying out to ocean liners from the barge office at the Battery in New York, and the association gave me a definite pleasure. Before boarding the landing craft, I had been briefed, along with twenty other correspondents, on the flagship of Rear Admiral John L. Hall, Jr., who commanded the task force of which our craft formed a minute part, so I knew where we were going and approximately when. Since that morning I had been sealed off from the civilian world, in the marshalling area, and when I went aboard our landing craft I knew that I would not be permitted even to set foot on the dock except in the company of a commissioned officer.

It was warm and the air felt soporific when I arrived. The scene somehow reminded me more of the Sheepshead Bay channel, with its fishing boats, than of the jumping-off place for an invasion. A young naval officer who had brought me ashore from the flagship took me over the landing craft's gangplank and introduced me to Lieutenant Rigg. Rigg, familiarly known as Bunny, was a big man, thirty-three years old, with clear, light-blue eyes and a fleshy, good-tempered face. He was a yacht broker in civilian life and often wrote articles about boats. Rigg welcomed me aboard as if we were going for a cruise to Block Island, and invited me into the wardroom to have a cup of coffee. There was standing room only, because Rigg's three junior officers and a Navy commander were already drinking coffee at the table. The junior officers— Long, Kavanaugh, and Williams—were all lieutenants (j.g.). Long, a small, jolly man with an upturned nose, was a Coast Guard regular with twenty years' service, mostly as a chief petty officer. He came from Baltimore. Kavanaugh, tall and straight-featured, was from Crary, North

Dakota, and Williams, a very polite, blond boy, came from White Deer, Texas. Kavanaugh and Williams were both in their extremely early twenties. The three-striper, a handsome, slender man with prematurely white hair and black eyebrows, was introduced to me by Rigg as the C.O. of a naval beach battalion that would go in to organize boat traffic on a stretch of beach as soon as the first waves of Infantry had taken it over. He was going to travel to the invasion coast aboard our landing craft, and since he disliked life ashore in the marshaling area, he had come aboard ship early. The commander, who had a drawl hard to match north of Georgia, was in fact a Washingtonian. He was an Annapolis man, he soon told me, but had left the Navy for several years to practice law in the District of Columbia and then returned to it for the war. His battalion was divided for the crossing among six LCILs, which would go in in pairs on adjacent beaches, so naturally he had much more detailed dope on the coming operation than normally would come to, say, the skipper of a landing craft, and this was to make conversations in the tiny wardroom more interesting than they otherwise would have been.

Even before I had finished my second cup of coffee, I realized that I had been assigned to a prize LCIL; our ship was to beach at H Hour plus sixty-five, which means one hour and five minutes after the first assault soldier gets ashore. "This ship and No. X will be the first LCILs on the beach," Rigg said complacently. "The first men will go in in small boats, because of mines and underwater obstacles, and Navy demolition men with them will blow us a lane through element C—that's sunken concrete and iron obstacles. They will also sweep the lane of mines, we hope. We just have to stay in the lane."

"These things move pretty fast and they make a fairly small target bow on," Long added cheerfully.

The others had eaten, but I had not, so Williams went out to tell the cook to get me up some chow. While it was being prepared, I went out on deck to look around.

Our landing craft, built in 1942, is one of the first class of LCILs, which have a rectangular superstructure and a narrow strip of open deck on each side of it. Painted on one side of the superstructure I noted a neat Italian flag, with the legend "Italy" underneath so that there would be no mistake, and beside the flag a blue shield with white vertical stripes and the word "Sicily." There was also a swastika and the outline of an airplane, which could only mean that the ship had shot down a German plane in a landing either in Sicily or Italy. Under Britain's double summer time, it was still light, and there were several groups of sailors on deck, most of them rubbing "impregnating grease" into shoes to make them impervious to mustard gas. There had been a great last-minute furor about the possibility that the Germans might use gas against the invasion, and everybody had been fitted with impregnated gear and two kinds of protective ointment. Our ship's rails were topped with rows of drying shoes.

"This is the first time I ever tried to get a pair of shoes pregnant, sir," one of the sailors called out sociably as I was watching him.

"No doubt you tried it on about everything else, I guess," another sailor yelled as he, too, worked on his shoes.

I could see I would not be troubled by any of that formality which has occasionally oppressed me aboard flagships. Most of the sailors had their names stenciled in white on the backs of their jumpers, so there was no need for introductions. One sailor I encountered was in the middle of a complaint about a shore officer who had "eaten him out" because of the way he was dressed on the dock, and he continued after I arrived. "They treat us like children," he said. "You'd think we was the pea-jacket navy instead of the ambiguous farce." The first term is one that landing-craft sailors apply to those on big ships, who keep so dry that they can afford to dress the part. "The ambiguous farce" is their pet name for the amphibious forces. A chief petty officer, who wore a khaki cap with his blue coveralls, said, "You don't want to mind them, sir. This isn't a regular ship and doesn't even pretend to be. But it's a good working ship. You ought to see our engine room."

A little sailor with a Levantine face asked me where I came from. When I told him New York, he said, "Me too—Hundred twenty-second and First." The name stenciled on his back was Landini. "I made up a song about this deal," he said, breaking into a kind of Off to Buffalo. "I'm going over to France and I'm shaking in my pants."

Through the open door of the galley, I could watch the cook, a fattish man with wavy hair and a narrow mustache, getting my supper ready. His name was Fassy, and he was the commissary steward. He appeared to have a prejudice against utensils; he slapped frankfurters and beans down on the hot stove top, rolled them around, and flipped them onto the plate with a spatula. I thought the routine looked familiar and I found out later that in his civilian days Fassy had worked in Shanty restaurants in New York.

While I was standing there, a young seaman stenciled Sitnitsky popped his head into the galley to ask for some soap powder so he could wash his clothes. Fassy poured some out of a vast carton into a pail of hot water the boy held. " 'Not recommended for delicate fabrics,' " the steward read from the carton, then roared, "So don't use it on your dainty lingerie!"

Since the frankfurters and beans were ready, I returned to the wardroom. There the board of strategy was again in session. The beach we were headed for was near the American line, only a mile or two from Port-en-Bessin, where the British area began. Eighteen years before, I had walked along the tops of the same cliffs the Americans would be fighting under. In those days I had thought of it as holiday country, not sufficiently spectacular to attract *le grand tourisme* but beautiful in a reasonable, Norman way. This illogically made the whole operation seem less sinister to me. Two pillboxes showed plainly on photographs we had, and, in addition, there were two houses that looked suspiciously like shells built around other pillboxes. Our intelligence people had furnished us with extraordinarily detailed charts of gradients in the beach and correlated tide tables. The charts later proved to be extraordinarily accurate, too.

"What worries me about landing is the bomb holes the Air Forces may leave in the beach before we hit," the commander was saying when I entered. "The chart may show three feet of water, but the men may step into a ten-foot hole anywhere. I'd rather the Air Forces left the beach alone and just let the naval guns knock out the beach defenses. They're accurate."

The general plan, I knew, was for planes and big guns of the fleet to put on an intensive bombardment before the landing. A couple of weeks earlier, I had heard a Marine colonel on the planning staff tell how the guns would hammer the pillboxes, leaving only a few stunned defenders for the Infantry to gather up on their way through to positions inland.

"We're lucky," the commander said. "This beach looks like a soft one."

His opinion, in conjunction with frankfurters and beans, made me happy.

We didn't get our passengers aboard until Saturday. On Friday I spent my time in alternate stretches of talk with the men on deck and the officers in the wardroom. Back in Sicily, the ship had been unable to get off after grounding at Licata, a boatswain's mate named Pendleton told me. "She got hit so bad we had to leave her," he said, "and for three days we had to live in foxholes, just like Infantrymen. Didn't feel safe a minute. We was sure glad to get back on the ship. Guess she had all her bad luck that trip."

Pendleton, a large, fair-haired fellow who was known to his shipmates as the Little Admiral, came from Neodesha, Kansas. "They never heard of the Coast Guard out there," he said. "Nobody but me. I knew I would have to go in some kind of service and I was reading in a Kansas City paper one day that the Coast Guard would send a station wagon to your house to get you if it was within a day's drive of their recruiting station. So I wrote 'em. Never did like to walk."

Sitnitsky was washing underclothes at a sink aft of the galley once when I came upon him. When he saw me, he said, "The fois' ting I'm gonna do when I get home is buy my mudder a Washington machine. I never realize what the old lady was up against."

Our neighbor LCIL, tied alongside us, got her soldier passengers late Friday night. The tide was low and the plank leading down to our ship from the dock was at a steep angle as men came aboard grumbling and filed across our deck to the other LCIL. "Didjever see a goddam gangplank in the right place?" one man called over his shoulder as he eased himself down with his load. I could identify a part of a mortar on his back, in addition to a full pack. "All aboard for the second Oran," another soldier yelled, and a third man, passing by the emblems painted on the bridge, as he crossed our ship, yelled, "Sicily! *They* been there, too." So I knew these men were part of the First Division, which landed at Oran in Africa in 1942 and later fought in Sicily. I think I would have known anyway by the beefing. The First Division is always beefing about something, which adds to its effectiveness as a fighting unit.

The next day the soldiers were spread all over the LCIL next door, most of them reading paper-cover, armed-services editions of books. They were just going on one more trip, and they didn't seem excited about it. I overheard a bit of technical conversation when I leaned over the rail to visit with a few of them. "Me, I like a bar [Browning automatic rifle]," a sergeant was saying to a private. "You can punch a lot of tickets with one of them."

The private, a rangy middleweight with a small, close-cropped head and a rectangular profile, said, "I'm going into this one with a pickaxe and a block of TNT. It's an interesting assignment. I'm going to work on each pillbox individually," he added, carefully pronouncing each syllable.

When I spoke to them, the sergeant said, "Huh! A correspondent! Why don't they give the First Division some credit?"

"I guess you don't read much if you say that, Sarge," a tall blond boy with a Southern accent said. "There's a whole book of funnies called 'Terry Allen and the First Division at El Guettar.'"

All three men were part of an Infantry regiment. The soldier who was going to work on pillboxes asked if I was from New York, and said that he was from the Bensonhurst section of Brooklyn. "I am only sorry my brother-in-law is not here," he said. "My brother-in-law is an M.P. He is six inches bigger than me. He gets an assignment in New York. I would like to see him here. He would be apprehensive." He went on to say that the company he was with had been captured near the end of the African campaign, when, after being cut off by the Germans, it had expended all its ammunition. He had been a prisoner in Tunis for a few hours, until the British arrived and set him free. "There are some nice broads in Tunis," he said. "I had a hell of a time." He nodded toward the book he was holding. "These little books are a great thing," he said. "They take you away. I remember when my battalion was cut off on top of a hill at El Guettar, I read a whole book in one day. It was called 'Knight Without Armor.' This one I am reading now is called 'Candide.' It is kind of unusual, but I like it. I think the fellow who wrote it, Voltaire, used the same gag too often, though. The characters are always getting killed and then turning out not to have been killed after all, and they tell their friends what happened to them in the meantime. I like the character in it called Pangloss."

Fassy was lounging near the rail and I called him over to meet a brother Brooklynite. "Brooklyn is a beautiful place to live in," Fassy said. "I have bush Number Three at Prospect Park."

"I used to have bush Number Four," the soldier said.

"You remind me of a fellow named Sidney Wetzelbaum," Fassy said. "Are you by any chance related?"

I left them talking.

Our own passengers came aboard later in the day. There were two groups—a platoon of the commander's beach battalion and a platoon of amphibious engineers. The beach-battalion men were sailors dressed like soldiers, except that they wore black jerseys under their field jackets; among them were a medical unit and a hydrographic unit. The engineers included an M.P. detachment, a chemical-warfare unit, and some demolition men. A beach battalion is a part of the Navy that goes ashore; amphibious engineers are a part of the Army that seldom has its feet dry. Together they form a link between the land and sea forces. These two detachments had rehearsed together in landing exercises, during which they had traveled aboard our LCIL. Unlike the Coastguardsmen or the Infantry on the next boat, they had never been in the real thing before and were not so offhand about it. Among them were a fair number of men in their thirties. I noticed one chief petty officer with the Navy crowd who looked about fifty. It was hard to realize that these older men had important and potentially dangerous assignments that called for a good deal of specialized skill; they seemed to me more out of place than the Infantry kids. Some sailors carried carbines and most of the engineers had rifles packed in oilskin cases. There were about a hundred and forty men in all. The old chief, Joe Smith, who was the first of the lot I got to know, said he had been on battleships in the last war and had been recalled from the fleet reserves at the beginning of this. He took considerable comfort from the fact that several aged battleships would lay down a barrage for us before we went in. You could see that he was glad to be aboard a ship again, even if it was a small one and he would be on it for only a couple of days. He was a stout, red-faced, merry man whose home town was Spring Lake, New Jersey. "I'm a tomato squeezer," he told me. "Just a country boy."

Cases of rations had been stacked against the superstructure for the passengers' use. The galley wasn't big enough to provide complete hot meals for them, but it did provide coffee, and their own cook warmed up canned stew and corned beef for them for one meal. The rest of the time they seemed simply to rummage among the cans until they found something they liked and then ate it. They ate pretty steadily, because there wasn't much else for them to do.

Our landing craft had four sleeping compartments belowdecks. The two forward ones, which were given over to passengers, contained about eighty bunks apiece. Most of the crew slept in the third compartment, amidships, and a number of petty officers and noncoms slept in the fourth, the smallest one, aft. I had been sleeping in this last one myself since coming aboard, because there was only one extra bunk for an officer and the commander had that. Four officers who came aboard with the troops joined me in this compartment. There were two sittings at the wardroom table for meals, but we managed to wedge eight men in there at one time for a poker game.

There was no sign of a move Saturday night, and on Sunday morning everybody aboard began asking when we were going to shove off. The morning sun was strong and the crew mingled with the beach-battalion men and the soldiers on deck. It was the same on board every other LCIL in the long double row. The port didn't look like Sheepshead Bay now, for every narrow boat was covered with men in drab-green field jackets, many of them wearing tin hats, because the easiest way not to lose a tin hat in a crowd is to wear it. The small ships and helmets pointed up the analogy to a crusade and made the term seem less threadbare than it usually does. We were waiting for weather, as many times the crusaders, too, had waited, but nobody thought of praying for it, not even the chaplain who came aboard in mid-morning to conduct services. He was a captain attached to the amphibious engineers, a husky man I had noticed throwing a football around on the dock the previous day. He took his text from Romans: "If God be for us, who can be against us?" He didn't seem to want the men to get the idea that we were depending entirely on faith, however. "Give us that dynamic, that drive, which, coupled with our matchless super-modern weapons, will ensure victory," he prayed. After that, he read aloud General Eisenhower's message to the Allied Expeditionary Force.

After the services, printed copies of Eisenhower's message were distributed to all hands on board. Members of our ship's crew went about getting autographs of their shipmates on their "Eisenhowers," which they apparently intended to keep as souvenirs of the invasion. Among the fellows who came to me for my signature was the ship's coxswain, a long-legged, serious-looking young man, from a little town in Mississippi, who had talked to me several times before because he wanted to be a newspaperman after the war. He had had one year at Tulane, in New Orleans, before joining up with the Coast Guard, and he hoped he could finish up later. The coxswain, I knew, would be the first man out of the ship when she grounded, even though he was a member of the crew. It was his task to run a guideline ashore in front of the disembarking soldiers. Then, when he had arrived in water only a foot or two deep, he would pull on the line and bring an anchor floating in after him, the anchor being a light one tied in a life jacket so that it would float. He would then fix the anchor—without the life jacket, of course—and return to the ship. This procedure had been worked out after a number of soldiers had been drowned on landing exercises by stepping into unexpected depressions in the beach after they had left the landing craft. Soldiers, loaded down with gear, had simply disappeared. With a guideline to hold onto, they could have struggled past bad spots. I asked the boy what he was going to wear when he went into the water with the line and he said just swimming trunks and a tin hat. He said he was a fair swimmer.

The rumor got about that we would sail that evening, but late in the afternoon the skipper told me we weren't going to. I learned that the first elements of the invasion fleet, the slowest ones, had gone out but had met rough weather in the Channel and had returned, because they couldn't have arrived at their destination in time. Admiral Hall had told correspondents that there would be three successive days when tide conditions on the Norman beaches would be right and that if we missed them the expedition might have to be put off, so I knew that we now had one strike on us, with only two more chances.

That evening, in the wardroom, we had a long session of a wild, distant derivative of poker called "high low rollem." Some young officers who had come aboard with the troops introduced it. We used what they called "funny money" for chips—five-franc notes printed in America and issued to the troops for use after they got ashore. It was the first time I had seen these notes, which reminded me of old-time cigar-store coupons. There was nothing on them to indicate who authorized them or would pay off on them—just *"Emis en France"* on one side and on the other side the tricolor and *"Liberté, Egalité, Fraternité."* In the game were three beach-battalion officers, a medical lieutenant (j.g.) named Davey, from Philadelphia, and two ensigns—a big, ham-handed college football player from Danbury, Connecticut, named Vaghi, and a blocky, placid youngster from Chicago named Reich. The commander of the engineer detachment, the only Army officer aboard, was a first lieutenant named Miller, a sallow, apparently nervous boy who had started to grow an ambitious black beard.

Next morning the first copy of the *Stars and Stripes* to arrive on board gave us something new to talk about. It carried the story of the premature invasion report by the Associated Press in America. In an atmosphere heavy with unavowed anxiety, the story hit a sour note. "Maybe they let out more than *Stars and Stripes* says," somebody in the wardroom said. "Maybe they not only announced the invasion but told where we had landed. I mean, where we *planned* to land. Maybe the whole deal will be called off now." The commander, who had spent so much time pondering element C, said, "Add obstacles—element A.P." A report got about among the more pessimistic crew members that the Germans had been tipped off and would be ready for us. The Allied high command evidently did not read the *Stars and Stripes*, however, for Rigg, after going ashore for a brief conference, returned with the information that we were shoving off at five o'clock. I said to myself, in the great cliché of the second World War, "This is it," and so, I suppose, did every other man in our fleet of little ships when he heard the news.

Peace or war, the boat trip across the English Channel always begins with the passengers in the same mood: everybody hopes he won't get seasick. On the whole, this is a favorable morale factor at the outset of an invasion. A soldier cannot fret about possible attacks by the Luftwaffe or E-boats while he is preoccupied with himself, and the vague fear of secret weapons on the far shore is balanced by the fervent desire to get the far shore under his feet. Few of the hundred and forty passengers on the LCIL I was on were actively sick the night before D Day, but they were all busy thinking about it. The four officers and twenty-nine men of the United States Coast Guard who made up her complement were not even queasy, but they had work to do, which was just as good. The rough weather, about which the papers have talked so much since D Day and which in fact interfered with the landing, was not the kind that tosses about transatlantic liners or even Channel packets; it was just a bit too rough for the smaller types of landing craft we employed. Aboard our LCIL, the Channel didn't seem especially bad that night. There was a ground swell for an hour after we left port, but then the going became better than I had anticipated. LCTs (Landing Craft, Tanks), built like open troughs a hundred feet long, to carry armored vehicles, had a much worse time, particularly since, being slow, they had had to start hours before us. Fifty-foot LCMs (Landing Craft, Mechanized) and fifty-foot and thirty-six-foot LCVPs (Landing Craft, Vehicles and Personnel), swarms of which crossed the Channel under their own power, had still more trouble. The setting out of our group of LCILs was unimpressive —just a double file of ships, each a hundred and fifty-five feet long, bound for a rendezvous with a great many other ships at three in the morning ten or fifteen miles off a spot on the coast of lower Normandy. Most of the troops traveled in large transports, from which the smaller craft transferred them to shore. The LCILs carried specially packaged units for early delivery on the Continent doorstep.

Rigg turned in early that evening because he wanted to be fresh for a hard day's work by the time we arrived at the rendezvous, which was to take place in what was known as the transport area. So did the commander of the naval beach battalion. I stood on deck for a while. As soon as I felt sleepy, I went down to my bunk and got to sleep—with my clothes on, naturally. There didn't seem to be anything else to do. That was at about eight. I woke three hours later and saw a fellow next to me being sick in a paper bag and I went up to the galley and had a cup of coffee. Then I went back to my bunk and slept until a change in motion and in the noise of the motors woke me again.

The ship was wallowing slowly now, and I judged that we had arrived at the transport area and were loafing about. I looked at my wristwatch and saw that we were on time. It was about three. So we hadn't been torpedoed by an E-boat. A good thing. Drowsily, I wondered a little at the fact that the enemy had made no attempt to intercept the fleet and hoped there would be good air cover, because I felt sure that the Luftwaffe couldn't possibly pass up the biggest target of history. My opinion of the Luftwaffe was still strongly influenced by what I remembered from June, 1940, in France, and even from January and February, 1943, in Tunisia. I decided to stay in my bunk until daylight, dozed, woke again, and then decided I couldn't make it. I went up on deck in the gray predawn light sometime before five. I drew myself a cup of coffee from an electric urn in the galley and stood by the door drinking it and looking at the big ships around us. They made me feel proletarian. They would stay out in the Channel and send in their troops in small craft, while working-class vessels like us went right up on the beach. I pictured them inhabited by officers in dress blues and shiny brass buttons, all scented like the World's Most Distinguished After-Shave Club. The admiral's command ship lay nearby. I imagined it to be gaffed with ingenious gimmicks that would record the developments of the operation. I could imagine a terse report coming in of the annihilation of a flotilla of LCILs, including us, and hear some Annapolis man saying, "After all, that sort of thing is to be expected." Then I felt that everything was going to be all right, because it always had been. A boatswain's mate, second class, named Barrett, from Rich Square, North Carolina, stopped next to me to drink his coffee and said, "I bet Findley a pound that we'd be hit this time. We most always is. Even money."

We wouldn't start to move, I knew, until about six-thirty, the time when the very first man was scheduled to walk onto the beach. Then we would leave the transport area so that we could beach and perform our particular chore—landing one platoon of the naval beach battalion and a platoon of Army amphibious engineers—at seven-thirty-five. A preliminary bombardment of the beach defenses by the Navy was due to begin at dawn. "Ought to be hearing the guns soon," I said to Barrett, and climbed the ladder to the upper deck. Rigg was on the bridge drinking coffee, and with him was Long, the ship's engineering officer. It grew lighter and the guns began between us and the shore. The sound made us all cheerful and Long said, "I'd hate to be in under that." Before dawn the transports had begun putting men into small craft that headed for the line of departure, a line nearer shore from which the first assault wave would be launched.

Time didn't drag now. We got under way sooner than I had somehow expected. The first troops were on the beaches. The battleship Arkansas and the French cruisers Montcalm and Georges Leygues were pounding away on our starboard as we moved in. They were firing over the heads of troops, at targets farther inland. Clouds of yellow cordite smoke billowed up. There was something leonine in their tint as well as in the roar that followed, after that lapse of time which never fails to disconcert me. We went on past the big ships, like a little boy with the paternal blessing. In this region the Germans evidently had no long-range coastal guns, like the ones near Calais, for the warships' fire was not returned. This made me feel good. The absence of resistance always increases my confidence. The commander of the naval beach battalion had now come on deck, accoutered like a soldier, in greenish coveralls and tin hat. I said to him cheerfully, "Well, it looks as though the biggest difficulty you're going to have is getting your feet in cold water."

He stood there for a minute and said, "What are you thinking of?"

I said, "I don't know why, but I'm thinking of the garden restaurant behind the Museum of Modern Art in New York." He laughed, and I gave him a pair of binoculars I had, because I knew that he didn't have any and that he had important use for them.

Our passengers—the beach-battalion platoon and the amphibious engineers—were now forming two single lines on the main deck, each group facing the ramp by which it would leave the ship. Vaghi and Reich, the beach-battalion ensigns, were lining up their men on the port side and Miller, the Army lieutenant with the new beard, was arranging his men on the starboard side. I wished the commander good luck and went up on the bridge, which was small and crowded but afforded the best view.

An LCIL has two ramps, one on each side of her bow, which she lowers and thrusts out ahead of her when she beaches. Each ramp is handled by means of a winch worked by two men; the two winches stand side by side deep in an open-well deck just aft of the bow. If the ramps don't work, the whole operation is fouled up, so an LCIL skipper always assigns reliable men to operate them. Two seamen named Findley and Lechich were on the port winch, and two whom I knew as Rocky and Bill were on the other. Williams, the ship's executive officer, was down in the well deck with the four of them.

We had been in sight of shore for a long while, and now I could recognize our strip of beach from our intelligence photographs. There was the house with the tower on top of the cliff on our starboard as we went in. We had been warned that preliminary bombardment might

remove it, so we should not count too much upon it as a landmark;
however, there it was and it gave me the pleasure of recognition. A path
was to have been blasted and swept for us through element C and the
mines, and the entrance to it was to have been marked with colored
buoys. The buoys were there, so evidently the operation was going all
right. Our LCIL made a turn and headed for the opening like a halfback
going into a hole in the line. I don't know whether Rigg suddenly became
solicitous for my safety or whether he simply didn't want me underfoot
on the bridge, where two officers and two signalmen had trouble getting
around even without me. He said, "Mr. Liebling will take his station on
the upper deck during action." This was formal language from the young
man I had learned to call Bunny, especially since the action did not seem
violent as yet, but I climbed down the short ladder from the bridge to the
deck, a move that put the wheelhouse between me and the bow. The
upper deck was also the station for a pharmacist's mate named Kallam,
who was our reserve first-aid man. A landing craft carries no doctor, the
theory being that a pharmacist's mate will make temporary repairs until
the patient can be transferred to a larger ship. We had two men with this
rating aboard. The other, a fellow named Barry, was up in the bow.
Kallam was a sallow, long-faced North Carolinian who once told me he
had gone into the peacetime Navy as a youth and had never been good
for anything else since. This was his first action, except for a couple of
landings in Nicaragua around 1930.

The shore curved out toward us on the port side of the ship, and
when I looked out in that direction I could see a lot of smoke from what
appeared to be shells bursting on the beach. There was also an LCT,
grounded and burning. "Looks as if there's opposition," I said to Kallam,
without much originality. At about the same time something splashed in
the water off our starboard quarter, sending up a high spray. We were
moving in fast now. I could visualize, from the plan I had seen so often
in the last few days, the straight, narrow lane in which we had to stay.
"On a straight line—like a rope ferry," I thought. The view on both sides
changed rapidly. The LCT that had been on our port bow was now on
our port quarter, and another LCT, also grounded, was now visible. A
number of men, who had evidently just left her, were in the water, some
up to their necks and others up to their armpits, and they didn't look as
if they were trying to get ashore. Tracer bullets were skipping around
them and they seemed perplexed. What I hate most about tracers is that
every time you see one, you know there are four more bullets that you
don't see, because only one tracer to five bullets is loaded in a machine-
gun belt. Just about then, it seems in retrospect, I felt the ship ground.

I looked down at the main deck, and the beach-battalion men were
already moving ahead, so I knew that the ramps must be down. I could
hear Long shouting, "Move along now! Move along!," as if he were
unloading an excursion boat at Coney Island. But the men needed no

urging; they were moving without a sign of flinching. You didn't have to look far for tracers now, and Kallam and I flattened our backs against the pilot house and pulled in our stomachs, as if to give a possible bullet an extra couple of inches clearance. Something tickled the back of my neck. I slapped at it and discovered that I had most of the ship's rigging draped around my neck and shoulders, like a character in an old slapstick movie about a spaghetti factory, or like Captain Horatio Hornblower. The rigging had been cut away by bullets. As Kallam and I looked toward the stern, we could see a tableau that was like a recruiting poster. There was a twenty-millimeter rapid-firing gun on the upper deck. Since it couldn't bear forward because of the pilot house and since there was nothing to shoot at on either side, it was pointed straight up at the sky in readiness for a possible dive-bombing attack. It had a crew of three men, and they were kneeling about it, one on each side and one behind the gun barrel, all looking up at the sky in an extremely earnest manner, and getting all the protection they could out of the gunshield. As a background to the men's heads, an American flag at the ship's stern streamed across the field of vision. It was a new flag, which Rigg had ordered hoisted for the first time for the invasion, and its colors were brilliant in the sun. To make the poster motif perfect, one of the three men was a Negro, William Jackson, from New Orleans, a wardroom steward, who, like everybody else on the LCIL, had multiple duties.

The last passenger was off the ship now, and I could hear the stern anchor cable rattling on the drum as it came up. An LCIL drops a stern anchor just before it grounds, and pays out fifty to a hundred fathoms of chain cable as it slowly slides the last couple of ship's lengths toward shore. To get under way again, it takes up the cable, pulling itself afloat. I had not known until that minute how eager I was to hear the sound of the cable that follows the order "Take in on stern anchor." Almost as soon as the cable began to come in, something hit the ship with the solid clunk of metal against metal—not as hard as a collision or a bomb blast; just "clink." Long yelled down, "Pharmacist's mate go forward. Somebody's hurt." Kallam scrambled down the ladder to the main deck with his kit. Then Long yelled to a man at the stern anchor winch, "Give it hell!" An LCIL has to pull itself out and get the anchor up before it can use its motors, because otherwise the propeller might foul in the cable. The little engine that supplies power for the winch is built by a farm-machinery company in Waukesha, Wisconsin, and every drop of gasoline that went into the one on our ship was filtered through chamois skin first. That engine is the ship's insurance policy. A sailor now came running up the stairway from the cabin. He grabbed me and shouted, "Two casualties in bow!" I passed this information on to the bridge for whatever good it might do; both pharmacist's mates were forward already and there was really nothing else to be done. Our craft had now swung clear, the anchor was up, and the engines went into play. She turned about and shot forward like a destroyer. The chief machinist's mate said afterward that the engines did seven hundred revolutions a minute instead of the six hundred that was normal top speed. Shells were kicking up water-spouts around us as we went; the water they raised looked black. Rigg said afterward, "Funny thing. When I was going in, I had my whole attention fixed on two mines attached to sunken concrete blocks on either side of the place where we went in. I knew they hadn't been cleared away—just a path between them. They were spider mines, those things with a lot of loose cables. Touch one cable and you detonate the mine. When I was going out, I was so excited that I forgot all about the damn mines and didn't think of them until I was two miles past them."

A sailor came by and Shorty, one of the men in the gun crew, said to him, "Who was it?" The sailor said, "Rocky and Bill. They're all tore up. A shell got the winch and ramps and all." I went forward to the well deck, which was sticky with a mixture of blood and condensed milk. Soldiers had left cases of rations lying all about the ship, and a fragment of the shell that hit the boys had torn into a carton of cans of milk. Rocky and Bill had been moved below decks into one of the large forward compartments. Rocky was dead beyond possible doubt, somebody told me, but the pharmacist's mates had given Bill blood plasma and thought he might still be alive. I remembered Bill, a big, baby-faced kid from the District of Columbia, built like a wrestler. He was about twenty, and the other boys used to kid him about a girl he was always writing letters to. A third wounded man, a soldier dressed in khaki, lay on a stretcher on deck breathing hard through his mouth. His long, triangular face looked like a dirty drumhead; his skin was white and drawn tight over his high cheekbones. He wasn't making much noise. There was a shooting-gallery smell over everything and when we passed close under the Arkansas and she let off a salvo, a couple of our men who had their backs to her quivered and had to be reassured. Long and Kavanaugh, the communications officer, were already going about the ship trying to get things ticking again, but they had little success at first.

Halfway out to the transport area, another LCIL hailed us and asked us to take a wounded man aboard. They had got him from some smaller craft, but they had to complete a mission before they could go back to the big ships. We went alongside and took him over the rail. He was wrapped in khaki blankets and strapped into a wire basket litter. After we had sheared away, a man aboard the other LCIL yelled at us to come back so that he could hand over a half-empty bottle of plasma with a long rubber tube attached. "This goes with him," he said. We went alongside again and he handed the bottle to one of our fellows. It was trouble for nothing, because the man by then had stopped breathing.

We made our way out to a transport called the Dorothea Dix, which had a hospital ward fitted out. We went alongside and Rigg yelled that we had four casualties aboard. A young naval doctor climbed down the grapple net hanging on the Dix's side and came aboard. After he had looked at our soldier, he called for a breeches buoy and the soldier was hoisted up sitting in that. He had been hit in one shoulder and one leg, and the doctor said he had a good chance. The three others had to be sent up in wire baskets, vertically, like Indian papooses. A couple of Negroes on the upper deck of the Dix dropped a line, which our men made fast to the top of one basket after another. Then the man would be jerked up in the air by the Negroes as if he were going to heaven. Now that we carried no passengers and were lighter, the sea seemed rough. We bobbled under the towering transport and the wounded men swung wildly on the end of the line, a few times almost striking against the ship. A Coastguardsman reached up for the bottom of one basket so that he could steady it on its way up. At least a quart of blood ran down on him, covering his tin hat, his upturned face, and his blue overalls. He stood motionless for an instant, as if he didn't know what had happened, seeing the world through a film of red, because he wore eyeglasses and blood had covered the lenses. The basket, swaying eccentrically, went up the side. After a couple of seconds, the Coastguardsman turned and ran to a sink aft of the galley, where he turned on the water and began washing himself. A couple of minutes after the last litter had been hoisted aboard, an officer on the Dix leaned over her rail and shouted down, "Medical officer in charge says two of these men are dead! He says you should take them back to the beach and bury them." Out there, fifteen miles off shore, they evidently thought that this was just another landing exercise. A sailor on deck said, "The son of a bitch ought to see that beach."

Rigg explained to the officer that it would be impossible to return to the beach and ordered the men to cast off the lines, and we went away from the Dix. Now that the dead and wounded were gone, I saw Kallam sneak to the far rail and be sicker than I have ever seen a man at sea. We passed close by the command ship and signaled that we had completed our mission. We received a signal, "Wait for orders," and for the rest of the day we loafed, while we tried to reconstruct what had happened to us. Almost everybody on the ship had a battle headache.

"What hurts me worst," Lechich said, "is thinking what happened to those poor guys we landed. That beach was hot with Jerries. And they didn't have nothing to fight with—only carbines and rifles. They weren't even supposed to be combat troops."

"I don't think any of them could be alive now," another man said.

As the hours went by and we weren't ordered to do anything, it became evident that our bit of beach wasn't doing well, for we had expected, after delivering our first load on shore, to be employed in ferrying other troops from transports to the beach, which the beach-battalion boys and engineers would in the meantime have been helping to clear. Other LCILs of our flotilla were also lying idle. We saw one of them being towed, and then we saw her capsize. Three others, we heard, were lying up on one strip of beach, burned. Landing craft are reckoned expendable. Rigg came down from the bridge and, seeing me, said, "The beach is closed to LCILs now. Only small boats going in. Wish they'd thought of that earlier. We lost three good men."

"Which three?" I asked. "I know about Rocky and Bill."

"The coxswain is gone," Bunny said. I remembered the coxswain, the earnest young fellow who wanted to be a newspaperman, who, dressed in swimming trunks, was going to go overboard ahead of everyone else and run a guideline into shore.

"Couldn't he get back?" I asked.

"He couldn't get anywhere," Rigg answered. "He had just stepped off the ramp when he disintegrated. He must have stepped right into an H. E. shell. Cox was a good lad. We'd recommended him for officers' school." Rigg walked away for the inevitable cup of coffee, shaking his big tawny head. I knew he had a battle headache, too.

A while afterward, I asked Rigg what he had been thinking as we neared the coast and he said he had been angry because the men we were going to put ashore hadn't had any coffee. "The poor guys had stayed in the sack as late as they could instead," he said. "Going ashore without any coffee!"

Long was having a look at the damage the shell had done to our ship, and I joined him in tracing its course. It had entered the starboard bow well above the waterline, about the level of the ship's number, then had hit the forward anchor winch, had been deflected toward the stern of the boat, had torn through the bulkhead and up through the cover of the escape hatch, then had smashed the ramp winch and Rocky and Bill. It had been a seventy-five-millimeter anti-tank shell with a solid-armor-piercing head, which had broken into several pieces after it hit the ramp winch. The boys kept finding chunks of it around, but enough of it stayed in one piece to show what it had been. "They had us crisscrossed with guns in all those pillboxes that were supposed to have been knocked off," Long said. "Something must have gone wrong. We gave them a perfect landing, though," he added with professional pride. "I promised the commander we would land him dry tail and we did." Long has been in the Coast Guard twenty years and nothing surprises him; he has survived prohibition, Miami and Fire Island hurricanes, and three landings. He is a cheerful soul who has an original theory about fear. "I always tell my boys that fear is a passion like any other passion," he had once told me. "Now, if you see a beautiful dame walking down the street, you feel passion but you control it, don't you? Well, if you begin to get frightened, which is natural, just control yourself also, I tell them." Long said that he had seen the commander start off from the ship at a good clip, run well until he got up near the first line of sand dunes, then stagger. "The commander was at the head of the line about to leave the ship when young Vaghi, that big ensign, came up and must have asked him for the honor of going first," Long said. "They went off that way, Vaghi out ahead, running as if he was running out on a field with a football under his arm. Miller led the soldiers off the other ramp, and he stepped out like a little gentleman, too." The space where the starboard ramp had once been gave the same effect as an empty sleeve or eye socket.

It was Frankel, a signalman who had been on the bridge, who told me sometime that afternoon about how the wounded soldier had come to be on board. Frankel, whose family lives on East Eighteenth Street in Brooklyn, was a slender, restless fellow who used to be a cutter in the garment center. He played in dance bands before he got his garment-union card, he once told me, and on the ship he occasionally played hot licks on the bugle slung on the bridge. "A shell hit just as we were beginning to pull out," Frankel said, "and we had begun to raise the ramps. It cut all but about one strand of the cable that was holding the starboard ramp and the ramp was wobbling in the air when I saw a guy holding on to the end of it. I guess a lot of us saw him at the same time. He was just clutching the ramp with his left arm, because he had been shot in the other shoulder. I'll never forget his eyes. They seemed to say, 'Don't leave me behind.' He must have been hit just as he stepped off the ramp leaving the ship. It was this soldier. So Ryan and Landini went out and got him. Ryan worked along the rail inside the ramp and Landini worked along the outside edge of the ramp and they got him and carried him back into the ship. There was plenty of stuff flying around, too, and the ramp came away almost as soon as they got back. That's one guy saved, anyway." Ryan was a seaman cook who helped Fassy in the galley, and Landini was the little First Avenue Italian who had made up the special song for himself.

Along about noon, an LCVP, a troughlike fifty-footer, hailed us and asked if we could take care of five soldiers. Rigg said we could. The craft came alongside and passed over five drenched and shivering tank soldiers who had been found floating on a rubber raft. They were the crew of a tank that had been going in on a very small craft and they had been swamped by a wave. The tank had gone to the bottom and the soldiers had just managed to make it to the raft. The pharmacist's mates covered them with piles of blankets and put them to bed in one of our large compartments. By evening they were in the galley drinking coffee with the rest of us. They were to stay on the ship for nearly a week, as it turned out, because nobody would tell us what to do with them. They got to be pretty amphibious themselves. The sergeant in command was a fellow from Cleveland named Angelatti. He was especially happy about being saved, apparently because he liked his wife. He would keep repeating, "Gee, to think it's my second anniversary—I guess it's my lucky

day!" But when he heard about what we thought had happened to the
men we put ashore, he grew gloomy. The tanks had been headed for that
beach and should have helped knock out the pillboxes. It hadn't been
the tankmen's fault that the waves had swamped them, but the sergeant
said disconsolately, "If we hadn't got bitched up, maybe those other guys
wouldn't have been killed." He had a soldier's heart.

On the morning of D Day-plus-one, our LCIL was like a ship with a
hangover. Her deck was littered with cartons of tinned rations. There
was a gap where the starboard ramp had been and there were various
holes in the hull and hatches to mark the path of the anti-tank shell.
Everybody aboard was nursing a headache. We hung around in the
Channel, waiting for orders and talking over the things that had happened to us. The men in the engine room, which was so clean that it
looked like the model dairy exhibit at the World's Fair—all white paint
and aluminum trim—had sweated it out at their posts during the excitement on deck and the engine-room log had been punctiliously kept. On
the morning of D-plus-one, Cope, the chief machinist's mate, a tall,
quiet chap from Philadelphia, told somebody that from the order "Drop
stern anchor" to the order "Take in on stern anchor," which included all
the time we had spent aground, exactly four minutes had elapsed. Most
of us on deck would have put it at half an hour. During those four
minutes all the hundred and forty passengers we carried had run off the
ramps into three feet of water, three members of our Coast Guard complement of thirty-three had been killed, and two others had rescued a
wounded soldier clinging to the end of the starboard ramp. The experience had left us without appetite. I remember, on the afternoon of D
Day, sitting on a ration case on the pitching deck and being tempted by
the rosy picture on the label of a roast-beef can. I opened it, but I could
only pick at the jellied juice, which reminded me too much of the blood
I had seen that morning, and I threw the tin over the rail.

By D-plus-one we were beginning to eat again. That morning I was
on the upper deck talking to Barrett, when we saw a German mine go
off. It threw a column of water high into the air and damaged a ship near
it. German planes had been fiddling around above our anchorage during
the night, without bombing us; evidently they had been dropping mines.
We had seen three of the planes shot down. Barrett looked at the water
spout and said, "If we ever hit a mine like that, we'll go up in the air like
an arrow." It was Barrett who had bet a pound, even money, that we
would be hit during the action. I asked him if he had collected the bet
and he said, "Sure. As long as we got hit whether I take the money or
not, I might as well take it." In the wardroom, Kavanaugh, the communications officer, talked to me about Bill, one of the Coast Guard boys
who had been hit. Kavanaugh, who had censored Bill's letters, said, "Bill
began every letter he ever wrote, 'Well, honey, here I am again.' " Long,

the engineering officer, told me about a patch he had devised that would expand in water and would close up any underwater holes in the hull, and seemed rather to regret that he had had no chance to try it out. Rigg kept repeating a tag line he had picked up from Sid Fields, a comedian in a London revue: "What a performance! What a performance!" But the most frequent subject of conversation among both officers and men was the fate of the fellows we had put on the beach. We had left them splashing through shallow water, with tracer bullets flying around them and only a nearly level, coverless beach immediately in front of them and with a beach pillbox and more of the enemy on a cliff inshore blazing away with everything they had. We had decided that hardly any of our men could have survived.

Late that afternoon our landing craft got an order to help unload soldiers from a big troopship several miles off the French shore. We were to carry the men almost as far as the beach and then transfer them to Higgins boats. One of our ramps was gone and the other one was not usable, and it would have been superfluous cruelty to drop a soldier with a full pack into five feet of water, our minimum draught. We gathered from the order that the Germans were no longer shooting on the beach; this, at least, represented progress.

The soldiers who lined the decks of the transport, all eager to get ashore at once, belonged to the Second Division; they wore a white star and an Indian head on their shoulder flashes. A scramble net hung down the port side of the vessel, and soldiers with full equipment strapped to their backs climbed down it one by one and stepped backward onto our landing craft. As each man made the step, two seamen grabbed him and helped him aboard. It often took as much time to unload the soldiers from a big ship as it did for the ship itself to get from Britain to the Norman coast, and it seemed to me that a small expenditure on gang-planks of various lengths and furnished with grapples, like the ones used in boarding operations in ancient naval battles, would have sped these transfers more than a comparable outlay for any other device could possibly have done. While we were loading the men, a thirty-six-foot craft approached us on the other side. There were two other thirty-six-footers there side by side already. The newest thirty-six-footer got along-side the outer one of the pair of earlier arrivals and the crew boosted up a man who had been standing in the stern of the boat and helped him on to the other craft. The man made his way unsteadily across both of the intervening thirty-six-footers to us, and men on the boats passed his gear, consisting of a typewriter and a gas mask, along after him. He was in a field jacket and long khaki trousers without leggings. The clothes were obviously fresh out of a quartermaster's stores. He wore the war correspondent's green shoulder patch on his field jacket. His face and form indicated that he had led a long and comfortable life, and his eyes betrayed astonishment that he should be there at all, but he was smiling.

Some of our Coastguardsmen helped him over our rail. He said that he was Richard Stokes of the St. Louis *Post-Dispatch*, that he had been a Washington correspondent and a music critic for many years, that he had wanted to go overseas when we got into the war, and that he had finally induced his paper to send him over. He had got airplane passage to Britain, where he had arrived two weeks before, and had been sent to the invasion coast on a Liberty ship that was to land men on D-plus-one. "It seems just wonderful to be here," Stokes said. "I can hardly believe it." He had been very much disappointed when he found out that because of the violence of the German resistance, the Liberty ship was not going to land her passengers for a couple of days. The ship's captain had said to him, "There's another crowd going ashore. Why don't you go with them?" Then the skipper had hailed a boat for him. "And here I am," said Stokes. "It's too good to be true." He was sixty-one years old, and the world seemed marvelous to him. He said he had never been in a battle and he wanted to see what it was like.

We got all our soldiers—about four hundred of them—aboard and started in toward the same stretch of shore we had left in such haste thirty-six hours before. The way in looked familiar and yet devoid of the character it had once had for us, like the scene of an old assignation revisited. The house with the tower on top of the cliff was now gone, I noticed. The naval bombardment, although tardy, had been thorough. Scattered along the shore were the wrecked and burned-out landing craft that had been less lucky than ours. Several of our men told me they had seen the LCT that had been burning off our port quarter on D Day pull out, still aflame, and extinguish the fire as she put to sea, but plenty of others remained. Small craft came out to us from the shore that had so recently been hostile, and soldiers started climbing into them, a less complicated process than the transfer from the troopship because the highest points of the small craft were nearly on a level with our main deck. I could see occasional puffs of smoke well up on the beach. They looked as if they might be the bursts of German shells coming from behind the cliff, and I felt protective toward Stokes. "Mr. Stokes," I said, "it seems to be pretty rough in there." He didn't even have a blanket to sleep on, and he didn't have the slightest idea whom he was going to look for when he got in; he was just going ahead like a good city reporter on an ordinary assignment. He watched two boats load up with soldiers and then, as a third came alongside—I remember that the name painted inside her ramp was "Impatient Virgin"—he said, "Mr. Liebling, I have made up my mind," and went down and scrambled aboard, assisted by everybody who could get a hand on him. He got ashore all right and did some fine stories. A couple of weeks afterward he told me, "I couldn't stand being within sight of the promised land and then coming back."

■

There was nothing for us to do during the daylight hours of D-plus-two, but toward eight o'clock in the evening we got an order to go out to another troopship and unload more Second Division soldiers, who were to be taken to a beach next to the one where we had landed on D Day. The ship was an American Export liner. Several other LCILs were also assigned to the job of emptying her. I was on our bridge with Rigg when we came under her towering side, and the smell of fresh bread, which her cooks had evidently been baking, drove all other thoughts from our minds. Rigg hailed a young deck officer who was looking down at us and asked him if he could spare some bread. The officer said sure, and a few minutes later a steward pushed six long loaves across to our bridge from a porthole at approximately our level. They were an inestimable treasure to us. Everything is relative in an amphibious operation; to the four-man crews who operate the thirty-six-foot LCVPs, which are open to the weather and have no cooking facilities, an LCIL seems a floating palace. They would often come alongside us and beg tinned fruit, which they would receive with the same doglike gratitude we felt toward the merchantman for our bread.

The soldiers came aboard us along a single narrow plank, which was put over from the port side of the troopship to our rail, sloping at an angle of forty-five degrees. We pitched continuously in the rough water, and the soldiers, burdened with rifles and about fifty pounds of equipment apiece, slid rather than ran down the plank. Our crew had arranged a pile of ration cases at the rail, right where the gangplank was fastened, and the soldiers stepped from the end of the plank to the top case and then jumped down. We made two trips between the merchantman and the small boats that night, and only one soldier fell, and was lost, between the ships during the whole operation. That, I suppose, was a good percentage, but it still seemed to me an unnecessary loss. On our first trip from ship to shore, while we were unloading soldiers into small boats a couple of hundred yards off the beach, there was an air raid. The soldiers standing on our narrow deck, with their backs to the deckhouse walls, had never been under real fire before, but they remained impassive amid the cascade of Bofors shells that rose from hundreds of ships. Much of the barrage had a low trajectory and almost scraped the paint off our bridge. On one ship some gunners who knew their business would hit a plane, and then, as it fell, less intelligent gun crews would start after it and follow it down, forgetting that when a plane hits the water it is at the waterline. An anti-aircraft shell traveling upward at an angle of not more than twenty degrees wounded a good friend of mine sleeping in a dugout on the side of a cliff ashore a couple of nights later.

A beach-battalion sailor came out to us on one of the first small boats from the shore. He was a big, smiling fellow whom we had brought from England on our first trip to the invasion coast, one of "those poor bastards" we had all assumed were dead. The cooks hauled him into the galley for sandwiches and coffee, and within a couple of minutes officers as well as men were crowding about him. Nearly everybody we asked him about turned out to be alive—the commander of the beach battalion; Miller, the Army lieutenant; little Dr. Davey; Vaghi and Reich, the poker-playing ensigns; Smith, the beach battalion's veteran chief petty officer; and others whom we had got to know on the ship. They had had a rough time, the sailor said. They had lain for five hours in holes they had scooped in the sand when they went ashore, while one or two American tanks that had landed shot at pillboxes and the pillboxes shot back. Then some infantrymen who had landed in small boats at H Hour worked their way up the beach and took the German positions, releasing our friends from the position in which they were pinned down. They were living on the side of a hill now and getting on with their work of organizing traffic between ship and shore. It was very pleasant news for us aboard the landing craft. We worked all night unloading soldiers, but the Coast Guard crew didn't mind; they were in a good mood.

Early the next day, D-plus-three, I thumbed a ride ashore to go visiting. I hailed a passing assault craft, a rocket-firing speedboat, which took me part of the way and then transferred me to an LCVP that was headed inshore. The LCVP ran up onto the beach, dropped her bow ramp, and I walked onto French soil without even wetting my feet. This was the moment I had looked forward to for four years minus nine days, since the day I had crossed the Spanish frontier at Irún after the fall of France. Then the words of de Gaulle—"France has lost a battle but not the war"—were ringing in my ears, for I had just heard his first radio speech from London, but I had not dared hope that the wheel would turn almost full circle so soon. There was the noise of cannonading a couple of miles or so beyond the cliffs, where the First Division was pushing on from the fingerhold it had made good on D Day, but on the beach everything was calm. Troops and sailors of the amphibious forces had cleared away much of the wreckage, so that landing craft coming in would not foul their hulls or anchor chains; metal road strips led up from the water's edge to the road parallel with the shore. Men were going about their work as if there were no enemy within a hundred miles, and this was understandable, because no German planes ever arrived to molest them as they unloaded vehicles and munitions for the troops up ahead. To men who had been in other campaigns, when a solitary jeep couldn't pass down a road without three Messerschmitts' having a pass at it, this lack of interference seemed eerie, but it was true all the same. During the first week after the invasion began, I didn't see one German plane by daylight. Almost in front of me, as I stepped off the boat, were the ruins of the concrete blockhouse that had fired at us as we ran in on D Day. The concrete had been masked by a simulated house, but the disguise had been shot away and the place gaped white and roofless. I had more a sense of coming home to the United States Army than to France, for the first M.P. of whom I inquired the way to the command post of the beach battalion said he didn't know. This is S.O.P., or standard operating procedure, because a soldier figures that if he tells you he knows, he will, at best, have trouble directing you, and if the directions turn out to be wrong you may come back and complain. He has nothing to lose by denying knowledge.

I walked along the beach and met a beach-battalion sailor. He was equally unknowledgeable until I convinced him that I was a friend of the commander. Then he led me two hundred yards up a cliff to the place I had asked about. The commander was not there, but a Lieutenant Commander Watts and a Lieutenant Reardon, both New Yorkers, were. They had gone ashore on another landing craft, but I had met them both while we were in port in Britain awaiting sailing orders. They had landed five hundred yards up the beach from us and had, of course, got the same reception we got. The command post was installed in a row of burrows in the face of the cliff from which the Germans had fired down on the incoming boats and the beach on D Day; now it was we who overlooked the beach. In the side of another cliff, which was almost at a right angle to this one, the Germans had had two sunken concrete pillboxes enfilading the beach, and I realized that the crossfire had centered on our landing craft and the others nearby. Meeting these men reminded me of what the First Division soldier had said to me a few days earlier about "Candide": "Voltaire used the same gag too often. The characters are always getting killed and then turning out not to have been killed at all, and they tell their friends what happened to them in the meantime." Watts said that after they had left their landing craft, they had run forward like hell and then had thrown themselves down on the beach because there was nothing else to do. The forepart of the beach was covered with large, round pebbles about the size, I imagine, of the one David used on Goliath, and when the German machine-gun bullets skittered among them the stones became a secondary form of ammunition themselves and went flying among the men. "We had infantry up ahead of us, but at first they were pinned down too," Watts said. "A couple of tanks had landed and one of them knocked out a seventy-five up on the side of the hill, but in a short while the Germans either replaced it or got it going again. Then, after a couple of hours, two destroyers came and worked close in to shore, although there were plenty of mines still in there, and really plastered the pillboxes. The infantry went up the hill in the face of machine-gun fire and drove the Germans out of the trench system they had on the crown of the hill. I'll show it to you in a couple of minutes. It's a regular young Maginot Line. By nightfall we felt fairly safe. We found out later from prisoners that the Three Hundred and Fifty-second German Field Division had been holding anti-invasion exercises here the day before we attacked. They had been scheduled to go back to their barracks D Day morning, but when scouts told them about the big fleet on the way in, they decided to stay and give us a good time. They did." It wasn't until a week later, in London, that I found out that because of this untoward circumstance our beach and those on either side of it had been the toughest spots encountered in the landings, and that the losses there had not been at all typical of the operation.

I was delighted to discover Smith, the old chief petty officer, reclining in a nearby slit trench. He was looking very fit. He was forty-seven, and I had wondered how he would do in the scramble to the beach. He had not only made it but had gathered a large new repertory of anecdotes on the way. "A guy in front of me got it through the throat," Smitty said. "Another guy in front of me got it through the heart. I run on. I heard a shell coming and I threw myself face down. There was an Army colonel on one side of me, a Navy captain on the other. The shell hit. I was all right. I looked up and the captain and the colónel was gone, blown to pieces. I grabbed for my tommy gun, which I had dropped next to me. It had been twisted into a complete circle. I was disarmed, so I just laid there."

While I was listening to Smitty, Reardon, talking over a field telephone, had located the commander somewhere on top of the cliff, along the German trench system, which had been taken over by the amphibious engineers as billets. Watts and I decided to walk up and find him. We made our way along the face of the cliff, on a narrow path that led past clusters of slit trenches in which soldiers were sleeping, and got up to the crest at a point where some Negro soldiers had made their bivouac in a thicket. We followed another path through a tangled, scrubby wood. The Germans had left numbers of wooden skull-and-crossbones signs on the tree trunks. These signs said *"Achtung Minen"* and *"Attention aux Mines."* Whether they indicated that we had taken the enemy by surprise and that he had not had time to remove the signs put up for the protection of his own and civilian personnel, or whether the signs were put there for psychological purposes, like dummy guns, was a question for the engineers to determine. Watts and I took care to stay in the path.

We found the commander, who was in good form. He said that he had lost only a couple of the forty-five beach-battalion men who had been on the landing craft with us but that in the battalion as a whole the casualties had been fairly heavy. "Not nearly what I thought they would be when I left that boat, though," he said.

The trench system was a fine monument to the infantrymen of the First Division who had taken it. I couldn't help thinking, as I looked it over, that the German soldiers of 1939–41 would not have been driven from it in one day, even by heroes, and the thought encouraged me. Maybe they were beginning to understand that they were beaten. There were no indications that the position had been under artillery fire and I could see only one trace of the use of a flamethrower. As I reconstructed the action, our fellows must have climbed the hill and outflanked the position, and the Germans, rather than fight it out in their holes, had cleared out to avoid being cut off. They had probably stayed in and continued firing just as long as they still had a chance to kill without taking losses. As the French say, they had not insisted. The trenches were deep, narrow, and so convoluted that an attacking force at any point could be fired on from several directions. Important knots in the system, like the command post and mortar emplacements, were of concrete. The command post was sunk at least twenty-five feet into the ground and was faced with brick on the inside. The garrison had slept in underground bombproofs, with timbered ceilings and wooden floors. In one of them, probably the officers' quarters, there was rustic furniture, a magnificent French radio, and flowers, still fresh, in vases. On the walls were cheap French prints of the innocuous sort one used to see in speakeasies: the little boy and the little girl, and the coyly equivocal captions.

An engineer sergeant who showed us through the place said that the Americans had found hairnets and hairpins in this bombproof. I could imagine an *Oberstleutnant* and his mistress, perhaps the daughter of a French collaborationist, living uneventfully here and waiting for something in which the *Oberstleutnant* had unconsciously ceased to believe, something that he wished so strongly would never happen that he had convinced himself it would happen, if anywhere, on some distant part of the coast. I thought of the Frenchmen I had known in 1939, waiting in a similar mood in the Maginot Line. The sergeant, a straight-featured Jewish fellow in his late thirties, said, "Those infantrymen were like angels. I tell you, I laid there on the beach and prayed for them while they went up that hill with nothing—with bayonets and hand grenades. They did it with nothing. It was a miracle." That made me feel good, because the infantry regiment involved had long been my favorite outfit. The commander was sardonic about one thing. "You remember how I used to worry about how my men would fall into bomb holes and drown on the way in because the Air Forces had laid down such a terrific bombardment?" he asked. "Well, I defy you to find one bomb hole on this whole beach for a mile each way."

The commander and Watts accompanied me back to the shore. On the way, we stopped at a field hospital that had been set up under canvas. There I talked to some Italian prisoners who were digging shelter trenches. They were fine, rugged specimens, as they should have been, because since the Italian surrender they had undoubtedly had plenty of exercise swinging pickaxes for the Todt organization. Their regiment of bridge-building engineers had been disarmed by the Germans in Greece and the men had been given the choice of enrolling in Fascist combat units or in labor service, they told me. They had all chosen labor service.

They seemed to expect to be commended for their choice. They had built many of the trenches in the district. "We wouldn't fight for Hitler," they assured me. I thought that the point had been pretty well proved. Now they were digging for us. They said that all Germans were cowards.

We went down to the shore, and the commander, who, being beach-master, was in charge of all traffic alongshore, hailed a Duck for me. The Duck put me on an LCVP, which took me back to my ship. On the way out, I realized that I had not seen a single French civilian the entire time ashore.

When I came aboard our landing craft, Long, the engineering officer, grinned at me.

"Did you notice a slight list, sometimes on one side, sometimes on the other, the last two days?" he asked.

I said, "You mean the one you said must be on account of the crew's all turning over in their sleep at the same time?"

"Yes," he said. "Well, today we found an open seam down in the stern. She started to list that night the big bomb dropped next to us, but you were sleeping too sound to get up. So maybe we'll go back to port. She has no ramps, the forward anchor winch is sheered in half, and she may as well go into the yard for a couple of days."

The morning of D-plus-four, Rigg signaled the command ship for permission to put back to Britain. As soon as the signalman blinked out the message, every man on board knew there was a chance we would go back, and even fellows who had expressed a low opinion of the British port at which our flotilla had been stationed looked extremely happy. While we were waiting for an answer to our request, an LCIL that acted as a group leader, a kind of straw boss among the little ships, passed near us, and the lieutenant on her bridge ordered us over to help tow a barge of ammunition. We were to be paired with another LCIL on this job. The barge, a two-hundred-and-fifty-tonner, was loaded with TNT, and the idea was for one LCIL to make fast on each side of her and shove her in to shore. The Diesel motors of an LCIL, although they can move their craft along at a fair speed, haven't the towing power of a tug. The two LCILs bounced about in the choppy sea for quite a while as we tried to get towing lines aboard the big barge that would hold. Even after we finally got started, every now and then the lines would snap; and we would bounce against the side of the barge, as we put more lines aboard her, with a crash that disquieted us, even though we had been told many times that the explosive was packed so carefully that no jouncing would possibly set it off. We were very happy when the barge grounded on the beach according to plan and we could cast off and leave her. Just before we had finished, the group leader came along again and an officer on her bridge shouted over to us through a megaphone, "Report to control-ship shuttle service!" This meant that we were going back to Britain; control ships organize cross-Channel convoys. We were not sorry to go.

By Sunday, D-plus-five, when we at last got started, the water had smoothed out so much that the Channel was like the Hyde Park Serpentine. The flat-bottomed LCIL will bounce about in the slightest sea, but today our craft moved along like a swanboat. The water was full of ration cartons, life jackets, and shell cases, and on the way over we picked up one corpse, of a soldier wearing a life jacket, which indicated that he had never got ashore. Since German planes were dropping mines every night, the lookout was instructed to keep a sharp watch for suspicious objects in the water, and this was almost the only thing it was necessary to think about as we loafed along. A seaman from Florida named Hurwitz was lookout on the bow in the early morning. "Suspicious object off port bow!" he would bawl, and then, "Suspicious object off starboard quarter!" Most of the suspicious objects turned out to be shell cases. Finally, Hurwitz yelled, "Bridge! The water is just full of suspicious objects!"

The main interest aboard now was whether we would get to port before the pubs closed, at ten o'clock in the evening. Long was getting unheard-of speed out of his motors and it seemed that we would make the pubs easily. Then we happened upon a British LCT that was all alone and was having engine trouble. She asked us to stand by in case her motors conked out altogether. We proceeded at four knots. When the British skipper signaled to us, "Doing my utmost, can make no more," which meant that our chance of beer had gone glimmering, Rigg made a gesture that for delicacy and regard for international relations must have few parallels in navy history. He ordered a signal that may someday be in schoolbooks along with Nelson's "England expects every man to do his duty." "Never mind," he signaled the crippled LCT. "We would have been too late for pub-closing time anyway."

# JOHN KEEGAN

---

THE MILITARY HISTORIAN John Keegan has written
*Six Armies in Normandy,* a classic account.

---

■

## FROM *Six Armies in Normandy*

### DESCENT

The static line of the American T-5 parachute, a broad webbing
strap hooked at one end to the anchor cable in the aircraft, tied at the
other to the top of the parachute canopy, was fifteen feet long. As the
parachutist emerged from the cabin of the DC-3, throwing himself outward towards the port wing with a pull of his hands on the edges of the
doorway, he was flicked by the slipstream—a combination of the propeller wash and the wind of the plane's own forward movement—to the
static line's end. The resulting tug ripped the cover off the pack tray,
exposing the canopy of the parachute which it began to pull free by a
thinner cord attached to the canopy's apex. At the same time the jumper's body, acting under the force of gravity, began to leave the slipstream
and fall earthward. In the opening sequence of the British X parachute,
under which the 6th Airborne Division's soldiers had just landed at the
other end of the bridgehead, this separation of jumper and canopy occurred at relatively low velocity, since the static line deployed the rigging
lines, twenty-two feet long, joining canopy and jumper's harness so that
he was at rest, relative to the canopy itself, when it began to deploy. With
the T-5, however, separation of canopy and jumper was dynamic, the
canopy itself pulling the rigging lines from his pack tray, and the resulting moment of arrest, as deploying canopy and falling body worked
against each other through the rigging lines, could be extremely severe.
Known as the "opening shock," and dreaded by all, it exerted a force of
up to five G on the human body and threatened to injure it if the harness
were not properly adjusted. As its apogee, it broke the tie at the end of
the static line and released parachutist and canopy to fall to earth together.

The sequence took three seconds and the descent, from seven
hundred feet, about forty. Burgett, who landed just north of St. Martin-
de-Varreville, gives a vivid account of his experience:

> Doubled up and grasping my reserve chute, I could feel the rush of
> air, hear the crackling of the canopy as it unfurled, followed by the

sizzling rigging lines, then the connector links whistling past the back of my helmet. Instinctively the muscles of my body tensed for the opening shock, which nearly unjointed me when the canopy blasted open. I pulled the risers apart to check the canopy and saw tracer bullets passing through it; at the same moment I hit the ground and came in backwards so hard I was momentarily stunned . . . The sky was lit up like the Fourth of July. I lay there for a moment and gazed at the spectacle. It was awe-inspiring. But I couldn't help wondering at the same time if I had got the opening shock first or hit the ground first; they were mighty close together.

Colonel Vandevoort, dropped by a flak-wary pilot at far above jumping speed, reported that "the opening shock popped lights in the back of your eye-balls and tore off musette bags, field glasses and anything else that wasn't tied down securely." Lieutenant Elmer Brandenberger, of the 1st Battalion, 502nd, was cradling a rifle in his arms. "The opening shock tore it from my grasp. I can still remember the thought flashing through my mind that it would hit some damned Kraut and bash in his head." Private Sherwood Trotter, of the 1st/506th, lost a '30 machine-gun to opening shock and Lieutenant Robert Matthews, of the 377th Parachute Artillery, was knocked out. "When I got that tremendous opening shock, my chin snapped down on my binocular case and out I went. Came to just off the ground and was knocked out again when I hit."

Some of the jumpers suffered more serious wounds in the air, though few of these were the result of aimed shots. Despite the moonlight, the falling parachutes showed up poorly against the sky and only in two places, at Angoville-au-Plain, where the Germans deliberately set fire to a house, and at Ste Mère-Eglise, where a building was ignited by the Allied preparatory bombing, did the Germans see well enough from the ground to pick off individuals. One of these was Colonel Wolverton. But there was a great deal of loose metal criss-crossing the parachutists' airspace, and some of it found a billet. Private Guerdon Walthall "saw tracer go through the fellow below me and I really started sweating about getting hit before I reached the ground," but he did so unharmed. Captain Felix Adams, medical officer of the 377th Artillery, was hit on the helmet ("good old helmet") by a piece of flak and landed unconscious, and another medical officer, Captain Hugh Caumartin, of the 2nd/506th, was hit twice, "once on the nose—and I worried about what my wife would think when I returned without a nose" and then in the leg. He landed on his unwounded leg near St Martin-de-Varreville, in a field lined with German machine-guns which sent "streams of tracer in cross fire only a few feet over my head . . . Others were dropping into the same field and they were being hit and hurt." After dosing himself with his own morphia, he disregarded his wounds, crawled off to a hedge and set up his aid post.

## LANDING

Medicine could do nothing for those injured in the way parachutists feared most—by landing with a malfunctioning or unfurled parachute. Malfunctions are always rare with a static-line parachute and, because the Americans carried a reserve (which the British then did not), even more rarely fatal. There are no surviving reports of fatal malfunctions from the 82nd or 101st on June 6th (though one gloriously unlucky private managed to open his reserve in his DC-3 as it approached the dropping zone, filling the cabin with billowing silk and driving his stick companions to flights of blasphemy unequaled even by the drill sergeants at Fort Benning). But a considerable number reported being dropped so low that their parachute scarcely had time to deploy or of seeing others whose canopies had not deployed at all. Burgett at St Martin-de-Varreville saw a DC-3, coming in low and diagonally across the field where he was struggling to unbuckle his harness, disgorge a stick of "vague, shadowy figures . . . Their chutes were pulling out of the pack trays and just starting to unfurl when they hit the ground. Seventeen men hit the ground before their chutes had time to open. They made a sound like large ripe pumpkins being thrown down to burst against the ground."

Some sticks fell to their deaths because their pilots gave them the green light when they had already crossed the east coast of the Cotentin, though at least one dropped close enough to the beach for most men in it to struggle ashore and hit a track through minefields and German strongpoints to dry ground—as hard a way of invading Europe as anyone found that day. Many who landed on the Cotentin drowned all the same, for the floods of the Douve and the Merderet, undetected on the aerial photographs and invisible from the flight path, stood two and three feet deep among the reeds and ripe hay of the water meadows. A man making the regulation sideways roll on landing finished beneath the surface and, if he could not free himself on one lungful of air from his imprisoning harness, breathed water and died. Private James Blue, an All American, just escaped that fate. A North Carolina farm-boy, he was strong as well as fit, had the good luck to find hard ground under the flood and managed to struggle to his feet. "Before he found his balance, his parachute dragged him over backwards and he went under again, weighed down by his equipment, fumbling at the buckles of his harness . . . he was half dead when he got clear, sick from the water he had swallowed and trembling from the shock."

All along the valleys of the two little rivers, other parachutists were fighting their own little battles with the unexpected enemy. Corporal Francis Chapman, of C Battery, 377th Artillery, "landed in water about five feet deep. Managed to stand up after a bit of swimming. Reached down, got my jump knife from the boot top and slashed my harness, cutting right through my jump jacket in the process. I managed to wade towards shallow water." Father Francis Sampson, Catholic chaplain of the 506th Infantry, landed in water over his head, cut free his equipment and was then dragged by his parachute to a shallow patch. He took ten minutes to free himself from his harness, crawled back exhausted to where he had touched first and, after five or six dives, recovered his Mass equipment. As he did so, he saw first one and then two other aircraft crash in flames near by, and offered prayers for the repose of the souls of the men within. Hugh Pritchard, a radio operator with a set in his leg bag, fell into water with 140 lbs of equipment securely fastened to his body and a back injured by "opening shock," lost his knife as he struggled to cut his way to the surface and was reprieved at his last gasp when his parachute collapsed and ceased to drag him along the bottom. "The terror of that first night," he recalled in 1967, "remains so vivid even today that sometimes I wake up in a cold sweat and nearly jump out of bed."

# JOHN HERSEY

THE JUNE 17, 1944, edition of *The New Yorker* carried this story of Lieutenant John F. Kennedy, the commander of a PT boat in the Pacific, and his survival. John Hersey heard it from Kennedy and at his suggestion interviewed three men on the boat for this piece.

■

## Survival

Our men in the South Pacific fight nature, when they are pitted against her, with a greater fierceness than they could ever expend on a human enemy. Lieutenant John F. Kennedy, the ex-Ambassador's son and lately a PT skipper in the Solomons, came through town the other day and told me the story of his survival in the South Pacific. I asked Kennedy if I might write the story down. He asked me if I wouldn't talk first with some of his crew, so I went up to the Motor Torpedo Boat Training Center at Melville, Rhode Island, and there, under the curving iron of a Quonset hut, three enlisted men named Johnston, McMahon, and McGuire filled in the gaps.

It seems that Kennedy's PT, the 109, was out one night with a squadron patroling Blackett Strait, in mid-Solomons. Blackett Strait is a patch of water bounded on the northeast by the volcano called Kolombangara, on the west by the island of Vella Lavella, on the south by the island of Gizo and a string of coral-fringed islets, and on the east by the bulk of New Georgia. The boats were working about forty miles away from their base on the island of Rendova, on the south side of New Georgia. They had entered Blackett Strait, as was their habit, through Ferguson Passage, between the coral islets and New Georgia.

The night was a starless black and Japanese destroyers were around. It was about two-thirty. The 109, with three officers and ten enlisted men aboard, was leading three boats on a sweep for a target. An officer named George Ross was up on the bow, magnifying the void with binoculars. Kennedy was at the wheel and he saw Ross turn and point into the darkness. The man in the forward machine-gun turret shouted, "Ship at two o'clock!" Kennedy saw a shape and spun the wheel to turn for an attack, but the 109 answered sluggishly. She was running slowly on only one of her three engines, so as to make a minimum wake and avoid detection from the air. The shape became a Japanese destroyer, cutting through the night at forty knots and heading straight for the 109. The thirteen men on the PT hardly had time to brace themselves. Those who saw the Japanese ship coming were paralyzed by fear in a curious way: they could move their hands but not their feet. Kennedy whirled the wheel to the left, but again the 109 did not respond. Ross went through the gallant but futile motions of slamming a shell into the breach of the 37-millimeter anti-tank gun which had been temporarily mounted that very day, wheels and all, on the foredeck. The urge to bolt and dive over the side was terribly strong, but still no one was able to move; all hands froze to their battle stations. Then the Japanese crashed into the 109 and cut her right in two. The sharp enemy forefoot struck the PT on the starboard side about fifteen feet from the bow and crunched diagonally across with a racking noise. The PT's wooden hull hardly even delayed the destroyer. Kennedy was thrown hard to the left in the cockpit, and he thought, "This is how it feels to be killed." In a moment he found himself on his back on the deck, looking up at the destroyer as it passed through his boat. There was another loud noise and a huge flash of yellow-red light, and the destroyer glowed. Its peculiar, raked, inverted-Y stack stood out in the brilliant light and, later, in Kennedy's memory.

There was only one man below decks at the moment of collision. That was McMahon, engineer. He had no idea what was up. He was just reaching forward to slam the starboard engine into gear when a ship came into his engine room. He was lifted from the narrow passage between two of the engines and thrown painfully against the starboard bulkhead aft of the boat's auxiliary generator. He landed in a sitting position. A tremendous burst of flame came back at him from the day room, where some of the gas tanks were. He put his hands over his face, drew his legs up tight, and waited to die. But he felt water hit him after the fire, and he was sucked far downward as his half of the PT sank. He began to struggle upward through the water. He had held his breath since the impact, so his lungs were tight and they hurt. He looked up through the water. Over his head he saw a yellow glow—gasoline burning on the water. He broke the surface and was in fire again. He splashed hard to keep a little island of water around him.

Johnston, another engineer, had been asleep on deck when the collision came. It lifted him and dropped him overboard. He saw the flame and the destroyer for a moment. Then a huge propellor pounded by near him and the awful turbulence of the destroyer's wake took him down, turned him over and over, held him down, shook him, and drubbed on his ribs. He hung on and came up in water that was like a river rapids. The next day his body turned black and blue from the beating.

Kennedy's half of the PT stayed afloat. The bulkheads were sealed, so the undamaged watertight compartments up forward kept the half hull floating. The destroyer rushed off into the dark. There was an awful quiet: only the sound of gasoline burning.

Kennedy shouted, "Who's aboard?"

Feeble answers came from three of the enlisted men, McGuire, Mauer, and Albert; and from one of the officers, Thom.

Kennedy saw the fire only ten feet from the boat. He thought it might reach her and explode the remaining gas tanks, so he shouted, "Over the side!"

The five men slid into the water. But the wake of the destroyer swept the fire away from the PT, so after a few minutes, Kennedy and the others crawled back aboard. Kennedy shouted for survivors in the water. One by one they answered: Ross, the third officer; Harris, McMahon, Johnston, Zinsser, Starkey, enlisted men. Two did not answer: Kirksey and Marney, enlisted men. Since the last bombing at base, Kirksey had been sure he would die. He had huddled at his battle station by the fantail gun, with his kapok life jacket tied tight up to his cheeks. No one knows what happened to him or to Marney.

Harris shouted from the darkness, "Mr. Kennedy! Mr. Kennedy! McMahon is badly hurt." Kennedy took his shoes, his shirt, and his sidearms off, told Mauer to blink a light so that the men in the water would know where the half hull was, then dived in and swam toward the voice. The survivors were widely scattered. McMahon and Harris were a hundred yards away.

When Kennedy reached McMahon, he asked, "How are you, Mac?"

McMahon said, "I'm all right. I'm kind of burnt."

Kennedy shouted out, "How are the others?"

Harris said softly, "I hurt my leg."

Kennedy, who had been on the Harvard swimming team five years before, took McMahon in tow and headed for the PT. A gentle breeze kept blowing the boat away from the swimmers. It took forty-five minutes to make what had been an easy hundred yards. On the way in, Harris said, "I can't go any farther." Kennedy, of the Boston Kennedys, said to Harris, of the same home town, "For a guy from Boston, you're certainly putting up a great exhibition out here, Harris." Harris made it all right and didn't complain any more. Then Kennedy swam from man to man, to see how they were doing. All who had survived the crash were able to stay afloat, since they were wearing life preservers—kapok jackets shaped like overstuffed vests, aviators' yellow Mae Wests, or air-filled belts like small inner tubes. But those who couldn't swim had to be towed back to the wreckage by those who could. One of the men screamed for help. When Ross reached him, he found that the screaming man had two life jackets on. Johnston was treading water in a film of gasoline which did not catch fire. The fumes filled his lungs and he fainted. Thom towed him in. The others got in under their own power. It was now after 5 a.m., but still dark. It had taken nearly three hours to get everyone aboard.

The men stretched out on the tilted deck of the PT. Johnston,

McMahon, and Ross collapsed into sleep. The men talked about how wonderful it was to be alive and speculated on when the other PTs would come back to rescue them. Mauer kept blinking the light to point their way. But the other boats had no idea of coming back. They had seen a collision, a sheet of flame, and a slow burning on the water. When the skipper of one of the boats saw the sight, he put his hands over his face and sobbed, "My God! My God!" He and the others turned away. Back at the base, after a couple of days, the squadron held services for the souls of the thirteen men, and one of the officers wrote his mother, "George Ross lost his life for a cause that he believed in stronger than any one of us, because he was an idealist in the purest sense. Jack Kennedy, the Ambassador's son, was on the same boat and also lost his life. The man that said the cream of a nation is lost in war can never be accused of making an overstatement of a very cruel fact. . . ."

When day broke, the men on the remains of the 109 stirred and looked around. To the northeast, three miles off, they saw the monumental cone of Kolombangara; there, the men knew, ten thousand Japanese swarmed. To the west, five miles away, they saw Vella Lavella; more Japs. To the south, only a mile or so away, they actually could see a Japanese camp on Gizo. Kennedy ordered his men to keep as low as possible, so that no moving silhouettes would show against the sky. The listing hulk was gurgling and gradually settling. Kennedy said, "What do you want to do if the Japs come out? Fight or surrender?" One said, "Fight with what?" So they took an inventory of their armament. The 37-millimeter gun had flopped over the side and was hanging there by a chain. They had one tommy gun, six 45-caliber automatics, and one .38. Not much.

"Well," Kennedy said, "what do you want to do?"

One said, "Anything you say, Mr. Kennedy. You're the boss."

Kennedy said, "There's nothing in the book about a situation like this. Seems to me we're not a military organization any more. Let's just talk this over."

They talked it over, and pretty soon they argued, and Kennedy could see that they would never survive in anarchy. So he took command again.

It was vital that McMahon and Johnston should have room to lie down. McMahon's face, neck, hands, wrists, and feet were horribly burned. Johnston was pale and he coughed continually. There was scarcely space for everyone, so Kennedy ordered the other men into the water to make room, and went in himself. All morning they clung to the hulk and talked about how incredible it was that no one had come to rescue them. All morning they watched for the plane which they thought would be looking for them. They cursed war in general and PTs in particular. At about ten o'clock the hulk heaved a moist sigh and turned turtle. McMahon and Johnston had to hang on as best they could. It was clear that the remains of the 109 would soon sink. When the sun had passed the meridian, Kennedy said, "We will swim to that small island," pointing to one of a group three miles to the southeast. "We have less chance of making it than some of these other islands here, but there'll be less chance of Japs, too." Those who could not swim well grouped themselves around a long two-by-six timber with which carpenters had braced the 37-millimeter cannon on deck and which had been knocked overboard by the force of the collision. They tied several pairs of shoes to the timber, as well as the ship's lantern, wrapped in a life jacket to keep it afloat. Thom took charge of this unwieldy group. Kennedy took McMahon in tow again. He cut loose one end of a long strap on Mc-Mahon's Mae West and took the end in his teeth. He swam breast stroke, pulling the helpless McMahon along on his back. It took over five hours to reach the island. Water lapped into Kennedy's mouth through his clenched teeth, and he swallowed a lot. The salt water cut into Mc-Mahon's awful burns, but he did not complain. Every few minutes, when Kennedy stopped to rest, taking the strap out of his mouth and holding it in his hand, McMahon would simply say, "How far do we have to go?"

Kennedy would reply, "We're going good." Then he would ask, "How do you feel, Mac?"

McMahon always answered, "I'm O.K., Mr. Kennedy. How about you?"

In spite of his burden, Kennedy beat the other men to the reef that surrounded the island. He left McMahon on the reef and told him to keep low, so as not to be spotted by Japs. Kennedy went ahead and explored the island. It was only a hundred yards in diameter; coconuts on the trees but none on the ground; no visible Japs. Just as the others reached the island, one of them spotted a Japanese barge chugging along close to shore. They all lay low. The barge went on. Johnston, who was very pale and weak and who was still coughing a lot, said, "They wouldn't come here. What'd they be walking around here for? It's too small." Kennedy lay in some bushes, exhausted by his effort, his stomach heavy with the water he had swallowed. He had been in the sea, except for short intervals on the hulk, for fifteen and a half hours. Now he started thinking. Every night for several nights the PTs had cut through Ferguson Passage on their way to action. Ferguson Passage was just beyond the next little island. Maybe . . .

He stood up. He took one of the pairs of shoes. He put one of the rubber life belts around his waist. He hung the .38 around his neck on a lanyard. He took his pants off. He picked up the ship's lantern, a heavy battery affair ten inches by ten inches, still wrapped in the kapok jacket. He said, "If I find a boat, I'll flash the lantern twice. The password will be 'Roger,' the answer will be 'Wilco.'" He walked toward the water. After fifteen paces he was dizzy, but in the water he felt all right.

It was early evening. It took half an hour to swim to the reef around the next island. Just as he planted his feet on the reef, which lay about four feet under the surface, he saw the shape of a very big fish in the clear water. Kennedy remembered what one of his men had said a few days before, "These barracuda will come up under a swimming man and eat his testicles." He had many occasions to think of that remark in the next few hours.

Now it was dark. Kennedy blundered along the uneven reef in water up to his waist. Sometimes he would reach forward with his leg and cut one of his shins or ankles on sharp coral. Other times he would step forward onto emptiness. He made his way like a slow-motion drunk, hugging the lantern. At about nine o'clock he came to the end of the reef, alongside Ferguson Passage. He took his shoes off and tied them to the life jacket, then struck out into open water. He swam about an hour, until he felt he was far enough out to intercept the PTs. Treading water, he listened for the muffled roar of motors, getting chilled, waiting, holding the lamp. Once he looked west and saw flares and the false gaiety of an action. The lights were far beyond the little island, even beyond Gizo, ten miles away. Kennedy realized that the PT boats had chosen, for the first night in many, to go around Gizo instead of through Ferguson Passage. There was no hope. He started back. He made the same painful promenade of the reef and struck out for the tiny island where his friends were. But this swim was different. He was very tired and now the current was running fast, carrying him to the right. He saw that he could not make the island, so he flashed the light once and shouted "Roger! Roger!" to identify himself.

On the beach the men were hopefully vigilant. They saw the light and heard the shouts. They were very happy, because they thought that Kennedy had found a PT. They walked out onto the reef, sometimes up to their waists in water, and waited. It was very painful for those who had no shoes. The men shouted, but not much, because they were afraid of Japanese.

One said, "There's another flash."

A few minutes later a second said, "There's a light over there."

A third said, "We're seeing things in this dark."

They waited a long time, but they saw nothing except phosphorescence and heard nothing but the sound of waves. They went back, very discouraged.

One said despairingly, "We're going to die."

Johnston said, "Aw, shut up. You can't die. Only the good die young."

Kennedy had drifted right by the little island. He thought he had never known such deep trouble, but something he did shows that unconsciously he had not given up hope. He dropped his shoes, but he held onto the heavy lantern, his symbol of contact with his fellows. He stopped trying to swim. He seemed to stop caring. His body drifted through the wet hours, and he was very cold. His mind was a jumble. A few hours before, he had wanted desperately to get to the base at Rendova. Now he only wanted to get back to the little island he had left that night, but he didn't try to get there; he just wanted to. His mind seemed to float away from his body. Darkness and time took the place of a mind in his skull. For a long time he slept, or was crazy, or floated in a chill trance.

The currents of the Solomon Islands are queer. The tides shoves and sucks through the islands and makes the currents curl in odd patterns. It was a fateful pattern into which Jack Kennedy drifted. He drifted in it all night. His mind was blank, but his fist was tightly clenched on the kapok around the lantern. The current moved in a huge circle—west past Gizo, then north and east past Kolombangara, then south into Ferguson Passage. Early in the morning the sky turned from black to gray, and so did Kennedy's mind. Light came to both at about six. Kennedy looked around and saw that he was exactly where he had been the night before when he saw the flares beyond Gizo. For a second time, he started home. He thought for a while that he had lost his mind and that he only imagined that he was repeating his attempt to reach the island. But the chill of the water was real enough, the lantern was real, his progress was measurable. He made the reef, crossed the lagoon, and got to the first island. He lay on the beach awhile. He found that his lantern did not work any more, so he left it and started back to the next island, where his men were. This time the trip along the reef was awful. He had discarded his shoes, and every step on the coral was painful. This time the swim across the gap where the current had caught him the night before seemed endless. But the current had changed; he made the island. He crawled up on the beach. He was vomiting when his men came up to him. He said, "Ross, you try it tonight." Then he passed out.

Ross, seeing Kennedy so sick, did not look forward to the execution of the order. He distracted himself by complaining about his hunger. There were a few coconuts on the trees, but the men were too weak to climb up for them. One of the men thought of sea food, stirred his tired body, and found a snail on the beach. He said, "If we were desperate, we could eat these." Ross said, "Desperate, hell. Give me that. I'll eat that." He took it in his hand and looked at it. The snail put its head out and looked at him. Ross was startled, but he shelled the snail and ate it, making faces because it was bitter.

In the afternoon, Ross swam across to the next island. He took a pistol to signal with, and he spent the night watching Ferguson Passage from the reef around the island. Nothing came through. Kennedy slept badly that night; he was cold and sick.

■

The next morning everyone felt wretched. Planes that the men were unable to identify flew overhead and there were dogfights. That meant Japs as well as friends, so the men dragged themselves into the bushes and lay low. Some prayed. Johnston said, "You guys make me sore. You didn't spend ten cents in church in ten years, then all of a sudden you're in trouble and you see the light." Kennedy felt a little better now. When Ross came back, Kennedy decided that the group should move to another, larger island to the southeast, where there seemed to be more coconut trees and where the party would be nearer Ferguson Passage. Again Kennedy took McMahon in tow with the strap in his teeth, and the nine others grouped themselves around the timber.

This swim took three hours. The nine around the timber were caught by the current and barely made the far tip of the island. Kennedy found walking the quarter mile across to them much harder than the three-hour swim. The cuts on his bare feet were festered and looked like small balloons. The men were suffering most from thirst, and they broke open some coconuts lying on the ground and avidly drank the milk. Kennedy and McMahon, the first to drink, were sickened, and Thom told the others to drink sparingly. In the middle of the night it rained, and someone suggested moving into the underbrush and licking water off the leaves. Ross and McMahon kept contact at first by touching feet as they licked. Somehow they got separated, and, being uncertain whether there were any Japs on the island, they became frightened. McMahon, trying to make his way back to the beach, bumped into someone and froze. It turned out to be Johnston, licking leaves on his own. In the morning the group saw that all the leaves were covered with droppings. Bitterly, they named the place Bird Island.

On this fourth day, the men were low. Even Johnston was low. He had changed his mind about praying. McGuire had a rosary around his neck, and Johnston said, "McGuire, give that necklace a working over." McGuire said quietly, "Yes, I'll take care of all you fellows." Kennedy was still unwilling to admit that things were hopeless. He asked Ross if he would swim with him to an island called Nauru, to the southeast and even nearer Ferguson Passage. They were very weak indeed by now, but after an hour's swim they made it.

They walked painfully across Nauru to the Ferguson Passage side, where they saw a Japanese barge aground on the reef. There were two men by the barge—possibly Japs. They apparently spotted Kennedy and Ross, for they got into a dugout canoe and hurriedly paddled to the other side of the island. Kennedy and Ross moved up the beach. They came upon an unopened rope-bound box and, back in the trees, a little shelter containing a keg of water, a Japanese gas mask, and a crude wooden fetish shaped like a fish. There were Japanese hardtack and candy in the box and the two had a wary feast. Down by the water they found a one-man canoe. They hid from imagined Japs all day. When night fell, Kennedy left Ross and took the canoe, with some hardtack and a can of water from the keg, out into Ferguson Passage. But no PTs came, so he paddled to Bird Island. The men there told him that the two men he had spotted by the barge that morning were natives, who had paddled to Bird Island. The natives had said that there were Japs on Nauru and the men had given Kennedy and Ross up for lost. Then the natives had gone away. Kennedy gave out small rations of crackers and water, and the men went to sleep. During the night, one man, who kept himself awake until the rest were asleep, drank all the water in the can Kennedy had brought back. In the morning the others figured out that he was the guilty one. They swore at him and found it hard to forgive him.

Before dawn, Kennedy started out in the canoe to rejoin Ross on Nauru, but when day broke a wind arose and the canoe was swamped. Some natives appeared from nowhere in a canoe, rescued Kennedy, and took him to Nauru. There they showed him where a two-man canoe was cached. Kennedy picked up a coconut with a smooth shell and scratched a message on it with a jackknife: "ELEVEN ALIVE NATIVE KNOWS POSIT AND REEFS NAURU ISLAND KENNEDY." Then he said to the natives, "Rendova, Rendova."

One of the natives seemed to understand. They took the coconut and paddled off.

Ross and Kennedy lay in a sickly daze all day. Toward evening it rained and they crawled under a bush. When it got dark, conscience took hold of Kennedy and he persuaded Ross to go out into Ferguson Passage with him in the two-man canoe. Ross argued against it. Kennedy insisted. The two started out in the canoe. They had shaped paddles from the boards of the Japanese box, and they took a coconut shell to bail with. As they got out into the Passage, the wind rose again and the water became choppy. The canoe began to fill. Ross bailed and Kennedy kept the bow into the wind. The waves grew until they were five or six feet high. Kennedy shouted, "Better turn around and go back!" As soon as the canoe was broadside to the waves, the water poured in and the dugout was swamped. The two clung to it, Kennedy at the bow, Ross at the stern. The tide carried them southward toward the open sea, so they kicked and tugged the canoe, aiming northwest. They struggled that way for two hours, not knowing whether they would hit the small island or drift into the endless open.

The weather got worse; rain poured down and they couldn't see more than ten feet. Kennedy shouted, "Sorry I got you out here, Barney!" Ross shouted back, "This would be a great time to say I told you so, but I won't!"

Soon the two could see a white line ahead and could hear a frightening roar—waves crashing on a reef. They had got out of the tidal current and were approaching the island all right, but now they realized that the wind and the waves were carrying them toward the reef. But it was too late to do anything, now that their canoe was swamped, except hang on and wait.

When they were near the reef, a wave broke Kennedy's hold, ripped him away from the canoe, turned him head over heels, and spun him in a violent rush. His ears roared and his eyes pinwheeled, and for the third time since the collision he thought he was dying. Somehow he was not thrown against the coral but floated into a kind of eddy. Suddenly he felt the reef under his feet. Steadying himself so that he would not be swept off it, he shouted, "Barney!" There was no reply. Kennedy thought of how he had insisted on going out in the canoe, and he screamed, "Barney!" This time Ross answered. He, too, had been thrown on the reef. He had not been as lucky as Kennedy; his right arm and shoulder had been cruelly lacerated by the coral, and his feet, which were already infected from earlier wounds, were cut some more.

The procession of Kennedy and Ross from reef to beach was a crazy one. Ross's feet hurt so much that Kennedy would hold one paddle on the bottom while Ross put a foot on it, then the other paddle forward for another step then the first paddle forward again, until they reached sand. They fell on the beach and slept.

Kennedy and Ross were wakened early in the morning by a noise. They looked up and saw four husky natives. One walked up to them and said in an excellent English accent, "I have a letter for you, sir." Kennedy tore the note open. It said, "On His Majesty's Service. To the Senior Officer, Nauru Island. I have just learned of your presence on Nauru Is. I am in command of a New Zealand infantry patrol operating in conjunction with U.S. Army troops on New Georgia. I strongly advise that you come with these natives to me. Meanwhile I shall be in radio communication with your authorities at Rendova, and we can finalize plans to collect balance of your party. Lt. Wincote. P.S. Will warn aviation of your crossing Ferguson Passage."

Everyone shook hands and the four natives took Ross and Kennedy in their war canoe across to Bird Island to tell the others the good news. There the natives broke out a spirit stove and cooked a feast of yams and C ration. Then they built a leanto for McMahon, whose burns had begun to rot and stink, and for Ross, whose arm had swelled to the size of a thigh because of the coral cuts. The natives put Kennedy in the bottom of their canoe and covered him with sacking and palm fronds, in case Japanese planes should buzz them. The long trip was fun for the natives. They stopped once to try to grab a turtle, and laughed at the sport they were having. Thirty Japanese planes went over low toward Rendova, and the natives waved and shouted gaily. They rowed with a strange rhythm, pounding paddles on the gunwales between strokes. At last they reached a censored place. Lieutenant Wincote came to the water's edge and said formally, "How do you do. Leftenant Wincote."

Kennedy said, "Hello. I'm Kennedy."

Wincote said, "Come up to my tent and have a cup of tea."

In the middle of the night, after several radio conversations between Wincote's outfit and the PT base, Kennedy sat in the war canoe waiting at an arranged rendezvous for a PT. The moon went down at eleven-twenty. Shortly afterward, Kennedy heard the signal he was waiting for —four shots. Kennedy fired four answering shots.

A voice shouted to him, "Hey, Jack!"

Kennedy said, "Where the hell you been?"

The voice said, "We got some food for you."

Kennedy said bitterly, "No, thanks, I just had a coconut."

A moment later a PT came alongside. Kennedy jumped onto it and hugged the men aboard—his friends. In the American tradition, Kennedy held under his arm a couple of souvenirs: one of the improvised paddles and the Japanese gas mask.

With the help of the natives, the PT made its way to Bird Island. A skiff went in and picked up the men. In the deep of the night, the PT and its happy cargo roared back toward base. The squadron medic had sent some brandy along to revive the weakened men. Johnston felt the need of a little revival. In fact, he felt he needed quite a bit of revival. After taking care of that, he retired topside and sat with his arms around a couple of roly-poly, mission-trained natives. And in the fresh breeze on the way home they sang together a hymn all three happened to know:

> Jesus loves me, this I know,
> For the Bible tells me so;
> Little ones to Him belong,
> They are weak, but He is strong.
> Yes, Jesus loves me; yes, Jesus loves me . . .

# HIROYUKI AGAWA

HIROYUKI AGAWA, a native of Hiroshima, graduated from Tokyo Imperial University in 1942 and then joined the Japanese navy, serving as an information officer in Taiwan. He won the Yomiuri Prize for his first novel, *Citadel in Spring,* from which I have taken this excerpt about the battle of the Marianas. In that battle, which the American Navy would later refer to as the Marianas Turkey Shoot, the Japanese lost three aircraft carriers and approximately four hundred carrier-based planes. Japanese gains were limited to one direct hit on the battleship *South Dakota,* one plane diving into the battleship *Indiana,* and 130 American aircraft shot down.

■

## FROM *Citadel in Spring*

Koji's friend Kuki, with the Mobile Fleet as it steamed northward through the Sulu Sea toward the battle zone in the western Pacific, was looking at the same message. His ship was the *Taiho,* flagship of both the First Mobile Fleet and the First Air Division. It was a new aircraft carrier which, unlike carriers converted from seaplane tenders or auxiliary carriers converted from merchantmen, had been designed from the keel up as an aircraft carrier. It had just been commissioned in March. Kuki had gone from Special Services in Tokyo to Kure, and had flown then to Singapore, where he reported to the *Taiho.* Its armor was thick and because there was little wasted space and few scuttles, the ship was hot and living quarters very cramped. Still, the wardroom and other common areas all had air-conditioning and fluorescent lighting, and the ship was fitted with the very latest that Japanese technology had to offer in radar, gyrocompasses, optical rangefinders, radios, anti-aircraft guns and the like. The First Air Division at this time was made up of three regular aircraft carriers: besides the *Taiho,* there was the *Zuikaku* and the *Shokaku.*

At the same time, 30 knots ahead, Yukio Ibuki stood on the flight deck of the aircraft carrier *Hiyo* in the Second Air Division and listened in the ranks at general formation as his captain read the statement initiating Battle Operation A. The Second Air Division consisted of three aircraft carriers, the *Junyo,* the flagship, the *Hiyo,* and the *Ryuho.* The *Ryuho* had been the submarine tender *Taigei* before it had been converted, and the auxiliary carriers *Junyo* and *Hiyo* had been, respectively, the *Kashihara-maru* and *Izumo-maru*, both with the Japan Mail Line.

The Third Air Division, the carriers *Chiyoda* (flagship), *Chitose*, and *Zuiho*—the first two converted seaplane tenders—was another thirty knots ahead. These three air divisions, in total a nine-carrier flotilla, were escorted in a ring defense by a large task force consisting of battleships, cruisers, and destroyers, and other ships, including the *Yamato*, the *Musashi*, the *Nagato*, and the *Kongo*. Thus the fleet flagship *Taiho* that Kuki was aboard was steaming at the end of a formation of ships strung out over a considerable distance. Commander Ezaki, who had been head of Special Services S Section, was aboard the *Zuiho* as executive officer. Just as Admiral Togo's victorious ships had done in the battle of the Japan Sea during the Russo-Japanese War, each vessel flew from its masthead the Z signal flag of combat. As for the aircraft on the nine carriers, there were Tenzan torpedo attack planes, Comet light bombers, and the Zero fighter, improved Model 52. Except for the Comets, though, the planes were now obsolete. Even the Zero, so feared at the time of the fierce fighting over Guadalcanal—and flown by superb pilots —was no longer a match for American aircraft because of its poor defensive capabilities and a reversal in the quality of pilots on the two sides. It was now dismissed as a "paper plane" or a "Zero lighter." The plane's glory days were epitomized by an often-told story of a message being sent in the clear to an advance command post that B-17s should avoid a particular area because Zeroes were there. And even in the case of the new Comet, the pilots had not achieved proficiency, so they were not able to fully exploit its capabilities.

While the *Taiho* was on maneuvers at its anchorage in the Singapore area, Comets stalled time and again thanks to the insufficient training of the pilots, and 50 lives were lost. The vast majority of the Naval Air Force's fine pilots flying at the onset of the war were now gone. The young, green pilots had been given an accelerated three-month training, and had been drilled in only one method of attack. Concern about this cast an ineffaceable unease over the warships steaming toward the decisive battle in the Marianas.

Kuki, aboard the *Taiho*, which had left its Lingga anchorage in April 1944 and put to sea for training, had seen countless young, ruddy-cheeked petty officers, fresh out of training, go to their deaths almost daily as the ship steamed back and forth across the equator for almost a month, until mid-May. The principal cause of the mishaps was underdeveloped flying skills. During landing practice the bridge presented a terrible psychological barrier for a pilot, who would, in his attempt to stay away from it, stall the bomber and plunge it into the sea. Once a plane was in the water it would sink as soon as the canopy was opened, taking its crew with it. Seeing all this with his own eyes, Kuki had become increasingly pessimistic, and wrote letters to Wada, Hirokawa, and Koji that were shot through with cynical comments on the utterly unfavorable progress of the war. He would stamp these personal communications with an official seal and enclose them with classified papers bound for Japan by air.

In mid-May all units, anticipating the battle, left their training areas and began to rendezvous off Tawi-Tawi Island, northeast of Borneo and southwest of Mindanao. Both Kuki's *Taiho* and Ibuki's *Hiyo* were part of this. There were five battleships, nine aircraft carriers, 13 cruisers, some 30 destroyers, many oilers and supply ships, practically all the ships left in the Japanese Imperial Navy. The waters off Tawi-Tawi were a bright and beautiful light blue, and Kuki, together with two fellow idlers from the junior officers' quarters, the paymaster and the medical officer, was constantly neglecting his duties to go to the bow of the ship to cool off and discuss the possibility of defeat and what that would mean. The bow was in the shade of the flight deck and provided a nice breeze, and when the carrier was sailing on maneuvers they could see silver flying fish flashing up out of the water before them and sailing over the waves like seagulls. The idlers enjoyed their inactivity, to which they gave the name "shade-bathing."

Immediately after the fleet had rendezvoused, however, enemy submarines began to swarm in Tawi-Tawi waters like schools of porpoises. Destroyers that went out to challenge them were themselves sunk, so exercises beyond where the carriers were anchored became impossible. Thus the carrier planes could not practice take-offs and landings. The half-trained flight crews futilely waited on standby, their level of proficiency dropping even more.

The U.S. Navy's Task Force 58 struck Saipan on June 11. The Japanese fleet off-loaded all inflammables from its ships, all hands drank to victory, and at 8 o'clock on the morning of the 13th set off from Tawi-Tawi, the whole of the Imperial Navy's surviving forces. That afternoon one of the three carrier-based bombers that had been out on anti-submarine patrol crashed on landing because of pilot error, coming in on top of the plane landing in front of it and bursting into flames. There were no injuries on the carrier itself, but since the bomber had been carrying bombs, they could not attempt to extinguish the fire because of the danger of explosion. All hands went below to wait for the fire to burn itself out, but this meant that five men and three officers perished in the flames. That evening the fleet temporarily dropped anchor in the channel northeast of Iloilo in the Philippines to take off the dead and take on provisions. Looking at the large, blue-black form of a nearby island, Kuki could not help but feel it was an omen of ill fortune.

As they were leaving the San Bernardino Channel the following day they could see a fire set by the natives on a headland on Samar Island. It appeared to be a signal to the American submarines, and, as if in response, a lookout on the *Taiho* reported sighting a periscope. Moments later Kuki's signal intelligence group in the First Mobile Fleet intercepted a transmission by what appeared to be the same sub of an O message, used for especially urgent tactical communication, in the BIMEC strip cipher employed by submarines. It was an extremely loud signal; the sub was apparently transmitting very close to the fleet, audaciously so. They could not break the cipher, but it seemed obvious the sub was reporting its discovery of the Japanese fleet. Kuki immediately notified the communications staff officers, but they were slow to take action and the Japanese side lost contact with the submarine. This was one of the immediate causes for the failure of Operation A.

An at-sea refueling was conducted on June 16. On the 18th the fleet arrived in the battle area, and in the afternoon information on at least part of the American task force became available, but since the sun was about to set, the attack was called off. Scout planes went out before dawn the next morning, the 19th, in several waves. These early sorties should have passed over the enemy task force, which was in the immediate area, but no sighting reports came back from them, and by the time the enemy's deployment became generally known, the sun had already risen. The initial attack, which should have begun at daybreak, thus suffered a delay of several hours. The American task force, centered on Saipan, was divided into several flotillas, each of which was virtually equivalent in firepower to the entire Japanese fleet. At seven o'clock the carriers turned their bows into the wind. By 8:30 the first wave of attacking planes had taken off from the *Taiho*. Preparations for sending off the second wave began immediately. But at that moment the last carrier-bomber in the first wave off the *Taiho* suddenly veered strangely, then abruptly dived into the sea, where it quickly sank beneath the waves. At almost the same instant a *Taiho* lookout spotted torpedo wakes 30 degrees off the starboard bow. The *Taiho* responded with a hard-over rudder, evading three torpedoes. One, however, struck the starboard bow. The bomber pilot had spotted the torpedo wakes as he took off and had tried to protect the carrier by crashing into the torpedoes, but had missed them.

Kuki was at his station, and felt a jolt, like a car riding up over a large rock. The *Taiho* did not catch fire, but the gas tanks at the bow ruptured, part of the flight deck was ripped up, planes in the second wave that were on deck were blown about, and the forward elevator jammed as it was descending to the hangar deck. Gasoline fumes spread through the ship and some of the men who inhaled too much became disoriented. The order was issued to open the side-scuttles and for those with hobnails on their soles to go up and down ladders carefully, since the fumes would be ignited if a hobnail created a spark against an iron ladder rung. The *Taiho*, without reducing its authorized top battle speed of 33 knots or its immediate standby status, was able to make headway unimpeded, but with the flight deck elevator dropped below deck level, leaving a gaping void above it, the next group of planes could not be sent off. A work crew in gas masks had gathered lumber together and hastened to repair the damage.

The First Air Division, however, was now caught in the net of the American submarines. Almost immediately afterward the *Shokaku*, close by the *Taiho*, was hit by a torpedo. A huge hole was opened amidships and she immediately started to burn and very quickly lost speed. At first, her crew was able to keep her afloat. She pulled out of the line and attempted to return to base at Yokosuka under destroyer escort, but in the end the 29,000-ton carrier sank beneath the waves.

Meanwhile, the *Taiho* had received no reports at all from the planes that had gone off to attack the American ships. Those back on the carrier waited uneasily. The planes were scheduled to skim over the water as low as possible, and when they had closed to 50 knots of the enemy they were to climb steeply, then, having achieved a high altitude, were to swoop down in a surprise attack. By making a low-level attack they would exploit the curvature of the earth and evade detection by the enemy's radar. They were to gain altitude before attacking because it was assumed that enemy fighters would be flying cover over their carriers. This was the only tactic the pilots who had gone through accelerated training had been taught. They would not have known what maneuver to adopt had they been called upon to respond to a different situation. They carried out the maneuver they had been taught faithfully and accurately. The enemy, however, had prepared a surprise for them. It was not clear whether the Americans' analysis of the situation was simply superior or they had broken an enciphered message. In any case, a large formation of enemy fighters was waiting above them as they began their climb— their speed lower because the climb was steep—50 knots short of the enemy carriers.

The Japanese losses were huge. Of the first and second wave of approximately 400 aircraft that had taken off from the nine carriers— excluding those planes that landed at airfields on Tinian, Guam, and Rota—no more than a hundred were able to return.

As the surviving planes began to return to the *Taiho* in small groups in the afternoon, Kuki was at his duty station, having had a late lunch in the officers' lounge next to the radio room. Suddenly a tremendous, rending explosion resounded through the ship. Kuki lost consciousness.

When he came to he was in utter darkness. He did not know how long he had been knocked out. Neither his vision nor his hearing had entirely returned to normal; he was still only semi-conscious. He had the sensation that he was lolling half asleep in bed, as he had during his tranquil student days. Then his consciousness, the feeling of having just awakened, seemed about to desert him once again. He could hear people groaning.

"Damn! We've been hit," he said, and in that instant tried to jump up. It was then he felt a spasm of pain from his legs to his back. Something held his legs; he couldn't move them. He heard the sound of something rolling about or burning, a powerful, rumbling sound, in the hangar at his back. A bright shaft of light shone through a crack in the steel bulkhead.

He gradually realized what had happened to him. The deafening explosion had knocked his heavy desk on top of him, something had hit him hard on the head, and he had fallen beside the desk, his legs pinned by it. When he realized this, he was able to calm himself somewhat. Flames were now leaping through the crack in the bulkhead behind him and he could smell his hair singeing.

*Well, so this is how I'm to die.*

He felt no sadness, nothing. Images of his family and people who had been close to him seemed to float before his eyes. He had no idea what was happening elsewhere on this huge carrier. It seemed to him that it was sailing along under its own power. Two men, seamen apparently, rushed out of the darkness, intending to flee toward the passageway through another bulkhead break through which light was visible, next to a bomb hoist.

"Hey! Wait!" Kuki shouted before he realized it. The two men ran off without so much as a glance in his direction.

"Is that you, Ensign Kuki?" a voice asked in the darkness from a corner of the room. It was Chief Petty Officer Tajima. "Petty Officers Kato and Yamada have had it."

"How are you? Can you get out of there?"

"I'm afraid I can't," the CPO answered. "It's my legs."

"My legs are caught too. And my hair is starting to burn, unfortunately." His own words struck him as extraordinarily casual. He did, however, shift himself around, pivoting on his legs, so that the flames could not get at his hair. It was an awkward position, so his abdomen was uncomfortably distended and, without really thinking about it, he put his hand on his belt. When he loosened it, his pants started to slip off. Surprised, he kicked his legs, and they slipped free of his pants. His pants cuff had been caught and he hadn't been able to pull it free, that was all. The desire to live surged within him like a raging river.

"Take off your pants!" he shouted at CPO Tajima. "Then you can escape."

He ran into the lounge. He had eaten lunch here only fifteen minutes before the explosion and now all the men he and others had relieved were dead. The bone of a broken leg, jutting up like a crutch, had pieces of dark red flesh adhering to it. Enameled plates and food, covered with blood, were scattered all about. As he was about to step through the hatch he noticed a man's head, split open like a pomegranate, wedged between the door and the jamb. He stepped on the head with his bare foot, then hopped to the passageway at the side of the ship. As soon as

he got to the passageway he saw an ensign-midshipman and two seamen
who were obviously confused. Black smoke rose from the carrier, which
was almost dead in the water.

"What the devil's happened?"

"Secondary explosions from the gasoline," the midshipman answered. "Shouldn't we lower the aft cutter?"

In that instant Kuki recalled hearing that when the mixture of gasoline fumes and air reaches a certain ratio, its explosive force is more
destructive than any bomb. He was still unable, however, to comprehend
the condition of the ship as a whole.

"The order to abandon ship hasn't been given yet, has it," Kuki said
sharply to the other three. "Let's go up on deck."

"But Ensign Kuki, you're badly injured."

For the first time Kuki realized something had happened to him. He
had a deep gash diagonally across his right leg. He had left behind his
shoes and pants, so only his *fundoshi* loincloth covered him. He put his
hand to his right ear; it was hanging from his head like a piece of meat.
One of the seamen improvised a bandage out of a hand towel and tied it
securely around his head. The four men headed for the flight deck. A
body was lodged between the rungs of the ladder, its arms dangling,
looking as though it would fall over the side of the ship at any moment.
Those who were not injured ran about aimlessly.

The huge flight deck had buckled down its middle, which had
heaved up, roof-like. Crimson flames wrapped in oily smoke leapt up
everywhere, and the bridge was already engulfed in smoke. When Kuki
saw this from the ladder he doubled back and made his way to the
quarterdeck, the only part of the ship that still remained intact. A helter-
skelter sort of abandon ship had already started and men were throwing
anything that would float into the water. The young, uninjured men
jumped boldly from the ship. Kuki looked over the side of the ship in
despair: he was so high up over the water; ever since training, high diving
into the water had been just about the hardest thing for him to do. His
leg and ear began to throb unbearably. The midshipman and the seamen
had gone their separate ways. A destroyer, apparently unable to approach because of the explosions, circled the *Taiho*, flashing its signal
light endlessly. Kuki made it down to the next lower deck. There he
found that the head of maintenance, a commander, had taken command
of the ship. He had had the men take off their shoes and was beginning
to put the men into the water.

He called out to Kuki as soon as he saw him.

"Hey, Ensign! You're hurt pretty bad, aren't you. Go first."

The seamen silently made way for Kuki. He saluted the commander,
took hold of the heavy line hanging over the side of the ship and slid
down it. As soon as he dropped into the water a huge swell washed over
him. He had cut his hands on the prickly rope and now they stung

painfully. As Kuki came back up to the surface he saw a sofa that he had often sat on floating nearby, and grabbed onto it. There was another man holding onto the other end, his face black with fuel oil. The man was bobbing up and down like a rubber ball, which Kuki found encouraging, but his wounds were now beginning to pain him horribly in the sea water, and because of the deep gash on his right leg it was difficult for him to kick; he could scarcely move the sofa along at all paddling only with his hands. He looked back when he was sure they had covered a good distance, but the huge vessel was still immediately behind him, looming over him as it listed. A severed hand floated toward Kuki and seemed about to trail after the sofa, then drifted away, horribly pale in the water as it was gently carried off by the current, palm down. It seemed to Kuki that the sinking of the *Taiho* was now only a matter of time. He had been desperately pushing the sofa as far away from the ship as he could get it and all the while it was gradually absorbing more water, so that finally each time he pushed against it, it would drop precipitously.

A destroyer came within about 200 meters of Kuki and he could see they were lowering a cutter. The current seemed to be taking the sofa in the opposite direction, so Kuki, after some hesitation, screwed up his courage and left it, swimming unaided toward the destroyer. He was tense and he was losing control of his legs. The *Taiho* grew more distant, but he was unable to get any nearer to the destroyer before him. He could see that it had lowered away the cutter, gone astern, then turned to its starboard and was now starting to get underway. The men in the cutter began rowing, taking the boat to his left and at a right angle to the direction Kuki was swimming. The sofa was gone now; he could see it nowhere. Kuki's spirits plummeted. The fuel oil was thick and black, and swells remorselessly hurled it and sea water into his mouth and nose. There was now almost no one to be seen on the deck of the *Taiho*. The carrier, still listing to port, red hull exposed, was about to sink, its stern in the air. An officer stood on the sloping deck waving his cap in farewell. The battle flag, which should have been lowered, still flew at the mast. On the destroyer, now fully underway, Kuki could see countless crewmen lining the railing on the *Taiho* side of the ship like statuettes, their arms raised in salute.

The actual sinking was over quickly. The 44,000-ton vessel thrust its stern up into space and slipped beneath the waves in the twinkling of an eye. Tears coursed down Kuki's cheeks, and these the oily seas washed away.

Kuki once again began to drift into unconsciousness, overcome by a not-unpleasant drowsiness. One hour after the *Taiho* went to the bottom, as the colors of evening deepened in the waters west of the Marianas, devoid now of ships, Kuki's body also disappeared quietly beneath the huge swells. He was 26.

# SIR HAROLD GEORGE NICOLSON

Sir Harold Nicolson writes to his sons Ben and Nigel about a story from Pierre Viénot, who had been the Under Secretary at the Quai d'Orsay before joining the Free French.

■

FROM *The Diaries and Letters of Harold Nicolson*

DIARY                                                             *26th June, 1944*

The doodle-bug attack became so serious last night that Viti [Vita Sackville-West, his wife] and I waited up in my room for the midnight news. There was nothing new. We are kept awake during the night by the rocket-bombs howling overhead, and we hear as many as twelve explosions. It gets better after 2 a.m. and we get a little sleep.

H.N. TO B.N. & N.N.                                              *27th June, 1944*
                                                                  Sissinghurst

[Pierre] Viénot told me the story of de Gaulle's visit to Bayeux.[1] On landing, they went straight to see Montgomery and spent an hour with him while he explained the situation. (De Gaulle was delighted by this, as his professional side, his Ecole de Guerre side, was aroused. He is amazed by the capacity which we and the Americans have shown, and his optimism on his return was unbounded.) On leaving Montgomery they got into two jeeps and drove in the direction of Bayeux. They then realized that they had so far not seen a single citizen of France. They determined to stop the first Frenchman whom they saw and engage him in conversation. Two kilometers on this side of Bayeux they saw coming towards them two gendarmes on bicycles. General Koenig hailed them: "*Hé, les gendarmes!*" Seeing two senior French officers, they got off their bicycles. Viénot then realized that no Frenchman in France would recognize de Gaulle, since they had never seen his portrait. He remarked on this to the General, who thereupon introduced himself. "*Le Général de Gaulle,*" he said stiffly. Not "*Je suis le Général . . .*" but just giving his name like a German introducing himself at a *Bierabend*. The gendarmes were completely taken aback. They dropped their jaws and almost dropped their bicycles. Then they sprang to attention and saluted

[1] On 14th June.

as they had never saluted before. The General said to them, "Where are you off to?" They answered that they were going to a village near the beach-head. "Turn round," said the General, "and go back to Bayeux. Tell the people I am coming. We will wait here for five minutes in order to give you time." So they turned round and bicycled back furiously. While they were waiting, Viénot said to de Gaulle, "Now you have really committed an act of a dictator. You have instructed two French gendarmes to disobey an order." "And they obeyed me," said de Gaulle, purring to himself.

They went to the *sous-préfecture*. The *sous-préfet*, a man called Rochat, had been secretary to Pucheu and was, as such, suspect. The door was opened by Madame Rochat who nearly dropped dead when she was told it was de Gaulle. She showed them to her husband's study. Evidently he had just heard that they were coming. He was standing with his back to them on a stool taking down Pétain's portrait from above the fireplace. "*Descendez, monsieur*," said de Gaulle. That was all. It is not true that he was sacked immediately.

# MARIE VASSILTCHIKOV

---

MARIE VASSILTCHIKOV, a White Russian princess stranded in Germany during the war, kept detailed diaries and is a unique eyewitness source for the 20th of July plot to assassinate Hitler. Among the conspirators were several of her close friends and associates.

---

■

FROM *Berlin Diaries*

*Thursday, 20 July*

This afternoon Loremarie Schönburg and I sat chatting on the office stairs when Gottfried Bismarck burst in, bright red spots on his cheeks. I had never seen him in such a state of feverish excitement. He first drew Loremarie aside, then asked me what my plans were. I told him they were uncertain but that I would really like to get out of the A.A. as soon as possible. He told me I should not worry, that in a few days everything would be settled and we would all know what was going to happen to us. Then, after asking me to come out to Potsdam with Loremarie as soon as possible, he jumped into his car and was gone.

I went back into my office and dialed Percy Frey at the Swiss Legation to cancel my dinner date with him, as I preferred to go out to Potsdam. While I waited, I turned to Loremarie, who was standing at the window, and asked her why Gottfried was in such a state. Could it be the *Konspiration*? (all that with the receiver in my hand!). She whispered: "Yes! That's it! It's done. This morning!" Just then Percy replied. Still holding the receiver, I asked: "Dead?" She answered: "Yes, dead!" I hung up, seized her by the shoulders and we went waltzing around the room. Then grabbing hold of some papers, I thrust them into the first drawer and shouting to the porter that we were "*dienstlich unterwegs*" ["off on official business"], we tore off to the Zoo station. On the way out to Potsdam she whispered to me the details and though the compartment was full, we did not even try to hide our excitement and joy:

Count Claus Schenck von Stauffenberg, a colonel on the General Staff, had put a bomb at Hitler's feet during a conference at Supreme H.Q. at Rastenburg in East Prussia. It had gone off and Adolf was dead. Stauffenberg had waited outside until the explosion and then, seeing Hitler being carried out on a stretcher covered with blood, he had run to his car, which had stood hidden somewhere, and with his A.D.C., Werner von Haeften, had driven to the local airfield and flown back to Berlin. In the general commotion nobody had noticed his escape.

On reaching Berlin, he had gone straight to the O.K.H. [Army Command H.Q.] in the Bendlerstrasse, which had meanwhile been taken over by the plotters and where Gottfried Bismarck, Helldorf and many others were now gathered. (The O.K.H. lies on the other side of the canal from our Woyrschstrasse.) This evening at six an announcement would be made over the radio that Adolf was dead and that a new government had been formed. The new Reichskanzler [Chancellor of the Reich] would be Gördeler, a former mayor of Leipzig. With a socialist background, he is considered a brilliant economist. Our Count Schulenburg or Ambassador von Hassell is to be Foreign Minister. My immediate feeling was that it was perhaps a mistake to put the best brains at the head of what could only be an interim government.

# SIMONE DE BEAUVOIR

AN EXCERPT from *Force of Circumstance,* De Beau-voir's third volume of autobiography, follows.

■

FROM *Force of Circumstance*

We were liberated. In the streets, the children were singing:

*Nous ne les reverrons plus,*
*C'est fini, ils sont foutus.*

And I kept saying to myself: It's all over, it's all over. It's all over: every-thing's beginning. Patrick Walberg, the Leirises' American friend, took us for a jeep ride through the suburbs; it was the first time in years that I'd been out in a car. Once again I wandered after midnight in the mild September air. The bistros closed early, but when we left the terrace of the Rhumerie or the smoky little red inferno of the Montana, we had the sidewalks, the benches, the streets. There were still snipers on the roofs, and my heart would grow heavy when I sensed the vigilant hatred overhead. One night, we heard sirens. An airplane, whose nationality we never discovered, was flying over Paris; V-1s fell on the suburbs and blew houses to bits. Walberg, usually well-informed, said that the Ger-mans were putting the finishing touches to new and even more terrifying secret weapons. Fear returned, and found its place still warm. But joy quickly swept it away. With our friends, talking, drinking, strolling, laughing, night and day we celebrated our deliverance. And all the others who were celebrating too, near or far, became our friends. An orgy of brotherhood! The shadows that had immured France exploded. The tall soldiers, dressed in khaki and chewing their gum, were living proof that you could cross the seas again. They ambled past, and often they stum-bled. Singing and whistling, they stumbled along the sidewalks and the subway platforms; stumbling, they danced at night in the bistros and laughed their loud laughs, showing teeth white as children's. Genet, who had no sympathy with the Germans but who detested idylls, declared loudly on the terrace of the Rhumerie that these costumed civilians had no style. Stiff in their black and green carapaces, the occupiers had been something else! For me, these carefree young Americans were freedom incarnate: our own and also the freedom that was about to spread—we had no doubts on this score—throughout the world. Once Hitler and Mussolini had been overthrown and Franco and Salazar driven out,

Europe would be cleansed of Fascism for good. Through the C.N.R. charter, France was taking the path of socialism. We believed that the country had been shaken deeply enough to permit a radical remodeling of its structure without new convulsions. *Combat* expressed our hopes by displaying as its motto: "From Resistance to Revolution."

This victory was to efface our old defeats, it was ours, and the future it opened up was ours, too. The men now in power had been in the Resistance and, to a greater or lesser extent, we knew them all. We could count many of the important figures in the press and the radio as close friends. Politics had become a family matter, and we expected to have a hand in it. "Politics is no longer dissociated from individuals," Camus wrote in *Combat* at the beginning of September, "it is man's direct address to other men." . . .

That evening, Hemingway, who was a war correspondent, had just arrived in Paris and had arranged for his brother to come and see him at the Ritz where he was staying; the brother had suggested that Lise come with him and bring Sartre and myself along. The room, when we went in, bore no resemblance at all to the idea I had always had of the Ritz; it was large but ugly, with its two brass bedsteads; Hemingway was lying on one of them in pajamas, his eyes shielded by a green eyeshade; on a table within easy reach stood a respectable quantity of Scotch, some bottles half empty, others entirely so. He heaved himself up, grabbed hold of Sartre and hugged him. "You're a general!" he said as he squeezed him. "Me, I'm only a captain; you're a general!" (When he'd been drinking he always pushed modesty a bit too far.) Our conversation, punctuated by numerous glasses of Scotch, continued in this enthusiastic vein; despite his flu, Hemingway was bursting with vitality. Sartre, overcome by sleep, tottered away at about three in the morning; I stayed until dawn.

# GENÊT

GENÊT was the pen name of Janet Flanner. Born in
Indianapolis, Genêt moved to Paris in 1922 and three
years later became *The New Yorker*'s regular correspondent from the city, a job she filled with distinction
for fifty years.

■

## FROM *Paris Journal 1944–1965*

Until the Renaissance gets under way, mouths and hands are more
important than intellects and hopes. The shortages of food and employment are equally great; there is a nice balance between the empty factories and the nearly empty stomachs. When the Germans disappeared
from Paris in August, the black market began to disappear, too. This has
not turned out to be the blessing one might have expected. The black
market, and even the gray market—the constant bartering, selling, and
haggling that went on among friends—devastated what was left of
French morale and cheapened the value of time, since it consumed
hours of each day, but it also saved French lives. The black market was
built upon the French peasant's classic cupidity and the Vichy government's stupidity in thinking that it is a farmer's social duty to grow things
whether they profit him or not. Because the French peasant was paid
parsimoniously low official prices in an attempt to keep consumer prices
down, he found that he was receiving only a fraction of what it cost him
to produce what he sold. Therefore, humanly, he not only lied to the
authorities about the quantity he could bring to market but, inhumanely,
he undersupplied even his assessed regional share for the needy. And
while the Parisian, in the four years of the occupation, was losing, on
the average, forty pounds in weight because of inadequate rations, the
peasant was selling his surplus on the black market at profits which, if he
had big herds, flocks, and fields, made him a franc millionaire. Now, as
one of the money-minded *nouveaux riches*, he fears the inflation he
helped to create. Thus nowadays a cow in the bush seems a better bet
than thirty thousand francs in the hand. The peasant has stopped selling,
the black market is drying up, and Parisians, who expected to fill up on
something more than freedom after the liberation, are still underfed.
This week's fat-and-flesh ration for a family of three in Paris is a half
pound of fresh meat, three-fifths of a pound of butter, and nine twenty-
fifths of a pound of sausage. On this much food the family of three will

not starve, but neither will any member of it feel full. Since the breakup of the excellently organized black market, substitute arrangements have come into being and with them have come hijacking, robberies, connivances, and Chicagoesque gangs drawn from the Mauvais Maquis, which was composed of thugs who had nothing to do with the original Maquis (the Communist Maquis Rouge) or the subsequent non-political Maquis Blanc and who have done the properly sacred Maquis legend harm. It is nothing now for helpless officials to announce that en route from Normandy to Paris two tons of butter have melted from a six-ton truckload. For that matter, whole trainloads of food have been reported lost, including the locomotive.

The first of the two major attacks by the Consultative Assembly on de Gaulle's Cabinet to date was made by slightly hungry Deputies, who asked questions about supplies. Last year, under the Nazis, the Deputies pointed out, there were turkeys for those who could pay a thousand francs for them. This year there were only bombed bridges, too few freight cars, and blasted railroad tracks. The Germans departed on and with two-thirds of the country's railway equipment and two-thirds of the country's trucks. This year, too, on the war maps, there is a great food-producing slice of France which even the Deputies may have forgotten about, since it is never mentioned and is still controlled by the Germans —from the lamb-grazing pasture lands above Bordeaux up into southern Brittany, secondary butter-and-egg basket of the country. Anyway, even if there were quantities of food in Paris, there would be nearly no fuel with which to cook it. The coal is in the north. There can be no transportation without coal and no coal without transportation. Two months of continuous rain have so swollen the rivers and canals that coal barges are tied up to the banks. Because of the lack of coal, there is no electric power for the city's factories, so they remain closed and the men have no work to do. But if they were open, who would fill all the jobs? Eight hundred thousand of the most skilled French factory workers are still labor slaves in Germany, working against the Allies. Because of the lack of electricity, a dozen of the Métro stations have been closed in an effort to force people to walk and reduce the number of passengers. The government has just announced that no public buildings will be heated before January 1st. The Academicians, old and wise men, have just announced that they will not hold their end-of-the-year annual meeting until some nice day next spring.

Then, because of the coal shortage, there is a gas shortage. Gas for cooking is rationed to an hour and a half for luncheon—it is on between noon and one-thirty—and an hour for supper, between seven and eight. There is no gas to heat the breakfast coffee of burned barley. Parisians rich enough to buy sawdust by the ton, and black-market gasoline for trucks to deliver it, can store a winter's supply of several tons of sawdust in half of an apartment and keep the other half warm with special saw-dust-burning stoves. With equally special low-current electrical attachments, the newly invented stone-lined stoves here can be heated during the night, after which the hot stones give warmth most of the next day. But these attachments are no longer available. For nearly everybody in Paris, the only available commodity is the cold. Except for the first winter after the defeat, this is the most uncomfortable winter of the war. Nevertheless, to the freed Parisians, dining in their overcoats on a meager soup of carrots and turnips, the only obtainable vegetables, Paris seems like home for the first time since the Christmas before the war.

# NORMAN LEWIS

IN 1944 Norman Lewis was in Naples. His *Naples '44*, a memoir written as a diary, captures that sad and desperate time.

■

## FROM *Naples '44*

*September 6*

The Canadians are generous and open-handed in every way. Bred in the freedom of limitless spaces, property, possessions and territorial rights of any kind seem to mean less to them than those things do to us. Anything they have is yours for the asking: their transport, their booze, or even a personally autographed picture of Rita. Unhesitatingly, and as a matter of course, a share is offered in the two dazed peasant girls picked up on one of their forays, whom they treat like pet monkeys, and feed with biscuits and scraps of bacon at odd times all through the day. They have run out of whiskey, and I have some misgivings about the sweet and ensnaring Strega. This they drink by the tumblerful, even for breakfast, after which, buckling on their guns, they go staggering off in search of adventure.

# FARLEY MOWAT

FARLEY MOWAT, one of Canada's most popular writers, served with the Canadian army in Italy during the
war and wrote *And No Birds Sang*, from which I have
taken the following excerpt, based on his experiences
in battle. His other books include *People of the Deer*
and *The Snow Walker*.

■

## FROM *And No Birds Sang*

During the night the Loyal Edmonton Regiment had reached the
Dittaino and established a bridgehead across it. Before dawn they were
relieved by our sister unit, the Royal Canadian Regiment, and, as the
sun rose, men of the R.C.R. crouched in hurriedly dug slit trenches and
stared up in awe at the mighty crag of Assoro.

The Germans on the promontory remained unperturbed. They had
little reason to be concerned, for it was obvious that a frontal attack up
the tortuous and twisting roadway that climbed laboriously from the
valley floor would be suicidal. Nor, apparently, could Assoro be outflanked. The only possible approach from westward was guarded by the
hill-crest town of Leonforte which occupied almost as strong a natural
defense position as Assoro itself. To the east lay a waste of gullies and
gorges of the kind we had faced at Valguarnera, but one that ended
at the foot of a nearly vertical rock face which soared almost a thousand feet to terminate at the ancient Norman castle crowning Assoro's
summit.

Assoro had been successfully defended four thousand years earlier
by men armed only with bronze swords, slings and spears. According to
Cockin, it had never been successfully stormed since. Now, in our time,
it was held by some of the world's best soldiers, armed with the most
modern weapons. Assoro appeared to be virtually impregnable.

So indeed it seemed to Brig. Howard Graham, commander of First
Brigade, who had been given the task of taking it. And so it must have
seemed to Lt.-Col. Bruce Sutcliffe when he in his turn received the order
to mount the actual attack.

Having told Jimmy Bird to have the battalion O-group waiting for
his return, and accompanied only by Cockin, Sutcliffe set out in mid-
morning of July 20 to make his reconnaissance. Reaching the Dittaino,
the two men crossed the dry riverbed on foot and made their way to a

forward observation post. This was no more than a shallow slit trench, barely sufficient to shelter the artillery observer who already occupied it. Sutcliffe and Cockin crouched in the open, map boards in front of them and binoculars leveled, the lenses winking in the sun as they anxiously scanned the mighty battlement looming ahead of them. They did not realize that they were being regarded in their turn.

On the Assoro scarp the crew of an Eighty-eight laid their gun over open sights. Seconds later a cloud of yellow dust and black smoke obscured the observation post in the valley below . . . and under its pall Sutcliffe lay dead and Cockin dying.

The loss of those who had been killed in the tumult and confusion of earlier actions had not yet been deeply perceived by us, but this new stroke of death was something else. It shredded the pale remnants of the illusion that real war was not much more than an exciting extension of battle games, and it fired us with rage against the enemy. This killing, before battle had been joined, seemed singularly vicious, almost obscene. When I heard news of it, I began to understand something of Alex Campbell's hatred of the Germans.

With Sutcliffe's death, command of the Regiment passed to Major Lord John Tweedsmuir. Barely thirty years of age, soft-spoken, kindly, with a slight tendency to stutter, he was a tall, fair-haired English romantic out of another age . . . his famous father's perhaps. "Tweedie," as we called him behind his back, had as a youth sought high adventure as a Hudson's Bay Company trader in the Arctic, then as a rancher on the African veldt, and finally as a soldier in a Canadian infantry battalion. But until this hour real adventure in the grand tradition had eluded him.

Going forward on his own reconnaissance that afternoon in company with the new second-in-command, Major "Ack Ack" Kennedy, Tweedsmuir looked up at the towering colossus of Assoro with the visionary eye of a Lawrence of Arabia, and saw that the only way to accomplish the impossible was to attempt the impossible. He thereupon decided that the battalion would make a right flank march by night across the intervening trackless gullies to the foot of the great cliff, scale that precipitous wall and, just at dawn, take the summit by surprise.

When Brig. Graham, a Hasty Pee himself and Lt.-Col. Sutcliffe's predecessor as the Regiment's commanding officer, heard the plan, his immediate reaction was to veto it. Years later he told me:

"It seemed like arrant madness. The likelihood that Tweedsmuir would lose the whole battalion seemed almost a dead certainty. I had a horrible vision of Balaklava and the Charge of the Light Brigade, and I was about to tell him: nothing doing! But then I thought, my God, he just *might* pull it off. So I let him go . . . but I sweat blood for the next twelve hours."

# DORIS LESSING

THE NOVELIST, short story writer, and playwright Doris Lessing was born in Persia and raised in what was then southern Rhodesia. She has been a resident of London for many years. Her books include *This Was the Old Chief's Country, Martha Quest, The Golden Notebook, The Good Terrorist,* and *The Habit of Loving.* "The Black Madonna" appears in *African Stories.*

■

## The Black Madonna

There are some countries in which the arts, let alone Art, cannot be said to flourish. Why this should be so it is hard to say, although of course we all have our theories about it. For sometimes it is the most barren soil that sends up gardens of those flowers which we all agree are the crown and justification of life, and it is this fact which makes it hard to say, finally, why the soil of Zambesia should produce such reluctant plants.

Zambesia is a tough, sunburnt, virile, positive country contemptuous of subtleties and sensibility: yet there have been States with these qualities which have produced art, though perhaps with the left hand. Zambesia is, to put it mildly, unsympathetic to those ideas so long taken for granted in other parts of the world, to do with liberty, fraternity and the rest. Yet there are those, and some of the finest souls among them, who maintain that art is impossible without a minority whose leisure is guaranteed by a hard-working majority. And whatever Zambesia's comfortable minority may lack, it is not leisure.

Zambesia—but enough; out of respect for ourselves and for scientific accuracy, we should refrain from jumping to conclusions. Particularly when one remembers the almost wistful respect Zambesians show when an artist does appear in their midst.

Consider, for instance, the case of Michele.

He came out of the internment camp at the time when Italy was made a sort of honorary ally, during the Second World War. It was a time of strain for the authorities, because it is one thing to be responsible for thousands of prisoners of war whom one must treat according to certain recognized standards. It is another to be faced, and from one day to the next, with these same thousands transformed by some international legerdemain into comrades in arms. Some of the thousands stayed where they were in the camps; they were fed and housed there at least. Others went as farm laborers, though not many; for while the farmers were as always short of labor, they did not know how to handle farm laborers who were also white men: such a phenomenon had never happened in Zambesia before. Some did odd jobs around the towns, keeping a sharp eye out for the trade unions, who would neither admit them as members nor agree to their working.

Hard, hard, the lot of these men, but fortunately not for long, for soon the war ended and they were able to go home.

Hard, too, the lot of the authorities, as has been pointed out; and for that reason they were doubly willing to take what advantages they could from the situation; and that Michele was such an advantage there could be no doubt.

His talents were first discovered when he was still a prisoner of war. A church was built in the camp, and Michele decorated its interior. It became a show-place, that little tin-roofed church in the prisoners' camp, with its whitewashed walls covered all over with frescoes depicting swarthy peasants gathering grapes for the vintage, beautiful Italian girls dancing, plump dark-eyed children. Amid crowded scenes of Italian life, appeared the Virgin and her Child, smiling and beneficent, happy to move familiarly among her people.

Culture-loving ladies who had bribed the authorities to be taken inside the camp would say, "Poor thing, how homesick he must be." And they would beg to be allowed to leave half a crown for the artist. Some were indignant. He was a prisoner, after all, captured in the very act of fighting against justice and democracy, and what right had he to protest? —for they felt these paintings as a sort of protest. What was there in Italy that we did not have right here in Westonville, which was the capital and hub of Zambesia? Were there not sunshine and mountains and fat babies and pretty girls here? Did we not grow—if not grapes, at least lemons and oranges and flowers in plenty?

People were upset—the desperation of nostalgia came from the painted white walls of that simple church, and affected everyone according to his temperament.

But when Michele was free, his talent was remembered. He was spoken of as "that Italian artist." As a matter of fact, he was a bricklayer. And the virtues of those frescoes might very well have been exaggerated. It is possible that they would have been overlooked altogether in a country where picture-covered walls were more common.

When one of the visiting ladies came rushing out to the camp in her own car, to ask him to paint her children, he said he was not qualified to do so. But at last he agreed. He took a room in the town and made some nice likenesses of the children. Then he painted the children of a great number of the first lady's friends. He charged ten shillings a time. Then one of the ladies wanted a portrait of herself. He asked ten pounds for it; it had taken him a month to do. She was annoyed, but paid.

And Michele went off to his room with a friend and stayed there drinking red wine from the Cape and talking about home. While the money lasted he could not be persuaded to do any more portraits.

There was a good deal of talk among the ladies about the dignity of labor, a subject in which they were well versed; and one felt they might almost go so far as to compare a white man with a kaffir, who did not understand the dignity of labor either.

He was felt to lack gratitude. One of the ladies tracked him down, found him lying on a camp-bed under a tree with a bottle of wine, and spoke to him severely about the barbarity of Mussolini and the fecklessness of the Italian temperament. Then she demanded that he should instantly paint a picture of herself in her new evening dress. He refused, and she went home very angry.

It happened that she was the wife of one of our most important citizens, a General or something of that kind, who was at that time engaged in planning a military tattoo or show for the benefit of the civilian population. The whole of Westonville had been discussing this show for weeks. We were all bored to extinction by dances, fancy-dress balls, fairs, lotteries and other charitable entertainments. It is not too much to say that while some were dying for freedom, others were dancing for it. There comes a limit to everything. Though, of course, when the end of the war actually came and the thousands of troops stationed in the country had to go home—in short, when enjoying ourselves would no longer be a duty, many were heard to exclaim that life would never be the same again.

In the meantime, the Tattoo would make a nice change for us all. The military gentlemen responsible for the idea did not think of it in these terms. They thought to improve morale by giving us some idea of what war was really like. Headlines in the newspaper were not enough. And in order to bring it all home to us, they planned to destroy a village by shell-fire before our very eyes.

First, the village had to be built.

It appears that the General and his subordinates stood around in the red dust of the parade-ground under a burning sun for the whole of one day, surrounded by building materials, while hordes of African laborers ran around with boards and nails, trying to make something that looked like a village. It became evident that they would have to build a proper village in order to destroy it; and this would cost more than was allowed for the whole entertainment. The General went home in a bad temper, and his wife said what they needed was an artist, they needed Michele. This was not because she wanted to do Michele a good turn; she could not endure the thought of him lying around singing while there was work to be done. She refused to undertake any delicate diplomatic missions when her husband said he would be damned if he would ask favors of any little Wop. She solved the problem for him in her own way: a certain Captain Stocker was sent out to fetch him.

The Captain found him on the same camp-bed under the same tree, in rolled-up trousers, and an uncollared shirt; unshaven, mildly drunk, with a bottle of wine standing beside him on the earth. He was singing an air so wild, so sad, that the Captain was uneasy. He stood at ten paces from the disreputable fellow and felt the indignities of his position. A year ago, this man had been a mortal enemy to be shot at sight. Six months ago, he had been an enemy prisoner. Now he lay with his knees up, in an untidy shirt that had certainly once been military. For the Captain, the situation crystallized in a desire that Michele should salute him.

"Piselli!" he said sharply.

Michele turned his head and looked at the Captain from the horizontal. "Good morning," he said affably.

"You are wanted," said the Captain.

"Who?" said Michele. He sat up, a fattish, olive-skinned little man. His eyes were resentful.

"The authorities."

"The war is over?"

The Captain, who was already stiff and shiny enough in his laundered khaki, jerked his head back frowning, chin out. He was a large man, blond, and wherever his flesh showed, it was brick-red. His eyes were small and blue and angry. His red hands, covered all over with fine yellow bristles, clenched by his side. Then he saw the disappointment in Michele's eyes, and the hands unclenched. "No it is not over," he said. "Your assistance is required."

"For the war?"

"For the war effort. I take it you are interested in defeating the Germans?"

Michele looked at the Captain. The little dark-eyed artisan looked at the great blond officer with his cold blue eyes, his narrow mouth, his hands like bristle-covered steaks. He looked and said: "I am very interested in the end of the war."

"*Well?*" said the Captain between his teeth.

"The pay?" said Michele.

"You will be paid."

Michele stood up. He lifted the bottle against the sun, then took a gulp. He rinsed his mouth out with wine and spat. Then he poured what was left on to the red earth, where it made a bubbling purple stain.

"I am ready," he said. He went with the Captain to the waiting lorry, where he climbed in beside the driver's seat and not, as the Captain had expected, into the back of the lorry. When they had arrived at the parade-ground the officers had left a message that the Captain would be personally responsible for Michele and for the village. Also for the hundred or so laborers who were sitting around on the grass verges waiting for orders.

The Captain explained what was wanted. Michele nodded. Then he waved his hand at the Africans. "I do not want these," he said.

"You will do it yourself—a village?"

"Yes."

"With no help?"

Michele smiled for the first time. "I will do it."

The Captain hesitated. He disapproved on principle of white men doing heavy manual labor. He said: "I will keep six to do the heavy work."

Michele shrugged; and the Captain went over and dismissed all but six of the Africans. He came back with them to Michele.

"It is hot," said Michele.

"Very," said the Captain. They were standing in the middle of the parade-ground. Around its edge trees, grass, gulfs of shadow. Here, nothing but reddish dust, drifting and lifting in a low hot breeze.

"I am thirsty," said Michele. He grinned. The Captain felt his stiff lips loosen unwillingly in reply. The two pairs of eyes met. It was a moment of understanding. For the Captain, the little Italian had suddenly become human. "I will arrange it," he said, and went off downtown. By the time he had explained the position to the right people, filled in forms and made arrangements, it was late afternoon. He returned to the parade-ground with a case of Cape brandy, to find Michele and the six black men seated together under a tree. Michele was singing an Italian song to them, and they were harmonizing with him. The sight affected the Captain like an attack of nausea. He came up, and the Africans stood to attention. Michele continued to sit.

"You said you would do the work yourself?"

"Yes, I said so."

The Captain then dismissed the Africans. They departed, with friendly looks toward Michele, who waved at them. The Captain was beef-red with anger. "You have not started yet?"

"How long have I?"

"Three weeks."

"Then there is plenty of time," said Michele, looking at the bottle of brandy in the Captain's hand. In the other were two glasses. "It is evening," he pointed out. The Captain stood frowning for a moment. Then he sat down on the grass, and poured out two brandies.

"Ciao," said Michele.

"Cheers," said the Captain. Three weeks, he was thinking. Three weeks with this damned little Itie! He drained his glass and refilled it, and set it in the grass. The grass was cool and soft. A tree was flowering somewhere close—hot waves of perfume came on the breeze.

"It is nice here," said Michele. "We will have a good time together. Even in a war, there are times of happiness. And of friendship. I drink to the end of the war."

Next day the Captain did not arrive at the parade-ground until after lunch. He found Michele under the trees with a bottle. Sheets of ceiling board had been erected at one end of the parade-ground in such a way that they formed two walls and part of a third, and a slant of steep roof supported on struts.

"What's that?" said the Captain, furious.

"The church," said Michele.

"Wha-at?"

"You will see. Later. It is very hot." He looked at the brandy bottle that lay on its side on the ground. The Captain went to the lorry and returned with the case of brandy. They drank. Time passed. It was a long time since the Captain had sat on grass under a tree. It was a long time, for that matter, since he had drunk so much. He always drank a great deal, but it was regulated to the times and seasons. He was a disciplined man. Here, sitting on the grass beside this little man whom he still could not help thinking of as an enemy, it was not that he let his self-discipline go, but that he felt himself to be something different: he was temporarily set outside his normal behavior. Michele did not count. He listened to Michele talking about Italy and it seemed to him he was listening to a savage speaking; as if he heard tales from the mythical South Sea islands where a man like himself might very well go just once in his life. He found himself saying he would like to make a trip to Italy after the war. Actually, he was attracted only by the North and by Northern people. He had visited Germany, under Hitler, and though it was not the time to say so, had found it very satisfactory. Then Michele sang him some Italian songs. He sang Michele some English songs. Then Michele took out photographs of his wife and children, who lived in a village in the mountains of North Italy. He asked the Captain if he were married. The Captain never spoke about his private affairs.

He had spent all his life in one or other of the African colonies as a policeman, magistrate, native commissioner, or in some other useful capacity. When the war started, military life came easily to him. But he hated city life, and had his own reasons for wishing the war over. Mostly, he had been in bush-stations with one or two other white men, or by himself, far from the rigors of civilization. He had relations with native women; and from time to time visited the city where his wife lived with her parents and the children. He was always tormented by the idea that she was unfaithful to him. Recently he had even appointed a private detective to watch her; he was convinced the detective was inefficient. Army friends coming from L—— where his wife was, spoke of her at parties, enjoying herself. When the war ended, she would not find it so easy to have a good time. And why did he not simply live with her and be done with it? The fact was, he could not. And his long exile to remote bush-stations was because he needed the excuse not to. He could not bear to think of his wife for too long; she was that part of his life he had never been able, so to speak, to bring to heel.

Yet he spoke of her now to Michele, and of his favorite bush-wife, Nadya. He told Michele the story of his life, until he realized that the shadows from the trees they sat under had stretched right across the parade-ground to the grandstand. He got unsteadily to his feet, and said: "There is work to be done. You are being paid to work."

"I will show you my church when the light goes."

The sun dropped, darkness fell, and Michele made the Captain drive his lorry to the parade-ground a couple of hundred yards away and switch on his lights. Instantly, a white church sprang up from the shapes and shadows of the bits of board.

"Tomorrow, some houses," said Michele cheerfully.

At the end of a week, the space at the end of the parade-ground had crazy gawky constructions of lath and board over it, that looked in the sunlight like nothing on earth. Privately, it upset the Captain: it was like a nightmare that these skeleton-like shapes should be able to persuade him, with the illusions of light and dark, that they were a village. At night, the Captain drove up his lorry, switched on the lights, and there it was, the village, solid and real against the background of full green trees. Then, in the morning sunlight, there was nothing there, just bits of board stuck in the sand.

"It is finished," said Michele.

"You were engaged for three weeks," said the Captain. He did not want it to end, this holiday from himself.

Michele shrugged. "The army is rich," he said. Now, to avoid curious eyes, they sat inside the shade of the church, with the case of brandy between them. The Captain talked, talked endlessly, about his wife, about women. He could not stop talking.

Michele listened. Once he said: "When I go home—when I go home —I shall open my arms . . ." He opened them, wide. He closed his eyes. Tears ran down his cheeks. "I shall take my wife in my arms, and I shall ask nothing, nothing. I do not care. It is enough to be together. That is what the war has taught me. It is enough, it is enough. I shall ask no questions and I shall be happy."

The Captain stared before him, suffering. He thought how he dreaded his wife. She was a scornful creature, gay and hard, who laughed at him. She had been laughing at him ever since they married. Since the war, she had taken to calling him names like Little Hitler, and Storm-trooper. "Go ahead, my little Hitler," she had cried last time they met. "Go ahead, my Storm-trooper. If you want to waste your money on private detectives, go ahead. But don't think I don't know what *you* do when you're in the bush. I don't care what you do, but remember that I know it . . ."

The Captain remembered her saying it. And there sat Michele on his packing-case, saying: "It's a pleasure for the rich, my friend, detectives and the law. Even jealousy is a pleasure I don't want any more. Ah, my friend, to be together with my wife again, and the children, that is all I ask of life. That and wine and food and singing in the evenings." And the tears wetted his cheeks and splashed on to his shirt.

That a man should cry, good Lord! thought the Captain. And without shame! He seized the bottle and drank.

Three days before the great occasion, some high-ranking officers came strolling through the dust, and found Michele and the Captain sitting together on the packing-case, singing. The Captain's shirt was open down the front, and there were stains on it.

The Captain stood to attention with the bottle in his hand, and Michele stood to attention too, out of sympathy with his friend. Then the officers drew the Captain aside—they were all cronies of his—and said, what the hell did he think he was doing? And why wasn't the village finished?

Then they went away.

"Tell them it is finished," said Michele. "Tell them I want to go."

"No," said the Captain, "no, Michele, what would you do if your wife . . ."

"This world is a good place. We should be happy—that is all."

"Michele . . ."

"I want to go. There is nothing to do. They paid me yesterday."

"Sit down, Michele. Three more days, and then it's finished."

"Then I shall paint the inside of the church as I painted the one in the camp."

The Captain laid himself down on some boards and went to sleep. When he woke, Michele was surrounded by the pots of paint he had used on the outside of the village. Just in front of the Captain was a picture of a black girl. She was young and plump. She wore a patterned blue dress and her shoulders came soft and bare out of it. On her back was a baby slung in a band of red stuff. Her face was turned towards the Captain and she was smiling.

"That's Nadya," said the Captain. "Nadya . . ." He groaned loudly. He looked at the black child and shut his eyes. He opened them, and mother and child were still there. Michele was very carefully drawing thin yellow circles around the heads of the black girl and her child.

"Good God," said the Captain, "you can't do that."

"Why not?"

"You can't have a black Madonna."

"She was a peasant. This is a peasant. Black peasant Madonna for black country."

"This is a German village," said the Captain.

"This is my Madonna," said Michele angrily. "Your German village and my Madonna. I paint this picture as an offering to the Madonna. She is pleased—I feel it."

The Captain lay down again. He was feeling ill. He went back to sleep. When he woke for the second time it was dark. Michele had brought in a flaring paraffin lamp, and by its light was working on the long wall. A bottle of brandy stood beside him. He painted until long after midnight, and the Captain lay on his side and watched, as passive as a man suffering a dream. Then they both went to sleep on the boards. The whole of the next day Michele stood painting black Madonnas, black saints, black angels. Outside, troops were practicing in the sunlight, bands were blaring and motor cyclists roared up and down. But Michele painted on, drunk and oblivious. The Captain lay on his back, drinking and muttering about his wife. Then he would say "Nadya, Nadya," and burst into sobs.

Towards nightfall the troops went away. The officers came back, and the Captain went off with them to show how the village sprang into being when the great lights at the end of the parade-ground were switched on. They all looked at the village in silence. They switched the lights off, and there were only the tall angular boards leaning like grave-stones in the moonlight. On went the lights—and there was the village. They were silent, as if suspicious. Like the Captain, they seemed to feel it was not right. Uncanny it certainly was, but *that* was not it. Unfair — that was the word. It was cheating. And profoundly disturbing.

"Clever chap, that Italian of yours," said the General.

The Captain, who had been woodenly correct until this moment, suddenly came rocking up to the General, and steadied himself by laying his hand on the august shoulder. "Bloody Wops," he said. "Bloody kaffirs. Bloody . . . Tell you what, though, there's one Itie that's some good. Yes, there is. I'm telling you. He's a friend of mine, actually."

The General looked at him. Then he nodded to his underlings. The Captain was taken away for disciplinary purposes. It was decided, however, that he must be ill, nothing else could account for such behavior. He was put to bed in his own room with a nurse to watch him.

He woke twenty-four hours later, sober for the first time in weeks. He slowly remembered what had happened. Then he sprang out of bed and rushed into his clothes. The nurse was just in time to see him run down the path and leap into his lorry.

He drove at top speed to the parade-ground, which was flooded with light in such a way that the village did not exist. Everything was in full swing. The cars were three deep around the square, with people on the running-boards and even the roofs. The grandstand was packed. Women dressed as gipsies, country girls, Elizabethan court dames, and so on, wandered about with trays of ginger beer and sausage-rolls and programs at five shillings each in aid of the war effort. On the square, troops deployed, obsolete machine-guns were being dragged up and down, bands played, and motor cyclists roared through flames.

As the Captain parked the lorry, all this activity ceased, and the lights went out. The Captain began running around the outside of the square to reach the place where the guns were hidden in a mess of net and branches. He was sobbing with the effort. He was a big man, and unused to exercise, and sodden with brandy. He had only one idea in his mind—to stop the guns firing, to stop them at all costs.

Luckily, there seemed to be a hitch. The lights were still out. The unearthly graveyard at the end of the square glittered white in the moonlight. Then the lights briefly switched on, and the village sprang into existence for just long enough to show large red crosses all over a white building beside the church. Then moonlight flooded everything again, and the crosses vanished. "Oh, the bloody fool!" sobbed the Captain, running, running as if for his life. He was no longer trying to reach the guns. He was cutting across a corner of the square direct to the church. He could hear some officers cursing behind him: "Who put those red crosses there? Who? We can't fire on the Red Cross."

The Captain reached the church as the searchlights burst on. Inside, Michele was kneeling on the earth looking at his first Madonna. "They are going to kill my Madonna," he said miserably.

"Come away, Michele, come away."

"They're going to . . ."

The Captain grabbed his arm and pulled. Michele wrenched himself free and grabbed a saw. He began hacking at the ceiling board. There was a dead silence outside. They heard a voice booming through the loudspeakers: "The village that is about to be shelled is an English village, not as represented on the program, a German village. Repeat, the village that is about to be shelled is . . ."

Michele had cut through two sides of a square around the Madonna.

"Michele," sobbed the Captain, *"get out of here."*

Michele dropped the saw, took hold of the raw edges of the board and tugged. As he did so, the church began to quiver and lean. An irregular patch of board ripped out and Michele staggered back into the Captain's arms. There was a roar. The church seemed to dissolve around them into flame. Then they were running away from it, the Captain holding Michele tight by the right arm. "Get down," he shouted suddenly, and threw Michele to the earth. He flung himself down beside him. Looking from under the crook of his arm, he heard the explosion, saw a great pillar of smoke and flame, and the village disintegrated in a flying mass of debris. Michele was on his knees gazing at his Madonna in the light from the flames. She was unrecognizable, blotted out with dust. He looked horrible, quite white, and a trickle of blood soaked from his hair down one cheek.

"They shelled my Madonna," he said.

"Oh, damn it, you can paint another one," said the Captain. His own voice seemed to him strange, like a dream voice. He was certainly crazy, as mad as Michele himself . . . He got up, pulled Michele to his feet, and marched him towards the edge of the field. There they were met by the ambulance people. Michele was taken off to hospital, and the Captain was sent back to bed.

A week passed. The Captain was in a darkened room. That he was having some kind of a breakdown was clear, and two nurses stood guard over him. Sometimes he lay quiet. Sometimes he muttered to himself. Sometimes he sang in a thick clumsy voice bits out of opera, fragments from Italian songs, and—over and over again—There's a Long Long Trail. He was not thinking of anything at all. He shied away from the thought of Michele as if it were dangerous. When, therefore, a cheerful female voice announced that a friend had come to cheer him up, and it would do him good to have some company, and he saw a white bandage moving toward him in the gloom, he turned over on to his side, face to the wall.

"Go away," he said. "Go away, Michele."

"I have come to see you," said Michele. "I have brought you a present."

The Captain slowly turned over. There was Michele, a cheerful ghost in the dark room. "You fool," he said. "You messed everything up. What did you paint those crosses for?"

"It was a hospital," said Michele. "In a village there is a hospital, and on the hospital the Red Cross, the beautiful Red Cross—no?"

"I was nearly court-martialed."

"It was my fault," said Michele. "I was drunk."

"I was responsible."

"How could you be responsible when I did it? But it is all over. Are you better?"

"Well, I suppose those crosses saved your life."

"I did not think," said Michele. "I was remembering the kindness of the Red Cross people when we were prisoners."

"Oh shut up, shut up, shut up."

"I have brought you a present."

The Captain peered through the dark. Michele was holding up a picture. It was of a native woman with a baby on her back smiling sideways out of the frame.

Michele said: "You did not like the haloes. So this time, no haloes. For the Captain—no Madonna." He laughed. "You like it? It is for you. I painted it for you."

"God damn you!" said the Captain.

"You do not like it?" said Michele, very hurt.

The Captain closed his eyes. "What are you going to do next?" he asked, tiredly.

Michele laughed again. "Mrs. Pannerhurst, the lady of the General, she wants me to paint her picture in her white dress. So I paint it."

"You should be proud to."

"Silly bitch. She thinks I am good. They know nothing—savages. Barbarians. Not you, Captain, you are my friend. But these people they know nothing."

The Captain lay quiet. Fury was gathering in him. He thought of the General's wife. He disliked her, but he had known her well enough.

"These people," said Michele. "They do not know a good picture from a bad picture. I paint, I paint, this way, that way. There is the picture—I look at it and laugh inside myself." Michele laughed out loud. "They say, he is a Michelangelo, this one, and try to cheat me out of my price. Michele—Michelangelo—that is a joke, no?"

The Captain said nothing.

"But for you I painted this picture to remind you of our good times with the village. You are my friend. I will always remember you."

The Captain turned his eyes sideways in his head and stared at the black girl. Her smile at him was half innocence, half malice.

"Get out," he said suddenly.

Michele came closer and bent to see the Captain's face. "You wish me to go?" He sounded unhappy. "You saved my life. I was a fool that night. But I was thinking of my offering to the Madonna—I was a fool, I say it myself. I was drunk, we are fools when we get drunk."

"Get out of here," said the Captain again.

For a moment the white bandage remained motionless. Then it swept downwards in a bow.

Michele turned towards the door.

"And take that bloody picture with you."

Silence. Then, in the dim light, the Captain saw Michele reach out for the picture, his white head bowed in profound obeisance. He straightened himself and stood to attention, holding the picture with one hand, and keeping the other stiff down his side. Then he saluted the Captain.

"Yes, *sir*," he said, and he turned and went out of the door with the picture.

The Captain lay still. He felt—what did he feel? There was a pain under his ribs. It hurt to breathe. He realized he was unhappy. Yes, a terrible unhappiness was filling him, slowly, slowly. He was unhappy because Michele had gone. Nothing had ever hurt the Captain in all his life as much as that mocking *Yes, sir.* Nothing. He turned his face to the wall and wept. But silently. Not a sound escaped him, for the fear the nurses might hear.

# JOSEPH HELLER

JOSEPH HELLER, who served as a bombardier with the American Air Force during the war, went on to write one of the few enduring novels about that conflict—*Catch-22*—and in the process gave the language a new phrase.

■

## FROM *Catch-22*

### THE SOLDIER IN WHITE

Yossarian ran right into the hospital, determined to remain there forever rather than fly one mission more than the thirty-two missions he had. Ten days after he changed his mind and came out, the colonel raised the missions to forty-five and Yossarian ran right back in, determined to remain in the hospital forever rather than fly one mission more than the six missions more he had just flown.

Yossarian could run into the hospital whenever he wanted to because of his liver and because of his eyes; the doctors couldn't fix his liver condition and couldn't meet his eyes each time he told them he had a liver condition. He could enjoy himself in the hospital, just as long as there was no one really very sick in the same ward. His system was sturdy enough to survive a case of someone else's malaria or influenza with scarcely any discomfort at all. He could come through other people's tonsillectomies without suffering any postoperative distress, and even endure their hernias and hemorrhoids with only mild nausea and revulsion. But that was just about as much as he could go through without getting sick. After that he was ready to bolt. He could relax in the hospital, since no one there expected him to do anything. All he was expected to do in the hospital was die or get better, and since he was perfectly all right to begin with, getting better was easy.

Being in the hospital was better than being over Bologna or flying over Avignon with Huple and Dobbs at the controls and Snowden dying in back.

There were usually not nearly as many sick people inside the hospital as Yossarian saw outside the hospital, and there were generally fewer people inside the hospital who were seriously sick. There was a much lower death rate inside the hospital than outside the hospital, and a much healthier death rate. Few people died unnecessarily. People knew a lot more about dying inside the hospital and made a much neater, more orderly job of it. They couldn't dominate Death inside the hospital, but they certainly made her behave. They had taught her manners. They couldn't keep Death out, but while she was in she had to act like a lady. People gave up the ghost with delicacy and taste inside the hospital. There was none of that crude, ugly ostentation about dying that was so common outside the hospital. They did not blow up in mid-air like Kraft or the dead man in Yossarian's tent, or freeze to death in the blazing summertime the way Snowden had frozen to death after spilling his secret to Yossarian in the back of the plane.

"I'm cold," Snowden had whimpered. "I'm cold."

"There, there," Yossarian had tried to comfort him. "There, there."

They didn't take it on the lam weirdly inside a cloud the way Clevinger had done. They didn't explode into blood and clotted matter. They didn't drown or get struck by lightning, mangled by machinery or crushed in landslides. They didn't get shot to death in holdups, strangled to death in rapes, stabbed to death in saloons, bludgeoned to death with axes by parents or children, or die summarily by some other act of God. Nobody choked to death. People bled to death like gentlemen in an operating room or expired without comment in an oxygen tent. There was none of that tricky now-you-see-me-now-you-don't business so much in vogue outside the hospital, none of that now-I-am-and-now-I-ain't. There were no famines or floods. Children didn't suffocate in cradles or iceboxes or fall under trucks. No one was beaten to death. People didn't stick their heads into ovens with the gas on, jump in front of subway trains or come plummeting like dead weights out of hotel windows with a *whoosh!*, accelerating at the rate of sixteen feet per second per second to land with a hideous *plop!* on the sidewalk and die digustingly there in public like an alpaca sack full of hairy strawberry ice cream, bleeding, pink toes awry.

All things considered, Yossarian often preferred the hospital, even though it had its faults. The help tended to be officious, the rules, if heeded, restrictive, and the management meddlesome. Since sick people were apt to be present, he could not always depend on a lively young crowd in the same ward with him, and the entertainment was not always good. He was forced to admit that the hospitals had altered steadily for the worse as the war continued and one moved closer to the battlefront, the deterioration in the quality of the guests becoming most marked within the combat zone itself where the effects of booming wartime conditions were apt to make themselves conspicuous immediately. The people got sicker and sicker the deeper he moved into combat, until finally in the hospital that last time there had been the soldier in white, who could not have been any sicker without being dead, and he soon was.

The soldier in white was constructed entirely of gauze, plaster and a thermometer, and the thermometer was merely an adornment left balanced in the empty dark hole in the bandages over his mouth early each morning and late each afternoon by Nurse Cramer and Nurse Duckett right up to the afternoon Nurse Cramer read the thermometer and discovered he was dead. Now that Yossarian looked back, it seemed that Nurse Cramer, rather than the talkative Texan, had murdered the soldier in white; if she had not read the thermometer and reported what she had found, the soldier in white might still be lying there alive exactly as he had been lying there all along, encased from head to toe in plaster and gauze with both strange, rigid legs elevated from the hips and both strange arms strung up perpendicularly, all four bulky limbs in casts, all four strange, useless limbs hoisted up in the air by taut wire cables and fantastically long lead weights suspended darkly above him. Lying there that way might not have been much of a life, but it was all the life he had, and the decision to terminate it, Yossarian felt, should hardly have been Nurse Cramer's.

The soldier in white was like an unrolled bandage with a hole in it or like a broken block of stone in a harbor with a crooked zinc pipe jutting out. The other patients in the ward, all but the Texan, shrank from him with a tenderhearted aversion from the moment they set eyes on him the morning after the night he had been sneaked in. They gathered soberly in the farthest recess of the ward and gossiped about him in malicious, offended undertones, rebelling against his presence as a ghastly imposition and resenting him malevolently for the nauseating truth of which he was bright reminder. They shared a common dread that he would begin moaning.

"I don't know what I'll do if he does begin moaning," the dashing young fighter pilot with the golden mustache had grieved forlornly. "It means he'll moan during the night, too, because he won't be able to tell time."

No sound at all came from the soldier in white all the time he was there. The ragged round hole over his mouth was deep and jet black and showed no sign of lip, teeth, palate or tongue. The only one who ever came close enough to look was the affable Texan, who came close enough several times a day to chat with him about more votes for the decent folk, opening each conversation with the same unvarying greeting: "What do you say, fella? How you coming along?" The rest of the men avoided them both in their regulation maroon corduroy bathrobes and unraveling flannel pajamas, wondering gloomily who the soldier in white was, why he was there and what he was really like inside.

"He's all right, I tell you," the Texan would report back to them encouragingly after each of his social visits. "Deep down inside he's really a regular guy. He's just feeling a little shy and insecure now because he doesn't know anybody here and can't talk. Why don't you all just step right up to him and introduce yourselves? He won't hurt you."

"What the goddam hell are you talking about?" Dunbar demanded. "Does he even know what you're talking about?"

"Sure he knows what I'm talking about. He's not stupid. There ain't nothing wrong with him."

"Can he hear you?"

"Well, I don't know if he can hear me or not, but I'm sure he knows what I'm talking about."

"Does that hole over his mouth ever move?"

"Now, what kind of a crazy question is that?" the Texan asked uneasily.

"How can you tell if he's breathing if it never moves?"

"How can you tell it's a he?"

"Does he have pads over his eyes underneath that bandage over his face?"

"Does he ever wiggle his toes or move the tips of his fingers?"

The Texan backed away in mounting confusion. "Now, what kind of a crazy question is that? You fellas must all be crazy or something. Why don't you just walk right up to him and get acquainted? He's a real nice guy, I tell you."

The soldier in white was more like a stuffed and sterilized mummy than a real nice guy. Nurse Duckett and Nurse Cramer kept him spick-and-span. They brushed his bandages often with a whiskbroom and scrubbed the plaster casts on his arms, legs, shoulders, chest and pelvis with soapy water. Working with a round tin of metal polish, they waxed a dim gloss on the dull zinc pipe rising from the cement on his groin. With damp dish towels they wiped the dust several times a day from the slim black rubber tubes leading in and out of him to the two large stoppered jars, one of them, hanging on a post beside the bed, dripping fluid into his arm constantly through a slit in the bandages while the other, almost out of sight on the floor, drained the fluid away through the zinc pipe rising from his groin. Both young nurses polished the glass jars unceasingly. They were proud of their housework. The more solicitous of the two was Nurse Cramer, a shapely, pretty, sexless girl with a wholesome unattractive face. Nurse Cramer had a cute nose and a radiant, blooming complexion dotted with fetching sprays of adorable freckles that Yossarian detested. She was touched very deeply by the soldier in white. Her virtuous, pale-blue, saucerlike eyes flooded with leviathan tears on unexpected occasions and made Yossarian mad.

"How the hell do you know he's even in there?" he asked her.

"Don't you dare talk to me that way!" she replied indignantly.

"Well, how do you? You don't even know if it's really him."

"Who?"

"Whoever's supposed to be in all those bandages. You might really be weeping for somebody else. How do you know he's even alive?"

"What a terrible thing to say!" Nurse Cramer exclaimed. "Now, you get right into bed and stop making jokes about him."

"I'm not making jokes. Anybody might be in there. For all we know, it might even be Mudd."

"What are you talking about?" Nurse Cramer pleaded with him in a quavering voice.

"Maybe that's where the dead man is."

"What dead man?"

"I've got a dead man in my tent that nobody can throw out. His name is Mudd."

Nurse Cramer's face blanched and she turned to Dunbar desperately for aid. "Make him stop saying things like that," she begged.

"Maybe there's no one inside," Dunbar suggested helpfully. "Maybe they just sent the bandages here for a joke."

She stepped away from Dunbar in alarm. "You're crazy," she cried, glancing about imploringly. "You're both crazy."

Nurse Duckett showed up then and chased them all back to their own beds while Nurse Cramer changed the stoppered jars for the soldier in white. Changing the jars for the soldier in white was no trouble at all, since the same clear fluid was dripped back inside him over and over again with no apparent loss. When the jar feeding the inside of his elbow was just empty, the jar on the floor was just about full, and the two were simply uncoupled from their respective hoses and reversed quickly so that the liquid could be dripped right back into him. Changing the jars was no trouble to anyone but the men who watched them change every hour or so and were baffled by the procedure.

"Why can't they hook the two jars up to each other and eliminate the middleman?" the artillery captain with whom Yossarian had stopped playing chess inquired. "What the hell do they need him for?"

"I wonder what he did to deserve it," the warrant officer with malaria and a mosquito bite on his ass lamented after Nurse Cramer had read her thermometer and discovered that the soldier in white was dead.

"He went to war," the fighter pilot with the golden mustache surmised.

"We all went to war," Dunbar countered.

"That's what I mean," the warrant officer with malaria continued. "Why him? There just doesn't seem to be any logic to this system of rewards and punishment. Look what happened to me. If I had gotten syphilis or a dose of clap for my five minutes of passion on the beach instead of this damned mosquito bite, I could see some justice. But malaria? *Malaria?* Who can explain malaria as a consequence of fornication?" The warrant officer shook his head in numb astonishment.

"What about me?" Yossarian said. "I stepped out of my tent in Marrakech one night to get a bar of candy and caught your dose of clap when that Wac I never even saw before hissed me into the bushes. All I really wanted was a bar of candy, but who could turn it down?"

"That sounds like my dose of clap, all right," the warrant officer agreed. "But I've still got somebody else's malaria. Just for once I'd like to see all these things sort of straightened out, with each person getting exactly what he deserves. It might give me some confidence in this universe."

"I've got somebody else's three hundred thousand dollars," the dashing young fighter captain with the golden mustache admitted. "I've been goofing off since the day I was born. I cheated my way through prep school and college, and just about all I've been doing ever since is shacking up with pretty girls who think I'd make a good husband. I've got no ambition at all. The only thing I want to do after the war is marry some girl who's got more money than I have and shack up with lots more pretty girls. The three hundred thousand bucks was left to me before I was born by a grandfather who made a fortune selling hogwash on an international scale. I know I don't deserve it, but I'll be damned if I give it back. I wonder who it really belongs to."

"Maybe it belongs to my father," Dunbar conjectured. "He spent a lifetime at hard work and never could make enough money to even send my sister and me through college. He's dead now, so you might as well keep it."

"Now, if we can just find out who my malaria belongs to we'd be all set. It's not that I've got anything against malaria. I'd just as soon goldbrick with malaria as with anything else. It's only that I feel an injustice has been committed. Why should I have somebody else's malaria and you have my dose of clap?"

"I've got more than your dose of clap," Yossarian told him. "I've got to keep flying combat missions because of that dose of yours until they kill me."

"That makes it even worse. What's the justice in that?"

"I had a friend named Clevinger two and a half weeks ago who used to see plenty of justice in it."

"It's the highest kind of justice of all," Clevinger had gloated, clapping his hands with a merry laugh. "I can't help thinking of the *Hippolytus* of Euripedes, where the early licentiousness of Theseus is probably responsible for the asceticism of the son that helps bring about the tragedy that ruins them all. If nothing else, that episode with the Wac should teach you the evil of sexual immorality."

"It teaches me the evil of candy."

"Can't you see that you're not exactly without blame for the predicament you're in?" Clevinger had continued with undisguised relish. "If you hadn't been laid up in the hospital with venereal disease for ten days back there in Africa, you might have finished your twenty-five missions in time to be sent home before Colonel Nevers was killed and Colonel Cathcart came to replace him."

"And what about you?" Yossarian had replied. "You never got clap in Marrakech and you're in the same predicament."

"I don't know," confessed Clevinger, with a trace of mock concern. "I guess I must have done something very bad in my time."

"Do you really believe that?"

Clevinger laughed. "No, of course not. I just like to kid you along a little."

There were too many dangers for Yossarian to keep track of. There was Hitler, Mussolini and Tojo, for example, and they were all out to kill him. There was Lieutenant Scheisskopf with his fanticism for parades and there was the bloated colonel with his big fat mustache and his fanticism for retribution, and they wanted to kill him, too. There was Appleby, Havermeyer, Black and Korn. There was Nurse Cramer and Nurse Duckett, who he was almost certain wanted him dead, and there was the Texan and the C.I.D. man, about whom he had no doubt. There were bartenders, bricklayers and bus conductors all over the world who wanted him dead, landlords and tenants, traitors and patriots, lynchers, leeches and lackeys, and they were all out to bump him off. That was the secret Snowden had spilled to him on the mission to Avignon—they were out to get him; and Snowden had spilled it all over the back of the plane.

There were lymph glands that might do him in. There were kidneys, nerve sheaths and corpuscles. There were tumors of the brain. There was Hodgkin's disease, leukemia, amyotrophic lateral sclerosis. There were fertile red meadows of epithelial tissue to catch and coddle a cancer cell. There were diseases of the skin, diseases of the bone, diseases of the lung, diseases of the stomach, diseases of the heart, blood and arteries. There were diseases of the head, diseases of the neck, diseases of the chest, diseases of the intestines, diseases of the crotch. There even were diseases of the feet. There were billions of conscientious body cells oxidating away day and night like dumb animals at their complicated job of keeping him alive and healthy, and every one was a potential traitor and foe. There were so many diseases that it took a truly diseased mind to even think about them as often as he and Hungry Joe did.

Hungry Joe collected lists of fatal diseases and arranged them in alphabetical order so that he could put his finger without delay on any one he wanted to worry about. He grew very upset whenever he misplaced some or when he could not add to his list, and he would go rushing in a cold sweat to Doc Daneeka for help.

"Give him Ewing's tumor," Yossarian advised Doc Daneeka, who would come to Yossarian for help in handling Hungry Joe, "and follow it up with melanoma. Hungry Joe likes lingering diseases, but he likes the fulminating ones even more."

Doc Daneeka had never heard of either. "How do you manage to keep up on so many diseases like that?" he inquired with high professional esteem.

"I learn about them at the hospital when I study the *Reader's Digest*."

Yossarian had so many ailments to be afraid of that he was sometimes tempted to turn himself into the hospital for good and spend the rest of his life stretched out there inside an oxygen tent with a battery of specialists and nurses seated at one side of his bed twenty-four hours a day waiting for something to go wrong and at least one surgeon with a knife poised at the other, ready to jump forward and begin cutting away the moment it became necessary. Aneurysms, for instance; how else could they ever defend him in time against an aneurysm of the aorta? Yossarian felt much safer inside the hospital than outside the hospital, even though he loathed the surgeon and his knife as much as he had ever loathed anyone. He could start screaming inside a hospital and people would at least come running to try to help; outside the hospital they would throw him in prison if he ever started screaming about all the things he felt everyone ought to start screaming about, or they would put him in the hospital. One of the things he wanted to start screaming about was the surgeon's knife that was almost certain to be waiting for him and everyone else who lived long enough to die. He wondered often how he would ever recognize the first chill, flush, twinge, ache, belch, sneeze, stain, lethargy, vocal slip, loss of balance or lapse of memory that would signal the inevitable beginning of the inevitable end.

He was afraid also that Doc Daneeka would still refuse to help him when he went to him again after jumping out of Major Major's office, and he was right.

"You think you've got something to be afraid about?" Doc Daneeka demanded, lifting his delicate immaculate dark head up from his chest to gaze at Yossarian irascibly for a moment with lachrymose eyes. "What about me? My precious medical skills are rusting away here on this lously island while other doctors are cleaning up. Do you think I enjoy sitting here day after day refusing to help you? I wouldn't mind it so much if I could refuse to help you back in the States or in some place like Rome. But saying no to you here isn't easy for me, either."

"Then stop saying no. Ground me."

"I can't ground you," Doc Daneeka mumbled. "How many times do you have to be told?"

"Yes, you can. Major Major told me you're the only one in the squadron who *can* ground me."

Doc Daneeka was stunned. "Major Major told you that? When?"

"When I tackled him in the ditch."

"Major Major told you that? In a ditch?"

"He told me in his office after we left the ditch and jumped inside. He told me not to tell anyone he told me, so don't start shooting your mouth off."

"Why that dirty, scheming liar!" Doc Daneeka cried. "He wasn't supposed to tell anyone. Did he tell you how I could ground you?"

"Just by filling out a little slip of paper saying I'm on the verge of a nervous collapse and sending it to Group. Dr. Stubbs grounds men in his squadron all the time, so why can't you?"

"And what happens to the men after Stubbs does ground them?" Doc Daneeka retorted with a sneer. "They go right back on combat status, don't they? And he finds himself right up the creek. Sure, I can ground you by filling out a slip saying you're unfit to fly. But there's a catch."

"Catch-22?"

"Sure. If I take you off combat duty, Group has to approve my action, and Group isn't going to. They'll put you right back on combat status, and then where will I be? On my way to the Pacific Ocean, probably. No, thank you. I'm not going to take any chances for you."

"Isn't it worth a try?" Yossarian argued. "What's so hot about Pianosa?"

"Pianosa is terrible. But it's better than the Pacific Ocean. I wouldn't mind being shipped someplace civilized where I might pick up a buck or two in abortion money every now and then. But all they've got in the Pacific is jungles and monsoons. I'd rot there."

"You're rotting here."

Doc Daneeka flared up angrily. "Yeah? Well, at least I'm going to come out of this war alive, which is a lot more than you're going to do."

"That's just what I'm trying to tell you, goddammit. I'm asking you to save my life."

"It's not my business to save lives," Doc Daneeka retorted sullenly.

"What is your business?"

"I don't know what my business is. All they ever told me was to uphold the ethics of my profession and never give testimony against another physician. Listen. You think you're the only one whose life is in danger? What about me? Those two quacks I've got working for me in the medical tent still can't find out what's wrong with me."

"Maybe it's Ewing's tumor," Yossarian muttered sarcastically.

"Do you really think so?" Doc Daneeka exclaimed with fright.

"Oh, I don't know," Yossarian answered impatiently. "I just know I'm not going to fly any more missions. They wouldn't really shoot me, would they? I've got fifty-one."

"Why don't you at least finish the fifty-five before you take a stand?" Doc Daneeka advised. "With all your bitching, you've never finished a tour of duty even once."

"How the hell can I? The colonel keeps raising them every time I get close."

"You never finish your missions because you keep running into the hospital or going off to Rome. You'd be in a much stronger position if you had your fifty-five finished and then refused to fly. Then maybe I'd see what I could do."

"Do you promise?"

"I promise."

"What do you promise?"

"I promise that maybe I'll think about doing something to help if you finish your fifty-five missions and if you get McWatt to put my name on his flight log again so that I can draw my flight pay without going up in a plane. I'm afraid of airplanes. Did you read about that airplane crash in Idaho three weeks ago? Six people killed. It was terrible. I don't know why they want me to put in four hours' flight time every month in order to get my flight pay. Don't I have enough to worry about without worrying about being killed in an airplane crash too?"

"I worry about airplane crashes also," Yossarian told him. "You're not the only one."

"Yeah, but I'm also pretty worried about that Ewing's tumor," Doc Daneeka boasted. "Do you think that's why my nose is stuffed all the time and why I always feel so chilly? Take my pulse."

Yossarian also worried about Ewing's tumor and melanoma. Catastrophes were lurking everywhere, too numerous to count. When he contemplated the many diseases and potential accidents threatening him, he was positively astounded that he had managed to survive in good health for as long as he had. It was miraculous. Each day he faced was another dangerous mission against mortality. And he had been surviving them for twenty-eight years.

# RIKIHEI INOGUCHI, TADASHI NAKAJIMA, and ROGER PINEAU

"KAMIKAZE" means "divine wind" in Japanese. A massive typhoon—considered a divine wind from heaven—had saved Japan from an attack by the Mongol Chinese emperor Kublai Khan in the thirteenth century. In the dying days of the war, the nation created its own "divine wind," Kamikaze pilots who crashed their planes into enemy ships. Before taking off on their missions, the pilots wrote letters home.

■

## Blossoms in the Wind

In blossom today, then scattered:
Life is so like a delicate flower.
How can one expect the fragrance
To last forever?
—VICE ADMIRAL OHNISHI,
    Kamikaze Special Attack Force

What, then, were the thoughts and feelings of suicide pilots themselves as they volunteered, waited their turn, and went out on their missions?

Mr. Ichiro Ohmi made a nationwide pilgrimage for four and a half years after the war to visit the homes of kamikaze pilots. The families showed him mementoes and letters of their loved ones. He has kindly provided [us] with copies of these letters, some of which express more clearly than could any other words the thoughts and feelings of the pilots about to die.

In general, what little the enlisted pilots wrote was of a simple, straightforward nature. Academy graduates also wrote very little—perhaps because they were thoroughly indoctrinated in the way of the warrior and thus accepted their fate matter-of-factly. It was the reserve officers from civilian colleges and universities, who had had only a hasty military training before receiving their assignments, who wrote the most.[1] A few typical letters serve to convey the spirit of kamikaze pilots.

The following letter is by Flying Petty Officer First Class Isao Matsuo of the 701st Air Group. It was written just before he sortied for a kamikaze attack. His home was in Nagasaki Prefecture.

*October 28, 1944*

*Dear Parents:*

*Please congratulate me. I have been given a splendid opportunity to die. This is my last day. The destiny of our homeland hinges on the decisive battle in the seas to the south where I shall fall like a blossom from a radiant cherry tree.*

*I shall be a shield for His Majesty and die cleanly along with my squadron leader and other friends. I wish that I could be born seven times, each time to smite the enemy.*

*How I appreciate this chance to die like a man! I am grateful from the depths of my heart to the parents who have reared me with their constant prayers and tender love. And I am grateful as well to my squadron leader and superior officers who have looked after me as if I were their own son and given me such careful training.*

*Thank you, my parents, for the twenty-three years during which you have cared for me and inspired me. I hope that my present deed will in some small way repay what you have done for me. Think well of me and know that your Isao died for our country. This is my last wish, and there is nothing else that I desire.*

*I shall return in spirit and look forward to your visit at the Yasukuni Shrine. Please take good care of yourselves.*

*How glorious is the Special Attack Corps' Giretsu Unit whose Suisei bombers will attack the enemy. Movie cameramen have been here to take our pictures. It is possible that you may see us in newsreels at the theater.*

*We are sixteen warriors manning the bombers. May our death be as sudden and clean as the shattering of crystal.*

*Written at Manila on the eve of our sortie.*

*Isao*

*Soaring into the sky of the southern seas, it is our glorious mission to die as the shields of His Majesty. Cherry blossoms glisten as they open and fall.*

[1] It must be borne in mind that for many hundreds of years while the code of the warrior (*Bushido*), which stressed as necessary a willingness to die at any moment, governed the conduct of the samurai, similar principles were concurrently adopted by merchants, farmers, and artisans, stressing the value of unquestioning loyalty to the emperor, other superiors, and the people of Japan. Thus, the introduction of the kamikaze principle was not so shocking to these Japanese as it would be to an Occidental. In addition, the belief that one continues to live, in close association with both the living and the dead, after death, generally causes their concept of death to be less final and unpleasant in its implications.

Lieutenant (jg) Nobuo Ishibashi, a native of Saga City in northern Kyushu, was born in 1920. He was a member of the Tsukuba Air Group before his assignment to the special attack corps. This is his last letter home.

*Dear Father:*

*Spring seems to come early to southern Kyushu. Here the blossoms and flowers are all beautiful. There is a peace and tranquillity, and yet this place is really a battleground.*

*I slept well last night; didn't even dream. Today my head is clear and I am in excellent health.*

*It makes me feel good to know that we are on the same island at this time.*

*Please remember me when you go to the temple, and give my regards to all of our friends.*

*Nobuo*

*I think of springtime in Japan while soaring to dash against the enemy.*

The following letter was written by Ensign Ichizo Hayashi, born in 1922 in Fukuoka Prefecture of northern Kyushu. He had been reared in the Christian faith. Upon graduation from Imperial University at Kyoto he joined the Genzan (Wonsan) Air Group, from which he was assigned to the special attack corps.

*Dearest Mother:*

*I trust that you are in good health.*

*I am a member of the Shichisei Unit of the special attack corps. Half of our unit flew to Okinawa today to dive against enemy ships. The rest of us will sortie in two or three days. It may be that our attack will be made on April 8, the birthday of Buddha.*

*We are relaxing in an officers' billet located in a former school building near the Kanoya air base. Because there is no electricity, we have built a roaring log fire and I am writing these words by its light.*

*Morale is high as we hear of the glorious successes achieved by our comrades who have gone before. In the evening I stroll through clover fields, recalling days of the past.*

*On our arrival here from the northern part of Korea we were surprised to find that cherry blossoms were falling. The warmth of this southern climate is soothing and comforting.*

*Please do not grieve for me, mother. It will be glorious to die in action. I am grateful to be able to die in a battle to determine the destiny of our country.*

*As we flew into Kyushu from Korea the route did not pass over our* home, but as our planes approached the homeland I sang familiar songs and bade farewell to you. There remains nothing in particular that I wish to do or say, since Umeno will convey my last desires to you. This writing is only to tell you of the things that occur to me here.

Please dispose of my things as you wish after my death.

My correspondence has been neglected recently so I will appreciate it if you remember me to relatives and friends. I regret having to ask this of you, but there is now so little time for me to write.

Many of our boys are taking off today on their one-way mission against the enemy. I wish that you could be here in person to see the wonderful spirit and morale at this base.

Please burn all my personal papers, including my diaries. You may read them, of course, mother, if you wish, but they should not be read by other people. So please be sure to burn them after you have looked at them.

On our last sortie we will wear regular flight uniforms and a headband bearing the rising sun. Snow-white mufflers give a certain dash to our appearance.

I will also carry the rising sun flag which you gave to me. You will remember that it bears the poem, "Even though a thousand men fall to my right and ten thousand fall to my left. . . ." I will keep your picture in my bosom on the sortie, mother, and also the photo of Makio-san.

I am going to score a direct hit on an enemy ship without fail. When war results are announced you may be sure that one of the successes was scored by me. I am determined to keep calm and do a perfect job to the last, knowing that you will be watching over me and praying for my success. There will be no clouds of doubt or fear when I make the final plunge.

On our last sortie we will be given a package of bean curd and rice. It is reassuring to depart with such good luncheon fare. I think I'll also take along the charm and the dried bonito from Mr. Tateishi. The bonito will help me to rise from the ocean, mother, and swim back to you.

At our next meeting we shall have many things to talk about which are difficult to discuss in writing. But then we have lived together so congenially that many things may now be left unsaid. "I am living in a dream which will transport me from the earth tomorrow."

Yet with these thoughts I have the feeling that those who went on their missions yesterday are still alive. They could appear again at any moment.

In my case please accept my passing for once and for all. As it is said, "Let the dead past bury its dead." It is most important that families live for the living.

There was a movie shown recently in which I thought I saw Hakata. It gave me a great desire to see Hakata again just once before going on this last mission.

*Mother, I do not want you to grieve over my death. I do not mind if you weep. Go ahead and weep. But please realize that my death is for the best, and do not feel bitter about it.*

*I have had a happy life, for many people have been good to me. I have often wondered why. It is a real solace to think that I may have some merits which make me worthy of these kindnesses. It would be difficult to die with the thought that one had not been anything in life.*

*From all reports it is clear that we have blunted the actions of the enemy. Victory will be with us. Our sortie will deliver a coup de grâce to the enemy. I am very happy.*

*We live in the spirit of Jesus Christ, and we die in that spirit. This thought stays with me. It is gratifying to live in this world, but living has a spirit of futility about it now. It is time to die. I do not seek reasons for dying. My only search is for an enemy target against which to dive.*

*You have been a wonderful mother to me. I only fear that I have not been worthy of the affection you have lavished on me. The circumstances of my life make me happy and proud. I seek to maintain the reason for this pride and joy until the last moment. If I were to be deprived of present surroundings and opportunities my life would be worth nothing. Standing alone, I was good for little. I am grateful, therefore, for the opportunity to serve as a man. If these thoughts sound peculiar, it is probably because I am getting sleepy. But for my drowsiness there are many other things I should like to say.*

*There is nothing more for me to say, however, by way of farewell.*

*I will precede you now, mother, in the approach to heaven. Please pray for my admittance. I should regret being barred from the heaven to which you will surely be admitted.*

*Pray for me, mother.*

*Farewell,*
*Ichizo*

(When his sortie was delayed, this flier added the following postscript to his letter.)

*"Strolling between the paddy fields the night is serene as I listen to the chant of the frogs." I could not help but think of this during my walk last evening. I lay down in a field of clover and thought of home. Upon my return to the barracks, my friends said that I smelled of clover and it brought them memories of home and mother. Several of them commented that I must have been a mamma's boy.*

*This did not disturb me at all; in fact, I was pleased by the remark. It is an index that people like me. When I am disturbed it is good to think of the many people who have been so kind to me, and I am pacified. My efforts will be doubled to prove my appreciation of the kindhearted people it has been my pleasure to know.*

*The cherry blossoms have already fallen. I wash my face each morning in a nearby stream. It reminds me of the blossom-filled stream that ran near our home.*

*It appears that we will go to make our attack tomorrow. Thus the anniversary of my death will be April 10. If you have a service to commemorate me, I wish you to have a happy family dinner.*

*Now it is raining, the kind of rain we have in Japan rather than what I experienced in Korea. There is an old organ in our billet and someone is playing childhood songs, including the one about a mother coming to school with an umbrella for her child.*

The departure was again postponed for this flier, and he had a chance to add yet another bit to the letter, which was finally mailed after he had taken off on his final flight:

*I have thought that each day would be the last, but just as with most things in life, one can never be certain. It is the evening of April 11, and this was not my day.*

*Do hope that I was photogenic today, for several newsreel cameramen were here, and they singled me out for a special series of pictures. Later the Commander in Chief of Combined Fleet greeted us in our billet and said to me, "Please do your best." It was a great honor for me that he would speak to so humble a person as myself. He is convinced that the country's fate rests upon our shoulders.*

*Today we gathered about the organ and sang hymns.*

*Tomorrow I will plunge against the enemy without fail.*

Ensign Heiichi Okabe was born in 1923. His home was Fukuoka Prefecture of northern Kyushu. Before enlisting he was graduated from Taihoku Imperial University. His first duty was in the Wonsan Air Group, and he was transferred thence to *Shichisei* Unit No. 2 of the special attack corps. He kept a diary which was sent to his family after his final sortie. The following is an excerpt from one of his last entries in that diary:

*February 22, 1945*

*I am actually a member at last of the Kamikaze Special Attack Corps.*

*My life will be rounded out in the next thirty days. My chance will come! Death and I are waiting. The training and practice have been rigorous, but it is worthwhile if we can die beautifully and for a cause.*

*I shall die watching the pathetic struggle of our nation. My life will gallop in the next few weeks as my youth and life draw to a close. . . .*

*. . . The sortie has been scheduled for the next ten days.*

*I am a human being and hope to be neither saint nor scoundrel, hero nor fool—just a human being. As one who has spent his life in wistful longing and searching, I die resignedly in the hope that my life will serve as a "human document."*

*The world in which I live was too full of discord. As a community of rational human beings it should be better composed. Lacking a single great conductor, everyone lets loose with his own sound, creating dissonance where there should be melody and harmony.*

*We shall serve the nation gladly in its present painful struggle. We shall plunge into enemy ships cherishing the conviction that Japan has been and will be a place where only lovely homes, brave women, and beautiful friendships are allowed to exist.*

*What is the duty today? It is to fight.*
*What is the duty tomorrow? It is to win.*
*What is the daily duty? It is to die.*

*We die in battle without complaint. I wonder if others, like scientists, who pursue the war effort on their own fronts, would die as we do without complaint. Only then will the unity of Japan be such that she can have any prospect of winning the war.*

*If, by some strange chance, Japan should suddenly win this war, it would be a fatal misfortune for the future of the nation. It will be better for our nation and people if they are tempered through real ordeals which will serve to strengthen.*

*Like cherry blossoms*
*In the spring,*
*Let us fall*
*Clean and radiant.*

# PRIMO LEVI

---

PRIMO LEVI, a chemist, was a member of the Italian antifascist resistance. Deported to Auschwitz in 1944, he survived to write two of the most memorable and beautifully written memoirs of camp life: *Survival in Auschwitz,* which is excerpted here, and *The Reawakening.*

---

■

FROM *Survival in Auschwitz*

### OCTOBER 1944

We fought with all our strength to prevent the arrival of winter. We clung to all the warm hours, at every dusk we tried to keep the sun in the sky for a little longer, but it was all in vain. Yesterday evening the sun went down irrevocably behind a confusion of dirty clouds, chimney stacks and wires, and today it is winter.

We know what it means because we were here last winter; and the others will soon learn. It means that in the course of these months, from October till April, seven out of ten of us will die. Whoever does not die will suffer minute by minute, all day, every day: from the morning before dawn until the distribution of the evening soup we will have to keep our muscles continually tensed, dance from foot to foot, beat our arms under our shoulders against the cold. We will have to spend bread to acquire gloves, and lose hours of sleep to repair them when they become unstitched. As it will no longer be possible to eat in the open, we will have to eat our meals in the hut, on our feet, everyone will be assigned an area of floor as large as a hand, as it is forbidden to rest against the bunks. Wounds will open on everyone's hands, and to be given a bandage will mean waiting every evening for hours on one's feet in the snow and wind.

Just as our hunger is not that feeling of missing a meal, so our way of being cold has need of a new word. We say "hunger," we say "tiredness," "fear," "pain," we say "winter" and they are different things. They are free words, created and used by free men who lived in comfort and suffering in their homes. If the Lagers had lasted longer a new, harsh language would have been born; and only this language could express what it means to toil the whole day in the wind, with the temperature below freezing, wearing only a shirt, underpants, cloth jacket and trou-

sers, and in one's body nothing but weakness, hunger and knowledge of
the end drawing nearer.

In the same way in which one sees a hope end, winter arrived this
morning. We realized it when we left the hut to go and wash: there were
no stars, the dark cold air had the smell of snow. In roll-call square, in
the gray of dawn, when we assembled for work, no one spoke. When we
saw the first flakes of snow, we thought that if at the same time last year
they had told us that we would have seen another winter in Lager, we
would have gone and touched the electric wire-fence; and that even now
we would go if we were logical, were it not for this last senseless crazy
residue of unavoidable hope.

Because "winter" means yet another thing.

Last spring the Germans had constructed huge tents in an open
space in the Lager. For the whole of the good season each of them had
catered for over a thousand men: now the tents had been taken down,
and an excess two thousand guests crowded our huts. We old prisoners
knew that the Germans did not like these irregularities and that something would soon happen to reduce our number.

One feels the selections arriving. "Selekcja": the hybrid Latin and
Polish word is heard once, twice, many times, interpolated in foreign
conversations; at first we cannot distinguish it, then it forces itself on our
attention, and in the end it persecutes us.

This morning the Poles had said "Selekcja." The Poles are the first
to find out the news, and they generally try not to let it spread around,
because to know something which the others still do not know can always
be useful. By the time that everyone realizes that a selection is imminent,
the few possibilities of evading it (corrupting some doctor or some prominent with bread or tobacco; leaving the hut for Ka-Be or vice-versa at
the right moment so as to cross with the commission) are already their
monopoly.

In the days which follow, the atmosphere of the Lager and the yard
is filled with "Selekcja": nobody knows anything definite, but all speak
about it, even the Polish, Italian, French civilian workers whom we
secretly see in the yard. Yet the result is hardly a wave of despondency:
our collective morale is too inarticulate and flat to be unstable. The fight
against hunger, cold and work leaves little margin for thought, even for
this thought. Everybody reacts in his own way, but hardly anyone with
those attitudes which would seem the most plausible as the most realistic,
that is with resignation or despair.

All those able to find a way out, try to take it; but they are the
minority because it is very difficult to escape from a selection. The Germans apply themselves to these things with great skill and diligence.

Whoever is unable to prepare for it materially, seeks defense elsewhere. In the latrines, in the washroom, we show each other our chests,

our buttocks, our thighs, and our comrades reassure us: "You are all right, it will certainly not be your turn this time, . . . *du bist kein Musel- mann* . . . more probably mine . . . " and they undo their braces in turn and pull up their shirts.

Nobody refuses this charity to another: nobody is so sure of his own lot to be able to condemn others. I brazenly lied to old Wertheimer; I told him that if they questioned him, he should reply that he was forty-five, and he should not forget to have a shave the evening before, even if it cost him a quarter-ration of bread; apart from that he need have no fears, and in any case it was by no means certain that it was a selection for the gas chamber; had he not heard the *Blockältester* say that those chosen would go to Jaworszno to a convalescent camp?

It is absurd of Wertheimer to hope: he looks sixty, he has enormous vericose veins, he hardly even notices the hunger any more. But he lies down on his bed, serene and quiet, and replies to someone who asks him with my own words; they are the command-words in the camp these days: I myself repeated them just as—apart from details—Chajim told them to me, Chajim, who has been in Lager for three years, and being strong and robust is wonderfully sure of himself; and I believed them.

On this slender basis I also lived through the great selection of October 1944 with inconceivable tranquillity. I was tranquil because I managed to lie to myself sufficiently. The fact that I was not selected depended above all on chance and does not prove that my faith was well-founded.

Monsieur Pinkert is also, a priori, condemned: it is enough to look at his eyes. He calls me over with a sign, and with a confidential air tells me that he has been informed—he cannot tell me the source of infor-mation—that this time there is really something new: the Holy See, by means of the International Red Cross . . . in short, he personally guar-antees both for himself and for me, in the most absolute manner, that every danger is ruled out; as a civilian he was, as is well known, attaché to the Belgian embassy at Warsaw.

Thus in various ways, even those days of vigil, which in the telling seem as if they ought to have passed every limit of human torment, went by not very differently from other days.

The discipline in both the Lager and Buna is in no way relaxed: the work, cold and hunger are sufficient to fill up every thinking moment.

Today is working Sunday, *Arbeitssonntag*: we work until 1 p.m., then we return to camp for the shower, shave and general control for skin diseases and lice. And in the yards, everyone knew mysteriously that the selection would be today.

The news arrived, as always, surrounded by a halo of contradictory or suspect details: the selection in the infirmary took place this morning; the percentage was seven per cent of the whole camp, thirty, fifty per cent of the patients. At Birkenau, the crematorium chimney has been smoking for ten days. Room has to be made for an enormous convoy arriving from the Poznan ghetto. The young tell the young that all the old ones will be chosen. The healthy tell the healthy that only the ill will be chosen. Specialists will be excluded. German Jews will be excluded. Low Numbers will be excluded. You will be chosen. I will be excluded.

At 1 p.m. exactly the yard empties in orderly fashion and for two hours the gray unending army files past the two control stations where, as on every day, we are counted and recounted, and past the military band which for two hours without interruption plays, as on every day, those marches to which we must synchronize our steps at our entrance and our exit.

It seems like every day, the kitchen chimney smokes as usual, the distribution of the soup is already beginning. But then the bell is heard, and at that moment we realize that we have arrived.

Because this bell always sounds at dawn, when it means the reveille; but if it sounds during the day, it means "*Blocksperre*," enclosure in huts, and this happens when there is a selection to prevent anyone avoiding it, or when those selected leave for the gas, to prevent anyone seeing them leave.

Our *Blockältester* knows his business. He has made sure that we have all entered, he has the door locked, he has given everyone his card with his number, name, profession, age and nationality and he has ordered everyone to undress completely, except for shoes. We wait like this, naked, with the card in our hands, for the commission to reach our hut. We are hut 48, but one can never tell if they are going to begin at hut 1 or hut 60. At any rate, we can rest quietly at least for an hour, and there is no reason why we should not get under the blankets on the bunk and keep warm.

Many are already drowsing when a barrage of orders, oaths and blows proclaims the imminent arrival of the commission. The *Blockältester* and his helpers, starting at the end of the dormitory, drive the crowd of frightened, naked people in front of them and cram them in the *Tagesraum* which is the Quartermaster's office. The *Tagesraum* is a room seven yards by four: when the drive is over, a warm and compact human mass is jammed into the *Tagesraum*, perfectly filling all the corners, exercising such a pressure on the wooden walls as to make them creak.

Now we are all in the *Tagesraum*, and besides there being no time, there is not even any room in which to be afraid. The feeling of the warm flesh pressing all around is unusual and not unpleasant. One has to take care to hold up one's nose so as to breathe, and not to crumple or lose the card in one's hand.

The *Blockältester* has closed the connecting-door and has opened the other two which lead from the dormitory and the *Tagesraum* outside. Here, in front of the two doors, stands the arbiter of our fate, an SS subaltern. On his right is the *Blockältester*, on his left, the quartermaster of the hut. Each one of us, as he comes naked out of the *Tagesraum* into the cold October air, has to run the few steps between the two doors, give the card to the SS man and enter the dormitory door. The SS man, in the fraction of a second between two successive crossings, with a glance at one's back and front, judges everyone's fate, and in turn gives the card to the man on his right or his left, and this is the life or death of each of us. In three or four minutes a hut of two hundred men is "done," as is the whole camp of twelve thousand men in the course of the afternoon.

Jammed in the charnel-house of the *Tagesraum*, I gradually felt the human pressure around me slacken, and in a short time it was my turn. Like everyone, I passed by with a brisk and elastic step, trying to hold my head high, my chest forward and my muscles contracted and conspicuous. With the corner of my eye I tried to look behind my shoulders, and my card seemed to end on the right.

As we gradually come back into the dormitory we are allowed to dress ourselves. Nobody yet knows with certainty his own fate, it has first of all to be established whether the condemned cards were those on the right or the left. By now there is no longer any point in sparing each other's feelings with superstitious scruples. Everybody crowds around the oldest, the most wasted-away, and most "muselmann"; if their cards went to the left, the left is certainly the side of the condemned.

Even before the selection is over, everybody knows that the left was effectively the "*schlechte Seite*," the bad side. There have naturally been some irregularities: René, for example, so young and robust, ended on the left; perhaps it was because he has glasses, perhaps because he walks a little stooped like a myope, but more probably because of a simple mistake: René passed the commission immediately in front of me and there could have been a mistake with our cards. I think about it, discuss it with Alberto, and we agree that the hypothesis is probable; I do not know what I will think tomorrow and later; today I feel no distinct emotion.

It must equally have been a mistake about Sattler, a huge Transylvanian peasant who was still at home only twenty days ago; Sattler does not understand German, he has understood nothing of what has taken place, and stands in a corner mending his shirt. Must I go and tell him that his shirt will be of no more use?

There is nothing surprising about these mistakes: the examination is too quick and summary, and in any case, the important thing for the Lager is not that the most useless prisoners be eliminated, but that free posts be quickly created, according to a certain percentage previously fixed.

The selection is now over in our hut, but it continues in the others, so that we are still locked in. But as the soup-pots have arrived in the meantime, the *Blockältester* decides to proceed with the distribution at once. A double ration will be given to those selected. I have never discovered if this was a ridiculously charitable initiative of the *Blockältester*, or an explicit disposition of the SS, but in fact, in the interval of two or three days (sometimes even much longer) between the selection and the departure, the victims at Monowitz-Auschwitz enjoyed this privilege.

Ziegler holds out his bowl, collects his normal ration and then waits there expectantly. "What do you want?" asks the *Blockältester*: according to him, Ziegler is entitled to no supplement, and he drives him away, but Ziegler returns and humbly persists. He was on the left, everybody saw it, let the *Blockältester* check the cards; he has the right to a double ration. When he is given it, he goes quietly to his bunk to eat.

Now everyone is busy scraping the bottom of his bowl with his spoon so as not to waste the last drops of the soup; a confused, metallic clatter, signifying the end of the day. Silence slowly prevails and then, from my bunk on the top row, I see and hear old Kuhn praying aloud, with his beret on his head, swaying backward and forward violently. Kuhn is thanking God because he has not been chosen.

Kuhn is out of his senses. Does he not see Beppo the Greek in the bunk next to him, Beppo who is twenty years old and is going to the gas chamber the day after tomorrow and knows it and lies there looking fixedly at the light without saying anything and without even thinking any more? Can Kuhn fail to realize that next time it will be his turn? Does Kuhn not understand that what has happened today is an abomination, which no propitiatory prayer, no pardon, no expiation by the guilty, which nothing at all in the power of man can ever clean again?

If I were God, I would spit at Kuhn's prayer.

# THOMAS BERNHARD

THE NOVELIST Thomas Bernhard spent the war in a boardinghouse for boys, an "educational prison" in Salzburg.

■

FROM *Gathering Evidence*

As a schoolboy I was haunted chiefly by two fears. One was the fear of everything and everybody at the boarding house, but especially of Grünkranz, who, with low military cunning, was always appearing from nowhere to hand out punishments. He was a model officer, of both the army and the SA, whom I hardly ever saw in civilian clothes but nearly always in his captain's uniform or his SA uniform, an archetypal Nazi who also conducted a male-voice choir in Salzburg and who was probably incapable, as I now realize, of coping with his sexual tensions and perverted sadistic urges. My other fear was fear of the war, with which we had long been familiarized by reports in the newspapers or from relatives on leave from the forces, such as my guardian, stationed in the Balkans, or my uncle, serving in Norway. The latter I always remember as a brilliant communist and inventor—he remained an inventor throughout his life—who always put extraordinary and dangerous thoughts into my head and confronted me with incredible and dangerous ideas, a truly creative spirit, though a flawed and unstable personality. We had been aware of the war as a *nightmare* at second hand which was being played out a long way away, engulfing the whole of Europe and devouring many human lives; but now it was suddenly brought home to us by the almost daily air-raid warnings. Caught up as I was *in and between* these two fears, this period at the boarding house inevitably became a time of mortal danger for me. What I studied in class was forced into the background, on the one hand by my fear of the National Socialist Grünkranz, on the other by my fear of war, in the shape of hundreds and thousands of droning, menacing aircraft which daily darkened the cloudless sky; for the greater part of our time was no longer spent working at our lessons in the Andräschule or the study rooms, but in the air-raid shelters, which we had seen being driven, over a period of months, into the two hills of the city by forced labor from abroad, mainly Russian, French, Polish, and Czech prisoners working under inhuman conditions. These shelters were enormous tunnels, hundreds of yards long, into which the populace streamed every day, at first hesitantly and out of curiosity but later, after the first air-raids on Salzburg, in their thousands out of fear and terror. In these dark caverns we witnessed the most terrible scenes, very often scenes of death, for the air supply was inadequate, and I often found myself sharing these dark, wet tunnels first with dozens and then gradually with hundreds of men, women, and children who had fainted. I can still see the thousands of people who had taken refuge in them anxiously standing, squatting, or lying there, pressed close together. The shelters underneath the hills afforded protection from the bombs, but many people died there of suffocation or fright, and I saw many of the victims being dragged out dead. Sometimes a whole succession of people fainted immediately after entering the shelter in the Glockengasse, the one we ourselves always used. All the pupils from the boarding house were marched there by boys who had been detailed to lead us—older boys from our school—together with hundreds and thousands of children from other schools. We were marched to the shelter along the Wolf Dietrich-Strasse, past the Hexenturm and along the Linzergasse and the Glockengasse. When people fainted in the shelter, they had to be dragged out immediately if their lives were to be saved. Several large buses containing stretchers and blankets were permanently parked by the entrances to the shelters. Those who had fainted were taken to the buses, but there was usually not enough room for all of them, and those who could not be accommodated in the buses were laid on the ground in the open air in front of the entrances, while those in the buses were driven through the city to the Neutor. Here the buses were parked, their occupants still inside, until the all-clear was sounded, by which time some of those inside were already dead. I myself fainted in the Glockengasse shelter on two occasions and was dragged into one of these buses and driven to the Neutor, but on each occasion I quickly recovered in the fresh air and was able to observe what went on at the Neutor—how helpless women and children gradually regained consciousness or quite simply failed to do so. It was never possible to ascertain whether those who did not recover had died of suffocation or of fear. These people who died of suffocation or fear were the first victims of the air attacks—or terror attacks, as they were called—even before a single bomb had fallen on Salzburg. By the time this happened, in mid-October 1944, at noon on a completely clear autumn day, a large number of people had already died in this way. They were the first victims of the air-raids, later to be joined by the many hundreds or thousands killed by the bombs. We schoolboys were afraid of an *actual* bombing raid on our city, which had been entirely spared until that day in October, yet at the same time we secretly longed for the *actual experience* of an air attack. We had not yet experienced such a terrible event, though we knew that hundreds of other towns in Germany and Austria had been bombed, many of them having been completely destroyed and obliterated. For the facts had not been concealed from us—indeed they had been forced upon our attention daily in all their terrible authenticity by countless personal accounts and newspaper reports—and the truth is that in our adolescent curiosity we wanted our city to be bombed too. Then it happened—I think it was the seventeenth of October. That day, as on hundreds of previous occasions, we had gone straight to the shelter in the Glockengasse by way of the Wolf Dietrich-Strasse, without entering or leaving the school. We had witnessed the by now familiar but still horrifying proceedings in the shelter with all the eagerness for sensation that is typical of the young: we had seen the fear of those standing, sitting, or lying there, mostly children, teenagers, women, and old men —all of them more or less bewildered, in spite of the fact that their lives had for so long been completely dominated by the terrible events of the war—suspiciously eying one another all the time in their universal helplessness, in that permanent state of watchfulness induced by the war, as if this were the only thing that kept them alive, apathetically watching everything with eyes dimmed by fear and hunger, the grown-ups accepting largely with indifference everything that happened, helpless to influence it. Like us, they had long since become accustomed to seeing people die in the shelter; they had long since come to accept the shelter, with all its horror and darkness, as their daily place of resort and come to terms with the continual humiliation and indignity to which they were subjected. That day, at a time when normally the all-clear would already have sounded, we suddenly heard a rumbling and felt an extraordinary shaking of the earth. This was followed by complete silence throughout the shelter. People looked at each other, saying nothing; but from the way they kept silent it was possible to gather that what they had been fearing for months had now happened—and in fact, after the tremor and the quarter of an hour's silence that followed it, word quickly spread that bombs had fallen on the city. After the all-clear, people pushed their way out of the shelter more urgently than usual, anxious to see for themselves what had happened. When we got into the open, however, nothing had changed, and we concluded that the talk of the town's being bombed had been just another rumor. We at once doubted the truth of what we had heard and once more persuaded ourselves that this city, described as one of the most beautiful in the world, would never be bombed—a conviction which many people in the town actually held. There was a clear grayish-blue sky, and I could neither see nor hear any evidence of an air attack. Suddenly it was reported after all that the old city—that is, the part of the city lying on the opposite bank of the Salzach—had been destroyed. *Everything* had been destroyed, it was said, and so we set off down the Linzergasse at a run. We could now hear all kinds of sirens and alarm bells from ambulances and fire engines; and after running across the Bergstrasse behind the Gablerbräu and into the Makartplatz, we saw the first signs of destruction. The streets were strewn with broken glass and rubble, and the air carried the distinctive smell of total war. A direct hit had turned the so-called Mozart House into a smoking pile of rubble, and the surrounding buildings, as we saw at once, were badly damaged. Terrible though the sight was, nobody stopped. We all ran on, expecting to find scencs of far greater destruction in the old city, where we suspected that most of the damage had taken place and from which there emanated all kinds of noises and unfamiliar smells indicating a greater degree of devastation. Until we had crossed the Staatsbrücke I had been unable to see any change in the familiar sights, but in the Old Market, as I could already see from some distance away, Slama's, the well-known and highly reputed gentlemen's outfitters, had been severely damaged. (This was the shop where my grandfather used to buy his clothes whenever he had the money and the opportunity.) All the windows, including the display windows, were smashed, and the clothes in the window display, which had still been highly desirable despite their inferior wartime quality, were all in shreds. To my amazement none of the people I saw in the Old Market took any notice of Slama's; they went on running in the direction of the Residenzplatz. I was with a number of other boys from the boarding house, and as soon as we turned the corner by Slama's, I knew what it was that had made people rush on without stopping: the cathedral had been hit by a so-called aerial mine, and the dome had crashed into the nave. We had reached the Residenzplatz at just the right moment: an enormous cloud of dust hung over the ruined cathedral, and where the dome had been there was a great gaping hole the size of the dome itself. From the corner by Slama's we had a direct view of the great paintings which had adorned the walls of the dome and were now for the most part savagely destroyed, what remained of them standing out against the clear blue sky in the light of the afternoon sun. It was as though this gigantic building, which dominated the lower part of the city, had had its back ripped open and were bleeding from a terrible wound. The whole square below the cathedral was strewn with fragments of masonry, and the people who had come running like us from all quarters gazed in amazement at this unparalleled and unquestionably fascinating picture, which to me seemed monstrously *beautiful* and not in the least frightening. Suddenly *confronted* with the absolute savagery of war, yet at the same time *fascinated* by the monstrous sight before my eyes, I stood for several minutes silently contemplating the scene of destruction presented by the square with its brutally mutilated cathedral—a scene created only a short while before, which had still not quite come to rest and was so overwhelming that I was unable to take it in.

# RANDALL JARRELL

THE AMERICAN poet, novelist, and critic Randall Jarrell served with the U.S.A.F. during World War II. His first book of war poems, *Little Friend, Little Friend,* was published in 1945.

■

## Losses

It was not dying: everybody died.
It was not dying: we had died before
In the routine crashes—and our fields
Called up the papers, wrote home to our folks,
And the rates rose, all because of us.
We died on the wrong page of the almanac,
Scattered on mountains fifty miles away;
Diving on haystacks, fighting with a friend,
We blazed up on the lines we never saw.
We died like aunts or pets or foreigners.
(When we left high school nothing else had died
For us to figure we had died like.)

In our new planes, with our new crews, we bombed
The ranges by the desert or the shore,
Fired at towed targets, waited for our scores—
And turned into replacements and woke up
One morning, over England, operational.
It wasn't different: but if we died
It was not an accident but a mistake
(But an easy one for anyone to make).
We read our mail and counted up our missions—
In bombers named for girls, we burned
The cities we had learned about in school—
Till our lives wore out; our bodies lay among
The people we had killed and never seen.
When we lasted long enough they gave us medals;

When we died they said, "Our casualties were low."
They said, "Here are the maps"; we burned the cities.


It was not dying—no, not ever dying;
But the night I died I dreamed that I was dead,
And the cities said to me: "Why are you dying?
We are satisfied, if you are; but why did I die?"

# EVELYN WAUGH

EVELYN WAUGH was one of the most brilliant comic novelists of his generation—some have said the most brilliant. What follows is a brief excerpt from his diary.

■

FROM *The Diaries of Evelyn Waugh*

*Saturday 11 November 1944*

Clissold and I went for a long walk, starting on crisp, frozen ground and returning, when the sun was up, through deep mud. In the afternoon a bath. Thinking the money well spent if it would keep Randolph quiet, Freddy and I have bet him £10 each that he will not read the Bible right through in a fortnight. He has set to work but not as quietly as we hoped. He sits bouncing about on his chair, chortling and saying, "I say, did you know this came in the Bible 'bring down my grey hairs with sorrow to the grave'?" Or simply, "God, isn't God a shit."

The first of a large party of escaped prisoners of war arrived here.

# ELIE WIESEL

FOLLOWING is an excerpt from *Night*, Elie Wiesel's Holocaust memoir. Wiesel's other books include *The Accident, The Town Beyond the Wall,* and *The Jews of Silence.*

■

## FROM *Night*

I witnessed other hangings. I never saw a single one of the victims weep. For a long time those dried-up bodies had forgotten the bitter taste of tears.

Except once. The *Oberkapo* of the fifty-second cable unit was a Dutchman: a giant, well over six feet. Seven hundred prisoners worked under his orders and they all loved him like a brother. No one had ever received a blow at his hands, nor an insult from his lips.

He had a young boy under him, a *pipel*, as they were called. A child with a refined and beautiful face, unheard of in this camp.

(At Buna, the *pipel* were loathed: they were often crueler than adults. I once saw one of thirteen beating his father because the latter had not made his bed properly. The old man was crying softly while the boy shouted: "If you don't stop crying at once I shan't bring you any more bread. Do you understand?" But the Dutchman's little servant was loved by all. He had the face of a sad angel.)

One day, the electric power station at Buna was blown up. The Gestapo, summoned to the spot, suspected sabotage. They found a trail. It eventually led to the Dutch *Oberkapo*. And there, after a search, they found an important stock of arms.

The *Oberkapo* was arrested immediately. He was tortured for a period of weeks, but in vain. He would not give a single name. He was transferred to Auschwitz. We never heard of him again.

But his little *pipel* had stayed behind in the camp, in prison. Also put to torture, he too would not speak. Then the SS sentenced him to death, with two other prisoners who had been discovered with arms.

One day when we came back from work, we saw three gallows rearing up in the assembly place; three black crows. Roll-call. SS all around us, machine-guns trained: the traditional ceremony. Three victims in chains—and one of them, the little *pipel*, the sad-eyed angel.

The SS seemed more preoccupied, more disturbed than usual. To hang a young boy in front of thousands of spectators was no light matter.

The head of the camp read the verdict. All eyes were on the child. He was lividly pale, almost calm, biting his lips. The gallows threw its shadow over him.

This time the *Lagerkapo* refused to act as executioner. Three SS replaced him.

The three victims mounted together on to the chairs.

The three necks were placed at the same moment within the nooses.

"Long live liberty!" cried the two adults.

But the child was silent.

"Where is God? Where is He?" someone behind me asked.

At a sign from the head of the camp, the three chairs tipped over.

Total silence throughout the camp. On the horizon, the sun was setting.

"Bare your heads!" yelled the head of the camp. His voice was raucous. We were weeping.

"Cover your heads!"

Then the march past began. The two adults were no longer alive. Their tongues hung, swollen, blue-tinged. But the third rope was still moving: being so light, the child was still alive. . . .

For more than half an hour he stayed there, struggling between life and death, dying in slow agony under our eyes. And we had to look him full in the face. He was still alive when I passed in front of him. His tongue was still red, his eyes were not yet glazed.

Behind me, I heard the same man asking:

"Where is God now?"

And I heard a voice within me answer him:

"Where is He? Here He is—He is hanging here, on this gallows. . . ."

That night the soup tasted of corpses.

# STUDS TERKEL

STUDS TERKEL'S *"The Good War"* is a major work of oral history, offering us a compelling picture of World War II through the voices of men and women who experienced it at firsthand. Here, the account of the poet John Ciardi, who served as an air force gunner in the Pacific.

∎

## The Bombers and the Bombed

I had no attraction to the military, yet we had to go out and do something. I was terribly innocent at twenty-six. I was the tanglefoot civilian who did not know what he was doing. I did not want to go in the navy. I would not under any circumstances get into a submarine. I didn't see any point in being a footslogger, sleeping in the mud.

I had dreams of being a pilot, so I signed up as an aviation cadet. The army decided I was not pilot material. The army was right. They sent me to navigation school. I would have come out as a navigator and been sent to the Eighth Air Force. As a graduate student, I had signed some petitions in favor of the Spanish Loyalists. When I came up for graduation from the navigation school, I was classified as a PAF—a premature anti-fascist. The Dies Committee had wired in. I did not get a commission. A year later, I heard that all forty-four men of my graduating class were either KIA or MIA, dead or missing in action.

When we got to Saipan, I was a gunner on a B-29. It seemed certain to me we were not going to survive. We had to fly thirty-five missions. The average life of a crew was something between six and eight missions. So you simply took the extra pay, took the badges, took relief from dirty details. Now pay up.

There was a way out. Any man who was tired of flying could report to the squadron CO and ground himself. He would be put on permanent garbage detail. Permanent garbage detail is better than burning to death. Yet in all the time we were there, most of a year, only two men in the whole squadron put themselves on permanent garbage detail. Not a one received any wisecracks from anybody. Everybody knew that if he dared, he'd be on that garbage truck with 'em.

I don't think it was patriotism. I think it was a certain amount of pride. The unit was the crew. You belonged to eleven men. You're trained together, you're bound together. I was once ordered to fly in the place of a gunner who had received a shrapnel wound. I dreaded that mission. I wanted to fly with my own crew. I didn't know those other people. I didn't want to run the risk of dying with strangers.

I was saved by two more flukes. The first was the Dies Committee.

We got to Saipan in November of '44, in time to fly the first raids over Tokyo. Those were long missions. We were in the air normally about fourteen hours. Most of it was over the open Pacific. We had to get over the coast, make our bombing run, and then make it back to Saipan. We took some rather heavy losses. Sixty-five percent of them, as I recall, were due to engine failures. The B-29 tended to catch fire. They finally flew the bugs out of this new plane.

At one time, one of the blisters on our plane was damaged—the plexiglass bubble out of which the gunner tracked. There were no spares on the island. We sat it out almost all the month of February of '45, waiting for a replacement. During that time, we lost a lot of crews. We were out surfing, playing in the ocean, spear fishing. I would give myself at least a forty percent chance of having been killed in February, except for this blister thing. Instead, it turned into a vacation.

The third time was a pure fluke. I was halfway through the tour of missions. I know it was over fourteen. You got an air medal for surviving five missions. If you survived eight more, you got another air medal. The next one was a DFC. I got two air medals, so I must have had fourteen or fifteen missions. I received orders to report to headquarters. The colonel in charge of awards and decorations said, "We've run into real trouble with our program. We need somebody with combat-crew experience who can write. You've taught college English, you've published a book. You're now working for me. You're going to take charge of the awards and decorations."

This program was raided by the brass, so that decorations were pointless after a while. Anybody up to the grade of a captain, you may assume earned it. Anybody from the grade of major up who has a high decoration *may* have earned it, but you don't have to believe it.

"Go to your squadron," the colonel said, "pick up your gear. We'll keep you on flying pay. You'll have to fly back and forth to Guam to report to the board. While you're at it, sew on an extra stripe." I was then a staff sergeant. I couldn't make tech for having been shot at, but I did it for grinding out words.

A few missions later, the crew I had been on took a direct hit over Tokyo Bay from an unexploded flake shell. It went right through the wing gas tank and the plane just blew up, disintegrated in midair. Just one of those flukes.

That's three times I should have been absolutely dead, except for flukes.

I feel sorry for the kids of Vietnam. They couldn't have figured out what it was they were fighting for. I knew why I was there. That doesn't mean I wasn't scared. I don't know what I would have done in Vietnam. I mean, I'm a botch as a killer, as a soldier. But as an American, I felt very strongly I did not want to be alive to see the Japanese impose surrender terms.

On the night before a mission, you reviewed the facts. You tried to get some sleep. The army is very good at keeping you awake forever before you have a long mission. Sleep wouldn't come to you. You get to thinking by this time tomorrow you may have burned to death. I used to have little routines for kidding myself: Forget it, you died last week. You'd get some Dutch courage out of that.

We were in the terrible business of burning out Japanese towns. That meant women and old people, children. One part of me—a surviving savage voice—says, I'm sorry we left any of them living. I wish we'd finished killing them all. Of course, as soon as rationality overcomes the first impulse, you say, Now, come on, this is the human race, let's try to be civilized.

I had to condition myself to be a killer. This was remote control. All we did was push buttons. I didn't see anybody we killed. I saw the fires we set. The first four and a half months was wasted effort. We lost all those crews for nothing. We had been trained to do precision high-altitude bombing from thirty-two thousand feet. It was all beautifully planned, except we discovered the Siberian jet stream. The winds went off all computed bomb tables. We began to get winds at two hundred knots, and the bombs simply scattered all over Japan. We were hitting nothing and losing planes.

Curtis LeMay came in and changed the whole operation. He had been head of the Eighth Air Force and was sent over to take on the Twentieth. That's the one I was in. He changed tactics. He said, Go in at night from five thousand feet, without gunners, just a couple of rear-end observers. We'll save weight on the turrets and on ammunition. The Japanese have no fighter resistance at night. They have no radar. We'll drop fire sticks.

I have some of my strike photos at home. Tokyo looked like one leveled bed of ash. The only things standing were some stone buildings. If you looked at the photos carefully, you'd see that they were gutted. Some of the people jumped into rivers to get away from these fire storms. They were packed in so tight to get away from the fire, they suffocated. They were so close to one another, they couldn't fall over. It must have been horrible.

I have one image of an early raid in which a Japanese fighter plane bored in. I saw his goggled face as he went over the top of our plane. I got a burst into him and he was gone. I got a probable for it. After the first raid, nothing came at us from behind. The Japanese lined up across the sky and came in to ram. They would all swarm on the B-29 and finish it off. That happened from time to time.

We were playing a lottery. A certain number of planes had to be lost. You were just hoping that by blind chance yours would not be. When news of that atom bomb came—we didn't know what it was—we won the lottery. Hey, we're gonna get out of here! We may survive this after all.

I never had any ambition to be a warrior. I had to condition myself, to sell myself against my own death. One measure of that is hatred. I did want every Japanese dead. Part of it was our own propaganda machine, but part of it was what we heard accurately. This was the enemy. We were there to eliminate them. That's the soldier's short-term bloody view.

I was never really a soldier. I was caught up in the army, a civilian putting in my service. When it was over, I had a longer view. It's anyone's universe. Anyone has as good a right to it as I have. Who am I to want to go out killing people?

I think the Germans of that era were guilty. On the other hand, I think any people subjected to a propaganda barrage, with their patriotic feelings worked on, could become savage.

When you're on a mission and you saw a Japanese plane go down, you cheered. This was a football game. When one of your guys went down, you sighed. It was miserable. One of the saddest things I ever saw, when we were flying wing on a plane that got hit, was the barber's-chair gunner in the big bubble at the very top. He was right there beside us in plain sight, beginning to go down. He just waved his hand goodbye. There was nothing you could do. You couldn't reach out to touch him. Of course, that got you.

You were under a compulsion to say nice things about the guy. You saw a plane break up. You saw it catch fire. You saw two chutes, one of them burning. Whatever it was, the truth is—the dark truth—you were secretly glad. It could have been you. It was a superstitious ritual we were playing. There were a certain number of blackballs to be passed out. Every time another plane went down, it was taken out of play. Somebody had to catch it, and somebody else caught it for you. It didn't make any sense, but that's the way we felt. That's a dirty, dark thing to say. When we go to funerals of old friends these days, in one corner of our minds we're saying, Well, I outlived that old bastard.

When the news came that so-and-so's crew had been hit and gone down over Tokyo, you made sounds: Oh, my God. But somewhere, very deep down in your psyche, is, It could have been me.

My first poems of any consequence, I feel, were war poems. I'm not a war poet, but just about that time they were beginning to come together. I found myself writing a lot of elegies for friends of mine who did not make it. Then it occurred to me that the way things were going, I might not make it. So I decided to write my own: "Elegy Just in Case . . .

*He recites:*

Here lie Ciardi's pearly bones
In their ripe organic mess.
Jungle brown, his chromosomes
Breed to a new address.

Here lies the sgt.'s mortal wreck
Lily spiked and termite kissed,
Spider pendant from his neck
And a beetle on his wrist.

Bring the tick and southern flies
Where the land crabs run unmourning
Through a night of jungle skies
To a climeless morning.

And bring the chalked eraser here
Fresh from rubbing out his name.
Burn the crew-board for a bier.
(Also Colonel what's-his-name.)

Let no dice be stored and still.
Let no poker deck be torn.
But pour the smuggled rye until
The barracks threshold is outworn.

File the papers, pack the clothes,
Send the coded word through air—
"We regret and no one knows
Where the sgt. goes from here."

▪ **1945** ▪

# PRIMO LEVI

---

PRIMO LEVI survived Auschwitz and went on to write
two of the most memorable memoirs of camp life: *Survival in Auschwitz* and *The Reawakening.* What follows
is an excerpt from a later work, *Moments of Reprieve,*
in which, once more, he describes and reflects upon
his experiences in the camp.

---

■

FROM *Moments of Reprieve*

### SMALL CHANGES

A few days ago in a group of friends we were talking about the
influence of small causes on the course of history. This is a classic con-
troversy, classically lacking a definitive and absolute solution: it can be
safely affirmed that the history of the world (well, let's be more modest
and say the history of the Mediterranean basin) would have been completely different if Cleopatra's nose had been longer, as Pascal would
have it, and just as safely you can affirm that it would have been exactly
the same, as Marxist orthodoxy and the historiography proposed by Tol-
stoy in *War and Peace* contend. Since it is not possible to reconjure up a
Cleopatra with a different nose but with the world around her exactly
the same as the historical Cleopatra's, there is no possibility of proving
or disproving either thesis; the problem is a pseudoproblem. Real problems sooner or later are resolved; on the contrary, pseudoproblems are
not. So, not being open to definitive solution, they are extremely long-
lived: the one under discussion is many centuries old, and destined to
live that long again.

We all agreed, at any rate, with the observation that small causes
can have a determining effect on individual histories, just as moving the
pointer of a railroad switch by a few inches can shunt a thousand-ton
train with two thousand passengers aboard to Madrid instead of Hamburg. A pistol bullet that severs a carotid artery has a very different effect
from one that only grazes it. And a casual encounter, a bet at roulette, a
lightning bolt . . .

At this point, everyone present insisted on telling about the small
cause that had radically changed his life, and I too, when the excitement
had abated, told mine, or, to be more precise, I refined the details, since
I had already told the story many times, both in conversation and in writing.

Exactly forty years ago I was a prisoner in Auschwitz, working in a chemical laboratory. I was hungry and on the lookout for something small and unusual (and therefore of high commercial value) to steal and exchange for bread. After various attempts (some successful, some not), I found a drawer full of pipettes. Pipettes are small glass tubes, precisely graduated, which are used to transfer exact amounts of liquid from one container to another. Nowadays more hygienic methods are employed, but at the time this was done by sucking up the liquid so that it rose exactly to the desired marking, then letting it descend by its own weight. There were a lot of pipettes. I slipped a dozen into a hidden pocket I had sewed inside my jacket, and took them back to the Camp. They are graceful, delicate objects, and on the way back several of them broke. Anyway, as soon as roll call was over and before the distribution of the evening soup began, I ran to the infirmary and offered the unbroken ones to a Polish male nurse whom I knew and who worked in the Contagious Ward, explaining that they could be used for clinical analyses.

The Pole looked at my booty with little interest and then told me that for that day it was too late; he no longer had any bread. All he could offer me was a bit of soup. He was a shrewd bargainer and knew that I had no choice. To carry those obviously stolen goods around in the Camp was dangerous, and there was nobody else I could offer them to. He enjoyed a monopoly and took advantage of it.

I accepted the proposed payment; the Pole disappeared among the patients of his ward and came back shortly with a bowl half full of soup, but half full in a curious way: vertically. It was very cold, the soup had frozen, and someone had removed half of it with a spoon, like someone eating half a cake. Who could have left half a bowl of soup in that reign of hunger? Almost certainly someone who had died halfway through the meal, and, given the sort of place this was, someone sick with a contagious disease. In the last weeks, diphtheria and scarlet fever had broken out in the Camp in epidemic proportions.

But at Auschwitz we didn't observe precautions of this kind. First came hunger, then all the rest; leaving something edible uneaten was not what is commonly called a "sin," it was unthinkable, indeed physically impossible. That same evening, my alter ego Alberto and I shared the suspect soup. Alberto was my age, had the same build, temperament, and profession as I, and we slept in the same bunk. We even looked somewhat alike; the foreign comrades and the Kapo considered it superfluous to distinguish between us. They constantly confused us, and demanded that whether they called "Alberto" or "Primo," whichever one of us happened to be closest should answer.

We were interchangeable, so to speak, and anyone would have predicted for us the same fate: we would both go under or both survive. But it was just at this point that the switch-point came into play, the small cause with the determining effects: Alberto had had scarlet fever as a child and was immune; I was not.

I realized the consequences of our rashness a few days later. At reveille, while Alberto felt perfectly all right I had a bad sore throat, I had trouble swallowing, and had a high fever, but "reporting" sick in the morning was not allowed, so I went to the lab as I did every day. I felt deathly sick but on that day of all days was given an unusual task. In that lab, half a dozen girls, German, Polish, and Ukrainian, worked, or pretended to work. The head of the lab called me aside and told me I must teach Fräulein Drechsel an analytical method which I myself had learned only a few weeks before. Fräulen Drechsel was a chubby German adolescent, clumsy, sullen, and dumb. Most of the time she avoided looking at us three slave-chemists. When she did, her dull eyes expressed a vague hostility, made up of mistrust, embarrassment, revulsion, and fear. She had never addressed a word to me. I found her disagreeable and distrusted her as well, because on preceding days I had seen her slink off with the very young SS man who watched over that department. And besides, she alone wore a swastika badge pinned to her shirt. She might have been a Hitler Youth squadron-leader.

She was a very bad pupil because of her stupidity, and I was a very bad teacher because I didn't feel well, didn't speak German well, and above all because I wasn't motivated; if anything, I was countermotivated. Why in the world should I have to teach that creature anything? The normal teacher-pupil relationship, which is a descending one, came into conflict with ascending relationships: I was Jewish and she was Aryan, I was dirty and sick, she was clean and healthy.

I believe it was the only time I have deliberately done someone wrong. The analytical method I was supposed to teach her involved the use of a pipette: a sister of those to which I owed the illness coursing through my veins. I took one from the drawer and showed Fräulein Drechsel how to use it, inserting it between my feverish lips, then held it out to her and invited her to do the same. In short, I did all I could to infect her.

A few days later, while I was in the infirmary, the Camp broke up under the tragic circumstances that have been described many times. Alberto was a victim of the small cause, of the scarlet fever from which he had recovered as a child. He came to say goodbye, then went into the night and the snow together with sixty thousand other unfortunates, on that deadly march from which few returned alive. I was saved in the most unpredictable way by that business of the stolen pipettes, which gave me a providential sickness exactly at the moment when, paradoxically, not being able to walk was a godsend. In fact, for reasons never clarified, at Auschwitz the fleeing Nazis abstained from carrying out explicit orders from Berlin—not to leave any witnesses behind. They left the Camp in a hurry, and abandoned us who were sick to our fate.

As for Fräulein Drechsel, I know nothing about what happened to her. Since it may be that she was guilty of nothing more than a few Nazi kisses, I hope that her intended assassination, the small cause set in motion by me, did not bring her grievous harm. At seventeen scarlet fever is cured quickly and leaves no serious aftereffects. In any case, I feel no remorse for my private attempt at bacteriological warfare. Later on, reading books on the subject, I learned that other people in other Camps had taken better-aimed and more systematic action. In places ravaged by exanthematic typhus—often fatal, and transmitted by lice in clothing—the prisoners who washed and ironed the SS uniforms would search for comrades who had died of typhus, pick lice off the corpses, and slip them under the collars of the ironed and spruced-up military jackets. Lice are not very attractive animals, but they do not have racial prejudices.

# I. F. STONE

ON APRIL 12, 1945, President Franklin D. Roosevelt,
who had led the United States through the war, died.
A nation sorrowed. In Washington, D.C., the radical
journalist I. F. Stone recorded the event.

■

FROM *The War Years*

FAREWELL TO F.D.R.

*April 21, 1945*

Mr. Roosevelt's body was brought back to Washington today for the
last time. The crowds began to gather early in Lafayette Park opposite
the White House, as they did all along the line of the procession from
Union Station. I got down to the park early and stood with many others
waiting. Some small boys climbed into a tree for a better view. The gray
tip of the Washington Monument showed above the White House. The
trees were in full green; tulips bloomed on the lawn. Outside on the
sidewalk there were soldiers in helmets every few feet, and we could hear
the harsh tones of command as the guard of honor lined up on the White
House lawn. Florists' trucks pulled up at the door, and huge wreaths
were taken inside. Cameras were set up on the front porch, and camera
men were perched on high ladders on the sidewalks and among us in the
park. Birds sang, but the crowd was silent.

In the park I recognized a group of girls from the C.I.O. offices in
nearby Jackson Place, Walter Lippmann, and an Army and Navy Club
bellboy with a sensitive Negro face. There were soldiers and sailors,
Waves and Wacs. There were many Negroes, some of them quite obviously housemaids. There were well-dressed women and men in shirt
sleeves. I noticed a small middle-aged priest, several grave and owlish
Chinese, many service men with their wives or sweethearts, a tired man
in overalls and blue-denim work cap. A tall gangling Negro boy in jitterbug jacket and pork-pie hat towered above the crowd in front of me. A
man who seemed to be a hobo, unshaven and dirty, jarred the silence
with a loud laugh at something a child behind him had said. There were
close-mouthed New England faces, Jewish faces, Midwestern faces;
workers and business men and housewives, all curiously alike in their
patience and in the dumb stolidity that is often sorrow's aspect.

A truck sped by on Pennsylvania Avenue. On the roof of the truck two navy men operated a movie camera, taking pictures of the crowd. Far above us, twenty-four Flying Fortresses roared across the skies in proud formation. One remembered the President's 50,000-plane speech, and choked. Motorcycle police heralded the procession's approach. The marching men, the solemn bands, the armored cars, the regiment of Negro soldiers, the uniformed women's detachments, the truck filled with soldiers, and the black limousine carrying officials and the President's family went by slowly. They seemed part of an unreal pageant by comparison with the one glimpse of what we had come to see—the coffin covered with a flag. Many faces in the crowd puckered as it went past. In that one quick look thousands of us said our goodbye to a great and good man, and to an era.

I was in the *PM* office in New York Thursday when it happened. There was a commotion in the newsroom. A copyboy ran out of the wire-room with a piece of United Press copy in his hand. That first flash, "The President died this afternoon," seemed incredible; like something in a nightmare, far down under the horror was the comfortable feeling that you would wake to find it was all a dream. The Romans must have felt this way when word came that Caesar Augustus was dead. Later, when work was done, I went to a meeting of liberals in an apartment on Washington Square. It was a gloomy gathering, much too gloomy to honor so buoyant a spirit as Mr. Roosevelt's. Some felt that with his passing the Big Three would split up, that hope of a new world organization was dim. One of those present reported, apropos, that an automobile-company official in Detroit had told a delegation of visiting French newspapermen, "Next we fight the Soviet Union." Some thought the Nazis would be encouraged to hold out, that the war had been lengthened by the President's passing. Everyone seemed to feel that trouble, serious trouble, lay ahead.

I don't want to sound like Pollyanna, but I can remember so many crepe-hanging sessions of this kind since 1932. The Roosevelt era, for folk who scare easily, was a series of scares. Just before he took office, when the bonus marchers were driven out of Washington, revolution seemed to be around the corner. There was the banking crisis. The NRA [National Recovery Administration] was suspected of being the beginning of fascism; one of my friends in New York cautiously erased his name from the volumes of Marx and Lenin he owned; he felt the men with the bludgeons might be in his apartment any day. The Supreme Court knocked one piece of reform legislation after another on the head, and Mr. Roosevelt, when he set out to fight back, showed a deplorable disrespect for the constitutional amenities. There were the Chicago massacre and the Little Steel strike. There was Hitler. France fell when our armed forces were in good shape for a war with Nicaragua. The Japs sank most of the fleet at Pearl Harbor. It was a lush era for Cassandras.

Somehow we pulled through before, and somehow we'll pull through again. In part it was luck. In part it was Mr. Roosevelt's leadership. In part is was the quality of the country and its people. I don't know about the rest of the four freedoms, but one thing Mr. Roosevelt gave the United States in one crisis after another, and that was freedom from fear. Perhaps his most important contribution was the example, the superlative example, of his personal courage. Perhaps some of us will feel less gloomy if we remember it. Perhaps some of us will be more effective politically if we also learn from Mr. Roosevelt's robust realism, his ability to keep his eye on the main issue and not worry too much about the minor details.

I found the mood of the intellectuals and New Dealers in Washington this week-end quite different from that in New York. There has been much swapping of information and sidelights, and there is a good deal of confidence in the new President. No one, least of all Mr. Truman, an impressively modest man, expects him fully to fill Mr. Roosevelt's shoes. But the general feeling among those who know Mr. Truman is that he will surprise the skeptical. I can only record my own impression for whatever it is worth. I talked with Mr. Truman several years ago and liked him immediately and instinctively. The Presidency is a terrific job, and it remains to be seen how he will stand up under its pressure. But he is a good man, an honest man, a devoted man. Our country could be far more poorly served. Mr. Truman is a hard worker, decisive, a good executive. He works well with people. He is at once humble about his own knowledge and capacities, as a wise man should be, and quietly confident about his ability to learn and rise to the occasion.

I hate to confess it, but I think Mr. Roosevelt was astute and far-sighted in picking Mr. Truman rather than Mr. Wallace as his successor. At this particular moment in our history, Mr. Truman can do a better job. Mr. Wallace's accession might have split the country wide open, not because of Mr. Wallace but because of the feeling against him on the right. Mr. Truman has the good-will of both sides and is in a position to capitalize on the sobering influence of Mr. Roosevelt's passing. The heaviest task of the President lies in the field of foreign relations, and the biggest obstacle to its accomplishment is in the Senate. It is fortunate that Mr. Truman's greatest and most obvious political assets are his relations with the Senate. He is a friendly person, and was well liked on both sides of the aisle. Isolationists like Wheeler and La Follette are among his friends, and he may be able to exert an influence with them that the circumstances and the momentum of past events denied to Mr. Roosevelt. The chances of a two-thirds' vote in the Senate for the new peace organization are improved by the shift in the Presidency. I say this with no disrespect to our great departed leader.

I think Mr. Truman will carry on Mr. Roosevelt's work. He had been very effective in support of Mr. Roosevelt in the Senate. I can authoritatively report that the famous B2H2 resolution[1] originated in Mr. Truman's office. Three of the sponsors, Senator Ball, Burton, and Hatch, were members of the Truman committee. Mr. Truman's closest personal friends in the Senate were Kilgore of West Virginia and Wallgren of Washington, both sturdy progressives and good New Dealers. There will be changes in the Cabinet, perhaps some for the better. On domestic policy Mr. Truman's record is an excellent one, and labor has nothing to fear from him. The shock of Mr. Roosevelt's death has created an atmosphere in which the new President may be able to unite the nation more closely than ever and carry it forward to that stable peace Mr. Roosevelt so deeply desired.

[1] The historic bi-partisan senate resolution of 1943, sponsored by Senators Ball, Burton, Hill and Hatch (hence B2H2) urging U.S. initiative in forming a United Nations.

# GENÊT

GENÊT, or Janet Flanner, *The New Yorker*'s correspondent in Paris, writes of FDR's death from France, where it touched the French on a very personal level.

■

## FROM *Paris Journal, 1944–1965*

*April 19 [1945]*

The death of President Roosevelt caused a more personal grief among the French than the deaths of their own recent great men. On the demise of both old Clemenceau and Marshal Foch, their grief was a nationalistic, patriotic emotion, since these men, the one with his sabre-sharp tongue, the other with his sword, had saved France. The sorrow the French felt at losing Roosevelt seemed like someone's private unhappiness multiplied by millions. Friday morning, when the news was first known here, French men and women approached the groups of Americans in uniform standing on street corners and in public places and, with a mixture of formality and obvious emotion, expressed their sorrow, sometimes in French, sometimes in broken English. On the Rue Scribe, a sergeant in a jeep held up traffic while he received the condolences of two elderly French spinsters. In the Jardin des Tuileries, an American woman was stopped beneath the white-flowering chestnut trees by a French schoolboy who, with trembling voice, spoke for his father, a dead Army officer, to express his father's love for the dead President. At the outdoor flower stalls of the Place de la Madeleine, a patriarchal flower vendor gave a passing and startled paratrooper a free pink tulip, with the statement "Today they will be sending beautiful flowers for your great man. How sad." A café waitress naïvely touched the sublime when she said of his death, *"C'est ennuyeux pour toute l'humanité."*

Since the American system for filling the Presidential chair when it is left vacant by death was unknown to most French citizens, the journals here carried an official explanatory paragraph headed *"Monsieur Truman Sera Président Jusqu'en 1948"* and quoted our Constitution.

The Paris press wrote of F.D.R. with sober magnificence and sincere superlatives. Under the spirited Gallic headline *"Vive Roosevelt!,"* the *Libération-Soir* spoke of "the unjust destiny and yet the ancient grandeur of the event." *Le Monde*, in an editorial entitled *"Après Roosevelt,"* began by saying, "The great voice which directed American political destinies has been silenced, but its echo continues in French souls." In conclusion, it praised "his charm, his beautiful and great words," and said, "Let us weep for this man and hope that his wise and generous conception of the human communities remains like a light to brighten the path for all men of good will." De Gaulle's Minister of Foreign Affairs said, "It is not only appropriate but necessary to express the depth of the sadness of the government and of the French people. Roosevelt was one of the most loved and venerated men in France. He takes with him the tenderness of the French nation."

The increasing malaise, now that Roosevelt must be absent from the peace, and the unexpected return last Saturday of thousands of French prisoners liberated from Germany, juxtaposed fear and happiness in a mélange that Parisians will probably always remember in recalling that historic weekend. On Saturday, eight thousand French male prisoners were flown back from Germany in American transport planes, which afterward tumultuously circled the city while the men were being unpacked from trucks outside the newly decorated reception center in the Gare d'Orsay. On its walls these weary men saw an astonishing series of modernistic bas-reliefs depicting their welcome return to the freedom of what explanatory signs called "*la liberté d'aimer*" and the liberty to play, to sleep, to work, to eat, to drink, and to breathe freely. Few of the prisoners, in their hasty flight from the German Army and their later flight with the Americans in the skies, had heard our sad news. When they did hear it, one thin, bitter blond Frenchman said, "*Voyez-vous.* We've come home too late."

The next day, the first contingent of women prisoners arrived by train, bringing with them as very nearly their only baggage the proofs, on their faces and their bodies and in their weakly spoken reports, of the atrocities that had been their lot and that of hundreds of thousands of others in the numerous concentration camps our armies are liberating, almost too late. These three hundred women, who came in exchange for German women held in France, were from the prison camp of Ravensbrück, in the marshes midway between Berlin and Stettin. They arrived at the Gare de Lyon at eleven in the morning and were met by a nearly speechless crowd ready with welcoming bouquets of lilacs and other spring flowers, and by General de Gaulle, who wept. As he shook hands with some wretched woman leaning from a window of the train, she suddenly screamed, "*C'est lui!*," and pointed to her husband, standing nearby, who had not recognized her. There was a general, anguished babble of search, of finding or not finding. There was almost no joy; the emotion penetrated beyond that, to something nearer pain. Too much suffering lay behind this homecoming, and it was the suffering that showed in the women's faces and bodies.

Of the three hundred women whom the Ravensbrück *Kommandant* had selected as being able to put up the best appearance, eleven had died en route. One woman, taken from the train unconscious and placed on a litter, by chance opened her eyes just as de Gaulle's color guard marched past her with the French tricolor. She lifted an emaciated arm, pointed to the flag, and swooned again. Another woman, who still had a strong voice and an air of authority, said she had been a camp nurse. Unable to find her daughter and son-in-law in the crowd, she began shouting "Monique! Pierre!" and crying out that her son and husband had been killed fighting in the resistance and now where were those two who were all she had left? Then she sobbed weakly. One matron, six years ago renowned in Paris for her elegance, had become a bent, dazed, shabby old woman. When her smartly attired brother, who met her, said, like an automaton, "Where is your luggage?," she silently handed him what looked like a dirty black sweater fastened with safety pins around whatever small belongings were rolled inside. In a way, all the women looked alike: their faces were gray-green, with reddish-brown circles around their eyes, which seemed to see but not take in. They were dressed like scarecrows, in what had been given them at camp, clothes taken from the dead of all nationalities. As the lilacs fell from inert hands, the flowers made a purple carpet on the platform and the perfume of the trampled flowers mixed with the stench of illness and dirt.

# KURT VONNEGUT, JR.

KURT VONNEGUT'S *Slaughterhouse-Five,* a novel inspired by his own experience of the firebombing of Dresden during the war, is a rare mixture of science fiction, satire, and black humor. Vonnegut's other novels include *Cat's Cradle; God Bless You, Mr. Rosewater; Breakfast of Champions;* and *Jailbird.*

■

## FROM *Slaughterhouse-Five*

The trip to Dresden was a lark. It took only two hours. Shriveled little bellies were full. Sunlight and mild air came in through the ventilators. There were plenty of smokes from the Englishmen.

The Americans arrived in Dresden at five in the afternoon. The boxcar doors were opened, and the doorways framed the loveliest city that most of the Americans had ever seen. The skyline was intricate and voluptuous and enchanted and absurd. It looked like a Sunday school picture of Heaven to Billy Pilgrim.

Somebody behind him in the boxcar said, "Oz." That was I. That was me. The only other city I'd ever seen was Indianapolis, Indiana.

Every other big city in Germany had been bombed and burned ferociously. Dresden had not suffered so much as a cracked windowpane. Sirens went off every day, screamed like hell, and people went down into cellars and listened to radios there. The planes were always bound for someplace else—Leipzig, Chemnitz, Plauen, places like that. So it goes.

Steam radiators still whistled cheerily in Dresden. Streetcars clanged. Telephones rang and were answered. Lights went on and off when switches were clicked. There were theaters and restaurants. There was a zoo. The principal enterprises of the city were medicine and food-processing and the making of cigarettes.

People were going home from work now in the late afternoon. They were tired.

Eight Dresdeners crossed the steel spaghetti of the railroad yard. They were wearing new uniforms. They had been sworn into the army the day before. They were boys and men past middle age, and two veterans who had been shot to pieces in Russia. Their assignment was to

guard one hundred American prisoners of war, who would work as con-
tract labor. A grandfather and his grandson were in the squad. The
grandfather was an architect.

The eight were grim as they approached the boxcars containing their
wards. They knew what sick and foolish soldiers they themselves appeared to be. One of them actually had an artificial leg, and carried not
only a loaded rifle but a cane. Still—they were expected to earn obedience and respect from tall, cocky, murderous American infantrymen
who had just come from all the killing at the front.

And then they saw bearded Billy Pilgrim in his blue toga and silver
shoes, with his hands in a muff. He looked at least sixty years old. Next
to Billy was little Paul Lazzaro with a broken arm. He was fizzing with
rabies. Next to Lazzaro was the poor old high school teacher, Edgar
Derby, mournfully pregnant with patriotism and middle age and imaginary wisdom. And so on.

The eight ridiculous Dresdeners ascertained that these hundred ridiculous creatures really *were* American fighting men fresh from the
front. They smiled, and then they laughed. Their terror evaporated.
There was nothing to be afraid of. Here were more crippled human
beings, more fools like themselves. Here was light opera.

So out of the gate of the railroad yard and into the streets of Dresden
marched the light opera. Billy Pilgrim was the star. He led the parade.
Thousands of people were on the sidewalks, going home from work.
They were watery and putty-colored, having eaten mostly potatoes during the past two years. They had expected no blessings beyond the mild-
ness of the day. Suddenly—here was fun.

Billy did not meet many of the eyes that found him so entertaining.
He was enchanted by the architecture of the city. Merry amoretti wove
garlands above windows. Roguish fauns and naked nymphs peeked down
at Billy from festooned cornices. Stone monkeys frisked among scrolls
and seashells and bamboo.

Billy, with his memories of the future, knew that the city would be
smashed to smithereens and then burned—in about thirty more days.
He knew, too, that most of the people watching him would soon be dead.
So it goes.

And Billy worked his hands in his muff as he marched. His fingertips, working there in the hot darkness of the muff, wanted to know what
the two lumps in the lining of the little impresario's coat were. The
fingertips got inside the lining. They palpated the lumps, the pea-shaped
thing and the horseshoe-shaped thing. The parade had to halt by a busy
corner. The traffic light was red.

There at the corner, in the front rank of pedestrians, was a surgeon
who had been operating all day. He was a civilian, but his posture was

military. He had served in two world wars. The sight of Billy offended him, especially after he learned from the guards that Billy was an American. It seemed to him that Billy was in abominable taste, supposed that Billy had gone to a lot of silly trouble to costume himself just so.

The surgeon spoke English, and he said to Billy, "I take it you find war a very comical thing."

Billy looked at him vaguely. Billy had lost track momentarily of where he was or how he had gotten there. He had no idea that people thought he was clowning. It was Fate, of course, which had costumed him—Fate, and a feeble will to survive.

"Did you expect us to *laugh*?" the surgeon asked him.

The surgeon was demanding some sort of satisfaction. Billy was mystified. Billy wanted to be friendly, to help, if he could, but his resources were meager. His fingers now held the two objects from the lining of the coat. Billy decided to show the surgeon what they were.

"You thought we would enjoy being *mocked*?" the surgeon said. "And do you feel *proud* to represent America as you do?"

Billy withdrew a hand from his muff, held it under the surgeon's nose. On his palm rested a two-carat diamond and a partial denture. The denture was an obscene little artifact—silver and pearl and tangerine. Billy smiled.

The parade pranced, staggered and reeled to the gate of the Dresden slaughterhouse, and then it went inside. The slaughterhouse wasn't a busy place any more. Almost all the hooved animals in Germany had been killed and eaten and excreted by human beings, mostly soldiers. So it goes.

The Americans were taken to the fifth building inside the gate. It was a one-story cement-block cube with sliding doors in front and back. It had been built as a shelter for pigs about to be butchered. Now it was going to serve as a home away from home for one hundred American prisoners of war. There were bunks in there, and two potbellied stoves and a water tap. Behind it was a latrine, which was a one-rail fence with buckets under it.

There was a big number over the door of the building. The number was *five*. Before the Americans could go inside, their only English-speaking guard told them to memorize their simple address, in case they got lost in the big city. Their address was this: "Schlachthof-fünf." *Schlachthof* meant *slaughterhouse*. *Fünf* was good old *five*.

# MARGUERITE DURAS

BORN IN Indochina, the novelist and filmmaker Marguerite Duras left for France at the age of seventeen to
study law at the Sorbonne. She has written many films,
the best known of which is *Hiroshima Mon Amour*. She
is also the author of fifteen novels, among them *The
Sea Wall* and *The Lover*. The excerpt that follows was
taken from *The War: A Memoir*. It is worth noting that
the "François Morland" referred to in the first paragraph was actually François Mitterrand, now president
of France.

■

## FROM *The War: A Memoir*

I can't remember what day it was, whether it was in April, no, it was
a day in May when one morning at eleven o'clock the phone rang. It was
from Germany, it was François Morland. He doesn't say hello, he's almost rough, but clear as always. "Listen carefully. Robert is alive. Now
keep calm. He's in Dachau. Listen very, very carefully. Robert is very
weak, so weak you can't imagine. I have to tell you—it's a question of
hours. He may live for another three days like that, but no more. D. and
Beauchamp must start out today, this morning, for Dachau. Tell them
this: they're to go straight to my office—the people there will be expecting them. They'll be given French officers' uniforms, passports, mission
orders, gasoline coupons, maps, and permits. Tell them to go right away.
It's the only way. If they tried to do it officially they'd arrive too late."

François Morland and Rodin were part of a mission organized by
Father Riquet. They had gone to Dachau, and that was where they'd
found Robert L. They had gone into the prohibited area of the camp,
where the dead and the hopeless cases were kept. And there, one of the
latter had distinctly uttered a name: "François." "François," and then his
eyes had closed again. It took Rodin and Morland an hour to recognize
Robert L. Rodin finally identified him by his teeth. They wrapped him
up in a sheet, as people wrap up a dead body, and took him out of the
prohibited part of the camp and laid him down by a hut in the survivors'
part of the camp. They were able to do so because there were no American soldiers around. They were all in the guardroom, scared of the
typhus.

Beauchamp and D. left Paris the same day, early in the afternoon.

It was May 12, the day of the peace. Beauchamp was wearing a colonel's uniform belonging to François Morland. D. was dressed as a lieutenant in the French army and carried his papers as a member of the Resistance, made out in the name of D. Masse. They drove all night and arrived at Dachau the next morning. They spent several hours looking for Robert L.; then, as they were going past a body, they heard someone say D.'s name. It's my opinion they didn't recognize him; but Morland had warned us he was unrecognizable. They took him. And it was only afterward they must have recognized him. Under their clothes they had a third French officer's uniform. They had to hold him upright, he could no longer stand alone, but they managed to dress him. They had to prevent him from saluting outside the SS huts, get him through the guard posts, see that he wasn't given any of the vaccinations that would have killed him. The American soldiers, blacks for the most part, wore gas masks against typhus, the fear was so great. Their orders were such that if they'd suspected the state Robert L. was really in, they'd have put him back immediately in the part of the camp where people were left to die. Once they got Robert L. out, the other two had to get him to walk to the Citroën II. As soon as they'd stretched him out on the back seat, he fainted. They thought it was all over, but no. The journey was very difficult, very slow. They had to stop every half hour because of the dysentery. As soon as they'd left Dachau behind, Robert L. spoke. He said he knew he wouldn't reach Paris alive. So he began to talk, so it should be told before he died. He didn't accuse any person, any race, any people. He accused man. Emerging from the horror, dying, delirious, Robert L. was still able not to accuse anyone except the governments that come and go in the history of nations. He wanted D. and Beauchamp to tell me after his death what he had said. They reached the French frontier that night, near Wissemburg. D. phoned me: "We've reached France. We've just crossed the frontier. We'll be back tomorrow by the end of the morning. Expect the worst. You won't recognize him." They had dinner in an officers' mess. Robert L. was still talking and telling his story. When he entered the mess all the officers stood up and saluted him. He didn't see. He never had seen that sort of thing. He spoke of the German martyrdom, of the martyrdom common to all men. He told what it was like. That evening he said he'd like to eat a trout before he died. In deserted Wissemburg they found a trout for Robert L. He ate a few mouthfuls. Then he started talking again. He spoke of charity. He'd heard some rhetorical phrases of Father Riquet's, and he started to say these very obscure words: "When anyone talks to me of Christian charity, I shall say Dachau." But he didn't finish. That night they slept somewhere near Bar-sur-Aube. Robert L. slept for a few hours. They reached Paris at the end of the morning. Just before they came to the rue Saint-Benoît, D. stopped to phone me again: "I'm ringing to warn you that it's more terrible than anything we've imagined . . . He's happy."

I heard stifled cries on the stairs, a stir, a clatter of feet. Then doors banging and shouts. It was them. It was them, back from Germany.

I couldn't stop myself—I started to run downstairs, to escape into the street. Beauchamp and D. were supporting him under the arms. They'd stopped on the first-floor landing. He was looking up.

I can't remember exactly what happened. He must have looked at me and recognized me and smiled. I shrieked no, that I didn't want to see. I started to run again, up the stairs this time. I was shrieking, I remember that. The war emerged in my shrieks. Six years without uttering a cry. I found myself in some neighbors' apartment. They forced me to drink some rum, they poured it into my mouth. Into the shrieks.

I can't remember when I found myself back with him again, with him, Robert L. I remember hearing sobs all over the house; that the tenants stayed for a long while out on the stairs; that the doors were left open. I was told later that the concierge had put decorations up in the hall to welcome him, and that as soon as he'd gone by she tore them all down and shut herself up alone in her lodge to weep.

In my memory, at a certain moment, the sounds stop and I see him. Huge. There before me. I don't recognize him. He looks at me. He smiles. Lets himself be looked at. There's a supernatural weariness in his smile, weariness from having managed to live till this moment. It's from this smile that I suddenly recognize him, but from a great distance, as if I were seeing him at the other end of a tunnel. It's a smile of embarrassment. He's apologizing for being here, reduced to such a wreck. And then the smile fades, and he becomes a stranger again. But the knowledge is still there, that this stranger is he, Robert L., totally.

He wanted to see around the apartment again. We supported him, and he toured the rooms. His cheeks creased, but didn't release his lips; it was in his eyes that we'd seen his smile. In the kitchen he saw the clafoutis we'd made for him. He stopped smiling. "What is it?" We told him. What was it made with? Cherries—it was the height of the season. "May I have some?" "We don't know, we'll have to ask the doctor." He came back into the sitting room and lay down on the divan. "So I can't have any?" "Not yet." "Why?" "There have been accidents in Paris already from letting deportees eat too soon after they got back from the camps."

He stopped asking questions about what had happened while he was away. He stopped seeing us. A great, silent pain spread over his face because he was still being refused food, because it was still as it had been in the concentration camp. And, as in the camp, he accepted it in silence. He didn't see that we were weeping. Nor did he see that we could scarcely look at him or respond to what he said.

The doctor came. He stopped short with his hand on the door handle, very pale. He looked at us, and then at the form on the divan. He didn't understand. And then he realized: the form wasn't dead yet, it was hovering between life and death, and he, the doctor, had been called in to try to keep it alive. The doctor came into the room. He went over to the form and the form smiled at him. The doctor was to come several times a day for three weeks, at all hours of the day and night. Whenever we were too afraid we called him and he came. He saved Robert L. He too was caught up in the passionate desire to save Robert L. from death. He succeeded.

We smuggled the clafoutis out of the house while he slept. The next day he was feverish and didn't talk about food any more.

If he had eaten when he got back from the camp his stomach would have been lacerated by the weight of the food, or else the weight would have pressed on the heart, which had grown enormous in the cave of his emaciation. It was beating so fast you couldn't have counted its beats, you couldn't really say it was beating—it was trembling, rather, as if from terror. No, he couldn't eat without dying. But he couldn't go on not eating without dying. That was the problem.

The fight with death started very soon. We had to be careful with it, use care, tact, skill. It surrounded him on all sides. And yet there was still a way of reaching him. It wasn't very big, this opening through which to communicate with him, but there was still life in him, scarcely more than a splinter, but a splinter just the same. Death unleashed its attack. His temperature was 104.5° the first day. Then 105°. Then 106°. Death was doing all it could. 106°: his heart vibrated like a violin string. Still 106°, but vibrating. The heart, we thought—it's going to stop. Still 106°. Death deals cruel knocks, but the heart is deaf. This can't go on, the heart will stop. But no.

Gruel, said the doctor, a teaspoonful at a time. Six or seven times a day we gave him gruel. Just a teaspoonful nearly choked him, he clung to our hands, gasped for air, and fell back on the bed. But he swallowed some. Six or seven times a day, too, he asked to go to the toilet. We lifted him up, supported him under the arms and knees. He must have weighed between eighty-two and eighty-four pounds: bone, skin, liver, intestines, brain, lungs, everything—eighty-four pounds for a body five feet ten inches tall. We sat him on the edge of the sanitary pail, on which we'd put a small cushion: the skin was raw where there was no flesh between it and the joints. *(The elbows of the little Jewish girl of seventeen from the Faubourg du Temple stick through the skin on her arms. Probably because she's so young and her skin so fragile, the joint is outside instead of in, sticking out naked and clean. She suffers no pain either from her joints or from her belly, from which all her genital organs have been taken out one by one at regular intervals.)* Once he was sitting on his pail he excreted in one go, in one enormous, astonishing gurgle. What the heart held back the anus couldn't: it let out all that was in it. Everything, or almost everything, did the same, even the fingers, which no longer kept their nails, but let them go too. But the heart went on holding back what it contained. The heart. And then there was the head. Gaunt but sublime, it emerged alone from that bag of bones, remembering, relating, recognizing, asking for things. And talking. Talking. The head was connected to the body by the neck, as heads usually are, but the neck was so withered and shrunken—you could circle it with one hand—that you wondered how life could pass through it; a spoonful of gruel almost blocked it. At first the neck was at right angles to the shoulders. Higher up, the neck was right inside the skeleton, joined on at the top of the jaws and winding around the ligaments like ivy. You could see the vertebrae through it, the carotid arteries, the nerves, the pharynx, and the blood passing through: the skin had become like cigarette paper. So, he excreted this dark green, slimy, gushing thing, a turd such as no one had ever seen before. When he'd finished we put him back to bed. He lay for a long time with his eyes half shut, prostrated.

For seventeen days the turd looked the same. It was inhuman. It separated him from us more than the fever, the thinness, the nailless fingers, the marks of SS blows. We gave him gruel that was golden yellow, gruel for infants, and it came out of him dark green like slime from a swamp. After the sanitary pail was closed you could hear the bubbles bursting as they rose to the surface inside. Viscous and slimy, it was almost like a great gob of spit. When it emerged the room filled with a smell, not of putrfaction or corpses—did his body still have the wherewithal to make a corpse?—but rather of humus, of dead leaves, of dense undergrowth. It was a somber smell, dark reflection of the dark night from which he was emerging and which we would never know. *(I leaned against the shutters, the street went by below, and as they didn't know what was going on in the room I wanted to tell them that here, in this room above them, a man had come back from the German camps, alive.)*

Of course he'd rummaged in trashcans for food, he'd eaten wild plants, drunk water from engines. But that didn't explain it. Faced with this strange phenomenon we tried to find explanations. We thought that perhaps there, under our very eyes, he was consuming his own liver or spleen. How were we to know? How were we to know what strangeness that belly still contained, what pain?

For seventeen whole days that turd still looks the same. For seventeen days it's unlike anything ever known. Every one of the seven times he excretes each day, we smell it, look at it, but can't recognize it. For seventeen days we hide from him that which comes out of him, just as we hide from him his own legs and feet and whole unbelievable body.

We ourselves never got used to seeing them. You couldn't get used to it. The incredible thing was that he was still alive. Whenever anyone came into the room and saw that shape under the sheets, they couldn't bear the sight and averted their eyes. Many went away and never came back. He never noticed our horror, not once. He was happy, he wasn't afraid any more. The fever bore him up. For seventeen days.

One day his temperature drops.

After seventeen days, death grows weary. In the pail his excretion doesn't bubble any more, it becomes liquid. It's still green, but it smells more human, it smells human. And one day his temperature drops—he's been given twelve liters of serum, and one morning his temperature drops. He's lying on his nine cushions, one for the head, two for the forearms, two for the arms, two for the hands, and two for the feet. For no part of his body could bear its own weight; the weight had to be swathed in down and immobilized.

And then, one morning, the fever leaves him. It comes back, but abates again. Comes back again, not quite so high, and falls again. And then one morning he says, "I'm hungry."

Hunger had gone as his temperature rose. It came back when the fever abated. One day the doctor said, "Let's try—let's try giving him something to eat. We can begin with meat extract. If he can take that, keep on giving it, but at the same time give him all kinds of other food, just small amounts at first, increasing the quantity just a little every three days."

I spend the morning going around to all the restaurants in Saint-Germain-des-Prés trying to find a meat-juice extractor. I find one in a fashionable restaurant. They say they can't lend it. I say it's for a political deportee who's very ill, it's a matter of life and death. The woman thinks for a minute and says, "I can't lend it to you, but I can rent it to you for a thousand francs a day." I leave my name and address and a deposit. The Saint-Benoît restaurant sells me the meat at cost price.

He digested the meat extract without any difficulty, so after three days he began to take solid food.

His hunger grew from what it fed on. It grew greater and greater, became insatiable.

It took on terrifying proportions.

We didn't serve him food. We put the dishes in front of him and left him and he ate. Methodically, as if performing a duty, he was doing what he had to do to live. He ate. It was an occupation that took up all his

time. He would wait for food for hours. He would swallow without knowing what he was eating. Then we'd take the food away and he'd wait for
it to come again.

He has gone and hunger has taken his place. Emptiness has taken
his place. He is giving to the void, filling what was emptied: those wasted
bowels. That's what he's doing. Obeying, serving, ministering to a mysterious duty. How does he know what to do about hunger? How does he
perceive that this is what he has to do? He knows with a knowledge that
has no parallel.

He eats a mutton chop. Then he gnaws the bone, eyes lowered,
concentrating on not missing a morsel of meat. Then he takes a second
chop. Then a third. Without looking up.
He's sitting in the shade in the sitting room near a half-open window,
in an armchair, surrounded by his cushions, his stick beside him. His
legs look like crutches inside his trousers. When the sun shines you can
see through his hands.
Yesterday he made enormous efforts to gather up the breadcrumbs
that had fallen on his trousers and on the floor. Today he lets a few lie.
We leave him alone in the room while he's eating. We don't have to
help him now. His strength has come back enough for him to hold a
spoon or a fork. But we still cut up the meat for him. We leave him alone
with the food. We try not to talk in the adjoining rooms. We walk on
tiptoe. We watch him from a distance. He's performing a duty. He has
no special preference for one dish over another. He cares less and less.
He crams everything down. If the dishes don't come fast enough, he sobs
and says we don't understand.
Yesterday afternoon he stole some bread out of the refrigerator. He
steals. We tell him to be careful, not to eat too much. Then he weeps.

# LOUIS-FERDINAND CÉLINE

THE BRILLIANT but cantankerous Louis-Ferdinand Céline is best known for two books: *Journey to the End
of the Night* and *Death on the Installment Plan.* He
was a doctor who set up his practice in a poverty-
stricken quarter of Paris in 1924. During the war, Céline supported the Vichy government. After the war, he
was imprisoned, tried for collaborating with the Nazis,
convicted, and then exonerated. The excerpt that follows was taken from Céline's memoir *Castle to Castle,*
which deals with his flight, along with other Vichy officials, including Pierre Laval, from the advancing Allied
armies late in the war.

■

FROM *Castle to Castle*

Maybe I shouldn't talk Siegmaringen up . . . but what a picturesque
spot! . . . you'd think you were at an operetta . . . a perfect setting . . .
you're waiting for the sopranos, the lyric tenors . . . for echoes you've
got the whole forest . . . ten, twenty mountains of trees! Black Forest,
descending pine trees . . . waterfalls . . . your stage is the city, so pretty-
pretty, pink and green, semi-pistachio, assorted pastry, cabarets, hotels,
shops, all lopsided for the effect . . . all in the "Baroque boche" and
"White Horse Inn" style . . . you can already hear the orchestra . . . the
most amazing is the Castle . . . stucco and papier-mâché . . . like a wedding cake on top of the town . . . And yet . . . if you'd take the whole
business . . . the Castle, the town, the Danube to the Place Pigalle! . . .
the crowd you'd draw! . . . the Ciel, the Néant and the Lapin à Gill
wouldn't hold a candle to it . . . Christ, the tourist buses you'd need . . .
the brigades of police . . . the crowd! . . . and all ready to pay!

In our time, I've got to admit, the place was gloomy . . . tourists,
sure . . . but a special kind . . . too much scabies, too little bread, and
too much R.A.F. overhead . . . and Leclerc's army right near . . . coming closer . . . the Senegalese with their chop-chops . . . for our heads
. . . nobody else's . . . right not I'm reading the paper . . . they're weeping over the fate of those poor Hungarians . . . if we'd been welcomed
like them . . . if anybody'd spilled so many tears over our misfortunes,
we'd have been very happy, I can tell you! we'd have danced the polka.
If those poor Hungarian refugees had had Article 75 on their asses, Coty

wouldn't have kept them for dinner . . . hell no! . . . if they'd been plain
Frenchmen from France, he'd have cut them in two on the spot . . . in
ten if they'd been war cripples . . . especially with the *Médaille Militaire*!
French sensibility is stirred by anything that's against France . . . the
heart of France goes out to its professed enemies! masochistic to the
death!

For us there in the attics, cellars, and broom closets, starving, I can
assure you there was no operetta . . . our stage was full of men condemned to death . . . 1,142 of us . . . I knew the exact number . . .

I'll have more to say about this picturesque spot! it wasn't just a
watering place and a tourist haven . . . tremendously historical! . . . A
Shrine! . . . take a bite out of that castle . . . stucco, bric-a-brac, ginger-
bread in every style, turrets, chimneys, gargoyles . . . unbelievable . . .
super-Hollywood . . . every period from the melting of the icecap, the
narrowing of the Danube, the slaying of the Dragon, the victory of St.
Fidelis down to William II and Goering.

Bichelonne had the biggest head of us all . . . not only a champion
of Polytechnique and the École des Mines . . . History! Geotechnics!
. . . He was an electronic brain! He had to tell us the which and the why!
explain the crotchets of the Castle! every last one! did he know why it
leaned south rather than north? . . . why those ramshackle chimneys,
those wormeaten battlements and drawbridges leaned more to the west?
. . . that goddam cradle of the Hohenzollerns! perched on its rock . . .
out of kilter! lopsided all over . . . inside, outside! every room and passageway . . . the whole business! all ready to topple into the water for
the last fourteen centuries! . . . go see for yourself . . . cradle and den
of the worst pack of rapacious wolves in Europe! some Shrine! and believe me it wobbled under the squadrons, the thousands and thousands
of Flying Fortresses bound for Dresden, Munich, Augsburg . . . by day
and by night . . . all the little stained-glass windows cracked and fell in
the river . . . you'll see!

All the same, this castle of Siegmaringen, this whole fantastic lop-
sided chunk of trompe-l'oeil managed to hold out for thirteen . . . fourteen centuries . . . Bichelonne didn't hold out at all . . . graduate of
Polytechnique, minister, amazing mind . . . he died at Hohenlychen in
East Prussia . . . pure coquetry . . . lunacy . . . went up there to be operated, have a fracture fixed . . . He had visions of himself going back to
Paris on the double beside Laval, triumphant . . . Arch of Triumph,
Champs-Elysées, the Unknown Soldier . . . he was obsessed by his leg
. . . it doesn't bother him anymore . . . the way they operated on him
up there at Hohenlychen, I'll tell you about it . . . the witnesses have
gone out of existence . . . so has the surgeon . . . Gebhardt, war criminal, hanged! . . . not for the way he operated on Bichelonne! . . . for all
sorts of genocides, little intimate Hiroshimas . . . oh, not that Hiroshima

makes me flip! . . . look at Truman, how happy he is, pleased with himself, playing the harpsichord . . . the idol of millions of voters! . . . the widower of millions of widows' dreams! . . . Cosmic Landru! . . . playing Amadeus' harpsichord . . . just wait a while . . . kill a lot of people and wait . . . that does it . . . not just Denoël! . . . Marion . . . Bichelonne . . . Beria . . . tomorrow B. . . . K. . . . H! the line forms to the right . . . shaking, stamping . . . yelling to get in . . . to be hanged quicker and shorter . . . roasted to a crisp . . . the whole National Assembly, the six hundred . . . listen to them, the state they're in, their impatience to be fed to the lions!

We 1,142 had other things to do besides looking at the landscape . . . we had to find our daily bread . . . myself, I've got to admit, I can get along on very little, but there, same as later in the north, we were really starving, not temporarily for the diet, no, this was serious . . .

All pretty miscellaneous! I read it over . . . How can I expect you to understand all this . . . not to lose the thread . . . my humblest apologies! . . . If my voice wavers, if I jibber-jabber, I'm no worse than most guides . . . you'll forgive me when you know the whole story . . . definitely! . . . so bear with me . . . I'm lying here . . . making my bed quake . . . all for you . . . getting my memories together . . . I need the fever to boil me up . . . to put the details in place . . . and the dates . . . I don't want to mislead you . . .

In that teetering lopsided barn . . . twenty manor houses one on top of the other . . . there was a library . . . that was really something . . . a treasure . . . amazing . . . we'll come back to that, I'll tell you . . .

For a while the 1,142 . . . Leclerc's army is coming closer . . . closer . . . were shaken with worry . . . with a desire to know more . . . more and more especially the intellectuals . . . and we had our quota of intellectuals in Siegmaringen . . . real cerebral types, serious . . . like Gaxotte could almost have been . . . none of your sad sacks from the café terraces, ambitious alcoholics, mental defectives with an idea now and then, squinting from charm to charm, from urinal to urinal, Slavs, Hungarians, Yankees, Mings, from commitment to commitment, from one Mauriaco-Tarterie to the next, from cross to sickle, from pernod to pernod, from coat to coat, from envelope to envelope . . . no, nothing in common! . . . all really serious intellectuals! . . . not the gratuitous, verbal kind . . . but ready to pay and paying . . . with Article 75 on their ass! . . . real lamppost fodder . . . flawless intellectuals . . . dying of hunger, cold, and scabies . . . Well, they were anxious to know if ever, down through the ages . . . there had ever been a clique, a caste, a gang as hated, as cursed as us, as furiously expected and searched for by hordes of cops (ah, lily-livered Hungarians!) to stick banderillas in us, fry us, or impale us . . .

It took a lot of research . . . and I can assure you that our intellectuals investigated . . . all the lousy stinking bastards that had been tor-

tured in one place or another . . . Spartacists . . . Girondins . . .
Templars . . . Communes . . . We examined all the Chronicles, Codes,
Libels . . . we weighed and sifted . . . we compared . . . were we . . .
could we be . . . as stinking . . . as fit to throw on the dump, to spit on
pitchforks, as Napoleon's friends? . . . after they'd shipped him to St.
Helena . . . were we? . . . Especially his Spanish friends . . . the hidalgo
collaborationists! . . . the *Josefins!* Good name to remember! . . . that's
what we were . . . *Adolfins!* . . . the *Josefins* got theirs all right . . . all
the Javerts[1] of the day on their ass! practically the same hue and cry . . .
as us, the 1,142 . . . with Leclerc's army in Strasbourg . . . and its chop-
chop Senegalese! . . . (and the Hungarians complaining about the Tar-
tars . . . Christ!)

Which shows you that that imperial library was rich, rich in everything . . . amazing what you could find there . . . fertilize your mind in
every field . . . manuscripts, memoirs, incunabula . . . you should have
seen our intellectuals climbing up ladders, Ph.D's, Academicians, graduates of the École Normale, all ages, expelled Immortals, rummaging
through all that . . . ardent! feverish! . . . Latin, Greek, French . . .
that was culture . . . and scratching their itch at the same time . . . on
top of every ladder . . . and each one wanting to be right . . . each
standing by his manuscript . . . his chronicle . . . that we were more
hated or less than Joseph's collaborators . . . that the price on our heads
was higher . . . or lower? . . . in francs . . . or in the escudos of the period . . . a Dean of the Faculty of Law inclined to "more" . . . an Immortal to "less" . . . We voted: fifty-fifty! The future is in the hands of
God! Hell! The Immortal was way off! The events have proved that . . .
the calvary of the *Adolfins* was infinitely more ferocious than all the
other vengeances end to end! as sensational as the H-bomb! . . . a
hundred thousand times more powerful than our piddling shells of '14!
Super-hunt! sensational kill! and forever . . . none of us will ever see the
end of it! . . . Saint Louis, the bum . . . it's for him we're expiating . . .
the brute! the torturer! . . . and they made him a saint . . . who baptized
a round million Israelis by force . . . in the beloved south of our beloved
France—that guy was worse than Adolf! . . . which shows you what you
can learn on the top of a ladder . . . ah, Saint Louis! . . . canonized in
1297 . . . We'll come back to him!

I was supposed to go to Laval's and I took you to Abetz's . . . that
little dinner . . . forgive me! . . . another little digression . . . I'm always
digressing . . . old age? . . . too full of memories? . . . I don't know . . .
I'll know later . . . or other people will know . . . about oneself it's hard
to tell . . . Anyway, to pick up where we left off . . . we were leaving the

---

[1] In Hugo's *Les Misérables*, Inspector Javert is the relentless pursuer and persecutor
of the hero, Jean Valjean.

music room . . . I was supposed to go see Laval . . . I'd wanted to go for
the last three days . . . since the skirmish at the station . . . when really
it was his doing if it hadn't ended in a general massacre . . . only one
dead! . . . I really had to go and congratulate him . . . and not discreetly!
loud and clear! it's no good treading lightly with politicians! heavy does
it! massive! . . . same as with dames! . . . politicians are debutantes as
long as they live . . . admiration! . . . admiration! votes! You don't tell a
young lady she's nice . . . no, you talk to her like Mariano: "Der's nobod
lika you in alla woil!" that's the least she'll stand for . . . same with your
politician! . . . besides I had a purpose . . . that he shouldn't raise a stink
about the Delaunys . . . Brinon wasn't the only power in the Castle . . .
I'd prepared my little spiel . . . at last I was on my way . . . from the
music room to Laval's, one floor . . . only one flight . . . I've explained
. . . I've told you what it was like . . . his setting, his office, his apartment, his floor . . . all First Empire . . . perfect First Empire! . . . you
won't find anything better in Malmaison . . . or I'd even say as good . . .
we know the terrible drawbacks of First Empire, that buttock-gouging
style . . . absolutely impossible to sit down! . . . chairs, armchairs, di-
vans! . . . resolutely "peach pit" . . . chairs for colonels, marshals! . . .
barely time to listen and take off! . . . to fly from victory to victory! no
connection with "Capuan delights!" but I was so tired, so much insomnia
to catch up on, that I made myself very comfortable on the peach pits
. . . I took a very nice rest . . . Naturally I started in with my compliment
. . . How splendid he had been! Laval of Auvergne and the Maghreb and
Alfortville! the incomparable! the attenuator-conciliator for whom London, New York, and Moscow envied us! . . . once I'd said my little piece,
there was nothing left for me to do but nod, wag my head amiably . . .
no need to talk . . . it was very comfortable at Laval's . . . he babbled all
by himself . . . he didn't ask anything of me . . . except to listen, that
was enough! . . . he was doing the talking . . . and he really threw himself into it! . . . he pleaded! . . . this . . . that . . . and then his case! . . .
his Cause! . . . you could only nod, he "incarnated" France much too
much to leave him time to listen . . . compliments or no compliments!
I'd come to tell him that it was thanks to him the massacre had been
nipped in the bud . . . that if not for him there would have been a
hecatomb! . . . the sincere truth! . . . he didn't give a shit! all he wanted
was for me to listen . . . he tolerated me as a listener! . . . not as a commentator! so I stowed my compliments . . . I sit down with my bag on
my lap, my instruments, and Bébert on my lap, too, in his game bag . . .
I knew his plea . . . he'd dished it out to me ten . . . twenty times . . .
"that under the present conditions . . . the weakness of Europe . . . only
one way of straightening everything out": his Franco-German policy!
. . . his! . . . without his collaboration no use trying . . . there wouldn't
be any History! or any Europe! that he knew Russia . . . etc. . . . etc.
. . . I could nod and wag away . . . this would go on for an hour . . . at

least . . . I knew all the variants, the mock objections, the impassioned appeals . . . he felt as if he were already buried! . . . in his family vault! . . . in Chateldon! . . . yes, but first . . . first! he'd demolish them all! all of them! . . . they wouldn't down him so easy! . . . he'd crush them first! . . . first . . . all of them! . . . all those jealous . . . envious deserters! all of his grotesque, slanderous detractors! yes! because he, Laval, he and nobody else, had France in his blood! . . . and all those idiotic midgets would have to admit that he had it in his pocket . . . and America, too . . . yes, America! . . . he could wind it around his finger . . . immense America! in the first place through his son-in-law! . . . and through his daughter, who was an American . . . and through Senator Taft, Roosevelt's Great Elector! . . .

"Ah, the High Court! . . . listen to me, Doctor!"

He made the High Court crawl on its belly! absolutely! . . . I tried to interrupt him just a little . . . give him a breathing spell . . . hopeless! . . . the way he was launched, not a chance of mentioning Delaunys . . .

Best way would be to let him talk . . . and slip out . . . I had plenty of things to do . . . the *Landrat* for Bébert's left-overs . . . then my patients at the *Milice* . . . then the hospital . . . then see Letrou . . . and then the *Fidelis* . . . even so I tried to interrupt him . . . a few words about my practice, my little troubles . . . maybe he could give me a little advice? . . . he knew more about it than I did . . . naturally! . . . he knew more than everybody . . . about everything . . . that greasy Arab with his ebony cowlick, nothing was missing but the fez . . . he was the real Abdullah of the Third Republic, who talks to everybody in the train, who knows better than anybody what they ought to do and don't . . . who knows more than the farmer about planting his alfalfa and clover, more than the notary about those little inheritance pettifoggeries, more than the photographer about those first communion pictures, more than the post office clerk about short-changing you on stamps, more than the hairdresser about permanent waves, more than election workers about ways of taking opposition posters down, more than the police about putting on handcuffs, and much more than the housewife about wiping the baby's ass . . .

You had a good rest listening as long as you watched your expression . . . He kept an eye on you . . . if you didn't seem quite convinced . . . he took another windup . . . he floored you for the count!

Ah, Mornet[2] and Co. wouldn't listen to him . . . they preferred to shoot him! . . . big mistake! . . . he had something to say . . . I know . . . I heard him ten times . . . twenty times . . .

"You can take if from me . . . I had the choice . . . they offered me the moon and the stars, Doctor . . . De Gaulle went looking for them . . . I made them wait! . . . the Russians too!"

I couldn't go on wagging the whole time . . .

"What did they offer you, Monsieur le Président?"

I had to seem to be paying attention.

"Anything I wanted! the whole Press!"

"Ah! Ah!"

That's all I said . . . no more . . . I knew the listener's role . . . he was pleased with me . . . not a bad listener . . . and especially . . . because I don't smoke . . . being a nonsmoker, he wouldn't have to offer me any . . . he could show me all his packages, two big drawers full of Lucky Strikes . . . you bummed a cigarette off him, he wouldn't see you again! . . . never! . . . or even a light! . . . a match!

"The English offered you all that, Monsieur le Président?"

"Absolutely . . . they begged me, Doctor!"

"Ah! . . . ah!" Amazement!

"I can even give you a name! . . . it won't mean anything to you! . . . an embassy name . . . Mendle! he offered to buy me twenty-five newspapers! and as many in the provinces!"

"Certainly, Monsieur le Président! . . . I believe you! . . . I believe you! . . ."

"I'm going to have a little fun,, Doctor! . . . you hear? . . . very well! Strike me down, I'll say to them! Strike! Strike hard! don't miss me the way you did in Versailles! . . . don't tremble! go right ahead! . . . but I'm warning you! . . . I've warned you! . . . you will be assassinating France!"

"Bravo, Monsieur le Président!"

The least I could do was show a little enthusiasm . . .

"Ah, you agree with me?"

"Completely, Monsieur le Président!"

He had me where he wanted me . . . straight to the gut!

"You agree with a Jew?"

Here we go! That word! The word Jew! . . . naturally he was going to bring it up! the stinker, he'd been biding his time!

He takes the offensive . . .

"You did call me a Jew, didn't you, Doctor? Yes, I know, you weren't the only one . . . There was also *Je suis partout!*" [3]

"Not in so many words, Monsieur le Président! . . . they didn't call you that in so many words! but I did, Monsieur le Président!"

"Ah, I like that! Right to my face!"

He bursts out laughing . . . he's not a bad sort . . . but he didn't take me by surprise, I knew what was going to happen . . . inevitable! . . .

"But you wrote the same thing yourself!"

"Oh, that was for my constituents . . . in Aubervilliers!"

"I know! I know, Monsieur le Président!"

Something else on his mind . . .

"But you, Doctor, why are you here? . . . why are you in Siegmaringen? . . . they tell me you complain a good deal . . ."

Who did he think he was fooling?

"If I'm here, Monsieur le Président, it's entirely thanks to you! you absolutely refused to send me anywhere else! You could have! Absolutely!"

I'm beginning to get sore! hell! his air of innocence! I know what I'm saying! . . . it would suit that scowling Arab for me to pay for the whole gang! to take the rap for all those lousy three-timing connivers! to foot the bill! and as long as we're talking frankly . . . and he's fooling around putting me on trial . . . it's my turn to bring up a few unpleasant truths! . . . I'm not dozing any more! . . .

"You found a spot for Morand! you found a spot for Maurois! . . . and Fontenoy![4] you found a spot for Fontenoy! . . . you found a spot for your daughter!"

"That's enough! That's enough, Céline!"

He stops me . . . I had a dozen more . . . a hundred!

"You found a spot for Brisson . . . Robert! you found a spot for Morand! I was right there . . . in his house!"

I don't pull any punches . . . I've got a memory like an elephant . . . people always think they can con me, my dumb look . . .

He has to have the last word . . .

"Then you know what people say about you?"

"Me? . . . I'm of no interest! . . . better talk about the big news . . . would you care to hear some really interesting news, Monsieur le Président?"

"Where did you get it?"

"In the street! . . . really hot! . . . and very convenient for you . . ."

"Spit it out! Quick!"

"Well . . . the story is that the Russians are going to fight the Americans! There you are, Monsieur le Président! . . ."

"That's what they're saying in Siegmaringen?"

"Absolutely!"

He thinks it over . . .

"The Russians fight the Americans? That's absolutely stupid and inept, Doctor! Have you stopped to think?"

"No . . . but that's what they're saying!"

"But that would mean chaos, Doctor! . . . chaos! do you know what chaos is?"

"Quite well, Monsieur le Président!"

"You've never been in politics?"

"Oh, so little . . . and really I'm so incompetent . . ."

"Then you can't understand! you don't know what chaos is!"

"I've some little idea . . ."

"No! . . . you don't know! I'll tell you! Chaos, Doctor, is a Julius Caesar in every village! . . . and twelve Brutuses to a country!"

"I believe you, Monsieur le Président!"

I won't let him have his last word!

"But I'm not Caesar, and you could perfectly well have found a spot for me . . . like Morand, Jardin, and the rest of them! . . . I wasn't asking you for much . . . I wasn't asking for an Embassy! . . . you didn't do a thing! . . . I wasn't Brutus either! . . . you'd have handed me over to the Fifis if I hadn't come to Germany!"

I stick to my guns! . . . I know my stuff . . . absolutely sincerely right! . . . I'm the rightest man in Europe! and the least appreciated! I've got fifty Nobel prizes coming to me!

"No, Monsieur le Président, I wouldn't be here!"

I want him to know!

He picks up his phone.

"I'm calling Bichelonne, I want him to hear you! . . . I want a witness! everybody's curious to know what you think! now everybody will know! . . . and not just me! . . . that I lured you into a trap here . . . an ambush?"

"Exactly, Monsieur le Président!"

He's got Bichelonne on the phone . . .

"Do you know what Céline has been telling me? . . . he says I'm a crook, a no-good, a traitor, and a Jew!"

"Not all that! you're exaggerating, Monsieur le Président!"

"No, Céline! . . . that's what you think! and you're entitled to your opinions! . . ."

He keeps on at the telephone . . . he talks . . . not about me any more . . . one thing and another . . . I watch him while he's talking . . . I see him on the slant, in profile . . . oh, I had the right idea! . . . if I wanted to compare him to somebody . . . I can still see him . . . somebody from now . . . I'd put him between Nasser and Mendès . . . the profile, the smile, the complexion, the Asiatic hair . . . one thing is sure! underneath the banter, he can't stand my guts . . . he was exactly in tune with present-day France, pure and sure,[5] and pro-flunkarino . . . they shouldn't have drilled him, he was worth at least ten Mendèses!

"Come on over!"

He insists . . . Bichelonne isn't in the mood . . . he needs coaxing . . .

"He's coming!"

And there he is . . . not the Afro-Asiatic type . . . oh no, not he! he was the big blond type . . . his head was really enormous! A giant spermatozoid! . . . all head! . . . Bonnard is the same . . . the giant spermatozoid type . . . giant tadpoles . . . one more millimeter they'd be on exhibit . . . in a jar! . . . oh, it's Bichelonne all right! . . . but say . . . I can hardly recognize him . . . so drawn and pale . . . a sad state . . . trembling . . . that's why he hadn't wanted to come . . . Laval doesn't give him time to recover . . . He starts right in . . . He wants Bichelonne to listen! he's too upset, he doesn't hear a thing . . .

"What are you trembling about, Bichelonne?"

Good reason . . . plenty good reason . . . he tells us . . . he's stammering with emotion! . . . they've broken a windowpane on him! . . . one of the windows in his room! . . . Laval has had ten broken! . . . he tells us all about it . . . he's kidding Bichelonne . . . nothing to tremble about! . . . but Bichelonne isn't joking . . . not at all! . . . he wants to know who? . . . how? . . . why? . . . a stone? . . . a bullet? . . . a plane? . . . propeller blast? . . . a cyclone? that's what kills him, not knowing who? . . . how? . . . why? . . . Bichelonne is no canary . . . not at all, but here all of a sudden he's panicked . . . not knowing why? and how? . . . flummoxed! . . . the planes come so near his window! . . . they practically graze it! . . . but maybe a bullet from the street? . . . maybe? . . . he hasn't found any! . . . he's looked all night! . . . meticulously! . . . the ceiling . . . the walls . . . nothing! . . . naturally he doesn't give a shit about what the President wants him to know! that I called him this! and that! he doesn't listen! his windowpane! his windowpane! . . . how? who? . . . that's what interests him! . . . Laval is wasting his breath . . . Bichelonne paces the whole length of the immense First Empire desk! . . . his hands clasped behind his back . . . thinking . . . thinking hard! . . . his problem! . . . Laval starts all over again: I've accused him of this . . . and that! . . . he gilds the lily! . . . I've called him a contemptible swine for saving Morand, Jardin,[6] "Guérard![7] and a hundred others! a thousand others! and deliberately sacrificing me! . . . a private racial grudge! . . . so the niggers of Leclerc's army would find me here! and chop me into small pieces! . . . absolutely premeditated!

I wasn't going to interrupt him! he was in full swing!

"Bravo, Monsieur le Président!"

Plea for the prosecution! I applaud! . . . He's prosecuting himself! . . . before another High Court! . . . the High Court of the imagination! . . . like the other . . . Both museums! . . .

"Bravo, Monsieur le Président!"

He's turned me into the Supreme High Court! . . . Bichelonne doesn't listen, not interested . . . he paces, he mutters . . . suddenly he fires a question at Laval!

"What do you think?"

He doesn't give a damn about what I've said . . . or not said! . . . his problem is his window! he goes on pacing . . . limping . . . not the "distinguished limp" in his case . . . a real claudication! . . . a fracture that hasn't knit right . . . in fact he wants to have it fixed, to be operated before our return to France! . . . operated right here in Germany! . . . by Gebhardt! . . . I know Gebhardt well . . . another character! A fraud, I'd thought at first . . . not at all! . . . he'd been a general on the Russian front for six months . . . in command of a *panzer* team . . . and for six months he'd been chief surgeon of the enormous S.S. hospital in Hohenlychen, East Prussia . . . you'd have taken him for a charlatan, too

. . . a clown! . . . I was mistaken . . . I sent a friend of mine . . . extremely anti-Boche . . . to watch him operate . . . this S.S. surgeon Gebhardt was very skillful! . . . nuts? . . . definitely! in his super-hospital in Hohenlychen there were six thousand surgery patients, a city, four times the size of Bichat! . . . he staged football games with one-legged teams . . . war cripples . . . he was cracked like the supermen of the Renaissance . . . he excelled in two, three rackets . . . tank warfare, surgery . . . ah yes, and singing! . . . I heard him at the piano . . . very amusing . . . he improvised . . . there I'm a good judge . . . during the Hitler period the Boches came close to developing a race of Renaissance men . . . this Gebhardt was one of them! . . . Bichelonne was another . . . in a different way . . . he was a Polytechnician! . . . There hadn't been a genius like him since Arago . . . what impressed me was his memory! . . . prodigious! . . . in the Vichy government he'd been in charge of the railroads . . . making them run come hell or high water! a labor of Hercules! . . . every line, switch, timetable, and detour in his head! . . . to the minute! . . . to the second! . . . with all the culverts, tracks, and stations that were blown up every night! It was no joke! and patching! and mending! and rerouting! and getting her moving again! . . . and two seconds later more dynamite . . . someplace else! The Fifis wouldn't let him sleep! Europe will never recover from that dynamiting mania! hysterics and pie crust! everything sky-high! . . . the habit has sunk in! . . . it'll take the atom bomb to make the place normal and livable again! and now this business with the windowpane . . . stone? bullet? propeller? Bichelonne couldn't take it . . . his nerves were on edge from Vichy . . . and now this windowpane was too much! . . . from the street? . . . from the air? . . . I understood . . . his nerves were shot . . .

It wasn't only his nerves they had wrecked! . . . his leg, too! . . . he'd been riding in a car . . . a little bomb! *plump!* happy landing, your Excellency! . . . he'd been on his way to the Ministry of Information . . . three fractures that hadn't knit right, they'd have to break his leg again to get it straight . . . and he wanted it done right away, in Germany! he didn't want to go back to Paris in this condition! he knew Gebhardt slightly . . . he was dead set on going up there to Hohenlychen . . . Gebhardt had offered . . . it didn't sound very good to me . . . I hadn't much faith in Gebhardt . . . he was sold on him . . . okay . . . he had the faith . . . okay . . . but this situation! . . . my goodness! he kept mumbling instead of listening to Laval . . . pacing the whole length of the big First Empire desk . . . mumbling the pros . . . and the cons . . . a bullet? . . . a propeller tip? . . . sunk in his meditations . . . he was pretty funny with his enormous head . . . but Laval wasn't amused! . . . in fact he was getting good and sick of him! . . . he hadn't sent for him to pace and mumble about a windowpane . . . he wanted him to listen! "Look at that! . . . are you looking, Doctor? . . . he's not listening! . . . his windowpane! . . . all he cares about is his windowpane! . . ."

Laval calls me to witness . . .

It couldn't go on like that! Laval knew the way . . . the one way to shake him out of his meditations: to ask him a stickler! no matter what! . . . put a different bee in his bonnet!

"Tell me, Bichelonne . . . I'd appreciate it . . . I used to know . . . I've forgotten . . . I need it for a little paper I'm doing . . . the capital of Honduras?"

Bichelonne pulls up sharp . . . now he's listening . . . he's not mumbling any more . . . he's going to answer . . .

"Tegucigalpa, Monsieur le Président!"

"No, no! I'm sorry, Bichelonne . . . British Honduras?"

"Belize, Monsieur le Président!"

"Area, Bichelonne?"

"21,000 square kilometers . . ."

"Principal products?"

"Mahogany . . . resin . . ."

"Fine! Thank you, Bichelonne!"

Bichelonne gets back to his window . . . pacing and limping again . . . but he's a little less preoccupied . . . Belize has done him good . . .

"Tell me, Bichelonne, as long as I've got you here . . . I need your help again . . . I used to know all those things! . . . I've forgotten! . . . tungsten, Bichelonne? . . . Rochat is always talking about it . . . he took some away with him . . ."

"Atomic weight 183.9 . . . density 19.3 . . ."

Once he'd got that off his chest, Bichelonne sat down . . . He's tired of pacing . . . he massages his leg . . . Laval sees his chance . . . he goes to the mirror, smoothes his cowlick . . . he straightens his tie . . . he's going to give us some more High Court! . . . ah, not so fast! not so fast! . . . I've got a few words to say too! always listening to other people . . . a little wave of pride comes over me! . . . not very bright of me! . . . I thought I'd shut them up once and for all! I was quick to regret it! I still regret it! I seldom let myself go . . . but I'd been listening to them too long! . . .

"Here," I said. "Take a look at this!"

I put my cyanide down on the table in front of them . . . on Laval's desk . . . my little phial . . . out of my pocket! . . . as long as they're talking about rare metals! . . . I've always got my cyanide on me! . . . ever since Sartrouville . . . here, they can see it . . . and the red label . . . they both look . . .

I was always being asked for cyanide . . . I always said I didn't have any . . . oh, they're not bashful . . . not these two . . . they're arguing already which one gets it! . . . it's all right with me . . . I've still got three phials . . . sealed the same way . . . same cyanide . . . the trouble is that they'll blab . . . sure to! . . . and I'd never mentioned it to anybody . . .

"Can I have it? Can I have it?"

Both of them . . . oh, they're not joking any more!

"Share it!"

Let them work it out between themselves . . . Then I change my mind . . .

"No . . . don't fight . . . I'll give you each one! Once it's open, you know, once it catches the humidity, it's no good!"

"But when? . . . but when?"

Ah, now they're beginning to take me seriously! I take another phial out of another pocket . . . and still another out of my lining! I don't tell them the whole story, my hems are full of little packets . . . I don't want to be caught without it . . . okay! . . . I can see they respect me now . . . they've stopped talking . . . but they're happy . . . they'll talk again . . . nothing good!

"What can I do for you, Doctor?"

"Monsieur le Président, if you'll kindly listen to me . . . in the first place don't open the phial . . . in the second place don't tell any-body . . ."

"Yes . . . that goes without saying! but yourself? . . . you must have some little wish?"

I get another little idea! I'd always refused everything! everything! . . . but the way things are . . . what difference does it make?

"Well, Monsieur le Président, you could appoint me governor of Saint-Pierre and Miquelon . . ."

No point in pussyfooting!

"Granted! . . . it's a promise! . . . you'll make a note of it, Biche-lonne?"

"Certainly, Monsieur le Président!"

Laval has a little question though . . .

"Who gave you that idea, Doctor?"

"Just like that, Monsieur le Président! the beauties of Saint-Pierre and Miquelon! . . ."

I tell him about them . . . not from hearsay . . . I'd been there . . . at that time it took twenty-five days from Bordeaux to Saint-Pierre . . . on the very frail *Celtique* . . . Saint-Pierre was still a fishing port . . . I know Langlade and Miquelon well . . . I know the road well . . . the only road from one end of the island to the other . . . the road and the memorial "milestone" . . . the road cut out of solid rock by the sailors of the *Iphigénie* . . . I'm not making it up . . . real memory, a real road! . . . and not only the sailors of the *Iphigénie*! convicts too! . . . they had a penal colony on Saint-Pierre . . . which left a memorial, too! . . .

"You ought to see it, Monsieur le Président! in the middle of the Atlantic Ocean!"

The main thing: I was appointed Governor . . . I'm still Gover-nor! . . .

# GEORGE CLARE

GEORGE CLARE, who started life in Vienna as Georg
Klaar, escaped to Ireland in 1938 and served with the
British army during World War II. He now lives in Lon-
don. The following selection is from *The Last Waltz*.

■

## FROM *The Last Waltz*

For many years I believed the report in *The Times* that Laval ordered
the deportations to make up to the Germans for the lack of French
volunteers for Germany's war industry. I also gave some credence to
another explanation I had read somewhere that he did it because the
Germans offered to return one French prisoner-of-war to France for
every two Jews handed over to them. For internal political reasons both
these deals could have been tempting for Pierre Laval, and the two
stories made sense.

It may seem difficult to understand, but for a very long time I hated
that stocky, swarthy petty bourgeois from the Auvergne even more than
Hitler. He was always immaculate with his inevitable white shirt and
whiter-than-white tie, as if he needed such outer purity over his breast
to hide something dirty underneath. I rejoiced and felt my parents to be
avenged when, after a trial serving more the cause of revenge than that
of justice, the half-alive Laval—he tried to poison himself and they
quickly pumped out his stomach—was dragged to the execution stake
and shot on 15 October 1945. I hated him so just because this former
socialist and eventual foreign and prime minister of the Third Republic,
unlike Hitler himself, was not a raving anti-semite. In my eyes he had
sacrificed my parents' lives not out of a conviction, however horrible,
but to curry favor with his German master and thus strengthen his own
position in the senile Marshal Pétain's government.

Eventually I overcame my reluctance to allow any aspect of my
parents' tragic fate to enter my consciousness and, first hesitantly, but
then with growing involvement, tried to discover its cause. And when I
knew more and remembered what vehement joy and satisfaction I had
felt when Laval was killed, I began to feel somewhat ashamed.

Laval was not innocent by any means. He did indeed make a deal
with Himmler's men, but it was not for the release of French prisoners-
of-war or the protection of Frenchmen who wanted to stay at home. It
was in order to save the lives of French Jews that he sacrificed the lives

of foreign Jews who had sought refuge in his country. The S.S.'s original target for Jews to be deported from France was 5,000. On 11 June 1942 Department IV-B4, Eichmann's office in the Reichs-sicherheits-Hauptamt (R.S.H.A.), the Berlin headquarters of the S.S., increased that figure to 100,000 and S.S. Captain Dannecker, Eichmann's twenty-seven-year-old representative in Paris, was told that the victims had to be taken from the occupied and unoccupied zones of France. Laval agreed to co-operate provided French Jews were spared. In that case he would give the orders for the arrest of foreign Jews in Vichy France. To some extent Laval succeeded, but as Geoffrey Warner points out in his book *Pierre Laval and the Eclipse of France* his attitude towards the foreign Jews was remarkably callous. Warner quotes Laval as saying to an American Quaker who had come to protest about the deportations that "these foreign Jews had always been a problem in France and the French government was glad that a change in the German attitude towards them gave France an opportunity to get rid of them."

The German's original demands specified that only Jews between the ages of sixteen and forty-five should be handed over to them. It was Laval who suggested to them that they should take younger children as well, as these should not be separated from their parents. Could he have said this from a humane motive? Warner cites André Guénier, Laval's wartime private secretary, who wrote: "Laval . . . never suspected the inhuman system and atrocities to which the people who were arrested and deported to the east were subjected . . ."

That, in spite of the great secrecy in which the S.S. shrouded their extermination policy, is hard to swallow. Laval may indeed not have known about Auschwitz, Treblinka and Maidanek in the summer and autumn of 1942, but more was known about Hitler's treatment of the Jews in France, which had had a free press until May 1940, than in Germany herself.

Was Laval worse informed than my father was when he wrote those despairing words, "What is going to happen is not difficult to guess"?

It is believable that he thought the Jews were taken to live in Polish spas at a time when a *Times* correspondent could report "that Jews still free in Vichy France feared that the erasure of names from the national register confirmed the rumors that the arrested Jews had been virtually sentenced to death"?

Did the Chief of Government know less than M. Reuter or Couve de Murville, his own official?

Did he have to order the arrest of Roman Catholic priests, who gave shelter to Jewish children? He was not an innocent by any means; but he did probably save Jewish lives. 61,000 Jews, men, women and children, arrived in Auschwitz from France, and 78.5 per cent of them were gassed on arrival; but while in other countries occupied by Germany nearly 90 per cent of their pre-war Jewish population was wiped out, only 50 per cent of all Jews in France, French and foreign, did not survive. According to some estimates between 80 and 90 per cent of native French Jews were alive at the end of the war. There was no need to gloat over the execution of Pierre Laval.

But after these questions about Laval another question must be asked. Why, by and large, did the French behave so differently from the Germans when the Jews were arrested and deported? Why did they protest so loudly and succor so many? Why, with very few exceptions—only one comes to mind, Berlin's brave Canon Lichtenberg—did the German Roman Catholic clergy, who forced Hitler to abandon his "Euthanasia Program" in 1941 when his power and popularity were greatest, remain so silent when the Jews were deported? Why did they not break that silence when rumors about the Jews' ultimate fate had become persistent in Germany, while so many of their French brethren, from bishop to village priest, spoke out and helped wherever they could?

France's anti-semitism had roots in history reaching just as far back as German anti-semitism. St. Agobard, Archbishop of Lyon, living in the ninth century, denounced the Jews as true enemies of God and the synagogue as the church of Satan where the Jews assembled, "a race cursed to their very bowels" with whom "contact should be avoided as a foul contamination." (How well the Austrian students' Waidhofer resolution echoed his sentiments!) In his book *God's First Love*, Friedrich Heer, that most remarkable Austrian historian and philosopher, relates that a Monsignor Bresolles of the Catholic Institute in Paris wrote a book in 1933 claiming that Agobard's polemic against the Jews displayed wisdom and good sense. That book—it seems unbelievable—was published in France in 1949. Heer also mentions St. Bernard of Clairvaux, another medieval French bishop, who preached against the "bestial" Jews and called them "lower than animals and murderers since the beginning of time."

In the nineteenth century, probably the most fruitful of all for sowing the seeds of Jew-hatred, not only Austrian and German, but also French politicians, writers and intellectuals, wrote down and spoke the thoughts which Hitler, by translating them into action, took to their "logical and final conclusion."

But to come back to our question. The point, often ignored yet obvious in human terms, which provides at least part of the answer, is that the French when helping the Jews knew themselves to be acting against their German enemy. The Germans closed their eyes for the opposite reason. They did not want, as the German saying goes, to "befoul their own nest" when their nation, as they saw it, was fighting for its survival. When the Roman Catholic clergy spoke out against euthanasia it knew that it had the support of its parishioners, even of Nazi officials, because the sick and mad that were killed were of their own kind. At least a decade of intensive anti-semitic propaganda, to which the French had not been exposed, had persuaded a great number of Germans that the Jews were "alien elements in their midst." But even so the public reaction would have been strong. If the German churches, Protestant and Roman Catholic alike, instead of keeping silent out of fear for their own institutions, had possessed the courage to say from the pulpits what they probably knew by 1943—and certainly by 1944—namely, that the Jews were being shot and gassed in their millions. Had Hitler during the years of his struggle for power openly said that the extermination of Jewish men, women and children was an integral part of his program, his share of the popular vote would never have reached even the miserable 2.6 per cent he obtained in 1928.

# HARRY MULISCH

THE NOVELIST, poet, and playwright Harry Mulisch is considered by many to be Holland's most important postwar writer. He was born to a Jewish mother whose family died in the concentration camps and a father who was jailed for collaborating with the Nazis. He lives in Amsterdam. The following comes from his novel *The Assault*.

■

FROM *The Assault*

In the silence that was Holland then, six shots suddenly rang out. First, one echoed through the street, then two more in rapid succession, and a few seconds later, a fourth and a fifth. After a moment came a kind of scream, followed by a sixth shot. Anton, about to throw the dice, froze and looked at his mother, his mother at his father, his father at the sliding doors; but Peter picked up the cover of the carbon lamp and put it over the flame.

Suddenly, all was dark. Peter stood up, stumbled forward, opened the sliding doors, and peered through a crack in the curtains of the bay window. Freezing cold air immediately streamed in from the parlor.

"They shot someone!" he said. "Someone's lying there." He hurried into the front hall.

"Peter!" cried his mother.

Anton heard her follow. He jumped up himself and ran to the bay window. Unerringly he dodged all the invisible furniture that he hadn't seen for months: the armchairs, the low, round table with the lace doily under the glass plate, the dresser with the ceramic platter and the portraits of his grandparents. The curtains, the windowsill, everything was icy cold. No one had breathed in this room for so long that there weren't even any frost flowers on the windowpanes. It was a moonless night, but the frozen snow held the light of the stars. At first he thought that Peter had been talking nonsense, but now he too saw it through the left side of the bay window.

In the middle of the deserted street, in front of Mr. Korteweg's house, lay a bicycle with its upended front wheel still turning—a dramatic effect later much used in close-ups in every movie about the Resistance. Limping, Peter ran along the garden path into the street. The last few weeks he'd had a boil on his toe that would not heal, and his mother had cut a piece out of his shoe to ease the pain. He knelt beside a man lying motionless in the gutter not far from the bicycle. The man's right hand was resting on the edge of the sidewalk, as if he had made himself comfortable. Anton saw the shimmer of black boots and the iron plates on the heels.

In a whisper that was surprisingly loud, his mother called Peter from the doorstep to come in at once. He stood up, looked to right and left along the quay and then back at the man, and limped home.

"It's Ploeg!" Anton heard him say a minute later in the hall, a tone of triumph in his voice. "Dead as a doornail, if you ask me."

Anton too knew Fake Plocg, Chief Inspector of Police, the greatest murderer and traitor in Haarlem. He passed by regularly on his way between his office and his house in Heemstede. A big, square-shouldered man with a rough face, he was usually dressed in a hat, a brown sports jacket, and a shirt with a tie. But he wore black riding pants and high boots, and he radiated violence, hate, and fear. His son, also named Fake, was in Anton's class. From the bay window Anton stared at the boots. He knew those, all right, because Fake had been brought to school a couple of times by his father on the back of that very bicycle. Each time they arrived at the school entrance, everyone fell silent. The father looked about with a mocking glance, but after he left, the son went in with downcast eyes and had to manage as best he could.

"Tonny!" His mother called. "Get away from that window!"

On the second day of school when nobody knew who he was yet, Fake had appeared in the pale-blue uniform and black-and-orange cap of the Nazi youth organization. That was in September, shortly after Mad Tuesday, when everyone thought the liberators were on their way and most National Socialists and collaborators had fled to the German border or beyond. Fake sat all alone at his desk in the classroom and pulled out his books. Mr. Bos, the science teacher, stood in the doorway, his arm against the doorjamb to keep out the other students; he had called back those who had already entered. He announced to Fake that there would be no teaching students in uniform, it hadn't gotten that far and would never get that far, and he should go home and change. Fake said nothing, did not look back at the doorway but remained motionless. After a while the principal edged through the students and began to whisper excitedly to the teacher, who wouldn't give in.

Anton stood in the front of the crowd and, under Bos's arm, stared at the back of the boy in the empty room. Then, slowly, Fake turned around and looked him straight in the eyes. All at once Anton was overcome by a strange pity for him. How could Fake possibly go home, with that father of his? Before he knew what he was doing, Anton dove under Mr. Bos's arm and sat down at his desk. This broke down the general resistance of the others. After school the principal stood waiting for him in the hall, caught him briefly by the arm, and whispered that he had probably saved Mr. Bos's life. Anton didn't quite know what to do with his compliment. He never told anyone at home about it, and the incident was never mentioned again.

The body in the gutter. The wheel had stopped turning. Above, the amazing starry sky. His eyes were used to the darkness now, and he could see ten times better than before. Orion lifting his sword, the Milky Way, one brilliant, shiny planet, probably Jupiter—not in centuries had Holland's skies been this clear. On the horizon two slowly moving searchlights crossed each other and fanned out, but no plane could be heard. He noticed that he was still holding one of the dice in his hand and put it in his pocket.

As he was about to move away from the window, he saw Mr. Korteweg come out of his house, followed by Karin. Korteweg picked Ploeg up by the shoulders, Karin by the boots, and together they began dragging him through the snow, Karin walking backwards.

"Look at that," said Anton.

His mother and Peter were just in time to see them deposit the body in front of Carefree. Karin threw Ploeg's cap, which had fallen off, onto his body. Her father moved the bicycle to the road in front of Carefree. The next moment they had disappeared into Home at Last.

Everyone was speechless in the bay window at the Steenwijks'. The quay was once more deserted, everything was as quiet as it had been, yet everything had changed. The dead man now lay with his arms above his head, the right hand clasping a gun, the long coat gathered at the waist, as if Ploeg had fallen from a great height. Now Anton clearly recognized the large face, its hair slicked down and brushed back, practically undisturbed.

"God dammit!" screamed Peter suddenly, his voice breaking.

"Hey, hey, watch it," came Steenwijk's voice from the darkness of the back room. He was still sitting at the table.

"They put him down in front of our house, the bastards!" Peter cried. "Jesus Christ! We've got to get him out of here before the Krauts come."

"Don't get involved," said Mrs. Steenwijk. "We had nothing to do with it."

"No, except that now he's lying in front of our door! Why do you suppose they did that? Because the Krauts are going to retaliate, of course. Just like before, at the Leidse Canal."

"We didn't do anything wrong, Peter."

"As if they care! You're dealing with Krauts." He left the room. "Come on Anton, hurry; you and I can do it."

"Are you crazy?" Mrs. Steenwijk cried. She choked, cleared her throat, and spat out the clove. "What do you want to do?"

"Put him back—or at Mrs. Beumer's."

"At Mrs. Beumer's? How can you think of such a thing?"

"Why not at Mrs. Beumer's? Mrs. Beumer had nothing to do with it either! If only the river weren't frozen . . . We'll see what we can do."

"No you don't!"

Mrs. Steenwijk rushed out of the room. In the dim light that fell through the transom into the front hall, Anton saw that his mother had posted herself in front of the door; Peter was trying to push her aside. He heard her turn the key as she called, "Willem, why don't you say something?"

"Yes . . . yes . . ." Anton heard his father's voice, still in the back room. "I . . ."

In the distance, shots rang out again.

"If he'd been hit a few seconds later, he'd be lying at Mrs. Beumer's now," called Peter.

"Yes . . ." said Steenwijk softly, his voice breaking in an odd way. "But that is not the case."

"Not the case! It wasn't the case that he was lying here, either, but now it *is* the case!" Peter said suddenly. "In fact, I'm going to take him back. I'll just do it alone."

He turned to run toward the kitchen door, but with a cry of pain tripped over the pile of logs and branches from the last trees his mother had chopped down in the empty lots.

"Peter, for God's sake!" cried Mrs. Steenwijk. "You're playing with your life!"

"That's exactly what *you're* doing, dammit."

Before Peter could pick himself up. Anton turned the key in the kitchen door and threw it into the hall, where it clattered and became invisible; then he ran to the front door and did the same with the house key.

"God dammit," cried Peter, almost in tears. "You're pathetic, pathetic, all of you."

He went to the back room, tore aside the curtains, and with his good foot pushed against the french doors. They burst open with a crash, sending strips of paper insulation flying, and suddenly Anton saw his father's silhouette outlined against the snow. He was still sitting at the table.

As Peter disappeared into the garden. Anton ran back to the bay window. He saw his brother appear around the house, climb over the fence, and grip Ploeg by the boots. At that moment he seemed to hesitate, perhaps because of all the blood, perhaps because he couldn't decide which direction to take. But before he could do anything, shouts echoed at the end of the quay.

"Halt! Stand still! Hands up!"

Three men approached, bicycling hard. They threw their bikes down on the street and began running. Peter dropped Ploeg's legs, pulled the gun out of Ploeg's hand, ran without limping to the Kortewegs' fence, and disappeared behind their house. The men screamed at each other. One of them, wearing a cap and an overcoat, took a shot at Peter and chased after him.

Anton felt his mother's warmth beside him.

"What was that? Are they shooting at Peter? Where is he?"

"Out in back."

With wide eyes Anton watched everything. The second man, who wore a Military Police uniform, ran back to his bicycle, jumped on, and rode away at full speed. The third, who was in civilian clothes, slid down the other side of the embankment and crouched on the towpath, holding a gun with both hands.

Anton dove below the windowsill and turned around. His mother had disappeared. At the table the silhouette of his father was a little more bent than before, as if he were praying. Then Anton heard his mother, in the backyard, whisper Peter's name into the night. It was as if the cold which now streamed into the house emanated from her back. There was no further sound. Anton saw and heard everything, but somehow he was no longer quite there. One part of him was already somewhere else, or nowhere at all. He was undernourished, and stiff now with cold, but that wasn't all. This moment —his father cut out in black against the snow, his mother outside on the terrace under the starlight—became eternal, detached itself from all that had come before and all that would follow. It became part of him and began its journey through the rest of his life, until finally it would explode like a soap bubble, after which it might as well never have happened.

His mother came in.

"Tonny? Where are you? Do you see him?"

"No."

"What should we do? Perhaps he's hiding somewhere." Agitated, she walked outside again and then came back. Suddenly she went to her husband and pulled at his shoulders.

"Will you ever wake up? They're shooting at Peter! Perhaps he's been hit already."

Slowly Steenwijk stood up. Without a word, tall and thin, he left the room. A moment later he returned wearing a scarf and his black bowler hat. As he was about to enter the garden from the terrace, he drew back. Anton could hear that he was trying to call Peter's name, but only a horse sound came out. Defeated, he turned back. He came in and went to sit, trembling, on the chair next to the stove. After a few moments he said, "Please forgive me, Thea . . . forgive me . . ." Mrs. Steenwijk's hands wrestled with each other.

"Everything has gone so well until now, and now, at the end . . . Anton, put on your coat. Oh God, where can that boy be?"

"Perhaps he went into the Kortewegs'," said Anton. "He took Ploeg's gun."

From the silence which followed his words he understood that this was something terrible.

"Did you really see that?"

"Just as those men came . . . Like this . . . as he ran away . . ."

In the soft, powdery light which now hung about the rooms, he acted out a short sprint and, leaning over, pulled an imaginary pistol out of an imaginary hand.

"You don't suppose he . . ." Mrs. Steenwijk caught her breath. "I'm going to Korteweg's right now."

She started to run into the garden, but Anton followed and said, "Watch out! There's another man out there somewhere."

As her husband had done before her, she drew back from the freezing silence. Nothing stirred. There was the garden, and beyond it the barren, snow-covered lots. Anton too stood motionless. Everything was still—and yet time went by. It was as if everything grew radiant with the passage of time, like pebbles at the bottom of a brook. Peter had disappeared, a corpse lay in front of the door, and all about them the armed men remained motionless. Anton had the feeling that by doing something which was within his power but which he could not quite think of, he could undo everything and return to the way they had been before, sitting around the table playing a game. It was as if he had forgotten a name remembered a hundred times before and now on the tip of his tongue, but the harder he tried to recall it, the more elusive it became. Or it was like the time when he had suddenly realized that he was breathing in and out continuously and must make sure to keep doing it or else suffocate—and at that moment he almost did suffocate.

Motorcycles sounded in the distance; also, he heard the noise of a car.

"Come in, Mama," said Anton.

"Yes . . . I'll close the doors."

He could tell from her voice that she stood on the edge of something she could not master. It seemed as if he was the only one who kept his wits, and that, of course, was as it should be, for a future aviator. In the Air Force difficult situations might also arise: at the eye of a cyclone, for instance, the wind is calm and the sun shines, but the pilot must fly out into the turmoil of weather, or else he'll get lost and run out of fuel.

Now the motorcycles and the car could be heard out front on the quay, while more cars—heavier ones—seemed to be approaching in the distance. So far, everything was still all right; nothing had changed, really —except of course that Peter had disappeared. How could anything really change?

Then there it was. Squeaking tires, shouting in German, the iron clatter of boots jumping onto the street. Now and then a bright light flashed through the split between the curtains. Anton tiptoed to the bay window. Everywhere soldiers with rifles and machine guns, motorcycles coming and going, trucks with still more soldiers; a military ambulance out of which a stretcher was being pulled. Suddenly he yanked the curtains closed and turned around.

"Here they are," he said into the darkness. At that moment there was a banging on the door, so unnecessarily loud, with the butt of a rifle, that he knew something terrible was about to happen.

"*Aufmachen!* Open at once!"

Involuntarily he fled to the back room. His mother went into the hall and called out with a trembling voice that the key was lost. But already the door was being broken down and slammed against the wall. Anton heard the mirror shatter, the one with the two carved elephants over the little side table with the twisted legs. Suddenly the hall and rooms were filled with armed men in helmets, wrapped in ice-cold air, all much too large for his mother and father's house. Already it was no longer theirs. Blinded by a lantern, Anton lifted one arm to his eyes. From beneath it he could see the shiny badge of the Field Police, and hanging from a belt, the elongated container of a gas mask, and boots caked with snow. A man in civilian dress entered the room. He wore a long black leather coat down to his ankles and on his head a hat with a lowered brim.

"*Papiere*, papers, *vorzeigen!*" he shouted. "*Schnell*, quick, all your papers, everything."

Steenwijk stood up and opened a drawer in the dresser, while his wife said: "We had nothing to do with all this."

"*Schweigen Sie*, silence!" snapped the man. He stood by the table and with the nail of his index finger flipped shut the book that Steenwijk had been reading. "*Ethica*," he read on the cover, "*Ordine Geometrico Demonstrata. Benedictus de Spinoza.* Ach so!" He looked up. "That's what you people read here; Jew books." And then to Mrs. Steenwijk, "Just take a few steps up and down."

"What should I do?"

"Walk back and forth! Do you have shit in your ears?"

Anton saw his mother trembling all over as she paced up and down with the puzzled expression of a child. The man aimed the flashlight at her legs.

"*Das genugt*, enough," he said after a while. Not till much later when he was in college did Anton learn that the man thought he could tell by her walk whether she was Jewish.

Steenwijk stood with the papers in his hand. "*Ich* . . ."

"You might take off your hat when you talk to me."

Steenwijk took off his bowler hat and repeated, "I . . ."

"Keep your mouth shut, you pig Jew-lover." The man studied the identity papers and ration cards, then looked about him.

"Where is the fourth?"

Mrs. Steenwijk tried to say something, but it was her husband who spoke.

"My oldest son," he began with a trembling voice, "confused by this dreadful accident, has rushed out of the parental home without taking his leave, and he went in that direction." With his hat he pointed in the direction of Hideaway, where the Beumers lived.

"So," said the German, shoving the papers into his pocket. "He rushed out, did he?"

"Yes indeed."

The man made a gesture with the head. "*Abführen*. Take them away."

# MARTHA GELLHORN

ST. LOUIS–BORN Martha Gellhorn has been to more than one war. She reported on the Spanish Civil War for *Collier's Weekly* in 1937–38, and then moved on to other battlefields in Finland, China, Italy, France, and Germany. Later she reported on the war in Vietnam and Israel's Six Day War in 1967. She has published many books, among them *The Face of War,* which includes the following report.

■

## Das Deutsches Volk

*April 1945*

No one is a Nazi. No one ever was. There may have been some Nazis in the next village, and as a matter of fact, that town about twenty kilometers away was a veritable hotbed of Nazidom. To tell you the truth, confidentially there were a lot of Communists here. We were always known as very Red. Oh, the Jews? Well, there weren't really many Jews in this neighborhood. Two maybe, maybe six. They were taken away. I hid a Jew for six weeks. I hid a Jew for eight weeks. (I hid a Jew, he hid a Jew, all God's chillun hid Jews.) We have nothing against the Jews; we always got on well with them. We have waited for the Americans a long time. You came and liberated us. You came to befriend us. The Nazis are *Schweinhunde.* The Wehrmacht wants to give up but they do not know how. No, I have no relatives in the Army. Nor I. No, I was never in the Army. I worked on the land. I worked in a factory. That boy wasn't in the Army either; he was sick. We have had enough of this government. Ah, how we have suffered. The bombs. We lived in the cellars for weeks. We refused to be driven across the Rhine when the S.S. came to evacuate us. Why should we go? We welcome the Americans. We do not fear them; we have no reason to fear. We have done nothing wrong; we are not Nazis.

It should, we feel, be set to music. Then the Germans could sing this refrain and that would make it even better. They all talk like this. One asks oneself how the detested Nazi government, to which no one paid allegiance, managed to carry on this war for five and a half years. Obviously not a man, woman or child in Germany ever approved of the war for a minute, according to them. We stand around looking blank and contemptuous and listen to this story without friendliness and certainly without respect. To see a whole nation passing the buck is not an enlightening spectacle. It is clear that all you have to do in Germany, in order to lead the country, is to be successful; if you stop being successful, no one will admit they ever heard of you. ⌉

At night the Germans take pot shots at Americans, or string wires across roads, which is apt to be fatal to men driving jeeps, or they burn the houses of Germans who accept posts in our Military Government, or they booby-trap ammunition dumps or motorcycles or anything that is likely to be touched. But that is at night. In the daytime we are the answer to the German prayer, according to them.

At the moment we are sitting on the west bank of the Rhine, facing the Ruhr pocket. The Germans here are peeved about the Ruhr pocket and wish us to push it back ten miles so that they will no longer be troubled by their own artillery, which fires into their villages whenever it can spare some shells. The 504th Regiment of the 82nd Airborne Division sent a company across the Rhine in landing craft one night and took and held a town for thirty-six hours. These landing craft are built like enlarged shoe boxes and are propelled forward by dint of paddles, and the current is swift, and the river is wide, and on the other side was the Wehrmacht, which was not giving up by any manner of means. The company of paratroopers drew onto themselves a great deal of armed attention—two German divisions, it was estimated. This small Airborne action relieved pressure at another part of the front, and the company lost many men.

In the afternoon of the day they got back, two officers and four sergeants were decorated with the Silver Star by General Gavin, who commands the division. This ceremony took place in a nondescript street, amidst brick rubble and fallen telephone wires. Some German civilians stuck their heads cautiously out of windows and watched with interest. It was very simple: one officer read the citations and General Gavin pinned on the medals. The six who received the medals were not dressed for the occasion; they had come directly from their work. Their faces were like gray stone and their eyes were not like eyes you will see every day and no one was talking about what had just been lived through across the river. It you had friends in the company who did not come back, that made it worse; if you knew no one personally it was bad enough.

The German civilians looked with wonder at this row of dirty silent men standing in the street. It makes little or no difference to anyone around there whether the Germans are Nazis or not; they can talk their heads off; they can sing "The Star-Spangled Banner"; they are still Germans and they are not liked. None of these soldiers has forgotten yet that our dead stretch back all the way to Africa.

The villages along the Rhine here are in pretty good shape. In the middle, of course, is Cologne, and Cologne is one of the great ruins of the world; but by and large these adjacent villages have nothing to complain of. The houses are well built and each one of them has a small cellar where large quantities of Germans sleep at night. As the soldiers say, they are not hurting for anything. There is food and clothing, coal, bedding, all household equipment, livestock. The Germans are nice and fat too, and quite clean and orderly and industrious. They carry on their normal lives within seven hundred yards of their Army, which is now their enemy.

The *Bürgermeister*, whom we appoint, rule the people by decrees which we publish and slap up on the walls. The Germans seem to love decrees, and they stand in line busily to read anything new that appears. We went to call on one *Bürgermeister* of a front-line village; he was, he said, a Communist and a half-Jew and he may be for all I know, but it is amazing how many Communists and half-Jews there are in Germany. He was a working man before and he says that plenty of people in the village are furious about his being *Bürgermeister*; he has got above himself, they think, because of the Americans. If the Americans fired him he would be killed, he said. He stated this in a matter-of-fact way, as if it were only to be expected.

We said, "Then that means the people here are Nazis."

"No, no," he said. "It is that they think I have too good a position."

We then told him we thought his fellow villagers must be lovely people; it was not regulation, we felt, to murder a man just because he had a good job.

He spoke with some despair about the future of Germany and finished by saying that America must help Germany to recover. We listened to this remark with surprise and asked him why; why did he imagine America was going to help Germany do anything? He admitted that perhaps we had a reason to hate Germany but they were relying on our well-known humanitarianism.

"Nuts," said the sergeant, who spoke German.

"Translate nuts," said the Lieutenant. "Where does he get these fancy ideas?"

The *Bürgermeister* went on to say that if the Americans did not occupy Germany for fifty years, there would be war again. Some man with a bigger mouth than Hitler, he said, will come along and promise them everything and they will follow and there will be war again.

"I believe him," said the Lieutenant.

After the tidy villages, Cologne is a startling sight. We are not shocked by it, which only goes to prove that if you see enough of anything you stop noticing it. In Germany, when you see absolute devastation you do not grieve. We have grieved for many places in many countries but this is not one of the countries. Our soldiers say, "They asked for it." Between two mountains of broken brick, and backed by a single jagged wall, a German had set up a push-cart and was selling tulips, narcissuses and daffodils. The flowers looked a little mad in this *décor,* and considering there are no houses to put flowers in, the whole set-up seemed odd. Two young men on bicycles rode up and one of them bought a bunch of tulips. We asked him what he wanted tulips for and he said he was Dutch. So of course he needed the tulips. He had been a slave laborer in this city for three years; his friend had been here only five months. They came from Rotterdam. Anything that happened to Cologne was all right with them.

The flower vendor came over to talk. Yes, this was his regular business; he walked eighteen kilometers a day to get the flowers. Now I think of it, he was allowed to travel only six kilometers from his dwelling place, so I wonder how he did it. He made very little money, but before we came he sold his flowers to the hospitals as well as to some old customers. He was alone in the world and he would go on with the flowers as long as there were any flowers and then he would probably sell vegetables. His family was dead. His whole family, forty-two of them, including his grandparents and parents, his wife and children, his sisters and their children and husbands. They had all been buried in one cellar during one air raid. He brought pictures out of his wallet. "Of this sister," he said, "we found only her torso. During the bombings, we prayed a great deal." The two soldiers and I sat in the jeep and wondered why he talked to us; if forty-two members of our families had been killed by German bombs we would not talk pleasantly to Germans.

A crowd gathered around us; since no one speaks to Germans, except on official business, you can collect a crowd anywhere simply by saying *"Guten Tag."* This desire to be chummy baffles us as much as anything. The crowd was varied and everyone talked at once. I asked them when things had started to go bad in Germany, because my editor wanted me to ask that. I had a private bet with myself on the answer, and I won. Things have been bad in Germany since 1933, they all said loudly. I said, No, I am talking about since the war. Since 1941 it has been bad. Why? Because of the bombs. *"Danke schön,"* I said. Then I asked what form of government they hoped for after the war. I had another bet with myself, and I won. Democracy, they cried. But one day in another village it came out much better than that, and much more truthfully. The women said that if they had enough to eat and could live quietly they did not care who ruled them. Note: *who.* The men said they had not talked politics for eleven years and no longer knew anything about government. However, democracy is a fine word and in frequent use in Germany. Then I asked them (for my editor) whether they had traveled during the war, had anyone made a side trip to Paris? No one had traveled anywhere at all; they were assigned their work and they stayed to do it, good and bad, twelve hours a day. After that the talk degenerated into the usual condemnation of the Nazis.

We decided to go and see friends for a change, so we went down to the riverfront to call on some Airborne pals. It is a stone jungle, through which the American soldiers roam on foot or bicycle. The Company CP was in a candy factory and we were taken to see the vast stocks of sugar, chocolate, cocoa, butter, almonds and finished candies that remained. Then we were led to a huge wine cellar, only one of three they had located. Next we visited a flour warehouse which had more flour in it than any of us had seen at one time. After this (and by now we were all in a temper, thinking how well off the Germans had been) we went through a jumble of factory buildings used as a general food depot, and we looked with anger on rooms full of Dutch and French cheese, Portuguese sardines, Norwegian canned fish, all kinds of jams and canned vegetables, barrels of syrup. We had seen the individual food supplies throughout Germany, and this small portion of wholesale food stock only convinced us further that the Germans had not given up butter for guns but had done very nicely producing or stealing both. We figured that the Germans could afford to starve for the next five years, just to catch up with the rest of Europe.

A row of German women sat outside the white tape which marked off the military zone. They were watching their houses. No roof or window remains and often there is not a wall left either and almost everything in those houses has been blown about thoroughly by high explosives, but there they sat and kept mournful guard on their possessions. When asked why they did this, they started to weep. We have all seen such beastly and fantastic suffering accepted in silence that we do not react very well to weeping. And we certainly do not react well to people weeping over furniture. I remember Oradour in France, where the Germans locked every man, woman and child of the village into the church and set the church afire, and after the people were burned, they burned the village. This is an extremely drastic way to destroy property, and it is only one of many such instances. The Germans themselves have taught all the people of Europe not to waste time weeping over anything easy like furniture.

Farther down the river, U.S. Military Government was registering German civilians in the villages. The Germans queued up in a line four deep and filed into a little house and made a thumbprint on a piece of paper and got the great pleasure of owning another bit of official printing matter, which said they lived in this village.

"It goes okay," said the young paratroop lieutenant who was in command here. "If they start shoving I just say something in a loud voice and boy, they snap right back into line."

During the war this village had lost ten civilian dead; during the last week German shells had killed seven more civilians. We talked with some German women about the horrors of the war. The bombs, they said, oh God the bombs. Two thousand eight hundred bombs fell on this village alone, they said. Do not be crazy, we told them, there would be no sign of a village if that were true. We are very near Cologne, they said (it was about ten miles away). That is not the same thing, we said. Ah, the bombs, they said, firmly convinced that their village was flat and they were all dead.

The bombs continue, though not now in this vicinity, but every day the bombers go over and while there is still that steady smooth roaring in the sky the Germans remember the war. However, it is only on this side of the river that the Germans are happy in defeat, and just across the river the German ack-ack continues to operate. Yesterday it operated effectively and a B-26 was shot down and a column of black smoke rose straight and mountain-high. It looked like a funeral pyre to all of us. Tanks of the Thirteenth Armored Division were moving up across the river, behind the burning plane, but the crew was there in a belt of Germans, and no one could reach them. From a 505th Regimental observation post, some paratroopers had seen four men get out of the plane. That was at about one o'clock on a soft clear day. At six o'clock began one of the strangest episodes anyone had yet seen in this war—and there were a few men present who had survived all four 82nd Airborne missions and the Battle of the Bulge and could be expected to have seen everything.

Across the Rhine on the green bank someone started waving a white flag. This was ignored, because it does not necessarily mean anything. Then a procession came down to a landing pier. They carried a Red Cross flag. Through binoculars, we could see a medic, a priest, and two German soldiers carrying a stretcher. A landing craft put out from our bank, well covered by our machine guns in case this was all a sinister joke. Presently on both banks of the Rhine there was an audience; normally no one would move in this area in daylight, and even at night you would be careful. Now we stood in the sun and gaped. Slowly three more stretchers were carried down to our boat. We could see civilians over there, children, German soldiers; everyone was out staring at everyone else. We could not quite believe it and were still prepared to dive for cover quickly. Then the little boat was launched into the current, but it drifted farther downstream and we followed it on our side, like people streaming along a racecourse to watch the horses come in. The boat landed and our medic, who had gone over to get these four wounded men, the survivors of the B-26 crew, shouted to clear the banks because the Krauts said they'd give the ambulance time to load and then they would open up. The war had stopped for approximately an hour on a hundred-yard front.

"I never saw the Krauts act so nice," one soldier said, as we wandered back to the buildings where we would not make such tasty targets.

"They know our tanks are coming up," another soldier said. "Krauts don't act nice for nothing."

The DPs (displaced persons, if you have forgotten) tell us that Krauts never act nice. There are tens of thousands of Russian and Polish and Czech and French and Yugoslav and Belgian slave laborers around here, and they pour in every day in truckloads to the camps which the 82nd Airborne now run. There is apparently an inexhaustible supply of human beings who were seized from their families and who lived in misery for years, with no medical care and on starvation rations, while working twelve hours a day for their German masters. They do not feel kindly toward the Germans. The only time I have seen a Russian cry was when a Russian nurse, a girl of twenty-five, wept with rage telling of the way her people were treated. They had all seen their dead thrown into huge lime-filled pits, which were the communal graves. "Everywhere the graves became as high as a mountain," she said. The anger of these people is so great that you feel it must work like fire in the earth.

British prisoners of war are starting to come through now, still joking, still talking in understatement, but with bitterness behind the jokes and the quiet words. The ones we saw had walked for fifty-two days from the Polish frontier to Hanover, where their tank columns freed them, and on that fearful march those who fell out, from hunger and exhaustion, died. Their Red Cross parcels kept them alive during five years but since last November no parcels had arrived. In one small group, nine men had died of starvation after the long march and their bodies lay for six days in the crowded barracks because, for some unknown reason, the Germans did not feel like burying them or allowing them to be buried.

"They're not human at all," a New Zealander said.

"I wish they'd let us take charge of the German prisoners," a boy from Wales said.

A man who was lying on the grass near him now spoke up thoughtfully. "You can't really learn to like those people," he said, "unless they're dead."

Meanwhile the Germans, untroubled by regret—because after all they did nothing wrong, they only did what they were told to do—keep on saying with energy, we are not Nazis. It is their idea of the password to forgiveness, probably followed by a sizable loan.

We are not Nazis; we are friends. Hundreds of thousands of people in khaki around here, and equal numbers of foreigners in rags, cannot see it that way.

# GÜNTER GRASS

GÜNTER GRASS, born in Danzig, was drafted into the
German army toward the end of World War II and captured by the Americans, who held him prisoner until
1946. The author of *The Tin Drum,* from which the following excerpt is taken, and other novels, Grass is
also an essayist, poet, playwright, and sculptor.

■

FROM *The Tin Drum*

## SHOULD I OR SHOULDN'T I?

First came the Rugii, then the Goths and Gepidae, then the Kashubes from whom Oskar is descended in a straight line. A little later the
Poles sent in Adalbert of Prague, who came with the Cross and was slain
with an axe by the Kashubes or Borussians. This happened in a fishing
village called Gyddanyzc. Gyddanyzc became Danczik, which was
turned into Dantzig, later written without the t, and today the city is
called Gdansk.

But before this orthographic development and after the arrival of
the Kashubes, the dukes of Pomerelia came to Gyddanyzc, They bore
such names as Subislaus, Sambor, Mestwin, and Swantopolk. The village became a small town. Then came the wild Borussians, intent on
pillage and destruction. Then came the distant Brandenburgers, equally
given to pillage and destruction. Boleslaw of Poland did his bit in the
same spirit and no sooner was the damage repaired than the Teutonic
Knights stepped in to carry on the time-honored tradition.

The centuries passed. The city was destroyed and rebuilt in turn by
the dukes of Pomerelia, the grand masters of the Teutonic Order, the
kings and anti-kings of Poland, the counts of Brandenburg, and the
bishops of Wloclawek. The directors of the building and wrecking enterprises were named Otto and Waldemar, Bogussa, Heinrich von Plotzke
—and Dietrich von Altenberg, who built the fortress of the Teutonic
Knights on the spot which became the Hevelius-Platz, where in the
twentieth century the Polish Post Office was defended.

The Hussites came, made a little fire here and there, and left. The
Teutonic Knights were thrown out of the city and the fortress was torn
down because the townspeople were sick of having a fortress in their city.
The Poles took over and no one was any the worse for it. The king who

brought this to pass was Kazimierz, who became known as the Great, son of Wladyslaw the First. Then came Louis of Hungary and after Louis his daughter Jadwiga. She married Jagiello of Lithuania, founder of the Jagellon dynasty. After Wladyslaw II came Wladyslaw III, then another Kazimierz, who lacked the proper enthusiasm and nevertheless, for thirteen long years, squandered the good money of the Danzig merchants making war on the Teutonic Knights. The attentions of John Albert, on the other hand, were more taken up by the Turks. Alexander was followed by Zygmunt Stary, or Sigismund the Elder. After the chapter about Sigismund Augustus comes the one about Stefan Batory, for whom the Poles like to name their ocean liners. He besieged the city and shot cannon balls into it for Lord knows how long (as we may read in our books), but never succeeded in taking it. Then came the Swedes and continued in the same vein. They got so fond of besieging the city that they repeated the performance several times. In the same period, the Gulf of Danzig also became exceedingly popular with the Dutch, Danes, and English, and a number of these foreign sea captains came to be heroes of the sea just by cruising around the Danzig roadstead.

The Peace of Oliva. How sweet and peaceful it sounds! There the great powers noticed for the first time that the land of the Poles lends itself admirably to partition. Swedes, Swedes, and more Swedes—Swedish earthworks, Swedish punch, Swedish gallows. Then came the Russians and Saxons, because Stanislaw Leszczynski, the poor King of Poland, was hidden in the city. On account of this one king, eighteen hundred houses were destroyed, and when poor Leszczynski fled to France because that's where his son-in-law Louis was living, the people of Danzig had to cough up a round million.

Then Poland was divided in three. The Prussians came uninvited and painted the Polish eagle over with their own bird on all the city gates. Johannes Falk, the educator, had just time to write his famous Christmas carol "O Du fröhliche . . ." when the French turned up. Napoleon's general was called Rapp and after a miserable siege the people of Danzig had to rap out twenty million francs to him. The horrors of the French occupation should not necessarily be held in doubt. But it lasted only seven years. Then came the Russians and the Prussians and set the Speicherinsel on fire with their artillery. That was the end of the Free State that Napoleon had dreamed up. Again the Prussians found occasion to paint their bird on all the city gates. Having done so with Prussian thoroughness, they proceeded to establish a garrison consisting of the 4th Regiment of Grenadiers, the 1st Artillery Brigade, the 1st Battalion of Engineers, and the 1st Regiment of Leib Hussars. The 30th Infantry Regiment, the 18th Infantry Regiment, the 3rd Regiment of Foot Guards, the 44th Infantry Regiment, and the 33rd Regiment of Fusiliers were all at one time or another garrisoned in the city, though none of them for very long. But the famous 128th Infantry Regiment did not leave until 1920. For the sake of completeness it may be worth mentioning that in the course of the Prussian period the 1st Artillery Brigade was expanded to include the 1st Battalion of Fortress Artillery, the 2nd Infantry Battalion, the 1st East-Prussian Artillery Regiment, and later the 2nd Pomeranian Foot Artillery Regiment, which was subsequently replaced by the 16th West Prussian Foot Artillery Regiment. The 1st Regiment of Leib Hussars was succeeded by the 2nd Regiment of Leib Hussars. The 8th Regiment of Ohlans, on the other hand, spent only a brief time within the city's walls, while the 17th West-Prussian Quartermaster Battalion was stationed outside the walls, in the suburb of Langfuhr.

In the days of Burckhardt, Rauschning, and Greiser, German authority was represented in the Free State only by the green uniformed security police. This changed in '39 under Forster. The brick barracks filled rapidly with happy lads in uniform, who juggled with every known weapon. We might go on to list all the units that were quartered in Danzig and environs from '39 to '45 or shipped out from Danzig to fight on the Arctic front. This Oskar will spare you and merely say: then, as we have already seen, came Marshal Rokossovski. At the sight of the still intact city, he remembered his great international precursors and set the whole place on fire with his artillery in order that those who came after them might work off their excess energies in rebuilding.

This time, strange to say, no Prussians, Swedes, Saxons, or Frenchmen came after the Russians; this time it was the Poles who arrived.

The Poles came with bag and baggage from Vilna, Bialystok, and Lwow, all looking for living quarters. To us came a gentleman by the name of Fajngold; he was all alone in the world, but he behaved as though surrounded by a large family that couldn't manage for one minute without his instructions. Mr. Fajngold took over the grocery store at once and proceeded to show his wife Luba, who remained invisible and unresponsive, the scales, the kerosene tank, the brass rod to hang sausages on, the empty cash drawer, and with the utmost enthusiasm, the provisions in the cellar. He engaged Maria as salesgirl and introduced her very verbosely to his imaginary Luba, whereupon Maria showed Mr. Fajngold our Matzerath, who had been lying in the cellar for three days under a square of canvas. We had been unable to bury him because the streets were swarming with Russians avid for bicycles, sewing machines, and women.

When Mr. Fajngold saw the corpse, which we had turned over on his back, he clapped his hands over his head in the same expressive gesture as Oskar had seen Sigismund Markus, his toy dealer, make years before. He called not only Luba his wife, but his whole family into the cellar, and there is no doubt that he saw them all coming, for he called them by name: Luba, Lev, Jakub, Berek, Leon, Mendel, and Sonya. He explained to them all who it was lying there dead and went on to tell us that all those he had just summoned as well as his sister-in-law and her other brother-in-law who had five children had lain in the same way, before being taken to the crematoria of Treblinka, and the whole lot of them had been lying there—except for him because he had had to strew lime on them.

Then he helped us to carry Matzerath upstairs to the shop. His family was about him again, and he asked his wife Luba to help Maria wash the corpse. She didn't stir a finger, but Mr. Fajngold didn't notice, for by now he was moving supplies from the cellar up to the shop. This time Lina Greff, who had washed Mother Truczinski, wasn't there to help us; she had a houseful of Russians and we could hear her singing.

Old man Heilandt had found work as a shoemaker. He was busy resoling the boots the Russians had worn out during their rapid advance and was unwilling at first to make us a coffin. But after Mr. Fajngold had drawn him into a business deal—Derby cigarettes from our shop for an electric motor from his shed—he set his boots aside and took up other tools and the last of his boards.

At that time—until we were evicted and Mr. Fajngold turned the cellar over to us—we were living in Mother Truczinski's flat, which had been stripped bare by neighbors and Polish immigrants. Old man Heilandt removed the door between the kitchen and living-room from its hinges, for the door between the living-room and bedroom had been used for Mother Truczinski's coffin. Down below, in the court, he was smoking Derby cigarettes and throwing the box together. We remained upstairs. I took the one chair that was left in the flat and pushed open the broken window. It grieved me to see that the old fellow was taking no pains at all with his work and turning out a plain rectangular box without the tapering characteristic of self-respecting coffins.

Oskar didn't see Matzerath again, for when the box was lifted on to the widow Greff's handcart, the Vitello Margarine slats had already been nailed down, although in his lifetime Matzerath, far from eating margarine, had despised it even for cooking.

Maria asked Mr. Fajngold to come with us; she was afraid of the Russian soldiers in the streets. Fajngold, who was squatting on the counter, spooning artificial honey out of a cardboard cup, expressed misgivings at first; he was afraid Luba might object, but then apparently his wife gave him permission to go, for he slipped off the counter, giving me the honey. I passed it on to Kurt, who made short shrift of it, while Maria helped Mr. Fajngold into a long black coat with gray rabbit fur. Before he closed the shop, bidding his wife to open for no one, he put on a top hat, considerably too small for him, which Matzerath had worn at various weddings and funerals.

Old man Heilandt refused to pull the cart as far as the City Cemetery. He hadn't the time, he said, he still had boots to mend. At Max-Halbe-Platz, the ruins of which were still smoldering, he turned left into Brösener-Weg and I guessed he was heading for Saspe. The Russians sat outside the houses in the thin February sun, sorting out wristwatches and pocket watches, polishing silver spoons with sand, experimenting to see how brassieres worked out as ear muffs, and doing stunt bicycle-riding over an obstacle course fashioned of oil paintings, grandfather clocks, bathtubs, radios and clothes trees. Enthusiastically applauded for their skill, they did figure eights, twists, and spirals, all the while dodging the baby carriages, chandeliers, and such like that were being thrown out of the windows. As we passed, they broke off their sport for a few seconds. A few soldiers with negligés over their uniforms helped us to push and tried to make passes at Maria, but were called to order by Mr. Fajngold, who spoke Russian and had an official pass. A soldier in a lady's hat gave us a birdcage containing a live lovebird on a perch. Kurt, who was hopping along beside the cart, tried to pull out its feathers. Afraid to decline the gift, Maria lifted the cage out of Kurt's reach and handed it up to me on the cart. Oskar, who was in no mood for lovebirds, put the cage down on Matzerath's enlarged margarine crate. I was sitting in the rear end of the cart, dangling my legs and looking into the folds of Mr. Fajngold's face, which bore a look of thoughtful gloom, suggesting a mind at work on a complicated problem that refused to come out.

I beat my drum a little, something sprightly, in an effort to dispel Mr. Fajngold's somber thoughts. But his expression remained unchanged, his eyes were somewhere else, maybe in faraway Galicia; one thing they did not see was my drum. Oskar gave up, and after that there was no sound but Maria's weeping and the rumbling of the wheels.

What a mild winter, I thought when we had left the last houses of Langfuhr behind us; I also took some notice of the lovebird, which was puffing out its feathers in consideration of the afternoon sun hovering over the airfield.

The airfield was guarded, the road to Brösen closed. An officer spoke with Mr. Fajngold, who during the interview held his top hat between his fingers, letting his thin, reddish-blond hair blow in the wind. After tapping for a moment on Matzerath's crate as though to determine its contents and tickling the lovebird with his forefinger, the officer let us pass, but assigned two young fellows, who couldn't have been more than sixteen, with caps that were too little and tommy guns that were too big, to escort us, perhaps for our protection or perhaps to keep an eye on us.

Old man Heilandt pulled, without ever once turning around. He had a trick of lighting his cigarette with one hand, without slowing down. Planes darted about overhead. The engines were so clearly audible because of the season, late February or early March. Only in the vicinity of the sun were there a few clouds which gradually took on color. The bombers were heading for Hela or returning from Hela Peninsula, where what was left of the Second Army was still holding out.

The weather and the droning of the planes made me sad. There is nothing so tedious, nothing that makes for such a feeling of surfeit and disgust, as a cloudless March sky full of airplane motors' crescendo and decrescendo. To make matters worse, the two Russian puppies kept trying, quite unsuccessfully, to march in step.

Perhaps some of the boards of the hastily assembled coffin had been jolted loose, first on the cobblestones, then on battered asphalt; we were heading into the wind and, as we have seen, I was sitting in the back; in any case, it smelled of dead Matzerath, and Oskar was glad when we reached Saspe Cemetery.

We couldn't take the cart as far as the iron gate, for the road was blocked shortly before the cemetery by the charred wreckage of a T-34. Other tanks, obliged to detour around it on their way to Neufahrwasser, had left their tracks in the sand to the left of the highway and flattened a part of the cemetery wall. Mr. Fajngold asked old man Heilandt to take the rear. They carried the coffin, which sagged slightly in the middle, along the tracks of the tank treads, traversed with some difficulty the stone pile into which the cemetery wall had been transformed, and finally, with their last strength, took a few steps among the tumble-down tombstones. Old man Heilandt tugged avidly at his cigarette and blew out smoke over the coffin. I carried the cage with the lovebird. Maria dragged two shovels behind her. Little Kurt carried or rather brandished a pickaxe, attacking the gray granite tombstones at the risk of his life, until Maria took it away from him and helped the men to dig.

How fortunate that the soil here is sandy and not frozen, I said to myself, while looking for Jan Bronski's place behind the northern wall. It must be here, I thought, or maybe there. I couldn't be sure, for the changing seasons had turned the tell-tale fresh whitewash a crumbling gray like all the walls in Saspe.

I came back through the hind gate, looked up at the stunted pines: So now they're burying Matzerath, I thought, for fear of thinking something irrelevant. And I found at least partial meaning in the circumstance that the two skat brothers, Bronski and Matzerath, should lie here in the same sandy ground, even if my poor mama was not here to keep them company.

Funerals always make you think of other funerals.

The sandy soil put up a fight, it probably wanted more experienced gravediggers. Maria paused, leaned panting on her pick, and began to cry again when she saw Kurt throwing stones at the lovebird in its cage. Kurt missed, his stones overshot the mark; Maria wept loudly and in all sincerity, because she had lost Matzerath, because she had seen something in Matzerath which in my opinion wasn't there, but which, as far as she was concerned, was to remain henceforth real and lovable. Mr. Fajngold said a few comforting words, which gave him a chance to rest, for the digging was too much for him. Old man Heilandt wielded his shovel with the regularity of a seeker after gold, tossed the earth behind him, and blew out puffs of smoke, also at measured intervals. The two

Russian puppies sat on the cemetery wall a few steps away from us, chatting into the wind. Overhead, airplanes and a sun growing steadily riper.

They may have dug about three feet. Oskar stood idle and perplexed amid the old granite, amid the stunted pines, between Matzerath's widow and a Kurt throwing stones at a lovebird.

Should I or shouldn't I? You are going on twenty-one, Oskar. Should you or shouldn't you? You are an orphan. Actually you should, it's high time. When your poor mama died, you were left half an orphan. That was when you should have made up your mind. Then they laid Jan, your presumptive father, under the crust of the earth. That made you a presumptive full orphan. You stood here on this sand named Saspe, holding a slightly oxidized cartridge case. It was raining and a Ju-52 was getting ready to land. Wasn't this "Should I? or shouldn't I?" audible even then, if not in the sound of the rain, then in the roaring of the landing transport plane? You said to yourself: it's the rain, it's the sound of airplanes' engines; uninspired interpretations of this sort can be read into any text you please. You wanted everything to be perfectly plain and not just presumptive.

Should I or shouldn't I? Now they are digging a hole for Matzerath, your second presumptive father. As far as you know, you have no more presumptive fathers. Why, then, do you keep juggling with two bottle-green bottles: should I or shouldn't I? Who else is there to question? These stunted pines, themselves so questionable?

I found a slender cast-iron cross with crumbling ornaments and encrusted letters adding up to Mathilde Kunkel—or Runkel. In the sand —should I or shouldn't I?—between thistles and wild oats—should I?— I found—or shouldn't I?—three or four rusty metal wreaths the size of dinner plates—should I?—which once upon a time—or shouldn't I?— were no doubt supposed to look like oak leaves or laurel—or should I after all?—weighed them in my hand, took aim—should I?—the top end of the ironwork cross—or shouldn't I?—had a diameter of—should I?— maybe an inch and a half—or shouldn't I?—I ordered myself to stand six feet away—should I?—tossed—or shouldn't I?—and missed—should I try again?—the cross was too much on a slant—should I?—Mathilde Kunkel or was it Runkel—should I Runkel, should I Kunkel?—that was the sixth throw and I had allowed myself seven, six times I shouldn't and now seven—*should*, the wreath was on the cross—*should*—wreathed Mathilde—*should*—laurel for Miss Kunkel—should I? I asked young Mrs. Runkel—yes, said Mathilde; she had died young, at twenty-seven, and born in '68. As for me, I was going on twenty-one when I made it on the seventh throw, when my problem—should I or shouldn't I?—was simplified, transformed into a demonstrated, wreathed, aimed, and triumphant "I should."

As Oskar, with his new "I should" on his tongue and in his heart, made his way back to the gravediggers, the lovebird let out a squeak and shed several yellow-blue feathers, for one of Kurt's stones had struck home. I wondered what question may have impelled my son to keep throwing stones at a lovebird until at last a hit gave him his answer.

They had moved the crate to the edge of the pit, which was about four feet deep. Old man Heilandt was in a hurry, but had to wait while Maria completed her Catholic prayers, while Mr. Fajngold stood there with his silk hat over his chest and his eyes in Galicia. Kurt, too, came closer. After his bulls's-eye he had probably arrived at a decision; he approached the grave for reasons of his own but just as resolutely as Oskar.

The uncertainty was killing me. After all, it was my son who had decided for or against something. Had he decided at last to recognize and love me as his only true father? Had he, now that it was too late, decided to take up the drum? Or was his decision: death to my presumptive father Oskar, who killed my presumptive father Matzerath with a Party pin for no other reason than because he was sick of fathers? Perhaps he, too, could express only by homicide the childlike affection that would seem to be desirable between fathers and sons.

While old man Heilandt flung rather than lowered the crate containing Matzerath, the Party pin in Matzerath's windpipe and the magazineful of Russian tommy-gun ammunition in Matzerath's belly, into the grave, Oskar owned to himself that he had killed Matzerath deliberately, because in all likelihood Matzerath was not just his presumptive father, but his real father; and also because he was sick of dragging a father around with him all his life.

And so it was not true that the pin had been open when I picked up the badge from the concrete floor. The pin had been opened within my closed hand. It was a jagged, pointed lozenge that I had passed on to Matzerath, intending that they find the insignia on him, that he put the Party in his mouth and choke on it—on the Party, on me, his son; for this situation couldn't go on forever.

Old man Heilandt began to shovel. Little Kurt helped him clumsily but with alacrity. I had never loved Matzerath. Occasionally I liked him. He took care of me, but more as a cook than as a father. He was a good cook. If today I sometimes miss Matzerath, it is his Königsberg dumplings, his pork kidneys in vinegar sauce, his carp with horse-radish and cream, his green eel soup, his Kassler Rippchen with sauerkraut, and all his unforgettable Sunday roasts, which I can still feel on my tongue and between my teeth. They forgot to put a cooking spoon in the coffin of this man who transformed feelings into soups. They also forgot to put a deck of skat cards in his coffin. He was a better cook than skat player. Still he played better than Jan Bronski and almost as well as my poor mama. Such was his endowment, such was his tragedy. I have never been able to forgive him for taking Maria away from me, although he treated her well, never beat her, and usually gave in when she picked a fight. He hadn't turned me over to the Ministry of Public Health, and had signed the letter only after the mails had stopped running. When I came into the world under the light bulbs, he chose the shop as my career. To avoid standing behind a counter, Oskar had spent more than seventeen years standing behind a hundred or so toy drums, lacquered red and white. Now Matzerath lay flat and could stand no more. Smoking Matzerath's Derby cigarettes, old man Heilandt shoveled him in. Oskar should have taken over the shop. Meanwhile Mr. Fajngold had taken over the shop with his large, invisible family. But I inherited the rest: Maria, Kurt, and the responsibility for them both.

Maria was still crying authentically and praying Catholically. Mr. Fajngold was sojourning in Galicia or solving some knotty reckoning. Kurt was weakening but still shoveling. The Russian puppies sat chatting on the cemetery wall. With morose regularity old man Heilandt shoveled the sand of Saspe over the margarine-crate coffin. Oskar could still read three letters of the word Vitello. At this point he unslung the drum from his neck, no longer saying "Should I or shouldn't I?" but instead: "It must be," and threw the drum where the sand was deep enough to muffle the sound. I tossed in the sticks too. They stuck in the sand. That was my drum from the Duster days, the last of those Bebra had given me. What would the Master have thought of my decision? Jesus had beaten that drum, as had a Russian with large, open pores and built like a bank safe. There wasn't much life left in it. But when a shovelful of sand struck its surface, it sounded. At the second shovelful, it still had something to say. At the third it was silent, only showing a little white lacquer until that too was covered over. The sand piled up on my drum, the sand mounted and grew—and I too began to grow; the first symptom being a violent nosebleed.

Kurt was the first to notice the blood. "He's bleeding, he's bleeding," he shouted, calling Mr. Fajngold back from Galicia, calling Maria from her prayers, and even making the two young Russians, who had been sitting on the wall the whole while, chattering in the direction of Brösen, look up in momentary fright.

Old man Heilandt left his shovel in the sand, took the pickaxe and rested my neck against the blue-black iron. The cool metal produced the desired effect. The bleeding began to subside. Old man Heilandt returned to his shoveling. There was still a little sand left beside the grave when the bleeding stopped entirely, but the growth continued, as I could tell by the rumbling and cracking and grinding inside me.

When old man Heilandt had finished shoveling, he took a dilapidated wooden cross with no inscription on it from a nearby tomb and thrust it into the fresh mound, approximately between Matzerath's head and my buried drum. "That does it!" said the old man and picked up Oskar, who was unable to walk, in his arms. Carrying me, he led the others, including the Russian puppies with the tommy guns, out of the cemetery, across the crushed wall, along the tank tracks to the handcart on the highway. I looked back over my shoulder toward the cemetery. Maria was carrying the cage with the lovebird, Mr. Fajngold was carrying the tools, Kurt was carrying nothing, the two Russians with the caps that were too small were carrying the tommy guns that were too big for them, and the scrub pines were bent beneath so much carrying.

From the sand to the asphalt highway, still blocked by the burned-out tank. On the tank sat Leo Schugger. High overhead planes coming from Hela, headed for Hela. Leo Schugger was careful not to blacken his gloves on the charred T-34. Surrounded by puffy little clouds, the sun descended on Tower Mountain near Zoppot. Leo Schugger slid off the tank and stood very straight.

The sight of Leo Schugger handed old man Heilandt a laugh. "D'you ever see the like of it? The world comes to an end, but they can't get Leo Schugger down." In high good humor, he gave the black tailcoat a slap on the back and explained to Mr. Fajngold: "This is our Leo Schugger. He wants to give us sympathy and shake hands with us."

He spoke the truth. Leo Schugger made his gloves flutter and, slavering as usual, expressed his sympathies to all present. "Did you see the Lord?" he asked. "Did you see the Lord?" No one had seen Him. Maria, I don't know why, gave Leo the cage with the lovebird.

When it was the turn of Oskar, whom old man Heilandt had stowed on the handcart, Leo Schugger's face seemed to decompose itself, the winds inflated his garments, and a dance seized hold of his legs. "The Lord, the Lord!" he cried, shaking the lovebird in its cage. "See the Lord! He's growing, he's growing!"

Then he was tossed into the air with the cage, and he ran, flew, danced, staggered, and fled with the screeching bird, himself a bird. Taking flight at last, he fluttered across the fields in the direction of the sewage land and was heard shouting through the voices of the tommy guns: "He's growing, he's growing!" He was still screaming when the two young Russians reloaded. "He's growing!" And even when the tommy guns rang out again, even after Oskar had fallen down a stepless staircase into an expanding, all-engulfing faint, I could hear the bird, the voice, the raven, I could hear Leo proclaiming to all the world: "He's growing, he's growing, he's growing . . ."

## DISINFECTANT

Last night I was beset by hasty dreams. They were like friends on visiting days. One dream after another; one by one they came and went after telling me what dreams find worth telling; preposterous stories full of repetitions, monologues which could not be ignored, because they were declaimed in a voice that demanded attention and with the gestures of incompetent actors. When I tried to tell Bruno the stories at breakfast, I couldn't get rid of them, because I had forgotten everything; Oskar has no talent for dreaming.

While Bruno cleared away the breakfast, I asked him as though in passing: "My dear Bruno, how tall am I exactly?"

Bruno set the little dish of jam on my coffee cup and said in tones of concern: "Why, Mr. Matzerath, you haven't touched your jam."

How well I know those words of reproach. I hear them every day after breakfast. Every morning Bruno brings me this dab of strawberry jam just to make me build a newspaper roof over it. I can't even bear to look at jam, much less eat it. Accordingly I dismissed Bruno's reproach with quiet firmness: "You know how I feel about jam, Bruno. Just tell me how tall I am."

Bruno's eyes took on the expression of an extinct octopod. He always casts this prehistoric gaze up at the ceiling whenever he has to think, and if he has anything to say, it is also the ceiling he addresses. This morning, then, he said to the ceiling: "But it's strawberry jam." Only when after a considerable pause—for by my silence I sustained my question about Oskar's size—Bruno's gaze came down from the ceiling and twined itself round the bars of my bed, was I privileged to hear that I measured four feet one.

"Wouldn't you kindly measure me again, Bruno, just to be sure?"

Without batting an eyelash, Bruno drew a folding rule from his back pants pocket, threw back my covers with a gesture that was almost brutal, pulled down my nightgown, which had bunched up, unfolded the ferociously yellow ruler which had broken off at five feet eleven, placed it alongside me, shifted its position, checked. His hands worked efficiently, but his eyes were still dwelling in the age of dinosaurs. At length the ruler came to rest and he declared, as though reading off his findings: "Still four feet one."

Why did he have to make so much noise folding up his ruler and removing my breakfast tray? Were my measurements not to his liking?

After leaving the room with the breakfast tray, with the egg-yellow ruler beside the revoltingly natural-coloured strawberry jam, Bruno cast a last glance back through the peephole in the door—a glance that made me feel as old as the hills. Then at length he left me alone with my four feet and my one inch.

So Oskar is really so tall! Almost too big for a dwarf, a gnome, a midget? What was the altitude of la Raguna's, my Roswitha's, summit? At what height did Master Bebra, who was descended from Prince Eugene, succeed in keeping himself? Today I could look down even on

Kitty and Felix. Whereas all those I have just mentioned once looked down with friendly envy upon Oskar, who, until the twenty-first year of his life, had measured a spare three feet.

It was only when that stone hit me at Matzerath's funeral in Saspe Cemetery that I began to grow.

# PRIMO LEVI

PRIMO LEVI, that most eloquent of concentration camp survivors, dealt with some of the questions put to him most often in the Afterword to *The Reawakening*.

■

FROM *The Reawakening*

### AFTERWORD

*2. Did the Germans know what was happening?*

How is it possible that the extermination of millions of human beings could have been carried out in the heart of Europe without anyone's knowledge?

The world in which we Westerners live has grave faults and dangers, but when compared to the countries in which democracy is smothered, and to the times during which it has been smothered, our world has a tremendous advantage: everyone can know everything about everything. Information today is the "fourth estate": at least in theory the reporter, the journalist and the news photographer have free access everywhere; nobody has the right to stop them or send them away. Everything is easy: if you wish you can receive radio or television broadcasts from your own country or from any other country. You can go to the newsstand and choose the newspaper you prefer, national or foreign, of any political tendency—even that of a country with which your country is at odds. You can buy and read any books you want and usually do not risk being incriminated for "antinational activity" or bring down on your house a search by the political police. Certainly it is not easy to avoid all biases, but at least you can pick the bias you prefer.

In an authoritarian state it is not like this. There is only one Truth, proclaimed from above; the newspapers are all alike, they all repeat the same one Truth. So do the radio stations, and you cannot listen to those of other countries. In the first place, since this is a crime, you risk ending up in prison. In the second place, the radio stations in your country send out jamming signals, on the appropriate wavelengths, that superimpose themselves on the foreign messages and prevent your hearing them. As for books, only those that please the State are published and translated. You must seek any others on the outside and introduce them into your country at your own risk because they are considered more dangerous than drugs and explosives, and if they are found in your possession at the border, they are confiscated and you are punished. Books not in favor, or no longer in favor, are burned in public bonfires in town squares. This went on in Italy between 1924 and 1945; it went on in National Socialist Germany; it is going on right now in many countries, among which it is sad to have to number the Soviet Union, which fought heroically against Fascism. In an authoritarian State it is considered permissible to alter the truth; to rewrite history retrospectively; to distort the news, suppress the true, add the false. Propaganda is substituted for information. In fact, in such a country you are not a citizen possessor of rights but a subject, and as such you owe to the State (and to the dictator who represents it) fanatical loyalty and supine obedience.

It is clear that under these conditions it becomes possible (though not always easy; it is never easy to deeply violate human nature) to erase great chunks of reality. In Fascist Italy the undertaking to assassinate the Socialist deputy Matteotti was quite successful, and after a few months it was locked in silence. Hitler and his Minister of Propaganda, Joseph Goebbels, showed themselves to be far superior to Mussolini at this work of controlling and masking truth.

However, it was not possible to hide the existence of the enormous concentration camp apparatus from the German people. What's more, it was not (from the Nazi point of view) even desirable. Creating and maintaining an atmosphere of undefined terror in the country was part of the aims of Nazism. It was just as well for the people to know that opposing Hitler was extremely dangerous. In fact, hundreds of thousands of Germans were confined in the camps from the very first months of Nazism: Communists, Social Democrats, Liberals, Jews, Protestants, Catholics; the whole country knew it and knew that in the camps people were suffering and dying.

Nevertheless, it is true that the great mass of Germans remained unaware of the most atrocious details of what happened later on in the camps: the methodical industrialized extermination on a scale of millions, the gas chambers, the cremation furnaces, the vile despoiling of corpses, all this was not supposed to be known, and in effect few did know it up to the end of the war. Among other precautions, in order to keep the secret, in official language only cautious and cynical euphemisms were employed: one did not write "extermination" but "final solution," not "deportation" but "transfer," not "killing by gas" but "special treatment," and so on. Not without reason, Hitler feared that this horrendous news, if it were divulged, would compromise the blind faith which the country had in him, as well as the morale of the fighting troops. Besides, it would have become known to the Allies and would have been exploited as propaganda material. This actually did happen but because of their very enormity, the horrors of the camps, described many times by the Allied radio, were not generally believed.

The most convincing summing-up of the German situation at that time that I have found is in the book *DER SS STAAT* (*The Theory and Practice of Hell*) by Eugene Kogon, a former Buchenwald prisoner, later Professor of Political Science at the University of Munich:

What did the Germans know about the concentration camps? Outside the concrete fact of their existence, almost nothing. Even today they know little. Indubitably, the method of rigorously keeping the details of the terrorist system secret, thereby making the anguish undefined, and hence that much more profound, proved very efficacious. As I have said elsewhere, even many Gestapo functionaries did not know what was happening in the camps to which they were sending prisoners. The greater majority of the prisoners themselves had a very imprecise idea of how their camps functioned and of the methods employed there. How could the German people have known? Anyone who entered the camps found himself confronted by an unfathomable universe, totally new to him. This is the best demonstration of the power and efficacy of secrecy.

And yet . . . and yet, there wasn't even one German who did not know of the camps' existence or who believed they were sanatoriums. There were very few Germans who did not have a relative or an acquaintance in a camp, or who did not know, at least, that such a one or such another had been sent to a camp. All the Germans had been witnesses to the multiform anti-Semitic barbarity. Millions of them had been present—with indifference or with curiosity, with contempt or with downright malign joy—at the burning of synagogues or humiliation of Jews and Jewesses forced to kneel in the street mud. Many Germans knew from the foreign radio broadcasts, and a number had contact with prisoners who worked outside the camps. A good many Germans had had the experience of encountering miserable lines of prisoners in the streets or at the railroad stations. In a circular dated November 9, 1941, and addressed by the head of the Police and the Security Services to all . . . Police officials and to the camp commandants, one reads: "In particular, it must be noted that during the transfers on foot, for example from the station to the camp, a considerable number of prisoners collapse along the way, fainting or dying from exhaustion . . . It is impossible to keep the population from knowing about such happenings."

Not a single German could have been unaware of the fact that the prisons were full to overflowing, and that executions were taking place continually all over the country. Thousands of magistrates and police functionaries, lawyers, priests and social workers knew generically that the situation was very grave. Many businessmen who dealt with the camp SS men as suppliers, the industrialists who asked the administrative and economic offices of the SS for slave-laborers, the clerks in those offices, all knew perfectly well that many of the big firms were exploiting slave labor. Quite a few workers performed their tasks near concentration camps or actually inside them. Various university professors collaborated with the medical research centers instituted by Himmler, and various State doctors and doctors connected with private institutes collaborated with the professional murderers. A good many members of military aviation had been transferred to SS jurisdiction and must have known what went on there. Many high-ranking army officers knew about the mass murders of the Russian prisoners of war in the camps, and even more soldiers and members of the Military Police must have known exactly what terrifying horrors were being perpetrated in the camps, the ghettos, the cities, and the countrysides of the occupied Eastern territories. Can you say that even one of these statements is false?

In my opinion, none of these statements is false, but one other must be added to complete the picture: in spite of the varied possibilities for information, most Germans didn't know because they didn't want to know. Because, indeed, they wanted *not* to know. It is certainly true that State terrorism is a very strong weapon, very difficult to resist. But it is also true that the German people, as a whole, did not even try to resist. In Hitler's Germany a particular code was widespread: those who knew did not talk; those who did not know did not ask questions; those who did ask questions received no answers. In this way the typical German citizen won and defended his ignorance, which seemed to him sufficient justification of his adherence to Nazism. Shutting his mouth, his eyes and his ears, he built for himself the illusion of not knowing, hence not being an accomplice to the things taking place in front of his very door.

Knowing and making things known was one way (basically then not all that dangerous) of keeping one's distance from Nazism. I think the German people, on the whole, did not seek this recourse, and I hold them fully culpable of this deliberate omission.

*3. Were there prisoners who escaped from the camps? How is it that there were no large-scale revolts?*

These are among the questions most frequently put to me by young readers. They must, therefore, spring from some particularly important curiosity or need. My interpretation is optimistic: today's young people feel that freedom is a privilege that one cannot do without, no matter what. Consequently, for them, the idea of prison is immediately linked to the idea of escape or revolt. Besides, it is true that according to the military codes of many countries, the prisoner of war is required to attempt escape, in any way possible, in order to resume his place as a combatant, and that according to The Hague Convention, such an attempt would not be punished. The concept of escape as a moral obligation is constantly reinforced by romantic literature (remember the Count of Montecristo?), by popular literature, and by the cinema, in which the hero, unjustly (or even justly) imprisoned, always tries to escape, even in the least likely circumstances, the attempt being invariably crowned with success.

Perhaps it is good that the prisoner's condition, non-liberty, is felt to be something improper, abnormal—like an illness, in short—that has to be cured by escape or rebellion. Unfortunately, however, this picture hardly resembles the true one of the concentration camps.

For instance, only a few hundred prisoners tried to escape from Auschwitz, and of those perhaps a few score succeeded. Escape was difficult and extremely dangerous. The prisoners were debilitated, in addition to being demoralized, by hunger and ill-treatment. Their heads were shaved, their striped clothing was immediately recognizable, and their wooden clogs made silent and rapid walking impossible. They had no money and, in general, did not speak Polish, which was the local language, nor did they have contacts in the area, whose geography they did not know, either. On top of all that, fierce reprisals were employed to discourage escape attempts. Anyone caught trying to escape was publicly hanged—often after cruel torture—in the square where the roll calls took place. When an escape was discovered, the friends of the fugitive were considered accomplices and were starved to death in cells; all the other prisoners were forced to remain standing for twenty-four hours, and sometimes the parents of the "guilty" one were arrested and deported to camps.

The SS guards who killed a prisoner in the course of an escape attempt were granted special leaves. As a result, it often happened that an SS guard fired at a prisoner who had no intention of trying to escape, solely in order to qualify for leave. This fact artificially swells the official number of escape attempts recorded in the statistics. As I have indicated, the actual number was very small, made up almost exclusively of a few Aryan (that is, non-Jewish, to use the terminology of that time) Polish prisoners who lived not far from the camp and had, consequently, a goal toward which to proceed and the assurance that they would be protected by the population. In the other camps things occurred in a similar way.

As for the lack of rebellion, the story is somewhat different. First of all, it is necessary to remember that uprisings did actually take place in certain camps: Treblinka, Sobibor, even Birkenau, one of the Auschwitz dependencies. They did not have much numerical weight; like the analogous Warsaw Ghetto uprising they represented, rather, examples of extraordinary moral force. In every instance they were planned and led by prisoners who were privileged in some way and, consequently, in better physical and spiritual condition than the average camp prisoner. This is not all that surprising: only at first glance does it seem paradoxical that people who rebel are those who suffer the least. Even outside the camps, struggles are rarely waged by *Lumpenproletariat*. People in rags do not revolt.

In the camps for political prisoners, or where political prisoners were in the majority, the conspiratory experience of these people proved valuable and often resulted in quite effective defensive activities, rather than in open revolt. Depending upon the camps and the times, prisoners succeeded, for example, in blackmailing or corrupting the SS, curbing their indiscriminate power; in sabotaging the work for the German war industries; in organizing escapes; in communicating via the radio with the Allies, furnishing them with accounts of the horrendous conditions in the camps; in improving the treatment of the sick, substituting prisoner doctors for the SS ones; in "guiding" the selections, sending spies and traitors to death and saving prisoners whose survival had, for one reason or another, some special importance; preparing, even in military ways, to resist in case the Nazis decided, with the Front coming closer (as in fact they often did decide), to liquidate the camps entirely.

In camps with a majority of Jews, like those in the Auschwitz area, an active or passive defense was particularly difficult. Here the prisoners were, for the most part, devoid of any kind of organizational or military experience. They came from every country in Europe, spoke different languages and, as a result, could not understand one another. They were more starved, weaker and more exhausted than the others because their living conditions were harsher and because they often had a long history of hunger, persecution and humiliation in the ghettos. The final consequences of this were that the length of their stays in the camps was tragically brief. They were, in short, a fluctuating population, continually decimated by death and renewed by the never-ending arrivals of new convoys. It is understandable that the seed of revolt did not easily take root in a human fabric that was in such a state of deterioration and so unstable.

You may wonder why the prisoners who had just gotten off the trains did not revolt, waiting as they did for hours (sometimes for days!) to enter the gas chambers. In addition to what I have already said, I must add here that the Germans had perfected a diabolically clever and versatile system of collective death. In most cases the new arrivals did not know what awaited them. They were received with cold efficiency but without brutality, invited to undress "for the showers." Sometimes they were handed soap and towels and were promised hot coffee after their showers. The gas chambers were, in fact, camouflaged as shower rooms, with pipes, faucets, dressing rooms, clothes hooks, benches and so forth. When, instead, prisoners showed the smallest sign of knowing or suspecting their imminent fate, the SS and their collaborators used surprise tactics, intervening with extreme brutality, with shouts, threats, kicks, shots, loosing their dogs, which were trained to tear prisoners to pieces, against people who were confused, desperate, weakened by five or ten days of traveling in sealed railroad cars.

Such being the case, the statement that has sometimes been formulated—that the Jews didn't revolt out of cowardice—appears absurd and insulting. No one rebelled. Let it suffice to remember that the gas chambers at Auschwitz were tested on a group of three hundred Russian prisoners of war, young, army-trained, politically indoctrinated, and not hampered by the presence of women and children, and even they did not revolt.

I would like to add one final thought. The deeply rooted consciousness that one must not consent to oppression but resist it instead was not widespread in Fascist Europe, and it was particularly weak in Italy. It was the patrimony of a narrow circle of political activists, but Fascism and Nazism had isolated, expelled, terrorized or destroyed them outright. You must not forget that the first victims of the German camps, by the hundreds of thousands, were, in fact, the cadres of the anti-Nazi political parties. Without their contribution, the popular will to resist, to organize for the purpose of resisting, sprang up again much later, thanks, above all, to the contribution of the European Communist parties that hurled themselves into the struggle against Nazism after Germany, in 1941, had unexpectedly attacked the Soviet Union, breaking the Ribben-trop-Molotov pact of September 1939. To conclude, reproaching the prisoners for not rebelling represents, above all, an error in historical perspective, expecting from them a political consciousness which is today an almost common heritage but which belonged at that time only to an elite.

# IAIN CHRICHTON SMITH

SCOTTISH-BORN Iain Chrichton Smith is a poet whose works have appeared in the *New Statesman, The Listener,* and *The Spectator.* He speaks and writes in Gaelic and has had Gaelic plays and stories broadcast by the BBC. He has published one collection of short stories, *The Beach and the Kid,* and several collections of poetry.

■

## For the Unknown Seamen
## of the 1939–45 War
## Buried in Iona Churchyard

One would like to be able to write something for them
not for the sake of the writing but because
a man should be named in dying as well as living,
in drowning as well as on death-bed, and because
the brain being brain must try to establish laws.

Yet these events are not amenable
to any discipline that we can impose
and are not in the end even imaginable.
What happened was simply this, bad luck for those
who have lain here twelve years in a changing pose.

These things happen and there's no explaining,
and to call them "chosen" might abuse a word.
It is better also not to assume a mourning,
moaning stance. These may have well concurred
in whatever suddenly struck them through the absurd

or maybe meaningful. One simply doesn't
know enough, or understand what came
out of the altering weather in a fashioned
descriptive phrase that was common to each name,
or may have surrounded each like a dear frame.

Best not to make much of it and leave these seamen
in the equally altering acre they now have
inherited from strangers though yet human.
They fell from sea to earth from grave to grave
and, griefless now, taught others how to grieve.

# SIR HAROLD GEORGE NICOLSON

---

HAROLD NICOLSON celebrates the surrender of Germany with his wife, Vita Sackville-West, and Ben, one of their sons. From his diaries, which were edited by his son Nigel.

---

■

FROM *The Diaries and Letters of Harold Nicolson*

*7th May, 1945*

At 3 comes the news that an hour ago Schwerin von Krosigk[1] had spoken on the wireless from Flensburg.[2] He has said that Germany was obliged to surrender unconditionally, crushed by the overwhelming might of her enemies. Ben and I dash to tell Vita who is in the courtyard. The three of us climb the turret stairs, tie the flag to the ropes, and hoist it in the soft south-west breeze. It looks very proud and gay after five years of confinement.

I decide to go up to London. The news of Schwerin's broadcast has apparently spread. In Staplehurst we see a handful of children fluttering little flags. When I get to London there are flags everywhere. At Cannon Street I see the B.B.C.'s Chief Engineer, Noel Ashbridge, escaping exhausted from London. He says that everything is completely tied up, that we cannot get Moscow to agree to a time for a simultaneous announcement and that everything is to be postponed until tomorrow.

I dine at Pratts, which is empty and dull. Coming back, I find a few instances of celebration. A Jewess in a paper cap is strolling down St. James's Street turning a rattle. A few drunken soldiers.

[1] He had been Minister of Finance continuously since his appointment by von Papen in 1932, and was Foreign Minister in the Doenitz Government.

[2] The town on the Danish border where Doenitz had set up his rump Government.

# EDMUND WILSON

EDMUND WILSON, born in New Jersey and educated at Princeton, was the most influential and wide-ranging critic of his time. The author of *Axel's Castle* and *To the Finland Station,* he also wrote novels, plays, and short stories. What follows is excerpted from his *Letters on Literature and Politics, 1912–1972.*

■

## FROM *Letters on Literature and Politics, 1912–1972*

May 28, 1945

*To Mamaine Paget*                                                              ROME

. . .I was interested in your account of VE day (this "VE" business is idiotic). It was just like that in 1914 during the bank holidays after the first war was declared: people rode around on the tops of taxis and gathered in front of Buckingham Palace and made the King and Queen come out on the balcony—they would yell, "Mary! Mary! We're wyting!" I think that the people are pathetic on occasions like this: they don't really know what they're cheering about, just that they're expected to make some demonstration. The ends of wars are never exciting: everybody has seen them coming and everybody is completely worn out. At the end of the last war I was in Chaumont, the American GHQ in France. A few French and American soldiers got drunk and walked through the streets brawling feebly. An American newspaperman in the army whom I'd been having dinner with kept saying, "Well, b' gosh, we beat Purdue!" by which he meant to compare the celebration to the excitement over a football victory in a very small Middle Western college. Here in Rome it was also on the Purdue level. —I've just had dinner with Dorothy Thompson and her husband, whom I'd never met before. I began by thinking how awful they were, but ended by deciding they were not so bad—though she is so ignorant and so silly that one wonders why anybody has ever let her go on in print about politics and he is one of those all too heavy jolly Viennese lightweights . . .

# THOMAS BERGER

THE GIFTED and prolific satirist Thomas Berger, author of *Little Big Man* among other novels, served with the U.S. Army in Germany during World War II. What follows is from his novel *Crazy in Berlin*.

■

## FROM *Crazy in Berlin*

Just as it had arrived in England after the great mass of troops assembled there for the Continental assault was gone, so did the 1209th cross the Channel and proceed eastward against the stream of real soldiers returning. At the outset, the assignment to Germany was seen as punishment cruel and perverse. For a year they had run an enormous Nissen-hut hospital in Devonshire, tending casualties flown straight there from the fields of battle, wounds yet hot and reeking. They were veterans of the European Theater and should have been let to cross the water and swagger before the slobs on Stateside duty, to mix undelineated with the repatriated combat regiments, back in the frame where the greater category enveloped the smaller, overseas versus home.

Instead, the score was to stay grievously unjust: for more than a year the 1209th had had to stand holding its portable urinals while patients lay smug with honorable wounds, relating the grand experiences denied to people of the rear areas. Charging the Siegfried Line; streetcars filled with explosives rolled down the hill into Aachen; the bridge at Remagen, with its sign: "You are crossing the Rhine by courtesy of the —th Infantry Division"; the bombs falling on the ball-bearing works at Peenemünde, courtesy of the Eighth Air Force; the Ardennes, where even company clerks and cooks took up their virgin rifles and joined the defense and even a general proved a hero, courtesy of the 101st Airborne Division; and at the very end, "Germany" itself made commonplace by courtesy of the Third Army, who got to Pilsen in Czechoslovakia and burst into the famous brewery to fill their helmets with beer. By courtesy of the 1209th General Hospital, Colonel Roy Fester commanding, one passed his water, told his stories, took a pain pill, and went to sleep.

Just at the point, though, where the responsible latrine intelligence had disqualified the hysterics who insisted the 1209th would any day be shipped to the Pacific, and established beyond a peradventure that it would settle in the Helmstedt field where the unit was then resting as an alleged transient, and stay there forever—just at this point where the wailing was loudest, there being nothing else to do except peer through the single set of field glasses at the nurses' tents across the meadow, came a courier of unquestioned authority with the word.

*Berlin*, it was to be Berlin, so long as something had to be accepted, a horse of a different hue from mere Germany; considerably better, in fact, since the combat forces had never got there. It would be at the courtesy of only the Russians, and the Russians themselves, with the Germans downed, were now a kind of enemy and face to face with their allies kept weapons at port arms. Already they had sealed the Helmstedt checkpoint, and when, after a week of negotiations, the colonel was permitted to pass with jeep, driver, and one aide, he made only fifteen miles before another Soviet unit arrested and held him twenty-four hours incommunicado.

All this, not to mention Berlin of the Nazi mythos: old Hitler screaming crazy garbage; creepy little Goebbels, dark and seamed, scraping along on his twisted foot; fat, beribboned Goering, more swollen joke than menace; swastikaed bruisers maltreating gentle little Jews; the Brandenburg Gate and Unter der Linden Trees; and acres of the famous blonde pussy, whom twelve years of Nazism had made subservient to the man in uniform: one heard that an SS trooper could bend down any girl on the street and let fly. And, once in the city, little work conjoined with a peculiar honor: the crap-house spokesmen who in England had been privy to a document from higher headquarters listing the 1209th as the biggest and best hospital in the Communications Zone, saw another now which said, approximately: the 1209th, selected because it was the biggest and best in the Communications Zone, would be the only general hospital in Berlin District.

Berlin was not the worst place to end a war; better, surely, than the gooks in the islands or France where pigs lived in the same houses as people.

# JOEL SAYRE

INDIANA-BORN Joel Sayre was a reporter, war correspondent, screenwriter and novelist. He covered the career of John Thomas "Legs" Diamond for the *New York Herald-Tribune* and, after moving out to Hollywood, worked on the screenplay of *Gunga Din.* After World War II, Sayre became a staff writer for *The New Yorker,* where the following report on Berlin, dated July 28, 1945, first appeared.

■

## Letter from Berlin

*July 14, 1945*

Some days ago, on Unter den Linden, I was staring through an iron gate barring the approach to what is left of the Ehrenmal, the Prussian equivalent of our Tomb of the Unknown Soldier, when two girls stopped beside me, also to stare. Each had a rucksack filled with wood on her back. There is no cooking gas in Berlin, no coal, no oil; householders burn wood from ruined buildings and dwellings, and they have no trouble finding plenty. The Ehrenmal, dedicated in 1931, is in the Alte Wache, or Old Guardhouse, a small, once handsome structure with walls of chaste limestone, built about a century and a quarter ago. For generations, at twelve-thirty in the afternoon every Sunday, Wednesday, and Friday, the guard outside the Alte Wache was changed while Berliners looked on with the same delight with which Londoners used to watch the changing of the guard at Buckingham Palace. The Ehrenmal, a slab of black granite bearing a wreath of silver and gold oak leaves and an inscription honoring the Prussians who died in the last war, was placed so that the illumination from a round skylight in the dome of the guardhouse shone on it. There is no guard outside the Alte Wache now. Its limestone walls are no longer chaste and the illumination from the shattered skylight is augmented by the light that comes through the jagged holes in the dome. The slab and the wreath of the Ehrenmal are still there, visible through the entrance, but the wreath has been jarred off the slab and both are littered with rubble, muck, and charred lumps of wood. "*Ach, ja,* poor Berlin," one of the girls said as they turned away. "How they beat us to pieces!"

The R.A.F. and our Eighth Air Force together dropped more than a hundred and fifty-six million pounds of bombs on Berlin. No one knows which section got it worst, for the complete figures on the damage won't be in for several months. Perhaps they will show that the parts worst hit were the workers' districts like Wedding and Köpenick. Nevertheless, Unter den Linden, the center of a target known to the Eighth Air Force as "Big B," or downtown Berlin, certainly got its share. The street, which, as everyone must remember, got its name from the rows of linden trees down its middle, is a hundred and ninety-eight feet wide and nearly a mile long, and it is the hub of Berlin's east-west axis. In prewar days, with its jewelry shops, bureaus for luxury travel, salesrooms for custom-made automobiles, hotels such as the Adlon and the Bristol, and restaurants whose food, drink, and service made you think of Ernst Lubitsch pictures, it was one of the world's great avenues. On it, too, were the University, the State Library, Frederick the Great's State Opera, the Ministries of Interior and Finance, and the American, French, and Soviet Embassies. Not much is left of these buildings; most of them are shells, at best.

Take the Adlon, down at the street's western end, close to the Brandenburg Gate. If you ignore the fact that its doors and windows are bricked up as a precaution against bomb blast, it looks from the outside as you might expect a first-rate metropolitan hotel to look. Inside, it is a fire-gutted shambles, a circumstance for which, it appears, the cupidity of the proprietor, Herr Adlon, is responsible. Before Berlin fell, on May 2nd, the Adlon had nearly four hundred thousand bottles of vintage wine in its cellar. As the Russian Army closed in on the city, somebody on the hotel's staff began worrying about these treasures and went to the boss. "*Um Gottes willen*, Herr Adlon," he is supposed to have said, "what are you going to do about all that wine? The Russians are coming and you don't want them to get it, do you? Give it to the people in the streets. Pour it down the sewers. *Um Christi willen*, Herr Adlon!" Herr Adlon replied that he would think it over. He thought it over so carefully, weighing and counterweighing every possibility with such thoroughness, that he had disposed of only a few gross of bottles, to his employees, at nine marks apiece, before the Red Army arrived in Berlin. Its enlisted men, as the enlisted men of any army in the world would have done, got into the wine cellar of the Adlon. They had succeeded in drinking only a few hundred bottles, however, when the hotel caught fire from, it is said, a lighted cigar dropped on a carpet by an exhilarated staff sergeant. Four hundred and ten of the Adlon's four hundred and fifty bedrooms and all of its two hundred and fifty-five baths were burned out, and the remainder of Herr Adlon's stock of bottled goods was turned into a pool of molten glass.

Or take the State Opera House, grandfather to the Scala in Milan and great-great-grandfather to the Metropolitan in New York. Its façade, including the Latin inscription on the lintel above its columns, announcing that Fredericus Rex gave the building to Apollo and the Muses, is intact. When you go inside, you realize that even a massed choir of Carusos and Chaliapins couldn't fill it with sound, for there is practically nothing left to fill. This is not the building's first bit of bad luck. It was opened in 1743, and its interior was burned out a century later; then it was restored, and in 1928 completely modernized. It was burned out again, by the R.A.F.'s incendiaries, two centuries after its erection, but was quickly restored by the Nazis and reopened. I suspect that Fredcricus Rex would have had some rather strong reactions had he been present on that reopening night. "Lohengrin," sung by the Reich's foremost artists, nourished the Führer's passion for Wagner and was at least a nod in Apollo's direction, but for those of the Party's leaders whose favorite muse was Terpsichore, there was a *Nackt-ballet*, or a posse of *Tanzgirls* with no clothes on, which performed fulsomely in each of the opera's intermissions. Later, the Eighth got the building again, for the third time, on one of its Big B operations.

With some friends, I walked one day down the short, narrow Oberwallstrasse, which runs off Unter den Linden. What we saw there can, with a few variations, be seen today in hundreds of Berlin side streets. There had been fighting in the Oberwallstrasse; a wrecked American half-track with S.S. license plates lay keeled over to starboard, and other military vehicles were strewn along behind it. A howitzer from the last war, which residents of the district told us had been taken from the Zeughaus, Berlin's military museum, and pressed into service, lay on its side. Clearly, the Russian heavy artillery had found the range. The Oberwallstrasse had also been bombed. Half of one large dwelling house had been sheared off, leaving four stories of rooms exposed to view. In one ground-floor room stood a small lathe which had doubtless been used to make parts of military instruments; during the war there was a great deal of *Heimarbeit*, or parlor manufacture, in Berlin.

Halfway up the street, an elderly woman and a little girl were foraging for fuel in another wrecked house. A sign on one wall of it said, in German, "Warning! As per order of the Herr Police President of Berlin, this property has been strewn with a highly poisonous rat exterminator. Children and domestic animals are to be kept at a distance." The old woman and the little girl hadn't read the sign or, more likely, didn't care. Under a fallen joist the child found a man's left shoe, in fairly good condition, and this she put into her rucksack. Single shoes are a commodity on Germany's black market.

In the gutter in front of another house we came across a soggy, coverless book that turned out to be Longfellow. "Life is real! Life is earnest!" and "Under a spreading chestnut tree" look funny in German; so does *"Auf den Ufern Gitschigummi sass der kleine Hiawatha."* Two youths who had been watching us came over. One said that in better days he had enjoyed Longfellow; the other had been fascinated by Edgar

Allan Poe. They were medical students waiting for the University to reopen and give them a chance to go on with their studies. That would not be for some time, I told them rather magisterially, as though I were a member of the Allied Control Commission. I pointed out that although we took Aachen last October, only the first four grades of its grammar schools had been opened so far and that nobody expected the university in Heidelberg to resume operation for at least another year. The two young men were surprised to learn that so little educational progress had been made elsewhere in Germany. Shortly after the capture of Berlin, they said, the Russians had reopened all the pre-University schools that were still standing. The only reason the University hadn't reopened, they said, was that it had been *ausgebombt*.

My friends and I walked back to Unter den Linden. A pale, bald man with protruding black eyes pedaled slowly by on a bicycle with no tires on its wheels. A hunchback, whose legs accounted for three-quarters of his height, trudged past in a blue windbreaker and checked trousers, pushing a handcart loaded with three empty barrels. Two trucks came along. One was a Studebaker 4 x 6, driven by a Russian soldier and carrying three Holstein cows, who looked poorly. The other was a German vehicle, painted black and powered by a wood-burning gas generator. Unter den Linden used to swarm with pedestrians and traffic, but now there was little of either. In front of the Brandenburg Gate a pretty Russian Wac, with the help of two flags, was directing what traffic there was. Above the gate's arches hung a Russian banner inscribed "Long live the Soviet Armies that planted their victory standards in Berlin!" On top of the gate, the outside right horse in the famous sculptured team of four steeds pulling Victory's chariot badly needed a veterinary.

A thin old man, who must have taken us for Russians, approached and said in a whining voice, "*Guten Tag*, comrades. Can you spare me a little tobacco?" He wore a black homburg that almost covered his ears, a wing collar and a string tie, a dark suit and overcoat that were very neatly brushed and pressed, and beautifully shined black shoes. We turned him down, and he sorrowfully walked on with his hands clasped behind him. A curly-haired, actorish-looking fellow in his thirties, wearing plus-fours and a canary pullover, came up to us and offered to pay cash for cigarettes. We said that we had all the cash we wanted, and he too went away. Next we got talking with a pale youth who was carrying a portfolio. He told us that he was a Jew and showed us his card to prove it. Jews and half-Jews in Berlin have identification cards issued by the Russians. Each card has the bearer's photograph, declares that he is a victim of National Socialism, and asks that he be given special consideration. This youth didn't mention tobacco. When one of us handed him a cigarette, he was overwhelmed.

No tobacco has been sold legally in Berlin since May 2nd. On the black market a single cigarette costs from fifteen to twenty marks (a dollar and a half to two dollars, at the official rate of exchange), depending on its quality. American cigarettes are considered the best, and the standard black-market price for a pack of twenty is three hundred marks, or thirty dollars. This ten-cent valuation of the mark is the arbitrary one set by our Army Finance Department, and the mark's actual purchasing power, even in the open market, is often two and a half to three times greater. The value of a pack of Chesterfields can thus run as high as seventy-five to ninety dollars.

The German word for the butt of a cigarette or cigar is *Kippe*. I'd conservatively estimate that at least two million of the three million Berliners left in the city that was once home for nearly four and a half million are now engaged in *Kippensammlung*, or butt collecting. The butt collecting in Berlin, I do not hesitate to say, is the most intensive on earth, and I am not forgetting the *Kippensammlung* on the Bowery and in the Middle East. Remain stationary on a Berlin street while you smoke a cigarette, and likely as not you will soon have around you a circle of children, able-bodied men, and whiskered old men, all waiting to dive for the butt when you throw it away. A riddle that has achieved wide circulation in the city runs as follows: If you can make one whole cigarette out of three butts, how many can you make out of ten butts? The answer is five. The explanation is that from nine of the ten butts you make three cigarettes, and from the butts of those three you make your fourth cigarette. You make the fifth cigarette from the butt of your fourth, plus the tenth original butt, *plus* a butt you borrow from a friend whom you pay back with the butt of the fifth cigarette after you've smoked it.

Butts are legal tender in the economic system that prevails in Berlin. The other afternoon, I was at the home of a woman who was having some glass put in the blown-out windows of her apartment. The glazier had been on the job all day, using old bent nails instead of putty. The woman's fifteen-year-old daughter came into the living room to say that the glazier had finished and was waiting to be paid. "*Na, wo hast du die Kippen gesteckt?*" ["Come now, where have you put the butts?"], the mother asked the child, who went out and shortly returned with a silver bowl containing about twenty butts. Her mother took the bowl into the next room, where the glazier had been working, and through the open door I could hear him expressing his ecstatic thanks. "They taste so *wunderschön* in my pipe!" he said. Plainly he was more than satisfied with his day's pay.

# J(AMES) G(RAHAM) BALLARD

BORN in Shanghai and educated at Cambridge, J. G. Ballard is best known for his science fiction writing. His novel *The Empire of the Sun* borrows heavily from his own wartime experiences in China.

■

## FROM *The Empire of the Sun*

A humid morning sun filled the stadium, reflected in the pools of water that covered the athletics track and in the chromium radiators of the American cars parked behind the goal posts at the northern end of the football pitch. Supporting himself against Mr. Maxted's shoulder, Jim surveyed the hundreds of men and women lying on the warm grass. A few prisoners squatted on the ground, their sunburned but pallid faces like blanched leather from which the dye had run. They stared at the cars, suspicious of their bright grilles, with the wary eyes of the Hungjao peasants looking up from their rice planting at his parents' Packard.

Jim brushed the flies from Mr. Maxted's mouth and eyes. The architect lay without moving, his white ribs unclasped around his heart, but Jim could hear his faint breath.

"You're feeling better, Mr. Maxted . . . I'll bring you some water." Jim squinted at the lines of cars. Even the small effort of focusing his eyes exhausted him. Trying to hold his head steady, he felt the ground sway, as if he and the hundreds of prisoners were about to be tipped out of the stadium.

Mr. Maxted turned to stare at Jim, who pointed to the cars. There were more than fifty of them—Buicks, Lincoln Zephyrs, two white Cadillacs side by side. Had they come to collect their British owners now that the war had ended? Jim stroked Mr. Maxted's cheeks, then reached into the cavern below his ribs and tried to massage his heart. It would be a pity for Mr. Maxted to die just as his Studebaker arrived to take him back to the Shanghai nightclubs.

However, the Japanese soldiers sat on the concrete benches near the entrance tunnel, sipping tea beside a charcoal stove. Its smoke drifted between the hospital trucks. Two young soldiers were passing pails of water to a weary Dr. Ransome, but the security troops seemed no more interested in the thousand Lunghua prisoners who occupied the football field than they had been during the previous day's march.

His legs trembling, Jim stood up and scanned the parked cars for his parents' Packard. Where were the chauffeurs? They should have been waiting by their cars, as they always did outside the country club. Then a small rain cloud dimmed the sun, and a drab light settled over the stadium. Looking at their rusting chrome, Jim realized that these American cars had been parked here for years. Their windshields were caked with winter grime, and they sat on flattened tires, part of the booty looted by the Japanese from the Allied nationals.

Jim searched the stands on the north and west slopes of the stadium. The concrete tiers had been stripped of their seats, and sections of the stands were now used as an open-air warehouse. Dozens of blackwood cabinets and mahogany tables, their varnish still intact, and hundreds of dining-room chairs were packed together as if in the loft of a furniture depository. Bedsteads and wardrobes, refrigerators and air-conditioning units were stacked above each other, rising in a slope toward the sky. The immense presidential box, where Madame Chiang and the Generalissimo might once have saluted the world's athletes, was now crammed with roulette wheels, cocktail bars and a jumble of gilded plaster nymphs holding gaudy lamps above their heads. Rolls of Persian and Turkish carpets, hastily wrapped in tarpaulins, lay on the concrete steps, water dripping through them as if from a pile of rotting pipes.

To Jim, these shabby trophies seized from the houses and nightclubs of Shanghai seemed to gleam with a show-window freshness, like the floors filled with furniture through which he and his mother had once wandered in the Sincere Company department store. He stared at the stands, almost expecting his mother to appear in a silk dress and run a gloved hand over these terraces of black lacquer.

Jim sat down and shielded his eyes from the glare. He massaged Mr. Maxted's cheeks with his thumb and forefinger, pinching his lips and hooking out the flies trapped inside his mouth. Around them the inmates of Lunghua Camp lay on the damp grass, staring at this display of their former possessions, a mirage that grew more vivid in the steepening August sunlight.

Yet the mirage soon passed. Jim wiped his hands on Mr. Maxted's shorts. The Japanese had frequently used the stadium as a transit camp, and the worn grass was covered with oily rags and the ash of small fires, strips of canvas tent and wooden crates. There were unmistakable human remains, bloodstains and pieces of excrement, on which feasted thousands of flies.

The engine of a hospital truck began to run noisily. The Japanese soldiers had come down from the stands and were forming themselves into a march party. Pairs of guards climbed the tailgates, cotton masks over their faces. Helped by three English prisoners, Dr. Ransome lifted down those patients either dead or too ill to continue the day's journey. They lay in the tire ruts that scored the grass, as if trying to fold the soft earth around themselves.

Jim squatted beside Mr. Maxted, working his diaphragm like a bellows. He had seen Dr. Ransome bring his patients back from the dead, and it was important for Mr. Maxted to be well enough to join the march. Around them the prisoners were sitting upright, and a few men stood beside their huddled wives and children. Several of the older internees had died in the night—ten feet away Mrs. Wentworth, who had played the part of Lady Bracknell, lay in her faded cotton dress, staring at the sky. Others were surrounded by shallow pools of water formed by the pressure of their bodies on the soft grass.

Jim's arms ached from the effort of pumping. He waited for Dr. Ransome to jump down from the hospital truck and look after Mr. Maxted. However, the three vehicles were already leaving the stadium. Dr. Ransome's sandy head ducked as the truck lumbered through the tunnel. Jim was tempted to run after it, but he knew that he had decided to stay with Mr. Maxted. He had learned that having someone to care for was the same as being cared for by someone else.

Jim listened to the trucks crossing the parking lot, their gear boxes gasping as they gathered speed. Lunghua Camp was at last being dismantled. A marching party formed itself beside the tunnel. Some three hundred British prisoners, the younger men with their wives and children, had lined up on the running track and were being inspected by a sergeant of the gendarmerie. Beside them, on the football pitch, were those prisoners too exhausted to sit or stand. They lay on the grass like battlefield casualties. The Japanese soldiers strolled among them, as if searching for a lost ball, uninterested in these British nationals who had strayed into a cul-de-sac of the war.

An hour later the column moved off, the prisoners plodding through the tunnel without a backward glance. Six Japanese soldiers followed them, and the rest continued their casual patrol of the blackwood cabinets and refrigerators. The senior NCOs waited by the tunnel and watched the American reconnaissance planes that flew overhead, making no attempt to mobilize the prisoners in the stadium. Within fifteen minutes, however, a second group had begun to assemble, and the Japanese came forward to inspect them.

Jim wiped his hands on the damp grass and put his fingers into Mr. Maxted's mouth. The architect's lips trembled around his knuckles. But already the August sun was driving the moisture from the grass. Jim turned his attention to a pool of water lying on the cinder track. He waited for the sentry to pass, and then walked across the grass and drank from his cupped hands. The water ran down his throat like iced mercury, an electric current that almost stopped his heart. Before the Japanese could order him away, Jim quickly cupped his hands and carried the water to Mr. Maxted.

As he decanted the water into Mr. Maxted's mouth, the flies scrambled from his gums. Beside him lay the elderly figure of Major Griffin, a retired Indian Army officer who had lectured in Lunghua on the infantry weapons of the Great War. Too weak to sit up, he pointed to Jim's hands.

Jim pinched Mr. Maxted's lips, relieved when his tongue shot forward in a spasm. Trying to encourage him, Jim said: "Mr. Maxted, our rations should be coming soon."

"Good lad, Jamie—you hang on."

Major Griffin beckoned to him. "Jim . . ."

"Coming, Major Griffin . . ." Jim crossed the cinder track and returned with a handful of water. As he squatted beside the major, patting his cheeks, he noticed that Mrs. Vincent was sitting on the grass twenty feet away. She had left her son and husband with a group of prisoners in the center of the football field. Too exhausted to move any further, she stared at Jim with the same desperate gaze to which she had treated him as he ate his weevils. The night's rain had washed the last of the dye from her cotton dress, giving her the ashen pallor of the Chinese laborers at Lunghua Airfield. Mrs. Vincent would build a strange runway, Jim reflected.

"Jamie . . ."

She called him by his childhood name, which Mr. Maxted, without thinking, had summoned from some prewar memory. She wanted him to be a child again, to run the endless errands that had kept him alive in Lunghua.

As he scooped the cold water from the cinder track, he remembered how Mrs. Vincent had refused to help him when he was ill. Yet he had always been intrigued by the sight of her eating. He waited while she drank from his hands.

When she had finished he helped her to stand. "Mrs. Vincent, the war's over now."

With a grimace, she pushed his hands away, but Jim no longer cared. He watched her walk unsteadily between the seated prisoners. Jim squatted beside Mr. Maxted, brushing the flies from his face. He could still feel Mrs. Vincent's tongue on his fingers.

"Jamie . . ."

Someone else was calling, as if he were a Chinese coolie running at the command of the European masters. Too light-headed even to sit, Jim lay beside Mr. Maxted. It was time to stop running his errands. His hands were frozen from the water on the cinder track. The war had lasted for too long. At the detention center, and in Lunghua, he had done all he could to stay alive, but now a part of him wanted to die. It was the one way in which he could end the war.

Jim looked at the hundreds of prisoners on the grass. He wanted them all to die, surrounded by their rotting carpets and cocktail cabinets. Many of them, he was glad to see, had already obliged him, and Jim felt angry at those prisoners still able to walk who were now forming a second march party. He guessed that they were being walked to death around the countryside, but he wanted them to stay in the stadium and die within sight of the white Cadillacs.

Fiercely, Jim wiped the flies from Mr. Maxted's cheeks. Laughing at Mrs. Vincent, he began to rock on his knees, as he had done as a child, crooning to himself and monotonously beating the ground. "Jamie . . . Jamie . . ."

A Japanese soldier patrolled the cinder track nearby. He walked across the grass and stared down at Jim. Irritated by the noise, he was about to kick him with his ragged boot. But a flash of light filled the stadium, flaring over the stands in the southwest corner of the football field, as if an immense American bomb had exploded somewhere to the northeast of Shanghai. The sentry hesitated, looking over his shoulder as the light behind him grew more intense. It faded within a few seconds, but its pale sheen covered everything within the stadium: the looted furniture in the stands, the cars behind the goalposts, the prisoners on the grass. They were sitting on the floor of a furnace heated by a second sun.

Jim stared at his white hands and knees, and at the pinched face of the Japanese soldier, who seemed disconcerted by the light. Both of them were waiting for the rumble of sound that followed the bomb flashes, but an unbroken silence lay over the stadium and the surrounding land, as if the sun had blinked, losing heart for a few seconds. Jim smiled at the Japanese, wishing that he could tell him that the light was a premonition of his death, the sight of his small soul joining the larger soul of the dying world.

# JOHN HERSEY

*HIROSHIMA* is one of the most memorable pieces of reporting to come out of the war. John Hersey visited Hiroshima in 1946 and re-created August 6, 1945—the day the first atomic bomb struck Hiroshima—in the lives of six survivors.

■

FROM *Hiroshima*

## A NOISELESS FLASH

At exactly fifteen minutes past eight in the morning, on August 6, 1945, Japanese time, at the moment when the atomic bomb flashed above Hiroshima, Miss Toshiko Sasaki, a clerk in the personnel department of the East Asia Tin Works, had just sat down at her place in the plant office and was turning her head to speak to the girl at the next desk. At that same moment, Dr. Masakazu Fujii was settling down cross-legged to read the Osaka *Asahi* on the porch of his private hospital, overhanging one of the seven deltaic rivers which divide Hiroshima; Mrs. Hatsuyo Nakamura, a tailor's widow, stood by the window of her kitchen, watching a neighbor tearing down his house because it lay in the path of an air-raid-defense fire lane; Father Wilhelm Kleinsorge, a German priest of the Society of Jesus, reclined in his underwear on a cot on the top floor of his order's three-story mission house, reading a Jesuit magazine, *Stimmen der Zeit:* Dr. Terufumi Sasaki, a young member of the surgical staff of the city's large, modern Red Cross Hospital, walked along one of the hospital corridors with a blood specimen for a Wassermann test in his hand; and the Reverend Mr. Kivoshi Tanimoto, pastor of the Hiroshima Methodist Church, paused at the door of a rich man's house in Koi, the city's western suburb, and prepared to unload a handcart full of things he had evacuated from town in fear of the massive B-29 raid which everyone expected Hiroshima to suffer. A hundred thousand people were killed by the atomic bomb, and these six were among the survivors. They still wonder why they lived when so many others died. Each of them counts many small items of chance or volition—a step taken in time, a decision to go indoors, catching one streetcar instead of the next —that spared him. And now each knows that in the act of survival he lived a dozen lives and saw more death than he ever thought he would see. At the time, none of them knew anything.

The Reverend Mr. Tanimoto got up at five o'clock that morning. He was alone in the parsonage, because for some time his wife had been commuting with their year-old baby to spend nights with a friend in Ushida, a suburb to the north. Of all the important cities of Japan, only two, Kyoto and Hiroshima, had not been visited in strength by B-*san*, or Mr. B. as the Japanese, with a mixture of respect and unhappy familiarity, called the B-29; and Mr. Tanimoto, like all his neighbors and friends, was almost sick with anxiety. He had heard uncomfortably detailed accounts of mass raids on Kure, Iwakuni, Tokuyama, and other nearby towns; he was sure Hiroshima's turn would come soon. He had slept badly the night before, because there had been several air-raid warnings. Hiroshima had been getting such warnings almost every night for weeks, for at that time the B-29s were using Lake Biwa, northeast of Hiroshima, as a rendezvous point, and no matter what city the Americans planned to hit, the Superfortresses streamed in over the coast near Hiroshima. The frequency of the warnings and the continued abstinence of Mr. B with respect to Hiroshima had made its citizens jittery; a rumor was going around that the Americans were saving something special for the city.

Mr. Tanimoto is a small man, quick to talk, laugh, and cry. He wears his black hair parted in the middle and rather long; the prominence of the frontal bones just above his eyebrows and the smallness of his mustache, mouth, and chin give him a strange, old-young look, boyish and yet wise, weak and yet fiery. He moves nervously and fast, but with a restraint which suggests that he is a cautious, thoughtful man. He showed, indeed, just those qualities in the uneasy days before the bomb fell. Besides having his wife spend the nights in Ushida, Mr. Tanimoto had been carrying all the portable things from his church, in the close-packed residential district called Nagaragawa, to a house that belonged to a rayon manufacturer in Koi, two miles from the center of town. The rayon man, a Mr. Matsui, had opened his then unoccupied estate to a large number of his friends and acquaintances, so that they might evacuate whatever they wished to a safe distance from the probable target area. Mr. Tanimoto had had no difficulty in moving chairs, hymnals, Bibles, altar gear, and church records by pushcart himself, but the organ console and an upright piano required some aid. A friend of his named Matsuo had, the day before, helped him get the piano out to Koi: in return, he had promised this day to assist Mr. Matsuo in hauling out a daughter's belongings. That is why he had risen so early.

Mr. Tanimoto cooked his own breakfast. He felt awfully tired. The effort of moving the piano the day before, a sleepless night, weeks of worry and unbalanced diet, the cares of his parish—all combined to make him feel hardly adequate to the new day's work. There was another thing, too: Mr. Tanimoto had studied theology at Emory College, in Atlanta, Georgia; he had graduated in 1940; he spoke excellent English;

he dressed in American clothes; he had corresponded with many American friends right up to the time the war began; and among a people obsessed with a fear of being spied upon—perhaps almost obsessed himself—he found himself growing increasingly uneasy. The police had questioned him several times, and just a few days before, he had heard that an influential acquaintance, a Mr. Tanaka, a retired officer of the Toyo Kisen Kaisha steamship line, an anti-Christian, a man famous in Hiroshima for his showy philanthropies and notorious for his personal tyrannies, had been telling people that Tanimoto should not be trusted. In compensation, to show himself publicly a good Japanese, Mr. Tanimoto had taken on the chairmanship of his local *tonarigumi*, or Neighborhood Association, and to his other duties and concerns this position had added the business of organizing air-raid defense for about twenty families.

Before six o'clock that morning, Mr. Tanimoto started for Mr. Matsuo's house. There he found that their burden was to be a *tansu*, a large Japanese cabinet, full of clothing and household goods. The two men set out. The morning was perfectly clear and so warm that the day promised to be uncomfortable. A few minutes after they started, the air-raid siren went off—a minute-long blast that warned of approaching planes but indicated to the people of Hiroshima only a slight degree of danger, since it sounded every morning at this time, when an American weather plane came over. The two men pulled and pushed the handcart through the city streets. Hiroshima was a fan-shaped city, lying mostly on the six islands formed by the seven estuarial rivers that branch out from the Ota River; its main commercial and residential districts, covering about four square miles in the center of the city, contained three-quarters of its population, which had been reduced by several evacuation programs from a wartime peak of 380,000 to about 245,000. Factories and other residential districts, or suburbs, lay compactly around the edges of the city. To the south were the docks, an airport, and the island-studded Inland Sea. A rim of mountains runs around the other three sides of the delta. Mr. Tanimoto and Mr. Matsuo took their way through the shopping center, already full of people, and across two of the rivers to the sloping streets of Koi, and up them to the outskirts and foothills. As they started up a valley away from the tight-ranked houses, the all-clear sounded. (The Japanese radar operators, detecting only three planes, supposed that they comprised a reconnaissance.) Pushing the handcart up to the rayon man's house was tiring, and the men, after they had maneuvered their load into the driveway and to the front steps, paused to rest awhile. They stood with a wing of the house between them and the city. Like most homes in this part of Japan, the house consisted of a wooden frame and wooden walls supporting a heavy tile roof. Its front hall, packed with rolls of bedding and clothing, looked like a cool cave full of fat cushions. Opposite the house, to the right of the front door, there was a large, finicky rock garden. There was no sound of planes. The morning was still; the place was cool and pleasant.

Then a tremendous flash of light cut across the sky. Mr. Tanimoto has a distinct recollection that it traveled from east to west, from the city toward the hills. It seemed a sheet of sun. Both he and Mr. Matsuo reacted in terror—and both had time to react (for they were 3,500 yards, or two miles, from the center of the explosion). Mr. Matsuo dashed up the front steps into the house and dived among the bedrolls and buried himself there. Mr. Tanimoto took four or five steps and threw himself between two big rocks in the garden. He bellied up very hard against one of them. As his face was against the stone, he did not see what happened. He felt a sudden pressure, and then splinters and pieces of board and fragments of tile fell on him. He heard no roar. (Almost no one in Hiroshima recalls hearing any noise of the bomb. But a fisherman in his sampan on the Inland Sea near Tsuzu, the man with whom Mr. Tanimoto's mother-in-law and sister-in-law were living, saw the flash and heard a tremendous explosion; he was nearly twenty miles from Hiroshima, but the thunder was greater than when the B-29s hit Iwakuni, only five miles away.)

When he dared, Mr. Tanimoto raised his head and saw that the rayon man's house had collapsed. He thought a bomb had fallen directly on it. Such clouds of dust had risen that there was a sort of twilight around. In panic, not thinking for the moment of Mr. Matsuo under the ruins, he dashed out into the street. He noticed as he ran that the concrete wall of the estate had fallen over—toward the house rather than away from it. In the street, the first thing he saw was a squad of soldiers who had been burrowing into the hillside opposite, making one of the thousands of dugouts in which the Japanese apparently intended to resist invasion, hill by hill, life for life; the soldiers were coming out of the hole, where they should have been safe, and blood was running from their heads, chests, and backs. They were silent and dazed.

Under what seemed to be a local dust cloud, the day grew darker and darker.

At nearly midnight, the night before the bomb was dropped, an announcer on the city's radio station said that about two hundred B-29s were approaching southern Honshu and advised the population of Hiroshima to evacuate to their designated "safe areas." Mrs. Hatsuyo Nakamura, the tailor's widow, who lived in the section called Nobori-cho and who had long had a habit of doing as she was told, got her three children—a ten-year-old boy, Toshio, an eight-year-old girl, Yaeko, and a five-year-old girl, Myeko—out of bed and dressed them and walked with them to the military area known as the East Parade Ground, on the northeast edge of the city. There she unrolled some mats and the children lay down on them. They slept until about two, when they were awakened by the roar of the planes going over Hiroshima.

As soon as the planes had passed, Mrs. Nakamura started back with her children. They reached home a little after two-thirty and she immediately turned on the radio, which, to her distress, was just then broadcasting a fresh warning. When she looked at the children and saw how tired they were, and when she thought of the number of trips they had made in past weeks, all to no purpose, to the East Parade Ground, she decided that in spite of the instructions on the radio, she simply could not face starting out all over again. She put the children in their bedrolls on the floor, lay down herself at three o'clock, and fell asleep at once, so soundly that when planes passed over later, she did not waken to their sound.

The siren jarred her awake at about seven. She arose, dressed quickly and hurried to the house of Mr. Nakamoto, the head of her Neighborhood Association, and asked him what she should do. He said that she should remain at home unless an urgent warning—a series of intermittent blasts of the siren—was sounded. She returned home, lit the stove in the kitchen, set some rice to cook, and sat down to read that morning's Hiroshima Chugoku. To her relief, the all-clear sounded at eight o'clock. She heard the children stirring, so she went and gave each of them a handful of peanuts and told them to stay on their bedrolls, because they were tired from the night's walk. She had hoped that they would go back to sleep, but the man in the house directly to the south began to make a terrible hullabaloo of hammering, wedging, ripping, and splitting. The prefectural government, convinced, as everyone in Hiroshima was, that the city would be attacked soon, had begun to press with threats and warnings for the completion of wide fire lanes, which, it was hoped, might act in conjunction with the rivers to localize any fires started by an incendiary raid; and the neighbor was reluctantly sacrificing his home to the city's safety. Just the day before, the prefecture had ordered all able-bodied girls from the secondary schools to spend a few days helping to clear these lanes, and they started work soon after the all-clear sounded.

Mrs. Nakamura went back to the kitchen, looked at the rice, and began watching the man next door. At first, she was annoyed with him for making so much noise, but then she was moved almost to tears by pity. Her emotion was specifically directed toward her neighbor, tearing down his home, board by board, at a time when there was so much unavoidable destruction, but undoubtedly she also felt a generalized, community pity, to say nothing of self-pity. She had not had an easy time. Her husband, Isawa, had gone into the Army just after Myeko was born, and she had heard nothing from or of him for a long time, until, on March 5, 1942, she received a seven-word telegram: "Isawa died an

honorable death at Singapore." She learned later that he had died on
February 15th, the day Singapore fell, and that he had been a corporal.
Isawa had been a not particularly prosperous tailor, and his only capital
was a Sankoku sewing machine. After his death, when his allotments
stopped coming, Mrs. Nakamura got out the machine and began to take
in piecework herself, and since then had supported the children, but
poorly, by sewing.

As Mrs. Nakamura stood watching her neighbor, everything flashed
whiter than any white she had ever seen. She did not notice what happened to the man next door; the reflex of a mother set her in motion
toward her children. She had taken a single step (the house was 1,350
yards, or three-quarters of a mile, from the center of the explosion) when
something picked her up and she seemed to fly into the next room over
the raised sleeping platform, pursued by parts of her house.

Timbers fell around her as she landed, and a shower of tiles pom-
meled her; everything became dark, for she was buried. The debris did
not cover her deeply. She rose up and freed herself. She heard a child
cry, "Mother, help me!," and saw her youngest—Myeko, the five-year-
old—buried up to her breast and unable to move. As Mrs. Nakamura
started frantically to claw her way toward the baby, she could see or hear
nothing of her other children.

# MARC KAMINSKY

MARC KAMINSKY, born during World War II, won the
New York Public Library Award in 1984 for *The Road
from Hiroshima,* from which the following poem was
taken. He has also written plays and translated Yiddish
poetry.

■

## The Soldier

1.
A bald head
on the body of a boy screaming, "Ichiro!"

its features so swollen
they had all run
into an anonymous mass

and gigantic!

I stared
at its awful roundness and size
and its brown covering
as the body ran toward me

the burnt head
mounted on top screaming my name.

2.
Whatever you hear
about Hiroshima
whatever wild stories you hear

all of it happened.

3.
I grabbed a stick
planted my feet under my shoulders
and crouched

why
had I been singled out by this weird
assailant?

then it crashed into me
coiled its arms around me
tried to bury its head
in my stomach

I raised my stick and began
to pummel
its legs and buttocks
crying, "Let me go!"

In horror he cried, "Ichiro!
It's me! Kyuzo! Your brother!"

# CLIVE JAMES

THE HISTORIAN Clive James recounts the end of the war, an ironic memory, from *Unreliable Memoirs*.

■

## FROM *Unreliable Memoirs*

After the first atomic bomb there was a general feeling that Japan had surrendered. The street was decorated with bunting. Strings of all the Allied flags were hung up between the flame trees. The Japanese missed their cue and all the bunting had to be taken in. Finally the Japanese saw the point and all the bunting was taken out again. Everybody was in ecstasies except my mother, who still had no news. Then an official telegram came to say that he was all right. Letters from my father arrived. They were in touch with each other and must have been very happy. The Americans, with typical generosity, arranged that all the Australian POWs in Japan should be flown home instead of having to wait for ships. My mother started counting the days. Then a telegram arrived saying that my father's plane had been caught in a typhoon and had crashed in Manila Bay with the loss of everyone aboard.

Up until that day, all the grief and worry that I had ever seen my mother give way to had been tempered for my ears. But now she could not help herself. At the age of five I was seeing the full force of human despair. There were no sedatives to be had. It was several days before she could control herself. I understood nothing beyond the fact that I could not help. I think that I was marked for life. I know now that until very recent years I was never quite all there—that I was play-acting instead of living and that nothing except my own unrelenting fever of self-consciousness seemed quite real. Eventually, in my middle thirties, I got a grip on myself. But there can be no doubt that I had a tiresomely protracted adolescence, wasting a lot of other people's time, patience and love. I suppose it is just another sign of weakness to blame everything on that one moment, but it would be equally dishonest if I failed to record its piercing vividness.

As for my mother, I don't presume even to guess at what she felt. The best I can say is that at least they got the chance of writing a few words to one another before the end. In one respect they were like Osip and Nadezhda Mandelstam in the last chapters of *Hope against Hope*— torn apart in mid-word without even the chance to say goodbye. But in another way they were not. My father had taken up arms out of his own free will. In Europe, millions of women and children had been killed for no better reason than some ideological fantasy. My father was a free human being. So was my mother. What happened to them, terrible though it was, belongs in the category of what Nadezhda Mandelstam, elsewhere in that same great book, calls the privilege of ordinary heart-breaks. Slowly, in those years, the world was becoming aware that things had been happening which threw the whole value of human existence into doubt. But my father's death was not one of them. It was just bad luck. I have disliked luck ever since—an aversion only increased by the fact that I have always been inordinately lucky.

# SHŪSAKU ENDŌ

THE JAPANESE NOVELIST and playwright Shūsaku
Endō is a Catholic who studied in France for three
years. His novels include *Obakasan* and *Wonderful
Fool*. The excerpt that follows is from *Stained Glass
Elegies*.

■

## FROM *Stained Glass Elegies*

I could still remember the day Father Bosch was taken away by the
military police. I did not see it happen. I had just returned home from
middle school, and two or three Catholic housewives were there, telling
my mother all the horrifying details. Plainclothes police and MPs had
stormed into the rectory without taking off their shoes, rifled through
every drawer in the place, and then taken the Father away. The housewives chattered timorously among themselves, unable to believe the ac-
cusation that the priest was a spy.

In those days every foreigner was suspect. The police and the military authorities kept an even closer watch on Catholic priests. Later we
learned that Father Bosch had been arrested because of a camera and a
photo album that he owned. They had come across a photograph of an
airplane factory in his album.

From that day, Mass was no longer celebrated at the church. Even
so, I heard that plainclothes detectives still came to survey the place
from time to time. Rumors circulated that Father Bosch was being
treated brutally by the military police. But we knew nothing of what was
really going on.

The church in my old friend's parish at Mikage was hardly an imposing structure. On a plot of land barely sixteen hundred square meters
stood the tiny church, the wooden rectory and a nursery school. While
he made some phone calls, I watched absently as some children tossed a
ball back and forth in the school playground.

One bespectacled boy was having trouble catching the balls flung at
him by a chubby little fellow. His awkwardness made me think of my
own youth. It had taken me until I was this old to realize that, at some
time or other in their lives, people all taste the same sorrows and trials.
Who could say that this boy was not experiencing the same grief I had
felt forty years before?

My friend finished his work and came in to say, "Everyone should be arriving between 5:40 and six o'clock. Do you want to wait here, or would you rather go into the chapel?"

To mark his anniversary, he was planning to celebrate Mass at six o'clock for his childhood friends who had been good enough to attend.

I entered the chapel alone and sat down. Two kerosene stoves had been placed in the aisle separating the men's pews from the women's; their blue flames flickered, but the chapel was still icy cold.

While I waited for the others to arrive, I thought about Father Bosch. It was now some thirty years since the end of the war, but he had remained here in Japan, laboring in the churches at Akashi and Kakogawa. He never thought of abandoning the people who had inflicted such cruel tortures upon him. Undoubtedly one day his bones would be laid to rest in this land.

These thoughts were prompted by the experiences I had had in Poland just two weeks earlier. A powdery snow had swirled through the sky over Warsaw each day, and at dusk a gray mist had enveloped the round domes of the churches and the squares gloomily overlooking the gates at the triumphal arch. People wearing fur caps shivered as they walked like livestock past the denuded trees in the squares. That dark, desolate vista had reminded me of the war, and in truth the scars of war were in evidence everywhere in that country. While I was in Poland I met a number of men and women who had survived the living hells at Auschwitz and Dachau. They rarely touched on their memories of those days, but there was one woman who rolled back the sleeve of her dress and showed me the convict number tattooed on her arm. "This is what it was like," she muttered sadly. The four digits clung to her slender forearm like ink stains. "Now perhaps you will understand."

As a child, she told me, she had spent a year in the Auschwitz camp. With the innocent eyes of youth she had looked on day after day as scores of her fellow prisoners were beaten, kicked, lynched, and slaughtered in the gas chambers.

"I am a Catholic, and I know I am supposed to forgive others . . . But I have no desire to forgive them."

Her eyes were riveted on mine as she spoke. Her breath reeked of onions.

"Never?"

"I doubt if I will ever forgive them."

Her despairing sigh echoed in my ears throughout my stay in Poland.

As I rubbed my hands together and waited in the unyielding pew for my old friend to celebrate the six o'clock Mass, I heard those words ringing in my ears once again. I could even smell the onions that fouled her breath.

Who is to say that Father Bosch doesn't feel the same way? I thought. Perhaps within the very depths of his heart there is one ineffaceable spot that will never be able to forgive the Japanese who flogged and trampled and tortured him.

Behind me the door to the chapel squeaked open. The sound of hesitant footsteps followed. I turned and saw three men standing with their overcoats over their arms. I had not seen them for many years, but I knew at a glance that they were Akira-san, Koike Yat-chan, and Eitarō. Layers of life and labor and age had piled up like dust on their youthful faces, too. Yat-chan saw me, raised a hand in greeting, and pointed me out to his companions. We merely exchanged glances; then they seated themselves in the cold chapel, where we maintained a respectful silence.

Our old friend appeared, dressed in his Mass vestments and reverently carrying the chalice swathed in a white cloth. At the altar decorated with two lighted candles, he began to intone the Mass. The chapel was silent, with just four of us in attendance, and the only other sound was an occasional cough from Akira-san.

Half-way through the Mass, where normally on the Sabbath he would deliver a sermon, our old friend blessed us with the sign of the cross and said:

"Thank you all very much. It is a great joy for me to be able to celebrate Mass for friends who once played in the same churchyard with me. Now twenty-five years have passed since I became a priest." His salutation was spoken in standard Tokyo speech laced with a bit of the Osaka dialect.

"I am the only one of our group who joined the priesthood, but I have continued to pray for the welfare of each one of you."

There were footsteps at the rear of the chapel; slowly, quietly they made their way forward, determined not to interrupt the priest's remarks. From the sound I visualized a bent old man. Father Bosch slipped into a seat at the front of the chapel and brought his palms together. His short-cropped hair was virtually white, and the shadows of physical debilitation and the loneliness of life were etched on his slender back. As I looked at his back, it occurred to me that shortly this priest would die here in Japan.

Sushi was served in the rectory dining-room. We clustered around Father Bosch, drinking beer and watered-down whiskey. Both Yat-chan, now the manager of an auto-parts factory, and Akira-san, a pharmacist, were flushed red with liquor, and they related one tale after another from their youthful days.

"Father. Shū-chan was really rotten, wasn't he?" Yat-chan called to Father Bosch. "Do you remember when he shinnied up the church steeple and pissed from up there?"

"Yes, I remember." He smiled in my direction and said, "I did have to reprimand you a lot."

"I was scared to death of you, Father."

"I would have had a mess on my hands if I'd let you go unchastened. As it was, I received a lot of complaints from the Women's Society. I really would have been in trouble if I hadn't scolded you."

"Shū-chan was definitely on the black list with those old ladies of the Women's Society. We never thought he'd turn out to be a novelist."

"I'm sure you didn't," I grinned sardonically. "I never dreamed I'd end up this way, either."

Father Bosch took only a sip or two of beer and swallowed down a few pieces of sushi. He had lived in Japan for many years, but there was still a trace of awkwardness in the way he used his chopsticks.

The kerosene stove warmed the room with a soft, tranquil blue flame. From the depths of my memory, the faces of each of the parishioners who had once come to church on Sundays, at Easter, and at Christmas, floated up. These were faces I had forgotten for a long while.

As I drank down my umpteenth glass of diluted whiskey, I remarked, "There was that university student named Komaki—do you remember? What's he doing these days? He used to play with us sometimes."

"Didn't you hear?" my old friend responded. "He was killed in the war."

I had heard nothing about it, since I had moved to Tokyo just after the defeat.

"Yamazaki and Kurita's father were killed too."

"I knew about them."

"The war was a terrible time," Yat-chan muttered, staring at the rim of his glass. "Just because we were Christians, they called us traitors and enemies at school and threw stones at us to torment us."

There was silence for a moment.

Then suddenly everyone's eyes turned toward Father Bosch. We had indeed been persecuted, but he alone had been subjected to torture.

For just an instant a look of confusion and embarrassment flashed across his face. Then he forced a smile for our benefit. To me it looked like a smile filled with pain. I thought of the oniony breath of the Polish woman when she had said, "I doubt if I will ever forgive them."

Someone asked, "Are you tired, Father?"

"No, I'm fine," he mumbled, his eyes fixed on the floor. "I only feel pain in the winter when it is cold. When spring comes, I am fine again. That is the way it always is."

# JOHN CHEEVER

MOST OF John Cheever's stories originally appeared in *The New Yorker,* and many of the best-known are assembled chronologically in *The Stories of John Cheever.* His novels include *Bullet Park* and *Falconer.* This excerpt is from *The Letters of John Cheever,* and was written to Josephine Herbst.

■

FROM *The Letters of John Cheever*

### MUSTERED OUT,
### NOVEMBER 21, 1945

*Thursday*

Dear Jo,

I got out of the army at three thirty on Tuesday. They played some organ music and gave us a very sensible address about our responsibilities as civilians and citizens and set us free. Everybody went running out of the chapel, shouting, like the last day of school, and now it's over. This at Fort Monmouth, New Jersey. Considering how comfortable my army life has been and how dismal the news in the Times still is, there is a fine, wonderful sense of liberation on getting out from under military jurisdiction.

New York isn't much these days. At least I don't think so. We seem to drink a lot of martinis, but the people are the people we've seen too much of and everybody's heard the jokes before. At night I read your copy of "The Ten Days that Shook etcetera" and it makes very pleasant reading.

Best,
John

# PETER PORTER

PETER PORTER, born and educated in Brisbane, Australia, came to England in 1951. His *Collected Poems* were published in 1983.

■

## Annotations of Auschwitz

I

When the burnt flesh is finally at rest,
The fires in the asylum grates will come up
And wicks turn down to darkness in the madman's eyes.

II

My suit is hairy, my carpet smells of death,
My toothbrush handle grows a cuticle.
I have six million foulnesses of breath.
Am I mad? The doctor holds my testicles
While the room fills with the zyklon B I cough.

III

On Piccadilly underground I fall asleep—
I shuffle with the naked to the steel door,
Now I am only ten from the front—I wake up—
We are past Gloucester Rd., I am not a Jew,
But scratches web the ceiling of the train.

IV

Around staring buildings the pale flowers grow;
The frenetic butterfly, the bee made free by work,
Rouse and rape the pollen pads, the nectar stoops.
The rusting railway ends here. The blind end in Europe's gut.
Touch one piece of unstrung barbed wire—
Let it taste blood: let one man scream in pain,
Death's Botanical Gardens can flower again.

V

A man eating his dressing in the hospital
Is lied to by his stomach. It's a final feast to him
Of beef blood pudding and black bread.
The orderly can't bear to see this mimic face
With its prim accusing picture after death.
On the stiff square a thousand bodies
Dig up useless ground—he hates them all,
These lives ignoble as ungoverned glands.
They fatten in statistics everywhere
And with their sick, unkillable fear of death
They crowd out peace from executioners' sleep.

VI

Forty thousand bald men drowning in a stream—
The like of light on all those bobbing skulls
Has never been seen before. Such death, says the painter,
Is worthwhile—it makes a color never known.
It makes a sight that's unimagined, says the poet.
It's nothing to do with me, says the man who hates
The poet and the painter. Six million deaths can hardly
Occur at once. What do they make? Perhaps
An idiot's normalcy. I need never feel afraid
When I salt the puny snail—cruelty's grown up
And waits for time and men to bring into its hands
The snail's adagio and all the taunting life
Which has not cared about or guessed its tortured scope.

VII

London is full of chickens on electric spits,
    Cooking in windows where the public pass.
This, say the chickens, is their Auschwitz,
    And all poultry eaters are psychopaths.

# STUDS TERKEL

AMONG THOSE who contributed to Studs Terkel's splendid oral history *"The Good War"* was Maxene Andrews of the Andrews Sisters. Here she describes her and her sisters' experiences entertaining the troops— those about to go off to war and those who had returned, wounded and shattered.

■

## Boogie Woogie Bugle Boy

Don't sit under the apple tree with anyone else but me,
Anyone else but me, anyone else but me, no, no, no,
Don't sit under the apple tree with anyone else but me
Till I come marching home.
Don't go walkin' down lover's lane with anyone else but me,
Anyone else but me, anyone else but me, no, no, no,
Don't go walkin' down lover's lane with anyone else but me
Till I come marching home.

I remember we sang it up in Seattle when a whole shipload of troops went out. We stood there on the deck and all those young men up there waving and yelling and screaming. As we sang "Don't Sit Under the Apple Tree," all the mothers and sisters and sweethearts sang with us as the ship went off. It was wonderful. The songs were romantic. It was a feeling of—not futility. It was like everybody in the United States held on to each other's hands.

I felt we were invincible. Right is right and we were right and we're gonna win. But the news was not encouraging. Remember Boak Carter, the commentator? My father would listen to him every night. We were in California, doing a picture with Abbott and Costello: *Buck Privates.* I would look on the set and see all those wonderful young men. It would go through my mind: am I ever gonna see them again? This was '39, '40. We were not yet in. But I had this great fear.

My sisters and I were so involved in our work, we didn't have much time to think of anything else. But oh, I remember the day war was declared. We were in Cincinnati. It looked like we were gonna break the house record in the theater. It didn't matter how cold it was or how high the snow, people were lined up for blocks. Every morning I'd walk over to the theater, seeing the lines already formed. This Sunday morning, I walked over and there were no lines. I thought, Now, this is funny. I walked onto the stage, which was very dark. The doorman and the stagehands were sitting around the radio. They had just one light on. They were talking about Pearl Harbor being bombed. I asked the doorman, "Where is Pearl Harbor?" Of course, the rest of the week there was no business.

But after that, as the war continued, attendance was tremendous. There was a sort of frenzy and a wonderful kind of gaiety. There was more money around then there had ever been. Our records became big sellers. Remember, during the Depression it was terrible. We closed every RKO theater in the country from north to south to east to west. We were doing three shows a day. With the war years, we did five, six shows a day. We toured almost fifty weeks a year in theaters.

No matter how many shows a day we did, we always went to the camps. We always made the hospitals when they started bringing the boys back. We were the only girls allowed in Oak Knoll Hospital when they were brought back from the Solomon Islands. They were known as basket cases.

We were working at the Golden Gate Theatre in San Francisco when a Red Cross nurse asked us if we'd come out and do a show. She kept us outside for a while. She said it would be something different from whatever we've seen. The most important thing was that we must not break down. The last thing the boys needed were tears.

We walked into the first ward and it was very quiet. When we were announced, there wasn't any applause at all. It was a very long ward. We were ushered into the middle. There were beds in front of us, beds behind us. We finally looked. The sight was terrible. We saw boys with no arms or legs, with half-faces. The three of us held on to each other, because we were afraid we were going to faint. The terrible thing is to hold back the tears.

We sang for about forty-five minutes. I think some of the fellas realized how we were feeling. One of the boys, all clothed in bandages, started to cry. He was crying throughout the numbers. Finally, one of the fellas yelled, "Don't pay any attention to him, he's just dreaming about his girlfriend." We stayed there for about three hours, going from ward to ward.

As we were leaving, a male nurse came over to us: "I have a young patient who would love to hear you sing." He asked us to sing something soft. Nice and easy and relaxed. We went down a long, long hallway and stopped in front of a door that two male nurses were guarding. We were ushered in. We were in a padded cell. The two guards closed the door behind us. We were alone.

In the corner, we saw a figure facing the wall. We started to sing "Apple Blossom Time." About halfway through, we began to hear this

hum. It was discordant and got louder and louder. When we came to the
end of the song, we didn't stop. We just kept singing. We repeated it and
repeated it. The figure turned around. He couldn't have been more than
nineteen years old. His eyes were looking at us, but he wasn't seeing us.
He was lost in another world. He was just humming and humming. He
was so handsome and so young.

A few months later, at the Golden Gate Theatre, the doorman came
to us: "You have a visitor." We were just about to do our last show. In
walked a serviceman. On his back was another serviceman, with no arms
and no legs. One we had seen in the ward. He had his artificial arms on.
He said, "I never asked you for your autograph, because I said that one
day I was going to give you mine." He leaned over on the dressing table
and he signed his name: it was Ted.

We went overseas for the USO. Our last date was in Naples. We
were billeted in Caserta, eighteen miles away. We did all our shows at
repo depots, where all the guys were being shipped out. We had one
more show to do. It was loaded with about eight thousand of the most
unhappy-looking audience you'd ever seen. They were hanging from the
rafters. All these fellas were being shipped out to the South Pacific. They
hadn't been home for four years, and it was just their bad luck. We were
trying to get them into good spirits.

We were pretty well through with the show when I heard someone
offstage calling me: "Pssst. Pssst." Patty was doing a little scene with
Arthur Treacher. The soldier said to me, "I have a very important message for Patty to tell the audience." I started to laugh, because they were
always playing tricks on us. He said, "I'm not kidding. It's from the CO."
I said, "I can't do it in the middle of the show." He said, "You're gonna
get me in trouble." So I took the piece of paper. I didn't read it. I walked
out on the stage, saying to myself I'm gonna get in trouble with Patty,
with Arthur, with the CO. I waited until the skit was over. Patty said,
"Stop your kidding. We can't read that here. We've got to finish the
show." I shoved the note at her. She finally said, "All right, I'll go along
with the gag."

So she said to the fellas, "Look, it's a big joke up here. I have a note
supposedly from the CO." Without reading it first, she read it out loud.
It announced the end of the war with Japan. There wasn't a sound in the
whole auditorium. She looked at it again. She looked at me. It was
serious. So she said, "No, fellas, this is from the CO. This is an announcement that the war is over, so you don't have to go." With that,
she started to cry. Laverne and I were crying. Still there was no reaction
from the guys. So she said it again: "This is the end, this is the end."

All of a sudden, all hell broke loose. They yelled and screamed. We
saw a pair of pants and a shirt come down from above. Following it was
a body. He came down and fell on the guys sitting downstairs. Patty said,

"You want to go out and get drunk? Or you want to see the show?" "No, no, no, we want to see the rest of the show." We made it very short.

We got into the jeep, and all of a sudden it hit us. Oh heavens, if this is a joke, they're gonna tar and feather us. We'll have to swim all the way back to the States. We suffered until we got to Caserta. They reassured us that the announcement was true.

A few years ago, Patty was working someplace in Cleveland. She checked into the hotel and was in the elevator. This elevator man said, "Don't you remember me?" He was a short, baldheaded guy. She said, "Should I?" He said, "Yeah, remember Naples? Remember the guy that fell off the rafter? That was me."


He was a famous trumpet man from out Chicago way,
He had a boogie sound that no one else could play,
He was top man at his craft.
But then his number came up and he was called in the draft.
He's in the army now ablowin' reveille.
He's the boogie woogie bugle boy of Company B.

# WILLIAM MANCHESTER

WILLIAM MANCHESTER, who served with the U.S. Marines during the war, wrote the definitive biography of General MacArthur, *American Caesar: Douglas MacArthur, 1880–1964.* An excerpt follows.

■

FROM *American Caesar: Douglas MacArthur, 1880–1964*

Early Sunday morning, two days later, a destroyer took Wainwright out to the slate-gray, forty-five-thousand-ton battleship *Missouri*, in Tokyo Bay. The ship, he thought, was "the most startling weapon of war I have ever seen. I simply could not believe that anything could be so huge, so studded with guns." As he climbed the starboard ladder he heard a familiar voice roar from above, *"Hello, Skinny!"* It was Halsey, whom he had not seen since the early 1930s, when he was a lieutenant colonel and Halsey a commander. The admiral reached down to pump his hand, led him to the quarterdeck, and showed him where he could stand during the coming surrender ceremony. Wainwright and Percival, the Briton who had surrendered Singapore, were to occupy positions of honor, flanking MacArthur and a step behind him. Behind them and on either side, forming a U, were Allied generals and admirals: red-tabbed Englishmen, Canadians, Australians, and New Zealanders; Russians in red-striped trousers; Chinese in olive-drab uniforms; the Dutch in their quaint caps; and row upon row of Americans in khaki. In the mouth of the U stood a microphone, an old mess table covered with green baize, and chairs on both sides of the table. The Japanese would stand on the far side, facing the General. Scaffolding had been erected for war correspondents and cameramen; every inch of the gun turrets and the decks overhead was crammed with gobs in immaculate white, many holding Kodaks and all craning their necks for a glimpse of MacArthur, who had come aboard earlier and was now striding in the admiral's cabin below. Overhead the General's five-star flag, with Nimitz's five stars beside it, floated beneath the American flag which had flown over the Capitol in Washington on December 7, 1941.

Afterward the memories of both victors and vanquished would agree about everything that happened that day except the weather and the date. Eichelberger, who was piped aboard a few minutes after 8:00 a.m., escorted by Commander Harold Stassen, thought the quarterdeck "as hot in the sunlight as the top side of a kitchen range," while the Japanese diplomat who had been appointed to draw up an official report of the day's events for the Imperial Palace, Toshikazu Kase, a gnomish graduate of Amherst and Harvard and the secretary to Foreign Minister Mamoru Shigemitsu, would remember it as a "surprisingly cool day for early September." To the Occidentals it was September 2, 1945, but Nipponese accounts referred to it as "the second day of the ninth month of the twentieth year of Showa, being the two thousand six hundred and fifth from the Accession of the Emperor Jimmu." It hardly mattered. By any reckoning the day would be memorable. As Eichelberger put it, "I had the eerie feeling that we were walking through the pages of history."

Naturally, the Allies were in a jolly mood. Holland's C.E.L. Helfrich, who had survived the desperate Battle of the Java Sea in 1942, was joking with Richmond Kelly Turner, whose amphibious force had put the marines ashore at Guadalcanal; Eichelberger was in an animated conversation with Kenney, Stilwell, and Carl "Tooey" Spaatz, the airman. It was the unenviable task of Commander Horace Bird, the *Missouri*'s gunnery officer, to silence all this brass before MacArthur and Nimitz came on deck. He despaired of getting their attention until, in exasperation, he cupped his hands to his mouth and yelled: "*Attention, all hands!*" That quieted them, but they couldn't help smiling. Then Bird informed them that the destroyer *Lansdowne* was approaching with the eleven-man Nipponese delegation. Teddy White noted a swift change in the expressions of the Allied officers: "Stilwell bristled like a dog at the sight of an enemy. Spaatz's chiseled face lines were sharp in contempt. Kenney curved his lips in a visible sneer."

The emotions of the Japanese were almost indescribable. At 5:00 a.m. they had assembled in the half-burned official residence of the new prime minister, Prince Toshihiko Higashikuni. The diplomats, led by Shigemitsu, who had been crippled years ago by a terrorist's bomb in Shanghai and limped on a wooden leg, wore tall silk hats, ascots, and cutaways. The ranking soldier was the chief of the imperial general staff, Yoshijiro Umezu, "his chest covered with ribbons and hung with gold braid," White would write, "his eyes blank and unseeing." Umezu had at first refused to participate in the surrender ceremony; Hirohito had brought him round with a personal appeal. Even the emperor had been unable to persuade Admiral Toyoda to attend, however. Toyoda had ordered his operations officer, Sadatoshi Tomioka, to take his place: "You lost the war," he told him, "so you go." Tomioka obeyed, but vowed to commit seppuku upon his return.

Before they left for Yokohama, the officers unbuckled their sabers and flags were removed from the hoods of the battered cars of their motorcade. "We had thus furled the banner and ungirt the sword," wrote Kase in his subsequent account. "Diplomats without flag and soldiers without sword—sullen and silent we continued the journey until we reached the quay." The first vessel they saw was the Japanese destroyer *Hatsuzabura*, with her three five-inch guns depressed, as though bowing. Then they mounted the pier and beheld the gleaming Allied armada, the greatest ever assembled, "lines on lines of gray battleships," a Japanese wrote afterward, ". . .anchored in majestic array. This was the mighty pageant of the Allied navies that so lately belched forth their crashing battle, now holding in their swift thunder and floating like calm sea birds on the subjugated waters."

At 8:55 a.m. the delegation reached the *Missouri*. Shigemitsu was first up the ladder, leaning heavily on his walking stick. He was struggling to mount the steps; Commander Bird stepped down and extended his hand; the foreign minister, his face wooden, shook it off and then briefly accepted it. An American newspaperman wrote that the waiting Allied commanders watched the foreign minister's plight "with savage satisfaction." Bird showed the Japanese where to stand, in four ranks. Kase felt "subjected to the torture of the pillory. A million eyes seemed to beat on us with the million shafts of a rattling storm of arrows barbed with fire. I felt their keenness sink into my body with a sharp physical pain. Never have I realized that the glance of glaring eyes could hurt so much. We waited . . . standing in the public gaze like penitent boys awaiting the dreaded schoolmaster. I tried to preserve the dignity of defeat but it was difficult and every minute contained ages." Actually only four minutes passed before the chaplain's invocation and the recorded playing of "The Star-Spangled Banner" over the ship's public address system. Then MacArthur appeared, walking briskly between Nimitz and Halsey, whose flagship this was. The two admirals peeled off to take their places in the U, and the General stepped straight to the microphone. He later wrote that he had "received no instructions as to what to say or what to do. I was on my own, standing on the quarterdeck with only God and my own conscience to guide me." His chest, unlike those of the other officers, was bare of medals. A U.S. sailor whispered: "Look at Mac. Ain't he got no ribbons?" The gob beside him whispered back: "If he wore them, they'd go clear over his shoulder."

His stance was a portrait of soldierly poise. Only his hand trembled slightly as he held a single sheet of paper before him and said: "We are gathered here, representatives of the major warring powers, to conclude a solemn agreement whereby peace may be restored." It would, he continued, be inappropriate to discuss here "different ideals and ideologies" or to meet "in a spirit of distrust, malice or hatred." Instead, both the conquerors and the conquered must rise "to that higher dignity which alone benefits the sacred purposes we are about to serve." It was his "earnest hope and indeed the hope of all mankind" that "a better world shall emerge," one "founded upon faith and understanding—a world dedicated to the dignity of man and the fulfillment of his most cherished wish—for freedom, tolerance and justice." At the end he said: "As Supreme Commander for the Allied Powers, I announce it my firm purpose, in the tradition of the countries I represent, to proceed in the discharge of my responsibilities . . . while taking all necessary dispositions to insure that the terms of surrender are fully, promptly, and faithfully complied with."

Listening to the mellifluous, sonorous voice, Lieutenant General Yatsuji Nagai marveled at MacArthur's youthful bearing, contrasting it with Umezu's stooped, senescent appearance. He wondered whether the outcome of the war could account for the difference. Tomioka was struck by the General's lack of vindictiveness. But the diminutive Kase was enraptured. He thought: "What stirring eloquence and what a noble vision! Here is a victor announcing the verdict to the prostrate enemy. He can exact his pound of flesh if he so chooses. He can impose a humiliating penalty if he so desires. And yet he pleads for freedom, tolerance, and justice. For me, who expected the worst humiliation, this was a complete surprise. I was thrilled beyond words, spellbound, thunderstruck. For the living heroes and dead martyrs of the war this speech was a wreath of undying flowers." It seemed to Kase that "MacArthur's words sailed on wings," that "this narrow quarterdeck was now transformed into an altar of peace."

Two copies of the instrument of capitulation lay on the table, one bound in leather for the Allies, the other, canvas-bound, for the Japanese. As cameras clicked and whirred, the signing now began. The General beckoned to Shigemitsu, who hobbled forward, sat down, and fumbled with his cane, gloves, and hat. Halsey, thinking he was stalling, wanted to slap his face and shout, "Sign, damn you, sign!" but MacArthur, realizing that the man was simply bewildered, said in a voice like a pistol shot, "Sutherland! Show him where to sign!" Next, Umezu, scorning the chair, leaned forward awkwardly and scribbled his name. After the Japanese, it was the turn of the victors. One Japanese, watching the representatives of nine great Allied nations parade to the green baize, could not help wondering "how it was that Japan, a poor country, had had the temerity to wage war against the whole world."

Not everything went well in this historic transaction. A drunken Allied delegate, not an American, made rude faces at the Japanese. The Canadian emissary wrote on the wrong line. At one point in the proceedings Carl Mydans, the *Life* photographer, ran out for a close-up of the erect, severe, solemn MacArthur. (As he was being hustled away, the General winked at him.) These were the only interruptions, however, and at the end of the eighteen-minute ritual MacArthur sat, pulled five fountain pens from his pocket, and affixed his own signature with them. He handed the first to Wainwright; the second, to Percival. The third would go to West Point and the fourth to Annapolis. The last, a cheap, red-barreled affair, belonged to Jean. He used it to write the "Arthur" in

his signature. She would save it for their son. Rising at 9:25 a.m., he said
in a steely voice, "These proceedings are now closed." As the Japanese
were led away, he put an arm around Halsey's shoulders and said, "Bill,
where the hell are those airplanes?" As if on signal, a cloud of planes—
B-29s and navy fighters—roared across the sky from the south. They
joined, Kenney wrote, "in a long sweeping majestic turn as they disappeared toward the mists hiding the sacred mountain of Fujiyama."

In that instant, World War II ended. But MacArthur meant to speak
the first words of the peace, too, and had spent most of the night working
and reworking them in his spiky handwriting. Now he returned to the
microphone for a broadcast to the American people. Jean, listening in
Manila, would never forget the vibrancy in his voice as he said: "Today
the guns are silent. A great tragedy has ended. A great victory has been
won. The skies no longer rain death—the seas bear only commerce—
men everywhere walk upright in the sunlight. The entire world is quietly
at peace. The holy mission has been completed. And in reporting this to
you, the people, I speak for the thousands of silent lips, forever stilled
among the jungles and the beaches and in the deep waters of the Pacific
which marked the way." He said, "Men since the beginning of time have
sought peace," but "military alliances, balances of power, leagues of
nations, all in turn failed, leaving the only path to be by way of the
crucible of war." Now "we have had our last chance. If we do not now
devise some greater and more equitable system, Armageddon will be at
our door. The problem basically is theological and involves a spiritual
recrudescence and improvement of human character that will synchronize with our almost matchless advances in science, art, literature and
all material and cultural developments of the past two thousand years. It
must be of the spirit if we are to save the flesh."

Nearly a century earlier, he observed, Matthew Perry had landed
here "to bring to Japan an era of enlightenment and progress, by lifting
the veil of isolation to the friendship, trade, and commerce of the world.
But, alas, the knowledge thereby gained of Western science was forged
into an instrument of oppression and human enslavement. Freedom of
expression, freedom of action, even freedom of thought were denied
through appeal to superstition, and through the application of force. We
are committed," he said, "to see that the Japanese people are liberated
from this condition of slavery." He believed that "the energy of the
Japanese race, if properly directed, will enable expansion vertically
rather than horizontally. If the talents of the race are turned into con-
structive channels, the country can lift itself from its present deplorable
state into a position of dignity. To the Pacific basin has come the vista of
a new emancipated world. Today, freedom is on the offensive, democracy is on the march. Today, in Asia as well as in Europe, unshackled
peoples are tasting the full sweetness of liberty, the relief from fear." He
concluded: "And so, my fellow countrymen, today I report to you that

your sons and daughters have served you well and faithfully with the calm, deliberate, determined fighting spirit of the American soldier and sailor. . . . Their spiritual strength and power has brought us through to victory. They are homeward bound—take care of them."

A third of a century later Kenney would still regard this as the General's "greatest speech." From Yokohama *Time* correspondent Shelley Mydans cabled, "The best adjective for MacArthur's attitude toward this peace and the Japanese is 'Olympian.' He is thinking in centuries and populations." But with few exceptions the other officers on the quarterdeck lacked his vision; they had enjoyed the mortification of the Japanese, and that, and the relief that it was all over, had been the extent of their emotional experience. After the General had left, Eichelberger joined a group of admirals for coffee and doughnuts in the wardroom. Some of the talk was shoptalk; they discussed future implications of modern war's three dimensions—ground, sea, and air. Mostly, however, they were merry. Early in the war Halsey had boasted that after the war he would ride Hirohito's white horse down the main street of Tokyo, and now, Eichelberger wrote Miss Em, "in Halsey's cabin is the most beautiful saddle I've ever seen. It is a donation from some town in Oklahoma and is cowboy type [sic] with a great deal of sterling silver. He said it cost $2,000. . . . I got a kick out of seeing Halsey when he scowled at the Japs as he stood behind Nimitz when the latter was signing the surrender document." One of the naval officers wondered aloud whether MacArthur might like to borrow the saddle for a ride on the emperor's mount.

ment, Inc. Reprinted by permission of Dutton, an imprint of New American Library, a division of Penguin Books USA Inc., and International Creative Management, Inc.

*Dutton, and Macmillan, London & Basingstoke*
Excerpt from *A Very Private Eye* by Barbara Pym. Copyright © 1984 by Hillary Walton. Preface and all editorial text © 1984 by Hazel Holt. Rights in U.K. administered by Macmillan, London & Basingstoke. Reprinted by permission of the publisher.

*Faber and Faber Limited*
"The conscript" and "Swing-song," from *Collected Poems* by Louis MacNeice. Reprinted by permission of Faber and Faber Limited.

*Farrar, Straus & Giroux, Inc.*
Excerpt from *Letters on Literature and Politics 1912–1972* by Edmund Wilson. Copyright © 1977 by Elena Wilson. Reprinted by permission of the publisher.

*Farrar, Straus & Giroux, Inc., and Jonathan Cape Ltd.*
"The Order," from *Babi Yar* by A. Anatoli (Kuznetsov). Copyright © 1970 by Jonathan Cape Ltd. Rights outside the U.S. administered by Jonathan Cape. Reprinted by permission of the publishers.
"Safe at Home" from *The Facts* by Philip Roth. Copyright © 1989 by Philip Roth. Rights in U.K. administered by Jonathan Cape Ltd. Reprinted by permission of the publishers.

*Farrar, Straus & Giroux, Inc., and Joan Daves Agency*
Excerpt from *The Casualty* by Heinrich Böll. Translation copyright © 1987 by the Estate of Heinrich Böll and Leila Vennewitz. Rights outside the U.S. administered by Joan Daves Agency. Reprinted by permission of Farrar, Straus & Giroux, Inc., and Joan Daves Agency.

*Farrar, Straus & Giroux, Inc., and Faber and Faber Limited*
"A Stone Church Damaged by a Bomb," from *Collected Poems* by Philip Larkin. Copyright © 1988, 1989 by the Estate of Philip Larkin. Rights outside the U.S. administered by Faber and Faber Limited. Reprinted by permission of the publishers.
"Losses," from *The Complete Poems* by Randall Jarrell. Copyright 1948, © 1969 by Mrs. Randall Jarrell. Rights in U.K. administered by Faber and Faber Limited. Reprinted by permission of the publishers.

*The Free Press and Virago Press Limited*
Excerpt from *Winter in the Morning: A Young Girl's Life in the Warsaw Ghetto and Beyond, 1939–1945* by Janina Bauman. Copyright © 1986 by Janina Bauman. Rights outside the U.S. administered by Virago Press Limited. Reprinted by permission of the publishers.

*David R. Godine, Publisher*
Excerpt from *Obasan* by Joy Kogawa. Copyright © 1981 by Joy Kogawa. Reprinted by permission of the publisher.

*Victor Gollancz Ltd.*
"For the Unknown Seamen of the 1939–45 War Buried in Iona Church-yard," from *Selected Poems* by Iain Crichton-Smith. Copyright © by Iain Crichton-Smith. Reprinted by permission of the publisher.

*Harcourt Brace Jovanovich, Inc., and A. M. Heath & Company Limited*
Excerpts from *The Collected Essays, Journalism and Letters of George Orwell*, volume II, 1940–1943, edited by Sonia Orwell and Ian Angus. Copyright © 1968 by Sonia Brownell Orwell. Rights outside the U.S. administered by A. M. Heath & Company Limited. Reprinted by permission of Harcourt Brace Jovanovich, Inc., and A. M. Heath & Company Limited, for the Estate of the late Sonia Brownell Orwell and Martin Secker & Warburg Ltd.

*Harcourt Brace Jovanovich, Inc., and The Hogarth Press*
Excerpt from *A Writer's Diary* by Virginia Woolf. Copyright 1954 by Leonard Woolf and © renewed 1982 by Quentin Bell and Angelica Garnett. Rights outside the U.S. administered by The Hogarth Press. Reprinted by permission of the publishers and the Estate of Virginia Woolf.

*HarperCollins Publishers Inc. and Hamish Hamilton Limited*
Excerpt from *Rumors of Peace* by Ella Leffland. Copyright © 1979 by Ella Leffland. Rights in U.K. administered by Hamish Hamilton Limited. Reprinted by permission of the publishers.

*HarperCollins Publishers Ltd.*
Excerpts from *Harold Nicolson's Diaries*, edited by Nigel Nicolson. Reprinted by permission of the publisher.

*William Heinemann Limited*
Excerpt from *The Great Fortune* by Olivia Manning. Reprinted by permission of William Heinemann Limited.

*David Higham Associates Limited*
"East Is West" by Dan Davin, from *Short Stories from the Second World War*, chosen by Dan Davin. Reprinted by permission of David Higham Associates Limited.

*Hill and Wang, and MacGibbon and Kee*
Excerpts from *Night* by Elie Wiesel. Translation copyright © 1960 by MacGibbon and Kee. Renewal copyright © 1988 by The Collins Publishing Group. Rights in U.K. administered by MacGibbon and Kee. Reprinted by permission of Hill and Wang, a division of Farrar, Straus and Giroux, Inc., and MacGibbon and Kee/Grafton Books, a division of HarperCollins Publishers Inc.

*The Literary Executor of Richard Hillary*
Excerpt from *The Last Enemy* by Richard Hillary. First published by Macmillan in the United Kingdom in 1942. Reprinted by permission of Macmillan London and the Literary Executor of Richard Hillary. All rights reserved.

*Henry Holt and Company, Inc., and Librairie Artheme Fayard*
"Solik" and "The Myechotka Musketeers" by K. S. Karol, from *Between Two Worlds*. Copyright © 1983 by Librairie Artheme Fayard, translation © 1986 by Henry Holt and Company, Inc., and Pluto Press. Rights in the U.K. administered by Librairie Artheme Fayard. Reprinted by permission of the publishers.

Michener, renewed © 1975 by James A. Michener. Reprinted by permission of Macmillan Publishing Company.

*Macmillan Publishing Company and Hamish Hamilton Ltd.*
Excerpts from *Scroll of Agony: The Warsaw Diary of Chaim A. Kaplan*, translated from the Hebrew and edited by Abraham I. Katsh. Copyright © 1965, 1973 by Abraham I. Katsh. Rights in U.K. administered by Hamish Hamilton Ltd. Reprinted by permission of the publishers.

*Macmillan, London and Basingstoke*
Excerpt from *The Last Waltz in Vienna* by George Clare. Reprinted by permission of the publisher.

*MCA Music Publishing and MCA Music Ltd.*
"Boogie Woogie Bugle Boy," words and music by Don Raye and Hughie Prince. Copyright © 1940, 1941; renewed by MCA Music Publishing, a division of MCA Inc., New York. © Leeds Music Corp. Reprinted by permission of MCA Music Publishing and MCA Music Ltd.

*Scott Meredith Literary Agency Inc.*
Excerpt from *The Naked and the Dead* by Norman Mailer. Copyright 1948, © renewed 1976 by Norman Mailer. Reprinted by permission of the author and the author's agents, Scott Meredith Literary Agency, Inc., New York.

*William Morrow & Company, Inc., and William Heinemann*
Excerpt from *A World Apart* by Gustave Herling. Copyright 1951, © 1986. Rights outside the U.S. administered by William Heinemann. Reprinted by permission of the publishers.

*William Morrow & Company, Inc., and David Higham Associates Limited*
Excerpt from *Chronicles of a Wasted Time*, vol. 2, *The Infernal Grove* by Malcolm Muggeridge. Copyright © 1973 by Malcolm Muggeridge. Rights outside the U.S. administered by David Higham Associates. Reprinted by permission of William Morrow & Company, Inc., and David Higham Associates Limited.

*William Morrow & Company, Inc., and The Hogarth Press*
"Casablanca," from *The Gallery* by John Horne Burns. Copyright 1947, 1949 by John Horne Burns. Copyright © renewed 1964. Rights in U.K. administered by The Hogarth Press. Reprinted by permission of the publisher.

*John Murray (Publishers) Ltd.*
"Letter to the Chairman, Aliens Tribunal" from *Letters of Max Beerbohm, 1892–1956*. Letter copyright © by Eva Reichman 1988. Reprinted by permission of the publisher.

*New Directions Publishing Corporation and David Higham Associates Limited*
"A Refusal to Mourn the Death by Fire of a Child in London," from *Poems of Dylan Thomas*. Copyright 1954 by the Trustees for the Copyrights of Dylan Thomas. Rights outside the U.S. administered by David Higham Associates Limited. Reprinted by permission of New Directions Publishing Corporation and David Higham Associates Limited.

*New Directions Publishing Corporation and Laurence Pollinger Limited*
Excerpts from *Confessions of a Mask* by Yukio Mishima. Copyright © 1966 by New Directions Publishing Corporation. Rights in U.K. administered by Laurence Pollinger Limited. Reprinted by permission of New Directions Publishing Corporation and Laurence Pollinger Limited.

*The New Yorker*
"Letter from Berlin," from *The New Yorker*, July 28, 1945. Copyright 1945, © 1973 by The New Yorker Magazine, Inc. Reprinted by permission of the publisher.

*Peter Owen Ltd: Publishers*
Excerpt from *Stained Glass Elegies* by Shūsaku Endō. Reprinted by permission of the publisher.

*Oxford University Press*
"Annotations of Auschwitz" from *Collected Poems* by Peter Porter. Copyright © 1983 by Peter Porter. Reprinted by permission of the publisher.

*Pantheon Books*
Excerpt from *Sketches from a Life* by George F. Kennan. Copyright © 1989 by George F. Kennan. Reprinted by permission of Pantheon Books, a division of Random House, Inc.
Excerpt from *The Assault* by Harry Mulisch, trans. by Claire White. Copyright © 1985 by Random House, Inc. Reprinted by permission of Pantheon Books, a division of Random House, Inc.
Excerpts from *"The Good War": An Oral History of World War II* by Studs Terkel. Copyright © 1984 by Studs Terkel. Reprinted by permission of Pantheon Books, a division of Random House, Inc.
Excerpt from *The War: A Memoir* by Marguerite Duras, trans. by Barbara Bray. Translation copyright © 1986 by Barbara Bray. Rights in the U.K. administered by Pantheon Books. Reprinted by permission of the publisher.

*Pantheon Books and Chatto & Windus*
Excerpt from *The Great World* by David Malouf. Copyright © 1990 by David Malouf. Rights in the U.K. administered by Chatto & Windus. Reprinted by permission of the publishers.

*Pantheon Books and Rogers, Coleridge & White Ltd.*
Excerpts from *Naples '44* by Norman Lewis. Copyright © 1978 by Norman Lewis. Rights outside U.S. administered by Rogers, Coleridge & White Ltd. Reprinted by permission of Pantheon Books, a division of Random House, Inc.; and Rogers, Coleridge & White Ltd.

*Pantheon Books and Martin Secker & Warburg*
Excerpt from *The Tin Drum* by Günter Grass. Copyright © 1961, 1962 by Pantheon Books, a division of Random House, Inc. Renewed 1989, 1990 by Random House, Inc. Reprinted by permission of the publishers.

*Pantheon Books and Verso Editions*
From *The War Diaries of Jean-Paul Sartre* by Jean-Paul Sartre, trans. by Quinton Hoare. English translation copyright © 1984 by Verso Editions.

*Random House, Inc., and Michael Joseph Ltd.*
Excerpt from *World's Fair* by E. L. Doctorow. Copyright © 1985 by E. L. Doctorow. Rights in U.K. administered by Michael Joseph Ltd. Reprinted by permission of the publishers.

*Random House, Inc., and Lucy Kroll Agency*
"Letter from James Jones to Jeff Jones," from *To Reach Eternity: The Letters of James Jones*, edited by George Hendrick. Copyright © 1989 by George Hendrick and Gloria Jones. Rights outside U.S. administered by Lucy Kroll Agency. Reprinted by permission of Random House, Inc., and Lucy Kroll Agency.

*Random House, Inc., and the Trustee for the Estate of John O'Hara*
"Graven Image," from *Collected Stories of John O'Hara* by John O'Hara, edited by Frank MacShane. Copyright 1943 by John O'Hara. Originally published in *The New Yorker*. Rights in U.K. administered by the Trustee for the Estate of John O'Hara. Reprinted by permission of Random House, Inc., and the Trustee for the Estate of John O'Hara.

*Random House, Inc., and Tessa Sayle Agency*
Excerpt from *Sophie's Choice* by William Styron. Copyright © 1976, 1978, 1979 by William Styron. Rights outside U.S. administered by Tessa Sayle Agency. Reprinted by permission of Random House, Inc., and Tessa Sayle Agency.

*Random House, Inc., and Sterling Lord Literistic, Inc.*
"The Voice," from *Collected Stories* by V. S. Pritchett. Copyright 1947, 1949, 1953, © 1956, 1959, 1960, 1961, 1962, 1966, 1969, 1973, 1974, 1979, 1982 by V. S. Pritchett. Rights outside U.S. administered by Sterling Lord Literistic, Inc. Reprinted by permission of Random House, Inc., and Sterling Lord Literistic, Inc.

*Residenz Verlag*
Excerpts from *Gathering Evidence* by Thomas Bernhard. Originally published in German: Thomas Bernhard, *Die Ursache* © 1975 Residenz Verlag, Salzburg und Wien. Thomas Bernhard, *Ein Kind*, © 1982 Residenz Verlag, Salzburg und Wien. Reprinted by permission of the publisher.

*Alan Ross*
"Night Patrol" by Alan Ross. Copyright 1944 by Alan Ross. First published in *Penguin New Writing 1944–1955*. Reprinted by permission of the author.

*Alan Ross Ltd.*
Excerpts from *Memoirs of the Forties* by J. Maclaren-Ross. Copyright © 1965 by Alan Ross Ltd. Reprinted by permission of Alan Ross Ltd.

*Russell & Volkening, Inc.*
"Hovering Above the Pit" and "Two Capsules of Cyanide," from *Hasidic Tales of the Holocaust* by Yaffa Eliach. Copyright © 1982 by Yaffa Eliach. Reprinted by permission of Russell & Volkening, Inc., as agents for the author.
"Cross Channel Trip," parts I, II, III, by A. J. Liebling from *The New Yorker*, July 1, 8, and 15, 1944. Copyright © 1944 by A. J. Liebling, renewed in 1972 by Jean Stafford. Reprinted by permission of Russell & Volkening, Inc., as agents for the author.

*Sheil Land Associates*

    Excerpt from *A Child of the War* by George MacBeth. Reprinted by permission of the Sheil Land Associates.

*Simon and Schuster, Inc.*

    Excerpt from *Catch-22* by Joseph Heller. Copyright © 1955, 1961, 1989 by Joseph Heller. Reprinted by permission of Simon & Schuster, Inc.

    Excerpt from *The Road from Hiroshima* by Marc Kaminsky. Copyright © 1985 by Marc Kaminsky. Reprinted by permission of Simon & Schuster, Inc.

*Simon & Schuster, Inc., and Jonathan Clowes Ltd.*

    "The Black Madonna" by Doris Lessing. From *African Stories* (U.S.) and *This Was the Old Chief's Country* (U.K.). Copyright © 1951, 1953, 1954, 1957, 1958, 1961, 1962, 1963, 1964, 1965 by Doris Lessing. Rights outside U.S. administered by Jonathan Clowes Ltd. Reprinted by permission of Simon & Schuster, Inc., and Jonathan Clowes Ltd.

*Simon & Schuster, Inc., and Victor Gollancz Ltd.*

    Excerpt from *The Empire of the Sun* by J. G. Ballard. Copyright © 1984 by J. G. Ballard. Rights outside U.S. administered by Victor Gollancz Ltd. Reprinted by permission of the publishers.

*Simon & Schuster, Inc., and Wylie, Aitkin & Stone Incorporated*

    Letter of November 21, 1945, from *Letters of John Cheever*, edited by Benjamin Cheever. Copyright © 1988 by Benjamin Cheever. Rights in U.K. administered by Wylie, Aitkin & Stone Incorporated. Reprinted by permission of Simon & Schuster, Inc., and Wylie, Aitkin & Stone Incorporated.

*The Society of Authors*

    Letters from *Collected Letters, 1926–1950*, by Bernard Shaw. Reprinted by permission of The Society of Authors.

*Summit Books*

    Excerpts from *Moments of Reprieve* by Primo Levi. Copyright © 1979, 1981, 1982, 1983, 1985 by Summit Books; © 1981, 1985 by Giulio Einaudi, editore s.p.a. Reprinted by permission of the publisher.

*Summit Books and Giulio Einaudi, editore s.p.a.*

    Excerpt from *The Reawakening* by Primo Levi. Copyright © 1986 by Summit Books. Rights in U.K. administered by Giulio Einaudi, editore s.p.a. Reprinted by permission of the publishers.

    Excerpt from *Survival at Auschwitz* by Primo Levi. Copyright © 1986 by Summit Books. Rights in U.K. administered by Giulio Einaudi, editore s.p.a. Reprinted by permission of the publishers.

*Unwin Hyman*

    "The Earth Is a Syllable," from *In the Green Tree* by Alun Lewis. Reprinted by permission of the publisher.

    "Raiders' Dawn" from *Raiders' Dawn* by Alun Lewis. Reprinted by permission of the publisher.

*Vanguard Press and David Higham Associates*

    From *Selected Letters of Edith Sitwell* by Edith Sitwell, ed. J. Lehmann and D. Parker. Letters copyright © 1970 by Frances Sitwell. Editorial Matter copy-

# A NOTE ON THE TYPE

The text of this book was set in Electra, a Linotype face designed by W. A. Dwiggins (1880–1956). This face cannot be classified as either modern or old style. It is not based on any historical model; nor does it echo any particular period or style. It avoids the extreme contrasts between thick and thin elements that mark most modern faces and attempts to give a feeling of fluidity, power, and speed.

Composed by Dix Type Inc.
Syracuse, New York
Printed and bound by The Haddon Craftsmen, Inc.,
Scranton, Pennsylvania
Designed by Helen Barrow